Crime and Spy Jazz
on Screen, 1950–1970

ALSO BY DERRICK BANG

*Crime and Spy Jazz on Screen Since 1971:
A History and Discography* (McFarland, 2020)

Vince Guaraldi at the Piano (McFarland, 2012)

Crime and Spy Jazz on Screen, 1950–1970

A History and Discography

Derrick Bang

Foreword by Cheryl Pawelski

McFarland & Company, Inc., Publishers
Jefferson, North Carolina

LIBRARY OF CONGRESS CATALOGUING-IN-PUBLICATION DATA

Names: Bang, Derrick, 1955– author.
Title: Crime and spy jazz on screen, 1950–1970 : a history and discography / Derrick Bang.
Description: Jefferson : McFarland & Company, Inc., Publishers, 2020. | Includes bibliographical references and index.
Identifiers: LCCN 2020011238 | ISBN 9781476667478 (paperback : acid free paper) ∞
ISBN 9781476639888 (ebook)
Subjects: LCSH: Motion picture music—History and criticism. | Jazz in motion pictures. | Jazz—History and criticism. | Crime films—History and criticism. | Spy films—History and criticism. | Television music—History and criticism.
Classification: LCC ML2075 .B289 2020 | DDC 781.5/42—dc23
LC record available at https://lccn.loc.gov/2020011238

BRITISH LIBRARY CATALOGUING DATA ARE AVAILABLE

ISBN (print) 978-1-4766-6747-8
ISBN (ebook) 978-1-4766-3988-8

© 2020 Derrick Bang. All rights reserved

No part of this book may be reproduced or transmitted in any form or by any means, electronic or mechanical, including photocopying or recording, or by any information storage and retrieval system, without permission in writing from the publisher.

Front cover images © 2020 Shutterstock

Printed in the United States of America

McFarland & Company, Inc., Publishers
Box 611, Jefferson, North Carolina 28640
www.mcfarlandpub.com

Table of Contents

Acknowledgments — vii
Foreword by Cheryl Pawelski — 1
Introduction — 5
Prologue: The Naked Truth — 11

1. Audition: 1947–1956 — 15
2. Dreamsville: 1957–1958 — 32
3. Blue Satin: 1959 — 54
4. Breezy Capers: 1960 — 72
5. Contract with Depravity: 1961 — 88
6. Jamaica Jazz: 1962 — 101
7. Champagne and Quail: 1963 — 113
8. Meet Mr. Solo: 1964 — 129
9. Mr. Kiss Kiss Bang Bang: 1965 — 144
10. Mission Blues: 1966 — 167
11. Home, James, Don't Spare the Horses: 1967 — 200
12. Shifting Gears: 1968 — 226
13. This Never Happened to the Other Fella: 1969 — 248
14. Soul Flower: 1970 — 257

Appendix A: Instrument Abbreviations — 265
Appendix B: Discography — 266
Chapter Notes — 291
Bibliography — 299
Index — 301

Acknowledgments

When it comes to writing a book—*any* kind of book—the wisdom of Buzzy Linhart and Mark "Moogy" Klingman's 1973 hit song definitely resonates: You've got to have friends.

On top of which, one never knows the true depth of such kindness, until just such a friend graciously exerts an undisclosed amount of time and effort, while chasing down an obscure something-or-other. Such treasure hunts obviously are a lot easier in our modern era, but some things still elude digital search techniques. Actually, quite a few things … at least, quite a few of the things *I* was looking for, while gathering the raw materials and data that ultimately led to the completion of this two-volume project.

Not that it began that way. When I initially pitched an analysis of film/TV crime and action jazz to my obligingly intrigued editor, the resulting contract was for a single book of somewhere in the neighborhood of 125,000 words; I naïvely assumed said page count would be sufficient. That was four years ago, during which time I considered a combined total of roughly 1,000 movies and television shows, ultimately discussing approximately 550 in brief or at considerable length. The result landed just shy of 600,000 words. Okay, fine; first drafts are overwritten. After some necessary pruning—and then additional judicious tightening—I wound up with 250,000 words. Trimming further would have cut into the "good stuff"; the text would have been compromised beyond repair, destroying the manuscript's design as a truly definitive study of this jazz subgenre.

The first note of thanks therefore goes to my editor, David Alff, and all others involved at McFarland, who agreed that the best solution was *not* to hack 'n' slash the manuscript to an all-but useless shadow of its former self, but to rewrite the contract for a two-volume set. Bless you all; my wife and I will name our subsequent cats and dogs after each and every one of you.

Moving on, many other people have been extraordinarily charitable with their time, expertise and patience, for which I'm profoundly grateful.

I couldn't have finished these books—heck, I couldn't have *started* them—without the research acumen of Scott McGuire, who constantly surprised me by ferreting out obscure recordings and video items from the most arcane sources. If somebody held a contest for sleuthing skills, I've no doubt he'd win.

Lee Riggs, of the University of California, Davis, Shields Library, also deserves an enthusiastic shout-out for research assistance, and for door-to-door book check-out service. (Talk about getting spoiled!)

Daniel Urazandi, of Bizarro World—an impressively diverse pop-culture shop, and our town of Davis's sole remaining DVD rental outlet—chased down quite a few obscure titles on my behalf. Much obliged.

A quick shout-out as well, to Thomas Film Classics (shop.thomasfilmclassics.com) and Robert's Hard to Find Videos (robertsvideos.com), for their amazing libraries of obscure films and television shows. Quite a few titles within these pages would have remained no more than tantalizing (and undiscussed) possibilities, absent their extensive catalogs.

A sweeping bow, tip o' the hat, and flourish of arms to Cheryl Pawelski, for her generous foreword. Long may Omnivore Recordings—her tiffany music label—reign.

Lukas Kendall, of Film Score Monthly, spent two decades wrestling with Hollywood studios and major record labels, to bring soundtrack fans quality debuts and resurrections of beloved film and TV scores. He generously granted permission for many of the album covers that appear within these pages.

Roger Feigelson, of Intrada—a companion label similarly dedicated to the restoration of such music—was equally kind to allow the use of their album covers.

I occasionally use the word *indefatigable* in the subsequent text, to describe the select few composer/performers with the preternatural ability to produce stunning quantities of quality music despite absurdly tight scheduling constraints. The same term applies to journalist, author and lecturer Jon Burlingame, whom I've never met, but who absolutely deserves his reputation as America's leading writer on the subject of film and TV music. He paved the way with wit, insight and thoughtful analysis—on top of which, he's fun to read—and his richly informative body of work is astonishing: commentary in all manner of publications (notably *Daily Variety* and the *Los Angeles Times*); detailed articles for the Film Music Society; lengthy oral history interviews on behalf of the Film Music Foundation and the Television Academy Foundation; enlightening liner notes for soundtrack reissues and debuts; and his three seminal books, *Sound and Vision: 60 Years of Motion Picture Soundtracks*, *TV's Biggest Hits* and *The Music of James Bond*. His *oeuvre* has been exceptionally helpful, and I humbly aspire to trail at the distant edge of his enormous shadow.

My deep gratitude to Lisa and Amy, of the Bernstein Family Trust, for allowing the generous use of the portrait of Elmer Bernstein within these pages.

Needless to say, this book wouldn't exist without the brilliant individuals who *created* that which is described herein: the many scores of scorers (sorry, couldn't resist) who wrote and performed all of this great music. They've brought me *such* pleasure over the years, and I couldn't begin to cite them all ... although a short list would include Elmer Bernstein, Henry Mancini, Edwin Astley, Quincy Jones, David Shire, John Barry, Earle Hagen and Lalo Schifrin. And Kenyon Hopkins and Nelson Riddle. Oh, Laurie Johnson and Mort Stevens. Jerry Goldsmith. Mike Post and Pete Carpenter. Did I mention Roy Budd? (Okay, stop. You get the idea.)

Finally, a bottomless pit of gratitude to my Constant Companion, Gayna: for her cheerful (well, mostly) willingness to proofread the gargantuan first draft, and—even more so—for being such a good sport, while forced to *listen* to this stuff, over and over and *over* again, during these past four years. Greater love hath no spouse, and—believe me—that is *not* taken for granted. To borrow one of John Barry's James Bond title songs—lyrics by Tim Rice and Stephen Short—you're my "All Time High."

That said, this book and its companion volume, *Crime and Spy Jazz on Screen Since 1971: A History and Discography*, are dedicated to my father, whose great frustration—for many years—was that his baby-boomer son displayed a typical 1960s teenager's dismissive disinterest in jazz ... until a concentrated exposure to Mr. Barry's early 007 scores, and Vince Guaraldi's anthems for Charlie Brown and the Peanuts gang, and a rapidly expanding diversity of jazz artists thereafter, put the kid on the proper path. (Dad was savvy enough to avoid using the "J-word"—not wanting to sabotage the evolving dynamic—until it was safe to do so.) He delighted in hearing the information and anecdotes that I dug up, as these two books took shape; he was captivated by occasional snatches of chapters-in-progress. My only regret, having now completed the journey, is that he didn't live long enough to see the results actually published. But I know—nonetheless—that he has been reading over my shoulder the entire time.

Foreword
by Cheryl Pawelski

Crime pays ... sometimes.

Especially when it's fiction, on television or the silver screen, and accompanied by a superb, swingin' soundtrack. That's just the truth, and probably the only example of criminal activity that won't get you locked up in the slammer. Crime actually *can* pay big: in entertainment value, advertising revenues, box office receipts and—especially, for our concerns here—hit theme songs, riveting scores and classic soundtracks.

Inspired by the shady corners, characters and cliffhangers that graced the TV shows and movies of the mid–20th century, this is the first book and discography that compiles and traces this music's history. For all the intense attention and cataloging of music inspired by the years spanning the 1940s to early '80s, crime/action jazz just wasn't among the genres covered. Why this hasn't been rectified until the second decade of the 21st century is a mystery to me. Storied labels like Blue Note, Chess, Atlantic and Stax; genres like doo wop, rockabilly, surf and hot rod; and any and all things Beatles, Dylan, Beach Boys, Sinatra, over and over, and then over again some more: All have been obsessively collected, dissected, scrutinized and anthologized.

In the 1990s, we even experienced renewed interest in what was then dubbed "lounge" music, starting with Capitol Records' super successful *Ultra-Lounge* series of CD compilations, and the use of Louis Prima's "Jump, Jive an' Wail" in a Gap TV commercial. Both of those cultural touch points skirted right up to—and sometimes included—some of the music covered in these pages, but no deep dives to anthologize materialized. Perhaps the oversight is explained because action/crime jazz might be considered too much of a sub-subgenre? Perhaps by definition, action/crime jazz must associate with film and television for inclusion in the genre, thus diluting the singular focus on music? Whatever the case, Derrick Bang has righted the wrong, and finally given action/crime jazz its due.

Crime jazz. For me, those two words sitting together conjure smoky cigarette whiffs of the *Mad Men* era, as stale and heavy as the air was in my parents' basement, when I pawed through their records to discover the album *The Best of Henry Mancini* for the first time. My brother and I devoured that album. At the time, we had none of the TV or film references; we just thrilled to music that was so different from the kid stuff we were fed in the '70s. "Peter Gunn," "March of the Cue Balls" and "Baby Elephant Walk" were super kid-friendly, with their huge melodic motifs and varied instrumentation. We wore that album out. It wasn't until later that we made the connections to the private eye world of TV's *Peter Gunn,* the casinos inhabited by *Mr. Lucky* on the boob tube, and the spies running around *Charade* on the big screen. (We viewed them all in reruns.)

While so much about that era was so very wrong—as *Mad Men* creepily captured—many things were very right, and very cool. Architecture, literature, film, art/design, TV and music ... all exploring and exploding out of the postwar pop culture boom. Film and television, two of this book's co-stars, were making technical and creative strides; the goods the broadcast world produced for the mass media frenzy were gulped down by insatiable audiences worldwide. The studio recording of music was making its own technical advances; musicians, engineers and producers worked 'round the clock to provide the musical bed to the soundtrack of the times.

I caught the first half of this cultural burst mostly through a backwards lens. While it felt almost close enough to touch, a lot of those calendar pages had turned by the time I got to the cocktail party. The music, film and television that predated me lingered in the form of LPs and reruns on UHF channels, and—later—on videotapes. It also lingered in its influence on what came after, and was built upon it. Obsessively, I traced it all—trying to peel back the layers of the influenced, to get to the essence of the original—but once one is familiar with what has been influenced, it's impossible to experience the original fresh, and for the first time.

I've tried. I've spent my professional life chasing the pre-digital-era music that so captured my imagination and drove me to my life's work. Just like you, I await the invention of the time machine.

I did have a front-row seat to the unlikely, vault-clearing, loungy boom, while working at Capitol Records throughout the '90s. I had a small bit to play in the Louis Prima/Gap ad, in particular, having provided the licensing department with the handful of songs—including that Prima tune—to send to the ad agency. I spent a dozen years crawling through those circular hallways and studios, where a lot of this music was captured on magnetic tape for the ages. If it wasn't recorded at Capitol, a whole lot more of this music was created just up the road at any number of legendary nearby studios; a few remain, most are long gone.

And talk about getting a whiff of another time! To walk down Capitol's photo-lined hallway, toward the lighted *"Quiet * Recording Area—Observe Recording Lights"* sign, and breathe the rarified air in Studio A ... it's *special*. I was privileged to tread where Billy May, Nelson Riddle, Plas Johnson, Miles Davis, Dean Martin, Peggy Lee, Les Baxter, Ray Anthony, Al Caiola—and so many more, who played and sang on these soundtracks—walked and worked. I even got to produce my way through compilations and reissues of the James Bond canon, since Capitol controlled the United Artists catalog on which a great deal of the John Barry 007 soundtracks were originally issued in the States. I've been very fortunate.

Of course, the amazing time I spent at Capitol still didn't allow me to reach through the time hole, but it was close as anyone is likely to come.

So, while private eyes, detectives, spies, cops, robbers and double-crossing agents all lurk in these pages, the musical themes that brought them to life are here to be truly appreciated in anthology form, for the first time. This is a curated work—one with a point of view and opinions—and it's a wonderful place to start exploring. Derrick's choices for inclusion in musical, film and TV citations are derived by sifting his subjects through various parameters. He employed a series of qualifiers to get to a very tasty center, and ultimately produce a comprehensive and choice genre overview. First, is it TV or movie music? Yes? Is the theme of the visual component action or crime? Cool, keep going. Is it jazz? Yes? Perfect.

Now, this last part is crucial: Is it *really* good, and can it stand on its own musically? Yes? Bingo! If you answered no to any of these questions, you won't find that music in this book.

Foreword by Cheryl Pawelski

Unlike other books that anthologize an era of music, this one is unusual in that Derrick draws connections to—and flips between—his three subjects; as a result, this is no dry discographical reference book of lists, nor is it just a book of prose reciting what we already know about the topic. He insightfully notes where film, TV and music crisscross and evolve, sometimes innovating together and, in some cases, *because* of each other. Toggling back and forth globally, Derrick also illustrates how cultures became more influential on each other, because of the accelerating connectivity delivered through the media growth, as the century wore on.

Derrick's exhaustive research also exposes many repeat names in the musician credits. For a musician of this era, a recording day might have yielded sessions for an album, a film score, a commercial jingle or a TV show. There was no snobbery among musicians, about the ultimate product of a day's work; you'll therefore find some of the same names in both film and TV credits. (And go look at your records *not* associated with scores or soundtracks; these same musicians certainly are there as well.)

Delivered with appropriate winks and nods, the information presented is detailed, dense (in the best possible way) and scholarly. Derrick's enthusiasm is addictive, and he has delivered a very entertaining read. Action/crime jazz finally gets its due, and it certainly does pay! While we're certain to be richer in our knowledge of the genre, if you're like I am, you'll be much poorer after tracking down all the wonderful music just waiting to be discovered.

While I deeply appreciate the road map for my future viewing and listening … the lighter wallet, maybe not so much.—Thanks a lot, Derrick.

Cheryl Pawelski is a Grammy Award–winning record producer and co-founder of the record label Omnivore Recordings. In her spare time, she collects records. She and her wife, Audrey Bilger, call Los Angeles and Portland home.

Introduction

Some of our most instantly recognized jazz melodies originated on the large and small screen.

The anxious trill that kicks off Lalo Schifrin's furious 5/4 "*Mission: Impossible* Theme" immediately evokes images of a lit fuse; smash-cut glimpses of mayhem to come; and a clinical, disembodied voice greeting Peter Graves—or Steven Hill, the first season—with the immortal phrase, "Good evening, Mr. Phelps (Briggs). Your mission, should you choose to accept it…"

The brick-through-plate-glass opening notes of Walter Schumann's "Theme to *Dragnet*"—dum-de-*dum*-dum—date to the show's origins on radio; they've since become an oft-mocked cliché, most (in)famously in the hands of versatile comedian Stan Freberg and late-night talk-show host Johnny Carson. Even so, that four-note phrase still evokes memories of a grimly methodical police procedural that began, each week, with tight-lipped Jack Webb intoning, "This is the city: Los Angeles, California. I work here. I'm a cop."

The hard-charging, brass-heavy "James Bond Theme" has promised flamboyantly staged spy craft ever since John Barry's propulsive orchestration debuted in 1962's *Dr. No*, with Vic Flick's throbbing guitar licks plucking out the smoldering main theme. The tune has become iconic, covered by scores (hundreds?) of other instrumentalists—even Barry refined the arrangement numerous times—but nothing compares to the original. Indeed, the explosive, four-chord motif that precedes the melody is just as memorable, and just as likely to raise a smile.

America's Eisenhower generation is just as likely to cite Henry Mancini's pounding "*Peter Gunn* Theme," while genre fans savvy enough to season their domestic viewing with British imports get equally giddy upon hearing the opening five notes of Laurie Johnson's exhilarating "*Avengers* Theme."

While most of what we can collectively term action/crime jazz has been attached to grim, crime-laden dramas populated by vicious characters—or inventive heist thrillers that get their suspense from the planning of seemingly impossible thefts—that isn't always the case. This allows us to drift into *spoof noir*, thereby acknowledging Mancini's seminal "Pink Panther Theme," with Plas Johnson's droll tenor sax giving such a whimsical bounce to *that* equally unforgettable tune.

Although such iconic examples are well known even to mainstream folks who otherwise don't pay much attention to jazz, serious buffs have long cherished the roughly three decades—from the early 1950s, more or less, to the early 1980s, less or more—that encouraged a wealth of great stuff from veteran and up-and-coming jazz cats eager to "shade" the adventures of cops, private eyes, crusading journalists, impassioned lawyers, spies and secret agents. Hundreds of albums and chart-placing singles emerged during those 30-ish years, and a great deal of that music is overlooked these days … along with the trends that fostered it.

Some of these themes have been resurrected, in this 21st century, as a rebranded and kitschy element of the so-called "lounge music" movement. Perhaps we should be grateful for any such exposure, since it has brought previously unavailable albums into the accessible digital realm. But the subtext is insulting: the implication being that this music is (at best) amusingly retro, and not really worth serious consideration.

I resist—even resent—such a pejorative view: no surprise, since this preface precedes what I hope you'll find is an enthusiastic appreciation for jazz scores that typically stand alone as an isolated listening experience—divorced from their source films or TV shows—far more successfully than most soundtracks. At the same time, the best albums and singles immediately evoke specific, exciting moments from their audio-visual origins.

That immediate music-to-image synergy also puts a lie to the condescending attitude of far too many Hollywood filmmakers, past and present, who arrogantly insist(ed) that film and TV scores are "successful" only when viewers *don't* notice them.

"[It's a] fallacious premise," observed contemporary classical composer Irwin Bazelon, "[that] the audience should not be aware of the music in films. The screen represented drama, action and dialogue; music was merely a subordinate detail, a window dressing. Anything that detracted from visual involvement was looked upon with suspicion."[1]

I ask you: Where's the fun in *that*?

* * *

Let's talk—as briefly as possible—about this book's methodology.

First of all, some essential terms:

- Title theme—the primary theme of a movie or TV show, generally heard behind the opening credits, and often repeated, perhaps in a different arrangement, during the end credits.
- Underscore—traditionally the music layered behind on-screen dialogue, although now more frequently referring to the bulk of a film or TV episode score: which is to say, everything except the title and end themes.
- Cue—a single portion of an underscore: a segment written for a specific scene or sequence.
- Motif—a brief series of notes that forms a core melody, from which the greater "whole" of a theme is constructed. The three sets of three descending flute notes, followed by two rising notes, form the fundamental 3-3-3-2 motif of Lalo Schifrin's "Mission: Impossible Theme."
- Leitmotif—a cue associated with a particular character, place or idea; Sean Connery's laconic entrance in the early moments of *Dr. No* ("Bond. James Bond.") is backed by "The James Bond Theme," a tune that subsequently signaled 007's derring-do in all future films.
- Ostinato—a phrase or motif that persistently repeats, somewhat in the manner of a vamp. The four-beat baseline that opens Henry Mancini's "Peter Gunn Theme" is an ostinato.
- Stinger—a fleeting cue often associated with sudden on-screen action.
- Bumper—a short cue often designed to take the action out (or back in) between scenes (in a film), or between commercials (on television).

- Diegetic music—that which exists in the realm inhabited by the story's characters, often heard from a radio, juke box, phonograph player or live nightclub combo. In other words, the *dramatis personae* always hear diegetic music; sometimes they even perform it.
- Non-diegetic music—that which exists as underscore shading, to enhance or serve as counterpoint to on-screen action. We viewers hear non-diegetic music, but the *dramatis personae* do not.
- "Mickey-mousing"—the act of writing an underscore cue that precisely duplicates, in terms of mood and/or syncopation, the on-screen action. It's equivalent to a drummer who needlessly hits a rim shot to punctuate a comic's on-stage joke: in both cases, considered lazy and redundant.
- Tracking—building an underscore from a library of existing cues, as opposed to composing an entirely fresh score.
- Cover—a rerecording of an original tune or theme, often (but not always) by a different musician.

Now, with that out of the way…

Most films are scored (composed) by a single individual—or sometimes a pair (or more) of collaborators—who handle everything: the main title, any necessary character themes, and all cues employed from the opening to closing credits. If the film generates a soundtrack album, that composer gets the name credit. Ergo, Elmer Bernstein wrote the score for 1955's *The Man with the Golden Arm*; he's the one credited on the resulting soundtrack album. He's also the one nominated for the Academy Award (which he lost to Alfred Newman's non-jazz score for *Love Is a Many-Splendored Thing*).

Television shows were a different animal from the beginning, because of the far greater musical burden involved. While some indefatigable and impressively creative composers—Mancini and Edwin Astley come to mind—followed the big-screen model, scoring every episode of a TV series during seasons that could last 30 weeks or more, they were rare exceptions. It was far more common for one person to help set a show's tone by writing the title theme and then scoring one or more early episodes, after which other composers would take over. The title theme (usually) was retained during the show's entire run; subsequent musicians were allowed to be creative to a point, while understanding the need to emulate the style as initially established.

On top of which, very few production companies had the luxury—or budget—to request wholly original underscores for a series that could deliver 38 episodes in a single season (as was the case with *Peter Gunn*). More typically, the first half-dozen to dozen episodes would get original underscores from one or more composers, and their various cues—for car chases, fistfights, gun battles, suspenseful skulking, romantic overtures, whatever—would establish an ever-expanding library then used to track subsequent episodes. Occasional future episodes might be partially scored with new material, if the script demanded culturally distinct or setting-specific cues. If the show proved successful enough to run for many years, specific episodes in subsequent seasons often earned entirely fresh underscores, thereby further enhancing the library of cues.

Sometimes the title theme composer also would write and record an hour or two of his own "generic" cues—as opposed to crafting one or more underscores for specific episodes—to be used as a given director saw fit.

Alternatively, some shows warranted *only* an original title theme, and otherwise were tracked almost entirely by "generic" cues taken from libraries created solely for that purpose (almost always supplied by composers and session musicians who worked anonymously). In some cases, a new series would be tracked by cues originally written for entirely different programs. Composers' and musicians' unions established strict rules, over time, regarding how such cues could and should be used, with specific percentages determining when a given composer would—or wouldn't—receive credit. (The often arcane details of such rules and contracts are beyond our purview here.)

Attribution often was spotty in the 1950s; it improved in the '60s, by which time the end credits would tell the story. "Music by Earle Hagen" means that he wrote the title theme and an original underscore (or most of it) for the episode. Shared credits are self-explanatory: "Theme by Morton Stevens" and "Music Composed and Conducted by Don B. Ray" acknowledges Stevens for the title theme, and Ray for the given episode's underscore. "Theme by Dave Grusin" with no other credit—except for a "Music Editor," "Music Supervisor" or something similar—means the episode was tracked.

The upshot: A title theme didn't necessarily indicate the quality of a given show's underscore. Some of the coolest TV show main themes are attached to programs with otherwise banal music.

The evolution of action jazz parallels the evolution of television itself, while at the same time responding (to a degree) to big-screen trends. Cross-pollination was common; unlike American film stars who turned down their noses at TV work—or TV actors who couldn't wait to abandon *their* medium, to become film stars—jazz musicians cheerfully jumped back and forth. And why not? A gig was a gig.

It's often assumed that early TV "crime jazz"—a reasonably accurate designation for the music that accompanied early dramas starring cops, sleuths and virtuous investigators from various professions—sprang from the big screen's post–World War II fascination with the scandalous characters and seamy behavior found in Hollywood's artfully moody *film noir* B pictures. It's commonly—but quite incorrectly—assumed that the atmospheric richness of most (all?) *film noir* entries was enhanced by jazz scores. For the most part, that's a fallacy.

Much as I'd love to wax poetic about the merits of (for example) 1941's *The Maltese Falcon*, 1944's *Double Indemnity* and *Laura*, 1946's *The Big Sleep* and 1947's *Out of the Past*, all have sweepingly melodramatic, string-based orchestral scores by, respectively, Adolph Deutsch, Miklós Rózsa, David Raskin, Max Steiner and Roy Webb. That said, the classic *noir* period extended to the conclusion of the 1950s, by which time jazz had indeed infiltrated the genre. The same was (and is) true of television: Plenty of otherwise nifty detective/crime shows are saddled with humdrum, plain-vanilla—and, frankly, dull—orchestral scores.

At the end of the day, of course, a label is only that. It's all great jazz—well, most of it—and well worth a listen.

Despite the degree to which action jazz blossomed on television sets and movie theater screens, for the most part (initially, at least) it was driven by the former. That informs the pages to follow, which begin with television's infancy and proceed chronologically through the evolutionary phases of network (and non-network) programming. Each chapter focuses on one or more years, and opens with significant small-screen developments, then segues to parallel big-screen activity. As British and Western European film and television companies begin to exert an influence—starting in the late 1950s—such activity also is acknowledged.

American and British coverage is intended to be comprehensive, but expediency had to intervene, with respect to the international scene, lest the result become overwhelming.

Introduction 9

As the most obvious example, an entire book could be devoted to 1960s and '70s Italian spy jazz alone. Lacking that much space, I focused on Italian entries that boast noteworthy scores and/or musicians. (Chet Baker, anyone?) Ergo, don't take it personally if I've omitted one of your favorite foreign films or TV shows, or completely "overlooked" a composer. Or two. Or three. It was a decision borne of practicality, not prejudice.

Besides which, you can't accuse me of sloth. During the four years that went into the research and writing of these two volumes, I considered 486 films from 1950 to the present day, and ultimately watched 350; each subsequently earned anywhere from a few paragraphs to several pages of discussion. The task was far more challenging on the small screen, where 750 shows were contemplated from 1947 forward; 206 ultimately made the cut, which meant watching up to half a dozen episodes of each, to discuss them in suitable detail.

That said, I'll undoubtedly get a few outraged letters wondering how the heck I *possibly* could have neglected *that* classic (American or otherwise). Or *that* masterpiece. To which I can only reply, One tries one's best. And that's why God invented second editions. Suggestions are welcome, and I can be reached at this book's companion website: screenactionjazz.com.

* * *

An apology: Spoilers are inevitable. This study isn't merely a shopping list of composer, film and/or TV series credits; it's important to specify the music's *context*, in terms of how individual cues—and an overall score—augment (or, in some cases, damage) the on-screen action. Although every effort has been made to avoid the frivolous disclosure of plot surprises, it's impossible to discuss some of the following films and TV show episodes *without* doing so. Ergo, this isn't the book to read, if you're gonna get vexed by narrative revelations. *Mea maxima culpa.*

* * *

Having now emerged at the far end of this jazz-laden journey, I can promise that the trip is intriguing, with plenty of swinging detours (and more than a few bad-note dead ends). I wasn't that sanguine going in; the topic—and the need to temper my often giddy admiration for this genre, with some balanced insight—frankly seemed overwhelming. But as often is the case with jazz, the investigative symphony eventually settled into a comfortable rhythm ... and my music library (and the groaning shelves in our small home) are all the richer for the process that led to this published result.

If the following pages similarly pique your curiosity—and correspondingly deplete *your* bank account—then I'll consider it a job well done.

Prologue:
The Naked Truth

The city's late-night mean streets were darker than a vengeful dame's soul when I hurried up the back stairs of the grimy, concrete-walled office building—my footsteps echoing the nervous thumping of my heart—and knocked timidly on the designated third-floor door. An unsuccessful attempt to decipher the faded name on the frosted glass window was interrupted by a grunt from within; I swallowed hard and opened the door in time to see a match flare from behind what appeared to be a shabby wooden desk. A cigarette sparked into life, and the waving match directed me to a wobbly slatted chair that faced the desk; as I sank into its recesses, it gave the protesting squeak of a mouse tossed into a meat grinder.

"So whaddya want?" growled a voice, with the throaty rasp of gravel crunching underfoot.

My mouth had grown dry as the fetid dust-bunnies in my pantry back home. Nothing emerged but wheezing swallows. With a phlegmy rumble that I took to be a contemptuous chuckle, the silhouetted figure moved; I heard the gargle of liquid splashing from an unseen bottle, and into a small glass that was scraped across the desk in my direction. Envisioning a tumbler that probably hadn't been washed since the city installed running water, but fearing the potential disrespect a refusal might prompt, I gamely hoisted the glass and downed the contents in a single panicked swallow. The liquid burned like the four-alarm spices Madame Cheng dumps on the kung pao chicken that I enjoy in her back-alley eatery every evening.

"Well?" my host enquired again, his outline barely silhouetted by the smoldering cigarette, his impatience slicing through the darkness like a sharpened razor dragged across an unsuspecting throat.

I finally found my voice. "I want the dope on the gumshoe who *didn't* become television's first prime-time detective."

"TV," he spat, contemptuously. "Chewing gum for the eyes."

He paused, then grunted. "But okay. Ya want the low-down, I got it."

And he proceeded to relate the following saga (his articulation, elocution and vocabulary suddenly adopting the sophistication of a university professor):

Hollywood tough-guy George Raft starred in a 1946 B-melodrama, *Mr. Ace*, as title character Eddie Ace, a sorta-kinda gangster and behind-the-scenes political mover and shaker. He's approached by society dame Margaret Wyndham Chase (Sylvia Sidney), who's willing to use any means necessary to maximize success in her run for state governor. Eddie initially refuses, scornful of a woman's place in politics. She stubbornly enters the race anyway; things go badly, but she and Eddie fall in love, and—miraculously—both decide to embrace a virtuous, honest-government campaign. Happy ending for all.

The midsummer release was modestly successful. A year later, Raft and the character were reunited for a short-lived ABC radio series titled *The Cases of Mr. Ace*; it was helmed by Jason James—a pseudonym for Jo Eisinger—who'd just won an Edgar Award for Best Radio Drama, as a scripter for *The Adventures of Sam Spade*. (Eisinger, a journalist turned film and—eventually—TV writer, is famed for scripting two of Hollywood's best-ever *film noirs*: *Gilda* and *Night and the City*. He'd win a second Edgar in 1984, for scripting an episode of HBO's *Philip Marlowe, Private Eye* ... about which, much more elsewhere.) James/Eisinger rebuilt the character, turning Eddie into a tough-talking Manhattan PI who shared his cases during weekly chats with Dr. Karen Gayle (Jeanette Nolan), a gorgeous "lady psychoanalyst" who devoured the details as essential research for her ambitious book on criminal behavior.

The radio show premiered June 25, 1947, and an enthusiastic *Billboard* review praised the "top Hollywood cast" and "top script," while also enthusing about the score: "And what music! Not an organ—a full orchestra!"[1] Despite such plaudits, the show ran only to the end of that summer, at which point Raft moved on to other projects. (Four episodes survive to this day, and are readily available online.) Movers and shakers in CBS' embryonic TV department liked the premise, so James/Eisinger was hired to shepherd the series to this new medium.[2] CBS took the adaptation seriously, fronting $300,000 for "a series of three 13-episode half-hour films [with a] budget per half-hour film given at $7,500." As a further indication of top quality, CBS planned to make the series on 35mm film, rather than the much cheaper (and early television-typical) videotape.[3] Suave Don Haggerty made the character a much more sophisticated gumshoe, who moved to Hollywood and changed his name to Eddie Drake; he became an easily recognized fixture motoring around in a distinctive, three-wheeled 1948 Davis D-2 Divan, which he dubbed "Dave." The role of gorgeous shrink Karen Gayle went to Patricia Morison.

Several months later, *Billboard* reported that CBS had completed the first five episodes of the newly christened *Cases of Eddie Drake*, and that four more were in final editing and dubbing: the remaining four of the initial 13-episode first series were to have begun filming three days earlier.[4]

Except that it didn't happen.

By the time that mid–November *Billboard* piece was published, Morison had jilted Eddie for a much more tempting lover: the stage. Cole Porter personally selected her to take the female lead role (Lilli Vanessi) in his new musical, *Kiss Me, Kate*. Rehearsals had begun immediately for a 3½-week Broadway tryout period, which anticipated the show's December 30 opening at the New Century Theater.[5]

Everybody knows what happened to *that* show.

Back at CBS, Eddie Drake was cast adrift. A minimum of 13 episodes was required to bring a series to fruition; *The Cases of Eddie Drake* was four short. What happened next remains the subject of considerable speculation: CBS shelved the series for several years, and then—at some point—somebody commissioned four more episodes, with Lynne Roberts taking over the female lead as "lady criminologist" Dr. Joan Wright. The 13-episode package *may* have aired in some big-city markets, after which the DuMont Network picked it up for a 13-week run starting March 6, 1952.

One of Patricia Morison's initial episodes survives and is readily viewable online; in all respects—acting, scripting, the witty repartee between Haggerty and Morison, and the quality afforded by the 35mm film stock—it's leagues ahead of anything else TV produced in the late 1940s.

Much too little, much too late. By then, Martin Kane had firmly established his rep as TV's first private eye, with an NBC series that debuted September 1, 1949. Had Morison hung around long enough to complete the initial set of 13 episodes, CBS easily could have debuted *The Cases of Eddie Drake* much earlier that same year.

"And dat was dat," my host concluded, reverting to his street-level argot, and noisily hawking a disgusting wad of phlegm into one corner of the office, where it landed with a wet *splat* that bespoke a pool of countless prior expectorations. After which, that corner seemed to undulate, as if occupied by something gelatinous. And alive.

"Eddie was done in by a two-timin' dame."

He lapsed into silence, and I knew that our interview was over. Muttering barely audible thanks, I rose from the chair—it gave another shrill bleat as the legs scraped against the pitted wood floor—and backed out the doorway, determined not to reveal my fear by bolting in sheer terror. But as I descended the steps back to the street, where dawn was breaking and the city was struggling to embrace another day, I knew that I hadn't gotten *quite* the full story.

True, Eddie was ill-treated by the duplicitous Patricia Morison, who had the bad taste to embrace an enormously successful career on stage, film and (yes, even) TV. But that wasn't the sole reason for the failure of his series. Despite all the money that CBS lavished on the show, one crucial element was given short shrift.

The music.

The culprits have been lost to history, but the lingering evidence revealed by that lone surviving episode is damning: Eddie's exploits are accompanied by needlessly frivolous and perky symphonic cues—probably CBS library cues—that often are at odds with on-screen events. In a word, the score is dreadful.

Martin Kane *deserved* first place, because he *had a better theme song.*

1

Audition: 1947–1956

American TV's origins were modest. Only two networks—DuMont and NBC—operated during the initial 1946/47 and 47/48 seasons, with just a handful of shows Sunday through Friday. Things expanded exponentially when ABC and CBS came on board the following year; all four networks delivered solid programming blocks from 7 to 11 p.m. each day.

After that, of course, things exploded…

The Small Screen

Barney Blake, Police Reporter became television's first mystery series, debuting April 22, 1948, but the honor seems ignominious. The *Billboard* reviewer was far from impressed by this NBC entry, noting that "if the caliber of the scripts show no improvement, [this series] will go down in history not only as the first but also the worst of its breed."[1] There's no way to gauge the accuracy of that dismissal, as none of the 13 live-to-air episodes has survived. The same is true of TV's second mystery series: ABC's similarly short-lived police drama *Stand By for Crime*, which debuted January 11, 1949. It's therefore impossible to discuss either show's theme song, although it's safe to assume that both followed the common practice of many early TV shows, with chirpy organ melodies similar to those that introduced radio mystery programs (and which sound, these days, like vapid public ice arena Muzak).

Next up—debuting the following season, on September 1, 1949—was NBC's *Martin Kane, Private Eye*. Unlike its two predecessors, this show became a hit, rotating four stars—William Gargan, Lloyd Nolan, Lee Tracy and Mark Stevens—during a run that continued for five years. The laid-back, New York–based sleuth initially enjoys a friendly relationship with cooperative Police Lt. Bender (Fred Hillebrand), but after the first season Kane adopts a Chandler-esque attitude less appreciated by subsequent law enforcement colleagues.

Charles Paul's title theme is consistent throughout; it, too, is a simple organ cue with a mildly anticipatory melody, as if shadowing somebody up a flight of stairs. It plays against a silhouette of Kane, as he fires a match and stokes his pipe. Episode underscores are unremarkable orchestral shading, with occasional reprises of the title theme. The show has a low-budget charm—with simple sets, occasionally muffed lines and plenty of stock footage—that keeps it a watchable guilty pleasure to this day.

Paul's title theme was released by MGM on a 10-inch 78 rpm disc, to little fanfare. That said, Martin Kane was the first TV private detective to have his theme subsequently covered, during the next few years, by several jazz artists: the Eddie Safranski Trio (Derby); Nelson Riddle and his Orchestra (Capitol); and guitarist Al Caiola (RCA Victor).

Sadly, America's first crime series with a strong jazz touch has been lost to the mists of time.

Hard-hitting Boston-based photojournalist Jack "Flashgun" Casey, created by author George Harmon Coxe, starred in a couple dozen *Black Mask* short stories between 1934 and '43. Casey leaped to the big screen in 1936's *Women Are Trouble* and 1937's *Meet Flash Casey*. A radio series was inevitable; it debuted in 1943 and ran on the CBS network for just over a decade. The radio series established the jazz element: During his off hours—and also when searching for tips—Casey hangs out at the Blue Note Café. Music is supplied by the house band, The Blue Note Musicians, actually a trio led by celebrated jazz pianist Teddy Wilson.[2]

The jazz touch was maintained when Casey transitioned to a CBS-TV series—*Crime Photographer*—on April 19, 1951. The hard-boiled photographer still hangs out at the Blue Note Café, sharing his adventures with Ethelbert the bartender. Guitarist Tony Mottola and his trio took over as The Blue Note Musicians; based on Mottola's other endeavors at the time, his sidemen likely were John Guarnieri (piano) and Herman Albert (bass). The trio supplies a lot of background music, and also performs the show's title theme.

The series initially starred Richard Carlyle and John Gibson, respectively, as Casey and Ethelbert; they were replaced, two months in, by Darren McGavin (the first of his many network series starring roles) and Cliff Hall. The show ultimately ran a season and a half and was broadcast live-to-air; no episodes are known to have survived. That may be tragic from the viewpoint of jazz fans, but—as McGavin once noted—perhaps not a bad thing in other respects.

"[When the show was canceled], the cast of *Crime Photographer* didn't go down fighting," he said. "They took off for the hills. It was so bad that it was never re-run, and that's saying something, when you recall the caliber of television programs in those days."[3]

* * *

Baby-boomers and their parents immediately recognize TV's first truly iconic title theme from its initial four-note fanfare, which *always* caught a listener's attention:

Dum ... dee-*DUM*-dum!

Dragnet debuted as a radio series on June 3, 1949; creator Jack Webb also starred as Los Angeles Police Department Det. Sgt. Joseph "Joe" Friday. The show broke ground with its realistic depiction of the methodical legwork required to investigate and solve crimes actually drawn from LAPD case files. ("Ladies and gentlemen: The story you are about to hear is true. Only the names have been changed, to protect the innocent.") Composer Walter Schumann's four-note fanfare blossoms into a military-esque march dominated by brass and timpani, heard in full during each episode's end credits.

All the key elements—the style, the stars and the music—were retained when the show was adapted for television, debuting December 16, 1951, as an episode of *Chesterfield Sound Off Time*. *Dragnet* became its own series a few weeks later, when its long NBC run began January 3, 1952. The television version outlasted the radio series, continuing through the summer of 1959.

Schumann handled all the music chores until his death in August 1958; he was replaced by Nathan Scott, who duly maintained the show's memorable title theme. Sadly, there's ample reason to believe that Schumann's death was accelerated by stress relating to a lawsuit regarding those unforgettable first four notes. Both the radio and TV series were going strong when the theme was covered by jazz trumpeter/bandleader Ray Anthony, in the summer of 1953. That's when film composer Miklós Rózsa's publisher "suddenly" noticed that its client had used those four notes, in precisely the same tempo and intensity, as a stinger cue called "Danger Ahead," which anticipates the restaurant gun battle toward the end of 1946's *The Killers* (95 minutes into the film, to be precise). Schumann lost the subsequent plagiarism suit; from that point forward, Rózsa's name was added to all *Dragnet*/"Danger Ahead" four-note cue sheets. Schumann retained ownership of the longer "Dragnet March" that concluded each TV episode.[4]

That controversy aside, neither the show's theme nor interior music could be considered jazz, but that wasn't true of the subsequent covers. The aforementioned Anthony, an alum of the Glenn Miller Orchestra, was first out of the gate; his smoking cover for Capitol—an arrangement credited to trombonist Dick Reynolds—blends both "Danger Ahead" and the "Dragnet March" into a sassy, big band ball of fire, highlighted by a ferociously swinging bridge that kicks off with dynamic, double-time drums, walking bass and a roar of brass. Anthony's disc entered *Billboard's* Ten Top Tunes Chart on August 29, 1953, and stayed there for 14 weeks, peaking at No. 5 for three weeks beginning October 3.

Additional jazz covers quickly came from Buddy Morrow and His Orchestra (RCA Victor); Grady Martin and the Slew Foot Five (Decca); and, in the UK, Jack Parnell and His Musicmakers (Parlophone). Novelty takeoffs were recorded by Spike Jones and His City Slickers (RCA Victor) and Stan Freberg (Capitol, a two-sider dubbed "Christmas Dragnet Part I and II"). You literally couldn't turn on the radio in late 1953 and early '54 without hearing *somebody* playing that tune. It was the first TV show theme to achieve pop radio success.

The other notable private-eye entry of 1952 was *The Cases of Eddie Drake*, the sad details of which are discussed in this book's prologue. This show's title theme is standard, radio-style orchestral melodrama; the composer is left unacknowledged.

The Lineup also began life as a popular radio series, debuting July 6, 1950, on the CBS network. The San Francisco–based crime drama partners Lt. Ben Guthrie (Bill Johnstone) with Sgt. Matt Grebb (Wally Maher), as they efficiently solve *noir*-ish cases that always conclude with a perp lineup.[5] The series continued through early 1953, and CBS revived it for television on October 1, 1954.

This new half-hour cop show had impressive technical credentials. Much like *Dragnet*, the semi-documentary series adapted its stories from San Francisco Police Department case files; that verisimilitude—along with the novelty of the Bay Area location shooting—helped make the show a hit that ran for six years. Acknowledging the setting's popularity, in syndication the show was rechristened *San Francisco Beat*: the title by which it remains best known today. Viewers appreciated the blossoming bond between Guthrie (Warner Anderson) and Grebb (Tom Tully). Over time, their clinical, *Dragnet*-style stoicism softened into an actual relationship; the show eventually settled into a style that served as a template, years later, for *The Streets of San Francisco*.

The Lineup's title theme, credited to Eddie Dunstedter, is an unadorned, mildly suspenseful melody with a repeated four-note motif. That theme and all interior music remained undistinguished during the first five seasons, much (all?) of it likely extracted from the CBS music library. Things would change during the sixth and final season, as we'll see in a subsequent chapter.

Highway Patrol warrants a brief mention, and not merely because it remains one of the most popular syndicated dramas ever produced for television. An entire generation of baby boomers grew up to star Broderick Crawford's gruff orders—"Ten-four. *Ten-four!*"—because the series was rerun for years after completing its initial four-season 1955–59 broadcast. David Rose's boldly melodramatic, march-style title theme is equally familiar to the show's many fans: An opening four-note fanfare repeats until the melody begins, at which point the volume drops beneath a foreboding voice-over announcer, and then rises again for a climactic blast of brass.

The theme isn't close to jazz, but the show's popularity prompted several mildly swinging covers, a couple of them coming from across the pond: Cyril Stapleton (Decca) and Ken Mackintosh (His Master's Voice). The Yanks finally honored their own in 1959, when Buddy Morrow included the theme on his RCA Victor album *Impact*.

* * *

Along with variety shows, situation comedies, an ever-expanding roster of Westerns—and, yes, cop and detective dramas—TV's "golden age" of the 1950s was dominated by high-profile anthology series that showcased top-flight actors, directors and writers. Most of these series began by adapting existing books, plays and even films; during later seasons, the content shifted to original scripts by heavyweight writers such as Rod Serling, Reginald Rose, Abby Mann and Paddy Chayefsky, all of whom occasionally dabbled in *noir*-ish material.

Unfortunately, the "prestige" attached to most of these series could have been subtitled "bereft of jazz."

NBC's *Kraft Television Theatre* was first out of the gate, debuting May 7, 1947. It soon was followed by *Westinghouse Studio One* (CBS; Nov. 7, 1948), *Suspense* (CBS; Jan. 6, 1949), *Robert Montgomery Presents* (NBC; Jan. 30, 1950) and roughly a dozen others.

As its title suggests, CBS' equally prestigious *Playhouse 90* expanded the format to 90 minutes during a four-season run that began October 4, 1956. A young jazz pianist/composer named Johnny Williams scored one second-season episode—"The Right Hand Man"—and garnered his first TV credit; Jerry Goldsmith scored 10 episodes during the final season. Two of his scores—"Marriage of Strangers" and "Tomorrow"—are included on the anthology album *Jerry Goldsmith: The Early Years, Volume One*. Neither can be considered jazz; both are gentle, harmonica-laden orchestral scores that blend nostalgia with Americana.

That was typical. If the surviving episodes from these various series are an indication, almost all their scores were string-laden, Hollywood-style melodrama: even when adapting stories by *noir* authors such as Raymond Chandler, Cornell Woolrich, Dashiell Hammett, Fredric Brown and others. That said, a few exceptions do exist.

CBS' *Four Star Playhouse* adopted its title from the four film celebrities—Charles Boyer, Ida Lupino, David Niven and Dick Powell—who took turns starring in all productions, during a four-season run that began September 25, 1952. The first season's second episode is noteworthy for an "original story and screen play" by Blake Edwards titled "Dante's Inferno," which introduces suave, witty Willie Dante (Powell), owner/manager of the titular swanky restaurant/nightclub, which conceals an illegal high-stakes gambling casino in a back room. The setting is late-night, often at the 2 a.m. closing hour; Dante frequently finds himself in the crosshairs of the dryly serious police Lt. Manny Waldo (Regis Toomey), with whom he exchanges snarky, Chandler-esque dialogue. The restaurant "front" features a band that entertains the crowd with some swinging dance jazz. (The underscore is strictly string-laden symphonia.) Dante proved popular enough to become *Four Star Playhouse*'s only recurring character and returned in seven more episodes during the series' run; the band in his restaurant soon yielded to an unseen solo pianist with a solid jazz touch. The character and setting clearly are prototypes for Edwards' later series, *Peter Gunn* and *Mr. Lucky*.

The syndicated series *The Star and the Story*—which ran in most markets from January 1955 through the spring of 1956—follows a similar format. Henry Fonda introduces each episode, explaining that its star has "personally selected" the story to be dramatized. One of the final episodes—"The Thin Line," based on a Fredric Brown chiller—stars David Niven as Johnny Marlin, a veteran sax/clarinet jazz musician institutionalized for having tried to kill his wife, Kathy (Joan Camden): a crime he cannot remember. The teleplay gives ample exposure to several big band jazz tunes, including one of Johnny's own platters.

Ray Anthony plays himself—and briefly demonstrates his trumpet chops—in the aptly titled "Take Five," one of the final episodes of the anthology series *Studio 57*, which debuted September 21, 1954, and ran four seasons. The story, set in the world of nightclub jazz, concerns an attractive singer whose eagerly anticipated club debut is delayed when she receives a suicide note from her boyfriend.

The Big Screen

The point can be debated, but John Huston probably deserves credit for introducing jazz to a dramatic film score.

Aside from its status as a *film noir* classic, 1950s *The Asphalt Jungle* also is Hollywood's first heist crime thriller: a subgenre soon to become a cinematic staple. The film earned a quartet of well-deserved Academy Award nominations, including one for Harold Rosson's gorgeous, shadow-laced, black-and-white cinematography. Huston and Ben Maddow based their script on W.R. Burnett's 1949 novel of the same title; the result is a lean, taut and well-acted drama of the crime-*definitely*-doesn't-pay school.

Miklós Rózsa's melodramatic "formal" score is heard only twice, as narrative bookends: a main theme behind the title credits, and a three-minute cue at the end, which adds poignant tension to the story's conclusion. The rest of the drama is bereft of music, except for twice: early on, when a diner radio plays about 40 seconds of gentle dance hall jazz supplied by an uncredited Alexander Hyde; and toward the end, when a hamburger joint jukebox delivers some energetic big band jitterbug by a similarly uncredited André Previn. It wasn't nearly enough music to warrant a soundtrack album.

(*The Asphalt Jungle* would lend its name to a 1961 TV police drama, with its own swinging jazz theme by no less than Duke Ellington: about which, more later.)

Movie studio moguls still regarded popular plays as surefire box-office winners during the early years following World War II, and that meant Tennessee Williams' *A Streetcar Named Desire* was destined for the big screen. But retaining the 1948 Pulitzer Prize-winning play's scandalous content—while satisfying blue-nosed censors and skittish Warner Bros. executives—became an ongoing battle for director Elia Kazan and Williams, who adapted his play with assistance from screenwriter Oscar Saul. In the end, the filmmakers succeeded with inference, suggestion, guile and their hope that viewers could connect some suggestive dots.

Streetcar, from 1951, also is significant as the first mainstream American film with a substantial jazz score, for which composer Alex North was Oscar-nominated (losing to

Franz Waxman's work on *A Place in the Sun*). North's role in letting the jazz genie out of the Hollywood bottle cannot be exaggerated; having his score attached to such a successful film immediately showed studio chiefs that box-office gold could be found in those jazz-laden hills.

Streetcar was the perfect vehicle for this musical uprising: not quite *noir* in the usual sense, as there's no "crime" on display, but Harry Stradling's shadow-infested, black-and-white cinematography—along with the story's moral decadence—are more than enough to qualify. With its hot, humid setting in New Orleans' French Quarter, along with its characters' slimy behavior, the narrative demands the sweltering ambiance of sultry horns and dirty saxes; North delivers them, and then some. The film's title theme opens with a fanfare of screaming, bluesy trumpet, which immediately suggests the scandalous behavior to come. Shrill strings shadow the horn, segueing suddenly to a fast-paced interlude of swinging piano, bass and drums, with brass pops accelerating the tension even further. Blanche DuBois (Vivien Leigh) has barely climbed onto the streetcar named Desire—traveling from Auriol, Miss., for an "extended visit" with her sister Stella (Kim Hunter) and her husband, Stanley (Marlon Brando)—and already audiences are revved up for the avarice and carnality to come.

North's score isn't the film's sole jazz element. Stella and Stanley live within shouting distance of the Four Deuces Café, which day and night pumps out a steady stream of Dixieland, Scott Joplin rags and jazz standards. We never enter the café, but its presence is felt in almost every scene.

Miles Davis waxed poetic on various aspects of jazz for a lengthy 1955 interview in *Down Beat* magazine, during the course of which he noted: "Do you know the best thing I've heard in a long time? Alex North's music for *A Streetcar Named Desire*. That's a wild record—especially the part Benny Carter plays. If anybody is going to be able to write for strings in the jazz idiom or something near to it, it'll be North. I'd recommend everyone hearing that music."[6]

The Capitol soundtrack album, credited to North and conductor Ray Heindorf, does not include any of the source cues emanating from the Four Deuces.

The year 1951 was also a banner year for MGM musicals, including *Show Boat*, *Royal Wedding* and the Academy Award-winning best picture, *An American in Paris*. Film historians invariably overlook another memorable title, perhaps because it was shot in monochrome by MGM's B-unit, for a modest $885,000 … or perhaps because director László Kardos' *The Strip* is a *noir* jazz musical, complete with gangsters, guns and gals of questionable repute. The film deserves recognition for an equally ambitious jazz score, particularly since it beat *Streetcar* to the box office by one month. Granted, all the jazz is played live as diegetic source cues, within a narrative context—often at full length—but that seems a minor quibble when one can watch so many sensational performances by heavyweights such as Louis Armstrong, Earl "Fatha" Hines, Jack Teagarden and Barney Bigard. (An uncredited George Stoll and Pete Rugolo supplied the unremarkable orchestral underscore elements.)

Allen Rivkin's original script opens in classic *noir* manner, with a voice-over narrator, a dead mobster, and a gorgeous dame fading fast, in a pool of her own blood. At first blush, the guilty party appears to be Stanley Maxton (Mickey Rooney), the drummer at a lively Los Angeles nightclub dubbed Fluff's Dixieland; details are revealed as the story emerges in flashback. Considerable screen time is spent in the club, starting when Fluff (William Demarest) introduces the house band: Armstrong (trumpet), Teagarden (trombone), Bigard

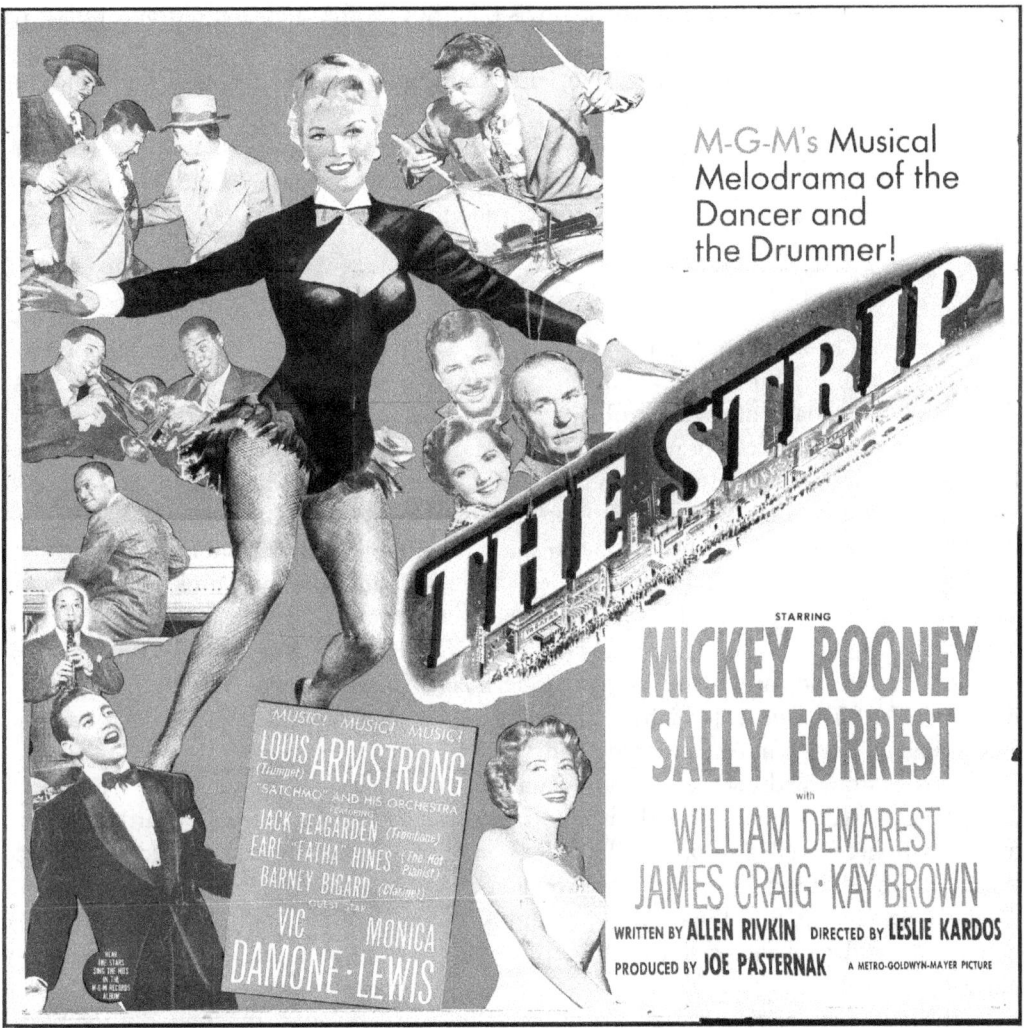

The banner proclamation notwithstanding, *The Strip* doesn't get much juice from the "melodrama" between dancer Jane Tafford and drummer Mickey Rooney (whose enthusiastic efforts are ghosted by Cozy Cole). The main attraction is the wall-to-wall music performed on camera by "Satchmo and his Orchestra," Earl "Fatha" Hines (The Hot Pianist!) and many other jazz greats.

(clarinet), Hines (piano), Lloyd Pratt (acoustic double bass, ghosted by Arvell Shaw) and Hal Stover (drums, ghosted by Cozy Cole).

After taking their bows, the band launches into an energetic reading of "Shadrack," with Armstrong doubling on trumpet and vocal; midway through the song, the musicians segue to a vibrant instrumental arrangement of "When the Saints Go Marching In." This is followed by some fast-paced dance jazz, after which Teagarden's smooth vocal introduces a rhythmic, midtempo reading of "Basin Street Blues." It's a terrific 15-minute sequence barely interrupted by plot exposition, and typical of what occurs each time the story returns to Fluff's. When the action briefly shifts to other trendy Sunset Strip nightspots of the early 1950s—Ciro's, Mocambo—the film obliges with performances by Vic Damone ("Don't

Blame Me") and singer/dancer Monica Lewis ("La Bota"), the latter backed by a pulsating Latin band.

MGM wasn't in the habit of authorizing soundtrack albums for its B unit, and *The Strip* was no exception. The closest one can get is the 1997 Rhino Movie Music anthology album, *Now You Has Jazz: Louis Armstrong at MGM*, which features all of the sextet's performances, along with several additional tracks—"Ain't Misbehavin'," "One O'Clock Jump" and "I'm Coming Virginia"—which were recorded for the film but left on the cutting-room floor.

* * *

Two years later, 1953's *The Wild One* plunged full-throttle into hard-charging bebop and Afro-Cuban rhythms: rather ironic, since early big-screen teen angst most often is associated with the nascent rock 'n' roll scores that emerged in 1955's *Blackboard Jungle* and subsequent youth-oriented dramas. But when Marlon Brando's Johnny—the original rebel without a cause—feeds the jukebox in the café/bar where much of the action takes place in *The Wild One*, he punches buttons for swinging tracks by emerging jazz talents gathered into two big band ensembles headed by (respectively) Shorty Rogers and Leith Stevens.

Unfortunately, director Laslo Benedek's modest B-flick initially took the blame for kick-starting the notion that jazz was the "ideal" genre for films that dealt with amoral and illicit behavior, a view summed up deliciously by K.C. Spence: "A plethora of films alloyed psychological friction and neurosis with modern jazz. The zenith may have been reached in 1953 with *The Wild One* ... [which] depicted youths as vagabond bikers, spoiling for a fight, disrupting a quiet town. And enjoying Shorty Rogers music."[7]

Stevens initially drew the scoring assignment, but Brando—although only a few years into his big-screen career—already was calling some shots. "Marlon had heard an album of Shorty Rogers' small group," recalled trombonist Milt Bernhart. "He wanted it as source music, [so] everything that came from the jukebox was by Shorty. Because of that [film], Shelly [Manne], me, Bud [Shank], Pete Candoli, Conrad Gozzo, and anybody who could play bebop and read music started to get calls on motion pictures. *The Wild One* really broke the ice."[8]

The film opens as cinematographer Hal Mohr focuses on an empty road, Brando heard in voice-over while Johnny confesses that he doesn't quite understand how matters got out of hand that day; his regretful tone is emphasized by a slow, melancholic blend of sax, flute and harp (a tune appropriately titled "Bewildered," on the soundtrack album). As Brando's confession concludes, Stevens abruptly shifts to an orchestral arrangement of the pounding title theme, with its insistent 2-2-2-2-3 motif repeated by urgent, angry horns. Brando and his fellow bikers burst onto the screen, Stevens' frenetic melody suggesting the disruption they're about to provoke.

Johnny immediately saunters up to the café/bar's jukebox, punches a button, and is rewarded with an uptempo ballad ("Windswept") that opens with 4-3 horn riffs before settling into a smoldering romantic melody. The juke is in continuous use during most of the film, cranking out one boisterous jazz track after another: whether the action takes place inside the café/bar, or on the street immediately outside the establishment.

Most of the arrangements on the Decca soundtrack album are significantly different than what is heard in the film, and Bill Perkins' tenor sax work is particularly lovely in this handling of "Blues for Brando." Shorty Rogers and his orchestra delivered their own concurrent release on RCA Victor, with yet again different versions of the various tunes.

This also was the year that Hollywood cemented the relationship between jazz and tough-talking private detectives.

By this point, 34-year-old ex-Army Air Corps flight instructor-turned-author Mickey Spillane had produced seven novels starring *very*-hard-boiled private detective Mike Hammer. Spillane's notoriously violent creation first hit the big screen in director/scripter Harry Essex's fitfully entertaining adaptation of *I, the Jury*. The film's strongest asset is its richly atmospheric look: late-night dark shadows, foreboding long shots and unsettlingly tight close-ups, all courtesy of veteran *noir* cinematographer John Alton. Too bad, then, that star Biff Elliott is such a disappointment as Hammer; his bearing and mush-mouthed line deliveries make Mike look and sound like a dim-bulb palooka who couldn't tie his own shoes, let alone solve a complicated murder mystery.

Although much of Franz Waxman's score is traditional symphonic melodrama, he supplies distinct jazz themes for three of the women who take up Hammer's time. (His loyal secretary—Velda, played with spunk by Margaret Sheridan—doesn't get a theme of her own. Waxman's jazz cues are reserved for the "bad girls," once again linking jazz with vice.) The first, a forlorn, bluesy clarinet cue, is introduced during an achingly sad encounter when Mike attempts to comfort reformed junkie Myrna (Frances Osborne). The mood is completely different when Hammer later quizzes the nymphomaniacal Mary Bellamy (Dran Hamilton); unsettling piano and accordion riffs back a somber muted trumpet melody against a slow and deliberate 4/4 beat, as she seductively evades his queries. The most ambitious cue is reserved for Charlotte Manning (Peggie Castle), the psychoanalyst who helped get Myrna straight, and who soon proves to be connected to all the other suspects. Her theme, once again via a bluesy solo clarinet, manages to sound romantic, mysterious and a bit foreboding.

The film didn't produce a soundtrack album *per se*, but Waxman included these three primary cues—in slightly reworked arrangements that enhance their jazz elements—on a Decca LP that features his score for 1956's *Crime in the Streets*.

Spillane also was involved with 1954's *Ring of Fear*, a truly dreadful attempt to turn a circus documentary into a *noir* thriller. It warrants mention solely because the score incorporates two jazz cues that pianist/composer/band leader Stan Purdy had written and performed (with his orchestra) for a vinyl "story album" titled *Mickey Spillane's Mike Hammer*, which featured the author narrating an original Hammer tale. Spillane actually co-stars in *Ring of Fear*, playing himself, as an amateur detective trying to determine the cause of various "accidents" designed to sabotage the Clyde Beatty Circus.

That same year, having dipped his toes in the jazz pool with *The Wild One*, Leith Stevens embraced the genre with a vengeance, with a solid jazz score for the luridly titled *Private Hell 36*.

Unfortunately, hardly anybody noticed.

This low-budget *noir* effort is helmed by Don Siegel, soon to impress sci-fi fans with his solid handling of *Invasion of the Body Snatchers*. *Private Hell 36* is co-written by star Ida Lupino; she plays Lilli, a fading nightclub singer who catches the attention of reckless LAPD cop Cal (Steve Cochran). He happens upon a pharmacy robbery that yields a $50 bill known to have been part of a $300,000 heist in New York, which resulted in the death of a guard. With Lilli's help, Cal and his partner Jack (Howard Duff) eventually track down the killer, who perishes during a car chase. They pocket what's left of the money, rather than turning it in; all the elements now are in place for the sort of grim climax destined for the morally bankrupt characters in *film noirs*.

Private Hell 36 doesn't unfold to pervasive symphonic backing. Instead, Stevens' score emerges as diegetic cues heard on car and apartment radios, or the jukebox at the club where Lilli performs. As such, this music gets louder or quieter as the characters move closer or further away from it, and—although the core theme repeats several times throughout the film—we never hear more than brief snatches in any given scene.

The Coral soundtrack album is an entirely different experience: eight tracks and 26 minutes of solid ensemble jazz that ranges from savage, Afro-Cuban bop to warmer, West Coast "cool" themes.

Alfred Hitchcock's *Rear Window*, also released in 1954, often gets overlooked during discussions of *noir* thrillers. That's puzzling; John Michael Hayes' enthralling script is a faithful adaptation/expansion of "It Had to Be Murder," a 1942 short story by famed crime author Cornell Woolrich (under the pseudonym William Irish). The narrative certainly possesses the essential *noir* elements, given that the protagonist—photojournalist L.B. "Jeff" Jeffries (James Stewart)—grows increasingly convinced that one of his neighbors has murdered his wife ... *and* chopped her up into easily transportable pieces (a rather grim scenario for its time!).

The title credits are cleverly superimposed over the rising blinds of the large, triple-paned picture window through which Jeff can observe everybody in his residential complex; composer Franz Waxman spots this sequence with a lively, Gershwin-esque rhapsody of orchestral chamber jazz, opening with uptempo timpani and expanding as a cheerful clarinet rises above celesta riffs and swinging, bluesy strings. The melody sets a buoyant mood; fluttering brass and reeds even leave space for the counterpoint *meowing* of a cat seen running up a flight of concrete stairs. The lengthy cue continues as Robert Burks' camera slowly pans along all of the complex's other open windows on this sweltering, 94-degree morning, while the various residents begin their day. One of those individuals, known only as "the composer," resides in a studio apartment with even larger windows; his grand piano becomes the source for many of the film's subsequent diegetic cues, as he struggles to compose a theme that ultimately takes shape as "Lisa." This cue is deliberately named after Jeff's girlfriend (Grace Kelly) and used by Hitchcock—in various arrangements and instrumental configurations—to further the story's suspense.

A bar across the street—barely visible through a walkway between two of the apartment buildings—generates additional diegetic cues, employed for a more sinister tone, as the film nears its final, fateful climax. We hear an uptempo piano/clarinet/vibes combo swinger—dubbed "Jukebox No. 6" by Waxman—followed by a jump-jazz arrangement of Livingston/Evans' "Red Garters." The studio-framed composer, meanwhile, has brought in a quartet of friends—guitar, harmonica, clarinet and trumpet—and they launch into a fully fleshed rendition of "Lisa," just as the actual Lisa is caught by the suspected killer.

Waxman's popularity notwithstanding, no soundtrack album was produced, although a sassy, full-length reading of "Juke Box No. 6" and the finished arrangement of "Lisa" have appeared on a few anthologies of music from Hitchcock films. The most comprehensive sampling of *Rear Window*'s score is a swinging, four-movement suite—"Prelude," "Rhumba," "Ballet" and "Finale"—on the 1990 compilation album *Hitchcock: Master of Mayhem*.

* * *

Hard-boiled movie dicks don't come much meaner, or crime thrillers more savagely *noir*, than director Robert Aldrich's muscular 1955 adaptation of Mickey Spillane's *Kiss Me Deadly*. The film has become something of a *noir* classic, primarily because of Ernest

Laszlo's idiosyncratic cinematography: cockeyed camera angles and ominous shadows that suit a doom-laden storyline straight out of Dante's *Inferno*. A.I. Bezzerides based his screenplay only loosely on the sixth Mike Hammer adventure, while turning the PI into a unapologetic sadist played with gusto by Ralph Meeker, who grins enthusiastically every time he savagely bitch-slaps an uncooperative suspect. Everything about the film is disorienting, starting with the title credits ... which unspool *backwards*.

The case begins with a barbarous death that points Hammer in the direction of a crime boss appropriately named Carl Evello (Paul Stewart); a sinister doctor (Albert Dekker); the waif-like Lily (Gaby Rodgers); and plenty of thugs and come-hither molls. They're all chasing after what Mike's secretary Velda (Maxine Cooper) calls "the great whatzit": a mysterious, lead-lined box that feels warm to the touch. The story builds to a frenzied, apocalyptic finale; when that Pandora's Box finally is opened, it symbolically sends the remaining baddies straight to hell. Quietly conservative, mid–1950s moviegoers must've choked on their popcorn.

Jazz emerges solely as source music. When Hammer stops to give a ride to a terrified young woman, his car radio plays Nat King Cole's "I'd Rather Have the Blues (Than What I've Got)." Later, as the morose detective takes comfort in whiskey shots at a favorite nightclub, the song is repeated by the chanteuse (Mady Comfort) who fronts the club's jazz combo. Given the maelstrom into which Hammer has been dragged, the symbolism is hard to miss. The film didn't generate a soundtrack album, but—decades later—Frank De Vol's darkly melodramatic orchestral title theme was included in anthology collections such as *Crime Scene USA*.

De Vol also scored 1955's *The Big Knife*, which—although identified as a *noir* by numerous film historians—barely qualifies; it's more accurately a cynical drama about Hollywood's sordid underbelly, with hints of infidelity, blackmail, betrayal and a veiled suggestion of murder. Director Robert Aldrich's insufferably talky (read: boring) film betrays its origins as an adaptation of Clifford Odets' 1949 Broadway play, with little to open up the action. Most of the film takes place in a single living room set.

Successful actor Charlie Castle (Jack Palance) has grown weary of the laughably melodramatic—but popular—films that he makes for autocratic studio boss Stanley Shriner Hoff (Rod Steiger). Charlie would prefer not to renew his contract, but Hoff and his right-hand man Smiley Coy (Wendell Corey) threaten him with a trump card: knowledge of a hit-and-run accident, with Charlie behind the wheel, that killed a child. The situation becomes more combustible when would-be starlet Dixie (Shelley Winters), tired of being treated by Hoff as little more than a prostitute, threatens to reveal the sordid truth; she was in the car with Charlie that fateful night. Smiley blandly proposes they "solve" this problem by involving Charlie in a scheme to kill Dixie (!), which finally pushes the actor into a drastic act that neither Aldrich nor Palance can make the slightest bit credible.

De Vol's standard-issue symphonic score is as overwrought as Steiger's ludicrous performance, but the film also employs occasional jazz source cues. The first occurs when Charlie is visited by Connie (Jean Hagen), the slutty wife of his best friend, who lustfully throws herself at him while a pair of big band jazz swingers play on his phonograph. The second tune climaxes with a screaming trumpet when the smug Connie, having successfully aroused Charlie's lust, heads upstairs to the bedroom.

Charlie's discovery that a drunken Dixie is becoming "incautious" comes a bit later, when a neighbor throws a noisy party that features plenty of big band swing. Finally, Eileen Wilson's sultry rendition of a mambo titled "Two's a Crowd" is heard when Charlie invites

Dixie over, hoping to persuade her into more discreet behavior; the party music shifts to some fast jazz when she arrives. When Smiley returns the next day, to calmly insist that Dixie "has to go," Charlie's phonograph plays a big band tune ironically dubbed "That's Love, That's Love," with Eddie De Marlo handling the vocal.

The film didn't generate a soundtrack album *per se*, but Columbia did release a gatefold "double pack" set of twin 45s.

Elsewhere in Hollywood, most workaholics would have been satisfied with one hit series, but Jack Webb was far from ordinary. Writing, producing, starring in—and occasionally directing—the weekly radio *and* TV versions of *Dragnet* apparently hadn't kept him busy enough; back in 1951, he indulged his passion for Dixieland jazz by headlining a second radio series, *Pete Kelly's Blues*. The setting is Kansas City in the 1920s; Webb stars as cornet player/bandleader Pete Kelly, who with his "Big Seven" combo is the featured act at a basement speakeasy. The stories find Kelly mixed up with gangsters, bent cops, forlorn dames and other folks of questionable virtue: wafer-thin plots that are merely an excuse for Kelly and the Big Seven to play lots of music. Each episode features at least two numbers by the combo, with famed Dixieland trumpet player Dick Cathcart ghosting Webb's performances.

In 1955, the industry respect resulting from *Dragnet* enabled Webb to mount a big-screen adaptation of *Pete Kelly's Blues*. The essential details are identical; the setting is 1927 Kansas City, where Webb's Pete Kelly and his Big Seven are the house band at 17 Cherry Street. The modest narrative again is mostly an excuse for plenty of music, and the film is an early landmark of great combo performances—not all of it Dixieland—and memorable jazz vocals by co-stars Ella Fitzgerald and Peggy Lee.

The film's soundtrack is an intriguing mix. The underscore is by Ray Heindorf and the Warner Bros. Orchestra: mostly standard symphonic texturing. But Heindorf also wrote the bluesy title theme, which debuts over the opening credits and is heard numerous times throughout the film, most notably as a cheerful vocal by Fitzgerald. The soundtrack's primary attractions are the numerous club performances—and one studio recording session—by Kelly and his Big Seven.

The film generated several albums: *Music from Jack Webb's Pete Kelly's Blues* (Columbia), an entirely instrumental affair with four tracks by Ray Heindorf and the Warner Bros. Orchestra, and the remaining eight by Matty Matlock and his Jazz Band (as the ersatz Pete Kelly and his Big Seven); *Pete Kelly's Blues* (RCA Victor), which blends some of Webb's narration with combo versions of the same tunes; and *Songs from Pete Kelly's Blues* (Decca), which showcases Lee and Fitzgerald.

(Webb still wasn't finished with *Pete Kelly's Blues*; the radio show-turned-movie would return one more time, as a short-lived 1959 TV series.)

All of which brings us to *The Man with the Golden Arm*.

Elmer Bernstein was hired to score this 1955 drama a mere four years into his Hollywood career. Director Otto Preminger already had stirred up trouble with 1953's sexually candid *The Moon Is Blue*, bravely—and successfully—released without the era's all-important Motion Picture Production Code Seal of Approval. No doubt emboldened by this, Preminger went looking for fresh controversy. He found it in Nelson Algren's 1949 novel, which depicts the downward spiral of World War II veteran-turned-illicit card dealer "Frankie Machine," with emphasis on his addiction to morphine. The film script changed the drug to heroin, but otherwise left the narrative's core beats in place.

Bernstein smelled opportunity.

"I went to the Preminger," he recalled, years later, "and said 'I have a kind of odd idea about what I want to do with this score.' He said, 'What is it?' I said, 'Well, this guy wants to be a jazz drummer. I think this should be a jazz-driven score.' He said, 'That's what you're here for. If you think that's what you want to do, do it.' So I went ahead and did it."[9]

Bernstein didn't stint with personnel. In one scene, when a jittery Frankie (Frank Sinatra) stumbles into an audition hall, he hears—and we see—Shorty Rogers and his Giants: Pete Candoli (trumpet/flugelhorn); Frank Rosolino and Milt Bernhart (trombones); Bob Cooper, Jimmy Giuffre, Bill Holman and Bud Shank (reeds); Ralph Peña (double bass); and Shelly Manne (drums).

Armed with that crew and many other jazz cats, Bernstein delivered the opening salvo in what would become jazz's transformational influence on the entire concept of film scoring. It's impossible to overstate Bernstein's impact; his work on *Golden Arm* was a game-changer.

Not that Bernstein had any notion of that.

In addition to providing the title credits sequence for *The Man with the Golden Arm*, graphic artist Saul Bass also designed the arresting poster art. His four-decade career was highlighted by equally imaginative title sequences for films such as *Around the World in Eighty Days*, *Vertigo*, *Anatomy of a Murder*, *Psycho*, *Walk on the Wild Side* and *It's a Mad, Mad, Mad, Mad World*.

"I had *no* idea," he admitted, decades later, "when I did *The Man with the Golden Arm*, that it was a ground-breaking score that was going to create the fuss it created."[10]

Theater audiences knew something was up immediately, as Bernstein's propulsive, exhilarating main theme literally explodes, in a wave of sinister strings and nervous horn riffs, against title designer Saul Bass' unsettling opening credits: stark white bars and a distorted white arm, along with white text against a coal-black screen. Bernstein's theme would become an obligatory part of countless crime jazz and *noir* soundtrack compilations over ensuing decades, and today remains a genre standard. But this melody is mere prelude to a score that exhibits as vibrant a presence as any other character in the story. This becomes clear as echoes of the title theme build to jangly, jazzy intensity when poor Frankie finally succumbs to temptation. Horns blare in pulse-beat syncopation when the neighborhood pusher removes drug paraphernalia from a drawer and places each item on top of the bureau: spoon (*blaaaaat!*), needle (*blaaaaaaaaat!!!*) and so forth. Rolling piano chords build to a crescendo as the needle slides into Frankie's arm—thankfully, off camera—and then ... release.

The soundtrack album proved unexpectedly popular, spending 16 weeks on *Billboard's* Top Pop Albums chart; Bernstein's single also was a hit, spending 13 weeks on the Hot 100 chart. Cover versions of the title theme also performed well, in some cases better than Bernstein's original (and *there's* the definition of a mixed blessing).

But such success was somewhat pyrrhic. The modest presence of jazz in the scores for *A Streetcar Named Desire*, *The Wild One* and *Private Hell 36* already had prompted viewers (and listeners) to associate this music form with crime and unsavory characters, and now jazz had the added burden of being linked with drug abuse. Small wonder, then, that churchgoing folks still regarded jazz as "the devil's music."

* * *

The box-office success of *The Wild One* and *Blackboard Jungle* prompted a wave of films about juvenile delinquents and teen gangs, most of which were low-rent drive-in junk. But *Crime in the Streets* boasts a fine pedigree: Reginald Rose's script began life as an episode of ABC's anthology series, *The Elgin Hour*, which starred John Cassavetes and was broadcast on March 8, 1955. When Allied Artists decided to expand the teleplay into a 1956 feature film, director Don Siegel staged all the action within a huge studio set built to encompass the story's locale: a once-bucolic New York City neighborhood now in thrall to the Hornets, a street gang led by hot-tempered Frankie Dane (Cassavetes). The film opens on a bloody rumble between the Hornets and a rival gang, after which Frankie's upstairs neighbor, Mr. McAllister (Malcolm Atterbury), tells the police that he saw one of the Hornets with a zip gun. The boy is arrested, which enrages Frankie; he plots to kill McAllister, with the aid of fellow gang members Lou Macklin (Mark Rydell) and Angelo "Baby" Gioia (Sal Mineo).

Franz Waxman delivered a taut, exciting score that at times sounds very much like George Gershwin's symphonic jazz rhapsodies.

"Whenever my father was asked which of his film scores were his favorites, he did not always give the same answer," noted John W. Waxman, decades later. "Most often his first choice would be either *Rebecca*, and sometimes *Sunset Boulevard* or *Taras Bulba*, but *Crime in the Streets* was always his second choice, because this score allowed him to bring forth his interest and background in jazz. It gave him the opportunity to write contemporary jazz much in the mold of Ellington."[11]

The Decca soundtrack album orchestrates Waxman's score into three mini-suites, although their titles are deceptive. "The Plot" actually is (mostly) the frantic title credits music heard over the street rumble, whereas "The Crime"—a veritable jazz symphony, at more than 13 minutes—gathers all the nervous cues heard as the seething Frankie plans his revenge against McAllister. "The Celebration," finally, is the jaunty rock 'n' roll number heard during a street dance.

Several of the films discussed in these pages were condemned by the Roman Catholic National Legion of Decency—including *Rififi*, *From Russia with Love* and *The Pawnbroker*, all discussed elsewhere—but none provoked the pulpit-fulminating fire and brimstone that greeted *Baby Doll*, released in December 1956. Director Elia Kazan's salacious slice of Southern gothic was notorious even before its arrival, thanks to a titillating New York City promotional billboard that featured the image of scantily dressed star Carroll Baker stretched out in a ramshackle crib, sucking her thumb.

Tennessee Williams expanded the story from his 1946 one-act play, *27 Wagons Full of Cotton*, which the playwright softened somewhat for the big screen. The central figure is Mississippi Delta cotton gin owner Archie Lee Meighan (Karl Malden), a middle-aged alcoholic at the brink of financial ruin, thanks to the recent arrival of Sicilian Silva Vacarro (Eli Wallach), whose modern "cotton syndicate" has put many of the local, family-run operations out of business. As the story begins, Archie Lee's efforts to restore his shambling wreck of a mansion—dubbed Fox Tail—have been halted by his crumbling assets: a situation so critical that all of the furniture has just been repossessed … except for that crib in the nursery. Viewing the revival of his business as the only means of salvation, Archie Lee sneaks out one night and sets fire to Vacarro's gin, burning the structure to the ground. Convinced of Archie Lee's guilt, but unable to prove it, the Sicilian orchestrates a revenge scheme that leaves him alone with Archie Lee's much younger, white trash wife (Baker) for an entire afternoon.

This combustible decadence demanded just the right musical touch; Kazan found it in Kenyon Hopkins, then midway through a 10-year stint as chief composer and arranger at New York's Radio City Music Hall, having earlier worked with conductors and bandleaders such as Paul Whiteman, Andre Kostelanetz and Raymond Paige.[12] Hopkins demonstrated a flair for the seamy, down-and-dirty jazz that so perfectly suggests amorality and licentious behavior, while also evoking the genre's very strong regional American roots. (Hopkins' obscurity, at this late date, is deplorable; many of his film and TV assignments are discussed in subsequent pages, their soundtrack albums in desperate need of revival and greater acknowledgment.)

Hopkins hits the perfect blend of smoky jazz and florid burlesque with the title credits theme; it opens with the sort of orchestral flourish quite common for Hollywood melodramas, but then shifts to saucy, lazy blues highlighted by a decadent, five-note sax motif, backed by equally debauched strings. Doleful sax introduces the decrepit shell of Fox Tail, with impish harmonica licks anticipating the infantile backbiting that erupts between Archie Lee and Baby Doll.

Hopkins' score, conducted by Ray Heindorf and performed by the Warner Bros. Orchestra, was released by Columbia.

Elsewhere in the World…

By the early 1950s, American film director Jules Dassin had become known for several of Hollywood's better *film noir* entries, notably *The Naked City* (later to become a TV series), *Thieves' Highway* and *Night and the City*. This promising career evaporated when he was blacklisted by the House Committee on Un-American Activities. How ironic, then, that Dassin wound up making the best film of his career—the classic for which he remains deservedly famous—after relocating to Europe.

Rififi (1955) is recognized as one of the finest *noir* crime dramas the genre produced, celebrated in great part because of its meticulous depiction of the heist planned and executed by the story's four protagonists: a nail-biting sequence that runs 25 minutes without dialog or music. The narrative is adapted from French novelist Auguste Le Breton's *Du rififi chez les hommes*; Dassin made the film on a modest budget, on location throughout Paris, and without any star-caliber players.

The story begins as career gangster Tony "le Stéphanois" (Jean Servais) returns to his old neighborhood after serving a five-year prison stretch. He immediately suggests the ambitious burglary of a high-end jewelry shop on the Rue de Rivoli. The caper includes long-time colleagues Jo "le Suédois" (Carl Möhner) and Mario Ferrati (Robert Manuel); they import Italian safecracker César "le Melanais" (Dassin, taking the part under the acting pseudonym Perlo Vita). The heist is executed flawlessly—with particular admiration reserved for the clever use of an umbrella—but César later gives a stolen ring to his lover, and … well … things turn ugly very quickly.

Georges Auric's string-oriented underscore is largely the classical-influenced stuff of Hollywood melodrama. But much of the story's action takes place within a nightclub called *L'Âge d'Or*, allowing numerous opportunities for tasty jazz by the club's stage combo. Dassin even grants the band an after-hours "solo" scene, as a sinuous dancer rehearses her moves by wordlessly coaxing musical accompaniment from, in turn, the players on bass, piano, guitar, vibes and muted trumpet. The erotic sequence has absolutely nothing to do with the rest of the story, but it's quite enchanting.

No soundtrack album appeared. The closest one can get is the 2001 Slovak Radio Symphony Orchestra rerecording, *The Classic Film Music of Georges Auric, Volume 4*; it features four lengthy tracks, including the main title, with its core melody introduced via a lazy clarinet line. But these are the orchestral cues; none of the club jazz is present (which suggests that Auric had nothing to do with the combo stuff).

France's next *noirish* heist drama was much more ambitious with its use of jazz. Thanks to the innovative techniques employed in 1956's engaging, character-driven *Bob le Flambeur*, director Jean-Pierre Melville (a *nom de film* adopted by Jean-Pierre Grumbach) often is credited with jump-starting the nascent French New Wave movement. Not one to be constrained by a low budget, Melville turned this potential shortcoming into a virtue, coaxing authentic performances from unknown actors, and giving cinematographers Maurice Blettery and Henri Decaë free rein to make a character out of Paris' bustling Montmartre district. Lacking expensive equipment, Melville achieved tracking shots by famously using a hand-held camera on a delivery bike.[13]

The story follows the title character, Bob Montagné (Roger Duchesne), an aging but still quite suave gambler who strolls with relaxed familiarity through Montmartre's bars, cafés, restaurants and gaming dens. Despite Bob's desire to remain legit after having served a prison term years earlier, he can't resist a passing comment made by a friend who works as a croupier at the nearby Deauville Casino, where—on Grand Prix Day—the establishment is known to have as much as 800 million francs in its safe. Bob assembles and rehearses a crew with meticulous care; unfortunately, one of them spills the beans and alerts the police. Everything builds to a climax at the casino, where an unexpected twist lends delicious irony to the story's conclusion.

The music was handled by French pianist, band leader and producer Eddie Barclay, who collaborated on the score with French trumpeter and orchestra leader Jo Boyer. The resulting score is a blend of orchestral texturing and jazz, particularly the swinging big band cues that emanate as source music from radios in bars, restaurants, cars and apartments. Barclay and Boyer also get heavy use from the film's signature cue—"Thème de Bob"—which is heard first, via Boyer's expressive trumpet solo, over the title credits. Variations on this theme subsequently appear at least a dozen times, often with different instrumentation (and Benny Waters' solos on alto sax and clarinet). Some of the action takes place in a jazz club, where a septet delivers several swing numbers and bossa nova tunes. Melville also employs music cleverly in spots. Toward the end of the film, one character strolls past a series of restaurants, one after another; the music shifts to reflect the ethnicity and ambiance of each establishment in turn. It's a simple but remarkably effective musical trick, which we'll encounter again in other films.

Despite its subsequent fame and reasonably busy score, *Bob le Flambeur* never produced a soundtrack album. And even though it's one of the 12 films highlighted in Jazz on Film's 2013 *The New Wave* box set, *Bob le Flambeur* is represented by only one track: the aforementioned "Thème de Bob."

2

Dreamsville: 1957–1958

Everything changed overnight, thanks to a jazz pianist/arranger who worked with the reformed Glenn Miller Orchestra following his World War II service, and who in 1952 became an extremely busy member of the Universal Pictures music department, where he was affectionately known as "Hank."

But that didn't happen until September 22, 1958.

The Small Screen

Few TV detectives have been reinvented more than Richard Diamond. The character debuted April 24, 1949, on a popular NBC radio series that continued through the summer of 1953. It was created by Blake Edwards: the first of his many suave, detective-type heroes. He initially envisioned Diamond as an ex-OSS agent who, following the conclusion of World War II, settled in New York City and hired himself out as a private gumshoe. Star Dick Powell added an intriguing touch by making Diamond a pianist and crooner, and he often closed an episode by warbling a song to girlfriend Helen (Virginia Gregg).[1]

Diamond—played by Don Taylor—made his TV debut on November 22, 1956, in "Double Cross," an episode of the syndicated anthology series *Chevron Hall of Stars*. Edwards then sold the character as a series; CBS debuted *Richard Diamond, Private Detective* on July 1, 1957, with the lead role going to David Janssen. The show's opening is pure *noir*: A shadowy figure walks down a darkened street and slowly approaches the camera, pausing to light a cigarette that reveals Janssen's ruggedly handsome face. Composer Frank De Vol's title theme and interior scores are typical of detective shows during this period: suspenseful but otherwise unremarkable string-laden orchestral cues … but this would change. (Stay tuned.)

Janssen's Diamond shared the investigative scene with Frank Lovejoy's lone wolf "good guy for hire," who took his time getting featured in a weekly series titled *Meet McGraw*. That suited the character's laid-back personality: He isn't really an official private detective, but merely a guy with an endless supply of friends in trouble. Lovejoy debuted the character—whose first name never is revealed—in a February 1954 episode of CBS' *Four Star Playhouse*, then reprised the role a year later, in a March 1955 episode of CBS' *Stage 7* anthology series. McGraw finally found a regular home on NBC, for a single season that began July 2, 1957.

The show's underscores are built entirely from library cues, but the title theme deserves mention: a bluesy, instrumental arrangement of the Harold Arlen/Johnny Mercer classic, "One for My Baby (and One More for the Road)." Although almost certainly a library cue as well—no music credit is given—the big band reading is a smooth slice of lonesome, melancholy jazz that aptly complements Lovejoy's portrayal of the character.

2. Dreamsville: 1957–1958

McGraw is calm and laid-back: characteristics that certainly can't be applied to Lee Marvin's Sgt. Frank Ballinger. Few early crime shows were more violent than NBC's *M Squad*, which debuted in a hail of bullets on September 20, 1957. The show made a star of gravel-voiced Marvin, whose Ballinger heads the eponymous Chicago plainclothes detective team—the "M" doesn't seem to stand for anything—that battles various organized crime factions. The tone is pure *noir*, from the late-night settings and shadowy cinematography, to Marvin's clipped, clinical and Chandler-esque narration: a grim alternative to Jack Webb's dry, by-the-book voice-overs in *Dragnet*.

The show's underscores are built from standard-issue library cues, although music director Stanley Wilson wrote suitably ominous title and end credit themes, the latter with a vaguely military vibe. And so matters remained throughout the first season ... but by the time summer reruns rolled around, change was in the air. (Stay tuned.)

Meanwhile, NBC resurrected a detecting couple who had become quite popular on the big screen. William Powell and Myrna Loy co-starred in six *Thin Man* movies between 1934 and '47 (although each successive entry moved further afield from the Dashiell Hammett novel on which the first one was based). An equally well-liked radio series ran from 1941 to '50, and a television adaptation was inevitable. The series debuted on September 20, 1957; the teaming of Peter Lawford, Phyllis Kirk—and, of course, Asta the dog—proved as larkishly entertaining as the films.

Johnny Green penned an appropriately light-hearted orchestral theme for the series' first season. The bubbly cue sounds like something that might have introduced *Leave It to Beaver* or *My Three Sons*: leagues removed from what would be expected of a mystery show, even one with such a droll tone. No matter: It wouldn't last. (Stay tuned.)

Falling just slightly behind what opened every episode of *Dragnet*, the second-most famous 1950s four-note fanfare belongs to the title theme for *Perry Mason*. The first two notes, sustained on unison strings, are heard as Erle Stanley Gardner's famous attorney—memorably played by Raymond Burr—walks toward a courtroom bench; the second note fades as the judge hands Mason some paperwork. The show's title materializes, followed by a startling orchestral explosion of the final two notes. There's a pause as Mason examines the file; he smiles thinly as the fanfare repeats, this time with a three-note epitaph. Another pause, then the remaining credits appear against some saucy R&B. A longer 60-second arrangement, with additional strings and a lot of rolling piano, closes each episode over the end credits.

Composer Fred Steiner had a long and enormously successful television career that stretched into the early 1990s, but that 40-second cue remains his most memorable undertaking.

"[CBS music director] Lud Luskin assigned me to it," Steiner recalled, decades later. "A lot of people have asked how I came up with that theme, and I really don't know. I've found some old sketches for the *Perry Mason* theme—some old pencil sketches—and they have no resemblance to what I finally came up with. It's a complete mystery to me. The original title was 'Park Avenue Beat.' I conceived of Perry Mason as this very sophisticated lawyer—eats at the best restaurants, tailor-made suits, and so on—and yet, at the same time, he's mixed in with these underworld bad guys, murder and crime, so the underlying beat is R&B, for the crazy reason that, in those days, jazz and R&B always were associated with crime. So it's kind of a piece of symphonic R&B; that's why it's called 'Park Avenue Beat.'"[2]

Aside from that stimulating weekly introduction, most of the episodes—during a 10-year run that concluded in September 1966—relied on undistinguished orchestral library cues for their underscores. But Steiner's title theme prompted a few tasty jazz covers: by Warren Barker's jazz ensemble, for the anthology album *Top Television Themes* (Warner Bros.); the UK's Tony Hatch Orchestra (Pye); and Johnny Gregory and his orchestra (Fontana).

Gardner's beloved legal eagle later returned to television for a single 1973–74 season, with Monte Markham starring as *The New Perry Mason*; Burr consented to a run of TV films between 1985 and '95, under the umbrella heading *Perry Mason Returns*. Steiner's title theme was retained, but all music was otherwise unremarkable.

* * *

In an alternate universe, Mike Hammer's television debut would have taken place in 1954, on the strength of a half-hour pilot episode directed and scripted by Blake Edwards, with Brian Keith starring as the often-snarling title character. But this version failed to sell in our universe—becoming *quite* obscure over time—and four years passed before Darren McGavin assumed the role in the syndicated series *Mickey Spillane's Mike Hammer*, which debuted January 7, 1958, and ran two seasons. Devoted secretary Velda is conspicuously absent, which gives the promiscuous Mike the freedom to conclude most episodes in the arms of a "chickie-baby" encountered during the course of a case. The violence-laden capers are given titles that could have been lifted from the covers of pulp magazines: "Just Around the Coroner," "Skinned Deep," "Crepe for Suzette," "Swing Low, Sweet Harriet" and many, many others.

Saxophonist, arranger and orchestrator Dave Kahn composed Hammer's memorable theme, dubbed "Riff Blues." The 20-second title credits version opens with an orchestral statement of the 5-6 motif, then repeats that melody on solo trumpet in a slower, bluesier vein, while McGavin turns and smiles toward the camera. The cue expands to 35 seconds during the end credits; the melody plays twice on trumpet—muted the first time—before the music builds to a triumphant brass finale.

The tune caught the attention of music publisher Dave Gordon. "Dave called me up one day and said, 'I've got an album at RCA. Write me up 12 tunes real quick,'" Kahn recalled, years later. "So we did this album, and none of that music was ever in [the show]."[3]

The resulting album, *The Music from Mickey Spillane's Mike Hammer*, is arranged and conducted by jazz saxophonist/clarinetist Skip Martin, best known at that time for arrangements he wrote for World War II-era big band units fronted by Glenn Miller, Benny Goodman, Count Basie and others. It's a sleekly swinging collection of tracks; while it's true that only "Riff Blues" was used in the series at the time the album was recorded—all first season underscores were built from library cues—most of Kahn's compositions eventually found their way into second season episodes, as fresh cues arranged and conducted by Martin.[4]

Despite the tune's popularity, "Riff Blues" didn't get much cover action. Buddy Morrow paired it with the *Richard Diamond* Theme for RCA Victor, and Ralph Marterie included "Riff Blues" on his 1960 Mercury LP *Music for a Private Eye*.

ABC's *Naked City* debuted September 30, 1958, loosely based on 1948's Academy Award-winning *film noir* of the same title; director Jules Dassin's documentary-style drama starred Barry Fitzgerald and Don Taylor as two New York City cops who investigate a murder. The TV version employs a similar format, with John McIntire and James Franciscus stepping into the shoes of Lt. Dan Muldoon and Det. Jimmy Halloran. They're a constant presence in a weekly series of *cinema-verité* dramas that adopt an intimate, street-level approach to criminals and victims, and the cops who navigate between the two extremes.

2. Dreamsville: 1957–1958

The show's bluesy, melancholy title theme, its melody carried by a forlorn solo trumpet, came from composer George Duning. Unlike most programs of its era, *The Naked City* doesn't have an opening credits sequence *per se*; its title merely appears on the screen, following a teaser sequence that sets up the conflict to follow. Orchestral arrangements of Duning's title cue weave in and around these prologues, but the full-bodied theme isn't heard until the end credits, at which point that lonely trumpet often serves as a wistful counterpoint to what has just concluded. ("There are eight million stories in the naked city. This has been one of them.")

Duning receives an intriguing acknowledgment during those closing credits, via a text block that reads "Theme music from the Colpix Record Album *The Naked City*, by George Duning and Ned Washington." Although history has labeled that LP a soundtrack album, it really isn't; it's more akin to a radio drama, with McIntire narrating the saga of a small-town woman named Judy, who heads to New York in search of singing fame and fortune. Her saga unfolds against Duning's soft orchestral jazz rhapsody during the course of the album's 12 tracks; the first one opens with a vocal version of the title theme—never heard on the TV series—as a chorus croons lyrics by Academy Award-winning songwriter Ned Washington. The LP wasn't released until late November 1958, after the series had aired for a couple of months; this strongly suggests that Duning and Washington wrote the theme for the album first, and then Duning reorchestrated it as a jazz-flavored instrumental for the show. (All episode underscores are sourced from library cues, so a traditional soundtrack album wouldn't have been possible anyway.) Despite quite positive reviews, *The Naked City* couldn't find an audience. It was canceled after a single season, but not before one of its final episodes—"Four Sweet Corners"—served as a successful pilot for *Route 66*, which would debut in the fall of 1960. (And as we'll see, *The Naked City* also would return.)

* * *

Peter Gunn solved his first case on September 22, 1958: a nasty little caper titled "The Kill," which revolves around a criminal gang's attempt to extort protection money from the owner of the club—Mother's—where Pete hangs out. Viewers were enchanted: not merely by star Craig Stevens, who epitomizes debonair sophistication, athletic grace and droll verbal wit; but also by the ultra-hip score that shadows his every step. The music isn't present merely in Mother's, where the resident jazz combo provides a steady succession of swinging tunes; the luxuriously vibrant aural tapestry turns non-diegetic and trails Pete as he follows leads, evades death and solves each case. Nor was this a collection of overexposed library cues; it was fresh jazz from the West Coast "cool" school. It stayed that way during the show's three-season run on NBC and ABC; composer Henry Mancini delivered original scores for *every single one of the 114 episodes*. They aren't sparse, either; many episodes feature up to 15 minutes of music.

The show's graphic title credits are rather bland: the music behind them, anything but. This brief version of Mancini's iconic "Peter Gunn Theme" runs barely 20 seconds, giving viewers just a taste of the captivating bass line and attention-grabbing melody; a more developed version, lasting close to a minute, plays behind each episode's end credits.

"The *Peter Gunn* title theme actually derives more from rock and roll than from jazz," Mancini explained. "I used guitar and piano in unison, playing what is known in music as an *ostinato*, which means obstinate. It was sustained throughout the piece, giving it a sinister effect, with some frightened saxophone sounds and some shouting brass."[5]

The show, based in an anonymous waterfront town, quickly established what became a predictable—but always entertaining—narrative pattern. Pete finds a reason to drop by Mother's, where he flirts with gal pal and club chanteuse Edie Hart (Lola Albright); she often sings most of a tune. They kiss; he nibbles her ear; they flirt as much as TV censors would allow; he then splits when duty calls, leaving her pouting, if amiably resigned. Pete's pursuit of clues usually crosses paths with a parallel investigation by the perpetually grumpy police Lt. Jacoby (Herschel Bernardi). The case is solved; Pete returns to Edie's embrace; much jazz is heard along the way.

Viewers ate it up.

Aside from its use during the title and end credits, the "Peter Gunn Theme" never is heard during the show. Instead, each episode begins with a dialogue-free teaser—usually a murder, or the commission of some crime—that takes place against the same throbbing, chromatic walking bass cue ("Fallout!"). Rising horns and ostinato drums add a mounting sense of dread, eventually hitting a jagged crescendo as the teaser concludes with whatever nefarious act prompts the subsequent storyline.

"[The score] had some unique sounds that people are still using," Mancini reflected, years later. "Unique kinds of playing techniques: fall-offs on the end of notes and things like that, that were used dramatically; the use of bass flutes and alto flutes, for dramatic uses, and to take the place of a string section."[6]

Several months before the show debuted—but well after the pilot episode had circulated throughout Hollywood—Mancini was encouraged to approach RCA with the notion of doing a soundtrack album. It was recorded during three sessions in August and September of 1958, by which point numerous TV episodes were in the can; most of the 12 tracks were developed from cues heard in these early episodes. Others, including "Dreamsville," were new compositions not heard on TV until toward the end of the first season.

Concerned that Mancini wasn't a "name," RCA pressed only 8,000 copies of the album, which was a huge miscalculation. It reached stores in mid–January 1959 and entered *Billboard's* Top LPs chart at No. 3 on February 9. It hit No. 1 two weeks later and held that position for 10 weeks, through April 27; the album remained on the chart for an astonishing 107 weeks. RCA couldn't begin to keep up with the demand. "In all, it sold more than a million copies," Mancini marveled, "which was unprecedented for a jazz album. Suddenly, out of nowhere, I was a successful recording artist."[7]

RCA's initial reluctance to put much force behind the album's release extended to their insulting treatment of the single that featured "The Peter Gunn Theme," which wasn't even taken from the LP. The assignment instead went to Ray Anthony, on the strength of his hit arrangement of the *Dragnet* title theme. Anthony's cover version of "The Peter Gunn Theme" landed in December 1958; it entered *Billboard's* Hot 100 chart on January 5 and rose to No. 8 during a 17-week run.

But that was merely the beginning.

In February 1959, just as Mancini's LP was climbing up the charts, drummer Shelly Manne covered most of the album on a Contemporary release titled *Shelly Manne & His Men Play Peter Gunn*. The "men" joining Manne's drums are Conte Candoli (trumpet), Herb Geller (alto sax), Victor Feldman (vibraharp, marimba), Russ Freeman (piano) and Monty Budwig (bass). Manne's arrangements lean more toward hard bop; his album is a more aggressive contrast to Mancini's "cooler" sound. Contemporary publicized the LP with a single that paired "The Peter Gunn Theme" with "Slow and Easy."

That same month, Mancini returned to the studio for the first of three sessions that produced *More Music from Peter Gunn*, which RCA released—amid a much more aggressive marketing campaign—in early summer. It entered *Billboard's* Top LPs chart on July 13 and remained there for 24 weeks. (Yes, both albums charted simultaneously.)

The Aaron Bell Orchestra covered Mancini's first album, also in February 1959, on the Lion label. Saxman Ted Nash delivered his version—simply titled *Peter Gunn*—a few months later, for Crown. The Joe Wilder Quartet—Wilder (trumpet), Hank Jones (piano), Milt Hinton (bass) and John Cresci, Jr. (drums)—got into the act with *Jazz from Peter Gunn* (Columbia); the Soundstage All-Stars—Pete Candoli (trumpet); Milt Bernhart, Dick Nash and Frank Rosolino (trombone); Ted Nash and Ronnie Lang (alto sax); Larry Bunker (vibes); Bob Howe and Vincent Terri (guitar); Russ Freeman and Jimmy Rowles (piano); Red Mitchell (bass); and Alvin Stoller and Frank Capp (drums)—covered all of Mancini's second album on *More Peter Gunn* (Dot).

Guitarist Duane Eddy followed Ray Anthony's version of "The Peter Gunn Theme" with a throbbing rock cover of his own; it spent nine weeks on *Billboard's* Hot 100 chart, peaking at No. 27 on November 14, 1960. The song became an integral part of Eddy's repertoire for decades thereafter. He enjoyed renewed association with it in 1986, when mixed with The Art of Noise for a new single that won a Grammy Award (and also produced a droll rock video). During the intervening years, the tune became a standard covered by scores (hundreds?) of pop and jazz artists.

In 2010, Mancini's first album was honored by the Library of Congress as an addition to the National Recording Registry, for being "culturally, historically or aesthetically significant."

Meanwhile—moving back to the summer of 1958—producers involved with other crime-themed programs took notice when Edwards' *Peter Gunn* pilot made the rounds prior to its on-air debut.

The Thin Man got a spanking-new theme when it returned for its second season in the autumn of 1958, courtesy of jazz newcomer Pete Rugolo; he had spent World War II in an Army band performing alongside Paul Desmond and, after the war, was a member of Stan Kenton's ensemble. Rugolo's lively blend of bongos and brass runs a scant 30 seconds, but nonetheless adds some sass to the show's opening credits. In a move that must've frustrated Johnny Green, Rugolo's new theme was layered atop the title credits of all first-season episodes, after the series concluded and went into syndicated reruns. Green's original theme remains during the end credits, which (now inaccurately) continue to acknowledge him for the title theme.

Rugolo's tune was covered by Les Brown and His Band of Renown (Coral); Pam Garner crooned Sammy Cahn lyrics that few people are even aware exist.

Over at *M Squad*, music director Stanley Wilson was savvy enough to make a similar shift, and he went straight to the top. "I approached [Count] Basie," he acknowledged, in a 1959 *TV Guide* interview.[8]

"This was to be the first black orchestra to do a theme for television," confirmed Basie's record producer, Teddy Reig. "The press came out in full force, along with all the wheels from the [musician's] union. The truth was, we had nothing. After about an hour and forty-five minutes, all the executives started looking at each other [dubiously]. So I took Bill [Basie] into the men's room, and said, 'We're f*king up.' He said, 'It's OK; don't worry about it.' He went back to the piano, gave one of his signals, and all the guys start running over to their chairs. Then he motioned to Thad Jones to come over. Basie played a couple of chords, mumbled something, and sent Thad back to the trumpet section. Then he conferred with

Marshall Royal, and he delivered the message to the saxes. The next thing you know, we had 'M Squad.'"⁹

The cue is a swinging, brass-heavy burner every bit as ferocious as Marvin's character. The theme opens with the 5-6-5-4-5 brass fanfare that remains well remembered to this day, as the show's title looms onto the screen. Basie injects a brief keyboard interlude when Marvin's car approaches the camera and roars to a stop; he bursts out, gun blazing, as the brass fanfare repeats. A longer, 45-second arrangement plays during the end credits, which acknowledges both Basie and the given episode's underscore composer. Basie expanded his arrangement and released it as a 45 single on the Roulette label.

"[Basie] made the recording that opens the show every week," Wilson continued. "But it was too large a sound to carry through the rest of the show. That's when I looked up two really top jazzmen, Benny Carter and Johnny Williams."¹⁰

Alto sax giant Benny Carter fronted numerous big bands from 1929 to the end of World War II, and then divided his time between arranging for big bands and writing and composing songs and scores for major Hollywood films. Wilson's offer allowed Carter to become the first African American to garner a composer's screen credit on a TV show, during the first of his many assignments for *M Squad*.¹¹ He wound up scoring 17 episodes during the show's second season; Williams scored eight. Carter then scored all 39 episodes of the third and final season.

The show's popularity, along with that of its new musical identity, prompted a soundtrack album, *The Music from "M Squad."* Basie wasn't involved; the arrangement of his title theme and 11 expanded underscore tracks were handled by Carter, Williams and Pete Carpenter (the latter destined to enjoy a fruitful collaboration, years later, with Mike Post).

(Numerous sources incorrectly insist that this recording won a Grammy Award for Best Soundtrack Album: Background Score from Motion Picture or Television. Although *The Music from "M Squad"* was indeed one of the nominees in this category, it lost to Duke Ellington's score for *Anatomy of a Murder*.)

Covers of Basie's title tune were inevitable. Piano is front and center on the single by Harry James and his New Swingin' Band (MGM); the Red Garland Trio—Garland (piano), Sam Jones (bass), Arthur Taylor (drums)—turned the tune into a gentler (but equally tasty) piano-driven swinger (Prestige).

(Ira Newborn's title theme for 1982's short-lived ABC spoof series, *Police Squad!*, is a deliberate riff on Basie's *M Squad* theme.)

Peter Gunn also affected CBS' *The Lineup*. In an effort to revive flagging ratings, the sixth and final season was expanded to an hour. More significantly, the show got a new title theme—"San Francisco

The fifth episode of *M Squad's* second season, "The Trap," is of particular significance. John Williams earned his first-ever on-screen credit—"Music Score [by] John T. Williams, Jr."—for a score that solidly established the show's subsequent "crime jazz" sound. He retained that billing for the next episode ("Force of Habit"), but modified his name to "Johnny Williams" thereafter.

Blues"—courtesy of Jerry Goldsmith. It's a richly atmospheric jazz cue: a moody, mildly ominous 1-4 motif on low-end piano, backed by sleek walking bass, startling brass jabs and bongos. Goldsmith also scored three episodes—starting with "Wake Up to Terror," the season debut—but neither his jazzy touch, nor the cast changes, could save the show.

David Janssen's Richard Diamond didn't merely get a new theme; his entire show was rebooted. He moved to Los Angeles and went upscale, working from a luxurious ranch house and driving a DeSoto Fireflite convertible that boasts a car phone. He also gained a steady gal pal (Barbara Bain) and the deliciously slinky Sam, who handles his answering service messages. Viewers never see more of Sam than her legs, which—for a time—belong to young Mary Tyler Moore.

The even bigger shift, however, concerned the show's music. Composing chores were handed to Pete Rugolo, after a strong recommendation by Janssen. "[David and I] went to ball games together," Rugolo recalled. "We were buddies, and he liked my work. He had all my albums; he was a jazz lover."[12] The title credits sequence remains roughly the same, but not the accompaniment. Growling percussion rumbles a 6-5 motif beneath a shrill, predatory trumpet that repeats three descending notes while Diamond approaches the camera; a ferocious wall of brass, with a suggestion of vibes, crescendo as his face is revealed by the match.

The new theme caught on quickly. Warren Barker and His Orchestra covered it two months later on a Warner Bros. single that sounds like a slowly grinding strip number; not to be outdone, Rugolo released his own version in midsummer for Mercury.

When the series went into syndication, it was retitled *Call Mr. D*; in a nod to the popularity of Rugolo's new theme, it replaced the title credits music in the older first- and second-season episodes (no doubt to Frank De Vol's displeasure).

Rugolo's involvement wasn't limited to the new title theme; he also scored all of the third-season episodes, building a library of delectable jazz cues that complement Diamond's new swinging bachelor lifestyle and surroundings. Traditionalists initially may have raised their eyebrows at Rugolo's frequent flute touches, along with occasional appearances by French horn or cello, but such instrumentation became memorable elements of the show's jazz palette. A soundtrack album was inevitable, and Rugolo obliged with Mercury's *The Music from Richard Diamond*. It offers 11 cool tracks on top of the title theme: soft ballads highlighted by vibes and soulful flute; bongo- and brass-fueled action jazz; impishly suspenseful stealth cues; and even some jazz-inflected, proto-rock 'n' roll. The album is to die for.

But wait; there's more. When *Richard Diamond* returned for its fourth and final season in October 1959, the show's music shifted again! The Four Star production company had opted to build new (cheaper) library music by recording the cues for all of its TV shows overseas; this decision was wholly incompatible with Rugolo's existing efforts, which had been recorded in Los Angeles. Four Star and his publisher couldn't come to an agreement, and so none of Rugolo's vibrant music was used during the fourth season, which instead employed a "new" title theme—"Nervous," by Richard Shores—that was part of the Four Star library.[13]

This brief, two-movement cue opens with twitchy brass and percussion, as a silhouetted figure runs and "climbs" along abstract rectangular white windows against a solid black background; this new title sequence was designed by Maurice Binder, who'd soon go on to tremendous fame for his work on (among many others) the James Bond films. A final horizontal bar opens as the cue shifts to a bluesy tenor sax solo; Janssen walks into view as the credits appear and smiles into the camera against a final flourish of horns. The entire season's interior music also was tracked from jazz-hued library cues, also by Shores.

* * *

Peter Gunn wasn't the only game-changing detective to debut in 1958.

Whereas his show and *Richard Diamond* spun the Chandler-esque private detective in a direction that emphasized dry wit and debonair coolness, ABC's *77 Sunset Strip* took an entirely different approach. The first of what became Warner Bros.' popular roster of "exotic" detective series debuted October 10, 1958, to the finger-snapping sound of a title song that quickly became a hit single. The pop-flavored tune reflects the show's frothy tone, and *77 Sunset Strip* also derived much of its popularity by shrewdly including a supporting character who instantly won the hearts and minds of younger viewers: Gerald Lloyd Kookson III, better known as Kookie, and played with teen-dream, hair-combing insolence by Edd Byrnes. As the show evolved during the course of five seasons, Kookie's antics increasingly overshadowed the only fitfully suspenseful cases investigated by former government agents-turned-private eyes Stuart Bailey (Efrem Zimbalist, Jr.) and Jeff Spencer (Roger Smith).

But those younger viewers would have been surprised—if not horrified—by Byrnes' role in the series' pilot episode, released theatrically the same month under the title *Girl on the Run*. Very little of the eventual breezy formula is present, aside from Zimbalist's Stuart Bailey operating—as a solo pee-eye—from an office at 77 Sunset Strip. He lands a case protecting a singer (Erin O'Brien) who witnesses a high-profile murder, and whose life is threatened repeatedly by a coldly smirking assassin: Byrnes (!), complete with hipster slang and ducktail haircut. The grim atmosphere is total *noir*, thanks to Harold E. Stine's shadow-laden cinematography. Howard Jackson's orchestral score is strictly string-laden suspense, although O'Brien warbles a few jazz-inflected torch songs. Clearly, creator Roy Huggins made *massive* changes between this pilot and the subsequent series.

After being deposited more benignly on the small screen, Stuart—now partnered with Jeff—operates from an office at the eponymous address, adjacent to Dino's Lodge. The latter—an actual restaurant co-owned by Dean Martin, nestled for 20 years at 8532 Sunset Blvd.[14]—is where Kookie works as a valet, when not otherwise helping or hindering his buddies. The series quickly became "hip" and "with it," and Byrnes had a lot to do with that; the pop-oriented Mack David/Jerry Livingston title theme also helped. The sassy blend of keyboard boogie-woogie and brass flourishes was covered by "The Big Sound of" composer/arranger Don Ralke, then known for jazz-hued exotica albums; the tune enjoyed a brief, five-week run on *Billboard's* Hot 100 chart in the spring of 1959, peaking at No. 69 on April 27.

Jazz saxophonist and arranger/conductor Warren Barker had better luck with the Warner Bros. "soundtrack album." It enjoyed a 28-week run on *Billboard's* Top LPs chart, which concluded well after the show began its second season. That said, the quotation marks are deserved, because the LP is something of a bait-and-switch. As was common practice with Warner Bros. shows at the time, all episode underscores were built from library cues during the initial five seasons. Modest jazz content was heard occasionally, courtesy of the Frankie Ortega Trio, the house band at Dino's Lodge.

Barker therefore didn't have much from which to draw, when it came time to assemble a soundtrack album. The 13 tracks include four (!) versions of the title theme; most of the remaining tracks are covers of jazz standards. Sharp-eared listeners also will recognize the first 12 bars of "Late at Bailey's Pad" as an Alex North cue ("Stan Meets Blanche"), from his score for 1951's *A Streetcar Named Desire*.

Ironically, the "soundtrack" designation more properly belongs to another 1959 album—all but forgotten today—also affiliated with the TV series. The aforementioned Frankie Ortega Trio—Ortega (piano), Bert Hanson (bass) and Walter Sage (drums)—released *77 Sunset Strip and Other Selections* on the Jubilee label, with their intimate trio sound given considerably more heft, thanks to arrangements and big band backing by jazz trumpeter/bandleader Sy Oliver. In addition to a piano-driven cover of the show's title theme, the album features numerous Ortega originals that his trio performed on camera as the series proceeded.

The title theme gained additional momentum in 1960, when the show's UK debut prompted fresh jazz covers from across the pond by Jack Parnell (Philips) and the Pinewood Studio Band and Chorus (JAR). Additional covers came from Bob Miller and the Millermen (Fontana), and Victor Sylvester and His Cha Cha Cha Rhythm (Columbia). Most notoriously, Warners allowed Mel Henki and His Orchestra to release a burlesque arrangement with drum pops, sound effects and cheers, all of which brought an entirely different meaning to the show's title.

The program's waning popularity during the fifth season prompted a radical overhaul by new executive producer Jack Webb. The entire cast was fired except for Zimbalist, whose Stuart Bailey was crafted into a solo gumshoe; the show's tone also turned darker. The finger-snapping David/Livingston song was dumped in favor of a new title theme by Bob Thompson: a sternly melodramatic orchestral cue that opens with sweeping strings, as Bailey takes an elevator within the famed Bradbury Building. The show's fans, feeling justifiably betrayed, abandoned ship; the series was canceled midway through this misguided sixth season.

The Big Screen

Elmer Bernstein built on his nervous, electrifying work in *The Man with the Golden Arm* with an equally arresting, brass-laden score for 1957's *Sweet Smell of Success*: a grim *noir* drama highlighted by Burt Lancaster's calmly reptilian lead performance as newspaper society/gossip columnist J.J. Hunsecker (a not at all veiled caricature of then-popular syndicated radio, TV and newspaper columnist Walter Winchell, who was similarly ruthless when it came to abusing his power to crush political and personal enemies). *Sweet Smell* takes place during a few tempestuous days in New York City, as unscrupulous press agent Sidney Falco (Tony Curtis)—a desperate schemer willing to function as Hunsecker's lap dog—concocts a Machiavellian plan to break up a sweet relationship between the columnist's younger sister, Susan (Susan Harrison), and up-and-coming jazz guitarist Steve Dallas (Martin Milner), whom Hunsecker despises.

Bernstein's opening orchestral splash, dubbed "The Street," plays against title credits that unfold over a montage of Manhattan's late-night club scene: a growling, edgy blast of vibrant jazz that immediately sets the mood for the manipulative unpleasantness to come.

"I don't remember how I was brought into *Sweet Smell of Success*," Bernstein admitted, many years later. "I suspect it was because of *The Man with the Golden Arm*, because it was city music. I was left completely on my own; I never discussed the music with anyone. The inspiration came from the picture. I saw a dark energy in the film, and that's where I was going with that."[15]

The film actually has a dual musical identity. Bernstein's orchestral flourishes are bookended by several combo sets taking place in the club where Dallas has a regular gig as a member of the Chico Hamilton Quintet. These sessions are delivered as approachably warm chamber jazz by Hamilton (drums), Paul Horn (reeds), Carson Smith (double bass), Fred Katz (cello) and John Pisano (ghosting Milner on guitar).

Director Alexander Mackendrick's decision to use Hamilton's combo was savvy for a couple of reasons. Aside from the obvious pleasure of listening to such great music from an up-and-coming West Coast group, film audiences were exposed to an interracial band … at a time when such a thing raised hackles in certain quarters.

"Being a mixed group was not too cool out there, at that time," Hamilton acknowledged, years later.[16]

The film produced two Decca soundtrack albums. *Sweet Smell of Success: Music from the Soundtrack*

Elmer Bernstein was in his mid–30s when he scored *Sweet Smell of Success*, having paid his dues only four years earlier, with soundtracks for notorious stinkers such as *Robot Monster* and *Cat-Women of the Moon*. He earned 13 Academy Award nominations during a career that continued until he died in 2004, but won only once: for 1968's *Thoroughly Modern Millie* (courtesy Bernstein Family Trust).

is dominated by Bernstein's orchestral themes and underscore, with four tunes each by Hamilton and Katz. *The Chico Hamilton Quintet: Sweet Smell of Success* offers seven additional Hamilton/Katz combo tunes on side A, with side B devoted to an ambitious "Concerto of Jazz Themes" from the entire film.

* * *

Mike Hammer's third cinematic outing, 1957's reasonably entertaining *My Gun Is Quick*, moved the hard-charging private dick into firm jazz territory. Granted, portions of the score are unremarkable orchestral mood music, particularly a frivolous track that accompanies an interminable automobile pursuit (as if co-directors Phil Victor and George White assumed viewers hadn't ever seen two cars following each other on a freeway). But the rest of the music is solid combo jazz, and it's a shame a soundtrack album never was released; it might have identified who wrote and/or performed which cues, since the score is credited to Marlin Skiles, with "additional music" by Alexander Courage and Johnny

Williams. Skiles was a prolific pianist and composer who got his start with big band jazz in the 1920s and early '30s, before becoming a Hollywood fixture in 1936. Courage had just begun his movie and TV scoring career; Williams needs no introduction.

My Gun Is Quick opens as Hammer (Robert Bray) has a chance café encounter with a young woman dubbed "Red" (Jan Chaney), who wears an unusual ring. A moody jazz theme adds a melancholy note to their conversation; in an odd touch, when Hammer excuses himself to call his secretary Velda (Pamela Duncan), back at the office, her radio is playing the same tune! Red is killed a few scenes later, the ring snatched in the process; Hammer subsequently is caught between rival factions determined to obtain an extensive set of matching priceless jewels. Double- and triple-crosses follow, with Hammer cozying up to several saucy dames before finally solving the case.

Several scenes take place in a seedy strip joint known as the Bluebell Nightclub. The house band, displaying lively chops that are significantly superior to the *bada-boom* drum pops one would expect in such an environment, features Russ Freeman (piano), Stu Williamson (trumpet), Charlie Mariano (alto sax), Leroy Vinnegar (bass) and Richie Frost (drums, although he's ghosted by Shelly Manne). In most cases—as also is true of the earlier café scene—the jazz shading is so obviously different from the rest of the score, that one suspects separate recording sessions: jazz combo vs. orchestral ensemble.

Williams' fans—and they are legion—have suggested that the melody heard behind Hammer's stairway descent, when he discovers the body of a mute French janitor, could be "proto-Williams." It's certainly possible, but (thus far) nobody has offered proof one way or the other.

Sexual tension, cruelty and duplicity also are front and center in *The Strange One*, a ferocious denunciation of macho bad behavior in military academies. Author/playwright Calder Willingham turned his 1947 novel into a play for New York's Actors Studio, where the off-Broadway cast included a young James Dean. Most of the stage cast reprised their roles when Willingham further adapted the material for the screen in 1957, but Dean's untimely death precluded his participation. The subject matter was quite raw for its time, and surprisingly blunt even when viewed through the lens of history. The story takes place at the fictitious Southern Military College; the place is in thrall to Jocko De Paris (Ben Gazzara), a sadistic bully who torments freshmen newcomers who, by virtue of academic rank, aren't able to fight back.

Kenyon Hopkins' score immediately unnerves viewers, with a jarring blast of horns that plays over the Columbia Pictures logo. This segues into the film's swinging, sax-driven title theme: an almost charming melody rendered disconcerting by long descending runs on edgy strings. It's the perfect statement of Jocko's dual personality—oddly charismatic on the outside, pure evil on the inside—and, in fact, it becomes his theme.

Saucy jump jazz—with a swinging sax solo—plays on a diner jukebox during one tense scene; the juke later shifts to boogie-style arrangement of the main theme, with some nasty sax and guitar licks intensifying viewer anxiety. When the cadets finally rebel, another reprise of the main theme dissolves into agitated horns when Jocko is confronted and then driven, blindfolded, to what he believes will be his own execution.

"I used a twelve-tone technique, which I don't use ordinarily in a theatrical film," Hopkins explained, when interviewed shortly after the film's release. "The commercial melodies and the juke-boxes and the twelve-tone chase which comes at the end of the picture are all related. The theme used in the final chase is the tune called 'The Strange One,' used in a twelve-tone form. If you listen to the album a couple of times, you can see the relationship of the whole thing."[17]

The soundtrack LP allowed Hopkins to expand his cues into full-length compositions. "We do a little editing," he noted, describing the process of rewriting music for an album release. "If we have a bridge where just one chord is heard to emphasize a truck falling over a cliff, naturally we don't put the chord in the album. Mostly, it's a matter of blending cues. We have long tails on cues in movies, so they can be mixed out. Then we just cut off those tails and put the cues next to each other, and—generally speaking—you've got development."[18] The album hasn't been digitized, which is a shame; it's one of Hopkins' best scores and deserves resurrection and wider exposure.

Director Fred F. Sears' *Escape from San Quentin* is an unremarkable *noir* thriller: one of few big-screen starring vehicles for pop singer Johnny Desmond, who seems wholly out of his element as a tough convict on the run. He plays Mike Gilbert, a San Quentin short-timer who gets talked into an ill-advised escape by the vicious Roy Gruber (Richard Devon) and Hap Graham (Roy Engel). Double-crosses eventually lead to an unexpectedly upbeat conclusion—hardly appropriate for a true *noir*—that implies Mike *might* live happily ever after.

The film warrants brief mention because of its unusual score, composed and performed entirely on solo guitar by famed jazz/classical maestro Laurindo Almeida. Alas, the score can't be called jazz; Almeida's occasional cues are best described as thoughtfully atmospheric, adding emotional texture that the undertrained actors aren't able to deliver themselves. Two big band jazz cues are heard as radio source music: a swinging arrangement of Stephen Foster's "Jeanie with the Light Brown Hair," and a second tune too brief to be identified. No soundtrack album appeared.

* * *

Following World War II service, Richard Markowitz paid his dues by performing in Parisian jazz clubs; he slid into film and TV scoring in the late 1950s, and likely will be remembered for his great title theme to television's *Wild Wild West* (discussed later). But he deserves equal recognition for his big-screen scoring debut: the excellent jazz soundtrack for 1958's luridly titled *Stakeout on Dope Street*. The film is one of the many low-budget quickies with which producer Roger Corman was involved and was made on a microscopic budget of $31,000; despite that, it looks reasonably polished, thanks to impressive efforts by director Irvin Kershner and cinematographer Haskell Wexler (also making their feature debuts). The latter supplies a rich *noir* atmosphere to the suspenseful third act, which is further enhanced by Markowitz's action jazz.

The story is frank for its time. Teenagers Jim (Yale Wexler), Ves (Jonathan Haze) and Nick (Steven Marlo, under the alias Morris Miller) find a briefcase that contains a two-pound can of uncut heroin: accidently overlooked during a police shoot-out with mobsters. The teens concoct an ill-advised scheme to make money by having a neighborhood addict—Allen Kramer, as Danny—slowly sell the stuff in small quantities. Unfortunately, their efforts catch the attention of mob gunsels seeking the missing heroin; the police also are working hard to find the can, to destroy it. Bad choices lead everybody to a violent, late-night climax in Los Angeles' Chavez Ravine.

Markowitz's score is one of the film's strongest assets. Kershner stages much of the action in lengthy montages bereft of ambient sounds or audible dialog, even when people are talking—no doubt to minimize costs—and this gives Markowitz plenty of "space" for lengthy cues that are solid compositions in their own right. Music is ubiquitous throughout, even when subtle: as with the soft, anticipatory cymbal brushes heard during the pre-credits sequence, when a mob drug courier is about to have a *very* bad night.

The subsequent title credits theme opens with an angry rumble of drums, brass and disorienting, low-end piano; this segues into a series of dissonant horn fanfares against a descending four-note piano ostinato. Jim, Nick and Ves are introduced in their hangout—the back room of the latter's father's store—as Markowitz supplies a sassy swinger, with muted trumpet and sax solos against sleek walking bass. The mood turns sweet when a gentle sax ballad backs Jim's visit with girlfriend Kathy (Abby Dalton); they dream about a future they're unlikely to enjoy, given limited financial means (thus setting up Jim's willingness to become a reluctant drug dealer).

One of the longest and most ambitious cues—primarily free jazz, with unsettling, dissonant horns against jagged rhythm elements—backs Danny's lengthy recollection of what it was like to endure the surreal agony of withdrawal in a jail cell. When the mob guys eventually catch up with Nick and Ves, Jim flees with the can—still almost full of heroin—while uptempo piano runs and frantic horns keep time with his pounding footsteps. In the aftermath, a funereal solo drum march accompanies the brief end credits.

RCA Victor put out a soundtrack EP with four tracks: no more than a tantalizing portion of the ambitious score, but it's better than nothing. Unfortunately, the disc has yet to be digitized.

Stakeout on Dope Street would have made a great double bill with the similarly low-budget *Screaming Mimi*, director Gerd Oswald's big-screen adaptation of Fredric Brown's 1949 novel. Burnett Guffey's rich, chiaroscuro-esque cinematography is by far the highlight of this flick, which has far more atmosphere than plot logic.

The main attraction is the considerable screen time given to famed jazz vibraphonist/xylophonist Red Norvo and his trio, who even get billing in the title credits. That said, the "Red Norvo Trio" actually is a quartet; his regular sidemen Jimmy Wyble (guitar) and Red Wooten (acoustic double bass) are joined by a drummer whose identity has been lost to history. Much of the story's action takes place at El Madhouse, a boisterous hipster nightclub run by Joann "Gypsy" Masters (Gypsy Rose Lee). As the story progresses, Oswald lingers on half a dozen lengthy, on-camera performances by Norvo's combo, which most frequently delivers the West Coast "cool" jazz for which he had become known.

The fast-paced thriller begins as the titillating Virginia Wilson (Anita Ekberg) emerges from a dip in the ocean and is confronted by a knife-wielding maniac who tries to kill her. The experience shatters her mind and prompts a stay at the Highland Sanitarium, where she falls under the unhealthy spell of Dr. Greenwood (Harry Townes). Flash-forward a bit, and Virginia—now using the stage name Yolanda Lange—has become an exotic dancer, and the main attraction at El Madhouse. Yolanda comes to the attention of tough-talking newspaperman Bill Sweeney (Philip Carey), who unwisely falls in love with her. Enter *another* knife-wielding assailant, whose signature is a small, sculpted figurine of a screaming, barely dressed woman. What does it all mean?

The film's symphonic underscore is lifted, without credit, from Leonard Bernstein's memorable score for *On the Waterfront*. (Much to Bernstein's displeasure, a lot of his work for that film wound up in Columbia's music library, where Oswald was free to extract and use it.) No soundtrack album was produced—Bernstein likely would have sued—nor did Norvo capitalize on his combo's performances. One must endure the film to enjoy the band's efforts.

The viewing experience is far superior in *I Want to Live!*, which broke the conventional Hollywood mold by using a wall-to-wall jazz score: not just partially jazz, and not merely as source music. Every note in the film—both underscore *and* source music—is solid jazz. "John Mandel, at 32, has made musical history," enthused *Down Beat* associate editor John Tynan, in his liner notes for the soundtrack LP. "No composer writing for films before him has employed the jazz idiom to such telling effect, in integrating music and dramatic action."[19]

Audiences were primed for just such an innovation: The film had its U.S. premiere on November 18, 1958, only two months after the television debut of *Peter Gunn*. Best of all, *I Want to Live!* isn't content to provide a routine "texture" score; it remains one of the finest jazz soundtracks ever composed for an American drama.

The fact-based drama traces the events that led to "good-time girl" Barbara Graham's arrest and conviction for the murder of 64-year-old Mabel Monohan, a widow who lived in Burbank, Calif. Graham and accomplices Jack Santo and Emmett Perkins were executed on June 3, 1955; she was only the third woman in California's history to be executed in the gas chamber.[20] Nelson Gidding and Don Mankiewicz adapted their screenplay from letters Graham wrote while in prison; and from newspaper coverage by Pulitzer Prize-winning *San Francisco Examiner* reporter Edward Montgomery (played in the film by Simon Oakland).

Director Robert Wise wanted a jazz score, for reasons of atmosphere and authenticity; at the suggestion of André Previn, he hired Mandel, who had extensive jazz experience, and had wanted to be a music arranger since childhood. ("Back then, nobody knew what an arranger was," he recalled, decades later. "They thought it was somebody who moved chairs around.")[21] Mandel became a sideman in big bands led by Count Basie, Jimmy Dorsey and Buddy Rich; and a session veteran in ensembles backing Frank Sinatra, Peggy Lee, Mel Tormé and many other singers. He accepted the scoring assignment, but made no secret of his apprehension: "I was really very nervous, until I realized, after I learned the language and how to sync everything, that essentially I'd been doing that for a long time, and I just didn't know it. [Scoring] married all the things I'd been doing previously."[22]

Graham's wild, hard-living lifestyle was spent in numerous jazz clubs up and down the California coast, and she was a longtime fan of baritone sax legend Gerry Mulligan. "I have *all* his records," she tells a prison attendant, at one point during the film. Wise and Mandel therefore constructed a jazz score in two parts: Mandel's 24-piece big band performs the extensive dramatic underscore, while the film's numerous source cues—heard on radios, record players and even live in a club—are played by a septet headed by Mulligan. The result is a jazz-lover's dream come true: Very little of the film is *without* music, and it all feels organic and absolutely essential to the deeply unsettling narrative. A pre-release *Los Angeles Times* feature dubbed the music "anxiety jazz."[23] Mood and atmosphere are conveyed with an unusual collection of instruments, many played in their "freak registers": E-flat clarinet, contra-bass clarinet, contra bassoon, bass trumpet and bass flute.[24]

Mandel's title theme opens with a sharp, unexpected horn blast, followed by bongos, a smoky bass line and a primary melody delivered by a lonely baritone sax. (Most unusual, then and now: The opening credits cite Mulligan's entire combo by name, after the stars are acknowledged.) Strings, piano and flute add color as the credits continue; the sax theme evaporates and cuts abruptly to some lively bop by Mulligan's septet. The combo is performing live at the "New Frisco Club," where the free-spirited Graham (Susan Hayward) and her fellow good-time gals are drinking and dancing to the furious beat. It's a totally swinging scene, on which Wise holds for quite some time, allowing Mulligan and several of his sidemen to deliver some kick-ass solos. Subsequent diegetic cues are granted equal respect.

But once we hit the lengthy third act—as the gas chamber is prepared, and as Barbara agonizes during her final hours—the drama is augmented solely by Mandel's slow, despondent underscore: a melody driven by quiet, countdown-style percussion. That drumbeat slows during two cues, until it finally stops, as do Barbara's heart and breathing. "When you see somebody die in a gas chamber, it's not like being electrocuted; it's more like the life seeping out of you, as the cyanide takes over," Mandel explained, years later. "I had to concoct something that felt like the scene looked. What you saw on the screen were clouds of smoke, so I used instruments weaving in and out of each other, creating an impressionistic texture. The instrument playing the melody in this case was something you never hear: Harry Klee playing a piccolo in its bottom register. It makes an eerie sound … almost like someone's dying gasp."[25]

Both *Johnny Mandel's Great Jazz Score: I Want to Live!* and Mulligan's *The Jazz Combo from I Want to Live!* were released simultaneously by United Artists.

* * *

Henry Mancini was concluding his six-year apprenticeship at Universal Pictures when he came to the attention of Orson Welles.[26] The famously eccentric auteur had just completed a five-week shoot on a modest $895,000 B-film loosely based on the 1956 crime novel *Badge of Evil*. Welles initially had been hired solely for an acting role, but Charlton Heston agreed to co-star only after insisting that Welles also take the director's chair.[27] Ultimately, Welles also wrote the script, and—as a result—what might have been a forgettable programmer blossomed into *Touch of Evil*, one of the final superlative *film noir* thrillers of Hollywood's post–World War II era. Mancini's score contributes greatly to the film's seamy, pulsating malevolence: a moody "touch of evil" that the exacting director described in several memos to his composer. "What we want is musical color, rather than movement," Welles wrote, "sustained washes of sound rather than a tempestuous, melodramatic operatic style of scoring." And, most crucially, "The emphasis should go on Afro-Cuban rhythm numbers."[28]

Mancini delivered precisely what Welles desired, resulting in the young composer's first solo credit on a serious film drama.

The story takes place in flyspeck communities on both sides of an immigration check point along the Mexican/American border. Welles establishes this setting with one of the most memorable tracking shots in Hollywood history: Mikes Vargas (Heston), a narcotics investigator for the Mexican Ministry of Justice, takes an evening walk with his new American bride, Susan (Janet Leigh). The camera follows this slow stroll, progressive bursts of music emanating from the clubs they pass. Mancini wrote different source cues for each venue—bossa nova, rockabilly, dance hall swing—and the music fades up and down, even overlapping, as Heston and Leigh leisurely pass each establishment in turn. Then a bomb suddenly explodes in the trunk of a car driven by an American millionaire, killing everybody inside. Vargas gets sucked into the subsequent investigation by local police captain Hank Quinlan (Welles), who seems disinclined to find the actual murderer, and more interested in pinning the crime on the nearest available Mexican. The waters are muddied further by a Mexican drug-running family determined to punish Vargas for having jailed their paterfamilias.

Mancini's score often has been described—mistakenly—as primarily (or even solely) source music originating from radios, juke boxes and dive clubs in the various seedy settings. While it's true that numerous bits of music do emerge from such diegetic sources—including a tune Mancini wrote for the player piano in the Mexican brothel run by Tana (Marlene Dietrich)—many of the film's most powerful sequences unfold against traditional background scoring cues. Some of these themes clearly echo what Mancini was writing for *Peter Gunn*, particularly "Reflection," a bluesy blend of bass, piano and muted trumpet, which boasts gorgeous sax, guitar and trumpet solos.

"*Touch of Evil* was one of the best things I did in that period of my life," Mancini noted, and then emphasized the point further: "It's one of the best things I've *ever* done."[29]

("Tana's Theme" would be resurrected, decades later, as part of the soundtrack for 1995's *Get Shorty*.)

The initial Challenge soundtrack album featured mostly diegetic cues and only three of Mancini's actual score cues. A later 1962 Challenge release, deceptively titled *The Wild Side of Henry Mancini*, actually is a second *Touch of Evil* soundtrack album; it concentrates almost exclusively on Mancini's actual score cues.

Meanwhile, Across the Pond…

Veteran British film editor Seth Holt made his directorial debut with *Nowhere to Go*, a moody, low-key drama highlighted by Paul Beeson's stylish black-and-white cinematography: replete with late-night shadows, deep focus and striking camera angles. The film also

Touch of Evil didn't really involve "the strangest vengeance ever planned," although Janet Leigh's character narrowly escapes a fate worse than death. Henry Mancini's score serves as a reminder that, however larkish most of his later Hollywood work would become, his solid big band jazz roots—having served previously as a pianist/arranger for Glenn Miller, among others—were firmly showcased in this *noir* classic.

boasts the sole scoring effort by Jamaican-born hard bop trumpeter Alphonso Son "Dizzy" Reece. "*Nowhere to Go* was the first modern jazz film made in England," Reece noted, years later. "The format was watch the film, and improvise with a quartet right there. I had [saxophonist] Tubby Hayes on it; we set up, watched the film, did [the music] in one take, and we got a masterpiece out of that."[30] Reece, obviously a believer in "less is more," delivered only a handful of cues that Holt employs sparingly, more often allowing Beeson's dazzling tableaux to speak for themselves.

The story opens as London-based con artist Paul Gregory (George Nader) tricks a wealthy widow into making him an agent for the sale of her late husband's valuable coin collection. He then willingly allows himself to be arrested, assuming—as a first-time offender—he'll get a light sentence, and then be free to retrieve the loot. But he's sent down for 10 years, a sentence that he's unwilling to serve; with the help of prison mate Victor Sloane (Bernard Lee), Gregory escapes. Everything subsequently goes wrong, starting when Sloane double-crosses him. Now wanted for murder, Gregory lucks into the sympathetic graces of lonely ex-debutante Bridget Howard (Maggie Smith, in her film debut), who drives him to her family home in rural Wales. A later encounter with a gun-wielding farmer leaves Gregory wounded, perhaps dying. Elsewhere, the solemn Bridget awaits the man she'll never see again.

Lloyd Thompson's smooth walking bass introduces Reece's main theme, which debuts over the title credits: bold, blocky white text against Beeson's striking, late-night montage outside the prison. Reece's trumpet kicks off the somber cue against a thoughtful 4/4 beat, the horn "fluttering" through the primary melody; Hayes' backing sax is barely discernable, until he takes a pensive solo at the bridge. Following the prison break, after Gregory's contacts rebuff him, he wanders London's late-night streets during a montage set to a melancholy arrangement of the title theme, with mournful trumpet and sax solos reflecting the man's frustration and isolation.

The bulk of the film's score was released as a double-disc 45 EP on the UK's Tempo label; they've subsequently been digitized and made available via iTunes and similar services. (Be advised: The misleadingly titled *Nowhere to Go: Bonus Tracks Version* does not contain any additional music from the film. The seven extra cuts are taken from other Dizzy Reece studio sessions.)

Elsewhere in the World

Director Roger Vadim's *Sait-on jamais*—retitled *No Sun in Venice* for its U.S. release, rather than the more accurately translated *One Never Knows*—is an unremarkable 1957 crime thriller that likely would have faded into obscurity, were it not for one key element.

As is typical of the women in Vadim's films, the free-spirited Sophie (Françoise Arnoul) is unapologetically promiscuous; she's the "kept woman" of an aging ex-Nazi-turned-forger, Baron Eric von Bergen (O.E. Hasse). She lives in his palatial Venetian estate, where she also has become the lover of his brutal, much younger lieutenant, Sforzi (Robert Hossein). During a typical evening out, she encounters nice-guy photographer/journalist Michel (Christian Marquand); he initially—and wisely—wants no part of her, but ultimately succumbs to her charms. Enter *plenty* of trouble.

The film's score more than compensates for all other shortcomings. Producer Raoul Lévy pitched the assignment to John Lewis, during the Paris portion of the Modern Jazz

Quartet's late 1956 European tour[31]; the pianist/composer accepted the challenge, making *Sait-on jamais* the very first mainstream film to have commissioned—and delivered—a full jazz score. (*I Want to Live!* followed a year later.)

"Jazz is often thought to be limited in expression," Lewis explains, in the original LP liner notes. "It is used for 'incidental music' or when a situation in a drama or film calls for jazz, but rarely in a more universal way apart from an explicit jazz context. Here it has to be able to run the whole gamut of emotions and carry the story from beginning to end."[32] Lewis definitely succeeded in that lofty goal, although one could wish that his music had anchored a better film.

Lewis and his MJQ colleagues—Milt Jackson (vibes), Percy Heath (double bass) and Connie Kay (drums)—deliver a sparkling chamber jazz score that is mostly texture and mood, frequently reflecting the Venetian setting; you'll not detect specific character themes. Indeed, the entire score sounds like a jazz symphony, divided into movements only by virtue of Vadim's editing choices. Although most of the score seems to be non-diegetic, this is deceptive; the music occasionally emanates from sources such as Sophie's phonograph player, which becomes obvious when she lifts the tone arm at one point, to repeat a passage she particularly likes. Vadim also catches us off-guard at times. When Sophie bids a formal farewell to the baron, Heath's ominous bass riffs cut off abruptly as she exits the room. Since Vadim hasn't thus far used his score in such a manner, the impact is quite startling.

The Atlantic soundtrack album is saddled with an overlong title that must have given cataloguers a fit: *The Modern Jazz Quartet Plays One Never Knows (Original Film Score for "No Sun in Venice")*.

Various people took credit for introducing rising jazz legend Miles Davis to 24-year-old cinematographer-turned-writer/director Louis Malle in late 1957; the truth is lost to imperfect memory, but the result of that fateful meeting has become the stuff of cinema legend. When Malle's debut feature, *Ascenseur pour l'échafaud*, was released in January 1958, it boasted an improvisational jazz score by Davis. (More than three years would pass before the film played U.S. theaters, under the title *Elevator to the Gallows*; in the UK, it was known as *Lift to the Scaffold*.)

The collaboration was unusual, to say the least. However their meeting was arranged, Davis agreed to score Malle's just-completed film, although not in the conventional manner. Malle arranged for a private screening, after which Davis noodled some thoughts in his hotel room, before showing up with his sidemen—Barney Willen (tenor sax), René Urtreger (piano), Pierre Michelot (bass) and Kenny Clarke (drums)—at Paris' Le Poste Parisien Studio for two sessions.[33]

"It was a great learning experience, because I had never written a music score for a film before," Davis recalled, in his autobiography. "I would look at the rushes of the film and get musical ideas to write down. Since it was about a murder and was supposed to be a suspense movie, I used this old, very gloomy, dark building where I had the musicians play. I thought it would give the music atmosphere, and it did."[34]

Malle remembers it differently. "I showed [Davis] the film twice, only twice. We agreed on the parts where we felt music was needed. We rented a sound studio in Paris on the Champs-Elysees, and started working, as musicians do, very slowly. We worked from something like 10 or 11 that night until 5 in the morning. In that one night, the whole score was recorded. It's one of the very few film scores which is completely improvised."[35]

However it went down, the resulting 10 tracks are richly moody, achingly lonely, and very much a precursor to the sound Davis would deliver on his soon-to-be-released albums

Milestones and *Kind of Blue*. As an isolated listening experience, these 26 minutes of music are positively haunting.

As employed in Malle's film, however, they're not much of a score.

Davis' efforts are used sparingly; lengthy chunks of the film progress without any music, including several segments that beg for melodic accompaniment. More tellingly, the tone of the music that *is* used sometimes clashes with on-screen events; the disconnect can be jarring. Nor does Malle use anywhere near all of what Davis supplied; the film has no more than 12 to 15 minutes of music, mostly in fleeting snatches.

Ascenseur pour l'échafaud is a casually brutal *noir* drama, opening with a premeditated murder orchestrated by lovers Florence Carala (Jeanne Moreau) and Julien Tavernier (Maurice Ronet). They've conspired to kill her husband—industrialist/arms dealer Simon (Jean Wall), who also happens to be Julien's boss—with a plan that is orchestrated flawlessly ... except that Julien gets stuck in an elevator when the building's power is cut for the weekend. Meanwhile, his car is stolen for a joy ride by an amoral young couple, Louis (Georges Poujouly) and Veronique (Yori Bertin). They're emblematic of the bored, casually cruel youth often showcased in French New Wave dramas: heartless monsters who eventually kill two people solely for kicks.

Malle's best use of music—the one time Davis seems to understand how to amplify a scene—comes with Michelot's slow, heartbeat-style bass notes, accompanied by a seemingly distant wail of muted trumpet, each time we cut back to Julien: stuck in the elevator, knowing full well that his chances of getting away with murder are ebbing with each passing hour. The film's ironic conclusion unfolds against another well-placed bass/heartbeat countdown theme, this time with Davis' horn and Urtreger's keyboard lending smugness to the clever means by which investigating detective Cherrier (Lino Ventura) wraps up the case.

Fontana released Davis' score throughout Europe as a 10-inch LP. In the States, it became side A of Davis' 1958 album, *Jazz Track*. The film wouldn't get its own dedicated U.S. soundtrack LP until a 1974 Mercury release. 2018's Criterion Collection Blu-ray release of the film includes archival footage of Davis and Malle, shot for the French television program *Cinepanorama*, during the music's recording session.

* * *

Once *Rififi* ignited interest in heist thrillers, the inevitable parody wasn't far behind. The surprise is that director Mario Monicelli's *I soliti ignoti*—known in the States as *Big Deal on Madonna Street*—was a massive hit with 1958's moviegoers, and today is recognized as a masterpiece of Italian cinema. It also became the first Italian film to be released with a pure jazz soundtrack, and marked the scoring debut of pianist/composer Piero Umiliani.

The story begins when small-time crook Cosimo (Memmo Carotenuto) hatches the "perfect" scheme to burgle a pawn shop: a plan that mushrooms to involve Peppe (Vittorio Gassman); Tiberio (Marcello Mastroianni); Capannelle (Carlo Pisacane); Mario (Renato Salvatori); and Michele (Tiberio Murgia), a hot-tempered fellow unduly protective of his attractive sister, Carmelina (Claudia Cardinale). Cosimo and his comrades never seem to take this caper seriously, and the actual heist becomes a comedy of errors.

Umiliani built a score from a few principal themes designed to evoke distinct moods, via specific instrumentation: drama (trumpet and sax), suspense (piano and vibraphone), romance (solo contralto sax) and melancholia (clarinet). The ensemble is tight, and Umiliani's cues are a delicious blast of swing and uptempo dance jazz. "Mario Monicelli asked me to write a lively and jazzy soundtrack," Umiliani recalled, decades later. "I took the job lightly, and proposed themes I had previously composed. The director listened to them, and within two weeks I had the whole soundtrack ready. The movie was having a hard time finding a distributor, and everybody thought it was going to be a flop; instead, it was a real blockbuster."[36]

The title theme—dubbed "Blues for Gassman, Part I"—debuts under the opening credits. The lively melody is introduced by the horns; Umiliani takes a keyboard solo during the bridge, and everybody plays against finger-snapping drums and brushed cymbals. This cue repeats many times during the film, always with a smaller subset of the full ensemble. A sentimental love theme, introduced with a sweet solo trumpet carrying the melody, is heard when Mario meets Carmelina.

RCA Italiana released portions of Umiliani's score on a 7-inch EP.

* * *

The year 1958 also marked the scoring debut of a composer destined to become *quite* famous in soundtrack circles.

Lalo Schifrin supplemented a standard grade school education in Argentina with private lessons in piano, harmony and counterpoint; in 1953, at age 20, he accepted a composition scholarship at the Paris Music Conservatory. By then he had become an accomplished jazz pianist who balanced his daytime classical instruction with evenings performing in combos with Europe's finest jazz musicians. Schifrin returned to Argentina in 1956 and assembled a concert jazz band that secured numerous performance contracts on radio and the nascent television industry. This enhanced visibility had two career-defining results. Most significantly, visiting trumpeter, composer and bandleader Dizzy Gillespie asked Schifrin to join him in the United States, as his pianist and arranger. Before leaving, Schifrin was hired to score director Fernando Ayala's *El Jefe* (*The Boss*).[37] It would become the first film score in a career that would last well over half a century.

Ayala's film is a thinly disguised indictment of former Argentinean President Juan Perón, who'd been overthrown in a *coup d'état* three years earlier. It's a taut bit of crime *noir*, with numerous nighttime scenes given an apprehensive atmosphere by Richard Younis' gorgeous monochrome cinematography. Alberto de Mendoza stars as a charismatic, Perón-esque gang leader dubbed "El Jefe," who commands—and bullies—a motley crew of larcenous thugs willing to do his bidding, under the naïve belief that they're advancing the social good (which they absolutely aren't). Loyalties crumble as the violence escalates, reaching a climax when El Jefe accidentally kills a young woman. When he tries to shift blame to the group's young protégé, the entire gang rebels and denounces him. Unable to talk or buy his way free, El Jefe collapses: a whimpering, shrieking coward deservedly guaranteed to be arrested and tried for murder.

Schifrin handled the piano himself. The main theme kicks off with strings; the melody's foreboding 2-6 motif is traded between dour sax and trumpet solos. A later confrontation gains suspenseful tension via furious piano and bass riffs, followed by a ferocious drum solo when El Jefe beats a victim senseless. A quiet piano solo then follows the gang, as they slowly leave the unconscious man behind. Schifrin's best opportunities to exercise his sizable jazz orchestra are used as source cues: some fast-paced Latin swing, to back a dancer at a nightclub; several lively trumpet- and sax-fueled bebop combo numbers, when the gang assembles on El Jefe's yacht one evening; and some threatening bebop, with a savage trumpet, when El Jefe and his young acolyte pick up two young women, prior to the third-act climax.

"I used some jazz instrumentation for that movie," Schifrin acknowledged, years later, "although I wouldn't call it a jazz score."[38]

He was far too modest. It's an excellent jazz score, even more impressive given that it was Schifrin's first stab at film work. A partial soundtrack was released as a 78 rpm double-disc EP on Argentina's Disc Jockey label. Sadly, the four tracks never have been digitized or included on any of Schifrin's various anthology albums.

3

Blue Satin: 1959

It was the golden year.

Never again would so much sensational jazz—by top-flight artists—be so prevalent in film and television, both in the States and Western Europe. Virtually every American detective/crime series of the 1959–60 season was armed with a sleek title credits sequence and a sassy swing theme.

Jazz fans were in clover.

The Small Screen

Jack Webb couldn't let go of 1920s-era bandleader and cornet player Pete Kelly, who he already had played in a 1951 radio series and 1955 big-screen adaptation.

With *Dragnet* about to conclude its final season on NBC, Webb persuaded network brass to green-light a TV adaptation of *Pete Kelly's Blues*. The show made a late-season debut on April 5, with its Kansas City "Roaring '20s" speakeasy setting intact, along with the hovering criminal element that did its best to make trouble. Such melodrama again is no more than a minor distraction during half-hour episodes that focus mostly on the music performed by Pete's Original Big Seven Band, along with occasional guest musicians and singers. Webb surrendered the starring role to William Reynolds—whose horn playing is ghosted, as before, by Dick Cathcart—and Pete gets a steady gal pal in club singer Savannah Brown (Connee Boswell).

Despite the terrific music and Webb's active, behind-the-scenes involvement, the series failed to catch; it was canceled after only 13 episodes. Warner Bros. nonetheless issued a soundtrack album under the amusingly descriptive title of *Pete Kelly's Blues: The Authentic Music from the Television Production* (to distinguish it from the earlier film soundtrack LPs).

Those who preferred their action grittier and modern likely gravitated toward CBS' *Tightrope*. Viewers never know the name of the character played by star Mike Connors; as a deep undercover agent, his identity changes each time he infiltrates a fresh faction of organized crime. The taut, half-hour *noir* thriller ran for a single season, beginning September 8. George Duning composed the terse title theme, which is dominated by a repeated four-note melody on brass and strings, against ominous bongos. It's not really jazz, but this TV season's rush of swing-enhanced cops and private detectives prompted solid covers by Vic Schoen (Kapp), The Volcanos (Philips) and Stan Reynolds (Decca).

Imitation may be the sincerest form of flattery; in Hollywood, it has long been a way of life. The elevator pitch for NBC's *Staccato* couldn't have sounded more like *Peter Gunn*: Title character Johnny Staccato spends his down time in a Greenwich Village basement jazz club called Waldo's, where most episodes pause long enough to enjoy some cool sounds from the resident combo. Although lacking a steady sweetie, Staccato "stumbles" into cases in much the same way, thanks to an endless parade of crooks, hustlers, desperate dames and other assorted low-lifes.

But the comparison stops with the broad strokes. Star John Cassavetes plays the much scruffier Staccato just like the character's name: feisty, feral, impatient and wound tighter than the combo's drums. Unlike Gunn, Staccato also is a jazz pianist in his own right, with a tendency to sit in with the house sextet. The show's scripts are aggressively *noir*, as are the late-night settings and lush, atmospheric cinematography. Staccato walks a much seamier street; you'd never see Gunn involved with two young lovers trying to sell their unborn child.

Staccato also takes greater pride in its musicians. Waldo's combo features Pete Candoli (trumpet), Barney Kessel (guitar), Red Norvo (vibes), Red Mitchell (bass), Shelly Manne (drums) and a youthful Johnny Williams (piano), all of them seen on camera during several episodes, and name-checked during the end credits. Guest musicians include alto saxman Ronnie Lang, drummer Milt Holland, flutist Paul Horn, singer Nora Evans, and percussionist Jack Costanzo. The show's powerful theme and underscores for all 27 episodes came from Elmer Bernstein. The title theme opens with forcefully rolling percussion, backing off just a touch as the melody—a hard-charging 2-4-7-2 motif—emerges via unison brass, then repeats on equally insistent saxes. The tempo shifts during a double-time swing bridge dominated by a ferocious sax solo and bass-end piano runs. The result is breathtaking: absolutely the most exciting piece of music to open a TV show during the 1959–60 season.

Manne's participation was invaluable. "Shelly was one of my favorite people in the whole world," Bernstein acknowledged, years later. "As a drummer, he was very inventive. Let me put it this way: Generally, I tend to be rhythmically very active, and Shelly got a big kick out of that."[1]

Bernstein took an intriguing approach to the Capitol soundtrack album. Four of the 12 tracks are small combo numbers performed by the Waldo's sextet; four other tracks are performed by a 12-man "little big band" unit—two trumpets, two trombones, three reeds, vibes and four rhythm players—and the remaining three tracks, along with "Staccato's Theme," display the richer, more atmospheric sound of a full-size 25-man ensemble. The title theme attracted a couple of covers: notably Buddy Morrow and His Orchestra (RCA), and Martin Slavin (Decca UK).

Sadly, *Staccato* wasn't long for this world, much to the chagrin of jazz fans who canceled appointments to park in front of their TV sets every Thursday evening. Cassavetes, his eyes on the big screen, quickly grew annoyed by the demands imposed by weekly television; NBC eventually tired of his disruptive antics, and the series came to an abbreviated conclusion on March 24, 1960.

Having struck gold with *77 Sunset Strip*, Warner Bros. wasted no time creating two clones set in other U.S. locales that still were considered "exotic" to TV viewers in 1959. *Bourbon Street Beat* arrived first, on October 5; it's set in New Orleans, city of Dixieland jazz and wailin' blues. Cal Calhoun (Andrew Duggan) and Rex Randolph (Richard Long) run a two-man detective agency from an office above a French Quarter restaurant dubbed the Old Absinthe House. Cal and Rex are assisted by Melody Lee Mercer (Arlene Howell) and younger, hunky, detective wannabe Kenny Madison (Van Williams). Musical authenticity is supplied by a pianist known as The Baron—actually Eddie Cole, brother of the more famous Nat King Cole—who entertains Old Absinthe House diners with sassy, Dixieland-style keyboard work.

Hawaiian Eye arrived two days later, on October 7. (Hawaii had become a state just a few months earlier, on August 21.) Private gumshoes Tom Lopaka (Robert Conrad) and Tracy Stele (Anthony Eisley) base their luxurious poolside office at the Hawaiian Village Hotel, where they can easily catch a cab driven by ukulele-wielding, comic-relief sidekick Kazuo Kim (Poncie Ponce). Cheesecake is supplied by ditzy photographer-cum-nightclub singer Cricket Blake (Connie Stevens); between her and Kazuo, the show quickly became even sillier than *77 Sunset Strip* ... although, like its parent, *Hawaiian Eye* proved quite popular, and survived for four seasons.

Both shows boast pop-oriented vocal theme songs by the *77 Sunset Strip* duo of Mack David and Jerry Livingston. "Bourbon Street Beat" offers a bit of rolling percussion behind infantile lyrics; that said, the theme is quite catchy. "Hawaiian Eye" is pure corn, with similarly silly lyrics chanted against island-style percussion.

The cheekiest part of Warners' PI franchise was the release of jazz-inflected "soundtrack albums," despite the fact—as with *77 Sunset Strip*—that virtually all episode underscores are built from library cues. Once again imitating the template established by the parent show, both albums rely heavily on multiple instrumental arrangements of the respective title themes, with the rest of each disc filled out by covers of standards. Aside from the title songs, neither contains music heard within the respective series.

Music director Don Ralke earned the cover credit for the *Bourbon Street Beat* album. The covers include a saucy midtempo reading of "Blues in the Night"; a dreamy arrangement of "The Birth of the Blues," which boasts fine keyboard work by Eddie Cole; and the latter's gorgeous solo piano reading of "I Cover the Waterfront."

Warren Barker orchestrated the *Hawaiian Eye* album, which offers more source tunes and relies less heavily on reprises of the title theme. That said, the larkish cues are mostly cocktail exotica; the Arthur Denny/Martin Lyman/Esquivel influence is particularly obvious on a percussion-heavy, island-hued expansion of the title theme. (*Surfside 6*, which debuted a year later and ran for two seasons on ABC, was the only one of the *77 Sunset Strip* clones that failed to generate a soundtrack album, faux or otherwise. Nor was its dreadful Livingston/David title theme deemed worthy of individual release.)

"Bourbon Street Beat" was covered—with far more brass snap, and a sizzling solo by trombonist Warren Covington—by the Tommy Dorsey Orchestra (Decca). Stevens parlayed her popularity into a Warner Bros. LP with the headline-challenging title of *The New Singing Sensation of Television: Connie Stevens, as "Cricket" in the Warner Bros. Series "Hawaiian Eye,"* although none of the dozen tracks has anything to do with the TV series. In the States, the only jazz cover of the *Hawaiian Eye* title theme came from keyboardist Ernie Freeman (Imperial), but it also popped up on the Werner Müller Orchestra's 1962 album, *Hawaiian Swing* (Decca UK).

Viewers who found the various Warner Bros. detectives too frivolous might have been heartened by the TV series debut of Raymond Chandler's famed private investigator, but the author's fans certainly weren't, and with good reason; ABC's *Philip Marlowe* sanitized the character to the point of utter blandness. Philip Carey's lackluster performance also brought little to the table. The show limped along for half a season after its debut on October 6, and nobody mourned its loss.

Well ... nobody except jazz fans. The show's many faults aside, it boasts a terrific jazz theme by Richard Markowitz, who also composed all episode underscores. The title theme opens with ominous percussion and jagged brass riffs, as Marlowe's car approaches along a deserted, late-night road; unison trumpets introduce the melody, while the rhythm section shifts into a tense "countdown" mode, then builds to a crescendo of brass. Markowitz filled each episode with an ambitious amount of music: edgy action jazz during car chases and gun-laden confrontations; suspenseful swing cues for late-night skulking or conversations with potential suspects; and sultry small combo numbers—often dominated by silky piano riffs—when a lascivious dame is involved (pretty much every week). None of the music survived its television origins, nor has the series been revived for home video.

Squeamish viewers who *did* enjoy Carey's mild Philip Marlowe must've choked on their corn flakes when *The Untouchables* hit ABC on October 15. The crime series immediately got tagged as the most sadistic show on the tube, thanks to frequent, body-slamming bursts of gunfire, and scripts that include reasonably overt (for their time) depictions of seamy topics such as prostitution and drug abuse. Series star Robert Stack had debuted as heroic Eliot Ness half a year earlier, battling Al Capone in a two-part pilot episode that ran on consecutive installments—March 27 and April 10—of the CBS anthology series *Desilu Playhouse*. When the pilot went to series, Ness and his incorruptible fellow agents set their sights on Capone associates Dutch Schultz, "Bugs" Moran and "Mad Dog" Coll, along with others—such as Ma Barker—who never crossed paths with the actual Ness.

The early 1930s setting—in and around Chicago—encourages the use of considerable jazz, but very little of this music (at least initially) was original. The title theme, however, is an entirely different story: It came from the jazz-hued pen of arranger, composer and bandleader Nelson Riddle, already quite famous for his collaborations with Frank Sinatra and Nat King Cole. The theme opens with a sustained single note on unison brass, followed by the 5-6-6 fanfare that anchors the melody. The extended end credits version includes a cluster of two-beat brass fanfares at heartbeat tempo, against forcefully hypnotic percussion that suggests a slow funeral march (rather appropriate, given the number of thugs executed during the course of an average hour). Riddle eventually composed original scores for the first season's penultimate episode ("Head of Fire, Feet of Clay"), along with the first two episodes of the second season ("The Rusty Heller Story" and "The Jack 'Legs' Diamond Story").

Thanks to that and the series' rising popularity, Riddle was encouraged to produce a soundtrack album. Alas, fans quickly realized they'd been conned by Capitol's *Original Music from the TV Show The Untouchables*; Riddle's memorable title theme is the only track actually taken from the show. He fabricated the remaining dozen tracks in various 1930s styles, from Joplin-esque tack piano and Charleston-style banjo riffs, to the tuba and C-melody sax riffs typical of Dixieland: many with deliberately "pun-ny" names such as "Dejected-Ness" and "Tender-Ness." (Yes, there's also an "Eliot-Ness.")

Covers of the title theme came from The Applejacks (Lee Gordon), Milton DeLugg and His Orchestra (Roulette) and Howard McGhee (Winley).

Riddle also became involved with another popular crime series. ABC and creator Stirling Silliphant revived *Naked City* after a one-year hiatus, this time as an hour-long drama that debuted October 12. Paul Burke became the new star, as Det. Adam Flint; Horace McMahon and Harry Bellaver returned as supporting characters Lt. Parker and Sgt. Arcaro. This version of the series was far more successful, running three full seasons. The semi-documentary storytelling and atmospheric monochrome palette were retained, but the music underwent a shift. George Duning's previous title theme was dropped, and a new tune was commissioned from arranger/composer Billy May, a veteran of the big band jazz era. The result, a torch ballad subtitled "Somewhere in the Night," became an immediate and much-covered hit, both as an instrumental and pop vocal (the latter featuring Milt Raskin's lyrics).

Choice arrangements—whether titled "Naked City Theme" or "Somewhere in the Night"—came from Paul Phillips and His Band (Medallion); Jack Costanzo and His Orchestra (London); the Tony Hatch Orchestra (Pye); and Laurindo Almeida and the Bossa Nova All Stars (Capitol). Jazz chanteuse Teri Thornton delivered the definitive vocal version—a leisurely, bluesy pleasure—for Dauntless. Riddle, not to be outdone on a theme that he was performing on TV each week, issued his own version for Capitol; it *just* "bubbled under" *Billboard's* Hot 100 Chart at No. 130, on October 20 and November 10, 1962.

May's involvement was much more ambitious than just the title theme, because producer Herbert B. Leonard insisted on new music for every episode. He desired a "sophisticated" touch, and May wove thematically appropriate cues into each fresh drama, along with signature themes for the stars and frequent co-stars. He soon found it difficult to meet the demands of roughly 20 minutes' worth of new music for each weekly episode. "Good God," he said, at one point, "there's only an eight-bar melody in there. How many times could I turn it around? If I'd known the show was going to be a hit, I'd have written a more complicated theme."[2]

Salvation came when Screen Gems music supervisor Eddie Forsyth shared May's growing fatigue with Riddle, who had just begun to churn out similarly new underscores for CBS' *Route 66*, also under the supervision of Leonard. "I want the job!" Riddle immediately insisted. "I told him, 'You're mad, man,'" Forsyth laughed. "'You can't do that. My God, that's double the load, 40 minutes of original music!'"[3]

Riddle persevered and got the assignment. When *Naked City* finally closed its final case, Riddle had written 52 original underscores, to May's 43. The distinction is generally obvious: May's cues have a stronger jazz flavor, whether gentle or uptempo, and a greater reliance on brass statements; Riddle's scores are softer and more orchestral, with a greater reliance on strings. But that's an oversimplification; Riddle was equally adept at delivering a solid jazz score when a storyline required one.

It's an eternal shame that no soundtrack albums emerged from this revived *Naked City*; May and Riddle's output easily could have filled a prestige box set.

As the show's second season drew to a close, Riddle—who had faithfully retained May's theme in each episode he scored—lobbied for permission to write his own theme for the upcoming third season. Leonard and Forsyth granted Riddle's request, but for some reason this "New Naked City Theme" never was used.[4] This may have been a shrewd, eleventh-hour judgment on Leonard's part; Riddle's fresh theme is a breezy, sax-anchored anthem that seems better suited to *Route 66* than *Naked City*. It survives today only because Riddle included it on one of his compilation albums of reorchestrated and jazzed-up TV themes.

May's title theme—usually performed by Costanzo or Riddle—continues to surface on crime jazz anthology albums.

Naked City's semi-anthology approach made it an apt companion for ABC's *The Detectives*—also known as *The Detectives, Starring Robert Taylor* or *Robert Taylor's Detectives*—a drama that cycled its stars from week to week. Taylor is the common element, as the dour, hard-charging Capt. Matt Holbrook, head of a metropolitan police force; his rotating investigators include burglary detective John Russo (Tige Andrews), homicide detective James Conway (Lee Farr) and bunco squad veteran Otto Lindstrom (Russell Thorson). Herschel Burke Gilbert composed both the military-esque title theme and the library of underscore cues used during the show's three-year run, which began October 16, 1959. The music is standard-issue symphonia, but fans who swear they recall a jazzy title theme aren't hallucinating.

When the series moved to NBC for its third and final year, execs asked Gilbert to recast the title theme. "They thought we should try a little jazz version," Gilbert recalled, decades later. "I said hey, that's a great idea. So I recorded it, brought it back, and we put it in. It didn't seem to sit too well … same theme, same music, but in a jazz style. It was used for the main title and end title, and a few places in the series. Nobody seemed to be crazy over it, including me. By the third week, we cut out the jazz main title and went back to the classical march main title. By the sixth week, we stopped it on the end title, and played [the show] out with the original, and never went back to the jazz. It just didn't work! Nobody cared for it."[5]

* * *

Writer/director Blake Edwards, apparently not satisfied with having Henry Mancini provide roughly 15 minutes' worth of music for each episode of *Peter Gunn*, doubled his friend's workload by starting a new weekly series on October 24, just as Pete 'n' Edie began their second season. CBS' *Mr. Lucky* was adapted *very* loosely from the 1943 Cary Grant film; Edwards borrowed little more than the title, and the notion that the main character likes to gamble. As personified by John Vivyan, Lucky—he's never given a first name—oversees a luxurious floating casino on the good ship Fortuna, which maintains its "legal" status by anchoring just outside the 12-mile limit from an unspecified municipal shore. Lucky's patrons are a blend of socialites and shady characters; he discourages the latter from hanging around too long. Lucky and best friend/business associate Andamo (Ross Martin)—never given a *last* name—frequently spar with local cop Lt. Rovacs (Tom Brown). In later episodes, Lucky acquires a sorta-kinda steady girlfriend (Pippa Scott, as Maggie).

"The music for *Mr. Lucky* was designed to have a sound as different from that of *Peter Gunn* as possible," Mancini explained. "I'd heard Wild Bill Davis play the Hammond organ. His playing was concise, swinging and energetic. Another keyboard player, Buddy Cole, was also an expert organist, with a distinctive sound. So I wrote the theme for strings and assigned the punctuations normally given the brass to the Hammond organ, with Buddy playing the part. In the second chorus, I had him take a solo on the melody."[6]

This "softer" approach notwithstanding, the theme and Mancini's underscore cues still employed the swing touch with which *Peter Gunn* fans were familiar. The composer's weekly agenda became quite punishing. "On Tuesdays, I would look at the next *Peter Gunn* episode in the schedule; that night I would go in to MGM and record the score for the episode before it. On Wednesday, I would go in and watch the next *Mr. Lucky*, and that night I would record the music for the current episode. Each show had roughly 15 minutes of music. I would write the music for both shows between Thursday and Sunday. Jimmy Priddy, whom I had first known when he was in the trombone section of Tex [Beneke's] band, and who was a regular member of that little *Peter Gunn* band, was also my copyist, and he would be standing by. I'd turn out my pages and give them to him, and he'd get the music ready to record."[7]

This new show's gentle bossa nova title theme radiates sophistication, and the first five notes became an anthem; Lucky's watch chimes that melodic phrase when he checks the time, and the theme also pops up as underscore (unlike the "Peter Gunn Theme," in its series). Jay Livingston and Ray Evans supplied romantic lyrics, and—once heard (although never during the series' run)—it became impossible *not* to associate those initial five rising notes with the first line.

Just as every episode of *Peter Gunn* opens with the same menacing walking bass cue, Mancini kicks off each *Mr. Lucky* teaser with a similarly slow and ominous four-beat on drums, adding low-end 2-2 horn riffs and a climactic brass stinger, as (frequently) an unlucky witness to some criminal behavior meets a bad end. Andamo's vaguely South American/Caribbean-esque heritage also gives Mancini an excuse to fill the underscores with sleek samba and gentle bossa nova cues, along with occasional light-hearted swingers.

The series proved quite popular, and likely could have run for several seasons; unfortunately, it ran afoul of real-world events. The steadily brewing "quiz show scandal" of the late 1950s came to a head when a U.S. congressional subcommittee investigation began in the summer of 1959. This climaxed on November 2, during a televised subcommittee session, when disgraced TV game show contestant Charles Van Doren confessed his willing participation in behind-the-scenes rigging on shows such as *Twenty One*.[8] The subsequent overreaction went too far in the opposite direction, particularly on the part of the easily intimidated sponsors of TV shows, who feared moral criticism and ruled artistic decisions with an iron hand. With no explanation, beginning with the 16th episode, Lucky and Andamo suddenly are hosting a floating *restaurant*, instead of a casino ship.

Viewership dropped dramatically. "No longer excellent, [the ratings] remained good enough to keep the show on the air," Mancini recalled, "but Blake was unhappy. At the end of the year, he said, 'I'm not going to lend my name to this,' and closed the show down."[9]

Ironically, RCA released the first soundtrack album in early spring 1960, just after this format change; Mancini expanded a dozen of the show's cues into a collection of smooth bossa nova tracks. The album had an impressively healthy run of 78 weeks on *Billboard*'s Top LPs chart, through September 18, 1961. By that time, the show had been off the CBS schedule for an entire year, and the album also had a companion; *Mr. Lucky Goes Latin*, released in February 1961, stayed on the chart for 29 weeks. As had been the case with the two *Peter Gunn* albums, both *Mr. Lucky* soundtracks charted simultaneously. As its title suggests, the second album has a stronger Latin flavor, thanks to the participation of guitarist/mandolin player Laurindo Almeida.

Mancini's *Mr. Lucky* albums didn't get near the attention that had followed his music for *Peter Gunn*, although the title theme generated cool covers by Francis Bay (Omega), Georgie Auld (Top Rank International), Wally Stott (Pye), the Modernaires (UA), Vince Guaraldi (Fantasy) and Quincy Jones (Mercury). Sarah Vaughan released what remains the definitive vocal version, also for Mercury. The tune soon became an established standard included on albums by just about every top-flight jazz artist one could name.

* * *

The rapidly rising number of jazz-based television scores prompted a wealth of compilation cover albums in 1959, starting with the Warren Barker/Frank Comstock collaboration, *TV Guide Top Television Themes* (Warner Bros.). The LP opens with a swinging, double-time arrangement of "The D.A.'s Man"; other highlights include a delightfully stern reading of "The Perry Mason Theme," and a sweetly melancholy handing of "Pete Kelly's Blues." Skip Martin summoned several familiar faces to join an ensemble dubbed the Video All-Stars, for *TV Jazz Themes* (Somerset); the players include Jimmy Rowles, Paul Horn, Frank Rosolino, Shelly Manne, Red Mitchell and Pete Candoli. The album's first side covers half a dozen cues from *Peter Gunn*; the flip side contains generously long arrangements of the title themes from *Richard Diamond, 77 Sunset Strip* and *The Thin Man*. Somerset also issued *Songs and Sounds from the Era of The Untouchables*, as performed by "Skip Martin and His Prohibitionists." This large, Dixieland-style ensemble includes Pete Candoli, Frank Rosolino, Stan Wrightson and Red Mitchell. It's an effects-laden concept album; aside from a smoky, clarinet-flavored cover of Nelson Riddle's main theme for *The Untouchables*, the remaining tracks are merely suggested by the ambiance of 1930s Chicago.

Coral's somewhat mis-titled *Jazz Themes for Cops and Robbers*, by Leith Stevens and His Orchestra, actually is built from two sessions. Eight tracks come from Stevens' score for the big-screen film *Private Hell 36*, while the other four are TV theme covers. The combo for the latter features Buddy Childers (trumpet), Herb Geller (alto sax), Bud Shank (alto sax/flute), Dave Pell (baritone sax/bass clarinet), Russ Freeman (piano), Joe Mondragon (bass) and Shelly Manne (drums). They deliver tasty readings of "The Thin Man," "Perry Mason," "Peter Gunn" and "M Squad." The "dazzling sound of Keith Williams and His Orchestra" is featured on Edison International's *Big Band Jazz Themes from Television & Motion Pictures*. Highlights include "Perry Mason," "M Squad," "Richard Diamond," "Peter Gunn" and big-screen title themes from *The Wild One, I Want to Live!* and *The Man with the Golden Arm*.

The jazz touch is equally pleasing on Mercury's *Music for a Private Eye*, courtesy of Ralph Marterie and His Marlboro Men. This tight-tight-*tight* ensemble features Don Fagerquist, Ray Linn, Uan Rasey and Joe Triscari (trumpets); Bob Fitzpatrick, Tommy Pederson and Frank Rosolino (trombones); George Roberts (bass trombone); Paul Horn and Bud Shank (alto saxes); Gus Bivona and Bob Cooper (tenor saxes); Dale Issenhuth (baritone sax); Jimmy Rowles (piano); Al Viola (guitar); Joe Mondragon (bass); Irv Kluger (drums); and Lou Singer (percussion). Basie-style piano filigrees introduce the album-opening "M Squad," which blends tight rhythm with sleek solos on sax and trombone; mysterious drums and percussion elements kick off a bluesy arrangement of "Richard Diamond," with the melody traded between a sweet trumpet and unison brass. The menu also includes "The Thin Man," "77 Sunset Strip" and a boisterous, double-time arrangement of "The D.A.'s Man."

The don't-*dare*-miss offering came from guitarist Mundell Lowe and His All Stars: an octet that features Donald Byrd (trumpet), Jimmy Cleveland (trombone), Herbie Mann (flute and tenor sax), Tony Scott (clarinet and baritone sax), Eddie Costa (piano and vibes), Don Payne (bass) and Ed Shaughnessy (drums). Their well-titled RCA release, *TV Action Jazz!*, opens with a rip-snortin' cover of "Peter Gunn" that showcases the first of Lowe's many fleet-fingered guitar solos. Mike Hammer never got a reading of "Riff Blues" this sweet during his TV run; the arrangement is bluesy jazz gold. Even "The Perry Mason Theme" gets reconstructed as a midtempo finger-snapper, with tasty solos on reeds, guitar and vibes.

That was a tough act to follow, but Buddy Morrow gave it a decent shot with RCA's *Impact*. His approach is more dance band—sometimes augmented by a string section—than high-intensity jazz, although his ensemble (no player is identified) delivers some tight and tasty work. "Riff Blues" is highlighted by a sweet piano solo; "Perry Mason" offers rumbling drums and the drawl of unison horns backed by the obligatory rolling rhythm section; and "Richard Diamond" displays plenty of big band jazz fire, from a double-time percussion prelude to the tasty roar of unison horns and a wailing sax solo at the bridge.

The Buddy Morrow and Mundell Lowe albums have been digitized; the others exist solely on hard-to-find vinyl.

The Big Screen

Director Otto Preminger's mesmerizing adaptation of *Anatomy of a Murder* earned seven Academy Award nominations—losing all of them, thanks to *Ben-Hur*—but the true Oscar outrage was the absence of a nomination for Duke Ellington's sensational soundtrack: the first of only four big-screen features that he scored. Apparently the Academy's Music Branch voters were too stuffy to acknowledge a progressive jazz score: arguably Hollywood's first full non-diegetic jazz score assigned to a well-known composer.

The screenplay is adapted from the 1958 novel of the same title by Michigan Supreme Court Justice John D. Voelker, who based the story on his experience as a defense attorney during a lurid 1952 murder trial. The crime is a *fait accompli* as the film opens: Small-town attorney Paul "Paulie" Biegler (James Stewart) accepts the challenge to defend U.S. Army Lt. Frederick "Manny" Manion (Ben Gazzara), a Korean War veteran who turned himself in after shooting and killing roadhouse owner Bernard Quill. Manny readily acknowledges his action, arguing that it was justified because his wife Laura (Lee Remick) had just been beaten and raped by Quill. Preliminary interviews and research ultimately climax in a courtroom duel between Biegler and visiting state prosecutor Claude Dancer (George C. Scott).

The bulk of the score is heard during the film's first hour, as Biegler and his associates prepare for the case. Once the action shifts to the actual trial, the soundtrack remains silent; no music is heard in the courtroom. Ellington clearly relished the challenge of his first film soundtrack, writing distinct character themes—particularly the one for Laura—and incorporating variations into later scenes, as appropriate.

"I like playing with music and its relationship to the theater, particularly in the supporting role," Ellington noted, on an open-end interview disc that was sent to media outlets across the country. (Such discs came with prepared questions, so—for example—a radio DJ could frame a query to get the appropriate canned response, thus conveying the impression that Ellington was in the studio for a live interview.) "Doing the score for a picture really calls for being along with the action, and absorbing all of the atmosphere [of] everything taking place in the picture."[10]

The film opens with an explosive bleat on muted trumpet, which leads to a full-blown orchestral blast when the title appears amid Saul Bass' credits sequence. Propulsive, mid-tempo 4/4 swing takes us from the credits to a late-night montage that shows Biegler arriving home after a day spent fishing; the wordless sequence allows the full majesty of Johnny Hodges' sweet clarinet solo. The cue concludes with some of Duke's soft piano work; this foreshadows Beigler's tendency to noodle on his own piano, while trying to work out various details of the case. (Stewart's keyboard efforts are ghosted by Ellington.)

Hodges' salacious alto sax highlights the sultry, hip-swinging theme that introduces Laura: a cue appropriately titled "Flirtibird," and first heard (briefly) as source music in the bar from which she telephones Biegler, asking him to defend her husband. The cue repeats—this time with Russell Procope taking the droll clarinet line—when Biegler subsequently meets Laura and is mildly intimidated by her brazen sexuality. "This particular theme was the one I felt I had to do first," Ellington acknowledged. "It flew into me, and sort of knocked me down, and sort of wrote itself: the theme that represents Laura. I saw the rushes the first Sunday, and the minute I saw her, leaning against that car, I *knew* that I was on the right track with my No. 1 theme."[11]

As far as Ellington's fans are concerned, the best scene comes at a roadhouse late one night, when Biegler shares a piano stool with no less than the Duke himself, in his brief role as "Pie-Eye," leader of the "P.I. Five" quintet that features Ray Nance, Jimmy Hamilton, Jimmy Woode and James Johnson. They roar through a chirpy, midtempo swinger ("Happy Anatomy") that offers solos by Nance and Hamilton, Stewart doing his best to look like he's actually keeping up. As the song concludes, Biegler looks around and spots Laura, drinking and flirting with abandon. The P.I. Five launch into another vibrant number as he drags her away and—once outside—lectures her on the importance of decorum and propriety.

After the trial, Biegler is surprised to discover that the Manion house trailer is gone, Manny and Laura having split under cover of darkness. The camera pulls back as a reprise of the title theme roars into life—with echoes of "Flirtibird"—and builds to a screaming crescendo, thanks to Cat Anderson's astonishing trumpet solo, while the screen fades to black.

The soundtrack LP includes full-length versions of all the primary cues, along with a slow, bluesy ballad ("Midnight Indigo")—barely heard in the film—that blends celeste (Duke) and piano (Billy Strayhorn) with Harry Carney's achingly beautiful bass clarinet.

Although the simultaneous Columbia single failed to achieve chart success, the main theme underwent an intriguing transformation when Ellington gave the charts to good friend Peggy Lee and suggested that she set it to lyrics.[12] The result was titled "I'm Gonna Go Fishin'"—a subtle reference to Lee Remick's restless sybarite—and it not only became a popular number during Lee's concerts, but an instrumental and vocal jazz standard covered by Gerry Mulligan, Ella Fitzgerald, Shorty Rogers, Mel Tormé, The Four Freshman, Maria Muldaur and many, many others.

Jerry Goldsmith lacked Ellington's name recognition, but he'd been working in television for roughly five years when he had the opportunity to score the low-budget *noir* thriller *City of Fear*. It was his second big-screen assignment—following a 1957 Western, *Black Patch*—and the first to demonstrate his facility for gritty, percussive action scores. Much of Goldsmith's work on *City of Fear* is dark texture music that reflects the unsettling storyline; portions of the percussion and nervous brass sound very much like the ominous, even eerie music he'd soon compose for Rod Serling's *Twilight Zone*. The *City of Fear* score is notable for its absence of violins or violas, resulting in a grim brutality that complements both the film's overall tone, and the story's vicious main character. Goldsmith includes a bit of genuine jazz, notably a theme for one of the drama's sidebar characters. (Gently swinging combo jazz emanates as source music from various car, motel and diner radios, but these snatches seem to be library music.)

The fast-paced, 81-minute drama feels quasi-documentary, with numerous montages that draw their intensity from Goldsmith's music, while police and scientists attempt to find a vicious con, Vince Ryker (Vince Edwards), who has busted out of San Quentin with a steel cylinder that he believes is filled with cocaine. In reality, the cylinder contains granulated cobalt-60, a radioactive dust capable of killing everybody in Los Angeles, should the stuff become airborne. It's the ultimate paranoia thriller, as Ryker keeps trying to open the damn thing, while failing to associate his growing illness to his proximity to the cylinder.

Goldsmith's standout jazz theme is assigned to one of Ryker's deadbeat buddies, a jittery stoolie named Pete Hallon (Sherwood Price) with a fondness for expensive shoes. The cue is a finger-snapping blend of drums, double bass, marimba, clarinet and flute, first heard when Hallon is introduced, and echoed each time he reappears. Goldsmith ratchets up a trumpet line and insistent percussion during the third act, when the increasingly sick Ryker fails to notice that the cylinder has rolled out of his car and been left behind when he stops briefly at a gas station (a plot contrivance guaranteed to raise a squawk from nervous viewers).

Goldsmith's score finally was digitized and released in 2011.

City of Fear would have played well alongside the lurid hyperbole and conspicuous overacting that fuel *Guns Girls and Gangsters*, a violent slice of *noir* that feigns factual authenticity via admonishments from a stern off-camera narrator. Director Edward L. Cahn's B-movie quickie gathers tough-talking ex-cons for a "foolproof" plan to hold up an armored car ferrying Las Vegas casino money to a Los Angeles bank. The scheme might have worked, too, were it not for jealousy over a bad-news gal: Mamie Van Doren's Vi Victor, a Vegas lounge singer introduced as she belts out an uptempo ballad—"Anything Your Heart Desires"—laden with prophetic overtones. She's backed by a swinging big band jazz orchestra; the song—and the film's underscore—are written by Buddy Bregman, an in-demand conductor, arranger and composer enjoying the busiest decade of a long and impressively star-laden career.

The caper is scheduled for the day after the massive haul expected from Vegas' New Year's Eve weekend; Chuck (Gerald Mohr) and Vi finalize details while pretending to be tourists staying at the bucolic Stage Coach Inn, near the Nevada/California border. The young married couple who run this establishment love jazz; their jukebox keeps cranking out swing hits, particularly during a New Year's Eve party thrown for all of the lodgers. Big band swing and jump jazz tunes keep the place hopping.

Although much of Bregman's score for *Guns Girls and Gangsters* is standard-issue orchestral melodrama, he can't help sneaking in some of the swing elements with which he was surrounded, as the recently hired A&R head of jazz impresario Norman Granz's fledgling Verve record label.[13] Most obviously, a saucy solo sax lends sultry emphasis to all of Van Doren's key scenes.

B-films rarely generated soundtrack albums, and this one was no exception.

When it came to *true* singers, Harry Belafonte's early fans knew him best as the wildly popular talent whose 1950s hits included "Matilda," "Day-O (The Banana Boat Song)" and the entire contents of his breakthrough album, *Calypso*. He also established a modest film career, with notable roles in 1954's *Carmen Jones* and 1957's *Island in the Sun*. The latter foreshadowed Belafonte's other passion, as a dedicated civil rights activist who'd spend his entire life confronting racial injustice. To that end, he formed his own company—HarBel Productions Inc.—and negotiated a six-film distribution deal with United Artists, which gave him *carte blanche* on all aspects of production: a first for an African American actor/producer.[14] His first project was *Odds Against Tomorrow*, based on William P. McGivern's gritty 1957 crime novel of the same name.

A bank heist is concocted by disgraced former cop Dave Burke (Ed Begley), who independently pitches the job to Southern racist Earle Slater (Robert Ryan) and nightclub entertainer Johnny Ingram (Belafonte). The larcenous dynamic is uncomfortable from the onset: Earle can't stand working with a black accomplice, and Johnny grows increasingly infuriated by his white partner's brazen bigotry. Dave's half-baked scheme to get into a small-town bank in upstate Melton, N.Y., succeeds to a point, but then goes awry; the climax turns unexpectedly apocalyptic, and must have shocked 1959 audiences to their shoes.

Film scholars often cite *Touch of Evil* as the last of Hollywood's "classic period *film noirs*," but that's ridiculous; *Odds Against Tomorrow* came out a year and a half later, and it's every bit as *noir* as the finest genre entries from the previous two decades. Director Robert Wise orchestrates this saga of doomed men and pathetic women with a foreboding atmosphere that gets plenty of symbolic heft from Joseph C. Brun's gritty, grimy, black-and-white cinematography.

The scoring assignment went to John Lewis and his Modern Jazz Quartet. Lewis' work here has been recognized as the earliest example of a "third stream" film score, a description introduced in 1957 by composer Gunther Schuller. He defined it formally in 1961, as "a new genre of music located about halfway between jazz and classical music."[15]

The term certainly fits this score, with its blend of then-modern jazz and chamber music. Lewis was brought onto the project during production—quite rare for a film composer, at the time—and his input was welcomed by Wise, who praised his collaborator in a letter, noting that he was "damned glad we have you doing it."[16] Lewis didn't disappoint, augmenting his quartet members with a 22-piece jazz ensemble that includes Bill Evans (piano) and Jim Hall (guitar), along with trumpets, French horns, trombones, tubas, flute, harp, cello, timpani and percussion.

Lewis often employs instruments in odd, even dissonant pairings—guitar and piano, guitar and vibes—with the two halves seeming to quarrel, much like Johnny and Earle. The resulting musical tapestry is unsettling throughout, as befits the film's ominous atmosphere, with Lewis deliberately blending the MJQ's lush, "sweet" sound with jarring, discordant orchestral counterpoint. This is evident with the unsettling trumpet fanfare, piano and vibes that kick off Lewis' opening theme, heard over the film's title credits, as a slow percussion *dum ... dum ... dum* suggests a slowly ticking time bomb.

The next cue—our introduction to the vicious Earle Slater—is a brilliant mélange of music and image. He strides down a wind-swept city street, looking more phantasm than mortal; Lewis' theme for this scene, appropriately titled "A Cold Wind Is Blowing," is an equally spooky mixture of single guitar notes and wailing trumpet, and we get the message: Something wicked this way comes. Even so, the musical atmosphere isn't *entirely* threatening. A charming waltz is heard briefly during an establishing shot of folks skating on a frozen pond: a tune that Lewis later expanded into "Skating in Central Park," which became both a hit for the MJQ, and, in later years, an oft-covered jazz standard.

Wise favors lengthy, dialogless montages that advance the action while Lewis' themes deliver the desired atmosphere. Once in Melton, Wise cuts between the three men as they separately wait for nightfall. Lewis' nervous, tick-tock blend of percussion and vibes builds to an intense crescendo that segues perfectly to the town square clock striking 6 p.m.: the signal for the men to act. As things go wrong, the music turns frantic, angry and chaotic: an anticipatory prelude to the surprise finale and its deliberately ironic exchange of dialog between two cops.

Lewis' soundtrack album is somewhat unusual. The 19 tracks are brief, some running scarcely more than a minute: all very much the way they're heard in the film. In tandem with this official soundtrack, the Modern Jazz Quartet also produced *Music from Odds Against Tomorrow*, with extended versions of "Skating in Central Park" and five other key themes.

* * *

Although the French New Wave movement resonated across the Atlantic, Hollywood mostly ignored the call; realism and nonconformity were left to the aggressive young filmmakers who kick-started the American independent cinema movement that eventually blossomed in the late 1960s. Actor-turned-filmmaker John Cassavetes beat them by at least a decade, with *Shadows*: an ultra-low-budget ensemble drama that began as an acting class exercise and then turned into a largely improvised 1958 film. But Cassavetes was unhappy with the results; he reworked and reshot most of the film, this time with a more scripted narrative.[17] This "new" version of *Shadows* was released in 1959.

As a rambling two weeks in the lives of disaffected Beat Generation twentysomethings, Cassavetes' relationship drama doesn't come close to qualifying for this book's theme; that said, it's necessary to mention the involvement of celebrated jazz bassist Charles Mingus. He accepted Cassavetes' request to score the film, and the music proved as improvisational as the shoot. But most of Mingus' efforts were left behind when Cassavetes discarded his original edit; the one surviving cue is a lengthy drum and percussion jam that fuels an increasingly combustible party sequence. One assumes Mingus didn't care for the experience; he never scored another American drama.

His original score recordings remain unreleased, although he expanded several fragments into three tracks recorded in 1959—"Nostalgia in Times Square," "Alice's Wonderland" and "Self-Portrait in Three Colours"—and released on two of his albums: *Jazz Portraits* and *Mingus Ah Um*.

Meanwhile, Across the Pond…

Five years before he began his decade-long stint as host of the first incarnation of the TV game show *Jeopardy!*, Art Fleming starred as undercover investigator Ken Franklin, the title character in the UK TV series *International Detective*. Each episode opens with a world globe that rotates slowly against a blast of brass-heavy, big band jazz: a 17-second hint of the main theme, with a 5-3 melody built from the syllables of the show's title. The week's adventure begins as Franklin is briefed on his new case; an aura of documentary-style authenticity is supplied by a title card that reads, "This story is based on the secret files of The William J. Burns International Detective Agency Inc." (Both Burns and his agency actually existed; he also ran the U.S. Bureau of Investigation—precursor to the FBI—from 1921 to '24.)[18]

Although the New York–based Franklin spends most of these fast-paced half-hour episodes dealing with crooks, forgers and kidnappers in various parts of the United States, he earns the "international" designation by occasionally flying to Paris, Switzerland, Rome, Spain, Pakistan and even Australia. The diverse settings lend themselves to a variety of musical moods, all of them given at least a modicum of jazz shading by a large ensemble—known only as the "TV All Stars"—headed by Edwin Astley, a songwriter/arranger/band leader well known for the theme music and underscores he had composed for Britain's *The Adventures of Robin Hood* and *Ivanhoe*.

International Detective is all but forgotten today, but the music has fared better. The title theme actually is credited to Hollywood composer/arranger LeRoy Holmes, but the execution is pure Astley: Following the brass fanfare that kicks off the spinning globe teaser, the arrangement blossoms into a ferocious big band melody powered by dueling banks of unison horns.

Astley handled all of the equally vibrant underscores, which earned a soundtrack album on the UK's Ember label. The 19 tracks include "The Badge," a droll, Mancini-esque swinger with a perky flute melody backed by a toe-tapping rhythm section; and "Shock Tactics," laden with the explosive brass and percussion stingers that would become Astley signatures. Somewhat oddly, Ember also released roughly half the score on an LP under the fuzzier title of *Action Themes*; in a move destined to confuse archivists for years to come, all tracks except the main theme were retitled!

Elsewhere in the World

Trust the French to beat Hollywood at its own game. Few films look more *noir* than writer/director Jean-Pierre Melville's *Deux Hommes dans Manhattan* (*Two Men in Manhattan*), a luxuriously atmospheric mood piece that wanders in the direction of a murder mystery. Nicolas Hayer's expressive, shadow-laden cinematography is matched by the exquisite blend of combo and orchestral jazz from composers Christian Chevallier and Martial Solal: the first feature scoring assignment for both.

The plot is simple. Eyebrows lift when the French delegate to the United Nations, M. Fèvre-Berthier, fails to attend an important meeting. Despite having worked a full day, Moreau (Melville), a journalist with the Manhattan branch of Agence France-Presse, is assigned to enquire about the man's possible whereabouts. He collects unscrupulous *France-Match* photographer Delmas (Pierre Grasset), who knows the city well. Their only clues are three photographs of Fèvre-Berthier, posed with three mistresses: Judith Nelson (Ginger Hall), a stage actress; Virginia Graham (Glenda Leigh), a jazz singer; and Bessie Reed (Michèle Bailly), a stripper in a burlesque show. Moreau and Delmas visit each in turn, but as the long night proceeds with no obvious leads, they begin to worry that something unpleasant may have occurred. They also aren't aware—although we viewers are—that an unknown individual in a car has been following them.

The film opens as Bernard Hulin's mournful trumpet accents a montage of late-night Manhattan streets, against which the title credits are superimposed in small quadrilaterals. The full orchestra kicks in a two-note fanfare, and then strings reprise the trumpet passage against Hulin's comping. As Hayer's credit hits the screen, the melody roars into an uptempo, Gershwin-esque jazz rhapsody; Albert Raisner's harmonica and Chevallier's vibes add perky flourishes. Brief excerpts and arrangements of this melody follow Moreau and Delmas throughout the night, with Hulin's horn adding an ominous flourish each time the mysterious car trails in their wake.

Smaller combo numbers are heard, often as source music, during each visit. Prior to linking up with Delmas, Moreau checks in with Fèvre-Berthier's secretary (Colette Fleury); their chat takes place while a vibes/piano combo plays a dreamy tune on her phonograph. A salacious sax melody is heard when Moreau then collects his colleague, reflecting the photojournalist's fondness for compliant bedmates. When they track down Virginia, at a Capitol Records recording studio, she's finishing a take of a melancholy tune dubbed "Street in Manhattan." She's backed by a soft and quite tasty quartet: Art Simmons (piano), Chevallier (vibes), Paul Rovère (acoustic bass) and Kansas Fields (drums). A subsequent stop at a posh brothel is backed by a slow, sexy horn anthem while Moreau and Delmas interview a blonde prostitute. Uptempo strip jazz trails them into the burlesque club, where Bessie proves equally unhelpful.

Eventually, having solved the mystery, Moreau is confronted with the need to protect Fèvre-Berthier's reputation; Delmas, smelling a fat payday for a scandalous story, is unwilling to play along. Their eventual confrontation takes place at a nightclub dubbed the Pike Slip Inn, where the house combo—a piano/trumpet quartet, with Solal at the keyboard—concludes its final set with a mournful dirge. Delmas' ethics surface as the film concludes; Raisner's harmonica adds an ironic touch, while the photojournalist discards the incriminating rolls of film. The full orchestra rises into a reprise of the title theme against the light of dawn, as the end credits roll up the screen.

The soundtrack album includes all the primary themes, along with Leigh's gorgeous reading of "Street in Manhattan." The score doesn't appear to have been issued on CD, but it's readily available via streaming sites such as Spotify and iTunes (although, vexingly, only in Europe).

The (regrettable) early link between jazz and scandalous behavior was never more blatant than in director Édouard Molinaro's *Des Femmes Disparaissent* (*The Road to Shame*), a suspenseful depiction of naïve young women victimized by a prostitution/slavery ring. The atmosphere is classic *noir*, given additional sinful sizzle by the (comparatively) explicit sexuality that was emerging in late 1950s French cinema. The action takes place in a single evening, granting cinematographer Robert Juillard ample opportunity for moody close-ups and shadow-laden tableaux.

Molinaro, an avid jazz fan, wanted no less than the best; thanks to an introduction facilitated by "jazz fixer" Marcel Romano, the director was able to entice Art Blakey, whose Jazz Messengers played at L'Olympia and Club St. Germain in late 1958. Blakey, intrigued by the offer, agreed to tackle *Des Femmes Disparaissent* as his first—and, as it turned out, only—feature film scoring assignment.[19]

The story begins early one evening, with a lover's tiff between Pierre (Robert Hossein) and his fiancée, Béatrice (Estella Blain); she wants to enjoy a dubious "girls' night out," and resents his concern for her safety. Pierre's apprehension is well founded; the young women naïvely travel to a large country estate, for an evening of dancing with—they've been told—successful businessmen who can secure them well-paid jobs. Alas, these immaculately dressed older "dates" actually are criminals in the employ of the ruthless Quaglio (Jacques Dacqmine); as the evening wears on, the women will be drugged, raped and subsequently transported to parts unknown for a fate worse than death. Fortunately, the resourceful Pierre makes his way to the mansion, and proves quite heroic during a crackling third act.

The stark title credits are accompanied by Blakey's quietly tense drumbeat, with unexpected bursts from Benny Golson (tenor sax) and Lee Morgan (trumpet) raising the anxiety level before the film even begins. The quintet then introduces a bluesy main theme that repeats, in several variations, as the story continues. Once the young women arrive at the mansion, Blakey supplies lengthy compositions that serve as source dance music from an unseen phonograph player; Molinaro lets these gorgeous cues proceed at length. One of these, "Blues Pour Marcel," opens with Bobby Timmons' beautiful piano melody, which he then hands off to Golson, and then to Morgan; it's achingly seductive, and an ironic antithesis to what we know is coming. The suspenseful saga concludes after an action-laden climax; Pierre and Béatrice embrace, and their happy reunion is accompanied by a victorious cue that finds Morgan's sweet trumpet line counterpointed by Golson's sax. The melody builds to a climactic flourish that resolves in perfect harmony: All is well.

The soundtrack album includes all the film cues, along with several more lovely compositions that Molinaro used only briefly, or not at all.

Molinaro adopted an even more brutal touch for *Un témoin dans la ville* (*A Witness in the City*), released only five days later (!). This is a taut, intensely suspenseful psychological depiction of the depths to which revenge will take a man, and the resulting toll on innocent civilians who get in his way. The film gets much of its tension from cinematographer Henri Decaë's foreboding monochrome tableaux, which are well served by a minimalist jazz score from French saxophonist Barney Wilen: his first big-screen credit as composer.

Molinaro opens his film with a scream—literally—as French industrialist Pierre Verdier (Jacques Berthier) kills his mistress by throwing her from a speeding train. He's acquitted during the subsequent courtroom trial—the woman's death is ruled a suicide—and he returns home late that night, smugly certain that he has gotten away with murder. But the woman's husband, Ancelin (Lino Ventura), waits inside, determined to obtain his own justice. He kills Pierre, meticulously staging the scene to look like suicide by hanging. But this scheme goes awry, forcing Ancelin to contemplate an additional murder ... or two. Everything builds to an exciting third act that takes place almost in real time, during a chaotic night that depicts the violent lengths to which the increasingly desperate Ancelin will go, once he becomes a snarling, cornered animal.

Many of Wilen's score cues are brief and atmospheric, often used by Molinaro as stingers to enhance tension: piano chords that don't quite achieve melody, unsettling trumpet riffs, anxious sax and bass, and a furious drum roll and dissonant blasts of brass and sax. In great contrast, the quintet supplies a gorgeous jazz ballad for the film's primary theme, which debuts as the title credits appear over the courtroom montage that concludes with Pierre's release. Kenny Dorham (trumpet) introduces the theme's 3-2-3-2 motif against the gentle rhythm section; the combo shifts to swing during the bridge, as the trumpet fades away and Wilen takes a melancholy solo.

The soundtrack album reveals the degree to which Molinaro truncated much of Wilen's music. The title theme is the sole melody employed at full length within the film; the director used only portions of several other tracks. "Mélodie pour les Radio Taxis" is a duet showcase for sax and piano: a lament highlighted by Wilen's achingly morose sax, with pianist Duke Jordan comping quietly until he gets an equally poignant solo at the bridge. Wilen's final cue also is more ambitious. The film employs only a brief drum roll and wandering sax, when the screen fades to black against the word *FIN*. On the album, that track continues with a lengthy, melancholy piano solo that restates Wilen's two primary melodies, until Dorham's trumpet surfaces for a fleeting finale.

Although Pierre Choderlos de Laclos' late 18th century epistolary novel, *Les Liaisons Dangereuses*, isn't a crime saga or *noir* in the usual sense, the decadent characters' scandalous behavior makes them sufficiently malevolent. French director Roger Vadim brought the story into the mid–20th century and moved the action to debauched revelries held in posh Parisian homes and a Swiss ski chalet, and he designed the film to bare ingénues Annette Stroyberg and Jeanne Valérie to a notorious degree (for the time). The film also boasts an amazing score by two legendary jazz combos, but Vadim didn't treat the music with much respect.

Music advisor Marcel Romano went after no less than Thelonious Monk, who—after some dithering—spent July 27, 1959, in a New York studio with Charlie Rouse (tenor sax), Sam Jones (bass) and Arthur Taylor (drums); the combo recorded one or two takes of 11 tunes.[20] Almost all of these tracks were existing Monk standards such as "Pannonia," "Light Blue" and "Crepuscule with Nellie"—the latter featuring Barney Wilen, replacing Rouse on sax—along with a lovely solo piano cover of the Charles Albert Tindley hymn, "We'll Understand It Better By and By." In other words, Monk did not compose any new material specifically for the film.

Vadim couldn't have been unhappy, since he used much of this music. Even so, Monk's contributions were too relaxed and thoughtful for the party scenes that are key settings; these sequences demanded more pizzazz. Vadim and Romano therefore hired jazz pianist Duke Jordan to write some uptempo sparklers, which were recorded during two sessions by Art Blakey and the Jazz Messengers, in the same New York studio Monk and his crew had occupied the previous day. A lively percussion section—Tommy Lopez and William Rodriguez (congas), and John Rodriguez (bongos)—added fire to one cut, "No Hay Problema."[21]

Vadim then incorporated this wealth of great jazz into his finished edit. The results proved ... well, rather random.

The film's title credits are superimposed over a chessboard; cinematographer Marcel Grignon's camera slowly moves among the various pieces as Monk's mostly solo piano reading of "Crepuscule with Nellie" sets a contemplative mood. The pawns clearly represent the hapless individuals soon to be ensnared by the callously cruel behavior of Valmont (Gérard Philipe) and Juliette de Merteuil (Jeanne Moreau), married sexual predators who delight in debasing their various conquests. The stage is set during one of their refined cocktail parties, where Juliette is dumped by her middle-age American lover, Court (Nicolas Vogel). He has decided to marry 16-year-old Cécile (Valérie). Juliette seeks revenge by asking her husband to seduce Cécile, thereby rendering her "impure."

After the guests depart, Juliette explains that Valmont will find Cécile enjoying a holiday at a Swiss ski chalet. Monk's dreamy "Light Blue" plays on the phonograph as the couple eagerly anticipates the "fun" to come, at which point the diegetic cue abruptly becomes non-diegetic, during a smash edit that finds Valmont on the ski slopes. The same thing happens in reverse shortly thereafter: Monk's "Pannonica" is a larkish backdrop when Valmont takes a mild tumble in the snow. When this scene cuts to Juliette, reading a letter he has sent to their home back in Paris, the tune smoothly becomes a diegetic source cue—without skipping a beat—heard from the phonograph.

Although Valmont proceeds confidently in his campaign to lure Cécile into bed, he's distracted by another vision of loveliness: Marianne (Stroyberg), a quiet young woman with a husband and young child. To Valmont's surprise, he falls genuinely in love with Marianne, a hiccup that Juliette doesn't like at all. Events build to a ghastly climax during a rowdy and debauched party, the atmosphere growing more lascivious as alcohol flows and guests shed their clothes. This gleeful bacchanalia is fueled by a vigorous on-camera performance by Jordan (piano), Barney Wilen (sax), Kenny Dorham (trumpet), Paul Rovère (bass) and Kenny Clarke (drums). Rather annoyingly, though, as this sequence proceeds Vadim brusquely cycles through fleeting snippets of five Jazz Messenger cues—"Weehawken Mad Pad," "Miguel's Party," "Prelude in Blue," "No Problem" and "Valmontana"—with no regard for pauses or transitions. It sounds like somebody drops a phonograph tone arm at random portions of an LP, lets it play for five seconds, and then picks up the tone arm and drops it elsewhere, again and again. At one point, it's blatantly obvious that Clarke's on-camera drumming isn't synched to the score.

The 16 tracks recorded by Monk and his combo weren't released commercially until the summer of 2017; in the meanwhile, folks had to be content with what could be heard in the film. The Jazz Messengers recordings fared better, with a Fontana LP: *Art Blakey's Jazz Messengers Avec Barney Wilen: Les Liaisons Dangereuses 1960*. But that wasn't the end of the film's tempestuous relationship with its musicians. For reasons unknown, Jordan was denied credit on camera, his name replaced by the alias "Jack Marray." Obviously irked, he gathered a new quintet and rerecorded all of his music for a 1962 LP, *Duke Jordan: Les Liaisons Dangereuses*. By way of twisting the knife further, Jordan retitled most of the tracks!

Sliding southeast across the border, the success of Italy's *I soliti ignoti* made a sequel inevitable. It arrived in December 1959, with director Nanni Loy replacing Mario Monicelli on what became *Audace colpo dei soliti ignoti* (re-titled *Fiasco in Milan*, when released in the States almost four years later). Loy's touch is somewhat broader, and the comedy therefore more burlesque, but the plot "bumps" are pretty much the same. Most of the first film's cast returned, as did soundtrack composer Piero Umiliani. The bonus is the added participation of rising American jazz star Chet Baker, who gets acknowledged—as "Chet Baker and his trumpet"—during the title credits.

The story begins in Rome, when Peppe (Vittorio Gassman) is approached by Virgilio (Riccardo Garrone), a Milanese gangster who has read the newspaper accounts of the previous heist. Virgilio has concocted a "foolproof" plan to rob the local offices of *Totocalcio*, the national football betting pool known to accumulate a lot of cash during the course of a given week; he requires a gang to handle the details. Peppe reunites with Mario (Renato Salvatori), Michele (Tiberio Murgia) and doddering sneak thief Capannelle (Carlo Pisacane). They're joined by newcomer Ugo Nardi (Nino Manfredi), a mechanic and driver; a sexy overtone is provided by Virgilio's lover, Floriana (Vicky Ludovisi), a free-spirited exotic dancer. The scheme involves joining a trainload of fans traveling to Milan for the football match, then orchestrating a "traffic accident" with the *Totocalcio* vehicle, snatching the suitcase full of cash, and—shifting to a souped-up car outfitted with Ugo's custom-designed engine—driving to Bologna, to "innocently" rejoin the sports fans returning to Rome. Ah, but nothing goes right.

The title credits unfold against Berto Pisano's walking bass, Umiliani's background piano and unison horns, all introducing a "cool" ambiance. The credits segue to Peppe, as he leaves work one day and does his best to evade a sinister-looking fellow: almost five full minutes without dialog. The "cool" jazz shifts during this sequence to uptempo bebop, which signals Baker's influence; it's a more suspenseful cue, highlighted by a vibrant trumpet solo, as Peppe does his best to escape his almost supernatural pursuer. Variations of this theme—dubbed "Relaxin' with Chet" on the soundtrack album—are heard later during the heist. Baker also dominates an uptempo bebop swinger ("Tensione") first heard when the suitcase filled with money leaves the *Totocalcio* office.

At other times, Marcello Boschi's alto sax sets an entirely different mood, such as the sensual cue inserted when the men meet Floriana, sunbathing nude on her apartment roof. Baker, in turn, establishes a forlorn tone with his haunting work on the melody heard when Floriana cajoles further assistance from a *Totocalcio* accountant.

Baker's fame notwithstanding, the film failed to produce a soundtrack album. Well over half a century passed before four tracks were digitized and included in 2013's three-disc box set, *Chet Baker—Italian Movies*. Three years later, fans finally got a limited-edition LP release of the full score.

4

Breezy Capers: 1960

Television's first memorable secret agent arrived, a full two years before James Bond debuted on the big screen. Patrick McGoohan and the UK's ITV Network couldn't have imagined that NATO's trouble-shooting John Drake would be regarded as a trend-setter in an adventure/suspense genre that soon would be laden with all manner of spies, gadgets and clandestine agencies: many of them plying their tradecraft while backed by sizzling big band jazz scores.

The Small Screen

Fans of *The Twilight Zone* don't associate Rod Serling's iconic anthology series with jazz; the weird, otherworldly elements of most episodes—and the frequently melancholy atmosphere—are better complemented by the sinister orchestral cues from established big-screen composers such as Franz Waxman, Fred Steiner, Bernard Herrmann and Leonard Rosenman, not to mention the still-chilling title themes from Herrmann and Marius Constant. But a few episodes do indeed boast *noir* story elements that favor jazz underscores.

Jerry Goldsmith's first *Zone* contribution arrived on New Year's Day 1960, in an episode titled "The Four of Us Are Dying." Twitchy percussion, unexpected brass explosions and smoky swing interludes blend with sleek cocktail piano and Dixieland struts, in the unsettling saga of a smarmy opportunist who can change his face at will; he first impersonates a combo trumpet player, which establishes the jazz palette Goldsmith employs throughout the episode.

"The Fever" (Jan. 29) spins a cautionary tale about gambling addiction. Hapless Franklin Gibbs (Everett Sloane) cannot resist the siren call of a particular slot machine … especially when it *follows* him throughout the hotel! Although the episode is scored with stock music, much of it comes from "Street Moods in Jazz," a swinging suite by René Garriguenc. Portions of that lengthy cue became a *Zone* staple, surfacing again in several future episodes.

"A Passage for Trumpet" (May 20) is the poignant saga of jazz musician Joey Crown (Jack Klugman) who, dismayed by a life that he feels has amounted to nothing, decides to end it all. His despairing suicide attempt attracts the sympathy of a very specific guardian angel with his own facility for trumpet. The Lyn Murray/Jeff Alexander score is laden with club jazz, blues riffs and mournful trumpet solos; a particularly forlorn cue is heard when Joey reluctantly hocks his horn.

Goldsmith returned for the second season's "Nervous Man in a Four-Dollar Room" (Oct. 14). The story focuses on Jackie Rhoades (Joe Mantell), a terrified little man who can't extract himself from the clutches of a local crime boss. Stuck in a cheap hotel room, he argues with his reflection in a mirror: a braver, smarter, in-all-ways superior version of himself. Goldsmith introduces edgy, tick-tock percussion as this confrontation begins, and soon adds flute and throbbing guitar; these bursts of dissonant jazz add a delirious, hypnotic tone to the already disquieting teleplay.

Goldsmith's jazz touch is heard again, albeit only briefly, in the third-season episode "A Game of Pool" (Oct. 13, 1961), which again features Klugman. He stars as pool player Jesse Cardiff, who—alone in the hall one night—vents his frustration at never having been able to play the late, great Fats Brown (Jonathan Winters). This angst is mirrored by some lazy trumpet blues, at which point Fats suddenly appears, summoned from heaven. The horns rise as Fats offers a match … at the ultimate stakes. The score is built from the CBS library; some of Goldsmith's contribution is drawn from a series of cues collectively known as "Jazz Theme 1" (actually remnants from a failed TV show pilot called *Man on the Beach*).[1]

Nathan Van Cleave delivered tasty jazz scores for a pair of *noir* episodes during the series' fifth and final season, beginning with "Steel" (Oct. 4, 1963). This sports-themed story takes place in a humanitarian future (1974!), when boxing has been restricted to robots. Van Cleave opens the episode with a saucy blast of bass-heavy swing, as down-and-out manager Steel Kelly (Lee Marvin), his mechanic Pole (Joe Mantell) and their outmoded B2 robot "Battling Maxo" disembark from a bus. This initial cue is followed—as the story proceeds— by a dour trumpet melody, an uptempo big band cue, and climactic mournful reeds.

"Black Leather Jackets" (Jan. 31, 1964) may be the all-time silliest *Zone* episode, but Van Cleave gives it some respect. Three black-clad bikers roar into a conservative neighborhood and rent a home, hoping to blend in (!); they're actually the first wave of invaders from an alien planet. Van Cleave introduces the episode with a lengthy, fast-paced swing anthem highlighted by some mean organ riffs; the cue hearkens back to the similarly disruptive arrival of Marlon Brando's gang in *The Wild One*.

Some of these scores were released in the five-volume set of *Twilight Zone* LPs issued between 1983 and 1985.

Sliding back to more familiar territory, 1960's first new detective series, *Johnny Midnight*, features the eponymous actor-turned-gumshoe; he mounts his shingle in New York's Times Square and Broadway, where once he'd had a stage career. Star Edmond O'Brien's single season syndicated run couldn't have been more *noir*, from the shadowy cinematography and late-night settings, to the hard-boiled dialogue and Chandler-esque voice-over narration.

Producer Jack Chertok paid much more attention to music than was true of most syndicated shows. The 39 episodes are laden with jazz cues of all shapes and sizes: ominous piano riffs, saxes both lonely and sultry, mournful trumpets and—for each show's fist- or gun-laden confrontations—brass-heavy blasts of big band action jazz. Pianist Joe Bushkin arranged and led the band that played the show's title theme: a swing arrangement of the Harry Warren/Al Dubin classic, "Lullaby of Broadway"; that tune also pops up, at various tempos and with differing instrumentation, in most episode underscores. Gerald Fried handled the pilot; most of the other episodes are shared between Bushkin and Richard Shores, and the jazz ambiance is fairly consistent.

Alas, *Johnny Midnight* never produced a soundtrack album, which is a shame; the music swings like crazy.

NBC's *Thriller* offered everything from straight crime stories to macabre shockers that occasionally dabble in supernatural elements. The series' first season leaned toward "rational" sagas, while the second slid more forcefully into the weird and paranormal. As befit every episode's status as a minimovie, each received an original underscore; first season music duties were shared between Pete Rugolo and Jerry Goldsmith. Rugolo favored the *noirish* crime capers, giving some of them a jazz ambiance; Goldsmith embraced the ghost stories, flavoring them with unsettling orchestral compositions. Rugolo was replaced by Morton Stevens during the second season, at which point the show's jazz component vanished.

Rugolo also delivered the title theme, which opens with a meter-less blast from the rhythm section; unison horns introduce the 3-4-2 motif, which repeats against bongos and chaotic percussion. Variations of this theme often echo within underscores. The series became destination viewing by early 1961, which led to a soundtrack album devoted exclusively to Rugolo's episodes. He expanded his title theme, gave it an even more metrically challenged preamble, and added a swing bridge dominated by trombones and a mysterious organ interlude. Each of the subsequent tracks is expanded from an underscore theme unique to 11 episodes. "Papa Benjamin" deals directly with jazz; it concerns an orchestra leader who travels to the Caribbean to learn what makes the native music so percussively hypnotic. Rich trombones, snare drums, timpani and trumpets fuel the mobster-laden saga of "The Guilty Men," while the beguiling big band swinger written for "Twisted Image"—sounding very Stan Kenton-ish—offers delectable solos on sax, trombone and trumpet.

In 2017, Goldsmith's contributions finally earned some respect with the release of *Jerry Goldsmith: Thriller* and *Thriller 2*, although none of the contents can be considered jazz.

Over at Revue Studios, music director Stanley Wilson had been impressed by the eight episodes that John(ny) Williams scored for *M Squad*. Wilson needed a composer for a new series created by celebrated crime/spy author/journalist Eric Ambler, who concocted a unique agency staffed by detectives trained to anticipate and *prevent* an impending tragedy, as opposed to (for example) attempting to identify a killer after a murder had been committed. The resulting show, *Checkmate*, debuted September 17 on CBS.

Many years later, Williams chuckled at the implications of what this workload actually meant. "[In the early 1960s] Universal Studios produced about 12 television series a year, and each series had [approximately] 39 segments. You can do the math: Hundreds of television shows had to be scored every week. There was a great need for people who could write fairly well, at least, and quickly, and conduct it. So on a Tuesday you'd take an assignment for an hour program that might have 25 minutes of music: write it, orchestrate it, have it copied and conduct it the following Tuesday. That's a lot of music, and it was a tremendous amount of work, but it was a great opportunity, and I was really young enough not to realize how difficult it was. I went in on Tuesday, got my assignments, went home and *did* them … not realizing that it might have been a superhuman task! The bliss of youth.… I guess it protects us, in so many ways."[2]

Although Williams was granted a good-sized ensemble for the show's all-important title theme, he had to settle for fewer players during the weekly scoring sessions. "The band on the main-title session was probably eight brass with some winds, maybe as many as 20 musicians. But the episodes were done with a small group; I think I had two flutes, two horns and two trombones, percussion and keyboard, [for an average of] six or eight musicians. Shelly Manne was the percussionist, and he could always be relied upon for imaginative sounds."[3]

Checkmate's 30-second title sequence seems laughably bland by today's standards, but it was cutting-edge at the time: multicolored dollops of paint slopping and swirling into each other—in black and white, mind you—as the superimposed credits appear against

Checkmate became the first series for which John(ny) Williams earned credit as the sole responsible composer; he wrote the title theme and full underscores for all 36 episodes during the first season. On top of which, he was scoring episodes of *Bachelor Father* and *Tales of Wells Fargo* at the same time (courtesy Film Score Monthly).

throbbing timpani. The 2-4-6-6-4 motif is heard first on French horns, and echoed by unison trumpets. The end credits arrangement runs twice as long, adding a bridge of expectant brass and percussion, before reprising the primary motif and building to an orchestral crescendo.

Ironically, given that Wilson had hired Williams on the basis of the action jazz he delivered for *M Squad*, the *Checkmate* underscores offered few opportunities for similarly swinging cues. The tone is more sophisticated and urbane, as befits the characters played by Anthony George, Doug McClure and the elegant Sebastian Cabot. Exceptions do exist, on occasion allowing Williams to arm a guest star's performance with a character-specific jazz theme.

The show was a quick hit; Columbia, which had just signed Williams, proposed a soundtrack album. But since this request came early in the series' run, Williams found only five cues—plus the title theme—that could be expanded into album-ready arrangements. He therefore wrote six new pieces in the show's style, to fill the LP. One of these ("Fireside Eyes") wound up being used in a later episode; the others simply sound like they *should* have come from the show.[4] The expanded title theme is a bit slower than its TV antecedent, with the melody again introduced by French horns and trumpets; the subsequent "expectant" section is followed by a saucy new swing bridge powered by trombones, after which the core melody builds to the same rising orchestral climax. The actual series themes include "Cyanide Touch," a peppy sax swinger originally used as a jukebox source tune; and "Queen's Sacrifice," a sensuous ballad dominated by piano and muted horn against soft bass comping. The "new" tracks include a soft ballad ("Far Out Place"); quietly suspenseful "skulking" music ("En Passant," sounding very much like something from *Peter Gunn*); and dynamic blasts of uptempo action jazz ("The King Swings").

The album was both popular and critically successful, garnering Williams his first Grammy Award nomination. (Ironically, he lost to former mentor Mancini, who won for *Breakfast at Tiffany's*.) Manne liked the music well enough to release a hard bop cover version of the album in April 1962, *Shelly Manne & His Men Play Checkmate*. The "men" are Conte Candoli (trumpet), Richie Kamuca (tenor sax), Russ Freeman (piano) and Chuck Berghofer (bass). Several of the arrangements are quite "out there," which may have raised eyebrows among mainstream listeners expecting something closer to what they heard on television.

Hollywood's Sunset Strip was a star-laden beat for Los Angeles County Sheriffs Department Det. Dan Raven (Skip Homeier), in a short-lived NBC series that took his name; the stories generally revolve around high-profile guest stars, such as Bobby Darin, who play themselves. Veteran jazz trumpeter/composer Billy May delivered the music for all 13 episodes of *Dan Raven*, although the underscores rarely rise above standard-issue orchestral fare. The title theme is different: a 30-second brass screamer with ferocious horns backed by an equally insistent, bongo-laden rhythm section. Sadly, that dynamic jazz theme couldn't attract viewers, even when the cast featured high-profile music celebrities such as Julie London and Paul Anka. Raven soon retired to the Home for Forgotten Television Characters.

Debonair Australian leading man Rod Taylor hopped, skipped and jumped through various TV anthology show roles before landing his first steady gig as the star of ABC's *Hong Kong*, an adventure/crime series set amid the "exotic" citizens of the eponymous region, which—at the time—still was known as the British Crown Colony of Hong Kong. Taylor plays American investigative journalist Glenn Evans, whose nose for news is well matched by his double-barreled fists for fighting. Although Evans finds his own way into numerous escapades, he also does favors for old friends, visiting Navy brass and local Police Chief Inspector Neil Campbell (Lloyd Bochner).

Indefatigable big-screen composer and (at the time) 20th Century–Fox music director Lionel Newman wrote the show's title theme and underscore cues for the single 26-episode season. The music falls into three distinct categories: standard-issue symphonic shading; Asian-flavored atmospheric cues highlighted by distinctive Chinese instruments, which in many cases sound culturally insensitive today; and good old-fashioned, American-style jazz. The latter generally is heard as source music in the mildly decrepit bar/nightclub run by Evans' good friend Tully (Jack Kruschen): sometimes solo jazz piano, sometimes small combo swingers.

Newman conducted the unidentified orchestra that performed on the soundtrack LP, *Exciting Hong Kong*; the album blends all three styles of music. Newman's melodramatic big-screen tendencies are evident in sweeping, string-enhanced tracks such as "The Jade Empress"; one expects the nearest guest actress to glance heavenward, raise a hand to her forehead, and expire on the spot. Although the album version of the title theme opens the same way, it soon blossoms into a midtempo bass- and horn-fueled swinger, courtesy of a finger-snapping Billy May arrangement that builds into a ferocious blast of big band jazz. Indeed, portions of the album display far more pizzazz than the show. The sassy, brass-fueled "Tully's Bar" offers tasty piano, trumpet and vibes solos; "A Toast to Joanna" features soft horns and vibes against the strong rhythm of a slowly comping bass; and "Chop Chop Waltz" is a double-time rhythmic treat, with sparkling solos on sax, trombone and vibes.

After sadly watching *Mr. Lucky* slide into the oblivion of enforced respectabilization, writer/director Blake Edwards gamely resurrected Lucky's prototype—Willie Dante, played by Dick Powell in the octet of *Four Star Playhouse* episodes—and persuaded NBC to book a fresh series. Howard Duff stars as this new but not entirely rehabilitated entrepreneur, owner/manager of Dante's Inferno, a San Francisco–based nightclub. Although still on speaking terms with all manner of unsavory characters from his illegal gambling days, Dante is determined to run a clean establishment; alas, his former cronies aren't convinced. Neither were viewers; the show lasted less than a full season, proving to be no luckier than *Mr. Lucky*.

Leith Stevens scored all 26 episodes of *Dante* and also wrote the fleeting title theme: a 15-second blast of rolling jazz percussion and rising brass that barely has time to build to a climax. Stevens was granted more space with the 30-second end credits theme: a slow dance band swinger akin to what would have been played toward the end of an evening. Given all the time that Dante spends in his club, dodging clinging dames and tough-talking mobsters, the resident combo provides Stevens with ample opportunity for swinging source melodies. Jazz also turns up frequently as background cues heard from radios or phonographs in the homes and haunts of Dante's criminal friends and foes. The show wasn't popular enough to warrant a soundtrack album. When *Dante* went off the air in April 1961, and *Peter Gunn* concluded its three-season run a few months later, Edwards abandoned television in favor of an increasingly successful big-screen career.

Willie Dante may have appeared too old-fashioned for TV

The year 1960 was a busy one for Nelson Riddle. In addition to scoring every episode of *Route 66*, he also scored three episodes of *The Untouchables* and three films: *The Gun of Zangara*, *Ocean's 11* and *Alcatraz Express*. During a career that continued until his death in 1985, he earned seven Emmy Award nominations, winning none; and five Academy Award nominations, winning for 1975's *The Great Gatsby* (Photofest).

viewers who hungered for more narratively provocative fare. Nomadic loners had roamed peripatetically for years in TV Westerns, pausing just long enough to right some wrong before moving on, but CBS' *Route 66* was the first contemporary series to make cross-country wandering a major element of its appeal. The series was TV's response to the 1957 publication of Jack Kerouac's *On the Road*; stars Martin Milner and George Maharis radiated a breezy insouciance that lured faithful fans to their weekly escapades. The series was groundbreaking in many respects, not least because it was a hybrid: Tod Stiles (Milner), Buz Murdock (Maharis, later replaced by Glenn Corbett's Linc Case) and their powder-blue 1960 Corvette convertible may have anchored each episode, but their brief encounters—with different people, week to week—were a holdover from the anthology dramas that dominated 1950s television.

The series' music was similarly novel. Every one of the 116 episodes, over the course of four successful seasons, was scored by Nelson Riddle, then dividing his time between television and celebrated studio sessions with Frank Sinatra and Ella Fitzgerald. Riddle also wrote the series' iconic title theme: a sassy little piano riff against a driving rhythm section, with rising brass counterpointed by sweeping strings that somehow don't detract from the finger-snapping swing. The tune is insistently, hypnotically infectious: one of TV's ultimate earworms.

"I think it [captures] the intriguing mysticism which often generates at the beginning of a trip," Riddle explained. "There's a big question mark: that notion that this is going to be a little different. There is the persistence of sound, of motion: the romance of seeing them drive down this highway."[5]

As was the case with *Naked City*, *Route 66* doesn't open with a formal credits sequence; the show's title simply appears a minute or two into the first act, over the action. The most fascinating touch is the way that Riddle began to modify the title theme. He stuck to the familiar big band arrangement during the first season, but by the second season started to play around with instrumentation, tempo and mood. A few episodes start with no trace of the theme behind the title; others open with lush orchestral cues that only gradually resolve into variations of the theme. (It became something of a game—in our home, at least—to be first to spot a chord progression that was undeniably a portion of Riddle's theme.)

Riddle's underscores vary in a similar manner, dictated by a given episode's tone. Tod and Buz's encounters are all over the emotional map: Some are grimly serious and/or dangerous; others are romantic (always with regrets); still others are playfully silly. Most of Riddle's background efforts therefore are either dramatic or whimsical orchestral cues, but he indulges in jazz stylings on occasion. One second season entry—"How Much Is a Pound of Albatross?" (Feb. 9, 1962)—opens as a bored young woman on a motorcycle (Julie Newmar, as Vicki) roars down an empty highway and heads into Tucson, Ariz., against a torrid bit of sultry brass; the rhythm section ramps up when she eyes a cop and makes an illegal turn. The cue rises into a ferocious big band swinger as the chase intensifies, involving numerous police cars and motorcycles. The music climaxes when she side-swipes Tod and Buz, who've just arrived in town, causing their Corvette to demolish a store front's plate glass window. A smoky piano combo lends pathos a bit later, as a jailed Vicki attempts to explain the demons chewing at her soul; the melancholy jazz ambiance continues throughout the episode, when Buz unwisely falls under her spell.

Riddle was encouraged to record a full-length version of his main theme; the only surprise is that he waited so long to do it. The tune became the centerpiece of a 1962 Capitol anthology album titled *Route 66 and Other Great TV Themes*, which spent nine weeks on

Billboard's Top LPs chart, peaking at No. 63 on November 24. Riddle expanded the familiar finger-snapping melody to include a terrific guitar solo by Bob Bain during the bridge, backed by a gently comping muted trumpet. The theme attracted covers by Jack Costanzo and His Orchestra (Liberty), and Billy Vaughn and His Orchestra (Dot). Teri Thornton recorded a charming vocal version—titled "Open Highway," with lyrics by Stanley Styne— released in October 1963 by Columbia.

It's a shame Riddle never produced an actual soundtrack LP; he certainly had more than enough material, and fans have mourned this decision ever since. On the other hand, his version of the title theme has become an essential part of countless crime jazz and TV theme anthology albums.

Clueless NBC execs attempted to revive/remake the series in the early summer of 1993; the ill-advised result failed to include Riddle's iconic title theme. No doubt that contributed to an embarrassingly short run that ran out of gas after four weeks.

Over on the Warner Bros. lot, the Suits hadn't yet abandoned the *77 Sunset Strip* recipe; their final clone was an effort to blend that formula with the crime-laden environment of *The Untouchables*. *The Roaring 20's* [sic] is set in Prohibition-era New York City, where intrepid *New York Record* journalists Scott Norris (Rex Reason) and Pat Garrison (Donald May) go after big scoops involving the rival criminal gangs vying for control. They spend a lot of time in the raucous Charleston Club, where headlining singer Pinky Pinkham (Dorothy Provine) is good for tips on the mobsters in their midst. Pinky quickly became far more popular than her hunky but unremarkable male co-stars, as reflected by Provine's enhanced placement in the second-season title credits sequence.

The Roaring 20's boasted another insipid Jerry Livingston/Mack David title song, and all the non-diegetic underscores were built from library cues during the show's two-season run. But because Pinky and Her Playboys are granted so much screen time, each episode is laden with live performances of terrific Jazz Age pop tunes and instrumentals, many of them strung together in clever medleys. Provine and the band had the good fortune to be overseen by music director Alexander "Sandy" Courage, a veteran composer, arranger and orchestrator who'd cut his teeth on numerous MGM musicals. (He'd likely be annoyed, these days, to be known chiefly for having written the title theme for the original *Star Trek*.)

The Roaring 20's went through a *lot* of music. Courage was kept busy selecting period-authentic pop and show tunes: plenty by the Gershwins, Cole Porter, Rodgers and Hart, and Vincent Youmans. The medleys are quite clever, as with one that slides from "I'm Looking Over a Four Leaf Clover" (Dixieland instrumental), to "A Cup of Coffee, a Sandwich and You" (chorus vocal), to "Tea for Two" and "The Girl Friend" (lively dance band instrumentals). Provine sparkles in whimsical numbers such as "Doin' the Sigma Chi" and "Don't Bring Lulu" and can just as easily slide into bluesy ballads such as "Hard-Hearted Hannah" or the forlorn pathos of "Bye Bye Blackbird." The unidentified band roars through instrumental hits such as "Sweet Georgia Brown" and "Limehouse Blues."

The inevitable soundtrack LP flickered only briefly on *Billboard's* Top LPs chart but proved a sensation in the UK; that prompted Warner Bros. to release a sequel in the summer of 1961. *Dorothy Provine: The Vamp from The Roaring 20's* made minimal noise in the States but spent seven weeks on the UK albums chart.

Back in the modern world, actor Rick Jason wasn't content to become network TV's first insurance investigator; he also was the first TV detective to defend himself with karate. *The Case of the Dangerous Robin* stars Jason as Robin Scott, a wealthy, debonair and freelance "negotiator extraordinaire" who, with the help of gal pal Phyllis Collier (Jean Blake), roams the world to solve cases of large-scale insurance fraud, in exchange for 10 percent of any recovered assets.

The syndicated single season's 38 episodes are scored solely with library cues, but the title theme is worth noting: It was written by David Rose, a prolific and Oscar-nominated composer and music director who'd soon embrace a successful television career on shows such as *Bonanza*, *The Red Skelton Hour* and *Highway to Heaven*. He nonetheless may wind up best remembered for having written "The Stripper," which—in his own arrangement—hit No. 1 on *Billboard's* Hot 100 chart in the summer of 1962. Music fans familiar with that tune's extravagantly lusty instrumentation would be surprised by the bargain-basement simplicity of his theme for *Robin*: a 25-second melody taken by one shrill horn, against equally rudimentary rhythm supplied by a single drummer. It qualifies as jazz, but sure didn't involve much effort on anybody's part.

Surprisingly, it was covered by Pete Rugolo, who included it on his 1962 anthology album, *TV's Top Themes*. Alas, the arrangement is buried beneath so much orchestral schmaltz that it's impossible to extract Rose's melody from the string-laden slush.

* * *

When you're successful once, it's wise to keep striking while the iron remains hot. Both Buddy Morrow and Mundell Lowe followed their initial TV theme compilation albums with 1960 sequels. Morrow's *Double Impact* (RCA) goes even further overboard with distracting sound effects and manages to make "Hawaiian Eye" and "Bourbon Street Beat" even sillier than their original TV versions. Fortunately, some of the other tracks are rock-solid, including a savagely swinging cover of "Staccato's Theme" and a playfully bluesy reading of the UK's "International Detective."

Lowe once again gathered the best ensemble for his RCA release, *Themes from Mr. Lucky, The Untouchables and other TV Action Jazz*: Clark Terry (trumpet, flugelhorn); Willie Dennis, Urbie Green and Frank Rehak (trombones); Dick Hixson and Rod Levitt (bass trombone); Phil Bodner (flute, tenor sax); Eddie Costa (piano, vibes); George Duvivier (bass); and Ed Shaughnessy (drums). This unit takes a much more serious instrumental approach to "Hawaiian Eye," with Lowe introducing the theme on guitar and then yielding to swinging solos by the horn players; and Henry Mancini couldn't have asked for a sweeter arrangement of "Mr. Lucky." The album closes with a breakneck arrangement of "Staccato's Theme," granting solos to each player, after which Shaughnessy's drum solo leads to an unexpected conclusion in 5/4 time.

Audio Fidelity issued Peter Appleyard's *Percussive Jazz* ("Doctored for Super-Sound"), which offers sleek vibes work backed by a 20-piece ensemble that includes Hammond organ, flutes and a pianoforte. The LP opens with a powerful arrangement of the main theme from *The Man with the Golden Arm*, and Appleyard's handling of the "Dragnet Theme" is a solid blend of rolling percussion and unison brass.

The Big Screen

The bloodthirsty exploits of Brooklyn's "Murder Incorporated" assassins, feared throughout the 1930s and early '40s, prompted two high-profile Hollywood films. *The Enforcer* (1951) fictionalized the events; 1960s far more realistic *Murder Inc.* fearlessly identified the organization's key players, along with the tenacious attorney (Burton Turkus) who led the charge to bring them down. Co-directors Burt Balaban and Stuart Rosenberg turn the saga into a documentary-style crime *noir*, complete with narrative montages and Gayne Rescher's striking monochrome cinematography. Frank De Vol's grimly atmospheric symphonic score is salted with numerous combo and big band jazz cues, all used as source music.

The story begins as organized crime kingpin Louis "Lepke" Buchalter (David J. Stewart) hires small-time Brooklyn killers "Bug" Workman (Warren Finnerty) and Abe Reles (Peter Falk) to become the syndicate's go-to hit men. Financial debt makes unemployed singer Joey Collins (Stuart Whitman) a reluctant accomplice, much to the horror of his singer/dancer wife, Eadie (May Britt). The couple soon become unwilling hosts to Lepke, when he's forced to hide out from the police: a precarious arrangement that continues for years, until Eadie finally works up the courage to confess all to Turkus (Henry Morgan). A climactic tragedy finally gives the fearful Joey sufficient motivation to testify, allowing Turkus to assemble enough courtroom evidence to have Lepke sentenced to death.

The bulk of De Vol's non-diegetic score is built from suspenseful, string-laden orchestral cues that anticipate and then heighten Reles' coldly brutal behavior. The one exception is the film's swinging title theme, which opens with rolling percussion and blossoms into a brass-laden jazz waltz, with sparkling trumpet fanfares backed by deft piano comping. The remaining jazz cues are diegetic, such as the piano-driven trio number that backs an on-stage dancer at a Catskill resort club run by Walter Sage (Morey Amsterdam). The biggest jazz surprise is Sarah Vaughan, cast as an unnamed club singer; the drama pauses long enough to let her croon the concluding bars of an uptempo finger-snapper ("Fan My Brow"), with big band backing, and a full rendition of a slower, smoldering ballad ("The Awakening").

Both of her songs are included on the soundtrack LP, along with two jazz source cues—"Brownsville Bounce" and "Happy Dancer"—and the "Main Title" jazz waltz.

Numerous films fail to produce soundtracks, but it's rare with one as popular and music-laden as director Lewis Milestone's buoyant *Ocean's Eleven*. Given the many great Nelson Riddle big band charts that propel the flippant action, the absence of an album is a crime even greater than the heist orchestrated by Frank Sinatra and his cronies. The film is wall-to-wall jazz, starting with Riddle's swinging instrumental arrangement of the Sammy Cahn/Jimmy Van Heusen tune "Eee-O-Eleven," first heard over Saul Bass' colorful, marquee-style title credits sequence.

Four screenwriters developed the high-concept notion of World War II veterans-turned-thieves who take on Las Vegas, but the screenplay was largely ignored when Rat Packers Frank Sinatra, Dean Martin, Peter Lawford, Sammy Davis Jr. and Joey Bishop ad-libbed most of their lines. The finished product is a bit bloated and creaky, but Riddle's swinging score is terrific (and by far the best part of the film). The caper comes together when Danny Ocean (Sinatra) assembles his fellow 82nd Airborne comrades and outlines a crazy plan to simultaneously rob five Vegas casinos a few minutes after capacity crowds sing "Auld Lang Syne" on New Year's Eve. Minor dramatic tension is created by Danny's estranged wife (Angie Dickinson) and reformed mobster Duke Santos (Cesar Romero), who—after the fact—tries to muscle in on the action.

Ocean and his pals spend plenty of time casing the casinos, granting an excuse for several live performances. Martin delivers a spirited version of "Ain't That a Kick in the Head," which gets plenty of swing from vibraphonist Red Norvo and his quintet. A conversation in a different casino takes place while Louis Prima and Keely Smith present a sassy rendition of "I'm Gonna Live Until I Die," on a small stage in the background. Riddle also delivers lively instrumental arrangements of the same songs, along with unique "casino cues" as Ocean's crew cases each establishment in turn. A bit later, Riddle and the orchestra power the five simultaneous heists with Basie-esque big band swing: a cue that climbs key signatures as each casino is robbed, one after the other.

Alas, all of Riddle's marvelous jazz covers and incidental cues—most undoubtedly recorded in longer versions than what's used in the film—appear to have been lost ... and ain't *that* a kick in the head.

Ocean and his buddies weren't 1960s sole heist-meisters. Director Henry Hathaway's *Seven Thieves* is a similarly larkish escapade with more star wattage than suspense. Meticulous planner Theo Wilkins (Edward G. Robinson) develops an ingenious scheme to plunder $4 million in French francs from the vault of a Monte Carlo casino. His confederates include exotic dancer Melanie (Joan Collins) and her "protector," beatnik sax player Poncho (Eli Wallach); jovial safe-cracker Louis (Michael Dante); brooding tough-guy "muscle" and driver Hugo (Berry Kroeger); the casino's timid assistant director, Raymond (Alexander Scourby); and the menacing Paul Mason (Rod Steiger), who keeps everybody in line. The caper's outcome produces the sole plot twist, but even that resolves mildly.

At first blush, we're led to believe that Dominic Frontiere's score will be a jazz romp. The clever title credits—each star's name emblazoned on a rectangular casino chip—open with energetic combo swing, as a writhing Melanie dances while superimposed atop a roulette wheel; banks of trumpets and reeds maintain the uptempo beat. The first act features the barely dressed Collins gyrating through two sexually charged numbers that get additional erotic energy from a smokin' quartet of piano, bass, drums and sax. In between these dance numbers, the gang members chat against a softly swinging piano trio. But that's it for the jazz content. We never visit the club again, and Frontiere's score becomes string-laden and symphonic. The heist would have benefited from some tense swing cues, but it unfolds silently.

No soundtrack album appeared, which isn't much of a loss.

Meanwhile, Across the Pond...

Man from Interpol became the first British TV show with a title theme and original underscore written—for every one of its 39 episodes—by a well-established jazz icon. The fellow tagged for the job was Anthony John Kronenberg, better known as Tony Crombie, a pianist, drummer and bandleader who cut his teeth playing in 1940s and '50s units fronted by Victor Feldman, Ronnie Scott, John Dankworth and Duke Ellington.[6] *Man from Interpol* was Crombie's sole TV assignment, and he took it just as seriously as any steady club gig.

Richard Wyler stars as London-based Interpol agent Anthony Smith, who tackles cases that elude conventional police agencies. He spends most of his time in England, but on occasion travels to Canada, Japan, France or Australia to investigate cases involving murder, counterfeiting, theft, blackmail, art fraud or drug smuggling. The series was broadcast to random sections of the UK in 1959, via the then-patchwork Associated-Rediffusion Network; NBC subsequently picked it up for U.S. broadcast, where it debuted January 30, 1960.

The title theme opens as a lone drum beats a 1-4-10-1-2 motif; that introductory "melody" is repeated by a double-time wall of brass, while the cue builds to a climactic finale. Underscore cues vary from explosive big band action jazz ("My Fair Laine") to softer, Latin-hued anthems ("Samba De Janeiro"); and from wildly swinging vibes cues—"Big Ben Bounce" is particularly droll—to Mancini-esque walking bass traveling music ("Domus"). Crombie favors unison brass but is just as likely to allow solos by saxes, flutes, vibes and any other instrument in the huge ensemble. The show's plots are fairly routine—Wyler isn't a charismatic performer—but the music is sensational.

The UK's newly formed Top Rank label immediately released a 45 single with Crombie's title theme and two underscore cues; an official soundtrack LP followed. The UK's Ember label also released a soundtrack album with a slightly different mix of cues. Rock 'n' roll fans will be amused to note that one of Crombie's cues, "Eastern Journey," was "lifted" by The Who's Keith Moon for a song he titled "Cobwebs and Strange," and which appears on the band's *A Quick One* album of 1966.

British actor Ian Hendry, adept at playing brooding, intelligent characters, got his first series starring role in ITV's *Police Surgeon*, which debuted September 10. His Dr. Geoffrey Brent is an inquisitive bloke attached to London Metropolitan's Bayswater precinct, where his curiosity and medical expertise help solve "baffling" cases ... but not before he gets into trouble. The series is best remembered today—if it's remembered at all—as a vague precursor to his follow-up role in the first season of *The Avengers*. (The shows aren't actually related beyond the fact that Hendry plays a doctor in both.) *Police Surgeon* might have developed into a successful series in its own right, but behind-the-scenes "contractual issues" halted production after 13 episodes. (Only one episode is known to have survived.) Wanting to keep Hendry in front of viewers, ABC Television producer Leonard White hastily developed the elements for a replacement series—dubbed *The Avengers*—which debuted a month later.[7]

As was the case with numerous British TV shows during this period, each half-hour episode of *Police Surgeon* was broadcast live: a rough-and-tumble process that did not lend itself to underscores. That said, the show does have a saucy big band title theme, although viewers never heard more than 30 seconds of it. Lacking funds for original music, creator/producer Julian Bond opted for a vibrant library track: a 90-second jazz cue—titled "Big Knife 2"—that composer Ivor Slaney wrote for a December 1958 televised adaptation of Clifford Odets' Broadway stage drama, *The Big Knife*. The cue opens with ominously slow 4-4 percussion, after which unison brass introduces the 6-5 motif: an unhurried strut punctuated by additional bursts of brass and briefly plucked strings. A second bank of horns supplies counterpoint, as the melody climbs up the scale, builds to a climax, and then fades against gentle percussion.

ITV entered the secret agent genre with a vengeance, with the game-changing debut of *Danger Man* on September 11, 1960. It marked the series debut of Patrick McGoohan, who quickly became one of Britain's most popular actors. *Danger Man* is a superb blend of spy-jinks and crime drama, highlighted by an opulent, crisply photographed *noir* look courtesy of cinematographer Brendan J. Stafford, who lensed all but one of the 39 episodes. The series also marked a transition for composer Edwin Astley, who embraced jazz full throttle. "I decided to use both a jazz-orientated theme and jazz-based background music," he recalled, decades later, "which was quite unusual at the time."[8]

McGoohan's NATO agent is introduced by his voice-over, which runs over the title sequence that follows each episode's teaser. Although ostensibly based in Washington, D.C., most of John Drake's cases take him elsewhere: London, Vienna, Sicily, Hong Kong, Singapore, India and a variety of fictitious countries in Africa, South America and the Middle East.

Astley worked with a sizeable ensemble, but their identities (sadly) have been lost to time. His compelling and heavily rhythmic main theme opens with six low notes followed by a three-note brass ostinato, drawn from the syllables of the show's title: *Daaan-ger Maaaaaan!* This is followed by several 5-1-4 "question and answer" statements by the same low horns, concluding with a shrill repeat of the three-note brass fanfare. Astley delivered full underscores for the series' first six episodes, developing a library of 81 cues; these were supplemented by 19 additional cues written, as needed, to properly "shade" another 11 episodes. The remaining 22 episode underscores were built from this library of 100 cues.

Aside from full-blown action cues that employ the entire orchestra, Astley often sets a mood with only a few instruments. Slow walking bass and flute accompany Drake's sleuthing activities; the peril often inherent in pre-credits teasers is amplified by rapid walking bass and brass stingers. The first act almost always concludes with a suspenseful rising brass fanfare. Astley also uses numerous variations of the title theme, at various tempos and with unusual instrumental configurations; sometimes he employs only the bass line for skulking activities. Numerous source cues also came from Astley's pen, including a soft cocktail piano trio heard from a radio toward the beginning of "View from the Villa"; and lively boogie-woogie performed by a solo pianist when clueless police escorts are lured to a raucous party in "The Sisters."

"Every government has its secret service branch," Patrick McGoohan explains in voice-over during *Danger Man's* title sequence. "America, CIA; France, Deuxième Bureau; England, MI5. NATO also has its own. A messy job? Well, that's when they usually call on me, or someone like me. Oh, yes: My name is Drake. John Drake." Note the manner in which Drake repeats his name, two years before Sean Connery would echo this as one of *his* signature lines (CBS/Photofest).

Although Astley's jazz library perfectly suits the series, very few of the cues are long enough—or developed well enough—to be expanded into melodies that could fill a soundtrack album; as a result, there wasn't one. That said, Astley's title theme was covered by Ted Heath & His Music (London) and the Red Price Combo (Parlophone); the latter boasts a particularly dirty sax that takes an extended solo during a lively swing bridge.

Proving that good things come to those who wait, *all* of the series' surviving cues and alternate takes were digitized and gathered into a two-disc tiffany package in 2008; the 91 tracks on *Danger Man: Original Soundtrack* provide an exhaustive examination of Astley's approach to the show.

Hollywood's Robin Scott may retain the distinction of being TV's first crusading insurance investigator, but he only barely earned that honor. Two short months later, the UK's ABC network debuted *The Cheaters*, which stars John Ireland as John Hunter, a claims investigator for the Eastern Insurance Company. The two-season half-hour show is barely remembered, and all but lost today; it has been dismissed for "painful lethargy [and] John Ireland's carefully sustained somnambulistic performance."[9]

That may have been true of the acting, but the music is something else again. The title theme came from jazz pianist, vibraphonist, arranger and bandleader William A. "Bill" Le Sage, who at that time was leading a quartet with equally well-known baritone saxman Ronnie Ross. The title sequence makes grim viewing: Brooding rhythm and an ominous 4-beat are heard against images of various atrocities—an earthquake, a plane crash, a raging conflagration, flooding, and smash-and-grab theft—as the words DESTRUCTION, DEATH, FIRE and ROBBERY loom across the screen. Tasty vibes and sax rise above the percussion, launching the melody as the scene shifts to a close-up of Ireland; he narratively introduces his character and occupation, and his loathing for "some joker [who] comes along with an attempt to defraud." The melody resolves into a thoughtful ballad as the show's title and Ireland's credit appear.

The Le Sage/Ross quartet—Spike Heatley (acoustic double bass) and Allan Ganley (drums)—also fill each episode with a wealth of cheerful improvisational cues. The music is almost ubiquitous, even when jazz seems incongruous: say, while backing a brief conversation with a (supposedly) famed orchestral violinist. *The Cheaters* thus became a terrific weekly jazz showcase, particularly at a time when most British TV shows—especially those filmed and transmitted live—weren't able to present much music. It's a shame that most of this music vanished with the show. Le Sage and Ross never produced a soundtrack album, although they did include an uptempo arrangement of the title theme on their 1964 World Record Club album, *The Bill Le Sage/Ronnie Ross Quartet* (once again alongside Heatley and Ganley). That track, and a few surviving variations, have been digitized and included on some anthology albums, such as Fantastic Voyage's *Big Sound: Ember Soundtracks & Themes*.

* * *

Moving to the big screen, crime and jazz are joined at the hip in director Joseph Losey's *The Criminal*, released in the States as *Concrete Jungle*. Alun Owen's original script is a grimly realistic depiction of the pecking order established by prison convicts: an uneasy society of friends, enemies, stoolies, fragile alliances and guards inclined to play favorites. *The Criminal* marks the first of Losey's four collaborations with celebrated clarinetist, saxophonist, composer and band leader John(ny) Dankworth, who had spent the 1950s fronting numerous units large and small. His jaunty big band swingers serve as ironic counterpoint to the harsh environment and larcenous activities of this story's protagonist.

Johnny Bannion (Stanley Baker) is mere days away from earning his freedom after time served. Once released, he takes up with a new girlfriend (Margit Saad, as Suzanne) and immediately plans a racetrack job with backing by Mike Carter (Sam Wanamaker). The heist is successful, netting $40,000; Johnny buries the cash in the middle of a barren snowy field. Alas, he's immediately caught and returned to the same prison, where the pecking order has shifted during his brief absence; he's now under the thumb of Frank Saffron

(Grégoire Aslan), who demands a large cut of the haul. Saffron "arranges" a prison break so that Johnny can recover the loot, but even that is a betrayal. During a grim climax, the message is unmistakable: Crime most definitely does not pay.

Dankworth built a band from the cream of Britain's jazz royalty, and the ensemble includes—on piano—a recent Oxford graduate named Dudley Moore. The title credits open with "Thieving Boy," a soulful vocal by Dankworth's wife, jazz chanteuse Cleo Laine, backed by quiet percussion and a wall of mournful horns. Very little music is heard during the subsequent first act, as Johnny and his prison cronies are introduced. The first uptempo swinger arrives when Johnny is released; he swaggers out of prison against a jaunty alto sax solo, backed by the entire horn section and Kenny Clare's furious drumming. Suzanne's theme is a lyrical jazz ballad with a sweet 3-5 motif delivered by the entire horn ensemble.

When the film builds to its grim conclusion, Dankworth spots a vehicular chase with a suspenseful blast of action jazz. Clare's drumming establishes an accelerated 2/2 beat as dueling saxes and trumpets climb through several key changes, the cue intensifying with each shift. In the aftermath of a shoot-out, Laine once again croons "Thieving Boy" as the camera pulls back to reveal the futility of the challenge that now faces Carter, who has *no* idea where the buried money might be, in this enormous snowy field.

Although the score proved popular, Dankworth was his own toughest critic. "*The Criminal* contained some quality music," he acknowledged, years later, "but I was learning my craft, and there were weaknesses as well as clichés."[10] He expanded four of the primary cues for a two-disc 45 EP issued on Columbia's UK label: a woefully brief hint of the entire score. Those tracks have been digitized and are available via iTunes and similar services.

Whereas most of the characters in *The Criminal* deserve their fates, director Wolf Rilla's *Piccadilly Third Stop* includes some innocents. This taut little heist thriller deftly sketches a crew of unsavory characters who hatch a plot clearly doomed to failure. Much of Ernest Steward's lush monochrome cinematography is pure *noir*, particularly third-act sequences that take place in the dangerous London Underground tunnels. Veteran film and television composer Philip Green abandoned his usual orchestral approach, instead granting this crime saga a saucy, big band jazz score that kicks off with a swinging title theme.

High-society playboy/hustler Dominic (Terence Morgan) has long steered potential marks into the clutches of underworld fence/casino owner Humphries (Dennis Price); the newest victim is brash, low-level American gangster Joe Preedy (John Crawford). Dominic is enjoying a clandestine affair with Preedy's wife (Mai Zetterling, as Christine); after meeting the young and naïve Seraphina (Yolo Tani) at an aristocratic gathering, he sets about wooing—and corrupting—her, as well. She's the daughter of a foreign ambassador and lets slip that the embassy safe is known to contain somewhere in the neighborhood of £100,000. Dominic assembles a crew that includes his foppish best friend Toddy (Charles Kay), Preedy and a veteran safecracker known only as The Colonel (William Hartnell). The subsequent heist doesn't work out as Dominic hopes.

Green's title theme is a rousing big band swinger that introduces the core 2-2-2-1-1 motif via piano and unison horns; the melody builds to a rousing blast as Rilla's credit hits the screen. Variations of this theme occur repeatedly, mostly to shade bad behavior by Dominic and various other characters (another example of the jazz-equals-crime equation). Additional cues include a soft, smoky swinger when Humphries warns Preedy that he'd better make good on a bounced check; and a rhythmic, suspenseful ostinato—with plenty of bass and muted trumpet—heard as the gang plans, plots and prepares for the heist. Green also gets numerous opportunities for cocktail/dance band source cues; folks frequently turn on radios or phonograph players. One highlight is an uptempo jazz/rock bopper to which Toddy's meek girlfriend—the aptly named Mouse (Ann Lynn)—dances, when she's alone in their flat; it sounds very much like something the John Barry Seven would have placed on the pop charts during that era.

Sadly, no soundtrack album appeared.

Elsewhere in the World

French filmmakers busily kick-started what became known as the "New Wave" (*nouvelle vague*) cinema movement, which eschewed Hollywood's glossy, rigorously choreographed spectacles in favor of a more naturalistic, *cinéma vérité* approach that borders on documentary. François Truffaut's *The 400 Blows* and Alain Resnais' *Hiroshima, Mon Amour* were first out of the gate, and Jean-Luc Godard's *À bout de souffle* (*Breathless*) followed quickly. The latter also qualifies as a *noir* crime drama, in part because its larcenous protagonist identifies strongly with Humphrey Bogart's darker film roles.

The largely improvised narrative focuses on Michel (Jean-Paul Belmondo), a coldly indifferent, small-potatoes criminal. The film opens as he steals a car in Marseille, then callously shoots and kills a police officer. Now on the run, he snatches some money from one casual girlfriend (Liliane Dreyfus), and then reunites with a second—American journalism student Patricia (Jean Seberg)—mostly to evade pursuing police by hiding in her tiny apartment. Godard spends his film's entire second act in that apartment; although Patricia eventually agrees to flee with him to Italy—briefly imagining herself as a Bonnie to his Clyde—she impulsively betrays him to the police.

When it came time to score the film, Godard accepted a suggestion from fellow director Jean-Pierre Melville, who was quite impressed by jazz pianist/composer Martial Solal. Godard didn't have any strong ideas about what Solal should write, but the latter's improvisational spirit perfectly suited the director's temperament; Solal, in turn, recognized the degree to which jazz could add a "disturbing theme" to Belmondo's *film noir* affectations.[11]

Most of Solal's score cues are variations on two primary themes. The first is Michel's character cue ("La Mort"), dominated by a rising five-note motif that repeats, with an additional two notes added to the echo (thus, 5-5-2). "I spent several days seeking a theme that would fit this plot, this anxiety, this central character," Solal recalled, years later. "Finally, by chance I hit that small group of five notes."[12] The contrasting love theme ("Thème D'amour") also is built upon a five-note motif, but this time descending the scale; the result is calmer, playful and somewhat melancholy. "Strangely enough," Solal admitted, "the [main theme] is scary, and the other is quite relaxing."[13]

Although Solal wrote precise cues for specific scenes, Godard didn't use them in that manner. Emulating the approach he employed while fine-tuning his film, the director extracted brief slices from various cues, and sprinkled them like spice: here, there and everywhere. The resulting edit is full of music, but the cues rarely run more than 10 or 15 seconds. Godard knew what he was doing: Those fleeting bursts of music are well placed, and deftly complement the story's unsettling atmosphere.

Columbia France issued four of Solal's themes in 1966 on a 7-inch EP; a full 10-track score finally was digitized in 2002.

5

Contract with Depravity: 1961

Mind-bogglingly short-sighted as it seems today, the British Broadcasting Corp. (BBC) spent 20 years destroying its own cultural heritage.

For most of the 1950s, TV dramas were aired live, in the manner of news broadcasts; ergo, there was nothing to save. Early crime shows—such as 1951's *The Inch Man*—exist today only on the basis of surviving scripts and publicity photographs. One would assume, with the benefit of hindsight, that 1958's industry-wide adoption of filming on two-inch tape would have begun the process of establishing a program library, particularly at the BBC ... but no. "Television meant being live, over and done with," explained BBC historian Richard Molesworth. "When videotape came about, it wasn't seen as a means of preservation, or as an archival format. It was [only] in case a program was to be repeated in a short period of time: days or weeks."[1]

Tapes were bulky; they quickly began to stack perilously high in hallways, dressing rooms and offices. More damningly, tape expense was a line item in a program's budget; erasing and reusing existing tapes was cheaper than purchasing new ones. As time passed, hundreds (thousands?) of hours of tapes were fed into the BBC's bulk-erasure machine each year: the shows in question doomed by the grim designation of "no further interest." But space and financial issues weren't the sole culprits; "old" programming simply wasn't perceived to have any value. The prevailing belief was that nobody would care. The arrival of color in the later 1960s made the problem even worse, given the corporate assumption that earlier black-and-white programming suddenly held even *less* significance.

(It should be noted, in fairness, that the BBC wasn't the sole culprit here. ITV and other British studios were equally culpable.)

The situation improved slightly in 1975, with the establishment of what soon became the BBC Film and Television Library. But things didn't really get better until 1979, when Sue Malden became the BBC's Television Archive Selector. By then home VCRs were creating an entirely new population of fans who desired to collect every episode of their favorite shows ... and were horrified to learn about the BBC's two decades of self-imposed obliteration in the name of thrift. Malden began what blossomed into the herculean task of attempting to recover "lost" episodes and entire programs by establishing a network with fans of the BBC's most beloved show: *Doctor Who*. Salvation came slowly, with the discovery of tape canisters long forgotten in storage rooms, or improperly hoarded by BBC employees, or via the 16mm film reels generated when a show was sold to foreign territories (including the United States). The *Doctor Who* network expanded to encompass any and all programming content; amazing things were discovered in basements, attics and—in many cases—television stations in Western Europe, the Middle East and Africa, where employees had neglected to discard them.

All that effort notwithstanding, many shows—some of them extremely popular—remain mostly, or even entirely lost. Some of the casualties belong to the genres covered within these pages, and the first prominent examples debuted this year.

On a different note, this is the last chapter—the final year—to showcase exclusively black-and-white TV programs and films. Color was a-comin,' and shadow-laden *noir* was on its way out.

The Small Screen

A title theme rarely outshines—and outlasts—the TV series that prompted its creation, but that's precisely what happened with *The Asphalt Jungle*. The ABC police series took little more than its title from the 1950 John Huston film, or the 1949 W.R. Burnett novel on which *it* was based. The show ran for a mere 13 weeks in the spring and summer of 1961; it wasn't dynamic enough to stand out from an increasingly crowded field of similar dramas.

Its title theme, however, was another story. MGM secured no less than Duke Ellington, who also scored the pilot episode, "The Lady and the Lawyer." It was a reasonable fit, as Ellington recently had scored the *noir*-laden legal thriller, *Anatomy of a Murder*. "Pop told me he liked doing the music for the pilot," Mercer [Ellington] recalled. "He had never done one before. [But he] had no interest in providing any music for the rest of the series."[2]

The 40-second title sequence is indeed memorable. Ellington's thoughtful solo piano is heard against quiet bass, as a helicopter camera scans a major metropolis in the dead of night; a lone swinging sax rises as the credits appear over this vista. Bluesy unison brass introduces the repeated 3-1 motif; the dynamic sax returns when the camera peers down, focusing on a warehouse roof, on which the show's title is superimposed. The brass 3-1 motif repeats as a stinger, when the episode title appears. Ellington and his band also supplied roughly 11 minutes of music for the pilot. Although his theme is retained throughout the short-lived series, subsequent underscores came from jazz pianist/composer Calvin Jackson: his sole television assignment, amid a largely uncredited big-screen scoring career that stretched from 1944 through '65.

The TV series quietly faded away on June 25, but Ellington wasn't finished with his *Asphalt Jungle* efforts. He already had revisited key themes during a studio session the previous summer, when he and his band recorded a three-movement *Asphalt Jungle Suite*: "Wild Car Chase"/"Cops"/"Robbers." The first movement opens with Ellington's soft keyboard strokes against gentle percussion—more like the *anticipation* of a vehicular chase—then kicks into gear with tense brass and rapid cymbal brushes, finally building to a furious drum roll and orchestral explosion. Ellington restates the title theme against quiet drumming as the thoughtful, slowly swinging second movement opens; the full orchestra bursts into brilliant glory while the cue develops. The final movement is tense and expectant; Ellington's piano suggests a caper with a lyrical melody, then the orchestra backs tasty solos—by Johnny Hodges, Ray Nance, Jimmy Hamilton, Willie Cook and Paul Gonsalves—prior to a joyous climax.

Roughly a year later, shortly after the TV series was canceled, a second studio session produced "Asphalt Jungle Theme" and "Asphalt Jungle Twist."[3] They were released as a Columbia single a month later. The A-side is a sassier, slightly faster arrangement than the TV version, anchored by strong 4/4 drumming and fueled by terrific unison horns; delighted shouts of "Yeah!" can be heard throughout. The theme builds to a rising crescendo of brass that ultimately (maddeningly!) fades out, rather than resolving. No such control board interference marred Ellington and his band's vastly superior 1963 performance of this theme, captured on his live album *The Great Paris Concert*. The 8-minute *Asphalt Jungle Suite* remained unreleased until the 1984 compilation album, *Duke Ellington: Duke 56/62, Volume 2*.

When it became clear that the program wouldn't survive even a single season, MGM rehired the cast and crew that had made "The Lady and the Lawyer," shot additional footage, and expanded the hour-length drama into a 79-minute feature released as *The Lawbreakers*. Ellington's contributions were left behind; the film is scored by Johnny Mandel (about which, more later).

Elsewhere, wanting to take advantage of the professional momentum garnered during five seasons of *Highway Patrol*, Broderick Crawford slid smoothly into the equally gruff starring role of the syndicated *King of Diamonds*, which ran for a single 38-episode season in 1961 and '62. Crawford's tough-talking, trench coat-clad John King is an investigator who owes much to Mike Hammer, with a hair-trigger temper and a tendency to solve problems via brawling or gunplay. As chief investigator for Continental Diamond Industries, King crisscrosses the globe alongside junior sidekick Al Casey (Ray Hamilton), often foiling operations masterminded by (I'm not making this up) the Illicit Diamond Buyers Syndicate.

The episode scripts are either hilariously melodramatic or as lackluster as Hamilton's supporting performance, but the music—at least initially—is several cuts above. Frankie Ortega, riding high on his connection to *77 Sunset Strip*, supplied a vibrant title theme that swings like crazy; it opens with rhythmic percussion and a melody built from repeated rising brass triplets, very much in the mold of Count Basie's *M Squad* theme. Warren Barker assembled the underscores from a library of tasty jazz cues. Moody walking bass and anxious flute riffs often are heard behind criminal activity; lascivious reed riffs and trumpet stingers herald the arrival of gorgeous dames; and King's hard-charging antics are backed by rising explosions of brass.

Crawford's status notwithstanding, the show wasn't finding viewers. Rather than correct the obvious problem—the poor scripts—some clueless ZIV/United Artists exec commissioned a new title song from William Donati: a thoroughly embarrassing cha-cha ditty—with simply dreadful lyrics—sung by a breathy, *Gilligan's Island*-style male chorus. This ghastly blunder precedes Ortega's swinging instrumental theme during an extended title credits sequence, and becomes the sole music played against the closing credits. As a result, putting *King of Diamonds* out of viewers' misery was an act of mercy.

Attention to detail was more evident on *The New Breed*, a procedural ABC drama that debuted October 3 and gave the typical TV cop a "progressive" makeover, capitalizing on the rising degree to which technology was replacing door-to-door interviews and old-fashioned surveillance. LAPD Lt. Price Adams (Leslie Nielsen) heads an elite Metropolitan Squad that often relies on new-fangled high-tech equipment to close cases that have eluded "regular cops." This was the first series overseen by Quinn Martin under the banner of his new company, QM Productions, which soon would be responsible for an impressive number of 1960s and '70s crime and drama shows. *The New Breed* thus debuts a number of elements that would become QM signatures: a semi-documentary style; a labeled, four-act structure, plus epilog; stoic performances by the lead actors; and an opening credits sequence dominated by a stern announcer—typically Dick Wesson or Hank Simms—who supplies the episode title and identifies the stars, co-stars and "special guest stars."

The series got a swinging title theme from composer/arranger and jazz accordionist Dominic Frontiere, just transitioning from his big band origins into what would become an enormously successful film and television scoring career. *The New Breed* was his first series assignment; he immediately became part of the QM team, after delivering a vibrant title theme that Martin clearly loved. All told, Frontiere wrote roughly an hour's worth of cues, including the main and end titles. "Dominic was a swinger," recalled postproduction supervisor John Elizalde. "He was a genius; he could do anything. He could produce a score in two or three days. Sometimes that was all the time we had. He was a melodist supreme."[4]

Unfortunately, it's difficult to appreciate Frontiere's efforts during the title credits sequence, because the announcer's voice masks too much of the music. The theme stands alone during the end credits: vibrant brass fanfares atop brisk percussion, with the primary 1-1-5 motif stated by strings, after which reeds introduce a B-theme against swinging electric bass. The two melodies coalesce as the orchestra builds to a brass-fueled crescendo.

The New Breed didn't find an audience and was canceled after its single season; no soundtrack album emerged. Frontiere and Martin had better luck with future collaborations, none of which are relevant to this text.

The Big Screen

Blast of Silence, all but forgotten these days, should be celebrated as the last truly great crime drama in American cinema's post–World War II *film noir* cycle. Producer/cinematographer Merrill S. Brody's luxuriously bleak—yet oddly poetic—camerawork creates a tangible, fatalistic mood, which is enhanced by the cast's wholly convincing performances. The film also boasts one of the most enjoyable and dynamic scores attached to any entry in this book: a veritable symphony of swing cues by jazz clarinetist-turned-composer Meyer Kupferman. Not bad, all told, for a guerrilla B-film made by director/co-writer/star Allen Baron for roughly $20,000 (and some deferred lab payments).[5]

The bare-bones plot finds Cleveland hit man Frankie Bono (Baron) in New York City during the week between Christmas and New Year's Day, to fulfill a contract to kill mobster Troiano (Peter Clune). Frankie's movements and inner thoughts are dissected, questioned and even ridiculed by an omniscient narrator (an uncredited Lionel Stander), who delights in mocking the man. Rarely has narration been employed to such striking effect, and so faithfully in the style of hard-boiled novelists such as Dashiell Hammett, Raymond Chandler and Ross Macdonald. Perhaps Frankie pays attention, because he succumbs to doubts about his chosen career: an epiphany triggered by an unexpected encounter with Lori (Molly McCarthy), a woman he knew and liked, back in the day. Alas, mob-affiliated assassins aren't allowed to walk away from their careers; impending doom hangs over these characters like a shroud.

The identities of Kupferman's sidemen remain unknown, but they sure do swing. The credits unspool to an edgy blast of combo jazz, with noisy trumpets shadowing Frankie's arrival in the Big Apple. His surveillance of Troiano takes place as montage sequences, all spotted with ambitious swingers that open with solos on vibes, trumpet, sax and piano. The off-camera narration aside, the film has scant dialog; Baron—as director—fills the lengthy silences by allowing Kupferman's cues to run at length. The tone softens when Frankie bumps into Lori, an encounter spotted by a gentle oboe solo. Tasty diegetic trio/quartet jazz is heard on the radio in Frankie's hotel room, when he calls Lori in an effort to see her again. Live source music is delivered by a quartet—fronted by vocalist/conga drummer Dean Sheldon—in residence at The Village Gate, the famed Greenwich Village nightclub that here becomes a "beatnik den" where Frankie has a fateful encounter.

There was no question of a soundtrack album; the budget never could have supported one. Kupferman subsequently became quite famous as an inventive composer of concertos, symphonies, chamber works, ballets, operas, electronic pieces and melodies developed from "found" music, in addition to his fondness for jazz and 12-tone technique.[6]

Baron wasn't the only indie filmmaker working the Big Apple's mean streets in 1961; indie/experimental film director Shirley Clarke also was busy that year. Her subject was Jack Gelber's controversial play *The Connection*, which made quite a splash during its 1959 Obie Award–winning premiere by New York's Living Theater troupe. Gelber's drama—and Clarke's film—are presented in a *stage verité* manner, set in a claustrophobic apartment; the story follows a cluster of heroin addicts, many of them jazz musicians, as they await a fix from their "connection." To relieve the tension, they periodically break into performance jams; as a further story-within-a-story touch, they're also being filmed by a small crew working on a *cinema verité* documentary.

Although the jams seem improvisational, the production's score was rigorously planned to coincide with the play's dramatic "beats." Jazz pianist/composer Freddie Redd collaborated closely with Gelber during the play's creation, fine-tuning the "character and tempo" of seven pieces that would parallel the performers' behavior. The play ran for a few months before Gelber and Redd found jazzmen who also could "act" in the necessary manner; the final quartet, which remained stable during the remainder of the New York run, featured Jackie McLean (alto sax), Michael Mattos (bass) and Larry Ritchie (drums).[7]

The quartet recorded Redd's seven compositions during a studio session on February 15, 1960—seven months into the play's 17-month run—for a Blue Note album. Shortly thereafter, the play became the first big-screen project helmed by Clarke, who retained most of the stage cast for a feature that premiered at the Cannes Film Festival in May 1961. Stateside release didn't occur until October 1962, thanks to a protracted censorship battle that climbed all the way to the New York State Court of Appeals, due to the film's repeated use of the word *shit*.[8]

The action is set in a squalid little apartment owned by Leach (Warren Finnerty), who tolerates a motley collection of friends, while serving as the go-between for the connection—Cowboy (Carl Lee)—who has promised to bring everybody a heroin fix. Redd's fingers wander aimlessly over the keys of a dilapidated piano, while a few stragglers show up. The group is being filmed continuously by Jim Dunn (William Redfield), a would-be Orson Welles who keeps urging everybody to "act natural." The quartet breaks into its first jam ("Who Killed Cock Robin?"), an uptempo, hard bop arrangement that reflects everybody's increasing agitation. Minor squabbles erupt; Dunn is scorned for his ignorance, since—never having tried smack—he can't possibly adopt the proper "mood" for his film. With that challenge hovering over the room, subsequent performances include a relaxed, piano-driven ballad ("Time to Smile") and an uptempo number ("Music Forever") dominated by McLean's lengthy sax solo. Everybody eventually gets high, one individual dangerously so; his fate remains uncertain as the group disperses, the wigged-out Dunn no longer caring about his film.

Clarke's film never achieved mainstream recognition, although cinema historians now extol its authentic, hard-edged depiction of drug addiction. Redd's score, on the other hand, was famous from the moment Blue Note released the album. (The LP's seven tracks are

5. Contract with Depravity: 1961

quite different, at times, from what viewers hear while watching the film; the two versions of "Wiggin'" barely resemble each other.) Once the play became available for performances elsewhere, each region's resident jazz musicians became part of the action; a San Francisco production—lost to history—involved pianist Vince Guaraldi.

During a brief rotation in the New York production, trumpeter Howard McGhee "led" a quintet that features Tina Brooks (tenor sax), Redd (piano), Milt Hinton (bass) and Osie Johnson (drums); this version of Redd's seven compositions also became an LP, *Music from The Connection*. Other touring productions generated their own original scores. Tenor saxman Dexter Gordon wrote several of the tunes featured during a Los Angeles run; they were included in his 1961 Blue Note album, *Dexter Calling*. Elsewhere, Cecil Payne and Kenny Drew wrote seven new tunes for a sextet that featured Clark Terry (trumpet), Payne (baritone sax), Bennie Green (trombone), Duke Jordan (piano), Ron Carter (bass) and Charlie Persip (drums); that 1962 album, also titled *The Connection*, was released by Charlie Parker Records.

A similar *noir* setting—albeit not as sleazy—made Paul Newman a star, thanks to *The Hustler*. Director Robert Rossen's drama garnered an impressive nine Academy Award

In a review published Dec. 27, 1961, a *New York Times* film critic called Kenyon Hopkins' score for *The Hustler* "appropriately nervous." It's an apt description of a melodic tapestry which superbly complements director Robert Rossen's equally unsettling atmosphere (courtesy Intrada Inc.).

nominations, with a win for Eugen Schüfftan's sumptuously moody, black-and-white cinematography. The story, adapted by Rossen and Sidney Carroll from Walter Tevis' 1959 novel, begins as California-based pool player "Fast Eddie" Felson (Newman) travels across the country to challenge the legendary Minnesota Fats (Jackie Gleason) in his hometown pool parlor. Eddie is long on talent and cockiness, but short on integrity and self-discipline; he ultimately loses after allowing the marathon competition to continue past the limits of his stamina. Even so, professional gambler Bert Gordon (George C. Scott) sees promise in Eddie and offers an arrangement: a proposal the latter initially declines. During the lengthy second act, Eddie meets and begins a relationship with the morose, self-loathing Sarah Packard (Piper Laurie), an alcoholic polio survivor and would-be poet. Eddie eventually crawls back to Bert, which leads to a second match with Fats: at best a pyrrhic victory, because of what is lost along the way.

The film's rich *noir* atmosphere is enhanced by an edgy, superbly nuanced jazz score by Kenyon Hopkins. Phil Woods' alto sax and Jimmy Cleveland's trombone highlight many of the various cues; the former's solos often are quite heartbreaking, as befits the storyline.

Rossen overlays the title credits against Eddie's cocky strut following an easy match; Hopkins delivers a fast-paced main theme dominated by double-time brushed drums, bongos and a killer walking bass, while a joyful sax handles the melody. But this is deceptive; while the early stages of the first match with Fats plays against a cue as buoyant as Eddie's arrogant swagger, a muted trumpet sounds a note of caution. Later, Hopkins' theme for Sarah is a lazy, mournful blend of sax and piano comping, introduced as she and Eddie flirt superficially. Subsequent arrangements of Sarah's theme become increasingly anguished, as she realizes that Eddie never can give her the one thing—genuine love—that she so desperately wants. Circumstances briefly force him to depend on her; the story dangles a ray of hope that is mirrored by a lovely, lyrical jazz ballad, ostensibly performed by the house band when Eddie treats Sarah to dinner at a fancy restaurant. But such simple happiness can't last.

Much of the third act takes place without music, although cuts on the soundtrack album—notably "Lipstick on a Mirror"—suggest that Hopkins wrote cues that Rossen chose not to use. The composer's touch isn't felt again until Eddie's second match against Fats, with tick-tock percussion and sax/muted trumpet melodies suggesting the passage of time, and the slow build of suspense. As the end credits roll, Hopkins' ensemble builds to a gloomy fanfare, reflecting Eddie's tainted victory, and the cost at which it was achieved.

Many of the soundtrack album's 15 tracks are stitched together from two or three short cues. The playlist is more or less in story sequence, allowing for the few that never found their way into the film. One of the MIA cues, "Bert's Theme," is an eyebrow-lifter: a lively, merry melody that's wholly at odds with the character's predatory venality.

Crime is much more blatant in *King of the Roaring 20s: The Story of Arnold Rothstein*. As had been the case with his work on *Rear Window*, composer Franz Waxman's score borrows a note (quite a few, actually) from the vibrant orchestral jazz stylings of George Gershwin, while also adding a touch of the darker Leonard Bernstein pizzazz from *West Side Story*. Director Joseph M. Newman's by-the-numbers melodrama depicts the rise and fall of the ruthlessly calculating Jewish-American racketeer, gambler and entrepreneur, although Jo Swerling's screenplay pays little attention to actual history. That said, the production is highlighted by Waxman's score; Carl E. Guthrie's richly *noir*, black-and-white cinematography; and a fascinating starring performance by David Janssen, fresh off his hit TV series *Richard Diamond*.

The main theme's 2-3-4 motif debuts as a thunderous unison horn fanfare, followed by buoyant, midtempo ragtime piano when the title credits appear. The melody expands via bluesy saxes and sultry brass, with strong echoes of *Rhapsody in Blue* or *An American in Paris*. An ominous rhythm section—highlighted by smooth bass licks—adds an atmosphere of wariness, and then the orchestra explodes into Bernstein's mode of joyful, dissonant jazz. Powerful piano anchors a vibrant brass reprise of the 2-3-4 motif, with cheerful horns adding droll touches that segue into a burst of Charleston-style swing; this abruptly halts when all the instruments mash onto a single note that fades into silence, followed by cacophonous piano left unresolved. It's a remarkable, three-minute mini-jazz symphony that characterizes the dogged ascent, years of giddy triumph, and violent climax of Rothstein's life.

That 2-3-4 motif becomes the film's through-line. The first significant reprise comes via playful vibes and a sweet muted trumpet, when Carolyn (Dianne Foster)—the woman Arnold is determined to marry—consents to a kiss. The relationship clearly is doomed; much later, forlorn cello and muted trumpet repeat the motif when she finally decides to leave him. His world crumbles thereafter, leading quickly to the fateful poker game during which he's shot: a suspenseful scene scored solely by menacing snare drum and timpani. Waxman also supplies some lively Charleston source cues, heard during Arnold's visits to a local speakeasy.

In his liner notes for *The Young Savages*' soundtrack album, composer David Amram explained, "[My score] makes a statement about the film itself, but it also represents my personal feelings about New York, where I've lived and worked for the past six years. As a matter of fact, I've worked in some of the neighborhoods portrayed in the film" (courtesy Intrada Inc.).

No soundtrack appeared until late 2017, with the lavish four-disc box set, *Captains Courageous: The Frank Waxman Collection*; it includes the 20-track score from *King of the Roaring 20s*, along with an unused cue ("Visit with Papa") and one of the dance band source cues ("Speakeasy Charleston 3").

Juvenile delinquency and street gangs were a combustible topic in the late 1950s and early '60s. Although 1961's most visible response was the musical *West Side Story*, a more thoughtful bit of advocacy drama emerged a few months earlier. Television director John Frankenheimer made an auspicious big-screen splash with *The Young Savages*, a persuasively acted adaptation of Evan Hunter's 1959 novel, *A Matter of Conviction*. (Hunter, actually Salvatore Albert Lombino, is better known by another of his pen names: Ed McBain.) As with *12 Angry Men*, a seemingly "obvious" crime yields hidden complexities, eventually leading to a courtroom trial that argues the case from both sides of a "bleeding heart" divide.

The scoring assignment went to David Amram, a jazz and "beat" musician who earlier had worked on a couple of Frankenheimer's anthology TV assignments. Amram also played French horn in jazz bands fronted by Dizzy Gillespie, Lionel Hampton and Charles Mingus, and had been composing the scores for Joseph Papp's *Shakespeare in the Park* productions since 1956. (He'd continue through 1967.)[9] *The Young Savages* was Amram's big-screen scoring debut, and his selection initially didn't sit well with producer Harold Hecht.

"[Hecht] didn't want me, and said, 'The guys' a nobody, he's nothing,'" Amram recalled, years later. "So, the whole time I did that score, they had someone else leaning over my shoulder, a famous old Hollywood composer. I thought, wow, isn't that a compliment, he's so interested in me, in my music. I found out later that Harold Hecht had him there in case he didn't like what I did; he could pay me, fire me, and have the other guy do it instead. Fortunately, that didn't happen."[10]

The film opens brutally, as three teenagers stride grimly through the streets of New York's Spanish Harlem and, without warning, viciously stab a blind Puerto Rican boy to death. The three assailants are quickly caught, arrested and identified as members of the Thunderbirds street gang. The case goes to assistant district attorney Hank Bell (Burt Lancaster), who intends to seek the death penalty for all three boys … until he realizes that one of them (Danny) is the son of his former girlfriend, Mary diPace (Shelley Winters). Hank also gets conflicting pressure from his wife, Karin (Dina Merrill), who argues for "big picture" compassion; and his boss, district attorney Dan Cole (Edward Andrews), who views a swift conviction as a means to enhance his reelection campaign. The narrative expands to encompass ethnic bias, poverty, gang loyalty, conformity, mental capacity and the desperate lengths to which the residents of squalid homes are driven.

The film opens with a mournful harmonica quote, backed by gentle guitar: a cue that will come to represent the story's themes of sorrow and social injustice. Amram then cuts abruptly to an angry, dissonant blast of drums and brass: a five-note march on timpani, the beats timed to the strides of the three knife-wielding thugs, as they approach their victim. Many subsequent cues continue in this dissonant, brass-and-percussion vein; alternatively, Amram selects somber orchestral strings for a solemn, late-night chat between Hank and Karin, on the roof of their apartment. Quartet combo cues pop up as source music: backdrops for Hank's interviews with members of the rival gangs.

"They let me use jazz as an integral part of the picture," Amram noted, "rather than employing it to underscore violence, sadism or narcotics—which is usually the case in pictures. Jazz is heard not in the fight scenes, but during sequences that showed the neighborhoods where the boys lived."[11]

The soundtrack LP is highlighted by expanded arrangements of the two aforementioned source cues: "True Blue" and "Harold's Way Out" (the latter after Harold Land). Another track, "Las Muchachas Delicadas," barely heard in the film, is a lively, uptempo swinger by the same quartet configuration, Land once again on tenor. Amram vividly remembered that recording session: "As we played, Harold's great, smoky, serpentine sound filled up the whole studio with a kind of soul and warmth and realness, that was not part of the Hollywood movie scene at all."[12]

Meanwhile, Across the Pond…

On the UK's small screen, a long-running trilogy of crime shows that featured Scotland Yard's Det. Supt. Tom Lockhart (Raymond Francis)—*Murder Bag* (1957–58), *Crime Sheet* (1959) and *No Hiding Place* (1959–67)—also spawned a short-lived series that gave supporting character Det. Inspector Harry Baxter (Eric Lander) his own starring role. *Echo Four Two* lasted only during the late summer and early autumn of 1961, its intended 13 episodes held to 10 by an actors' strike.[13]

Nothing is known about the music for *Murder Bag* and *Crime Sheet*, as both shows are believed lost. Composer/arranger and big band veteran Laurie Johnson delivered a crisp, military-style anthem for *No Hiding Place*, but took a far jazzier approach to *Echo Four Two*. This theme has a vigorous sense of urgency, opening with a startling blast of brass and bold, march-style percussion. Low-end horns introduce the 1-3-1-3 melodic statement, followed by a reprise against shrill brass fanfares. Screaming trumpet and sax solos take over during the bridge; the entire band builds to a crescendo, pulls back to repeat the core melody, and then climaxes with a breathtaking orchestral blast. It's a terrific theme, sadly wasted on such a short-lived show.

Even so, Johnson's theme earned release as a Pye single, albeit as the B-side of his Top 10 hit, "Sucu Sucu" (about which, more momentarily). His *Echo Four Two* theme was covered by Johnny Gregory and His Orchestra (Fontana); this arrangement eschews the military cadence for rolling percussion on kettle drums and adds entirely different instrumentation during an equally swinging bridge.

Echo Four Two lasted fewer than three months. That wasn't the case with *The Avengers*.

Numerous books have been written about the evolution, popularity and lasting impact of this series, which became a cultural phenomenon during the 1960s: initially in Britain, and then throughout the world. Considering how the program developed during the decade—with changes in cast, tone and (for our purposes) music—it makes sense to treat each transition as a separate entity, starting with series 1, which debuted January 7, 1961. These 26 episodes pair Chelsea-based GP David Keel (Ian Hendry) with the mysterious John Steed (Patrick Macnee), a debonair agent working for some vaguely defined department of British Intelligence. Early scripts focus on routine criminal activity such as drug runners and diamond smugglers, but subsequent episodes delve more deeply into espionage and spycraft, with occasional traces of the macabre and fantastic elements for which the show soon would be known.

As the series was being developed, producer Leonard White got in touch with Johnny Dankworth. He accepted the assignment to write and perform a title theme for White's new series, along with "mood bridges and background music."[14] The resulting 35-second credits sequence is surprisingly crude, with static title cards that sometimes aren't even aligned properly. At first blush, Dankworth's theme is a mildly suspenseful, midtempo swinger, but it quickly grows redundant; the rising pairs of low horn couplets repeat incessantly against synchronous drums, and then are echoed via unison brass. An identical arrangement is heard six times (!) during every episode: under the aforementioned title sequence; as exit and entry bumpers behind the title cards delineating the show's three acts; and finally behind the closing credits. It also occasionally pops up as part of the underscore.

As was common in numerous British shows during this period, most of the drama takes place on sound stages and was transmitted "as live" while being shot on videotape; music almost never is heard during these sequences. When location work proved necessary, to reveal action taking place "out in the world," such brief footage was shot on 35mm film and inserted "on the fly" as the episode was broadcast. Since these filmed sequences were produced in advance, they could be augmented by Dankworth's mood bridges and background music. These are brief but swinging little four-, eight- or 12-bar combo vamps which—again—sometimes are repeated two, three or more times in succession.

As the series approached its midpoint, White requested a further set of atmospheric underscore cues and "longer stings" from Dankworth, to accompany the final batch of episodes.[15] It's impossible to know how much the series' "back end" may have benefited from the additional music, because only three full episodes are known to exist; just one of them—"Tunnel of Fear"—was produced following Dankworth's second visit to the studio. All the rest are believed lost.

Shortly after delivering these additional tracks, Dankworth further obliged White by recording an extended arrangement of his *Avengers* title theme with a full-blown jazz band, for a Columbia single. This version begins as TV viewers heard it during the end credits, and then Dankworth shifts into a terrific swing bridge with plenty of brass and keyboard action against bongo-laden percussion; a tasty flute solo introduces rising unison brass, and then the orchestra concludes the core melody in the usual manner.

Dankworth's theme was covered by John Gregory and His Orchestra for a Fontana four-track EP titled *The TV Thrillers*. This arrangement opens in the familiar manner, but the rhythmic elements appear sooner and segue to an instrumentally rich swing bridge with tense piano riffs, vibrant unison brass, cool walking bass and a nifty trumpet solo. (Frankly, it's superior to Dankworth's original.)

Dankworth's version became harder to find after he cut a fresh arrangement in 1963. Fans desiring the 1961 original should seek a 2015 compilation CD on Europe's Él label: *Escape in Time: Popular British Television Themes of the 1960s*.

The Avengers—and Dankworth's music—would undergo some changes before returning in the fall of 1962.

Slim as the remnants may be, at least we have *some* examples of what *The Avengers* looked like during its first season. The same cannot be said of *Top Secret*, which had an unusual premise for an early 1960s British spy show. Intelligence agent Peter Dallas (William Franklyn) requests a lengthy sabbatical from his London assignments to spend a year in Argentina, where he was raised. Once comfortably situated, he's hired by wealthy businessman Miguel Garetta (Patrick Cargill) to investigate—and close—organized crime activities that have eluded or overwhelmed the local constabulary. Such cases take Dallas all over the country, often accompanied by Garetta's nephew, Mike (Alan Rothwell).

The show's producers were drawn to the Laurie Johnson Orchestra's cover of "Sucu Sucu," a dance tune written and recorded in 1959 by Bolivian singer/composer Tarateño Rojas, which subsequently became quite popular all over the world. The tune became even better recognized in the UK when Johnson's version became the title theme for *Top Secret*, during a two-season run that debuted August 11, 1961. His heavily percussive arrangement opens with a roll of bongos—which anticipates the similar prelude he'd later use for his iconic *Avengers* theme—and then unison horns deliver the infectious 3-5-3-4-1 melody that prompted people throughout the globe to hit the dance floor. Unison reeds add a cheerful countermelody; solo brass and guitar supply an even stronger Latin flavor during the bridge. The result is beyond catchy, as it builds to a climactic, three-note orchestral flourish.

Unfortunately, Johnson's title theme is all that remains of *Top Secret*. All 26 episodes are lost.

* * *

On the big screen, the script and acting are quite tight in director Sidney Hayers' *Payroll*, released in the States as *I Promised to Pay*. At first blush, this UK entry unfolds like a crisply assembled heist thriller, as four crooks meticulously plot how best to steal the weekly employee wages from a local factory. But the aftermath becomes pure *noir*, as thieves fall out, and dogged police detectives tighten their investigation. All the elements are top-notch: Ernest Stewart's gorgeous, shadow-laden cinematography; a vindictive *femme fatale*; and a dour outcome that brings joy to almost nobody. The riveting cinematic package also benefits from Reg Owen's terrific big band jazz score.

Owen took up sax as a teenager and blossomed while studying with Benny Goodman's big band. While a member of the RAF Band during World War II, he taught himself arranging by transcribing charts by Goodman, Tommy Dorsey and Artie Shaw. Postwar activities included a lengthy stint with Ted Heath's jazz band, and a tenure with Cyril Stapleton's Show Band, before heading his own unit and taking a sideways detour into film scoring.[16]

Owen's 8/4 main theme, introduced over the title credits, begins as a midtempo cha-cha with a hypnotically rhythmic bass; a mildly exotic flute melody rises as wayward bongos surface. Unison horns take over, punctuated by brass fanfares; the entire orchestra picks up the pulsating tune, the intensity building to a final two-note blast. Variations of this theme recur often during the first act, as Johnny Mellors (Michael Craig) and his gang surveil an armored vehicle, to clock its route; later, in the aftermath of a heist gone awry, the crooks drive away to a fast swing cue, barely evading scores of shocked witnesses who try to stop their getaway car. At this point, Hayers all but eliminates music for a bit, allowing viewers to digest the awful implications of what just went down. A salacious sax introduces an entirely new mood when the avaricious—and married—Katie (Françoise Prévost) succumbs to Johnny's feral charm. The main theme blossoms into a vibrant action cue in anticipation of the climax and final confrontations between various characters.

Sadly, *Payroll* failed to produce a soundtrack album. Fans must be content with the Reg Owen Orchestra's 1961 Palette single, which features a rousing rendition of the film's title theme.

Elsewhere in the World

MGM-Television's decision to transform its *Asphalt Jungle* pilot into a feature film resulted in *The Lawbreakers*, which was released solely in Western Europe and Mexico. It's surprisingly risqué and quite violent by American standards of the era, which likely explains the absence of a Stateside release. This big-screen version boasts a sleek jazz score by Johnny Mandel, still a few years away from the name-brand fame that would come from *The Americanization of Emily* and *The Sandpiper*; his cues definitely echo Henry Mancini's *Peter Gunn* touch.

Vera Miles steals the show as a cold-hearted *femme* most definitely *fatale*. The story focuses on shady New York City lawyer Allen Bardeman (Robert Douglas) and his secretary, Angela Walsh (Miles), also his mistress. Bardeman is one link in a chain of individuals funneling numbers racket cash to an omnipresent crime syndicate; he collects the money weekly from bag man Sam Henry (Robert Henry), a corrupt City Hall administrator who picks up the cash from shady nightclub owner Ed Rackin (Ken Lynch). Angela encourages Bardeman to steal one of the weekly cash hauls; he embraces the idea, not realizing that she is double-timing him with Rackin, and that they intend to snatch the money and run off together. A parallel plot concerns newly appointed police commissioner Matthew Gower (Jack Warden, the TV show's star); he and his colleagues work their way up the food chain, as Bardeman, Rackin and Angela systematically betray each other.

Mandel complements the stark title credits with a smoky, atmospheric cue that trades the melody between clarinet and trumpet, while a background bank of horns supplies additional urgency. Much of the story action subsequently takes place in the sleazy Gaiety Nightclub run by Rackin; a mostly unseen vibes and trumpet combo shifts from bluesy ballads to raucous strip cues, while exotic dancers peel off their clothes or wander backstage in various stages of undress. Vibrant action jazz lends plenty of suspense to the climax, when Gower and his men surround Rackin and Angela at the city's busy transit station.

The patchwork film definitely benefits from Mandel's efforts, but the composer didn't think much of the assignment; no soundtrack album surfaced. "I did some TV movies and a few pictures in the early '60s I'd just soon forget," he recalled, decades later, "like *The Lawbreakers*, *The 3rd Voice* and *Drums of Africa*."[17]

6

Jamaica Jazz: 1962

Everything changed again, thanks to a shaken-not-stirred secret agent with a license to kill, and a British composer/arranger who'd been placing pop hits with his own rock 'n' roll/jazz septet since late 1957.

John Barry Prendergast developed his fondness for film music quite young, while spending time in the small chain of movie theaters managed by his father. Early influences included film composers Bernard Herrmann, Erich Korngold and Max Steiner, along with the "sharp attack" style of Stan Kenton's big jazz band. Barry studied piano and composition, played trumpet with an Army band during his military service, and in 1957 formed the John Barry Seven. Two years later, he composed his first film score for the Adam Faith rock 'n' roll pot-boiler, *Beat Girl*.[1]

A few years after that, Barry ignited the fuse of a musical subgenre soon to be known as spy jazz.

As an unrelated sidebar—and of far less consequence—nothing that concerns us debuted on American television in 1962.

The Small Screen

After seven successful years as a half-hour anthology series on CBS and NBC, *Alfred Hitchcock Presents* bounced back to the former network for an eighth season that debuted September 20, with a new title—*The Alfred Hitchcock Hour*—that reflected its expanded length. The familiar elements were retained: Hitchcock's droll introductions and postscripts, along with Charles Gounod's "Funeral March of a Marionette" as the memorable title theme. But the series changed its approach to episode music: Whereas all half-hour episodes had been scored from library cues, composers were hired to create original scores for slightly more than half of the 93 hour-length episodes unveiled during the new format's three-year run. These new cues were tracked into the remaining episodes.

Almost all of these new scores relied heavily on string-laden orchestral suspense cues: the old-style Hollywood approach taken by established composers such as Lyn Murray and frequent Hitchcock colleague Bernard Herrmann. But two third-season episodes are jazz oriented, as befits their storylines.

"Memo from Purgatory" (Dec. 21, 1964), adapted by Harlan Ellison from his own memoir of roughly the same title—*Memos from Purgatory*—details the harrowing 10 weeks he spent in 1954, posing as a member of street gang, to research his first novel, *Web of the City*. James Caan stars as Ellison's surrogate, Jay Shaw; key gang members are played by Walter Koenig, Tony Musante and Zalman King. Director Joseph Pevney opted for a vibrant jazz score; the assignment went to Lalo Schifrin, just beginning what would blossom into an enormously successful Hollywood film and television career.

The episode's credits unfold against a tense swing cue, with anxious horn fanfares backed by walking bass and midtempo percussion. Schifrin maintains this unsettling tone with all of his non-diegetic cues; brass, bluesy sax and his signature flutes anxiously duel against pensive percussion when Shaw insinuates himself into the gang, unwisely falling for the leader's ex-girlfriend, Philene (Lynn Loring). Alternatively, jukebox and phonograph source tunes—given titles such as "Malt Shop Twist," "Purgatory Twist" and simply "Jukebox"—are dance-friendly blasts of horn- and guitar-fueled jazz/rock. The story's ironic conclusion unfolds against a slow, mournful ballad appropriately titled "Baron's Blues."

The tone is more light-hearted in "Crimson Witness" (Jan. 4, 1965), which concerns a successful business executive (Peter Lawford, as Ernie Mullett) whose perfect life slides into chaos when his job, wife and girlfriend are taken over by his scheming brother (Roger C. Carmel, as Farnum Mullett). The sibling rivalry becomes progressively more violent and—ultimately—lethal. Celebrated jazz saxophonist Benny Carter delivers a whimsical, Ellington-esque score on his sole assignment for *The Alfred Hitchcock Hour*. The cues slide from mocking sax or muted trumpet against swirling strings, as Ernie is confronted by the escalating series of betrayals; to gently rhythmic swing cues, often punctuated by lyrical piano filigrees, when he subsequently plots the means to get even.

Both scores—along with numerous others—are included in the three-volume, seven-disc *Alfred Hitchcock Hour* sets.

The Big Screen

Following the light-hearted *High Time* and *Breakfast at Tiffany's*, director Blake Edwards and composer Henry Mancini's third high-profile film collaboration was the suspenseful *Experiment in Terror*, a taut crime thriller adapted by Gordon and Mildred Gordon from their 1961 novel, *Operation Terror*. Although lovingly crafted in the classic *noir* mode—late-night settings are given chilling *frisson* by Mancini's disconcerting score and Philip H. Lathrop's moody, documentary-style, monochrome cinematography—the film also is a compelling investigative procedural. It must've been a terrific FBI recruitment tool.

The story begins with a creepy jolt, as San Francisco bank teller Kelly Sherwood (Lee Remick) is ambushed one evening, by a killer who instructs her to steal $100,000 from her cash drawer at some future date. Should she fail to comply, or contact the police, he promises to kill her or her 16-year-old sister, Toby (Stefanie Powers). Kelly nonetheless calls the FBI, where she's placed under the calm and methodical guidance of John "Rip" Ripley (Glenn Ford). A few clues and a seemingly unconnected murder allow Rip and his colleagues to identify the killer as Garland "Red" Lynch (Ross Martin), a psychopath with a string of convictions for rape, assault, armed robbery and murder. He finally gives Kelly the date for her theft, and—to further ensure her cooperation—kidnaps Toby. Everything builds to a nerve-racking climax at Candlestick Park, during a night game between the San Francisco Giants and Los Angeles Dodgers, where Lynch has arranged to collect the money.

Wanting to concoct a main theme that would be as unnerving as possible, Mancini became intrigued by the autoharp. "I got one of these things and started playing with it, and I saw that it could only hit certain chords. It was not chromatic—I don't even know if it had a dominant seventh—but at any rate I strummed it, and I said, geez, this is a very chilling instrument. What I liked was that the decay [the length of time a note 'hangs' in the air] was forever."[2]

"While experimenting with it, I discovered I could get the notes with a guitar pick. This was the basis for the music for the opening of *Experiment in Terror*. I used two autoharps, with Bob Bain on one and Jack Marshall on the other, one plucking out the chords and the other playing the melody. It was very effective."[3]

The result is seriously unnerving. The title credits appear while Kelly drives home late one night, the theme introduced by a gentle triplet pattern on cymbals and an almost subsonic, low-D organ rumble; the twin autoharps chart her progress through darkened streets. Bowed bass adds additional tension as she gets closer to home, at which point the theme expands to include bass flutes, electric guitar, organ and the rest of the orchestra. When she pulls into her garage, a final autoharp strum lends alarming emphasis when *somebody else* closes the garage door.

The bulk of Mancini's subsequent underscore is dissonant and atmospheric: ominous blends of bass, strings, low-end piano runs, sustained tenor sax notes and those disorienting autoharp touches. This shifts during the climax at Candlestick Park, set to a welcome jolt of solid action jazz. Pulsating drums and shrill horns follow Lynch's unsuccessful attempt to get the money; a lone sax takes the title theme as the killer flees onto the now-empty field, Rip and scores of other agents closing in from all sides.

Mancini's underscore hardly exercised the talents of his jazz colleagues. They stretch instead on a series of source cues, the first of which is heard on Kelly's car radio, early in the film: a swinging, flute-driven shuffle with Jimmy Rowles' piano comping in the background. Later in the story, during a montage as FBI agents seek leads in various bars and restaurants, Mancini inserts a few brief combo cues: a bouncy piano/sax quartet in one establishment, and a tasty solo cocktail pianist in a second. A much livelier dance cue—with an organ introduction that anticipates Mancini's "Baby Elephant Walk"—is heard in the third act, from the jukebox at a teen-oriented venue called The Hangout. Mancini even includes an inside joke: As the crowd disperses from Candlestick Park, the stadium organ can be heard playing a few bars of the title theme from TV's *Mr. Lucky*.

The RCA soundtrack LP is a buoyant showcase for expanded and reorchestrated arrangements of the various diegetic cues. The brief car radio snippet blossoms into a mid-tempo swinger titled "Fluters Ball," with a pair of lovely flute solos at the bridge. Two public pool radio cues are expanded into the uptempo "Golden Gate Twist," with saucy unison saxes and a wicked guitar solo; and "Experiment in Terror (Twist)," with its *Peter Gunn*-esque walking bass and percussion, and a terrific sax solo. The album also includes a lovely sax theme intended for Remick—"Kelly's Tune"—which opens with some finger-snapping walking bass; sadly, the cue went unused in the film.

RCA also released the title track and a moody autoharp theme dubbed "Tooty Twist" as a 45. The former achieved additional fame in Pennsylvania's greater Pittsburgh area, where Al Caiola's cover version became the beloved opening to "Chilly Billy" Cardille's Saturday night horror movie program, *Chiller Theater*, from 1963 through '83.[4] Decades later, Mancini's title theme also became a popular item on lounge and exotica collections, covered by La Muerte, The Lounge-O-Leers, Impala, Laika and the Cosmonauts, The Blue Hawaiians and many others.

Richard Condon's *The Manchurian Candidate* was a hot-button political thriller upon publication in 1959, with its frightening saga of an American infantry platoon captured during the Korean War, and one soldier—Raymond Shaw—brainwashed by Chinese and Soviet intelligence operatives into becoming a lethal "sleeper assassin." Condon's novel also is a scathing indictment of the 1950s "red scare," with Shaw's step-father, John Iselin, a fascist U.S. senator in the Joseph McCarthy mold; Iselin is being groomed by Shaw's mother—Eleanor, a deep-cover Communist agent—to become a puppet Soviet dictator after Shaw is programmed to assassinate the U.S. presidential candidate.

A big-screen adaptation was inevitable, and director John Frankenheimer's scorching drama is a sinister *noir* classic, in great part due to Lionel Lindon's moody monochrome cinematography. Laurence Harvey is appropriately robotic as the repressed Shaw, who struggles to shake off his programming; Frank Sinatra is equally strong as hard-charging Bennett Marco, one of the other platoon members, whose nightmare flashbacks slowly unravel the Communist plot.

Frankenheimer wanted the music to blend jazz with classical influences, all with an unsettling undertone; composer David Amram responded with a score that perfectly reflects the film's paranoid atmosphere. "I had a chance to use contra-bass clarinets, hecklephones, three piccolos, bass flutes, a harpsichord and many other instruments I had not used before," Amram recalled.[5] As befit this mingling of genres, the large orchestra included chamber musicians, symphony soloists and plenty of jazz friends.

"I wrote a lot of jazz for the movie which never was used, partially just to have all the guys get together to have a session. Producer Howard Koch and the people connected with the film tried to make it easy for me to do a good job, rather than to impress me with the strength of their position. As a result, the music for *The Manchurian Candidate* came out better than any film score that I had ever done."[6]

That said, very little of the music in Frankenheimer's final edit can be considered jazz. The haunting main theme, debuting behind the title credits, is an orchestral lament, with strings carrying the melody; only during subsequent reprises does it blossom into a quiet jazz ballad of sorts, with sax and/or trumpet taking the lead. On the other hand, several source cues are solid swingers, starting with the blast of Latin-tinged big band jazz heard as the story begins: when Shaw, Marco and the rest of their platoon enjoy some raucous R&R in a bar located near their Korean military base. Much later, similarly brief bursts of big band jazz serve as party music during a Washington, D.C.-based costume ball.

No soundtrack LP was produced, although Amram's main theme was covered by Les Baxter on a 1962 Reprise single. Fans had to wait 35 years before the score was digitized, revealing the extent to which Frankenheimer discarded most of Amram's luxurious, richly swinging jazz cues. "Some Soul from Seoul" and "Mesopotamian Mambo (Cantina Latina)" are pulsating, toe-tapping jump jazz, with solid solos on sax, trumpet, piano and Amram's signature French horn. "Dare to Dream," a gorgeous ballad intended to spot Marco's chance introduction to Rose (Janet Leigh), offers a romantic theme traded between alto sax, piano and flute. Amram shifts to piano for "Slightly Manchurian Blues," an Asian-hued variation on traditional 12-bar blues, which boasts killer bass and sax work.

The Manchurian Candidate was remade in 2004, with Denzel Washington, Meryl Streep and Liev Schreiber; Rachel Portman's orchestral score hasn't a trace of jazz.

At the other end of the quality scale, *Satan in High Heels* is a hilariously tawdry bit of low-budget sleaze. Director Jerald Intrator and cinematographer Bernard Hirschenson miss no opportunity to leer at the well-endowed assets of their various starlets, and the sordid saga focuses on promiscuity, drug addiction and lesbianism. The story's frankness is provocative from an historical standpoint, and some of the performances—notably

Grayson Hall, as a butch nightclub owner—are better than one would expect. But the film's strongest asset is jazz guitarist Mundell Lowe's big band score: a terrific collection of swing cues performed by a truly hot ensemble.

Meg Myles, a 1950s pin-up model, stars as Stacey Kane, a singer and burlesque dancer stuck in a seedy carnival. Long-unseen junkie husband Rudy (Earl Hammond) turns up one evening, trying to win her back with a wad of cash; she tricks him out of the money and flies to New York, where she gets a job at an upscale nightclub/strip palace run by the sophisticated Pepe (Hall). The gold-digging Stacey latches onto club owner Arnold Kenyon (Mike Keene), bedding him in exchange for an apartment and a lavish wardrobe; she also sleeps with his deadbeat playboy son, Larry (Robert Yuro). This combustible triangle explodes when Rudy tracks her down, at which point Stacey decides to "solve" her problems by having him kill Arnold (!).

"It was pretty trashy," Lowe acknowledged much later, when asked about his involvement. "But I wanted to write for film, and this one was as good as any, to try out new things, musically. [The biggest challenge was] musician fatigue. Too many takes to finish on the dot causes musicians to start screwing up. So I decided to create breaks in extended pieces of music, by overlapping the cues. If I had three separate segments that made up a 4½-minute piece of music, I'd write an easy-going chord, like a C-7, at the end of each segment. At the end of the first cue, a sax, say, would run down the C-7 chord. Then we'd take a break. When we returned, the sax would then start the next segment by running down the same chord. This would allow the segments to be spliced together later seamlessly, without the music sounding chopped up or low-energy."[7]

Lowe must have relied on that technique a lot; the film is laden with lengthy montages that employ music in place of dialogue. Quite a few of his cues therefore run long, as full-blown compositions; the first is the title theme, which propels credits that play over Stacey's journey to New York. This rip-snortin' swinger opens with dynamic brass fanfares that quickly segue to a call-and-response melody traded between alternating banks of horns. Latin touches and a saucy sax melody fuel the next montage, when Stacy is taken under Arnold and Pepe's wing, and given a total makeover at various Manhattan salons and clothing shops. Eddie Costa's cool vibes are prominent in this cue, and also in the slower, flute-driven ballad that later shadows Stacey and Larry, while they flirt. That cue's gentleness is in deliberate contrast to the double-time blast of swingin' jump jazz that follows the avaricious Stacey, when she allows Arnold to drive her through the city.

The film's most "scandalous" sequence occurs when Stacey strips for a swim in a lake near the cabin where she and Larry have spent the night. Lowe backs this scene with a gentle melody dominated by flute, vibes and guitar, granting Stacey a degree of uninhibited happiness that makes her seem innocent (if only briefly). Once back in Manhattan, Lowe's music turns more aggressive when Rudy shows up; Costa's low-end piano runs and George Duvivier's bass add a threatening element to uptempo rhythmic cues that erupt with unsettling blasts of brass. Ultimately, Stacey is banished to an uncertain future on New York's mean streets. Lowe backs her forlorn departure with another brass-heavy swinger, as the screen fades to black.

Lowe's industry cred—as a composer, arranger and staff musician with the NBC Orchestra, and as a former sideman in units headed by Benny Goodman, Red Norvo, Charlie Parker and numerous others—likely facilitated the release of a soundtrack album: quite rare, for a low-budget production. Lowe reorchestrated all the film cues, turning them into even longer, jazzier melodies (oddly, with less emphasis on Costa's vibes). The initial pressing, with a sleeve bearing an image from the film's poster art, must not have sold well; it was reissued the following year with a sexier image and a new title—*Blues for a Stripper*—that gives no indication of the contents being a soundtrack. It subsequently was digitized under both titles.

Meanwhile, Across the Pond…

A lengthy British actors' strike delayed production on the second season of *The Avengers*, which prompted co-star Ian Hendry to leave the show and pursue a big-screen career. The producers took this opportunity to overhaul the entire series when it resumed on September 29, 1962. Patrick Macnee's John Steed became the star, and this 26-episode second series found him shuttling between three new companions. Honor Blackman's Cathy Gale earned the lion's share of episodes, and her leather motorcycle garb and "kinky boots" quickly made the character a fan favorite. Her adventures alternated with others featuring Dr. Martin King (Jon Rollason) and nightclub singer Venus Smith (Julie Stevens), both best forgotten.

Johnny Dankworth returned as the show's composer. His title theme was retained, along with his existing collection of stingers, mood bridges and background themes. He further expanded this library by composing some additional "linking music" and "tension links." Thanks to improved technology, these second series episodes display a greater musical presence; Dankworth's efforts often are supplemented by library cues from other composers. The series' jazz element is more pronounced, particularly in Blackman's episodes; her judo-laden skirmishes with incidental baddies often take place against Dankworth's vibrant brass stingers.

After Series 2 concluded, work began immediately on Series 3, which debuted on September 23, 1963. Martin King and Venus Smith avenged no more; Blackman's Cathy Gale became Steed's full-time partner. Dankworth celebrated this welcome shift by re-recording the show's title theme, adding rat-a-tat percussive "ticking" behind the rising pairs of low horn couplets. The swing interlude is smoother, with a tasty horn counterpoint. These changes were even more apparent when Dankworth and his band cut a fresh 45 single; an entirely new bridge is pure bebop brass against a 4-beat bass vamp, building to a crescendo of shrieking horns, before returning to the core theme and its explosive final orchestral note.

The Avengers was a UK phenomenon when Series 3 concluded on March 21, 1964, by which time Blackman had dropped her devastating bomb. She wouldn't return for Series 4, having accepted the offer to play a similarly rough 'n' tumble role on the big screen: Pussy Galore, in the film adaptation of *Goldfinger*. And, so, it was back to the drawing board for *The Avengers*, which would remain off the air for a year and a half, while many things—including the music—changed yet again.

Meanwhile, UK television viewers had become equally transfixed by a charming rogue with a venerable background: Simon Templar, better known as The Saint, who debuted in author Leslie Charteris' 1928 novel, *Meet the Tiger*. During the next three decades and change, as Charteris continued to feature The Saint in three dozen novels and short story collections, the character also became a popular fixture in big-screen films, radio shows, comic books and serialized newspaper adventures. By the early 1960s, he was ready to conquer television; *The Saint* debuted on October 4, 1962. Roger Moore proved sublime as the debonair and mockingly larcenous Templar, and the show became a popular phenomenon that ultimately produced 118 episodes during a six-series run that finally concluded on March 9, 1969.

The indefatigable Edwin Astley was along for the entire ride, as the series' sole composer. His title theme is constructed from a brief whistled "signature theme" that Charteris had devised and introduced in 1939's big-screen adventure, *The Saint Strikes Back*. Astley arranged this into a 25-second tune dominated by a 6-6-7 brass motif over slow percussion and throbbing guitar; it kicks off each episode as a sidebar character recognizes "the famous Simon Templar," prompting Moore to glance heavenward as a superimposed halo appears over his head. The melody repeats over the title credits, then climbs the scale for a final orchestral flourish.

Astley wrote numerous underscore cues designed specifically for early adventures, thereby building a music library that could be tracked into subsequent episodes with which he wasn't directly involved. Because *The Saint* was a filmed series—as opposed to "shot as live" on videotape, as was the case with initial seasons of *The Avengers*—Astley's music could play a much more prominent role in even the earliest episodes. Whimsical soprano reeds back Templar when he "breaks the fourth wall" to address the viewing audience; an astonishing number of title theme arrangements—in various tempos, instrumentations, moods and cultural shadings—also pop up in every episode. Several types of cues became ubiquitous. Staccato explosions of brass back fight scenes, particularly when The Saint beats a couple of baddies into submission; the weekly "damsel in distress" often is introduced with a mildly saucy sax cue; Simon's visits to various Western European or vaguely defined South American countries are flavored with cues that convey the appropriate cultural touch. Astley also supplied plenty of source cues for radios, phonographs and even live bands; they range from combo swing and orchestral dance music to—as the decade wore on—vibrant bits of jazz-inflected rock 'n' roll.

Ironically, Astley wasn't even close to being the first to release his *Saint* theme as a 45 single; that honor fell to the Les Reed Brass, which delivered a kick-ass swing version on the Piccadilly label. Astley finally responded with his own expanded version, which conveys The Saint's blend of mystery and whimsy, via rising big band horns, a dynamic bridge highlighted by comping vibes, and a flute-driven finale that steps up the scale for a final orchestral flourish.

When Series 5 debuted in the autumn of 1966, production shifted from black-and-white to color. Astley took this opportunity to update his title theme, with an accelerated tempo and far stronger brass elements. In the course of composing new underscores for 14 early color episodes, he built a new library of 200 cues, along with roughly three dozen alternate takes; all subsequent episode underscores were constructed from this library. Very little can be considered jazz; most cues are string- and flute-laden orchestral suspense riffs, with occasional brass stingers. The best exceptions are source cues: a sweet bossa nova version of the revised title theme, heard on a radio toward the end of "Interlude in Venice"; a brassy action cue with Neal Hefti–style percussion, heard as Simon watches a TV show at the beginning of "The Fiction-Makers"; a jazz-rock swinger performed by a nightclub combo, in "Escape Route"; and some cool brass against fast walking bass during a climactic fight in "Vendetta for the Saint."

Over in the States, RCA quickly okayed a full-length *Saint* soundtrack album. Highlights include the bossa-flavored "Chaise-Lounge," with its cool sax line; a sexy piano and muted trumpet ballad titled "Slinky"; and the finger-snapping, bongo- and brass-laden "Swinging Simon."

Astley reworked the title theme one more time, when the series returned for its sixth and final season, on September 29, 1968. This version no longer references Charteris' original "signature theme," instead introducing an entirely new seven-note motif via female vocalese against dynamic brass and percussion. Astley worked numerous variations of this new theme into subsequent underscores; a bold, brass-heavy arrangement midway through "The Organization Man" is particularly choice.

Nearly three decades later, coinciding with the release of 1997's ill-advised big-screen update of *The Saint*—which has virtually nothing to do with Charteris' character—the electronica dance band Orbital covered Astley's original theme as part of the film's soundtrack album. After all that time, an FFRR CD single of Orbital's arrangement lingered for 11 weeks on Britain's Top 40 chart, rising to No. 3 on April 19, 1997.

TV's Simon Templar would be resurrected in 1978, for *Return of the Saint*. (See this book's companion volume.)

On the big screen, a modest B-film thriller—with an unexpectedly influential score—was about to have an outsized impact on the movie industry.

Few pieces of music have garnered the recognition of "The James Bond Theme." It's arguably the world's best-known film score cue: as iconic as the gun-barrel montage that opened every 007 thriller for more than four decades, until the format was rebooted with 2006's update of *Casino Royale*. Unlike most movie cues, though, this theme had a difficult gestation and somewhat contentious afterlife, proving the old adage: Failure may be an orphan, but success has many fathers.

Dr. No producers Albert R. "Cubby" Broccoli and Harry Saltzman initially hired singer/songwriter Monty Norman to score their film. Norman and his wife, actress/singer Diana Coupland, spent the second half of January 1962 in Kingston, Jamaica, where they soaked up the region's vivacious musical essence while the film began shooting. Norman delivered a calypso-flavored score dominated by three songs: the seductive "Under the Mango Tree," a droll patter-song titled "Kingston Calypso," and the lively jazz-dance "Jump Up." He also wrote atmospheric orchestral cues, many of them instrumental arrangements of the aforementioned songs. But as the weeks passed, Norman was unable to come up with a main theme—something suitable for Bond himself—that was energetic enough to satisfy the producers. The composer ultimately dipped into his trunk of discarded songs, selecting one—"Bad Sign, Good Sign"—that had belonged to an unproduced musical. The tune has the unmistakable core melody that any Bond fan would recognize—*Dum-di-di-dum-dum, dum dum dum dum-di-di-dum-dum*—but it lacked … well … pizzazz.[8]

Enter John Barry, whose score for *Beat Girl*—dominated by shrill brass, robust guitar and hypnotic percussion—became England's first full-length soundtrack LP. His assignment on *Dr. No* was modest: to spruce up Norman's song, and turn it into a jazz anthem. Barry added a rhythmic bass line, Stan Kenton–style brass, a bit of countermelody and—most significantly—the pulsating, swing-oriented bridge.

"It was very Dizzy Gillespie," Barry explained. "The bridge of 'The James Bond Theme,' it's totally bebop. It was this crazy mixture of stuff that filtered through one entity and came out like it did, and the funny thing was, it all held together. It sounded like it all came out the same hole—you know, complete—but it was really a ragbag of ideas."[9]

"I didn't see any film," he added. "I worked on the weekend. I did this theme, went into the studio, recorded it, and that was it. No strings, just five saxes, nine brass, solo guitar and rhythm section. I got paid £200, and that was that."[10] But not just *any* solo guitarist. Barry turned to bandmate Vic Flick, whose throbbing licks had played a key role in the *Beat Girl* score. For *Dr. No*, Flick used a "big, blond, f-hole Clifford Essex Paragon cello-bodied guitar, fitted with a DeAmond Volume Pedal into a Vox 15-watt amplifier."[11]

"The original [Norman] theme was scored an octave higher," Flick explained. "I suggested to John that it would have a more ominous feel if I played it down the octave, starting on the sixth string. We tried it, and it turned out to be very effective.[12]

"I overplayed it," Flick added. "I leaned into those thick, low strings with the very hard plectrum, played it slightly ahead of the beat, and it came out exciting, almost 'attacking,' which fit the James Bond image."[13]

"We recorded it at EMI with lots of reverb," Barry added, "and lots of echo."[14]

Norman never could have imagined what Flick and Barry would do to his gentle ditty.

James Bond's debut film assignment begins in Jamaica, when he investigates the disappearance of the local British Intelligence station chief. Bond suspects a potential link to the recent radio-jamming disruption of Cape Canaveral rocket launches, a hunch shared by CIA colleague Felix Leiter (Jack Lord). Evidence points to Crab Key, an offshore island that supposedly supports only a bauxite mine, but which has a reputation for causing trespassers to "vanish." Bond heads to the island, accompanied by a Cayman Islander dubbed Quarrel (John Kitzmiller); they chance upon Honey Ryder (Ursula Andress), a young woman who is gathering shells. Quarrel is killed by the island's paramilitary squad; Bond and Honey are captured and taken to Dr. No (Joseph Wiseman), a metal-handed Chinese/German scientist who plans to sabotage Cape Canaveral's upcoming Project Mercury space launch, on behalf of the global criminal organization SPECTRE. Can a lone British secret agent foil this diabolical plot?

Both Norman and Barry were surprised, when they saw the finished film. Director Terence Young and editor Peter Hunt filled the score with Norman's three calypso-hued songs, both as vocals and instrumentals, but ignored his underscore cues; the sole exception is a sinister theme written for Dr. No, a blend of unsettling percussion and unison strings with a rising/falling 7-5 motif. Barry, in turn, expected that his "enhanced" main theme would be used solely during the film's title credits: a hypnotic display of multicolored circles "spawned" by the gun barrel opening, and developed by designer Maurice Binder (whose Bond title credits sequences would become as famous as this theme). But Young and Hunt loved Barry's two-minute cue and employed snatches of it half a dozen times throughout the film: most famously early on, at a private London club, where frustrated baccarat player Sylvia Trench (Eunice Gayson) demands to know the name of the man who keeps beating her. "Bond," Sean Connery replies dryly, "James Bond," as the soon-to-be-famous theme swells in the background.

The film's only other bit of swing is source music: a terrific jazz/rock arrangement of "Under the Mango Tree," performed by Byron Lee and the Dragonaires, and heard softly in the background while Bond, Leiter and Quarrel interrogate a spiteful photographer (Marguerite LeWars) in Puss Feller's nightclub.

The soundtrack album is a curious affair. Barry isn't cited anywhere, and Norman's name is buried in very tiny print on the jacket back. No mention is made of Byron Lee and the Dragonaires, or Coupland, who sings one of the vocal versions of "Under the Mango Tree." The LP claims that all tracks are "composed and conducted" by Norman, which absolutely isn't true. But that's not the strangest part. Only seven of the album's 18 tracks come from the film; all the others are Norman's discarded instrumental cues ... one of which, also confusingly called "The James Bond Theme," is an entirely different piece of music! (Neither Barry nor Norman had a hand in preparing the album.)

The John Barry Seven and Orchestra covered "The James Bond Theme" as a single released on Columbia's UK label. Astonishingly, the tune never cracked the U.S. *Billboard* charts, although it did occupy the UK's Top 40 Singles Chart for eight weeks. The *Dr. No* soundtrack album fared better in the States, spending 10 weeks on *Billboard's* Top LPs Chart in the summer of 1963. (Although *Dr. No* was released in the UK in October 1962, it didn't reach the States until May 1963.)

That slow start was no indication of staying power. Barry's arrangement of "The James Bond Theme" subsequently was covered by hundreds of pop, jazz and instrumental artists: from Glen Campbell to the Ventures, from Ferrante and Teicher to Brian Setzer, from Count Basie to John Zorn, from Meco to Moby. And, of course, it continues to appear in every new James Bond film.

The tune also generated several lawsuits regarding its creation, as Norman repeatedly had to defend his authorship against publications that gave sole credit to Barry (who compounded the problem by claiming as much during several interviews). The issue finally was resolved during a 2001 High Court jury trial that ruled for Norman. The song—and credit—would forever remain his. But Barry arguably fared better, back in the early 1960s, when his arranging and orchestration efforts won him the lucrative, high-profile gig of becoming *the* Bond composer for the next several decades.

Elsewhere in the World

Scripter Mel Goldberg's gritty drug melodrama, *The Murder Men*, has an intriguing back-story. It began life as "Blues for a Junkman: Arthur Troy," an episode of television's single-season *noir* crime drama series *Cain's Hundred*, and was broadcast on February 20, 1962. Possibly because of the guest-starring appearance by famed actress/jazz chanteuse Dorothy Dandridge, MGM expanded director Robert Gist's original cut with additional footage for release theatrically in Europe later that same year, now titled *The Murder Men*. (The 1961 release year indicated by the Internet Movie Database and numerous other sources is incorrect.) Given broader European sensibilities, the inserted footage is dominated by grittier content: several nasty executions and a fleeting glimpse of bared breasts (but not belonging to Dandridge, as also has been claimed erroneously).

The additional length also grants a lot more exposure to both Dandridge and composer Jeff Alexander's terrific jazz score. Much of the drama takes place in Club Troy, a big-city jazz nightspot owned by brothers Arthur and Maury Troy (James Coburn and Joe Mantell). Once upon a time, Norma Sherman (Dandridge) was the club's star attraction, appearing with a backing combo fronted by her trumpeter husband, Joe (Ivan Dixon). But that was before Norma got hooked on heroin, slid into the desperate life of a full-time junkie, and was arrested and sent to prison. This drama begins the day she's released, hoping to resume her former career, with help from lawyer and longtime friend Nicholas Cain (Mark Richman, the ongoing star of *Cain's Hundred*.) Although Arthur initially is willing to champion Norma's cause, he's being squeezed by mob boss Dave Keller (Edward Asner) into moving drugs himself. Keller doesn't want a high-profile former junkie anywhere near his operation, which sets up several conflicts guaranteed to turn out badly.

The film opens with montages that depict Norma's earlier fall from grace, amid a police round-up that nets numerous junkies and pushers. Ominous bass and bongos accompany her arrest; a sleek vibes solo highlights the brass-heavy title theme, heard over the opening credits. The musical mood lightens as we flash-forward; a jubilant swing theme shadows Norma when she leaves prison and returns to the apartment that has been maintained carefully, during her two-year absence. Her elation fades quickly as the story proceeds, her dismay enhanced by a somber, bluesy cue that mirrors her increasingly shattered expression.

These non-diegetic cues are balanced by a wealth of terrific source tunes, most taking place within Club Troy. The action pauses long enough to feature Joe's combo in a cool instrumental, granting a bit of camera time to the pianist's flying fingers. And nothing compares to Dandridge's sublime performances: "The Man I Love" and "I'll Get By (as Long as I Have You)," both backed by Joe's combo; and "Taking a Chance on Love," rehearsed with a different combo, when Norma attempts to get a job elsewhere. And while this marked an unexpected end to her acting career—Dandridge died under mysterious circumstances in September 1965—it was a high note on which to leave the stage.

Like most low-budget films, *The Murder Men* failed to generate a soundtrack album. (The 2009 Film Score Monthly release of an album devoted to *Cain's Hundred* focuses mostly on Jerry Goldsmith's episode scores, along with one by Morton Stevens.)

The Murder Men wasn't much competition for *Le Doulos*, adapted from Pierre Lesou's 1957 novel of the same title. French filmmaker Jean-Pierre Melville's richly atmospheric crime *noir* is highlighted by Nicolas Hayer's moody, monochrome cinematography: as genre-distinctive as the contribution by jazz pianist/composer Paul Misraki. Ominous orchestral cues complement the grim on-screen events, while swinging combo jazz melodies pop up as source cues in bars and nightclubs, and on apartment radios.

Newly released from prison, Maurice Faugel (Serge Reggiani) plans a fresh robbery with accomplices Silien (Jean-Paul Belmondo) and Rémy (Philippe Nahon). The job goes awry when the cops arrive, having been tipped off by an unknown informant; Rémy is killed, and the furious Maurice is convinced that Silien must be the informant. An additional subplot revolves around cold-blooded gangster Nuttheccio (Michel Piccoli), who runs a jazz nightclub and orchestrated an earlier jewel heist. Melville's script keeps the informant's identity secret until a clever third-act twist, which forces Maurice—and us viewers—to reevaluate earlier assumptions about honor and betrayal, as both apply to various individuals.

Misraki immediately gets our attention with ominous orchestral blasts, as stark white title credits blaze onto a black screen; a contemplative melody emerges on vibes and trumpets, when the screen brightens to show Maurice heading for a rendezvous with a criminal colleague, the drumbeat syncopated perfectly to his footsteps. Another orchestral blast cues the film's title, after which mournful horns deliver what will become the primary narrative cue. From this point forward, Melville uses music sparingly, and most of the non-diegetic cues are atmospheric strings and woodwinds; the one notable exception is a lazy, sultry blend of sax and guitar, heard after Silien charms his lover Fabienne (Fabienne Dali) into bed.

All the diegetic cues, in striking contrast, are tasty combo jazz numbers. Two emanate from a bedroom radio early on, in the apartment that Maurice shares with his lover. Silien's visit to the Cotton Club, where he discovers that Fabienne has become Nuttheccio's girlfriend, unfolds against a terrific 5/4 swinger performed by the venue's live band. The drum and piano work suggest the iconic Brubeck/Desmond "Take Five," but the trumpet/sax/guitar melody and interplay are, instead, a bluesy variation of the cue first heard during the title credits. Later, Maurice meets Jean (Phillipe March) and Silien in a piano bar, where the latter describes what *actually* has happened during the past few days. This recitation, running more than seven minutes and intercut with flashbacks, is shaded by tasty improvisational jazz played by a solo pianist occasionally glimpsed as the conversation proceeds.

The film didn't generate a soundtrack, although a sleek vibes and muted trumpet cue—titled "Le Doulos"—popped up on a few compilation albums of French gangster movie themes. But this is an entirely different piece of music; although the instrumentation and atmospheric mood are similar, the melody is nothing like the film's opening theme or any interior cue. The situation became even more confusing in 2015, with the arrival of Larghetto's "official" soundtrack album for *Le Doulos*, but its contents are equally suspect. Both radio source tracks are present—"Jazz Rapide" and "Slow pour vibraphone et trombone"—and a third cue, "Essuie-glace," spots a portion of the film's climactic finale. But the remaining tracks include the ersatz "Le Doulos," and the instrumentation isn't right on the others. It feels like Larghetto assembled a bunch of random Misraki cues and arbitrarily pretended the result is a soundtrack.

Purchase options ultimately were far superior for 1962's *Nóz w wodzie*, released the following year in the States as *Knife in the Water*. Roman Polanski put Polish cinema on the map with this solid feature debut. Although not larcenous, the script qualifies as *noir* intrigue, with its manipulative characters, disquieting atmosphere and omnipresent threat of danger. The simple story concerns a bored suburban couple—Andrzej (Leon Niemcyzk) and Krystyna (Jolanta Umecka)—who, on a whim, invite a young hitchhiker (Zygmunt Malanowicz) to join them on a one-day sailing excursion. The passive-aggressive Andrzej wants somebody to humiliate; the repressed Krystyna blossoms as the day proceeds, becoming a voluptuous tease who plays the men against each other. Polanski slowly enhances the simmering sexual conflict until it explodes, leading to a delectably ambiguous final scene.

Polanski desired a "cool" jazz score that would complement Jerzy Lipman's moody black-and-white cinematography; it was a brave decision, since jazz had been banned in Poland until Joseph Stalin's death in 1953. Even years thereafter, it remained barely tolerated by the Communist regime, despite being embraced by music fans—Polanski among them—who couldn't get enough of American-style swing. Composer and jazz pianist Krzysztof Komeda helped break the implicit barrier, with his 1956 album *I Sopot Jazz Festival*; Polanski deemed him the perfect choice, and Komeda rose to the occasion.[15]

Komeda composed a buoyant score for jazz quartet. Tenor saxman Bernt Rosengren takes melodic lead on the leisurely, melancholy title theme, while Komeda comps gently on piano; this cue tells us everything we need to know about the stifled relationship between Andrzej and Krystyna. The mood turns more cheerful when, now accompanied by the (never named) young hitchhiker, their sailboat slowly glides into the huge lake. Rosengren's sax riffs are less melodic and more celebratory: "free" jazz that complements the trio's delight at being on open water. Rosengren's sax later suggests the subtle struggle for dominance building between the two men; the inevitable brawl unfolds against a disconcerting bass solo, Roman Dylag's fingers walking randomly up and down his bass. Subsequent developments occur quickly—and without music—until Polanski pulls back from the final ambiguous scene, against a mildly disturbing reprise of the main theme.

Komeda expanded and rearranged the film's four primary cues for a monaural EP on Poland's Polskie Nagrania Muza label. Decades later, several labels released increasingly comprehensive digital versions of the score.

7

Champagne and Quail: 1963

This is an artistically bountiful year, particularly for Henry Mancini, whose sophisticated jazz stylings highlight two hit caper entries, one of which kicked off a subgenre that could be dubbed "spoof *noir*." As a result, Sean Connery's James Bond shared his rapidly increasingly popularity with an animated, salmon-hued feline whose antics made *his* title credits sequences just as legendary as those designed for 007's adventures.

The Small Screen

Bad enough that poor Richard Kimble (David Jannsen) had to stay one step ahead of dogged police pursuer Philip Gerard (Barry Morse) over the course of four seasons and 120 episodes of *The Fugitive*; imagine how distressed Kimble might have been, had he anticipated the degree to which CBS would add insult to injury.

But that came much later. *The Fugitive* was a hit right out of the gate, from its debut on September 17: the perfect marriage of creator Roy Huggins' concept, producer Quinn Martin's execution, suspensefully taut scripting, Jannsen's sublime performance, and Pete Rugolo's music. ("I was a great fan of Pete's," Huggins later admitted. "I had been a fan of Stan Kenton, and I realized that the 'Kenton sound' was really Pete Rugolo. I went out of my way to meet him.")[1] Viewers were mesmerized by the despair of this innocent physician, wrongly blamed for the murder of the wife he adored, forever looking over his shoulder, as he tried to clear his name by finding the "one-armed man" actually responsible for the crime. Despite his anxiety, Kimble always plays Good Samaritan while moving from town to town, adopting unremarkable identities that he'd put at risk while helping somebody else. As with *Route 66*, *The Fugitive* is essentially an anthology drama with a peripatetic main character. When Kimble's *Les Miserables*-themed plight eventually concluded on August 29, 1967, the final installment became the most-watched TV series episode to date.[2]

Fans loved Janssen's Dr. Kimble; they also loved everything about the way the series was assembled, including the music that perfectly suited each week's melodrama. The iconic 5/4 title theme boasts a strong snare drum line with a fast-paced sense of urgency, but most fans remember it for the initial 2-2 brass fanfare (which seems to "speak" the show's title: "The *few*…juh-tive!").

"I looked at the pilot and liked it, and decided to do it," Rugolo recalled. "They had me write about two or three hours of music; they showed me the main title, how Kimble would be running a lot during the series. So I came up with the idea of the *Fugitive* theme music at the beginning. [Then] I wrote several cues based on the theme: sad versions, neutral music, chases, a love theme, 'story' music (music you hear while the radio's playing), every possible kind of theme and variations. I also wrote a theme for Lt. Gerard; it was like a police theme—bah-bah-bah-*bumm*!—so that any time you saw Gerard, they'd start it off."[3]

What's interesting—and was somewhat unusual, at the time—is that Rugolo didn't custom-score *any* individual episodes; all 120 underscores are built from his initial efforts, and supplemented with other CBS library cues by different composers (in many cases, material that Jerry Goldsmith had written for *The Twilight Zone*). Few fans noticed this cross-pollination, because music supervisor Ken Wilhoit did such a fine job crafting each score, and also because variations of Rugolo's title theme are ubiquitous. Many elements "made" *The Fugitive* what it was, and music is high on that list.

Ironically, given the show's popularity, Rugolo wasn't able to cash in on the resulting fame. "That's a sad story," he recalled. "I was asked by Warner Bros. to make an album. The producer called me, and I wrote all the different arrangements, and I had set up a recording date with him.

Although *The Fugitive* remains one of Pete Rugolo's most iconic assignments, it didn't bring him any Emmy Award nominations; in great contrast, he was nominated during each of *Run for Your Life*'s three seasons. He ultimately won twice: for 1970's primetime special *The Challengers* and for a 1972 episode of *The Bold Ones: The Lawyers* (Photofest).

But the producer got fired at the last minute, and for some reason Warners didn't want to go through with it! I probably should have called some companies to see if they were interested, but I never followed through."[4]

Decades passed, until master tapes containing many of Rugolo's original cues were found in his garage. With a bit of engineering legerdemain, a digital album finally was released in 2000. Many of its 24 tracks are stitched together from multiple cues, all a treasure trove for fans.

The series hit home video in the early 1990s, most memorably with a Nu Ventures Video 20-volume series that offered two episodes per tape; each episode was as it had been aired "night of broadcast," a quarter-century earlier (which people would logically expect, right?). CBS/Paramount subsequently began to issue the complete series on DVD in 2007, breaking each season into two volumes. Sharp-eared listeners with excellent memories (and/or homemade off-air copies) noticed that some source music—stuff heard on jukeboxes and radios—had been changed in the first-season sets: odd, but only a minor eyebrow-lift.

But the *merde* hit the fan in the summer of 2008, with the arrival of Season 2: Volume 1.

7. Champagne and Quail: 1963

Fans *immediately* realized that each episode's *entire underscore* had been retracked with new cues by Mark Heyes, Sam Winans and Ron Komie. These individuals also were added to each episode's end credits, where their names were placed *above* Rugolo, now relegated to a lesser "theme by" listing. CBS/Paramount repeated this felony with the next three sets, through the end of Season 3 ... by which point the relentless letters, bad publicity and diminished sales no longer could be ignored. Both volumes of Season 4, arriving in late 2010 and early '11, were (thankfully) again almost "night of broadcast" accurate.

So what happened? The story is both complicated and stupid. In a nutshell, confusion relating to the library cues written by other composers, hindered by clumsy studio cue sheets—properly identifying who had composed which cue, and where it had originated—made it difficult for CBS to "legally clear" the music. Rather than take the time to research proper identification—for the purposes of royalty payments—some network suit(s) adopted the easier (cheaper?) alternative, by replacing the underscores. Only Rugolo's title and end themes remained.[5] It was an act of artistic insanity: A moment's logic dictates that the potential (sole?) market for a series that venerable, would be the fans who remember it from back in the day, and therefore *expect it to be as it was.*

In theory, CBS eventually came to its corporate senses, with the 2012 release of the complete series in a box set titled *The Fugitive: The Most Wanted Edition*. Except that early incarnations of this set merely repeated the Season 2/3 fiascos. Until they eventually didn't. As of this writing, Rugolo's original underscore cues—and most of those from other sources—have been restored to newer editions of the *Most Wanted* box sets. (*Caveat emptor*: A lot of "bad" sets continue to haunt the secondary market.)

CBS rebooted the series for a single 22-episode season that debuted October 6, 2000. Tim Daly was a poor substitute for David Janssen, and James Newton Howard's new orchestral title theme—although appropriately suspenseful—doesn't come within shouting distance of jazz.

While Richard Kimble did his best to avoid Lt. Gerard, an entirely different breed of police detective motored through the streets of Los Angeles.

The pre-credits teaser formula rarely changed: A body is found, often under highly unusual circumstances; the call goes out to LAPD Homicide Capt. Amos Burke (Gene Barry), invariably caught at a swanky party or *in flagrante almost delicto* with a half-dressed lovely who hopes to become a permanent houseguest at his palatial estate. Business first, pleasure later: Burke changes into a tailored three-piece suit, slides into the Rolls-Royce Silver Cloud II driven by butler/cook/personal chauffeur Henry (Leon Lontoc), and they head off to the crime scene. Cue a rumble of percussion, an effervescent 5-4 fanfare in unison brass, followed by a 4-note echo from a salacious alto sax, after which a breathy female voice coos, "It's *Burke's Law!*" Brief pause, and then one of the 1963–64 television season's most striking jazz themes roars into full orchestral fury. Following a commercial break, the show's title—always "Who Killed So-and-So?"—appears over the action as the title theme repeats, while viewers learn about the "Special Guest Stars in Alphabetical Order." The credits often run long, allowing plenty of time for the feisty orchestration of Herschel Burke Gilbert's swinging title theme.

"Aaron Spelling asked me if I'd like to write it, and I said yes," Gilbert recalled. "I got an idea of using a semi-jazz sound with an alto saxophone for the theme. And then I had another idea, and I had the theme go doe-*ree*-dah ... doe-da-dee-*dah* ... and then *stop*. And I went to Aaron and said, 'That's where you get some very sexy gal to go *It's Burke's Law.*' [So] they had a contest, and they were bringing girls to the studio by threes and fours, all trying to say 'It's *Burke's Law*!' And they chose the most sensuous of the voices, and it paid off: Everybody knew that series the moment they heard that little theme. And then the music picked up right after that, and you never heard that voice again."[6]

Burke isn't an average police detective; he's a millionaire who (somehow) attained the position because, well, he needs something to do. The character debuted in an episode of *The Dick Powell Show*, a 1961–63 anthology series that concluded just three days before Gene Barry assumed the role in ABC's *Burke's Law*. Powell starred as the first Burke, but Barry is more elegantly sophisticated in the role: essential characteristics, given the number of times—in each episode—that Burke must remain politely imperturbable while interviewing suspects who take eccentricity to jaw-dropping extremes.

Gilbert also began a library of the show's underscore cues: many of them variations of the title theme, all of which deftly complement Barry's debonair performance. Each episode's cuties are introduced with slinky horns that practically beg them to undress, but the cues always include a whimsical, soft jazz counterpoint that reflects Burke's inability to enjoy what's on offer, because … well … duty calls.

The popular title theme generated quite a few covers: jazz guitarist Al Caiola (Verve); Tommy Watt and His Orchestra (Columbia UK); Wynton Kelly (Verve UK); the Colin Frechter Orchestra (Summit); and Robin Garton and His Band (Martello). Blue Beat even released a ska version by Jamaica Greatest (although one must listen intently, to extract Gilbert's theme from the arrangement). Not wanting to be left behind, Barry—backed by Gilbert's arrangements and orchestrations—released his own album of torch songs: *Gene Barry Sings of Love and Things*. (His many hit TV shows notwithstanding, it must be remembered that Barry got his start as a stage song-and-dance man.)

Shortly before the show began its second season, Gilbert released a soundtrack album: a nifty collection of tracks by Gilbert and fellow TV colleague/composer Joseph Mullendore (albeit occasionally with too many strings for jazz purists). "Tuesday's Tune," "Blues Downstairs," "4:30 a.m." and "Bridget" are typical of the slinky piano, sax and trumpet melodies heard when Amos exchanges soft words with his weekly female companions; "Meeting at PJ's" and "Live!" are uptempo action jazz anthems akin to what Mancini wrote for *Peter Gunn*.

In a desperate bid to retain viewers after the show's ratings sagged toward the end of its second season, the producers dumped the formula and Barry's co-stars, removed Amos from his easy-going LAPD surroundings, and transformed him into a globe-trotting espionage agent who answers to "The Man" (Carl Benton Reid). It was a blatant ploy to cash in on the TV spy craze that had been ignited by *The Man from U.N.C.L.E*. Gilbert reworked his title theme, removing the breathy female announcer and relying entirely on a faster, more brass-forward arrangement that vamps over a montage of Barry shooting, punching, ducking and generally trying to out-cool all of TV's other secret agents. But ABC's Hail Mary play flopped; *Amos Burke: Secret Agent* solved his final case midway through the abbreviated third season.

That wasn't the last we'd seen of Amos. Three decades later, Barry slid back into the role for two seasons that ran on rival CBS, starting January 7, 1994. Everything is as it was during the original *Burke's Law*, except that Amos is older, presumably wiser, and works cases with his son, Peter (Peter Barton). Everything, that is, except for the music. For some bizarre reason, CBS chose not to revive Gilbert's iconic theme, and instead went with a wholly unmemorable new cue by John E. Davis Jr.

* * *

East Side/West Side remains must-see TV today; back in the autumn of 1963, it probably seared the eyeballs off unsuspecting viewers. Gritty, authentic, impeccably directed, written and performed—and frequently heartbreaking—the show was a shining diamond in a television landscape dominated by cubic zirconia. The notion of George C. Scott consenting to a weekly series is astonishing enough; the courageous, real-world scripting was even more unusual. *Too* unusual, as it turned out; viewers couldn't handle such depressing topics on a regular basis, and the show expired after its single season. The stories are set in the slums of New York City, where idealistic social worker Neil Brock (Scott) confronts clients enmeshed in crime, alcoholism and drug addiction, child abuse, homelessness, welfare fraud, race and age discrimination, and the frustrating limitations of a flimsy social safety net too frequently tangled by convoluted government bureaucracy. (How little things have changed....) He answers to sympathetic but practical agency head Frieda Hechlinger (Elizabeth Wilson); their lone staff member is secretary Jane Foster (Cicely Tyson). Guest stars drew from the cream of rising and established Hollywood/stage talent: Gene Hackman, Martin Sheen, Jessica Walter, James Earl Jones, Alan Alda, Colleen Dewhurst, Carroll O'Connor, Lee Grant and many, many others.

East Side/West Side became the first of Kenyon Hopkins' three TV series projects. In addition to writing a memorably edgy title theme, he composed original underscores for most of the 26 episodes, all of which fulfilled his brief to convey the mood, pulse and heartbeat of New York City. These aren't merely short, atmospheric cues and stingers, but in many cases—following Mancini's approach to *Peter Gunn*—fully developed melodies: character themes for guest stars, unique anthems for specific episodes, and a variety of lengthy cues for the establishing montages that often open an episode or divide interior acts.

The title theme kicks off with tense bongos, as Scott's face is superimposed over a late-night subway train; he fades from view when unison brass introduces the core 4-4 motif. The horns further develop that theme as subsequent credits flash onto the screen; the effect is jarring and suspenseful, foreshadowing grim tidings. An unexpectedly cheerful piano and string bridge augments the theme's longer end credits arrangement, which concludes with a similar blast of rising horns.

The must-have soundtrack album is a great showcase for Hopkins' efforts, starting with an even longer arrangement of the jittery title theme. Other tracks reflect a sometimes smothering sense of isolation, as with the mournful saxes of "Central Park West"; alternatively, "Traffic Jam" is a clever acoustic depiction of vehicular chaos, with saxes approximating car horns, and a jolly flute hovering above the melody. Strutting percussion and lazy unison horns kick off "Who Do You Kill," which gets its name from a particularly heartbreaking episode concerning a young African American couple struggling to make ends meet.

If *East Side/West Side* represented progressive television, NBC's *Bob Hope Presents the Chrysler Theatre* was a last gasp of a dying breed. This old-style anthology series split its content between comedies, variety shows and solid dramas; the latter included an impressive number of crime, spy and private detective thrillers. Scoring assignments went to numerous musicians, many inhabiting the jazz world: from big band leaders such as Les Brown and Dizzy Gillespie, to future superstars such as Quincy Jones and Lalo Schifrin. Unfortunately, almost none of the jazz scores were developed for *noir* entries; most were attached to dramas or comedies. John(ny) Williams wrote the symphonic theme that opens each installment; he also contributed original underscores—none referencing his jazz roots—to at least 10 episodes during the show's four-year run, which began September 27.

Benny Carter also provided numerous scores, the most jazz-oriented being the first season's second episode—"Something About Lee Wiley"—which profiles the highs and lows of a 1930s blues singer's career. Since some time is spent in jazz nightclubs, the episode boasts some excellent combo work, but the storyline is straight melodrama. Stanley Wilson composed a terrific jazz score for season four's "Free of Charge," with the music performed by Bud Shank (alto sax), Jimmy Rowles (piano), Ray Brown (bass) and Louis Bellson (drums); alas, the story concerns a musician swanning through Los Angeles while trying to compose an ode to the city. Schifrin's sole contribution is the second season's "Clash of Cymbals," a romantic melodrama about an aspiring concert pianist who falls in love with a self-absorbed conductor. Gillespie supplies an almost jazz-less backdrop to the third season's "After the Lions, Jackals," a doomed love affair between a secretary and a cynical novelist.

The sole entry that suits our purposes arrived during the third season: "The Faceless Man," which stars Jack Lord as an undercover intelligence agent. Quincy Jones supplies a sleek jazz score, which was retained when the 60-minute episode was augmented with additional footage in 1968 and released on the big screen as *The Counterfeit Killer* (about which, more later).

The Big Screen

Roughly the same time that spy jazz began to catch the public's fancy, Henry Mancini playfully spiked the genre with his larkish, swinging score to *The Pink Panther*. The iconic title theme is another of the world's most instantly recognizable instrumental jazz compositions: a slinky E-minor romp that owes much to Plas Johnson's ultra-cool tenor sax chops. This contribution was notable enough to warrant his own acknowledgment in the film's title credits (rare for a jazz soloist at *any* point in time, let alone in 1963).

"This is one instance where I heard the sound in my mind before I heard the actual melody," Mancini noted. "I wanted that breathy, low-register tenor sax sound, a cross between Lester Young and Ben Webster; and Plas Johnson had exactly that quality to contribute, along with a kind of saucy attitude and a nice attack. When I wrote [it] for the movie, I thought of it in the same way that writers used to contribute specialties for individuals within a big band. In fact, this had big band written all over it."[7]

"Hank had a talent for picking the right musicians for the mood he was trying to present," Johnson added, decades later. "He wanted a blues player. He liked the way I played it. I don't think we did more than two takes."[8]

Director Blake Edwards' handling of *The Pink Panther* is the quintessential heist spoof, with an unerring blend of bedroom farce, minor slapstick and an international cast of scene-stealers, led by Peter Sellers' memorable debut as bumbling Police Inspector Jacques Clouseau. Mancini's score deserves equal credit for the film's success, thanks to his delectable blend of swinging jazz and gentle bossa nova. Alongside Mancini's music, all the films in what became a lengthy series are remembered for their hilarious animated title sequences. DePatie-Freleng Enterprises set the tone, with this initial film's droll depiction of the title character trying to add his name to the credits, as they hit the screen. The pink pussycat's increasingly frantic antics are choreographed purr-fectly to Mancini's theme and Johnson's sax riffs, and the credits easily stand on their own as a mirthful mini-cartoon.

As the story begins, Princess Dala of the fictional country of Lugash is on a skiing holiday in Northern Italy's Cortina d'Ampezzo, where she—and her fabled Panther Diamond—are targeted by English playboy Sir Charles Lytton (David Niven). Lytton's breezy reputation is a cover for his clandestine activities as "The Phantom," a veteran jewel thief who always leaves a white glove at the scene of his crimes. Ah, but Lytton's luck may have run out. French police Inspector Clouseau, convinced that the thief will try for the diamond, has traveled to the same ski resort, hoping to catch The Phantom in the act. Matters are complicated further by the unexpected arrival of Lytton's ne'er-do-well American nephew, George (Robert Wagner). Romantic entanglements spiral in crazy comic fashion, and everything climaxes during a costume party—the action having moved to Princess Dala's villa in Rome—as both Sir Charles and George attempt to steal the diamond.

Prior to the climax's chaotic hijinks, calmer moments are given a cool spin by several Mancini compositions. Sir Charles' efforts to extract information from Princess Dala are assisted by a slow, sensuous sax and piano cue ("Royal Blue"), a gentle flute and alto sax samba ("Champagne and Quail") and a languid bit of fluff highlighted by Jimmy Rowles' keyboard work ("Piano and Strings"). Larcenous activities are conducted against a suspensefully tasty blend of bossa nova accordion, scratcher and percussion ("The Village Inn").

The soundtrack album spent an astonishing 87 weeks on *Billboard's* Top LPs chart, and the score was nominated for an Academy Award (losing to *Mary Poppins*). The title theme was nominated for six Grammy Awards, winning for Best Instrumental Composition, Best Instrumental Arrangement, and Best Instrumental Performance (Other Than Jazz). In 2001, the tune's ongoing popularity was cemented with a Grammy Hall of Fame Award. The title theme has been covered hundreds of times, by everybody from The Ventures and Bobby McFerrin, to jazz cats such as Quincy Jones, James Moody and Royce Campbell.

Mancini then teamed with director Stanley Donen for *Charade*, which has it all: intrigue, suspense, sparkling star wattage and a terrific narrative laden with witty *bon mots*, all delivered with impeccable timing by Cary Grant and Audrey Hepburn. Mancini's score, sliding from lite spy jazz to frothy pop, has much to do with the film's successful blend of mystery and romance. It's no surprise that *Charade* often is regarded as the best Hitchcock thriller that Hitchcock never made.

The Paris–based story begins as Regina "Reggie" Lampert (Hepburn) learns that her frequently absent husband Charles has been murdered, after he desperately converted all their assets into

Henry Mancini and lyricist Johnny Mercer shared an Academy Award nomination for their title song for *Charade*, but (alas) they lost to "Call Me Irresponsible," from *Papa's Delicate Condition* (Intrada Inc.).

$250,000 in cash, and then tried to flee from unknown assailants. But there's no trace of the money, which places Reggie in the crosshairs of three dangerous men: Tex Panthollow (James Coburn), Herman Scobie (George Kennedy) and Leopold W. Gideon (Ned Glass). Reggie gains the back-story after a briefing from CIA administrator Hamilton Bartholomew (Walter Matthau), stationed at Paris' U.S. Embassy; further intrigue is supplied by Peter Joshua (Grant), a debonair American who charms his way into Reggie's heart, and seems willing to help … or does he? (It's Cary Grant. What do *you* think?)

Mancini wrote and recorded the score in London, enhancing his large orchestra with a sizeable brass section and Latin-inflected percussion by Bobby Midgeley and Barry Morgan. The latter two enhance the captivating Latin jazz waltz title theme, which opens the film against a hypnotically swirling, colorful assemblage of title credits designed by Maurice Binder. Mancini's theme begins mysteriously, with rhythmic wood blocks, then accelerates with bass and bongos; the melody emerges via the distinctive sound of a cimbalom (a few years before John Barry would make that instrument famous, with *The Ipcress File*). After the first verse, Mancini shifts to heavy swing that hearkens back to his *Peter Gunn* days; the cimbalom returns for another refrain that fades out as the final credit—belonging to Donen—appears amid Binder's rotating circles of color. It's one of the best jazz film themes ever written, and it nimbly sets the tone and atmosphere for what follows.

As arresting as this fast-paced arrangement is, it's not the way Mancini initially conceived the tune. He was inspired after viewing an early scene where Reggie returns to her stripped apartment, shattered by the way stability has been ripped from beneath her feet. Mancini wrote this theme as a slow, solemn, solo piano A-minor waltz that poignantly conveys her loneliness and isolation (and, indeed, that's the way the melody is heard during that particular scene).[9] The score boasts a lot more. Many of Mancini's cues are fully realized melodies in their own right, often employed as diegetic tunes that exemplify the stylish bounce of the story's various settings: a skiing holiday at Megève; and a nightclub party game of "pass the orange." The film's suspenseful climax is spotted with an extended ostinato dominated by the title theme's throbbing rhythm section, as explosive brass fanfares and rising strings enhance the tension.

As had become his practice, Mancini reorchestrated and rerecorded the primary cues to turn the soundtrack album into a radio-friendly "party album." *Billboard* granted the album a Pop Spotlight shout-out, predicting that "the Mancini touch, coupled with a strong motion picture tie-in, should hurl this one on the best-seller list in short order."[10] The prediction proved accurate: The album charted for 42 impressive weeks. Crooner Andy Williams was first out of the gate with a vocal cover of the title theme, which also hit the Top 100 Chart—at No. 100—for one week concurrent with Mancini's instrumental version, on January 18, 1964. The tune subsequently was covered by scores of pop and jazz vocalists and instrumentalists: from Bobby Darin and The Four Freshmen, to Monica Mancini and Miranda Sage; from the Baja Marimba Band and the Anita Kerr Quartet, to the Oranj Symphonette and Terence Blanchard.

Mancini's 28-cue film score finally was issued in 2012; comparing it to the 1963 soundtrack album is a fascinating primer in the arts of arrangement and reorchestration.

Glossy, wide-screen "travelogue thrillers" such as *Charade* were quite the rage in the early to mid–1960s; audiences were captivated by watching romantic sparks ignite between marquee stars who face (comparatively) mild-mannered peril in a variety of international settings. *The Prize* delivers on that successful formula, with its undercurrent of Cold War espionage set against the pomp and circumstance of the annual Nobel Prize ceremony.

7. Champagne and Quail: 1963

Scripter Ernest Lehman drew the assignment to adapt Irving Wallace's 1962 best-seller, and his attempt to replicate what he had created for Hitchcock's *North by Northwest* is quite obvious.

The scoring assignment went to Jerry Goldsmith, just as his soon-to-be-famous career was transitioning from television work to A-list movie projects. His cues for *The Prize* are quite a mix, given director Mark Robson's constantly shifting moods: sweeping orchestral flourishes, suspenseful atmospheric bursts of strings and percussion, some gentle jazz for the primary romantic theme, and even some broadly larkish touches for the script's comic moments. There's also a strong foreshadowing of the action cues he'd soon write for TV's *The Man from U.N.C.L.E.*, although most of the jazz cues in *The Prize* are source music, rather than elements of the non-diegetic score.

The action takes place in Sweden, during the week leading up to the presentation of the various Nobel Prizes. Subplots involve marital discord between the two laureates for chemistry, and professional jealousy between the two men sharing the prize for medicine; but our focus is on Andrew Craig (Paul Newman), a cynical, hard-drinking American writer who has won the Nobel Prize for literature. The Swedish Foreign Department has assigned him a keeper, Inger Lisa Andersson (Elke Sommer), who finds him quite a handful. He's

Some of Jerry Goldsmith's moodier cues for *The Prize* sound very much like the work he was doing for Rod Serling's *Twilight Zone*, particularly the descending two-note motif employed for that show's pre- and post-commercial bumpers (courtesy Film Score Monthly).

nonetheless quick to notice that the aging laureate for physics, Dr. Max Stratman (Edward G. Robinson), seems an inexplicably changed man, from one day to the next. What Andrew doesn't yet know—although we viewers do—is that the Americanized Stratman has been kidnapped by the former Iron Curtain associates from whom he fled, and replaced with a double. Andrew grows increasingly convinced of the skullduggery afoot, but nobody believes the "outlandish" ravings of an imaginative writer with a reputation for alcoholism.

Goldsmith opens his dynamic title theme with a bold orchestral flourish; the striking jazz syncopation—alternating bars of 9/8 and 12/8—is fueled by brass fanfares, slashing strings and some lyrical foreground piano. Andrew's first visit to a jazz club dubbed The Golden Crown is backed two terrific source cues performed by the house jazz band: a trumpet-fueled swinger written by André Previn, and an uptempo combo cover of the standard "Just You, Just Me." Three swinging source cues also backstop Andrew's quiet chat with Emily (Diane Baker) in the hotel lounge the next day. But Emily isn't destined to become Andrew's love interest; that role falls to Inger, introduced via a lyrical, softly swinging romantic theme later repeated as seductive solos on piano and trumpet.

MGM decided the film score wasn't sufficiently "commercial" to warrant full-album treatment, so Goldsmith was limited to reorchestrating four cues—the title theme and three others—that shared space on a compilation LP titled *The Prize Plus Music from These Other Great Motion Pictures*. Goldsmith's full score wasn't released until 2002.

The jazz stylings are more intentionally prominent in *Johnny Cool*; indeed, prolific composer/arranger Billy May's swinging, big band soundtrack is far better than the film itself, which is a sloppy, laughably awful cheapie. *Johnny Cool* gave a rare starring role to character actor Henry Silva, reasonably well cast as a Sicilian assassin sent to the United States to dispatch the various mob bosses believed to have betrayed the exiled underworld kingpin (Marc Lawrence) who sees great potential in his vicious young protégé. Things get more complicated when Johnny bumps into bored society girl Darien "Dare" Guiness (Elizabeth Montgomery), whose ill treatment by low-level thugs adds further fuel to the hit man's fire.

May's vibrantly sophisticated score often is used in place of expository conversation, turning numerous sequences into montages (likely because this was faster and cheaper than looping dialog in postproduction). The percussion-laden "Borrow a Knife" kicks into gear when Johnny, having just discovered that Dare has been raped, charges out of her apartment, armed with a kitchen knife, and carves up the responsible parties. The band is equally adept on quieter selections, such as Montgomery's theme ("Dare's Affair"); the gently danceable "Morning in Balboa"; and the finger-snapping, *Peter Gunn*-esque touches of "The Coolest Pad" and "Nice Quiet Saloon."

May is known to have been accompanied by Bud Brisbois and Don Fagerquist (trumpets) and Justin Gordon (tenor sax); the rest of the ensemble members have been lost to history. Sammy Davis Jr. swings his way through the expository Jimmy Van Heusen/Sammy Cahn title tune, "The Ballad of Johnny Cool." Despite the film's glaring shortcomings, May's soundtrack is terrific.

Johnny Cool tried for *noir* ambiance but emerged as just plain silly. Although the golden age of such crime thrillers had concluded by the early 1960s, studios didn't entirely abandon the genre. Whit Masterson's 1961 crime thriller, *Evil Come, Evil Go*, was developed at 20th Century–Fox as a starring vehicle for pop singer Pat Boone. Unfortunately, it suffered from a minuscule budget and abbreviated shooting schedule. It's clear from what emerged—ultimately titled *The Yellow Canary*—that Rod Serling's script adaptation was seriously compromised.[11] Even so, the film isn't the total bomb that some reviews claim.

Floyd Crosby's menacing black-and-white cinematography gives the story an appropriately threatening atmosphere, and Kenyon Hopkins' jazz soundtrack is excellent.

The plot slightly evokes the 1932 Lindbergh baby kidnapping. Boone stars as Andy Paxton, a self-centered jazz/pop singer in the Frank Sinatra mold, whose insufferable behavior has pushed wife Lissa (Barbara Eden) to the brink of divorce. Such marital issues are shunted aside when their infant son is abducted by kidnappers who demand a ransom of $200,000. Police detective Lt. Bonner (Jack Klugman) cautions against submitting to this ultimatum, but the hot-headed Andy prefers to keep the situation "in house" with his bodyguard, Hub (Steve Forrest); his valet and longtime friend, Bake (Steve Harris); and his manager, Vecchio (Milton Selzer). It soon becomes clear that the kidnapping was an inside job, at which point Andy and Lissa—reunited by shared concern—take matters into their own hands.

Hopkins' vibrant title theme evokes the brass-heavy intensity of Henry Mancini's *Peter Gunn* theme, with Clark Terry's wailing trumpet backed by solid comping on flute and piano. This primary cue repeats often: in one case as jukebox source music, when Milt Hinton's pulsating walking bass and Lalo Schifrin's ferocious keyboard chops lend urgency to the on-screen action. Other notable cues include a bluesy midtempo waltz, with mischievous horn solos backed by Kenny Burrell's guitar and Schifrin's tasty keyboard comping; a lovely, lonely flute solo that accompanies Andy's effort to comfort Lissa; and the ominous rumble of horns, bass and percussion heard when Bake confesses to having embezzled some of Andy's money.

The soundtrack LP is even better than what can be heard in the film. Hopkins expanded many of the tracks, shifting tempos and even solos, allowing everybody in the band to shine. Terry and Schifrin benefit the most, but the album also grants enhanced exposure to Bill Costa's work on vibes. The album hasn't yet been released on CD, although in 2016 Disques Cinémusique did make it available as downloadable AAC files.

* * *

Following her *noir verité* depiction of the drug culture in *The Connection*, guerrilla filmmaker Shirley Clarke turned her attention to the predatory, appallingly disenfranchised Harlem slum youths who band together in street gangs, in *The Cool World*. Her template was Warren Miller's 1959 novel of the same title, which he transformed into a short-lived Broadway play; it ran for only two nights—February 22–23, 1960—at the Eugene O'Neill Theatre.[12]

Clarke's subsequent film adaptation has endured far better, having been selected for permanent preservation in 1994 by the Library of Congress' National Film Registry, for being "culturally, historically or aesthetically significant."[13] Low-budget limitations notwithstanding, the film is highlighted by the manner in which on-screen action is complemented, amplified and sometimes mockingly undercut by pianist/composer Mal Waldron's sumptuous jazz score. The music is raw, energetic and ubiquitous: performed by an outstanding bebop quintet that features Dizzy Gillespie (trumpet), Yusef Lateef (tenor sax), Waldron, Aaron Bell (acoustic double bass) and Art Taylor (drums).

The threadbare, documentary-style narrative focuses on 15-year-old Richard "Duke" Custis (Hampton Clanton), a member of the Royal Pythons street gang; the boy hopes to earn "respect" by purchasing a gun from Priest (Carl Lee), a former member now turned neighborhood gangster. But raising the necessary $50 proves impossible, so instead Duke simply challenges gang leader Blood (Clarence Williams III) for the top spot; the latter, a hopeless junkie, proves no competition. Now firmly in charge, Duke readies his fellow Pythons for a violent showdown with a rival gang: a lethal rumble that climaxes the film.

Music is absent for the first 10 minutes, while Clarke introduces characters and sets the stage; Gillespie's trumpet then erupts into manic fury—a cue titled "Duke on the Run"—when the boy snatches a purse from an unsuspecting victim. Clarke periodically interrupts the subsequent story for Harlem montages that show passersby, people at work, and children at play; these sequences are choreographed to a lively, lightning-paced waltz ("Street Music") introduced by Gillespie's perky trumpet, followed by Lateef's improvisational riffs and Waldron's silky keyboard comping. A raucous gathering of the Pythons at their apartment "clubhouse," and their subsequent ramble through the neighborhood streets, is set against some lively R&B jump jazz supplied by a supplementary quartet glimpsed fleetingly on camera: Charlie Jackson (guitar), Hal Singer (tenor sax), Julian Evell (acoustic double bass) and Herbie Lovelle (drums).

Duke's subsequent "relationship" with the Pythons' token girl, Luanne (Yolanda Rodríguez), bottoms out after she abandons him during a Coney Island excursion. Duke wanders back and forth along the deserted beach, calling her name, while Waldron supplies a haunting, calliope-style cue set against a lonely wail of 4/4 trumpet and sax couplets. The film ultimately circles back to the earlier cue—"Duke on the Run"—as a reminder that nobody has survived unscathed.

Gillespie was asked to perform the score on a soundtrack album, but he demurred, preferring an alternative option. "On the soundtrack of the movie, all I did was play," he recalled. "They hired me to play the music, which was written by Mal Waldron. Mal was so nervous and everything, he was almost depending on me to get it together, to assemble the different stages of it for the film. I told him, 'No, man, you get it together, and you tell me what to do, because this is yours, and I'll do what you want.' He finally put it together, but he was pretty nervous about it. Then they wanted to make an album from the soundtrack, and I told them I wouldn't go for that. I would go into the studio and make an album of the music. But I wouldn't be responsible for the soundtrack of the movie; I would be responsible for the album. We added some things; the album wasn't just like the film; I put a little Gillespiana in there, you know. So that's why it came out very well, beautifully."[14]

Gillespie assembled his own combo for the resulting LP: James Moody (sax and flute), Kenny Barron (piano), Chris White (bass) and Rudy Collins (drums). The resulting 11 tracks will be recognized by anybody familiar with the film, but the solos and instrumentation often vary.

Meanwhile, Across the Pond...

Mickey Spillane never lacked chutzpah.

When the tough-guy crime novelist revived his infamous series character after the 10-year hiatus that followed 1952's *Kiss Me, Deadly*, Mike Hammer's resurrection in *The Girl Hunters* became both a literary and cinematic event. The movie deal was struck in England—rather oddly—and Spillane assumed the roles of co-producer and co-scripter. Since Spillane was dissatisfied with the previous actors who had portrayed Hammer, he *starred* in the film as well, as his own literary creation. Although the resulting low-budget thriller is a plodding affair with too much talking and too little action, there's no denying Spillane's charisma; he makes a credible Mike Hammer. The film also is highlighted by co-star Shirley

Eaton, most often garbed in scant bikinis, a year before she became famous as James Bond's gilded companion in *Goldfinger*.

The exposition-heavy plot gets its momentum from Hammer's search for his long-missing secretary, Velda. She vanished years earlier and is presumed dead; despair has driven Hammer into a long bender. (This back-story explains Hammer's long absence from books and movies.) A suggestion that she's still alive prompts Hammer into fresh action, and he quickly embraces a case that links Velda with a dying FBI informant and a U.S. senator who was murdered awhile back. The plot thickens to include a hulking assassin, a helpful federal agent (Lloyd Nolan), a "Commie conspiracy" and the deceased senator's wife (Eaton). The case builds to a climax that concludes with a pair of grisly acts quite typical of the way Spillane's novels frequently end.

The mostly unremarkable music comes from veteran British film composer Philip Green, whose orchestral contribution better suits weepy 1950s melodramas. That said, the score is highlighted by a bluesy, oft-heard "Hammer theme" given a mournful jazz lilt by English trumpeter Eddie Calvert. It's a fairly simply theme—usually two sets of five melancholy notes—and sounds somewhat like the opening bars of Dave Kahn and Melvyn Lenard's "Riff Blues," which introduced Darren McGavin's TV *Mike Hammer* series each week. Brief bursts of big band jazz also pop up as source cues: on a radio when Hammer examines some of the dead senator's papers; and in a restaurant where Hammer gains additional information from the fed.

Spillane's lofty ambition to parlay this film into a series crashed on the shoals of lackluster box office; a rerelease the following year, in an effort to capitalize on Eaton's post–*Goldfinger* fame, was equally unsuccessful. The low budget precluded the possibility of a soundtrack album, but Calvert does bring plenty of swing to a pair of Green's cues, released as a 45 single.

James Bond, on the other hand, clearly was en route to a successful franchise. John Barry's arrangement of the iconic "James Bond Theme" is the first thing heard in *From Russia with Love*, during the debut of the image-and-music gun barrel stride, swivel and shoot. The 25-second arrangement is slightly faster and considerably more powerful than any of the versions heard in *Dr. No*, with Vic Flick's muscular guitar promising even more excitement.

"I was a big, big fan of Stan Kenton," Barry admitted, explaining the distinctive jazz approach that debuted with this sequel. "The genesis of the 'Bond sound' was most certainly that Kenton-esque sharp attack: extreme ranges, top C's and beyond, and on the low end you'd go right down to the low F's and below, so you'd have a wall of sound. The typical thing, that Bond thing, is very much this brass sound."[15]

He gives this sequel a vibrant, full-throttle score built around three primary cues: a lyrical title song/love theme; the already famous "James Bond Theme"; and a suspenseful action theme the composer dubbed "007," which would resurface in numerous subsequent films.

"['007'] was a lighter, more airy, uplifting kind of theme," Barry explained, years later. "It had a great, driving sense, too. And then I just wrote this big, 16-bar open melody, like a feel-good adventure theme, with the trumpets and the horns: that staccato accompaniment."[16]

From Russia with Love is impressively faithful to Fleming's 1957 novel. Operatives of the worldwide criminal organization SPECTRE—led by an as-yet-concealed man with a white cat—concoct a plan to trick Bond (Sean Connery) into assisting Soviet cipher clerk

James Bond wasn't merely back, in *From Russia with Love*; he was well on his way to becoming an international phenomenon. Producers Cubby Broccoli and Harry Saltzman saw no reason to alter a winning formula, and this second entry employed numerous veterans from *Dr. No*: director Terence Young, scripters Richard Maibaum and Johanna Harwood, editor Peter Hunt, cinematographer Ted Moore, art director Syd Cain and—of course—composer John Barry.

Tatiana Romanova (Daniela Bianchi), who wishes to defect to the West. She insists on Bond's involvement because—supposedly—she has fallen in love with his photograph; the added enticement is her promise to secure a Soviet Lektor cipher machine. She and Bond meet in Istanbul, where his efforts are assisted by local station head Kerim Bay (Pedro Armendariz). They "successfully" steal the Lektor and board the Orient Express to reach their planned escape route back to England, little realizing that unseen assassin Red Grant (Robert Shaw) has been clandestinely "helping" to facilitate SPECTRE's actual plan: to retrieve the Lektor while killing Bond and humiliating the British Secret Service.

Grant's methodical stalking and murder of a faux Bond, during what would become a series staple—the pre-credits sequence—is scored against a slow, moody reading of "The James Bond Theme," with startling explosions of brass punctuating the assassin's ultimately successful kill. This segues abruptly into the film's title theme: a forceful jazz instrumental that opens with an eye-popping explosion of machine-gun brass and percussion. Bongos signal a robust arrangement of the melody, spiced further by Alan Haven's jazz organ improvisations. The credits sequence concludes with a smooth transition to the swing bridge of "The James Bond Theme," followed by a reprise of the staccato intro. (Matt Monro's vocal version of the title song doesn't debut until later, when an excerpt is heard on a portable radio.)

Director Terence Young relies heavily on "The James Bond Theme," to heighten suspenseful anticipation. Barry scores a gypsy camp cat fight between two women with recurring, slashing bass notes, tick-tock percussion and blasts of brass and string-enhanced xylophone. This sexy display is interrupted when a gun-toting squadron of Kerim Bay's enemies storms the camp: the perfect setting to introduce Barry's new "007" theme. The eventual Orient Express trip is fraught with peril; Grant finally reveals himself against sinister strings and brass. Rather oddly, the subsequent action scenes are left unscored: the famous, close-quarters train compartment brawl between Grant and Bond; 007's hillside efforts to dodge a SPECTRE helicopter, once he and Tatiana flee from the train; and the subsequent water-bound chase involving three pursuing SPECTRE speedboats. (Barry definitely wrote music for the train compartment skirmish; one of the soundtrack album's cues is titled "Death of Grant.") Once past these and another last-minute obstacle, Bond and Tatiana take a romantic gondola ride as a full-length version of Monro's title song vocal swells over the end credits.

The soundtrack album has a few surprises. Many of the 18 cues are quite short, and a few aren't heard in the film, such as "Death of Grant" and "The Golden Horn." An alternate reading of the instrumental title theme is disappointing, because it fails to include Haven's cool jazz organ comping. (Barry's original score cues are believed lost.) The album nonetheless charted for 28 weeks in the States. Covers of the title theme were released by Craig Douglas (Decca UK); The Temperance Seven (Parlophone); Kenny Ball and his Jazzmen (Pye Jazz); and The Village Stompers (Epic).

Barry's alternate arrangement of his "007" theme—titled "007 Takes the Lektor" on the album—gained additional exposure in the States, when it was used extensively to introduce TV news programs in major markets during the mid-'60s.[17]

This was merely one of the first acknowledgments of how incredibly popular—and soon to be frequently imitated—Barry's ferociously rhythmic, brass-heavy impact would become. He *was* the Bond sound. In very short order, secret agent music wasn't merely regarded as "Bondian"; it also became "Barry-esque."

"Everything John did defined what spy music should be," composer David Arnold acknowledged, decades later, when he inherited the scoring franchise for a time.[18]

"Music is of the essence," agreed David Picker, former president of United Artists, which had signed the deal with Cubby Broccoli and Harry Saltzman, "and John made an *enormous* contribution."[19]

He would continue to do so, for many years.

Elsewhere in the World

French-Armenian filmmaker Henri Verneuil's caper thriller *Mélodie en sous-sol*—released in the States as *Any Number Can Win*—is based on American crime author Zekial Marko's 1959 novel *The Big Grab*, with the West Coast setting shifted to the French Riviera. *Mélodie en sous-sol* proved enormously successful throughout the world; it even won an Edgar Award, presented by the Mystery Writers of America, as the year's best foreign mystery film.

The story opens as debonair aging criminal Charles (Jean Gabin), freshly released from prison, plans an historic, career-capping caper: emptying the vault of Cannes' Palm-Beach Casino. Charles liaises with working-class petty thief Francis (Alain Delon), who establishes a cover as a high-rolling playboy; he romances a casino dancer (Carla Marlier, as Brigitte) to become a frequent backstage visitor, and thus—when the crucial night arrives—have ready access to the ventilation system that leads to the elevator shaft that is the sole access to the basement vault. The heist is successful; the two masked thieves escape with $1 billion francs in two large satchels, and then resume their cover identities. But police detectives arrive much too quickly. In one of the genre's most agonizing finales, Charles watches helplessly, on one side of the casino's large outdoor pool, as Francis—on the other side—sits helplessly with the two satchels, listening while a casino cashier describes those very bags to nearby inspectors. What can he do?

Verneuil gave the music assignment to jazz/experimental composer Michel Magne, who built the score around a single repeating theme. Source versions lean toward big band blues and swing; atmospheric variations play with percussion, brass elements and "prepared" keyboard. The melody debuts in full-blown, big band glory during a stylish opening credits sequence: The recurring six-note motif is heralded by a wall of trumpets that follows Charles, while he attempts to find his tiny home amid the high-rise apartments now surrounding it. Subsequent versions include a dance band swing arrangement introduced by a graceful piano solo; a Gershwin-esque reading, heard as Brigitte and the other dancers rehearse a routine; and the veritable symphony of arrangements, in distinct movements, that spots the half-hour heist sequence (which takes place against no dialog). The tense poolside finale stretches on as Magne enhances this ghastly denouement with a robust orchestral reprise of the main theme: an ironic counterpoint to the sickened frustration evident on Francis and Charles' frozen faces, while they stare powerlessly at each other.

Magne's title theme caught the attention of American jazz organist Jimmy Smith, who released a Verve single under the film's American title, "Any Number Can Win." The tune landed on *Billboard's* Hot 100 chart for a single week, hitting No. 96 on November 2, 1963. A 2006 digital release finally did justice to the full score; bonus tracks include Smith's version of the title theme, and a remix of the climactic cue ("Hymne a l'argent") by French jazz composer/musician/arranger Fred Pallem.

8

Meet Mr. Solo: 1964

Britain's now-established James Bond film series lit the fuse of secret agent fan frenzy, and American television's *Man from U.N.C.L.E.* supplied the dynamite. Well-timed marketing tie-ins also played a crucial role. Every boy on both sides of the Atlantic—but only a few girls (alas!)—had to possess MPC Multiple Toys' replica James Bond 007 Secret Shooting Attaché Case, loosely based on its "authentic" cousin in *From Russia with Love*; Ideal's copycat Napoleon Solo Spy Gun and Briefcase, complete with U.N.C.L.E. section badge; and Mattel's line of "Agent Zero M" gadgets, particularly the "Snap-Shot," which—with the quick flip of a button—changed from a camera into a pistol, and the (seemingly) innocent radio that turned into a cap rifle (long before Transformers were even a gleam in anybody's eye).

The resulting wave of hard-charging spy jazz also helped, as junior operatives pretended to "Open Channel D" on their ballpoint pens.

Pop-culture accouterments hadn't been this ubiquitous since Daniel Boone's coonskin caps, back in the mid–1950s. And the secret agent craze got even wilder, once low-budget foreign flicks begat a fresh genre category dubbed "Eurospy."

The Small Screen

But not *everything* had gone to the spies.

The Rogues is an occasional example of a soundtrack album that's far superior to the music originally heard in the TV series. Despite a beguiling premise and a cast of veteran scene-stealers—headed by David Niven, Charles Boyer, Gladys Cooper and Gig Young—the NBC entry ran only a single season of 30 episodes, beginning September 13. The larcenous Fleming and St. Clair families are practitioners of hereditary skullduggery that extends back generations and centuries. These modern descendants—Alec (Niven) in England, Tony (Young) in New York, and Marcel (Boyer) in France—maintain tradition by conning unscrupulous aristocrats and business types out of their wealth.

The title theme and almost all underscores were composed by Nelson Riddle, as he was coming off his assignments for *Naked City* and *Route 66*. "I was enamored of the way [Riddle] wrote," reflected Herschel Burke Gilbert, then music director of the production company that helmed *The Rogues*. "He wrote right in the parts: I could never do that; most composers can't do that. In other words, he wrote a trumpet part, wrote a second trumpet part, and wrote a third trumpet part, and kept it all in his head. That's a highly advanced way of scoring. You can count the number of people in our business—in any given year—at five, if that many, who can do that. It seemed to pour out of him."[1]

Unfortunately, most of Riddle's jazz/swing elements vanished in the hands of orchestrator Gil Grau and music supervisor Alfred Perry; all the televised cues became breezy orchestral numbers. Riddle took a different approach with his soundtrack LP; it has a much stronger cocktail jazz vibe, very much in the mold of Mancini's two *Peter Gunn* albums. The LP version of the title theme is a droll march, fairly close to the TV arrangement, with flutes and unison horns taking the melody against orchestral backing. The variant "From Rogues to Riches" is a saucy swing number, with a sleek piano solo by Jimmy Rowles. Mancini-style flute takes the lead against rhythmic bass on the midtempo "Gig"; trumpet and baritone sax solos highlight the mambo-flavored "A Rogue in Rio"; gentle piano, bass trombone and flute filigrees back Gene Cipriano's tenor sax in the dreamy "Latin Lady."

The Rogues wouldn't have pleased fans of socially conscious, *cinema-verité* dramas such as *East Side/West Side*; they'd have gravitated instead toward CBS' *The Reporter*, Pulitzer Prize-winning playwright/novelist Jerome Weidman's equally grave series about hard-charging newspaper reporter Danny Taylor (Harry Guardino), and his idealistic crusades against social injustice. In addition to similarly bleak scripts and a dour, big-city atmosphere, both series also feature vibrant jazz title themes and underscores by Kenyon Hopkins. Alas, *The Reporter* was far better at scaring up headlines than viewers; it lasted only 13 episodes before Danny filed his final exposé.

Jazz fans must've mourned.

Hopkins concocted a title theme with a terrific sense of presses-are-running urgency: sharp unison horns against rambunctious, teletype-style percussion, which pause long enough to uncork a blazing (if brief) alto sax interlude. The series has become a forgotten obscurity, but Hopkins nonetheless coaxed a soundtrack LP out of Columbia. It earned a Special Merit accolade from *Billboard*: "[The] score written by Kenyon Hopkins provides the kind of musical excitement that [comes from] a pulsating beat and enough good jazz-based touches to help it stand up without the benefit of video values."[2]

The title theme's intensity is surpassed by the even more frantic "Headline," with dueling brass and reeds against Ed Shaughnessy's ferocious drumming. Other notable tracks include "Are You Busy?" with Phil Woods' alto sax and some tasty trombone licks rising above a heavy 4/4 beat; the enchanting, flute-driven run at "Bossa Blu Nova"; and the 6/8 "Stop the Presses!," which Bernie Leighton's terrific piano chops and more cool sax turn into an R&B swinger that demands a dance floor.

On a lighter note, *Mr. Broadway* barely qualifies for this book's genre focus, unless one associates press agent hyperbole with duplicitous or outright nefarious activity. But it's true that New York City public relations specialist Mike Bell—played by Craig Stevens, radiating the debonair grace he brought to *Peter Gunn*—occasionally consorts with unsavory characters. In one episode, a gangster applies "pressure" to get his niece a booking as an opera singer; in another, Mike winds up accused of industrial espionage. The CBS show was a flop and ran only three months, despite a roster of high-profile guest stars such as Lauren Bacall, Art Carney, Liza Minnelli, Jason Robards and Stevens' former *Gunn* co-star, Lola Albright.

Mr. Broadway nonetheless merits attention, because it's the sole weekly TV assignment undertaken by jazz giant Dave Brubeck, who composed both a title theme and underscores for all 13 episodes. "I did not want to write fragmented themes and hours of cues which did not develop into tunes," Brubeck later explained. "Musical producer Robert Israel assured me ... that I should feel free to write full-length tunes from which cues and other background material could be developed. Once involved, I got carried away with the project and wrote enough material for several record albums."[3]

He didn't exaggerate. The Brubeck Collection, archived at California's University of the Pacific, includes a meticulous listing of the composer's recordings and cues relevant to *Mr. Broadway*. Over the course of 22 studio sessions that took place during the spring and summer of 1964, Brubeck recorded an astonishing number of cues, from fully formed songs—such as "Railroad Boogie," "Quiet Midnight," "Lonely Mr. Broadway" and "Whistle Stop Blues"—to dozens of miscellaneous bridges, curtains, inserts and stingers at a variety of tempos. Depending on script and mood, the finished cues were performed as piano solos, quartet numbers or full-blown orchestral ballads. The title theme, heard against simple credits as Stevens stares out at the New York City skyline, is a polyrhythmic waltz that opens with finger-snapping bass (Gene Wright) and drums (Joe Morello); Paul Desmond's alto sax takes the melody as Brubeck's piano comps merrily behind it.

Stevens didn't achieve much with *Mr. Broadway*, but Brubeck got a successful album, albeit under the "stealth" title of *Jazz Impressions of New York*; it debuted a few weeks after the show had been canceled. The title theme is much as it was heard on television, albeit with a more dynamic alto sax/piano bridge. Many of the other 10 tracks evoke a general sense of New York, particularly four lovely jazz waltzes which reflect the changing seasons that viewers never got to experience. "Autumn in Washington Square" opens with a long, lazy piano solo that eventually yields to Desmond's sweet alto sax; the shorter, more playful "Winter Ballad" feels like ice skating at Rockefeller Center. The bouncy, uptempo "Spring in Central Park" has the vibrant intensity of that season's sense of renewal; and Morello's slick drumming and Brubeck's joyful keyboard work give "Summer on the Sound" the excitement of beach volleyball and other hot weather sports.

Character-driven themes include the lighthearted "Broadway Bossa Nova"; and the somber "Lonely Mr. Broadway," with Brubeck comping behind Desmond's mournful sax. One additional track, "Toki's Theme," appeared on an earlier album—*Jazz Impressions of Japan*—which was released prior to the show's debut. It's a whimsical melody for Bell's pert Japanese assistant, played by co-star Lani Miyazaki: intended to reflect how, at that time, "in their own 'pop' music, the Japanese seem to parody themselves, using parallel fourths and other Western ideas of how the Oriental should sound, performed with a 'rock-a-billy' beat."[4]

* * *

The soundtrack world's first explosive revolution occurred in December 1955, when Frank Sinatra became *The Man with the Golden Arm*; the second innovation hit during the autumn of 1958, when *Peter Gunn* strolled into town; the third took place in late 1962, with the cinematic arrival of James Bond.

The fourth tectonic shift rattled Hollywood at 8:30 p.m. Tuesday, September 22, 1964, when Robert Vaughn first barked "Open Channel D" into his cigarette box communicator. (The antenna fountain pens came a bit later.) *The Man from U.N.C.L.E.* had arrived, and within a year television would be awash in gadget-toting secret agents, many of them plying their craft to jazz-hued soundtracks. Vaughn's Napoleon Solo and David McCallum's Illya Kuryakin were by no means television's first secret agents, nor were they the first to play with high-tech toys. But timing can be everything, and—with the world certifiably Bond crazy, in the wake of *Goldfinger* (released just five days earlier, in the UK)—there's little doubt that the American-born Solo, his Russian friend Kuryakin and their international spy agency chose the right moment to save the world on a weekly basis. Détente, indeed!

Jerry Goldsmith wrote the soon-to-be-iconic title theme and supplied a full score for the debut episode ("The Vulcan Affair") and two later episodes. The dramatic prelude of "Vulcan" opens with an ominous percussion ostinato and drum roll, after which Goldsmith's distinctive 5/4 theme kicks in, with its bold, four-bar brass statement. The "Vulcan" underscore also introduces two cues that would become series mainstays: a secondary four-bar action cue ("The Invaders"), with a core melody first stated by brass, then repeated by unison flutes; and the bossa nova romantic theme ("Meet Mr. Solo") designed for Solo's come-hither encounters with the "civilian assistant of the week" (usually an attractive young woman).

"If you noticed," Goldsmith recalled, years later, "every one of the themes I wrote for television, including U.N.C.L.E., had two elements: a main theme and a secondary theme, a countermelody. [In the scores], I milked the hell out of them; that's how I could do those shows so fast. That, I believed, was the way to do it. In those days, we took pride in what we did for television."[5]

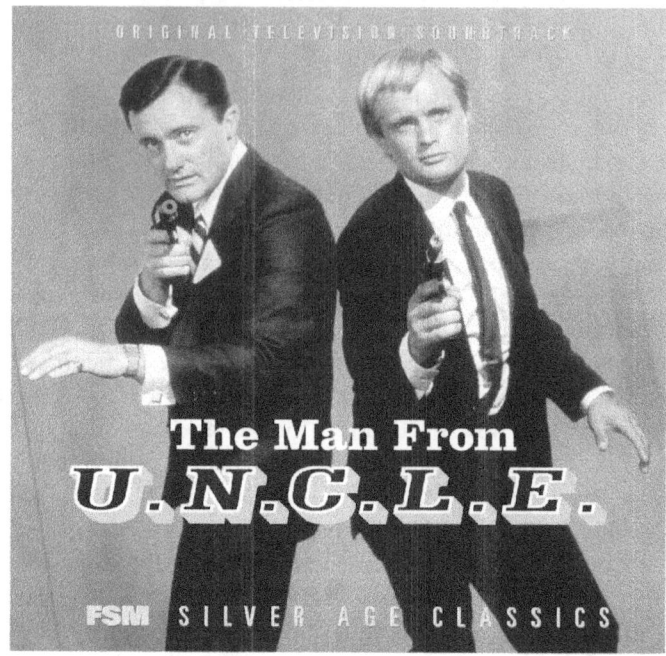

The Man from U.N.C.L.E. debuted with Jerry Goldsmith's killer title theme—in 5/4 time, two years before Lalo Schifrin would debut his even more memorable *Mission: Impossible* theme in that unusual meter—and a rich tapestry of underscores laden with swing melodies in their own right (courtesy Film Score Monthly).

MGM, hoping to mine more spy gold, expanded "The Vulcan Affair" with additional footage, retitled the result *To Trap a Spy*, and released it theatrically overseas. Goldsmith's score was retained and enhanced, by repeating some of his existing cues in the new footage. The result proved financially successful, and during the next several years MGM "built" seven more theatrical releases, in most cases from two-part episodes that became more frequent during later seasons. Most of these big-screen productions retained their original scores; the two exceptions—*One of Our Spies Is Missing* and *The Karate Killers*—were expanded from episodes with tracked underscores, and therefore earned new music by Gerald Fried.

Goldsmith's busy film schedule prohibited his future involvement with *U.N.C.L.E.*, although his title theme was used throughout the show's entire run (albeit in strikingly different arrangements). His efforts were supplemented during the first season by fellow composers Mort Stevens, Walter Scharf and Lalo Schifrin. The studio sessions featured well-established jazz talent: Manny Klein and Uan Rasey (trumpet); Dick Nash (trombone); Artie Kane (keyboards); Laurindo Almeida and Tommy Tedesco (guitar); Red Mitchell (bass); Shelly Manne (drums); and Larry Bunker and Emil Richards (percussion).

Although Schifrin drew only one episode ("The Fiddlesticks Affair"), his influence was felt strongly. His score included two Latin-flavored melodies that also became signatures: the jaunty "Roulette Rhumba," constantly reused within episodes that travel south of the border; and the gentler, bossa-flavored "Illya," designed to give Kuryakin his own theme. Ironically, Schifrin's most famous *U.N.C.L.E.* theme never was used in the show: In response to producer Norman Felton's request for "a THRUSH theme that would have possibility as a dance number,"[6] Schifrin came up with "The Man from THRUSH," a slinky bossa number that blends ultra-cool piano with growling, low-end brass. It was released as a Verve single in October 1965 and received considerable airplay, but never quite cracked the charts ... and never got tracked into any TV episodes.

The series was a hit when it returned—now in color—for its second and most successful year. Schifrin, asked to "improve" Goldsmith's title theme, produced a swinging, bongo-backed arrangement in standard 4/4 time, with the melody presented on flute. (Ironically, this version earned Goldsmith an Emmy Award nomination, for Best Individual Achievement in Music: Composition. He lost to David Rose, for his title theme to *Bonanza*.) Given that color filming was more expensive, budgets were drained from other departments; scoring orchestras were cut from (generally) 16 musicians to only eight. The first season's lavish underscores gave way to a "smaller" combo sound. Schifrin scored one more episode—"The Ultimate Computer Affair"—and all the other second season original scores were handled by Robert Drasnin and Gerald Fried. Their "tone" slid in a different direction; many cues seemed designed to elicit a smile, if not outright laughter. Episode plots also began to veer into more outlandish territory.

Although multiple composers alternated assignments from week to week, the schedule could be brutal: particularly since a freshly edited episode could be previewed only once, to assess a given story's tone.

"There were no videos to take home," Fried pointed out. "You had to make your decisions—get the feel of the show—just from that one viewing. And it was terrifying."

Even talented composers couldn't necessarily adjust to such punishing demands.

"Studying Beethoven's notebooks, he wasn't a 'first idea' man," Fried added. "He'd work a theme, and finally it would emerge as something you'd recognize from the symphonies. He worked *hard* on his themes.

"Mozart would have been a natural for television. He *was* a first-idea man; it came out of his head full-blown."[7]

U.N.C.L.E.'s escalating trend toward wink-wink-nudge-nudge mockery accelerated exponentially during the lamentable third season, when poor writing and limited budgets produced truly dreadful results. Fried contributed to the disaster with deliberately comic scores that rely heavily on electric guitar and organ. He still supplied cool action jazz at times—notably in "The Her Master's Voice Affair"—but many of his cues are as overblown and "hammy" as the cartoon villains. This is particularly true of his new arrangement of Goldsmith's title theme—yes, it was changed again—with its obnoxious blasts of brass behind the melody. *U.N.C.L.E.'s* musical style began to emulate that of the deliberately campy *Batman*, which had overtaken Solo and Kuryakin for pop-culture prominence. This suspicion became downright fact when Nelson Riddle—then busy with the caped crusader's show—agreed to score the two-part "Concrete Overcoat Affair." His cues sound *exactly* like *Batman* music.

U.N.C.L.E.'s ratings tanked, so fourth-season producers returned to basics: stronger, more dramatic plots accompanied by music in the style Goldsmith had established. His title theme was reworked yet again, this time as a fast-paced, no-nonsense jazz cue. Richard Shores became the go-to underscore composer, supplying plenty of tense action cues, notably in "The 'J' for Judas Affair." But it was too little, too late; Solo and Kuryakin battled THRUSH one final time—in the two-part "Seven Wonders of the World Affair"—which concluded January 15, 1968. The following week, unsuspecting viewers found the 8 p.m. Monday timeslot occupied by *Rowan & Martin's Laugh-In*.

Considering how much effort Felton put into the series' music, it's surprising that MGM wasn't more aggressive about tie-in singles or albums. Nothing happened until first-season shooting was nearly completed, when a jazz quartet dubbed The Gallants—H.B. Barnum (sax), Gerald Wiggins (piano), Jimmy Bond (bass) and Earl Palmer (drums)—appeared in "The See-Paris-And-Die Affair." As the episode concludes, the quartet performs a quiet arrangement of "Meet Mr. Solo." The Gallants therefore became the first group to cover the series title theme, on a Capitol single. Surf rock covers subsequently became ubiquitous, and they all sound rather awful: The Challengers (GNP Crescendo), The Clee-Shays (Triumph); and The Ventures (Liberty).

Jazz fans had better luck on the LP front. MGM finally made a fitful attempt to cash in on its own property, but *The Man from U.N.C.L.E. and Other TV Themes* offers only three covers by Milton DeLugg and His Orchestra. RCA was more ambitious, with *Original Music from The Man from U.N.C.L.E.* ... although, technically, it's a cover album. The jazzy, uptempo arrangements came from band leader and occasional film/TV composer Hugo Montenegro, soon to become famous for his cover of the title theme from *The Good, the Bad and the Ugly*. He adapted and expanded three cues each by Goldsmith, Stevens, Schifrin and Scharf, and the result proved quite popular; the album spent 20 weeks on *Billboard's* Top LPs chart. By the end of that run, Montenegro already had released a sequel: *More Music from The Man from U.N.C.L.E.* features equally vibrant jazz/pop covers of eight themes by Fried, and four by Drasnin.

Vaughn's Napoleon, McCallum's Illya and Fried returned for a 1983 TV movie appropriately titled *The Fifteen Years Later Affair* (aka *Return of The Man from U.N.C.L.E.*). Fried opens the film with yet another arrangement of Goldsmith's title theme, and supplies an underscore that feels just like old times (as does the film's clumsy plot).

The Big Screen

Although Peter Sellers' Inspector Jacques Clouseau debuted in *The Pink Panther*, many of the character's signature traits weren't introduced until the 1964 sequel, *A Shot in the Dark*. It's definitely the second entry in the official series—reuniting Sellers, director/co-scripter Blake Edwards, and Henry Mancini—but this film lacks a heist element and the iconic "Pink Panther Theme." Mancini instead concocted a new big band jazz anthem specifically suited to Clouseau's bumbling behavior and set to a fresh set of DePatie-Freleng's animated title credits. Throbbing bass guitar kicks off this swinger: As a cartoon Clouseau's face is blasted by repeated gunshots, the theme—primarily on harmonium, augmented by a solid trumpet line and plenty of larkish percussion riffs—perfectly complements the hilarious credits, the core melody occasionally pausing for rim shots and musical jokes that punctuate the animated antics. The credit sequence runs just shy of four minutes, and every second—visually and musically—is priceless.

Clouseau is sent to investigate the murder of a chauffeur employed by millionaire

Benjamin Ballon (George Sanders); one of his maids, Maria Gambrelli (Elke Sommer), is found standing over the body, with a still smoking gun. Despite all the evidence that points to her, Clouseau refuses to believe that Maria is guilty ... particularly since he quickly falls in love with her, and she with him. Victims pile up as the story proceeds; Clouseau's dogged effort to identify the true murderer eventually draws the attention of a shadowy assassin, who further increases the incidental body count.

This film is nowhere near as musically diverse as its predecessor. Mancini relies solely on two melodies: the title theme and sensual instrumental arrangements of "The Shadows of Paris," introduced as a vocal during the pre-credits teaser. The title theme is reprised in full-length glory twice, in equally swinging alternate arrangements: when Clouseau follows Maria to a nudist colony—this source version performed by a live jazz octet, the instruments carefully concealing any of the musicians' naughty bits—and as the end credits roll.

There wasn't enough distinct music to justify a soundtrack LP, although the two primary cues are included on Mancini's 1967 album, *Mancini Plays Mancini (And Other Composers)*, albeit in significantly different arrangements. More recently, the title theme has become a favorite on lounge compilations, with new "retro" covers by Whisky Biscuit, the Oranj Symphonette and The Lounge-O-Leers.

On a more serious note, director Don Siegel phoned in *The Hanged Man*, a flat update of Robert Montgomery's richly atmospheric 1947 *noir* classic, *Ride the Pink Horse*, itself adapted from Dorothy B. Hughes' 1946 crime novel of the same title. Siegel's laughably melodramatic retread is notable for only two reasons: It was the second original made-for-television film produced, debuting on NBC on November 18, 1964 (following *See How They Run*, which aired October 7).[8] The more important feature: The film's blend of diegetic and nondiegetic cues grants considerable screen time to Stan Getz and Astrud Gilberto, most notably when they perform "The Girl from Ipanema" on camera.

The plot finds loner Harry Pace (Robert Culp) traveling to New Orleans, to avenge the death of his friend Whitey Devlin (Gene Raymond) by goons under orders from corrupt union boss Arnie Seeger (Edmond O'Brien). But the unsuspecting Harry has been set up to take the fall for a blackmail scheme orchestrated by Arnie's duplicitous wife, Lois (Vera Miles), and Whitey; the latter is very much alive, having feigned his execution. Harry's journey to New Orleans is made in the company of Celine (Brenda Scott), a 16-year-old fortune teller traveling with her Uncle Picaud (J. Carrol Naish); they're hauling a float for the upcoming Mardi Gras parade. Celine falls hard for Harry, who gently keeps her at arm's length; the simmering melodrama builds to a violent climax during the parade, much to the delight of FBI agent Gaylord Grebb (Norman Fell).

Benny Carter built a complete score around his song "Only Trust Your Heart," a ballad that debuts in this film and quickly became a hit. Soft instrumental jazz arrangements of this tune accompany various scenes of ill-fated romance, and mournful strings are heard each time Celine warns that her tarot cards have foretold a grim fate for Harry; she keeps turning up the "hanged man" card, which gives this film its title. His wanderings through New Orleans streets, on the eve of Mardi Gras, provide an excuse for all manner of Dixieland source music emanating from various bars and restaurants; recognizable tunes include "When the Saints Come Marching In," Louis Armstrong's "Struttin' with Some Barbecue" and Paul Barnes' "Down by the Riverside." Cornet player Teddy Buckner leads a combo in one bar scene.

But Getz and Gilberto get the lion's share of the musical action; they even earn a spot in the opening credits, acknowledged as "The Stan Getz Quartette with Astrud Gilberto."

They first appear as the house band at a nightclub where Harry encounters Grebb; the action virtually ceases as Siegel allows Gilberto to sing the entire first verse of "The Girl from Ipanema," after which Getz takes a lovely tenor sax solo. Gary Burton can be seen on vibes; the other two musicians remain unknown. Harry and Grebb continue their chat as Gilberto concludes the song, after which the quartet segues into a tasty instrumental reading of "Quiet Nights." As the film nears its third act, Arnie and Lois attempt to enjoy a drink at the same nightclub; in the background, Getz's combo backs Gilberto as she sings "Only Trust Your Heart."

No soundtrack album was produced, although Getz and Gilberto subsequently performed "The Girl from Ipanema" and "Only Trust Your Heart" during countless concert and television appearances; both songs became bossa nova classics.

Elsewhere, director Sidney Lumet's unsettling adaptation of *The Pawnbroker* was far more successful. While tackling the challenge of filming Edward Lewis Wallant's harrowing 1961 novel, Lumet knew that he needed a score that would reflect both the story's East Harlem setting, and the traumatic Holocaust flashbacks that haunt the title character. (This was the first American film to depict the Holocaust from the viewpoint of a survivor.) Although the narrative is almost unbearably bleak, it concludes on a celebratory note: Sol Nazerman (Rod Steiger), who has endured by repressing his emotions, finally learns how to *feel* again.

"The concept of the score was 'Harlem triumphant!'—that the life, pain and energy of [Sol's] life there forced him to feel again," Lumet explained. "I decided I wanted two musical themes: one representing Europe, the other Harlem. The European theme was to be classical in its nature, precise but rather soft, a feeling of something old. The Harlem theme, by contrast, would be percussive, with lots of brass, wild in feeling—containing the most modern jazz sound that could be created."[9]

Lumet contacted John Cage, Gil Evans and John Lewis, all of whom seemed not quite right. "Then someone suggested Quincy Jones. I knew some of his jazz work from records he'd made on a big band tour of Norway. We met. It was love at first sight. His intelligence and enthusiasm were inspiring. I found out that he'd studied with Nadia Boulanger in Paris, which meant that his classical background was firm. He'd never done [an American] movie score, but that made him even more interesting to me."[10]

Jones studied trumpet while growing up in Seattle, and then attended Boston's Berklee College of Music. He toured with Lionel Hampton's band, as a trumpeter, arranger and occasional pianist. During the 1950s he worked with Duke Ellington, Count Basie, Sarah Vaughan, Ray Charles and a host of other jazz greats. He became vice-president of Mercury Records in 1961: the first upper-echelon black executive of a major record company. By this point he had a dozen albums to his credit, and soon would spend three years as Frank Sinatra's arranger and conductor.[11] Despite all this industry prestige and popular success, Jones' heart was set on working in cinema ... but Hollywood had its own entrenched notions about which composers were "appropriate" for movies.

"Blacks couldn't write string dates," Jones famously said, while itching to get a film scoring assignment. "They wouldn't let you. You could only write for big bands."[12]

Lumet came to the rescue.

"I showed him the movie. He loved it. We laid out a musical plot that was almost mathematical in its precision. It was a magnificent score, and the recording sessions were the most exciting I've ever been to. Because it was Quincy's first movie score, the band that turned out for him rivaled Esquire's All-Star Jazz Band."[13]

"I got the best players I knew," Jones acknowledged. "Trumpeter Freddie Hubbard, drummer Elvin Jones, Dizzy Gillespie, Oliver Nelson, Bobby Scott, a harpist, a woodwind and string section, percussionists—including Don Elliott on mouth percussion—everyone I could find. I wrote the score in two months and recorded it in two days. I wrote the last cue with 50 musicians sitting around yawning, as orchestrator Billy Byers and I scratched out pages furiously, but we got it done, and the picture really worked on all levels."[14]

The story is set in the early 1960s. Sol hasn't forgiven himself for surviving the Holocaust, after losing his wife and two children in the concentration camps. He has carved out a living as a pawnshop owner in East Harlem, where—having completely stifled his emotions—he handles customers with brutal detachment. He's indifferent to the cheerful enthusiasm of young assistant Jesus Ortiz (Jaime Sanchez), and blatantly hostile to friendly advances made by social worker Marilyn Birchfield (Geraldine Fitzgerald). Sol doesn't even mind his shop being used as a front by a local racketeer (Brock Peters, as Rodriguez). Sol's stiff façade finally cracks when he learns that Rodriguez earns some of his money through prostitution, which triggers a memory of Sol's wife being raped by Nazi soldiers. But this epiphany can't stop a climactic tragedy.

As Lumet desired, Jones' score is a blend of European classical influences (mostly somber violin cues) and hot-blooded big band jazz. The latter kicks off during the title credits, which flash over Sol's typical early morning journey to his shop: an automobile trip punctuated by walking bass and drums, trumpet fanfares, keyboard noodling and fast 4/4 solos—by Hubbard and J.J. Johnson—of the main theme's six-note motif. The tone turns mildly festive as Sol gets closer to his shop, concluding with a brief blast of bongos; this is, after all, *Spanish* Harlem. That vibrant bliss cuts off abruptly when he enters the shop and closes the door: Harlem, and its lively jazz, are *outside*.

Fortunately, Jesus has his own life: a happy relationship with his mother, and after-hours club-hopping with his girlfriend (Thelma Oliver). When the latter two make love one evening, the source music emanating from her radio is Jones' then-recent composition, the buoyant "Soul Bossa Nova" (eventually to achieve much greater fame as the "Austin Powers Theme"). Later, when Jesus charges into a pool hall and racks up the balls, while agonizing over whether to help a local gang rob Sol's shop, this montage is choreographed to a disconcerting 7/4 cue of enraged bongos, keyboard riffs and Elliot's whispered *chkk-chkk-cachaaaaa* vocal shadings. When that burglary goes awry and Jesus is shot, Jones switches to discordant free jazz, punctuated by sax and trumpet solos, as the boy's life drains away. The agonized Sol raises his face to heaven but cannot vocalize his despair; the scream comes instead from Jones' shrieking trumpets. Even so, this crisis yanks Sol from his emotional stupor; with blood literally on his hands, he stumbles down the street to an uncertain—but more hopeful—future.

The soundtrack album is significantly different than what is heard in the film; Jones rearranged much of the music and recorded it with a slightly different band. The album nonetheless reflects the film's blend of jazz and orchestral string cues; the latter include an overwrought vocal version of the title theme by Marc Allen and a mixed-voice chorus, singing lyrics that Jack Lawrence penned, to create a radio-friendly pop tune (a ghastly betrayal of the film's dramatic content). The jazz tracks are much better, with Jones supplying two ultra-cool, full-ensemble versions of the main theme ("Harlem Drive" and "End Title"), both dominated by driving percussion, Tommy Williams' terrific walking bass, and some vigorous horn work. The album's nicest surprise, though, is a leisurely quartet ballad—"The Naked Truth"—that isn't detectable in the film; Bobby Scott's sexy piano solo, at the bridge, is fabulous.

Sarah Vaughan sang a far more palatable version of the title song for a Mercury 45, paired with her cover of "Bye Bye," from TV private detective Peter Gunn's 1967 big-screen adventure, *Gunn* (discussed elsewhere).

Meanwhile, Across the Pond...

Patrick McGoohan's John Drake apparently took an extended leave of absence after the half-hour *Danger Man* series concluded in early 1962, but he was far from retired. Thanks to the big-screen Bond explosion, creator/producer Ralph Smart sensed the time was right for a revival; as a result, *Danger Man* reappeared on October 10, 1964, not quite a month after the London premiere of *Goldfinger*. McGoohan and the show's title were retained, with a few shifts in operational details; the expanded hour-length timeslot allows for better developed scripts, and the taciturn spy now works exclusively for British Intelligence, in a department dubbed M9. Drake's adventures once again are set to Edwin Astley's jazz-laden scores; assignments still take him to all parts of the world, although he also deals with garden-variety espionage in his London-based back yard.

Over the course of 47 episodes broadcast during slightly more than two years by ITV, Astley wrote just north of 400 new cues. Many employ the fresh sound of a harpsichord, which he decided would be one of Drake's musical signatures. Astley composed full scores for 13 episodes, along with incidental cues for another five built mostly from existing library cues. All remaining episodes are tracked from the library, except for Drake's final two adventures, which are a special case. "Koroshi" and "Shinda Shima" were filmed in color and later released in Europe, as a big-screen feature simply titled *Koroshi*. Both "halves" received fresh scores from Astley, who added Asian instruments and arrangements that suited the Japanese setting.[15]

Earlier, as the revived series began, the musical shift was immediately apparent. Four descending harpsichord notes repeat while a photo-reversed Drake approaches the camera; the image flips to "positive" as his face fills the screen against a three-note brass fanfare, and superimposed titles proclaim that "Patrick McGoohan is.... *Danger Man*." Suspenseful harpsichord elements remain prominent during the subsequent pre-credits sequence; brass fanfares build to a climax, after which Astley's new title theme kicks into life. This lively melody—dubbed "High Wire"—is introduced via harpsichord and rapid-fire percussion, then augmented by unison horns, as Drake drives his Mini Cooper through oddly deserted London streets.

"I remember the excitement," admitted Astley's son Jon, years later, when thinking backing to the studio session that produced this theme. "The harpsichord player was talking to my dad and saying, 'What sort of thing should we do?,' and my dad said, 'Well, some sort of boogie-woogie.'"[16]

This new theme *immediately* caught the attention of other musicians. Two weeks before the show debuted, the Bob Leaper Orchestra slowed the tempo for a cover on the Pye label; Ivor Slaney and His Orchestra weren't far behind, with an arrangement for His Master's Voice.

Astley frequently referenced this new theme—in various moods, tempos and instrumental combinations—within the underscores. Fast-paced action cues often employ the full orchestra; at other times, Astley relies on only a few instruments—often with mysterious harpsichord elements—to set a mood. Slow walking bass and unison horns accompany

Drake's sleuthing activities; peril is amplified by rapid walking bass and brass stingers. And, yes, each act once again concludes with a rising brass fanfare.

Unlike its half-hour predecessor, this version of *Danger Man* made it across the pond, and quickly became a Saturday evening staple after its debut on April 3, 1965. But nervous CBS execs, worried that American viewers wouldn't embrace a British show that lacked a hummable title theme, commissioned a fresh song from Steve Barri and P.F. Sloan. They succeeded beyond their wildest expectations: "Secret Agent Man," as recorded by Johnny Rivers, spent 11 weeks on *Billboard's* Hot 100 Chart, climbing all the way to No. 3 on April 23, 1966.

Astley, meanwhile, made his own mark with RCA's *Secret Agent Meets the Saint*. The album kicks off with a ferocious reading of "High Wire," with the harpsichord riffs backed by energetic brass and a unison trumpet reprise of the core melody at the bridge. Roughly a year later, in September 1966, RCA granted *Secret Agent* its own solo soundtrack album. Astley contributed five additional score tracks, which include a fast-paced action cue ("Cliff Hanger") powered by rapid walking bass, frantic bongos and edgy brass riffs; and a gentle horn lament ("Mal au Coeur") frequently used during episodes with melancholy resolutions.

The American UPN network unleashed a spoof-laden series titled *Secret Agent Man* in 2000. It "borrowed" the Sloan/Barri title theme, with an updated performance by Supreme Beings of Leisure. That aside, this series has nothing to do with McGoohan's *Danger Man/Secret Agent*, and it mercifully vanished after 12 gawdawful episodes.

Drake had serious competition on the big screen. When radio, television and newspaper ads proclaimed "James Bond back in action!" in late 1964, the team behind 007 could just as easily have bragged that John Barry was back. The incandescent Sean Connery may have been the obvious marquee draw, but Barry—who once again orchestrated Bond's exploits with such brassy, boldly swinging panache—was the producers' secret weapon. Barry's touch is more obvious with *Goldfinger*, as it's the first time a key character theme is woven so energetically throughout an entire Bond adventure.

"Everything came together," Barry acknowledged, "the song, the score, the style."[17]

And it wasn't just *any* character theme; for its time, this one was quite unusual. "That structure—two eights, a middle eight or bridge, and a last eight—that's classic song structure from the 1920s. It's probably the most successful songwriting structure that anyone's ever come up with, but it's so weird that it still doesn't sound that pat."[18]

After 007 dispatches a would-be assassin during the pre-credits teaser, Barry's orchestra roars into what arguably is the superlative Bond power anthem. Shirley Bassey's lusty delivery of the title theme—lyrics by Anthony Newley and Leslie Bricusse—kicks off with two explosive notes, followed by a five-note echo via muted trumpets.

"[That] wasn't in the original orchestration," Barry admitted, years later. "We'd been rehearsing with Shirley and the orchestra for about an hour and a half; they broke for a 20-minute tea break. And I just *heard* that *by-yah-yah-yah-yah*, I don't know why. I went to the piano, and I put it down; I got the copyist to put it on the trumpet parts with the *wah-wah* mute. And thank God, because it was the hook, the thing that really grabbed you."[19]

Numerous instrumental echoes of this theme are heard throughout the film: suspensefully, or as a call to danger, or sometimes only contemplatively. Barry employs it interchangeably with "The James Bond Theme," as hooks that drive not only action scenes, but the quieter, character-developing encounters. (Barry chose not to use his secondary "007" theme in this film.) The title credits sequence concludes when Bond flies into Miami to liaise with CIA buddy Felix Leiter (Cec Linder); this arrival in the States is accompanied by a blast of big band swing, powered by John Scott's deliciously dirty alto sax solo. "It's only a short cue," notes Eddi Fiegel, in her biography of Barry, "but with its enticing saxophone and its cocktail hour swish, it sets the whole film up fantastically."[20]

Felix informs Bond of their mission: to investigate the shady activities of international bullion magnate Auric Goldfinger (Gert Fröbe), believed to be smuggling gold illegally. Initial skirmishes—at a Miami resort, and then during a tense game of golf—lead to Goldfinger's factory in Geneva, and subsequently back to the States, at the villain's Kentucky stud farm. The enormity of Goldfinger's scheme then becomes clear: Backed by Red Chinese spies, he intends to invade nearby Fort Knox, not to steal the gold within, but to make it radioactive—and therefore worthless—with a particularly dirty atomic bomb. The U.S. and world economies will slide into chaos, and Goldfinger will wield incalculable influence with his own personal gold reserve.

Barry's showpiece cue kicks off the third-act climax: a lengthy, seven-minute jazz symphony that plays over the raid on Fort Knox. The cue begins softly, with military-style snare drums; the tempo and intensity build with crescendos of crashing cymbals and shrill brass echoes of the main theme. The drumbeat becomes hypnotic; unsettling reeds join the musical fray, as the villain's plan appears to succeed.

The UK and U.S. soundtrack albums are notably different. The former is significantly longer, with four tracks not present on the U.S. LP. On the other hand, the American pressing includes Barry's aggressive, jazz/rock instrumental arrangement of the title theme—boasting Flick's guitar licks, and also released as a UA single, backed by "James Bond Back in Action Again"—which isn't on the UK LP. Bassey's version of the title song (a different take than the one used on the LP)—was a chart success on both sides of the Atlantic.

The soundtrack album spent an astonishing 70 weeks on *Billboard's* Top LPs chart, and shot all the way to No. 1 on March 20, 1965, edging out *Beatles '65* (!) and the soundtrack albums for *Mary Poppins* and *My Fair Lady*. It remained in the top spot for three weeks and stayed in the Top 10 through early summer. (Starting December 11, 1965, it shared the chart each week with Barry's soundtrack album for *Thunderball*.) Barry and Bassey were photographed together, sharing twin gold records, reflecting sales of more than 1 million units.

But wait; there's more! Britain's Roland Shaw Orchestra delivered roaring big band jazz covers of the music from all three films, in *Themes from the James Bond Thrillers*; that album spent 25 weeks on *Billboard's* Top LPs chart in 1965, starting February 27. It was slightly outperformed by the anthology LP *Music to Read James Bond By*, which blends some of all three films' soundtrack cuts with jazz covers by LeRoy Holmes, Al Caiola and other artists; it spent 27 weeks on the *Billboard* Top LPs chart at roughly the same time. Clearly, fans couldn't get enough of James Bond movie music, and record labels happily obliged; both Shaw and the *Music to Read* producers later delivered two more LPs, as more films emerged.

Goldfinger's title song subsequently was covered by hundreds of pop and jazz artists, both as vocals and instrumentals: from Billy Preston and Jimmy Smith, to Chaka Khan and Tom Petty & The Heartbreakers; from Billy Strange and Sounds Orchestral, to Eric Winstone and the Earl Klugh Trio.

Elsewhere in the World

Alain Delon had become a European sensation by the time MGM distributed *Mélodie en sous-sol* (*Any Number Can Win*) in the States; he subsequently starred in celebrated French director René Clément's big-screen adaptation of American thriller author Gunnar Hjerstedt's provocative 1954 novel, *Joy House*. In France, this twisty little roundelay was released as *Les félins*, which translates to "The Felines," a title far more appropriate to the delectably sordid story.

The film opens as a New York–based gangster, furious that his wife has been seduced by a French playboy—Delon, as Marc—sends a quartet of goons to Monte Carlo, to find and kill the young man. Marc barely escapes with his life; while hiding in a charity mission, he's hired to become a chauffeur for Barbara (Lola Albright), a wealthy widow who lives in a luxurious chateau with her niece, Melinda (Jane Fonda). Alas, Marc has jumped from the frying pan and into the fire, because these two women—and the chateau—conceal a weird and dangerous secret. The acting is stilted by modern standards, and Fonda isn't yet talented enough to persuasively depict Melinda's erratic behavior; even so, viewers are kept guessing by the twisty script, which builds to a climax laden with poetic justice.

The scoring assignment went to Lalo Schifrin, newly hired by MGM after concluding a three-year stint in Dizzy Gillespie's quintet. *Les félins* allows Schifrin to flex his jazz chops with style. Sharp-eared fans will detect plenty of prototype riffs that he'd bring to fruition in later scores for (among others) *Bullitt* and *Dirty Harry*.

The terrific title theme is an enticing blend of plucked bass, reeds and brushed cymbals that build to a fast two-beat, as flute and horns add suspenseful color. During the New York prologue, Schifrin employs sinister walking bass and drums—somewhat akin to Henry Mancini's "Fall Out," for *Peter Gunn*—to convey the vicious intent of the gangsters sent to kill Marc. This "bad guys" theme reprises each time these four thugs get close to the beleaguered playboy, most notably when he barely escapes their clutches during a pell-mell foot chase along the Mediterranean coast. A later tumultuous pursuit incorporates what would become another Schifrin signature: human voices.

"I scored a chase with an ensemble of singers that started pianissimo, with closed mouths," he explained. "An electric bass and percussion help to penetrate the rhythm of the scene. The music was aleatoric. Each member of the vocal group was instructed to sustain their lowest possible note until they ran out of air. After they breathed, they returned one step higher and louder. At around a third of the way into the cue, they opened their mouths and sang 'AH!'—and continued the same procedure until they were screaming toward the end of fortissimo."[21]

Schifrin's primary character theme will make longtime jazz fans smile with recognition. We get a brief hint of this cue when Barbara attempts to seduce Marc; the theme later becomes a sexy, Latin-hued dance number when a purring Melinda seductively teases the chateau's mysterious *fourth* occupant.

Schifrin's soundtrack didn't get full release until issued on CD in 2004. By that time, however, a key portion of the score had been famous for decades. Schifrin reworked that character theme into a hard-charging jazz instrumental called "The Cat," which became a hit when Jimmy Smith recorded it as a Verve single. The tune spent six weeks on *Billboard's* Hot 100 Chart in September and October 1964, peaking at No. 67.

"It became his first million seller on disc," Schifrin proudly noted, years later.[22]

Better still, the tune won Schifrin his first Grammy: the 1965 award for Best Original

Jazz Composition. It also became a genuine jazz hit, covered by everybody from Henry Mancini to Papa John DeFrancesco.

* * *

James Bond's success inspired what quickly became a tsunami of often cheap imitations—most from Italy, and often starring bottom-rung American actors—soon given their own Eurospy designation. One of the first was *Agent Secret FX-18*, a laughably awful French/Italian/Spanish co-production highlighted solely by bits of tasty big band jazz. Grade-Z American actor Ken Clark is dreadful as secret agent Francis Coplan, based on a popular series character created by Belgian authors Gaston Van den Panhuyse and Jean Libert. The film's clumsy plot finds Coplan and beefy associates Fondane (Amédée Doménech) and Legay (Ramón Centenero) sent to Rome, to bust up a ring of traitorous French spies led by Barter (Claude Cerval). The secondary assignment is to snatch the special device with which the baddies have been passing top-secret information to Communists: a gadget that can transmit "5,000 words per second beamed vertically to a satellite." Considerable time is spent in a plaster-of-Paris cave set that appears left over from a bargain-basement pirate flick, where Coplan, Fondane and Legay repeatedly battle bad guys during poorly staged fistfights.

The Eddie Barclay/Michel Colombier score is wildly uneven; swinging big band jazz cues alternate with the sort of regional orchestral fluff one would expect from a Spanish travelogue. That said, Barclay and Colombier back the title credits sequence with a lively, drum-laden blast of big band bossa nova; later, a pleasantly lazy jazz ballad follows Fondane and Legay, when they're duped by two attractive women, and subsequently captured by Barter. *Agent Secret FX 18* failed to generate a soundtrack album—no surprise—but 2005's expanded CD edition of Colombier's 1969 album, *Capot Pointu*, includes three tracks from the film. They're worth seeking.

Director Romano Ferrara's *Intrigo a Los Angeles* (*Intrigue in Los Angeles*) is considerably better, although it looks and feels more like a late 1950s *noir* melodrama than a slice of mid–1960s Eurospy glamour. Adalberto Albertini's sinister monochrome cinematography contributes to that atmospheric distinction, as does a morbid third act that evokes Georges Franju's infamous 1960 French chiller, *Les Yeux Sans Visage* (*Eyes Without a Face*). But the set-up and first act are pure spyjinks with a soupçon of sci-fi, and Piero Umiliani's swinging jazz score demands our attention.

The bonkers plot begins as Professor Weiss (Stefano Pfau), a scientist believed killed in a lab explosion, is kidnapped by his former assistant, Jean (Carole Walker); she has trapped him in a bunker-like research facility concealed behind a Los Angeles strip club. Weiss has developed a substance that makes all living creatures immune to atomic radiation poisoning (!); Jean plans to sell this process to the highest bidder. CIA agents David Blair (Luciano Marini) and Thelma Avery (Mary Luger) investigate, alerted by the fact that several of the club's exotic dancers have died under mysterious circumstances. At this point, the irrational Jean becomes more insistent that Weiss fix her disfigurement—from the aforementioned lab explosion—with a "face transplant." As it happens, Thelma appears to be the perfect "donor." (Yikes!)

Intrigo a Los Angeles is noteworthy as one of Umiliani's several collaborations with trumpeter Chet Baker. The resulting score falls into four categories: brief bass and percussion ostinatos, for suspenseful encounters; full-blown jazz melodies, for occasional montages; frivolous tunes, for an eyebrow-lifting number of lengthy strip sequences; and eerie, jangly cues for the third act's descent into medical horror. Baker's presence is prominent early on, during his sparkling solo—against Umiliani's keyboard comping—in the lengthy swinger heard while David and Thelma are prepped for their assignment; sharp-eared listeners will realize that Umiliani borrows this tune from his earlier collaboration with Baker in 1959's *Audace Colpo Dei Soliti Ignoti*. Additional tasty cues include the big band melody that spots Thelma's efforts to evade the strip club owner's lecherous advances; and the fast-paced action jazz that propels a climactic car chase, when David tries to prevent the hopelessly insane Jean from escaping.

Fans had to wait until 2015 for a complete soundtrack album.

9

Mr. Kiss Kiss Bang Bang: 1965

Nothing succeeds like excess.

After undiscriminating European audiences devoured the dozen or so James Bond imitations and parodies mounted in 1964 by studios in Italy, Spain and France—or some combination of all three—opportunistic filmmakers *really* jumped on the Bondwagon this year. Roughly 50 secret agent projects got thrown in front of studio cameras, with an equal number following in 1966 and '67; most are low-budget quickies, often toplined by fading American or British actors willing to suffer incomprehensible plots and embarrassing action sequences. Shameless scripters concocted suspiciously similar names for their debonair spies (James Tont, Charles Bind, etc.), who were assigned equally analogous three-digit code numbers: 008, 077, 777 and so forth. (These thinly veiled imitations came into use only after United Artists threatened to sue French and Italian filmmakers who "borrowed" the 007 designation outright.)[1]

Such derivative plotting and shoddy production values notwithstanding, some Eurospy entries—even the most laughably inept, in every other respect—boasted solidly swinging action jazz scores. As we'll discover.

The Small Screen

Kelly Robinson (Robert Culp) and Alexander "Scotty" Scott (Bill Cosby) aren't the usual secret agents, and *I Spy* isn't the usual secret agent show. Gadgets and world-threatening megalomaniacs are conspicuously absent. While on assignment for an unspecified American Intelligence outfit, Kelly and Scotty generally deal with intimate situations that require careful negotiations: infiltrating revolutionary cells, identifying traitorous moles, safeguarding (often uncooperative) heads of state, or navigating the complexities of Cold War tensions. Their cover—Kelly a top-seeded tennis player, Scotty his trainer—gives them an excuse to travel the world; the show delivers on such international settings, with location filming in Japan, Mexico, Italy, Hong Kong, Greece, Spain and other countries. Missions aren't always successful; Kelly and Scotty often wind up with (to quote Marilyn Monroe) the fuzzy end of the lollipop, and little to show for their life-threatening efforts.

Every *I Spy* adventure—82 episodes over the course of three seasons—received an original underscore. (Producer Sheldon Leonard famously quipped that using "tracked" library cues was "like wearing someone else's underwear.)[2] The lion's share came from composer/arranger and big band veteran Earle Hagen, with an assist—on roughly one-third of them—by Hugo Friedhofer. The workload was huge: "*I Spy* averaged more than of 20 minutes of music in a 51-minute show," Hagen pointed out. "We had one that was 37 minutes; that's like wall to wall!"³

Hagen also wrote the kick-ass, waltz-time main theme, which opens with a throbbing, two-bar bass ostinato; reeds softly state the descending four-note melody, as a silhouetted graphic of Culp plays tennis on the screen. Tempo and volume accelerate when the figure slowly turns; his tennis racket transforms into a gun, and he "shoots" the show's title onto the screen. Brass and strings take over when Culp appears on camera; he tosses a bomb toward the viewer, and then peers over superimposed

"*I Spy* was the first real challenge for me," composer Earle Hagen admitted when interviewed in the September 2001 issue of *Film Score Monthly*. "The changing panoramas of countries and plot lines were extremely daunting. It never occurred to [producer] Sheldon [Leonard] that I might not be able to deliver that kind of product. But, then, it never occurred to *me*, either. I tried to write a self-contained score for each episode; it was like scoring an hour movie a week. That kind of show will never happen again in television" (courtesy Film Score Monthly).

excerpts of the episode to come. It's one of the jazziest music-to-image TV title credits sequences ever created.

"That was innovative," Hagen acknowledged, years later. "It was the first main title that I know of, that used graphic art, live action *and* superimposition. It was put together in 10-frame increments, which locked me into the tempo. That made it easy, because in the first part of the theme I was able to stall around until the gunshots, and that swept into the beginning of the theme, and I had it timed out to catch the bomb, and all that. It wasn't episodic; it was done to a beat. Having a pre-fixed tempo wound up being a great plus, because I didn't have to worry about matching something to picture."⁴

The show's travelogue nature demanded scores that suited a given locale. "I wrote a special theme for each of the countries. The theme I used for Hong Kong, or Japan, was presented in the opening of all the shows in that country. It was modified, re-arranged and re-orchestrated to suit the picture values being shown. Once we left that country, I would write a new one for the next locale."⁵ The nature of a story—dramatic, suspenseful, comedic, melancholy—would determine the tone of Hagen's music from week to week, but he rarely neglected to include at least a few jazz cues. (He called it "semi-jazz.")⁶

Hagen's attention to detail included "casting" an ensemble to suit a given script's artistic tone. As one example, he used an extremely unusual configuration—two harps, two pianos, 10 percussion, three horns and three basses—for the third-season episode "Home to Judgment."

"It was an unusual episode," he admitted. "Probably as stylized as anything we ever did on *I Spy*."[7]

Following Henry Mancini's approach to *Peter Gunn*, many of Hagen's cues are catchy, fully developed melodies in their own right, often allowed to run at length behind a montage. Echoes of the title theme are worked into underscore cues, often to promote suspense. Hagen also could be quite clever with source music. "The scene in [the episode] 'So Long Patrick Henry,' with the four of them in the boat, had one of the best music cues in that show. I had a theme for Ivan Dixon that played straight through the montage of them in the boat, then in a nightclub with them dancing a samba, then into a bar with the four of them sitting around talking, while a piano player played in the background. The theme went straight through and never changed tempo, while the background continuously changed to the samba, and then to the slow jazz piano background."[8]

A soundtrack album arrived in April 1966, shortly before the show concluded its first season. Hagen's busy schedule didn't grant him much studio time, so many of the tracks were lifted "as is" from his score cues recorded for the pilot and several early first-season episodes. These include location-setting themes such as the mariachi-hued "Away We Go to Mexico," a fast-paced swinger in 3/4 time; and the rhythmic, 5/4 "Away We Go to Tokyo," with Japanese instrumentation lending a cultural spin to the show's title theme. At the opposite end of the emotional spectrum, "Angel"—arranged by Warren Barker—is an achingly wistful ballad dominated by soft bass, piano, trumpet and strings, written for Eartha Kitt's heroin-addicted character in "The Loser." The album didn't chart, but the show's popularity prompted a sequel in December 1967 (confusingly sharing the same title as its predecessor). A shrill horn and saucy organ bridge power Hagen's fresh arrangement of the title theme; this version was issued on a single released in January 1968.

Hagen earned Emmy Award nominations for Music Composition all three years. He lost the first two, but the third time was the charm; he collected the 1968 honor for his work on the episode "Laya."

Their low-key, laid-back approach notwithstanding, Kelly and Scott are typical—in one important respect—of this era's secret agents and PIs: They're *men*. Honey West therefore was a rarity when introduced in 1957 as a private investigator conceived by novelist G.G. Fickling (actually husband-and-wife writers Forrest E. "Skip" and Gloria Gautraud Fickling). Anne Francis debuted as the "private eyeful" in an episode of *Burke's Law*—"Who Killed the Jackpot," broadcast April 1, 1965—wherein she upstages her male co-stars by solving the case. When she gained her own half-hour ABC series five months later, Honey had become a self-assured judo expert often garbed in black cat suits: a look clearly stolen from Honor Blackman and Diana Rigg, in Britain's *The Avengers*. Honey and love-struck partner Sam Bolt (John Ericson) work from a high-tech surveillance van, and she often sports Bondian gadgets such as tear-gas earrings, a lipstick radio and an exploding compact.

The scoring assignment went to Joseph Mullendore: a logical choice, since he had worked on numerous *Burke's Law* episodes. He gave *Honey West* a more vibrant jazz edge, starting with an exciting, brass-forward main theme. Bursts of unison trumpets introduce the title credits, which unfold over a beehive of hexagonal images of Francis; the core 3-4 motif debuts over a close-up of Honey's lips, leading to a rhythmic ostinato behind a montage of action stills. These climax with a blast of brass over a quick shot of Honey's pet ocelot, Bruce; an orchestral expansion of the melody then repeats over glamour shots of Francis and Ericson. Mullendore's end credits theme is completely different: a saucy sax number backed by a repeated string of five descending notes on unison horns.

Mullendore also wrote underscores for all but two of the single season's 30 episodes, and his scores are extremely "busy"; even sequences traditionally bereft of music—such as a conversation between two or three people—often are backed by soft swing cues. As with *Peter Gunn*, pre-credits teasers gain suspenseful heft from a twitchy jazz cue. Scripters constantly put Francis in glamorous or revealing outfits, and such sequences often take place against slinky piano cues or leering arrangements of the title theme's 3-4 motif; climactic fight scenes are choreographed to uptempo action jazz. Plenty of time is spent in bars, restaurants and nightclubs, all laden with equally swinging source music.

Mullendore also produced one of the decade's best—and most undersung—jazz TV soundtrack LPs. The album opens with an even more ferocious arrangement of the title theme—appropriately titled "Wild Honey"—which features sizzling unison brass and a nifty countermelody at the bridge. The romantic "Wait and See" blends tasty piano riffs and a sensuous sax melody, and even Bruce gets a theme: a slinky, midtempo swinger that feels *just* like a feline stalker, down to brass "meow-meow" elements.

Honey wasn't the only West prowling 1965's television's back lot alleyways. *The Wild Wild West* is one of the more unusual entries in the wave that followed *The Man from U.N.C.L.E.* Set during the post–Civil War United States, the show follows the adventures of James T. West (Robert Conrad) and Artemus "Artie" Gordon (Ross Martin), undercover agents working on behalf of President Ulysses S. Grant. While traveling the country in a tricked-out train car, they confront all manner of anarchists, radicals, revolutionaries and just plain criminals attempting to rob, sow dissent within, or take over various parts of the still not-so-United States. The show delivers just the right blend of derring-do, sly social commentary and cleverly contrived situations, and Conrad and Martin make a captivating team.

The Wild Wild West also boasts a terrific main theme synchronized to a clever title credits sequence. Richard Markowitz had cut his teeth scoring *Philip Marlowe* and *Johnny Yuma*, which serendipitously prepared him for a secret agent western. "What I did, essentially, was write two themes," he explained, years later. "One had a rhythmic contemporary feeling, and at that time was a new sound. I used an electronic bass, brushes and a vamp sound for when West was getting out of trouble; and the heraldic kind of western/outdoor theme over that, so that the two worked together … a kind of A/B formula."[9]

The enticing vamp kicks off with a brass statement of the 7-note fanfare that viewers quickly came to adore, set against throbbing Fender bass and drum brushes; an animated sequence begins as a heroic good guy, positioned in the central vertical rectangle of a segmented screen, "strides" into dangerous encounters with figures in the four corner squares. Brushes, brass and harmonica trade riffs over the bass as the vamp continues, the hero ultimately kissing—or decking, in later seasons—a knife-wielding hussy. As he then strides out of frame, Markowitz brings up the full orchestra for the "Americana" reprise of the full theme: the triumphant climax of what feels like a mini-movie in its own right. Although Markowitz eventually supplied only 11 full underscores, his musical "stamp" is evident throughout the show's four-year run. The vamp portion of his title theme is ubiquitous when West "suits up" in his train car, or when he employs some cleverly concealed gadget to escape a death trap.

Markowitz shared most of the first season underscore duties with Robert Drasnin;

others were contributed by Richard Shores and Russell Garcia. The four of them established the library of cues subsequently tracked into many later episodes. One original assignment went to newcomer Dave Grusin, making his "espionage score" debut. It became one of the series' rare jazz underscores; other exceptions include Shores' "The Night of the Firebrand," with plenty of uptempo action jazz very much in the *Man from U.N.C.L.E.* mode; jazz guitarist Mundell Lowe's "The Night of the Amnesiac"; and Walter Scharf's Latin-inflected cues for "The Night of the Assassin," which feature Laurindo Almeida's guitar licks and some sly percussion work by Victor Feldman.[10]

Conrad and Martin returned for a pair of lamentably campy TV movie sequels in 1979 and '80—*The Wild Wild West Revisited* and *More Wild Wild West*—but, aside from Markowitz's title theme, Jeff Alexander's underscores fail to capture the original jazz/Americana vibe. A comedic 1999 big-screen remake, with Will Smith and Kevin Kline, is an aberration best forgotten.

Rather surprisingly, the show didn't produce a soundtrack album until 2017, with the release of a sumptuous four-disc set boasting full or partial scores from 26 episodes.

James and Artie kidded around a lot, but their adventures remained semi-serious. That wasn't the case with one of the decade's most successful spy knockoffs: the *way*-over-the-top *Get Smart*, with its weekly antics by bumbling CONTROL agent Maxwell Smart, played by stand-up comic-turned-actor Don Adams. He's perfect in the role: forever stoic despite the utter chaos he unintentionally provokes, while battling the nefarious minions of KAOS. Max often gets rescued by his far more intelligent and resourceful colleague, Agent 99 (Barbara Feldon); they both report to a long-suffering superior dubbed The Chief (Edward Platt).

The scoring assignment went to former big band arranger Irving Szathmary, who had worked with units fronted by (among others) Benny Goodman, Artie Shaw and Jack Teagarden. *Get Smart's* credits sequence is comedy genius; Szathmary's jazzy, 12/8 title theme, backed by a twanging electric guitar ostinato, is the icing on the cake. The sequence begins as Max roars to a curbside stop in his bright red V8 Sunbeam Tiger; a repeating five-note vamp layered atop that guitar ostinato introduces the 3-1/3-1 brass motif as Max descends a flight of stairs and then strides through a series of heavy metal doors that part and *clang* shut—on the supporting cast credits—in his wake. The theme concludes with a two-note orchestral blast when he reaches a phone booth, dials a number, and plunges somewhere underground, into the bowels of CONTROL.

Szathmary also scored all 138 episodes during the show's five-season run. His whimsical, gag-laden cues are a virtual potpourri of instrumental madness: very much in the mold of novelty and avant-garde musicians such as Spike Jones and Raymond Scott (for whom Szathmary had done arrangements, early in his career). Almost nothing could have been built into an actual melody: no doubt the reason for the absence of a soundtrack album. The title theme nonetheless attracted numerous covers, the most famous from actor/drummer Bob Crane (Epic); others came from Billy Strange (Vocalion) and The Ventures (Liberty).

When Max and Agent 99 solved their final case in the spring of 1970, Szathmary unexpectedly retired, abandoning Hollywood—and music—entirely. His *Get Smart* theme lived on: first with a 1989 TV movie revival, then a fleeting 1995 series revival, and ultimately with a 2008 big-screen adaptation.

Just as Max had a series of signature phrases—notably "Missed it by *that* much" and "Would you believe…"—everybody associates Peter Falk's disheveled appearance and inquisitive "Just one more thing…" with Los Angeles Police Lt. Columbo. Ah, but the actor test-drove these quirky mannerisms in 1965's short-lived CBS series, *The Trials of O'Brien*.

At first glance, Falk's Shakespeare-quoting Daniel J. O'Brien looks like the last attorney anybody would hire. His personal life in shambles; he's constantly in debt; and he's eternally hectored by an ex-wife, landlord and long-unpaid secretary (hence the show title's clever dual meaning). Once inside a courtroom, though, O'Brien's quick intelligence and sharp eye for detail make him a mesmerizing—and thoroughly persuasive—advocate.

The show's music was assigned to composer, arranger and orchestrator Sid Ramin, whose eclectic credits included having written the theme and lyrics for television's *Candid Camera*; and as co-orchestrator of the music for *West Side Story*, alongside Leonard Bernstein and Irwin Kostal. Ramin gave *O'Brien* a terrific jazz title theme, along with memorably swinging underscores for all 22 episodes. The show doesn't have a title sequence *per se*; the credits appear over a different weekly montage—silent, except for Ramin's music—of O'Brien getting sucked into a new case. Falk's antics during these teasers are always droll, but Ramin's theme is jazz-serious: a 60-second swinger that opens with a blast of brass against a throbbing Fender bass ostinato, then settles into a chirpy melody carried by unison reeds. A brief string bridge leads to another brass semi-climax as the episode title appears, after which Ramin builds to a final explosive blast from the entire band.

Ramin also supplied plenty of droll swing cues beneath O'Brien's travails in the outer world, particular when confronted by folks to whom he owes money, or while accepting a case from often unusual clients. Meetings and conferences take place in restaurants and bars, always enlivened by jazzy combo source cues.

Ramin never recorded his title theme for commercial release, nor did *The Trials of O'Brien* produce a soundtrack album. Ray Martin covered the theme on his 1965 LP, *Thunderball and Other Thriller Music*; ordinarily, that would have been the end of the story. But less than a year after the show went off the air, Ramin modified his melody slightly and—with an assist from songwriter Tony Velona—turned it into a jingle for Diet Pepsi. We know it today as the incredibly famous "Music to Watch Girls By," which became a pop and jazz standard.

The Big Screen

Alain Delon had become hot stuff in his native France, but he failed to ignite MGM's entirely American production of *Once a Thief*. The raw ingredients *seemed* promising: Delon shares the screen with veteran actor Van Heflin and rising starlet Ann-Margret, in a crime thriller adapted by Zekial Marko (aka John Trinian) from his 1961 heist novel, *Scratch a Thief*. Unfortunately, all concerned are ill-served by Ralph Nelson's clumsy direction; both Delon and Ann-Margret overact atrociously, and the former often looks uncomfortable on camera. Time also hasn't been kind; to modern eyes, Delon's character constantly behaves like an abusive, sexist jerk.

On a happier note—indeed, lots and lots of happy notes—Lalo Schifrin adds plenty of carefully applied sizzle to the otherwise overcooked steak. We follow the unhappy saga of San Francisco–based career criminal Eddie Pedak (Delon), who—having done his prison time, and now trying to go straight—gets sucked into a caper orchestrated by older brother Walter (Jack Palance). Eddie's return to these larcenous roots greatly upsets his wife, Kristine (Ann-Margret), who veers from devoted compassion to betrayed hostility in the unpersuasive blink of an eye. Police inspector Mike Vido (Heflin) supplies an additional layer of tension by mercilessly dogging the ex-con.

The film's oddly bizarre title credits splash atop the patrons of a beatnik-laden jazz club, accompanied by a ferocious, jaw-dropping drum solo by Russell Lee (not a part of Schifrin's score). The drum solo grows ever more frantic as, elsewhere in the city, two unseen thugs rob a convenience store, killing one of the proprietors. Everything about this job—the vintage car used, the style of coat worn by the killer—is designed to frame Eddie. Schifrin's score jolts into life as we meet the poor guy and his happy family, against a cheerfully swinging piano, drum and horn-laden melody; this segues into the film's main theme, introduced as a gentle flute lament. This theme reprises frequently, with arrangements that give the melody line to muted trumpet, electric guitar and—during a love scene—a particularly sexy blend of flute and bass. Additional cool cues include a smokin' jump jazz track ("The Joint") that roars off the screen, when Kristine takes a job as a cocktail waitress in a noisy nightclub; a furious chase cue, after the heist goes down; and a final flute/guitar reading of the main theme, with wordless vocal shading by Marie Vernon, which backs the story's grim conclusion.

MGM decided against a traditional soundtrack album, opting instead for an anthology release: *Music from the Motion Picture "Once a Thief" and Other Themes*. Schifrin reorchestrated the film's three key cues—the main title, "The Joint" and a flute lament titled "Return to Trieste"—but a conspicuous string section compromises the result. The full score finally appeared in 2011's box set, *Lalo Schifrin Film Scores: 1964–68*.

Although Schifrin's early big-screen scoring assignments remain fairly obscure, that isn't true of his debut team-up with star Steve McQueen. Director Norman Jewison's handling of *The Cincinnati Kid* is a masterful adaptation of Richard Jessup's 1963 novel, with each of its colorfully memorable characters cast to perfection. The Depression–era story, set in New Orleans, concerns a long-anticipated poker match between debonair veteran player Lancey Howard (Edward G. Robinson) and scruffy, self-assured upstart Eric "The Kid" Stoner (McQueen). All the locals favor The Kid, but a shady, old-money gambler—Rip Torn, as Slade—intends to guarantee such success by blackmailing the dealer—The Kid's best friend, Shooter (Karl Malden)—into rendering occasional "assistance."

Schifrin had the misfortune to float into the deep end of conflicting opinions between Jewison and producer Martin Ransohoff. "The two of them had totally different concepts. … I realized that I was swimming in dangerous waters. But my instinct for self-preservation kicked in and forced me to do something that I have never again done in my career: I wrote two scores, one for the producer and one for the director. Just in case, I composed six different versions for the ending."[11]

Schifrin's electrifying main theme debuts as McQueen dodges trains in a vast switching yard; harmonica maestro Tommy Morgan carries the melody against driving percussion, with horns giving the rhythm a vibrant assist. The Kid's sweet but unsophisticated girlfriend, Christian (Tuesday Weld), is introduced against an achingly poignant, guitar-driven melody; Shooter's bad-news wife, Melba (Ann-Margret, at her slutty best), is given a sultry, disconcerting anthem. Interludes include a neighborhood cock fight, which Schifrin sets to a raucous blend of tack piano, banjo and Ozark mouth harp; and a slow, solo harmonica arrangement of the title theme, heard when The Kid visits Christian at her parents' farm. Later, as the two card warriors "suit up" in their respective hotel rooms, Howard does so to a mildly unsettling melody that conveys his calm skill and lengthy career; The Kid spruces up to a walking-bass variation of his theme. As both men apply the finishing touches, Schifrin blends the two themes to become one: Despite their differing backgrounds, these two opponents are equal. The marathon game unfolds without music. Its outcome prompts a reprise

In a move that was unusual for its time, the soundtrack LP for *The Cincinnati Kid* blended fuller, re-orchestrated versions of Lalo Schifrin's primary themes with some cues lifted directly from the film score. The album reviewed and sold well, prompting *Billboard* to tag it a breakout "New Action LP" on Jan. 29, 1966 (courtesy Film Score Monthly).

of the film's signature line—"You just ain't ready for me yet!"—as the main theme rises again.

A 2011 box set—*Lalo Schifrin Film Scores: 1964–68*—devotes an entire 77-minute disc to Schifrin's 14 original score cues, the initial MGM album contents, and 14 bonus tracks.

Schifrin's themes are infectiously melodic and easily hummable: characteristics that cannot be ascribed to the Eddie Sauter/Stan Getz score for *Mickey One*, which is as abstract as the existential film itself. The frequent wanderings into free jazz flawlessly complement the nerve-jangling terror that drives the title character. The mood is pure *film noir*: French New Wave by way of Kafkaesque paranoia, and a cinematic experience not to be embraced casually. Many find director Arthur Penn's handling of Alan Surgal's original screenplay unwatchably obtuse; at the very least, it must be viewed as allegory, fairy tale or—quite possibly—one man's descent into madness. All that said, Penn's extemporaneous approach is ideally matched by Sauter's meticulously composed jazz score, and then layered with Getz's ad-libbed tenor sax work; the latter even gets a shout-out in the opening credits ("Improvisations by Stan Getz"). *Mickey One* is the sole feature film score written by Sauter, a swing-era composer/arranger who worked with Red Norvo, Benny Goodman, Woody Herman, Artie Shaw and numerous other jazz greats.

The threadbare story opens on an unnamed stand-up comic (Warren Beatty) at the peak of his career, relishing a hedonistic lifestyle laden with booze, broads and betting. He somehow incurs the wrath of the organized crime bosses who control the Detroit clubs—the transgression remains unspecified—and, fearing for his life, flees to Chicago. He lands a stand-up gig at a seedy, vaudeville-throwback nightclub; he falls in love with Jenny Drayton (Alexandra Stewart), the film's sole "ordinary" character. But Mickey remains fearful that Mob assassins wait around every corner, and the film concludes when he reluctantly accepts a lucrative booking at an upscale restaurant/club dubbed Xanadu, where he's abruptly blinded by a harsh spotlight that conceals he knows not what: perhaps the eye of God.

The title credits unfold over a lengthy, wordless montage that efficiently depicts Mickey's fall from grace: a sequence spotted by a bossa nova cue typical of the albums Getz recently had made with Antônio Carlos Jobim, João Gilberto and Luiz Bonfá. Jarring shrieks on brass and Getz's agitated sax blasts signal Mickey's downward spiral, as his behavior grows ever more reckless. His decision to flee is accompanied by dissonant, echoing and overlapped sax solos, thanks to the magic of multi-tracking: an effect that Getz felt the scene deserved. "If it's musical and it's interesting," he explained, years later, "I say, 'Let it go down.' But nothing false. That's not false—it's just three me's."[12]

Mickey's subsequent effort to "make good" with the Mob begins with a taxi ride to a dangerous part of town, where a veritable United Nation of nightclubs occupies a single street. Bursts of conflicting source jazz emanate from each establishment—soloists include Clark Terry (trumpet and flugelhorn), Harvey Estrin (alto sax) and Tommy Mitchell (bass trombone)—and the result is a mélange of stride piano, trumpet combo jazz, aggressive rock and other genres, all overlaid to heighten Mickey's disorientation. After Mickey's "debut" at the Xanadu takes its disorienting turn, the end credits are accompanied by some uptempo combo swing from Getz—the melody strongly evoking the folk tune "Billy Boy"—with backing by Roger Kellaway (piano), Mel Lewis (drums) and Richard Davis (bass).

The score was rerecorded for the soundtrack album, with short cues often stitched into long single tracks. The fresh arrangement of the title credits theme ("Once Upon a Time") is particularly lush, and more strongly reminiscent of Getz's bossa nova albums; conversely, the album version of the end credit swing theme ("Is There Any Word? So This Is the Word") is cluttered by unnecessary strings.

The album's initial obscurity notwithstanding, it remained a favorite of the composer who put so much effort into marrying sound with image. "Most of the stuff I do, I can't listen to," Sauter admitted, years later, "but I can listen to that. What I try to do is string [the cues] together in such a way that it made one big piece. The ability to pick up on a theme and work it through was always a ball … maybe that's why I like *Mickey One*."[13]

* * *

Quincy Jones' second big-screen assignment was veteran director Edward Dmytryk's *Mirage*, an adaptation of novelist Howard Fast's *Fallen Angel*. The premise is a mind-bender: During a building-wide blackout in New York City, longtime company employee David Stillwell (Gregory Peck) follows the engaging Shela (Diane Baker) down the darkened stairs to street level, then watches her vanish down four more flights to an underground sub-basement. The following morning, those lower stairs aren't present in the building, which doesn't *have* any sub-basements. Various chillingly polite individuals start trying to kill David, who realizes that he can't remember much about himself. In desperation, he hires a novice private investigator (Walter Matthau) to help figure out what the heck is going on.

Despite his success on *The Pawnbroker*, Jones almost didn't get this job. When he first met the producer at Universal Studios, the guy took one look—obviously not having realized that Jones was black—and said, "I'll get back to you."

"He called Henry Mancini, an old and close friend," Jones recalled, "and asked him, 'Can Quincy Jones handle a score for Gregory Peck and Walter Matthau? This is not a black film.' Mancini said, 'C'mon, guys! He just did *The Pawnbroker*, and he was a student of Nadia Boulanger. This is the 20th century … you think the guy's gonna write the blues for Greg Peck? Hire him!'

"Way before and after *Mirage*, Mancini was a friend till the day he died, God bless him forever."[14]

Jones' score is delectably disorienting. A plucked harp, sinister flute riffs, harpsichord lines and unexpected trumpet pops echo David's increasing unease; a terrified daytime pursuit through an underground garage and public park gains intensity from a propulsive, bongo-laden cue with frantic brass stings. The most prominent cues are variations of the gentle main theme, which often accompany Shela's appearances.

The reorchestrated soundtrack album grants longer and more satisfying renditions of elaborate themes that are no more than fleeting cues during the film. The two best album tracks—"Kinda Scary" and "Boobie Baby"—aren't heard in the film at all. On the negative side, Jones again was compelled by studio mandate to provide a radio-ready title song. The gawpy result—sung by Johnny Mathis—opens the album but isn't used anywhere in the film (definitely a wise decision).

Mirage was a high-profile "A" picture; the laughably inept *Young Dillinger* is anything but. This revisionist depiction of how the notoriously violent gangster began his career is grade-Z drive-in fare at its worst. Clumsy stock footage alternates with mismatched film stock, and much of the "action" appears to have been shot on the same stretch of hillside roadway just outside Los Angeles. Scripters Arthur Hoerl and Donald Zimbalist blame girlfriend Elaine (Mary Ann Mobley) for the initial crime that puts John Dillinger (Nick Adams) on a downward spiral, when she encourages him to rob her father's safe, so they can elope. The atrociously corny dialogue is complemented by hilariously overwrought performances; Robert Conrad—co-starring as "Pretty Boy" Floyd—has one of the hammiest death scenes ever captured on camera.

(Shortly after the 17 days spent on this shoot, Conrad lucked into the role that cemented his career, when he made the pilot episode of *The Wild, Wild West*.)

Rather surprising—for schlock of this nature—the scoring assignment was accepted by famed trumpet player, arranger and composer Shorty Rogers, who had performed in big bands fronted by Woody Herman and Stan Kenton, and was one of the pioneers of the 1950s West Coast jazz movement.[15] Rogers delivered a powerful, brass-laden swing score that virtually overwhelms the movie, and director Terry O. Morse frequently uses cheerfully vibrant jazz cues that are wholly at odds with the grimly violent scenes they support.

Rogers built his score around three primary themes: a slow, bluesy ballad—the melancholy melody usually taken by sax or flute—that initially plays behind the title credits; a lively blast of Dixieland, with plenty of piano and clarinet, used during montage sequences; and a ferocious roar of trumpet-fueled action jazz, employed during car chases, shoot-outs and crime spree montages. Unfortunately, Morse uses the latter cue so frequently that it devolves into cliché, turning much of the third act into something out of the Keystone Kops.

No soundtrack album was produced.

Meanwhile, Across the Pond...

Frank Marker is the antithesis of a tough-talking, Chandler-esque private investigator. As developed by star Alfred Burke during the lengthy run of the ABC/Thames TV series *Public Eye*, he's an honorable white knight whose armor long ago faded to a disheveled gray, and whose clients, colleagues and police contacts rarely—if ever—accord him the proper respect. He's a lonely, middle-aged London bloke with no friends; he constantly struggles to make ends meet, but nonetheless does his best on behalf of those seeking help. His life slowly improves as the show progresses from its modest black-and-white origins—debuting January 23, 1965—to the full-color cases he tackled during the final 1975 season.

One thing remained constant, during the show's lengthy run: the relaxed and aptly melancholy jazz main theme by pianist, composer, conductor and bandleader Robert Sharples, concealed behind his occasional pseudonym of Robert Earley. It's a smoky, heartbreaking, muted trumpet melody backed by plucked bass and gentle cymbals, with lone piano notes comping softly in the background. The melody deftly conveys all the isolated, dispirited and beaten-down qualities that Burke portrays so well. The longer end credits arrangement reverses the instrumentation; the melody is taken on piano, with a trumpet comping in the background. The episodes themselves contain almost no music, except for brief echoes of the title theme, which accompany the between-act bumpers.

That beloved title theme eluded fans for decades, until Network's 2015 release of the compilation album *Themes for TV Drama: The Music of Robert Earley*.

Frank Marker spends a lot of time out in the world; the opposite is true of the detectives in Granada TV's *The Man in Room 17*. Jacques Futrelle's "Thinking Machine" short stories—which feature the analytical Augustus S.F.X. Van Dusen, most famously in "The Problem of Cell 13"—may have been on novelist/playwright Robin Chapman's mind, when he created this show. Much of the action takes place in Room 17 of the clandestine Department of Social Research, where former espionage agent-turned-criminologist Edwin G. Oldenshaw (Richard Vernon) and colleague Ian Dimmock (Michael Aldridge) tackle cases that have eluded police and Special Branch investigators. Oldenshaw and Dimmock never leave the room; they generally play Go while solving the case purely via deductive reasoning. This information is passed to plain-vanilla investigators doing the legwork in the outer world; glimpses of their progress—or lack thereof—are intercut with the theoretical brainstorming taking place in Room 17.

The show's catchy title theme came from English musician/composer Derek Hilton, a longtime Granada music director who—during an impressively prolific career—wrote well north of 200 TV themes. *Room 17*'s title cue is classic big band swing: It opens with rhythmic bass and bold brass statements, then segues to a 4/4 strut via unison horns. Fleeting organ riffs and frequent brass explosions power the theme to a dynamic conclusion. The longer end credits arrangement is slower and initially calmer, the horns kept to a low roar against more thoughtful percussion, until Hilton once again builds to a climactic burst of brass. Underscores are sparse—because of the show's live-to-film production—and confined primarily to atmospheric reeds, rumbling drums and staccato jazz stingers.

Hilton never recorded this theme for commercial release. Oldenshaw and Dimmock returned a year later in a sequel series—*The Fellows (Late of Room 17)*—about which, more later.

ITV's *Riviera Police* also was somewhat unusual, and decades ahead of its time, with a travelogue premise of four police detectives based in France's luxurious Cote d'Azor. The 13-episode series debuted August 2, and countless future American programs—most of them not very good—would use similar coastal settings as an excuse to focus mostly on women in skimpy bikinis. But although the coppers of *Riviera Police*—Supt. Adam Hunter (Geoffrey Frederick), Lt. Col. Constant Sorel (Frank Lieberman), Inspector Legrand (Brian Spink) and Supt. Bernie Johnson (Noel Trevarthan)—have nothing against admiring the female form, they dutifully concentrate on the investigative aspects of cases that take them to locations such as Monaco's Grand Prix or the Cannes Film Festival.

Producer/story editor Jordan Lawrence selected an existing Laurie Johnson tune as his show's title theme: "Latin Quarter," one of the interior movements from the composer's *Two Cities Suite*, available on the album of the same title. It's a rollicking melody that begins as the entire orchestra slides up several scales against a sassy rhythmic ostinato, at which point unison horns introduce the bouncy 5/5-2/5-2/4/4 melody. The style is full-blown big band swing, with a wicked flute solo at the bridge; the melody then repeats, climaxing with a furious four-note orchestral blast.

Almost all episodes are believed lost, although two of them—"Take It Sideways and Pray" and "Who Can Catch a Falling Star"—circulate via the Internet gray market.

Mention of Johnson brings us back to *The Avengers*. When the popular series returned in early October 1965, Patrick Macnee's John Steed had a new partner—Diana Rigg's Emma Peel—and a more specifically defined back-story; the show itself boasts an entirely new tone, along with a fresh jazz theme. Johnson's lusty, invigorating bursts of orchestral jazz perfectly suit the increasingly wild and sometimes science fiction-y challenges now facing Steed and Mrs. Peel. The show had become *fun*, and the same is true of Johnson's music. Aside from a kick-ass title theme that ranks as one of the decade's best on either side of the pond, he also supplied original underscores for every one of the 50 episodes that ran through November 1967.

Most people assume that Johnson created this title theme expressly for *The Avengers*. He actually modified an existing tune, "The Shake," which had debuted on his February 1965 album, *The Big New Sound Strikes Again*. "The Shake" pretty much *is* the new *Avengers* theme, although Johnson added an introductory drum roll and four-note brass statement, and also expanded the swing bridge. A staccato eight-note ostinato kicks off the lush orchestral melody as the show's title appears, followed by monochrome stills of Macnee and Rigg (filming still wasn't in color). Bold unison horns carry the melody to a triumphant climax, after which Johnson repeats the initial drum rolls and brass statements: all told, 45 seconds of pulse-quickening magic. The end credits version runs longer, allowing Johnson to include a more dynamic swing bridge.

The episodes—an increasingly wild blend of mod spy jinks and heightened reality, always addressed with proper British reserve by Macnee and Rigg—quickly became famous for their bizarre villains, crazed killers, mad scientists, deranged inventors and vengeful secretaries, all out to decimate Britain's upper-class movers and shakers. "All this presented me with each episode requiring its own special musical landscape and atmosphere," Johnson lamented.[16]

The prolific and inventive composer delivered an astonishing variety of jazz cues.

Patrick Macnee's John Steed and Diana Rigg's Emma Peel brought charm, sophistication and wit to the secret agent scene during two glorious years in the mid–1960s. The show became even more of an international pop culture sensation than it had been during Honor Blackman's previous run; *everybody* **stayed home to watch** *The Avengers* **(Photofest).**

Rolling drums and dramatic horns introduce a frantic action theme during the final fight sequence of "A Funny Thing Happened on the Way to the Station"; a slow brass march accompanies the students at a most unusual school for gentlemen's gentlemen, in "What the Butler Saw"; fast-paced "traveling music" anchors the road rally that sends Steed and Mrs. Peel roaring throughout the countryside, in search of "Dead Man's Treasure"; a droll 4/4 flute and horn cue suggests the back-and-forth sway of an elephant howdah, in

"Hidden Tiger." Every episode concludes with a droll little ballad—the melody traded between muted trumpet and keyboards—for the quirky tag scenes.

"Sometimes there would be as much as 30 minutes of music to be recorded and synchronized every week," Johnson added. "Over the whole series, I must have composed around 50 hours of music, in addition to the theme."[17]

The series came to the States on March 28, 1966. Worried that American viewers wouldn't understand it without some back-story, nervous ABC execs requested a new 30-second teaser to air prior to each episode's opening credits. Johnson supplies a rhythmic drum ostinato for this "chessboard opening," as a narrator introduces "agents extraordinary" John Steed ("top professional") and Emma Peel ("talented amateur"). When the next season shifted to color filming in January 1967, Johnson reused this vamp to kick off a fresh title credits sequence—as Emma shoots the cork off a champagne bottle held by Steed—that played on both sides of the pond.

Surprisingly, nothing approaching a soundtrack album appeared until 1982's *Original Television Scores: The Avengers*. With the advent of digital, Johnson began to include incidental *Avengers* cues on anthology albums such as *...With a Vengeance* (Sequel, 1997), *The Professional: The Best of Laurie Johnson* (Redial/PolyGram, 1998), *Cult TV Themes* (Castle Music, 2004) and *...You're Needed* (Él, 2007). The show finally got its own full-length soundtrack disc in 2007.

Moving to the big screen...

...John Barry was stumped.

Auric Goldfinger was a colorful villain; Russia was a familiar country. But what, precisely, was Thunderball? Within the context of this fourth James Bond outing, "Operation Thunderball" is the joint MI6/CIA task force assembled to recover the atomic bombs stolen by SPECTRE. But that didn't lend itself to lyrics, so Barry proposed an alternative that occurred to him during a trip to the Bahamas.

"On the plane out to Nassau, I picked up a newspaper," he recalled, "and *Goldfinger* was everywhere. The Bond thing was in full stride by then, and one article said that the Italians called Bond 'Mr. Kiss Kiss Bang Bang.' All I knew was that 'Thunderball' was the most horrendous title for a song, so I said to Cubby Broccoli, 'Let's use Mr. Kiss Kiss Bang Bang' as the title for the song instead. And he said, 'Yeah, go ahead.'"[18] With lyricist Leslie Bricusse at his side, Barry wrote a slinky jazz waltz that's as suave and smug as Bond himself. Both Dionne Warwick and Shirley Bassey recorded the song; Barry went to work and built much of the film's underscore from variations of the tune.

But at the last moment, American distributor United Artists insisted on a title theme that included the actual *title*. Forced back to the drawing board, Barry and new lyricist Don Black concocted a song that conceals its illogical lyrics beneath bombastic brass and Tom Jones' lusty vocal chops.

Thunderball was 1965's third most popular film in the United States, trailing only *The Sound of Music* and *Doctor Zhivago*. Barry's suspenseful action jazz played a major role in that success. His score for *Thunderball* is arguably one of his best, with cues built from four distinct themes—the title theme, "Mr. Kiss Kiss Bang Bang," "The James Bond Theme" and "007"—that weave in and out of each other, as the film proceeds. Musical high points include a furious, percussion-driven restatement of "The James Bond Theme"—the familiar four introductory notes resyncopated as an edgy statement repeatedly answered by a shrill blast of *wah-wah* brass—during the pre-credits' vicious, tautly choreographed *mano a mano* brawl; a thunderous 2/2 blast of percussion and brass, when 007 is nearly killed on a health clinic's spinal traction machine; and numerous deep-sea cues that evoke bits and bobs of "Mr. Kiss Kiss Bang Bang" and the swing bridge from "The James Bond Theme," along with a "floating" sensation created via vibes, alto flutes, harp and strings.

After the exciting climax, Bond and the nubile Domino (Claudine Auger) climb onto a large life raft; a cheeky hint of "The James Bond Theme" leads to a final blast of the title theme, as they get airlifted to safety in a *most* improbable manner.

Because of UA's last-minute waffling, no music from the film's final third made it onto the initial soundtrack album. The American LP is odd in another respect: The mono and stereo discs have different versions of the final instrumental arrangement of "Mr. Kiss Kiss Bang Bang." The "missing" portions of Barry's score remained unheard until 1992, when the digitized, double-disc *Best of James Bond 30th Anniversary Edition* included a 21-minute "Thunderball Suite" built from eight previously unreleased instrumental cues, along with both unused vocal versions of "Mr. Kiss Kiss Bang Bang." The title song was covered by Billy Strange (GNP Crescendo) and Jimmy Sedlar (Kapp). "Mr. Kiss Kiss Bang Bang" also garnered some attention, with vocal covers by Ann-Margret (RCA) and Buddy Greco (Columbia). The soundtrack album enjoyed a 27-week run on *Billboard's* Top LPs chart.

The escalating spy jazz craze also prompted several more Bondian compilations. Britain's Sounds Orchestral trio, which had covered Vince Guaraldi's "Cast Your Fate to the Wind" to impressive chart success, released *Impressions of James Bond* (aka *Sounds Orchestral Meets James Bond*) in late 1965 on the Pye label; Latin jazz percussionist Ray Barretto gave his inimitable spin to 10 themes on *Señor 007* (UA). The Roland Shaw Orchestra delivered the second in its 007 series, on London's *More Themes from James Bond Thrillers*; UA's *Music to Read James Bond By: Volume Two* followed in the summer of 1966. Count Basie got into the act that same year, on UA's *Basie Meets Bond*.

Bondmania had become as huge a cultural force as Beatlemania. The result—imitation being the sincerest form of flattery—was a gaggle of British spoofs, homages and outright rip-offs. *Licensed to Kill* was one of the first, introducing secret agent Charles Vine, played with tight-lipped irony by Tom Adams. The film is directed indifferently by Lindsay Shonteff, who also co-wrote the incomprehensible script. Vine is assigned to protect visiting Swedish scientist Henrik Jacobsen (Karel Stepanek), who has promised to share his invention of "Re-Grav"—which promises to "reverse the center of gravity"—with the British in exchange for £2 million. (Who said scientists are altruistic?) Multiple attempts are made on Jacobsen's life, by a bewildering assortment of thugs; Vine repeatedly saves the day via fine shooting with his wicked-looking handgun. The double- and triple-crosses are impossible to follow, and the plot expands to include an evil Russian doppelganger who looks just like our hero.

The film's cheap production values notwithstanding, it boasts a reasonably solid jazz score by Herbert Chappell (aka Bert or Bertram Chappell). He gives Vine's escapades plenty of rhythmic vigor, often with a bass- and guitar-driven main theme that frequently serves as a bridge between scenes. Solid action jazz accompanies the many traps that Vine and Jacobsen narrowly escape, including two car ambushes given a veneer of excitement by some aggressive trumpet and sax riffs. Much later, a bare-knuckle fight between Vine and a cross-dressing assassin (Paul Tann) is backed by vibrant jazz. Chappell goes all-out during this finale, augmenting the primary theme with a furious assault of horns, bongos and weird percussion effects.

Hollywood producer Joseph E. Levine imported the film for American release. That prompted a new Sammy Cahn/Jimmy Van Heusen title song, "The Second Best Secret

Agent in the Whole Wide World," performed with sassy enthusiasm by Sammy Davis Jr. The song also gave its name to the film's U.S. release title.

No soundtrack album was produced, but two score tracks were released in Japan, on a Seven Seas 45.

Despite its microscopic production values, washed-out film stock and a wooden supporting cast, Vine's debut was successful enough to warrant two sequels (discussed later).

The entertainment value is vastly superior in *The Liquidator*, based on the first of John Gardner's eight Boysie Oakes spy thrillers. The running gag is that Oakes only feigns being a tough mercenary type; he's actually a gutless sybarite horrified by the mere thought of violence. Scripter Peter Yeldham adapted the 1964 novel faithfully, and director Jack Cardiff delivers just the right blend of action, female pulchritude and tongue-in-cheek humor. It's a shame the anticipated series never came to fruition; it would have been a great ongoing role for the underappreciated Rod Taylor.

British Intelligence Col. Mostyn (Trevor Howard), grappling with a series of embarrassing security leaks, decides on a radical solution: He'll hire an assassin to quickly—and illegally—terminate (liquidate) all known moles, double agents and compromised department personnel. Remembering Boysie from their shared World War II service, Mostyn recruits him with the promise of a fat salary, lavish apartment, fancy car and ample wine, women and song ... without explaining what he'll be doing to earn this opulent lifestyle. By the time Boysie finds out, he's unwilling to abandon the posh goodies; he secretly hires an amiable freelance hit man (Eric Sykes, as Griffen) to carry out the liquidations. All goes well until Boysie is kidnapped by enemy agents, escapes and then is duped into what he believes will be a fake assassination attempt—for "training purposes"—on the Duke of Edinburgh.

The sizzling score came from Lalo Schifrin—his first big-screen spy flick—and he delivers plenty of action cues that evoke the energetic Bondian tone *without* sounding like John Barry.

"I was aware of the James Bond music," Schifrin acknowledged, much later, "but this was a

Some of composer Lalo Schifrin's best cues for *The Liquidator* are diegetic, such as the raucous, jazz/rock melody—punctuated by plenty of swinging percussion, electric guitar and a sweet trumpet solo—heard on the jukebox at the café where Rod Taylor's Boysie Oakes gets an offer he probably should have refused (courtesy Film Score Monthly).

satire on James Bond, so they let me do whatever I wanted to. I understood the movie, and I understood the satire, and I didn't want to use the Bond sound."[19]

Schifrin recruited some of London's top session players, and the result is swinging spy jazz shaded by Schifrin's bossa nova sensibilities. Not wanting to miss a Bondian beat, the film's producers secured Shirley Bassey—fresh from her knockout vocal for *Goldfinger*—to deliver an equally dynamic title theme for Boysie. The joke is that Schifrin's vigorous music, and Bassey's lusty performance, are at odds with Peter Callander's hilariously embroidered lyrics.

"[Bassey's] voice was the only connection to Bond," Schifrin laughed. "[The theme] was funny in a way, almost like a tango, and they all liked it."[20]

Once Mostyn gets Boysie's signature on various dotted lines, the latter is taken to his opulent bachelor pad: the first time we hear the bouncing Latin tune—"Boysie's Bossa," with a lovely vibes line—that becomes one of the film's signature themes. Later, after Boysie has been apprised of his lethal responsibilities—and has turned them over to Griffen—Schifrin contributes a droll, percussive tune for a hilarious montage, as the hired assassin calmly takes care of business. This cue climbs the octave and gets a bit faster, as each new victim is identified and dispatched. During an interlude at the French Rivera, Boysie wanders along the beach, eyeing all the babes; this montage gets some bounce from a flute-driven 3/4 cue ("Bikini Waltz") with a sexy bossa nova beat.

Schifrin reorchestrated, restructured and lengthened the primary themes for the soundtrack album.

Despite the mushrooming debuts of ersatz 007s, Bond co-producer Harry Saltzman opted for an entirely different approach while developing his new series; he wanted a serious secret agent akin to the thoughtful protagonists created by authors such as Graham Greene and John Le Carré. Saltzman settled on thriller novelist Len Deighton, who introduced an anonymous, working-class spy in 1962's *The Ipcress File*. Ah, but mainstream movie characters must have names, and—contrary to Deighton's preference—this reluctant spy now remains best known as Harry Palmer. Saltzman wisely surrounded himself with colleagues from the Bond franchise, including John Barry, production designer Ken Adam, editor Peter Hunt, and cinematographer Otto Heller. Palmer became Michael Caine's first starring role, following his breakout supporting performance in 1964's *Zulu*.

He plays Palmer as a saucy bloke who disdains authority and suffers through interdepartmental squabbling and a relentless barrage of bureaucratic forms. Things get more interesting when his boss, Col. Ross (Guy Doleman), loans him to Ministry of Defense colleague Major Dalby (Nigel Green), in order investigate the troubling string of top British scientists who've disappeared and/or abandoned their fields. Dalby suspects they may have been ransomed off to East German or Soviet enemies. Palmer's investigation proves *too* successful; he gets framed for the murder of a CIA agent, then kidnapped and—over the course of two weeks—subjected to insidious brainwashing. He escapes before the conditioning takes full effect and orchestrates a confrontation with Ross and Dalby: one of whom, he realizes, must be a traitor.

"With Bond, I concentrated on the action and adventure," Barry later explained, "whereas with *Ipcress* I built the score around the hero—or anti-hero—Harry Palmer."[21]

Barry took note of the fact that Palmer is a brooding, quiet individual who puts as much faith in intuition as the plodding minutia of research and surveillance. This demanded a thoughtful primary theme that sounds both melancholy and slightly ominous; such an atmospheric approach necessitated exotic instrumentation. Barry immediately thought of one of his favorite films, 1949's *The Third Man*. "It's the most extraordinary score ever," he enthused, "played on one instrument: the ultimate lesson in simplicity and character. *The Ipcress File* is my homage to *The Third Man*. I knew that was how I wanted to do it from the start, but obviously I wasn't going to use a zither."[22]

Barry thus became the first mainstream film composer to create an entire score around the sound produced by a cimbalom, a Central/Eastern European instrument akin to a hammered dulcimer. Its sound is both mysterious and lonely, even forlorn: characteristics that certainly epitomize Palmer. The instrument was played by Barry's good friend John Leach, who later also collaborated on the title theme for the TV series *The Persuaders*.

The primary theme for *The Ipcress File*, heard in whole or part throughout the film, opens with a gentle shimmering statement of five notes on vibes, answered by three descending bass notes on piano; an inquisitive flute introduces a 1-3-3 motif, while gently brushed cymbals establish a languid 4/4 beat. The cimbalom enters, trading riffs with the flute; the entire orchestra swells as the cimbalom takes over the melody, assisted after the first verse by gentle comping from a muted trumpet. The effect is hypnotic, as if anticipating something sinister and secretive. This theme debuts during the title credits, which appear over a wordless montage of Palmer's morning routine. In a particularly droll bit of editing, Barry allows a cimbalom note to fade into the interrupting *whirrrrr* of Harry's coffee grinder; the sound of the grinder then seems part of the melody, as the next flute note rises. Although this melody becomes ubiquitous as the story proceeds, Barry mixes things up a bit; when Harry catches the eye of Jean Courtney (Sue Lloyd), the sole woman working within his department, their wary romance eventually ignites against a slow, sultry trumpet combo cue.

Barry supplied some distinct, reorchestrated variations of the primary theme for the soundtrack LP: among them a silky combo waltz titled "Alone in Three-Quarter Time"; and the slow, laid-back and sexy "Alone Blues," which favors flute and piano, and includes a lazy trumpet solo. The theme subsequently was covered by numerous pop and jazz artists and became a staple on spy and lounge anthology albums.

Not *every* 1965 British thriller dealt with spies. Director J. Lee Thompson's *Return from the Ashes* is a dark three-hander: a psychological cat-and-mouse game based on French crime author Hubert Monteilhet's 1961 novel, *Le Retour des Cendres*. The story begins in pre–World War II Paris, when Stanislaus Pilgrin (Maximilian Schell), a shameless gigolo, meets medical professional Michele "Mischa" Wolf (Ingrid Thulin). She's enchanted by his free-spirited candor; he's interested only in her considerable wealth. They marry, but the union is brief; war breaks out, and—being Jewish—she's arrested and sent to a concentration camp. Years pass; the war ends. Pilgrin continues to live in their house, his bed now shared with Mischa's spoiled, sullen stepdaughter, Fabi (Samantha Eggar). But then Mischa returns, having survived her camp experience; this derails Pilgrin's plan to inherit her sizable estate. Greed, lust and betrayal lead to a murder plot and a suspenseful climax.

John Dankworth's primary theme is a slow, lyrical mambo with the melody's five-note motif traded between harpsichord, sax and strings: a delicate ballad that eventually becomes ironic, during later reprises, when juxtaposed against the contemptible behavior by Pilgrin and Fabi. Other jazz cues are diegetic: an unseen trio heard as Mischa and Pilgrin have drinks in a café, during their initial meeting; and several vibrant big band swing tunes played by an ensemble at a hotel bar, late in the story, when Pilgrin establishes an alibi by dancing with a compliant prostitute.

No soundtrack album was produced, although two cues were released on a 45 single, and later digitized on 2009's two-disc *Johnny Dankworth: Let's Slip Away—Film and TV 1960-1973*.

Claustrophobic paranoia is even stronger in director Roman Polanski's first English-language film, fueled by Catherine Deneuve's mesmerizing performance as a fragile, sexually insecure young woman who suffers from androphobia—a pathological fear of men—and literally loses her mind when left alone for 12 days. *Repulsion* is laced with brilliant Hitchcockian flourishes, from unsettling sound effects to the disorienting, ever-expanding landscape of the apartment in which Deneuve's Carol barricades herself, as her madness intensifies.

The film also features the first big-screen, solo-credited score by jazz drummer Chico Hamilton, although his effort scarcely can be regarded as "music." Nor does Polanski use much of it, preferring to enhance suspense through silence and disconcerting ambient sounds.

Hamilton delivers a slow, steady da-*bump*, da-*bump* of solo drums, over Maurice Binder's imaginative title sequence, as the credits slide across an extreme close-up of Carol's right eye. She's introduced at work, as a manicurist in a fancy beauty salon; Jimmy Woods contributes a doleful solo flute cue as she daydreams while attending to a client. The film's sole genuinely elegant theme ("Carol's Walk") is heard each time Carol strolls to and from work and the apartment that she shares with her sister, Helen (Yvonne Furneaux); it's a lovely, lyrical jazz ballad that blends flute, arranger Gabor Szabo's guitar and some gentle percussion. The rest of the score is defiantly unmusical: throbbing drums, sometimes laced with flute touches; Albert Stinson's nervous, bowed bass; and explosive "shock cues" of the sort found in horror movies.

Four of Hamilton's *Repulsion* cues were issued on a 1966 LP on the Italian CAM label. But that's misleading; two of those tracks—"Seduzione Al Buio" and "Repulsione Notturna"—aren't heard in the film, although it's possible Polanski chose not to use them. All four were digitized in 2008, along with a full-length, bonus track arrangement of "Carol's Walk," lifted from Hamilton's 1965 album, *Chic Chic Chico*.

Elsewhere in the World

Few films employed combo jazz as expansively as French director/scripter Raoul Lévy's *Je vous salue, mafia!*—released in the States as *Hail, Mafia*—which is as *noir*-drenched a crime thriller as anything Hollywood ever produced. The unsettling monochrome tableaux of New Wave cinematographer Raoul Coutard have much to do with that atmosphere; so does the wall-to-wall jazz score by clarinetist, tenor saxman and composer Hubert Rostaing, best known for his 1940s affiliation with Hot Club de France, and later as a member of Django Reinhardt's famed quintet.

The story, based on Pierre Lesou's 1964 novel of the same title, focuses on the manhunt for ex-pat American businessman Rudy Hamburg (Eddie Constantine); he has fled to the Bouches-du-Rhône region of Southern France, to avoid being called as a witness in a U.S. Senate investigation against the Mafia. New York–based Cosa Nostra bosses dispatch hit men Schaft (Henry Silva) and Phil (Jack Klugman) to kill him. The bulk of the film details the road trip Schaft and Phil take through France, as they close in on their prey; the unlikely partners establish a tenuous bond during matter-of-fact discussions about their vicious profession.

Rostaing performed with a small combo that features trumpet, keyboards, bass and drums; the players' identities are lost to time. There's a strong sense that the score was composed spontaneously, as the musicians watched the film, although many of the resulting cues are too cheerful; they don't fit the story's increasingly threatening tone. That said, the music would have stood alone quite well as a jazz album; alas, none was produced.

The film opens with a shriek of brass, which segues to slow, rhythmic drumming, when Rudy takes a late-night stroll along Parisian streets; he's backed by a melody (of sorts) on reeds, the 5/4 tempo set by drums and walking bass. A failed attempt on his life prompts an agitated trumpet solo; the film's title appears as fast-paced action jazz accompanies Rudy's panicked drive out of a parking garage. Once Phil and Schaft arrive in France, Rostaing backs their movements with all manner of vibrant jazz cues, some at odds with Schaft's vicious behavior. In one of Lévy's odder tableaux, the killers stop for gas at a station adjacent to some sort of dance club; tasty combo jazz emanates from the place, and couples dance outside. A muted trumpet solo keeps time as the dancers sway in and out of shadows that are caught superbly by Coutard's chiaroscuro cinematography. Uptempo sax and piano subsequently spot a tourism-style travel montage, when Phil and Schaft make the long drive to Marseille.

Double-time cymbals ramp down to a languid clarinet and muted trumpet cue, as the two assassins navigate the final few miles between them and Rudy. A single drum repeats a hypnotic 4-beat against agitated trumpet riffs, while—just up ahead, awaiting the inevitable—Rudy cleans his gun and prepares for unwanted visitors. In the aftermath, a solo flute delivers a forlorn dirge, as only one man is left standing.

Surprise twists also abound in French novelist Sébastien Japrisot's *Compartiment Tueurs*. Its big-screen adaptation—titled *The Sleeping Car Murders* in the States—marked an impressive directorial debut by Greek filmmaker Costa-Gavras. The film is equal parts character drama and police procedural, with a rumpled police detective—Yves Montand's Inspector "Grazzi" Grazziani—scrambling to stay ahead of an unseen assassin who is determined to kill all the witnesses to an earlier murder. The mounting tension is accelerated by composer Michel Magne's twitchy jazz cues, often backed by unsettling, surf rock-style guitars.

The story begins as a passenger train rockets into the Marseille station; travelers settle into five of the six berths in a sleeping compartment, for the overnight run to Paris. The unoccupied upper berth allows Bambi (Catherine Allégret) to sneak in a cute stowaway, Daniel (Jacques Perrin). He quietly slips off the train when it arrives early the next morning; after everybody else departs, he returns to the compartment to retrieve his suitcase, and discovers that the woman in one berth has been murdered. The subsequent investigation is assigned to Grazzi and his assistant, Jean-Lou Gabert (Claude Mann); they must identify the compartment's other occupants. Costa-Gavras eschews music during all the scenes involving police work, which grants that portion of the film the atmosphere of a methodical documentary. The case blossoms into a deadly race, as most of the compartment's other passengers are systematically murdered, one by one.

Elsewhere, Bambi and Daniel's budding courtship unfolds against a slow, sweetly romantic version of Magne's main theme. The police aren't even aware of Daniel's existence until the suspenseful finale, when Grazzi and the police dash across the city in an effort to rescue both young people. Magne supplies two groovy source cues during Daniel's anxious plight in a restaurant phone booth: a guitar-driven blast of midtempo surf rock that would have been right at home on a California beach; and a bluesy jazz swinger in slow 4/4, with agitated organ riffs comping behind an unhurried guitar melody. Once the killer's identity is revealed, a furious pursuit through Paris' late-night streets is choreographed to an even faster reprise of the suspenseful main theme.

The title theme and three of Magne's lengthier cues were issued on a vinyl EP, and eventually digitized in 2004.

At first blush, French director Pierre Granier-Deferre's *La Métamorphose des Cloportes* also feels like classic *noir*; it opens with a brazen daytime heist, during a sequence given urgency by Nicolas Hayer's moody black-and-white cinematography. But the subsequent meeting between twitchy, low-level crooks Edmond (Charles Aznavour), Rouquemoute (Georges Géret) and Arthur (Maurice Biraud) is laden with bluster and comic dialog, at which point we realize that this adaptation of Alphonse Boudard's debut 1962 novel blends farce with unexpected flashes of violence.

The film is best known—at least in music circles—as the only big-screen feature scored by jazz organist Jimmy Smith, who's joined on his beloved Hammond B3 by Quentin Warren (guitar) and Billy Hart (drums). The entire score was improvised during a one-night spotting session at Paris' Studio Europa-Sonor.[23] The result is uneven and not entirely successful, mostly because Grainer-Deferre employs the cues to excess; he also extracts bits and pieces from the trio's longer takes. But the director doesn't deserve sole blame. Smith is guilty of repetition and an overreliance on random, dissonant passages: perhaps enticing to those who adore free jazz, but often distracting and unsatisfying as employed within the film.

The story begins as Edmond, Rouquemoute and Arthur scheme to burglarize a safe believed to contain a fortune in francs; they persuade the far more sophisticated Alphonse (Lino Ventura)—a career criminal who specializes in stolen paintings—to bankroll their endeavor. The effort goes awry; Alphonse is arrested and jailed for five years. Seething with fury after being abandoned by these three *cloportes* (woodlouses), Alphonse seeks revenge upon his release. He further discovers that the others have stolen his stash of paintings, which during his incarceration have become quite valuable. He gradually tracks down Edmond and the others, but despite careful planning, Alphonse is duped by a clever plot twist. He winds up jailed again, this time for 20 years ... and determined, more than ever, to somehow even the score for this *new* betrayal.

The title credits burst onto the screen against a droll improvisational cue, as Smith noodles on his Hammond B3 against Hart's lively drumming; both are backed by a repeating 2-2 motif on Warren's guitar. This segues to an uptempo swinger that introduces the three conspirators. After the heist goes south and Alphonse later is released from prison, he wanders down a street and stops, stunned, when he sees one of his (stolen) paintings hanging in a gallery window. When he enters the establishment, Smith supplies a tasty romantic cue—with lush B3 chords—that introduces gallery supervisor Catherine (Irina Dernick), whose glance holds considerable promise. Their flirty banter takes place against another soft organ melody, which segues into Smith's official "Love Theme" (although it sounds more like a church hymn than a prelude to romance). The film's final surprise twist unfolds against a long, edgy blend of nervous drumming and sustained organ notes, the latter building mild suspense as they climb the scale.

The initial soundtrack album was digitized in 2002, on a compilation disc that includes Smith's covers of title themes from *Goldfinger*, *Mission: Impossible* and other crime/action films.

In neighboring Italy, 007-obsessed filmmakers busily churned out an endless stream of cheap, hastily mounted spy flicks, most of them quite embarrassing. Case in point: *Agente X1–7 Operazione Oceano*. Composer Piero Umiliani shamelessly mimics John Barry during this laughably inept Eurospy entry, with a primary cue that relies heavily on a throbbing guitar ostinato that sounds just like Vic Flick's rhythm line in "The James Bond Theme." And because director Tanio Boccia repeatedly employs variations of this brass-heavy melody during action sequences, familiarity definitely breeds contempt.

The film doesn't have much else to offer. American agent George Collins (Lang Jeffries) is assigned to protect a scientist—Rafael Bardem, as Professor Calvert—who has developed a means to affect the world's oceans. Various bad guys wish to control this process; they kidnap Calvert and threaten his attractive daughter (Eleanora Bianchi), frequently right under Collins' nose. He's a remarkably sloppy agent, forever getting tricked, drugged or attacked by slinky babes ... each of whom subsequently melts in his arms, after a few seductive phrases. Collins eventually rescues Calvert from a castle stronghold, after which the story takes a *truly* bizarre turn.

The film opens with a brass-heavy power ballad ("Danger's Waiting"), sung very much in the Shirley Bassey style. Collins is introduced as a dozen beach babes applaud his clumsy water-skiing technique; Umiliani supplies a cheerful bit of guitar-driven bossa nova for this eye-rolling sequence. The Barry-esque cue debuts thereafter, when Collins is ambushed by a gaggle of thugs. Umiliani's best cues are source music: notably a terrific unseen quartet—vibes, piano, bass and drums—performing in a hotel bar, when Collins spots a likely *femme fatale*. A bit later, a nightclub combo delivers several tasty bossa nova numbers, while he watches a feather fan dance, and otherwise does nothing of consequence. (This lackluster flick features plenty of "nothing of consequence.")

A digitized version of Umiliani's score finally debuted in 2013; it's vastly superior to the film.

Agente X1–7 Operazione Oceano is mostly dull and uninspired; writer/director Marco Vicario's *7 uomini d'oro* (*Seven Golden Men*) is jaw-droppingly silly: a gleeful riff on *Rififi* that boasts "special" effects which hearken back to the era of wire-supported spaceships in 1940s Hollywood serials. The bonkers plot opens as a criminal mastermind—Albert, mostly known as The Professor (Philippe Leroy)—and his crew agree to an assignment on behalf of international authorities: to "kidnap" the Castro-like leader of a Cuban-esque island nation, to gain information about missiles being supplied by Russians. Armed with an improbable selection of sci-fi gadgets, The Professor oversees a flawless mission undertaken by his diverse minions ... although the caper is nearly blown by the unpredictable behavior of his sexpot girlfriend, Giorgia (Rossana Podestà), whose matching eyes and hair change color "when she loves somebody."

Inane as the film is—it can be appreciated only as a live-action comic book—Armando Trovajoli's jazz-oriented score is an occasional treat. He relies on two primary cues, both repeated in numerous arrangements: a wildly swinging title theme with a dynamic unison brass melody against vibrant percussion; and a romantic ballad heard every time Podestà is on screen. This melody—whistled, taken by organ, or in a bossa nova mode—becomes more sensuous as she slithers through a series of increasingly revealing outfits.

Trovajoli's rather redundant soundtrack LP was reissued digitally in 1992.

Mercifully, director Luciano Martino's *Le spie uccidono a Beirut* (*Our Man in Beirut*, *The Spy Killers*, *Secret Agent Fireball*) is a cut above the previous two, because Ernesto Gastaldi's reasonably comprehensible script is well-grounded in genre spycraft. Carlo Savina's vibrant jazz/pop score is a nice bonus, particularly since Martino understands how to employ the music for proper dramatic impact (a weakness of many Eurospy efforts, where the application of score cues often feels random).

American actor Richard Harrison is solid as CIA Agent X-117 Bart Fleming (or Agent 077 Bob Fleming, depending on how the print is dubbed). He's assigned to recover Russian H-bomb details, which a few scientists have stolen and concealed on microfilm; the scientists are systematically killed, as Fleming races against Soviet agents desiring the same prize. Our hero is outfitted with all manner of improbable gadgets—a blowtorch pen, aspirin tablets containing microtransmitters that can be tracked by a wristwatch receiver—and he's frequently distracted by one slain scientist's daughter, Liz (Dominique Boschero). The caper builds to a surprisingly effective climax, when Fleming "borrows" a helicopter to pursue Liz and the microfilm, snatched by baddies attempting to escape in a motorboat.

Savina's score hovers between saucy action jazz and sinister, atmospheric splashes of percussion, solo reeds and harpsichord; one of the latter cues is heard when the first scientist is dispatched by a tiny tobacco pipe dart gun brandished by the slimy Yuri (Luciano Pigozzi). The credits unspool against a deliciously swinging, brass-heavy main theme backed by slick guitar comping and a way-cool rhythm section: a tune with more than a passing resemblance to Irving Szathmary's title theme for TV's *Get Smart* (a potentially suspicious coincidence, since this movie's release preceded that show's debut by half a year). As the story proceeds, Liz is showcased by several arrangements of a sexy romantic melody alternately played by sax and muted trumpet. Captivating diegetic cues include an unseen flute/brass quintet playing poolside at a hotel where Fleming briefly stays. Savina returns to a propulsive arrangement of the main theme during the climactic helicopter/boat chase, as Fleming desperately tries to save Liz from the clutches of Yuri and a nasty *femme fatale* (Wandisa Guida).

To the chagrin of spy jazz fans, the swinging soundtrack LP quickly went out of print. Hopes for CD release remain unfulfilled, but the CAM label did make the album available as a digital download in August 2008.

10

Mission Blues: 1966

Talk about an embarrassment of riches!
Never again would a single year deliver so much bounty.

The Small Screen

Pop-culture status is fleeting; the public is fickle. *The Man from U.N.C.L.E.* barely had time to enjoy name-brand visibility when a new hero swooped into town, with tongue firmly in cheek. ABC's *Batman* was a hit from its debut on January 12, thanks to exaggerated camp sensibilities; loopy camera angles and imaginative, full-color sets; the absurdly stoic performances from Adam West (Bruce Wayne/Batman) and Burt Ward (Dick Grayson/Robin); and—in no small part—Neal Hefti's energetic jazz theme (with or without its silly lyrics).

"That came very hard to me," Hefti admitted, decades later. "It took me a couple of months to write. I had seen some footage, and I knew how outrageous it had to be. So I needed to write a piece of music that was equally so. Well, when I first took the theme in to demonstrate it for Lionel Newman and the series producer at Twentieth Century–Fox, I had to sing it and play it on the piano. Well, I'm no singer, and I'm no pianist. But I had Lionel and the producer, Bill Dozier, listening to me. My first thought was that they were going to throw me out, very quickly, but as I was going through it, I heard them both reacting with statements like, 'Oh, that's kicky. That will be good in the car chase.' My father, (a salesman) once told me, 'If they say okay, get out of there before they change their mind.' When I saw Bill smiling, then I knew we had it."[1]

That title theme opens with a strident brass fanfare, as animated versions of the Caped Crusader and Boy Wonder race toward the viewer; a pulsating rhythm section kicks in with bass guitar and aggressive drumming, while the heroes deck a few villains. A mixed chorus of four tenors and four sopranos sings "*Bat-man*" in harmony with a trumpet line, when the title appears. The same few bars essentially repeat over and over, with occasional dissonant brass stingers augmenting *Whap! Biff! Ooof!* word balloons when additional baddies get thrashed: roughly 45 seconds of camp craziness, set to a vigorous jazz beat.

Unfortunately, Hefti wasn't able to come along for the subsequent bat-ride. Nelson Riddle stepped in to score 93 of what became 120 episodes during a wild three-season run. He set the show's tone, establishing numerous secondary themes and character cues, such as a slinky, midtempo sax and muted trumpet cue for Catwoman. (Nelson Riddle composing a theme for The Riddler. Could anything be more perfect?) Hefti's two-bar ostinato became a signature cue for the Batmobile, particularly when Batman and Robin roar out of the Batcave en route to foiling some nefarious plot (or getting caught in the preposterous weekly death trap). The music always feels "fast," which adds to the show's feverish momentum.

Riddle saves the best for fight scenes, all of which are choreographed with the frantic flamboyance of a Broadway musical. They're staged to fast-paced swing cues highlighted by occasional brass/woodwind glissandos timed to accompany the animated *Pow!/ Thud!* "sound effects" whenever our heroes smack someone in the kisser (or get smacked in return).

Riddle expanded many of these themes when the series generated a big-screen companion, released in the summer of 1966. With all four core villains in attendance, he had plenty of fun with *Batman: The Movie*, which feels like a TV three-parter. Musical high points include a slow, breezy ballad written for Bruce's romantic encounters with Miss Kitka (actually the Catwoman); a hilarious, brass-heavy suspense cue that spots Batman's frantic effort to dispose of a bomb before it goes off; and the uptempo swing numbers for numerous melees, particularly the dog-nuts final battle atop the Penguin's tricked-up submarine.

Hefti added an instrumental countermelody—guitar, organ and brass—when he recorded a full-length version of his title theme for a 45 single; despite the show's popularity, the disc never charted. He followed that with the LPs *Batman Theme and 11 Hefti Bat Songs* and *Hefti in Gotham City*. All the other songs are uptempo jazz/surf rock originals "suggested by" the series, but never used in the show. Riddle and his orchestra get top billing on *Batman (Exclusive Original Television Soundtrack Album)*, although the music cues are interrupted by plenty of dialogue excerpts.

Hefti's catchy theme inspired numerous covers during the first two months of 1966 alone: Al Caiola (UA); the Ronnie Kole Trio (White Cliffs); The Marketts (Warner Bros.); The Gallants (Capitol); Link Wray and The Raymen (Swan); the Peter De Angelis Orchestra and Chorus (ABC-Paramount); and quite a few others.

ABC wasn't about to limit its schedule to a single crime-fighting duo. When *The Green Hornet* debuted on September 9, everybody viewed it as a companion to *Batman*: same production team, same wildly colorful sets, same richly melodramatic narrator (executive producer William Dozier). These days, however, *The Green Hornet* is revered as the TV series that introduced American audiences to martial arts superstar Bruce Lee, cast as Kato: best friend, chauffeur and adept crime-fighting sidekick to Van Williams' domino-masked Green Hornet, whose civilian identity is *Daily Sentinel* publisher Britt Reid. *The Green Hornet* was treated a bit more seriously, without the high-camp tone of its companion show.

That didn't stop composer Billy May from filling every episode with wall-to-wall big band jazz themes: everything from seductive romantic ballads to brass-laden action cues. The show's title theme—May's jazzed-up arrangement of Nikolai Rimsky-Korsakov's "Flight of the Bumblebee"—immediately became iconic, thanks to New Orleans superstar Al Hirt's breathlessly aggressive trumpet solo. May frequently references the title theme throughout his underscores, notably when the Green Hornet and Kato roar out of their secret headquarters in a gimmick-laden sedan dubbed the Black Beauty. Each episode boasts fully developed jazz themes, such as "Horneted House," a fast-paced 4/4 blast of drums and brass that includes a terrific piano solo; and "Casey," a tasty vibes and horn ballad that alternates between 3/4 and 5/4 time—with a standard-time bridge—that was written for Lenore "Casey" Case (Wende Wagner), Reid's secretary.

Covers of the title theme came from The Ventures (Dolton), guitarist Buddy Merrill (Accent) and the drolly named B. Bumble and The Stingers (Mercury). Nothing touched

Hirt's original. (Despite its title and cover photo, Hirt's *The Horn Meets the Hornet* isn't a soundtrack album, but a compilation of various TV themes.)

The characters were revived for a 2011 big-screen comedy that bastardized their honorable tradition and deserves no further mention here.

Unfortunately, *Batman* had a lot to answer for. Embracing that show's camp tone hastened the demise of *The Man from U.N.C.L.E.*, and NBC's September debut of the even sillier *Girl from U.N.C.L.E.* was no less than ill-advised overkill. What could have been a rare 1960s example of gender emancipation, along the lines of *Honey West*, instead turned the supposedly smart and resourceful April Dancer (Stefanie Powers) into an embarrassment. She got stuck with—and frequently was humiliated by—joke villains played by comedians such as Stan Freberg, Shelley Berman and Dom DeLuise. Along with Boris Karloff. In drag. Although Powers deserves credit for having anchored the first hour-long American TV show starring a woman, it's at best a dubious honor.

The scoring assignments were shared by Dave Grusin and Richard Shores, and both served two masters with impressive skill. Their music is appropriately frivolous, as suits the show's tone; at the same time, they follow the *Man from U.N.C.L.E.* tradition of fully developed jazz themes, rather than relying on choppy action cues. Their music is far superior to the show for which it was written.

Grusin deserves most of the credit. His first assignment was to provide yet another fresh arrangement of Jerry Goldsmith's iconic *Man from U.N.C.L.E.* theme, for this companion show's title sequence; Grusin responded with an electrifying 9/8 chart that presents the melody in brass against bongos and harpsichord counterpoint. He also scored three of the first four episodes, establishing many of the secondary themes that would be tracked into subsequent adventures. He opens "The Dog-Gone Affair" with a hip-swaying big band sizzler and adds a second swing theme for an assemblage of Thrush agents. "The Mother Muffin Affair" features two cookin' action jazz themes: the first fueled by brass and harpsichord, the second with a vibrant flute melody against sizzling percussion and harpsichord counterpoint. Shores' swinging "traveling music," which opens "The Prisoner of Zalamar Affair," became another of the series' signature cues; the same is true of the suspenseful blend of percussion and brass in that episode's "stealth cue."

Unfortunately, neither Grusin nor Shores was involved with the soundtrack album; the project was given to arranger/producer Teddy Randazzo, who delivered appropriately swinging big band arrangements of Goldsmith's familiar title theme, along with numerous underscore themes by Grusin and Shores. Unfortunately, several tracks are compromised by irritating female vocalese. When the album was digitized in 2008, Randazzo's sole cover credit was replaced—much more appropriately—by shared credit with Grusin and Goldsmith.

Batman, the Green Hornet and various U.N.C.L.E. agents were media darlings all year, but Burt Reynolds was struggling to be noticed when he made his television starring debut in ABC's *Hawk*, as a hard-charging New York City detective assigned to the district attorney's office. Aside from confronting the usual roster of killers, psychopaths, arsonists, embezzlers and dope dealers, Hawk's full-blooded Iroquois heritage prompts constant discrimination and racism, both from department colleagues and random folks encountered on the streets. The scoring assignment went to Kenyon Hopkins, whose funkified title theme is a vibrant slice of street jazz. A drum roll kicks off a rhythmic *ba*-bum, *ba*-bum, ba-*BUM* that climbs the scale against cool sax counterpoint, as a tight close-up shows Reynolds driving the city's late-night streets. Hopkins expands the sax/brass duel during the longer end credits arrangement.

The series features equally ambitious jazz underscores, all but two of them from Hopkins. The pilot episode—"Do Not Mutilate or Spindle"—concludes with a lengthy inner city foot chase between a religious lunatic (Gene Hackman) and the terrified woman he's determined to "punish" (fatally); the tense, 10-minute sequence allows Hopkins to deliver a terrific mini-symphony of exciting brass- and woodwind-fueled action jazz. Shorty Rogers contributes an equally terrific jazz score for "Death Comes Full Circle," which finds Hawk trying to nail a hit-and-run driver for murder; the story concludes as Reynolds—always eager to do his own stunts—bursts through a door to chase down the killer, against a similarly lengthy, high-octane action jazz cue.

The show survived only 17 episodes, and no soundtrack emerged.

Cop shows were prevalent by the mid–1960s, and none could have gotten more violent than *The Felony Squad*, where bad guys frequently met their end in a lethal hail of bullets. The series is another entry in the veteran cop/rookie partner subgenre, with Sgt. Sam Stone (Howard Duff) doing his best to bring Det. Jim Briggs (Dennis Cole) up to speed. Both men regard desk Sgt. Dan Briggs (Ben Alexander), Jim's father, as a guiding influence. The action takes place in a deliberately unidentified American metropolis; creator Richard Murphy clearly wanted to demonstrate that police work is far more dangerous than what had been depicted in most shows, while also acknowledging the rising youth movement that was adding civic unrest to a cop's challenges.

Pete Rugolo supplied both a title theme and a library of cues for the bulk of the series' 73 episodes. The arresting 50-second theme demands attention from its initial electric guitar ostinato, heard as a helicopter camera pans a late-night metropolis. Superimposed title cards tell us "The place: a city," as unison horns introduce the primary melody; still shots of the stars appear, as we learn "The time: now." The melody builds to a crescendo against a swing countermelody, and we get the final message: "The story of…. The Felony Squad." Unison horns repeat the signature melody as the cast is introduced, and then the entire ensemble builds to a vibrant finale.

Unfortunately, the title theme's jazz stylings didn't migrate to the episode underscores. Most of Rugolo's cues rely on suspenseful orchestral strings and reeds, ascending brass riffs, and descending brass runs. The show's fast-paced half-hour format didn't permit montages that would have allowed cues to expand into actual melodies, which explains the absence of a soundtrack album.

Not all of this TV season's action was restricted to modern times; CBS' World War II-era *Jericho* blends spycraft with period espionage. The stories, set in war-torn Europe, concern the activities of a three-man "impossible missions" squad: American Capt. Franklin Sheppard (Don Francks), an explosives expert; Free French Lt. Jean-Gaston André (Marino Masé), a weapons specialist; and British Royal Navy Lt. Nicholas Gage (John Leyton), a former circus performer handy in situations that require physical dexterity and prowess. Their adventures involve clandestine activities behind enemy lines: sabotaging a Nazi submarine base; destroying a German radar installation; stealing military plans; and—in one memorable case—smuggling an entire symphony orchestra out of occupied Paris.

Lalo Schifrin was hired to score the pilot episode, but executive producer Norman Felton didn't like the result.[2] His second choice was Jerry Goldsmith, who wrote a slick title theme in waltz time: an action-oriented brass melody against suspenseful percussion, with a woodwind countermelody that suggests the show's lighter elements. Goldsmith's sole episode underscore lacks jazz, but Mort Stevens made up for that with "Dutch and Go"; it features several brass-heavy swing cues, a couple of which sound very much like what he'd

10. Mission Blues: 1966

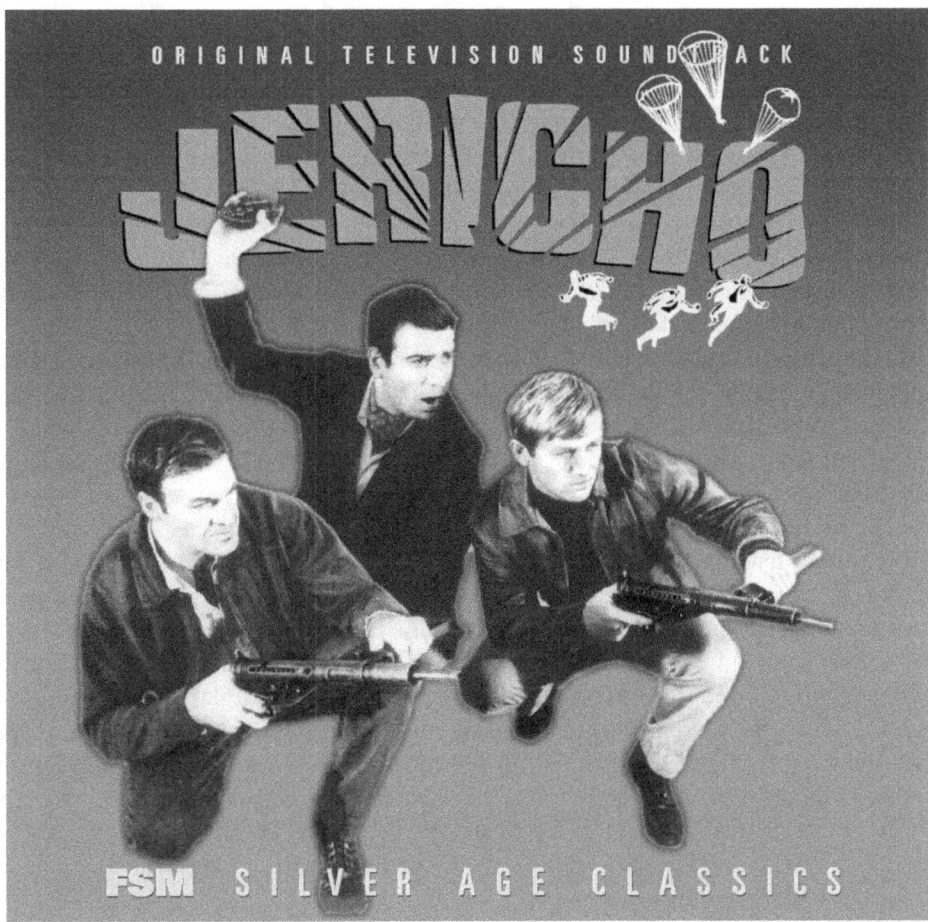

Although Lalo Schifrin's proposed title theme for *Jericho* was rejected, he successfully delivered a heavily percussive underscore for the episode "Upbeat and Underground," which includes a tense cue that clearly anticipates "The Plot," soon to become the secondary signature theme in *Mission: Impossible* (courtesy Film Score Monthly).

later write for *Hawaii Five-O*. Richard Shores' efforts for "Four O'Clock Bomb to London" also are noteworthy, with a blend of cool swing cues and fast-paced action jazz.

The show failed to find an audience and vanished after 16 episodes. Half a century later, a soundtrack album paired suites from 10 *Jericho* episodes—alongside Schifrin's rejected title theme—with John(ny) Williams' score for the failed TV pilot *The Ghostbreaker*.

The year 1966 was staggeringly busy for Schifrin; he delivered scores for five feature films, five TV documentaries, one TV movie and isolated episodes of *Jericho* and two other TV shows, along with title themes and multiple underscores for three *more* TV shows. Ironically, the first of the latter also is set during World War II.

Well-plotted action and nail-biting suspense fuel *Blue Light*, an espionage series that lasted only 17 episodes on ABC. Robert Goulet is persuasive as American journalist David March, planted early as one of 18 "sleeper agents" inside Germany, before the Nazis began their advance across Europe. Only a few upper-echelon American officials know of March's risky assignment; everybody else believes that he has betrayed his country. Unfortunately, the Nazis learned about this operation and killed the other 17 sleepers; only March remains.

His precarious position leaves him vulnerable both to Allied operatives who view him as a traitor and Gestapo investigators determined to expose him: all while he attempts to infiltrate German weapons bases, delay Hitler's planned invasion of England, and other clandestine missions designed to help the Allies.

The show's intensity gave Schifrin ample opportunities for underscore action cues, many of which anticipate the sizzling swing he'd soon bring to *Mission: Impossible* and *Mannix*. Schifrin also composed the title theme: a taut, military-style march powered by a bold 5-8 brass motif. He scored the pilot episode and the bulk of those that followed; the remainder went to Joseph Mullendore, Dave Grusin and Pete Rugolo. Everybody's approach is the same: propulsive jazz cues that reflect the show's fast-paced suspense.

The first four episodes were stitched together and released theatrically as *I Deal in Danger*, four months after the show went off the air. Schifrin expanded his title theme, giving it a more ominous touch and adding a percussion element that again anticipates "The Plot." Unfortunately, none of the music for *Blue Light* exists outside of its television (and big screen) origins.

Schifrin's next assignment was NBC's superlative *T.H.E. Cat*, an undersung, quasi-detective series that deserves resurrection both for its entertainment value, and for its music. It's one of Schifrin's all-time best TV assignments. *T.H.E. Cat* screams for a prestige album, but—thus far—none of the music exists outside of its television origins.

The show is styled very strongly in the *Peter Gunn* mold. Thomas Hewitt Edward Cat (Robert Loggia) is a onetime circus aerialist and former cat burglar turned professional bodyguard. He never carries weapons, relying instead on physical prowess and quick reflexes to take out bad guys determined to kill his clients. When not working, Cat hangs out in the Casa del Gato nightclub, where he spends many enjoyable hours chatting with owner and best friend Pepe (Robert Carricart), while various combos perform piano- and guitar-driven bossa nova tunes from the stage (Schifrin sometimes is visible as the pianist). The bands also back visiting singers.

Schifrin's saucy title theme, the melody shared by jazz flute and brass, has the swinging, swaggering insolence of a four-legged feline; it plays against gently animated title credits that convey the title character's athletic grace. This theme is referenced throughout Cat's adventures, often as the foundation of lengthy swing cues that accompany otherwise silent, late-night prowling montages. Every episode is laden with cool jazz: both as source performances at Casa del Gato, and as non-diegetic cues during Cat's suspenseful investigative activities and athletic fight scenes. Schifrin favors flutes, tense piano runs and bold brass cues for the latter, all of which are performed in deliciously swinging arrangements. The music is terrific: the best TV jazz showcase since *Peter Gunn* and *Johnny Staccato*.

It's therefore bewildering that Schifrin never recorded *any* of this series' music. (He might have worried that folks would confuse this title theme with his earlier composition, "The Cat," which is an entirely different tune.) Even the show is hard to find; it hasn't been issued on home video, and only a few random episodes are available via the Internet. (More's the pity.)

As for Schifrin's third and final 1966 series assignment…

Three pieces of film and TV espionage music evoke instant recognition from listeners of all ages, in great part because each has been ubiquitous for half a century: "The James Bond Theme," "The Pink Panther Theme" and Schifrin's "Mission: Impossible Theme." The latter arguably is the most famous TV espionage theme of all time, attached to the best espionage *show* of all time. Listeners hearing that 50-second tune for the first time, on September 17, 1966, *knew* they were in for something special.

Creator/producer/writer Bruce Geller concocted a format that defied television convention, by making his continuing characters beholden to a rigorously maintained *modus operandi*, rather than the other way around. We never knew anything about Daniel Briggs (Steven Hill), James Phelps (Peter Graves), Rollin Hand (Martin Landau), Cinnamon Carter (Barbara Bain), Barney Collier (Greg Morris) or Willie Armitage (Peter Lupus), beyond the fact that they're resourceful experts in various aspects of spy craft. All that matters is the way in which they operate, as a team, to deconstruct and then execute an "impossible mission." They do so with style, verve, cunning and ingenious creativity: and with added momentum provided by the dynamic music.

Schifrin immediately understood the formula-over-personality inversion after viewing the pilot episode, at which point he resisted Geller's suggestion to compose unique themes for each character. "I said I thought that would be wrong," Schifrin recalled. "There are so many [characters], it would be confusing. What we should do is have one theme, like a march, suspense, intrigue, tension ... it's like a paramilitary operation. What we're playing is the *mission*, no matter what the different members are doing."[3]

Applying this suggestion led Schifrin to develop what became the show's *secondary* theme, as he set about scoring the pilot: a "working the problem" cue anchored by stuttering snare drums and powered by a taut, pensive melody shared by muted brass and bottom-end strings. Brief snare drums stingers are ubiquitous as linking cues for sequences involving planning, prepping and ultimate execution; the music bridges scenes and draws viewers more intensely into the action. And because much of the action takes place as wordless montage—dialogue customarily is sparse and clipped—music's role as the show's "voice" is even more crucial. "['The Plot'] has the sense of a march, but it is a march with suspense," Schifrin explained. "It was easy; it came fast."[4] (No surprise, since he found a home for a cue that he'd written for two earlier failed series.)

Although Schifrin now had a strong sense of what the underscore needed to accomplish, the show still lacked a title theme. It had to be "very dynamic music that promised adventure, action and danger," Schifrin noted.[5] "In television, in those days, people were in the kitchen, having a soft drink. Then all of a sudden, in the living room, the TV set is playing the theme over a new show. And [it would make people think] 'Oh, I have to go and see this.' It's like a logo."[6]

All ears were drawn to a cue that he wrote for the pilot episode's triumphant finale, when—the mission complete—the team escapes in the nick of time, amid relieved grins and adrenaline afterburn. It's an intense 5/4 theme dominated by Schifrin's signature bongos and flutes; urgency is supplied by *duhn ... duhn.... DAH-dum* percussion, while flutes develop the melody from a trio of descending three-note phrases, followed by an ascending two-note phrase.

"5/4 is an unpredictable rhythm." Schifrin pointed out, years later. "It doesn't telegraph the next beat."[7]

Geller pounced on this cue. "When the main title of *Mission: Impossible* was made," he later explained, "it was built around the music, not scored afterwards. Many times since then whole sequences of film have been handled the same way: the music dictating the editing. Lalo Schifrin is the sixth member of the Impossible Missions Force. His face may not be visible among [the] dossiers, but you can hear him every week, holding together by main strength and melody an intricate, cross-cut tale of tension."[8]

The resulting title sequence is as iconic as the music. The cue opens with a trill of unison flutes and percussion elements, as a match lights a horizontal fuse that bisects the screen; the rhythmic beat kicks in as the fuse repeatedly runs from left to right against fleeting clips from the episode to follow (much the way Robert Culp peers at a similarly assembled montage during *I Spy* title credits). Schifrin introduces the flute melody halfway through this sequence, adding even more urgency with a jagged brass reprise of the rhythmic bass beat. The melody continues as the word MISSION is typed one letter at a time across the screen; still images of the stars appear in silhouettes of individual letters. They vanish when the word MISSION reappears, now partially obscured by the word IMPOSSIBLE, as if ink-stamped; the theme builds to a double-note orchestral finale and fades out. Leaving viewers breathless.

Schifrin recorded a new arrangement of the title theme as season five began, accelerating the tempo and modifying the instrumentation, but this new version is "softer" and less exciting than its predecessor. Calmer heads prevailed and brought back to the original arrangement for season six. Season seven's different heads weren't content to leave well enough alone, so Schifrin was asked to redo the theme again; this arrangement modifies the melody slightly while retaining some of its original intensity.

Schifrin also scored some first-season episodes, supplying a great start to what became an ambitious library of tense, jazzy and atmospheric *Mission* cues. Cimbalom elements add an Eastern European flavor to "Memory" and "Operation Rogosh," the latter also benefiting from the unsettling placement of harpsichord touches. The first season's biggest musical surprise is "A Cube of Sugar," partially scored by avant-garde jazz trumpeter/drummer/composer Don Ellis. His bizarre, highly disturbing free jazz cues are an ideal backdrop to a story that focuses on drug addiction. This marked Ellis' scoring debut, and he'd soon shift to the big screen for memorable work on *The French Connection* and other thrillers.

The second season found Jerry Fielding and Robert Drasnin joining a scoring team that also included Walter Scharf, Jack Urbont and *U.N.C.L.E.* veteran Gerald Fried.

"We went through a lot of composers," recalled Desilu music supervisor Jack Hunsaker. "No composer in town could do what Lalo did. A lot of them didn't agree with what Lalo did, thought that his music was repetitious, and that his arrangements disturbed people. They would come in and do their own thing, and we would throw out anything that did not have to do with *Mission*. No matter who wrote what, Lalo's music always dominated every episode, and that went on for almost the entire series. Of all the composers who worked on the show in subsequent years, only Jerry Fielding came close to creating the suspense which worked so well for the show."[9]

One of Fielding's assignments—the second season's two-part episode, *The Council*—was reedited and released in Western Europe as a feature film titled *Mission Impossible Versus the Mob*.

When released as a single, Schifrin's title theme enjoyed a healthy 14-week run on *Billboard's* Hot 100 Chart. A few covers subsequently were released by Alan Copeland (weirdly mashed together with The Beatles' "Norwegian Wood," on ABC), the Kane Triplets (a vocal version for UA) and Jimmy Smith (Verve).

Schifrin's single drew attention to the first of his two soundtrack albums. Because the series didn't really have memorable "themes" aside from the primary two, most of the dozen tracks are original compositions that hadn't been heard on television; that said, Schifrin ultimately dropped them into future episodes. The album enjoyed an impressive 47-week run on *Billboard's* Top LPs Chart, and was nominated for three Grammy Awards, winning two.

The album's sequel also introduced original tunes not yet used in the series; again, some of them landed in future episodes.

Although Phelps and his associates executed their final assignment on March 30, 1973, Schifrin wasn't yet finished with the show. A decade and a half later, a lengthy Writers Guild strike ran from March 7 through August 7, 1988, and brought television and movie production to a standstill.[10] Networks sought creative ways to mount fresh programming; one solution involved "recycling" old shows and their scripts. ABC therefore revived *Mission: Impossible* for two seasons that began that October 23. Peter Graves' Jim Phelps was the sole returning character, but Schifrin also returned to the fold; he updated his two iconic cues and fully scored three of the first four episodes. The title credits sequence is much the same; Schifrin's new arrangement is characterized by heavy rhythmic touches and a slight disco beat: plenty of heavy bass, synth and electric guitar.

Most of the other original scores are handled by John E. Davis, with Ron Jones picking up the balance. 1992's *Mission: Impossible–Then and Now* features excerpts from five of Schifrin's original series scores, along with excerpts from five of Davis' revival scores; that album was followed by a pair of even more lavish box sets.

Tom Cruise began a popular big-screen revival in 1996, which has run six films and counting, but—aside from the wise retention of Schifrin's title theme—none of the scores can be considered jazz. That said, the first film includes a cover of the title theme by U2's Adam Clayton and Larry Mullen, Jr.; it was released as a PolyGram single and became a 20-week hit on *Billboard's* Hot 100 Chart, peaking at No. 7 on June 22, 1996: far higher than Schifrin's original single climbed.

The Big Screen

Schifrin's first splashy Hollywood production gives no indication of the thrilling jazz scores he had been doing for television. *Blindfold*, a failed attempt to mimic the *Charade* formula, is based *very* loosely on the 1960 novel of the same title by Lucille Fletcher. By the time director Philip Dunne and co-scripter W.H. Menger got done with it, the film had devolved into a ludicrous, farcical mess, serving mostly as a vehicle for Italian sex bomb Claudia Cardinale. Worse yet, Schifrin's score was transformed into bland orchestral mush by music supervisor Joseph Gershenson, who removed almost every trace of jazz. The only vibrant exceptions are two voluptuous, horn-laden cues for the strip club where Vicky Vincenti (Cardinale) works as an exotic dancer.

She's the worried sister of Arthur Vincenti (Alejandro Rey), a scientist of supreme importance to the U.S. intelligence community. When he goes missing, Vicky arranges an "accidental" encounter with psychiatrist Bartholomew Snow (Rock Hudson), hired by clandestine government spook George Prat (Jack Warden) to treat Vincenti, who is suffering from a nervous breakdown. Security protocols demand that Snow can't know where Arthur is sequestered, so he's blindfolded every time he's taken to treat his patient. The situation grows murkier as various other alphabet agencies get involved; Snow begins to worry about who can be trusted. Once allied with Vicky, he must find the hidden location by relying on the sounds and sensations he experienced during each blindfolded trip (a gimmick stolen for numerous subsequent thrillers).

Plas Johnson's tenor sax gets some nice (if brief) exposure during a romantic arrangement of the title theme, heard during a flirty taxi ride shared by Snow and Vicky; their first kiss prompts a mildly sexy blend of piano and muted trumpet. Toss in a bluesy trumpet reprise of the title theme, during the end credits, and that's the extent of what could be considered jazz. *Blindfold* failed to produce a soundtrack album—mercifully—but the title theme was covered by Tullio Gallo, for a 45 on Italy's GTA label.

Director Stanley Donen also hoped to replicate the elements that had made *Charade* such a hit, and the result was *Arabesque*. He hedged his bet byreuniting with composer Henry Mancini and screenwriter Peter Stone, but—rather oddly—saddled the latter with hack co-scripters Julian Mitchell and Stanley Price. The film's subsequent problems aren't limited to its poor narrative; stars Gregory Peck and Sophia Loren are a *far* cry from Cary Grant and Audrey Hepburn.

The bewildering saga begins when Oxford University professor and hieroglyphics expert David Pollock (Peck) is asked to translate a message possessed by sinister shipping magnate Nejim Beshraavi (Alan Badel). David initially refuses but is persuaded to change his mind after a clandestine meeting with Hassan Jena (Carl Duering), prime minister of some Middle Eastern country; he believes that Beshraavi is up to no good, and so David becomes a reluctant spy. Beshraavi lives in a palatial estate owned by his lover, Yasmin Azor (Loren), whose apparent allegiance to good or evil shifts as frequently as her lavish outfits. Peck has no facility for the script's dumb one-liners, all of which land with thuds that nearly drown out the frothy score.

The music, at least, is up to Mancini's high standards. The lively main theme, driven by Shelly Manne's Eastern-flavored drum work and three English horns, debuts during a vibrant title credits sequence designed by Maurice Binder. This theme reprises frequently, but most of the remaining, string-laden cues are orchestral texture. Ah, but Mancini once again reorchestrated sometimes fleeting film cues into lengthier melodic tracks for the soundtrack album, and several are much jazzier than their on-screen counterparts. "Something for Sophia" boasts solid solos on trumpet (Jack Sheldon), alto sax (Ted Nash) and de-tuned piano (Jimmy Rowles). "Façade," a lovely, Latin-flavored track featuring French horn (Vincent de Rosa), flute (Ethmer Roten) and mandola (Bob Bain), would have been right at home alongside Mancini's many themes for TV's *Peter Gunn* or *Mr. Lucky*. As usual for this time period, the album also includes a vocal version of "We've Loved Before (Yasmin's Theme)," intended solely for radio play.

(Did this promotional gimmick *ever* work? Mushy, "easy listening" love songs wouldn't have been on an AM radio DJ's playlist in a post–Beatles world increasingly dominated by rock 'n' roll. Can you even imagine it? "Here's a catchy little number that'll send you out to see *Arabesque*, playing now at a theater near you." Not likely.)

Dunne and Donen should have realized there was no substitute for Audrey Hepburn. She personified glossy Hollywood productions during much of the 1960s, and director William Wyler's *How to Steal a Million* makes perfect use of her talents (and her gorgeous Givenchy outfits). The lighthearted script focuses on a rather unusual museum heist: a caper given just the right bounce by rapidly rising composer Johnny Williams (still a few years from dropping the second syllable of his first name). This was one of Williams' first big-deal, mega-star assignments, and—having learned much while apprenticing with Henry Mancini—he responded with a lush orchestral score that stealthily slides into light jazz.

The story is set in Paris, where aristocratic Nicole Bonnet (Hepburn) has long been dismayed by her father's larcenous ways. The world celebrates Charles Bonnet (Hugh Griffith) as a prosperous art collector, but in fact his wealth derives from selling forged paintings. Such fraudulent talent runs in the family; he has long prized a supposed Cellini statuette of Venus, actually sculpted by Nicole's grandfather. Charles impishly allows the Venus to be displayed at the Kléber-Lafayette Museum, little realizing that this will trigger an insurance-mandated examination that is certain to expose the statuette as a fake, resulting in a likely prison sentence. By coincidence, Nicole has gotten to know high-society burglar Simon Dermott (Peter O'Toole); she begs him to help steal the well-protected Venus, before it can be scrutinized.

The film's title credits appear against a lively orchestral melody that Williams later described as a "French boulevard piece [with a] Gallic flavor."[11] It opens with upper-register piano flourishes and impudent brass responses, before settling into a sumptuous melody shared by horns and strings. Williams recasts this melody, at a slower tempo, as the love theme that eventually unites Nicole and Simon. When they eventually spend several cramped hours in the museum janitor's closet, awaiting the opportunity to put their plan into action, Williams delivers a jovial, midtempo suspense cue powered by throbbing bass and a droll organ melody.

"There's a little chase scene at the end, where Peter O'Toole and Audrey Hepburn come out of the closet," Williams recalled, a few years later. "There's a chase in the museum, and I treated it in a very burlesque way: sort of slipping on banana skins, followed by a crash from the orchestra, and running semiquavers all over the place. I thought I'd gone too far, but Wyler loved it."[12]

The soundtrack album is a far superior showcase for Williams' score; it's also the first LP generated by a big-screen feature score that he composed entirely on his own. Williams expanded and reorchestrated the primary themes to produce a listener-friendly party album. One brief film cue, heard while Simon and Nicole drive outside the museum, blossoms into a frothy jazz waltz ("Simon Says") with impish byplay between reeds, strings and a seductive electric guitar; a soft source cue ("Nicole") opens with call-and-response between piano and flute, after which a muted trumpet delivers a tender melody very much in the Mancini-esque mold of "Dreamsville."

Further in the vein of star-wattage larceny, *Gambit* is both a clever heist flick and a delightful romantic comedy; it's fueled by the incandescent pairing of Michael Caine and Shirley MacLaine, who navigate an ingeniously twisty script. British con man Harry Dean (Caine) and art forger Emile Fournier (John Abbott) have their eyes on a priceless sculpture owned by Ahmad Shahbander (Herbert Lom), a reclusive industrialist who lives in the fictitious Middle Eastern country of Dammuz. Harry and Emile hire Eurasian chorus girl Nicole Chang (MacLaine) as their ticket into Shahbander's penthouse home, due to her striking similarity to the man's late, beloved wife. Unfortunately, Harry's information about Shahbander is 10 years out of date; the man is nothing like he was portrayed in a lavish magazine article, nor is Nicole a politely docile woman quietly willing to follow all instructions to collect a $5,000 inducement. Everything goes wrong ... until, miraculously, it all goes right again.

Composer Maurice Jarre never wrote a jazz score during a career that spanned half a century, and—for the most part—*Gambit* is no exception. Most of the non-diegetic cues sounds suspiciously close to the music that brought him an Academy Award for *Lawrence of Arabia*. That said, the larkish title theme is quite catchy, and is given a bit of swing by some sleek walking bass. A rowdy Hong Kong nightclub, where Harry and Emile meet Nicole, also is the perfect setting for some raucous big band action; Jarre obliges with a saucy strip number and two lively jump jazz cues. In the third act, when Nicole allows Shahbander to "show her the city" as a means of keeping him away from his penthouse, they dine in a lavish restaurant while a house quartet delivers a lyrical jazz cover of "Strangers in the Night."

The film failed to produce a soundtrack album, but the title theme earned a captivating jazz/pop cover by Sammy Kaye and his Orchestra, on a Decca single.

Director Jack Donohue's yawningly sluggish *Assault on a Queen* is an impressively clumsy heist adventure, despite an A-list roster of talent that includes screenwriter Rod Serling. Frank Sinatra toplines the cast, which also features rising star Tony Franciosa and Italian sexpot Virna Lisi. But Serling's dialogue is hilariously corny, the interpersonal melodrama absurd, and the performances either overwrought or stiff as a board. Most damningly, the core plot isn't the slightest bit credible.

On the other hand, this badly bungled brew features some terrific music by Duke Ellington. But as a further indication of the artistic clumsiness at work, most of the swinging big band cues are wholly inappropriate for a so-called thriller that spends much of its time on or beneath the ocean waves. Rarely has a score been so at odds with story action.

Ellington's involvement came as a favor to Sinatra, but the famed composer was forced into less than optimal circumstances and given only a few weeks to write and record the entire score. Numerous cues were laid down during two studio sessions, but this wasn't enough music to fully spot the film; Ellington's other commitments precluded additional work within the narrow time frame. Paramount composer/orchestrator Nathan Van Cleave and arranger/orchestrator Frank Comstock were hired to "stretch" Ellington's dozen cues into a broader orchestral underscore.[13]

The far-fetched plot finds Bahamas-based fishing guide Mark Brittain (Sinatra) and longtime friend Linc Langley (Errol John) hired by obnoxious treasure hunter Vic Rossiter (Franciosa); his lover/financial backer, Rosa Lucchesi (Lisi); and their German partner, Eric Lauffnauer (Alf Kjellin). The commission to find a sunken Spanish galleon is abandoned when Mark happens upon a long-missing World War II-era German submarine. This prompts a new plan to rob the bank on board the Queen Mary during one of its passenger-laden pleasure cruises. The sub is raised and put into working order with the assistance of expert engineer Tony Moreno (Richard Conte), at which point the sextet sets off to rendezvous with the massive ocean liner. Mark, uneasy all along about both the scheme and some of his colleagues, finds his worst fears realized.

Ellington's efforts include several character and "situational" themes: a slow, sexy swinger for Rosa ("She Walks Well"); a cue employed for Mark's various underwater activities and the raising of the sub ("The First Dive"); and a cute blend of steel drums, Latin percussion and soprano woodwinds ("Mama Bahama"), heard during occasional visits to the bar where our heroes gather after a hard day's work. The disconnect hits during Mark's first dive, and the subsequent raising of the sub, because the spotting cues don't say "ocean" or "underwater" to *any* degree; they sound more like midtempo dance music for a bossa nova nightclub, with plenty of bongos and brass. Back on shore, Mark and Rosa eventually fall into each other's arms, against Ellington's gorgeous ballad, "Blessings on the Night." A first reading is highlighted by a lyrical jazz flute solo, backed by bossa nova percussion; Ellington's coltish piano runs kick off a second arrangement, which includes another seductive flute solo.

Once Mark, Vic and Eric finally board the Queen Mary, armed with a cover story, the unfolding heist takes place against a lengthy suspense/action suite built by Comstock from several of Ellington's cues, notably the "Queen Theme" and the underwater theme (the latter much more appropriate for this above-water sequence). But the caper dissolves into failed chaos, leaving the few survivors adrift at sea, far from land and with no food or water: a gloomy conclusion spotted by a cheerful, uptempo reading of "She Walks Well." This is a happy ending?

Ellington, clearly displeased by the way his music was tampered with, deserved the final word: He dismissed the film as a "bad Western."[14]

No soundtrack album appeared until 2016. The disc includes the score's 18 cues, precisely as they're heard in the film; liner notes explain which are "pure Ellington," and which are enhanced by Cleave or Comstock. A bonus track, Ellington's original arrangement of the cue intended to be heard behind "The Big Heist," is a terrific six-minute blast of big band jazz that boasts a cool flute solo from Bud Shank; it's far more exciting than the bland orchestral version used in the film.

As heist films go, writer/director Bernard Girard's *Dead Heat on a Merry-Go-Round* is an oddity: We're never sure whether to root for the scheme to succeed or hope that it fails. James Coburn's character charms, bluffs and cons his way through a series of preliminary scams, to finance an audacious plan; it unfolds during a mildly suspenseful third act. Earlier, moving across the country as convenience demands, Coburn's Eli Kotch—merely one of many aliases adopted during the course of the story—slides into relationships with women who can help him, or who own valuables that can be stolen and fenced for working capital. Each woman is callously abandoned in turn. Then he meets Inger Knudsen (Camilla Sparv), whose devotion proves useful. The ultimate goal is to empty the vault of a bank located at the Los Angeles International Airport: a scheme scheduled during the chaos resulting from the U.S. arrival of the Soviet premier.

The score came from Stu Phillips, soon to become a go-to composer for hit TV shows in the 1970s and '80s. His work here is dominated by numerous arrangements of the captivating title theme: a catchy 5/4 jazz anthem that slides into waltz time during its bridge. It opens mischievously, with tentative percussion; unison reeds and keyboards then deliver the lyrical melody against droll orchestral flourishes dominated by strings for the 3/4 bridge. Subsequent arrangements alter the tempo, with slightly different instrumentation, but always as impish as Coburn's ear-splitting grin. As the story moves toward its climax, Phillips injects rhythmic drums, expectant flourishes and suspenseful riffs from the unison reeds. Then comes the twist finale, accompanied by a close-up of Inger's stricken face; the end credits roll as Phillips repeats the main theme in its original exuberant glory. Alas, no soundtrack album was produced.

Coburn fared far better when he slid into his secret agent shoes.

Most of James Bond's early cinematic imitators were one-offs that came and went in a couple of weeks and deserve to be forgotten. A few of these faux 007s generated sequels and series, but only two have stood the test of time: James Coburn's Derek Flint duet, and Dean Martin's Matt Helm quartet. (More's the pity, when it comes to the latter.)

Coburn's brash Derek Flint remains the best. His stylish debut in *Our Man Flint* is an effervescent example of 1960s spy spoofery at its finest, thanks to its lavish sci-fi sets and well-staged action sequences. Director Daniel Mann also makes excellent use of Jerry Goldsmith's slick, kitschy, action-oriented jazz score, powered by a main theme that's the equal of John Barry's best 007 cues.

The world's nations are shattered by an unprecedented wave of weather-related disasters: clearly the work of some diabolical agency. Anxious members of the United Nations-esque Zonal Organization for World Intelligence and Espionage (ZOWIE) turn to U.S. representative Lloyd Cramden (Lee J. Cobb), who agrees that the only man for the job is ex-agent Derek Flint. At the mention of his name, a three-note blast of brass kicks off a Bondian title credits sequence; those first three notes are answered by three more, slightly subdued, after which vibrant percussion signals a hypnotically swinging, conga-style melody powered by dueling electric guitarists Bob Bain and Al Hendrickson. Strings and a wall of brass kick the tune into even higher gear during the bridge, with a final melodic filigree provided by a Thomas organ.

Goldsmith frequently reprises this theme: often via action-jazz arrangements that make ample use of session musicians Plas Johnson (tenor sax), Ronnie Lang (alto sax), Dick Nash (trombone), Red Mitchell (bass) and Shelly Manne (drums). When Flint takes his live-in quartet of voluptuous female companions out for dinner at a fancy Manhattan restaurant, he dances with each in turn; the source jazz band supplies four different versions of the main theme, instrumentally modified—thanks to a French-ified accordion, Italian-esque mandolins and Asian accents—to reflect each young woman's heritage. Additional notable cues include a main theme arrangement carried by balalaika, accordion and soft, sexy sax, when Flint and bad gal Gila (Gina Golan) seduce each other; a gentle, flute-driven bossa nova waltz, heard when Flint explores the "pleasure section" of the villains' Mediterranean island headquarters; and—most particularly—the bold, fast-paced burst of 4/4 action jazz powered by dynamic percussion and throbbing guitar, which backs Flint's annihilation of said headquarters.

Goldsmith added a bit more electronic dash while arranging his primary cues into orchestral jazz/pop for the soundtrack album. The only way to hear all of Goldsmith's original cues is via the isolated score on the film's 2013 Blu-ray.

Goldsmith's primary "Flint Theme" became an oft-covered staple of spy jazz, with Hugo Montenegro delivering a particularly catchy version that blends the melody with the memorable electronic ring of the red "hot phone" that connects Cramden to the U.S. President (a sound effect that also found its way into 1997's *Austin Powers: International Man of Mystery*). Other covers came from Billy Strange (GNP Crescendo), The Silvertones (Treasure Isle), Tommy McCook and the Supersonics (Peckings), and famed jazz flutist Herbie Mann (Atlantic).

As for Matt Helm…

American author Donald Hamilton wrote 27 novels featuring the U.S. government counteragent, starting with 1960s *Death of a Citizen*. The books are grim, gritty and realistic; Helm is cynical, pragmatic and unapologetically ruthless, as circumstance demands. The big-screen adaptations are jokey, pun-laden burlesques; Dean Martin's handling of the character is based on his own lackadaisical, booze-swilling playboy image. The tone is set in *The Silencers*, which is little more than a cartoon frequently punctuated by Martin's crooning; he sings 10 (!) songs during the course of the imbecilic screenplay. At this late date, the film's unapologetic sexism is repugnant; the humiliation endured by co-star Stella Stevens is particularly disgusting.

Hamilton's fans were horrified, but he was pragmatic. The film was a hit, despite its juvenile tone, and that translated into stronger book sales.

The plot, such as it is, finds Helm on semi-permanent leave from Intelligence & Counter-Espionage (ICE), having forsaken spydom for life as a fashion photographer for male-oriented magazines. He's coaxed out of retirement by former partner Tina (Daliah Lavi), to prevent a global criminal organization dubbed "Big O" from firing a missile into one of New Mexico's underground atomic bomb test sites; the bad guys hope the Americans will blame the Russians, thereby initiating a nuclear war. (How this outcome would be

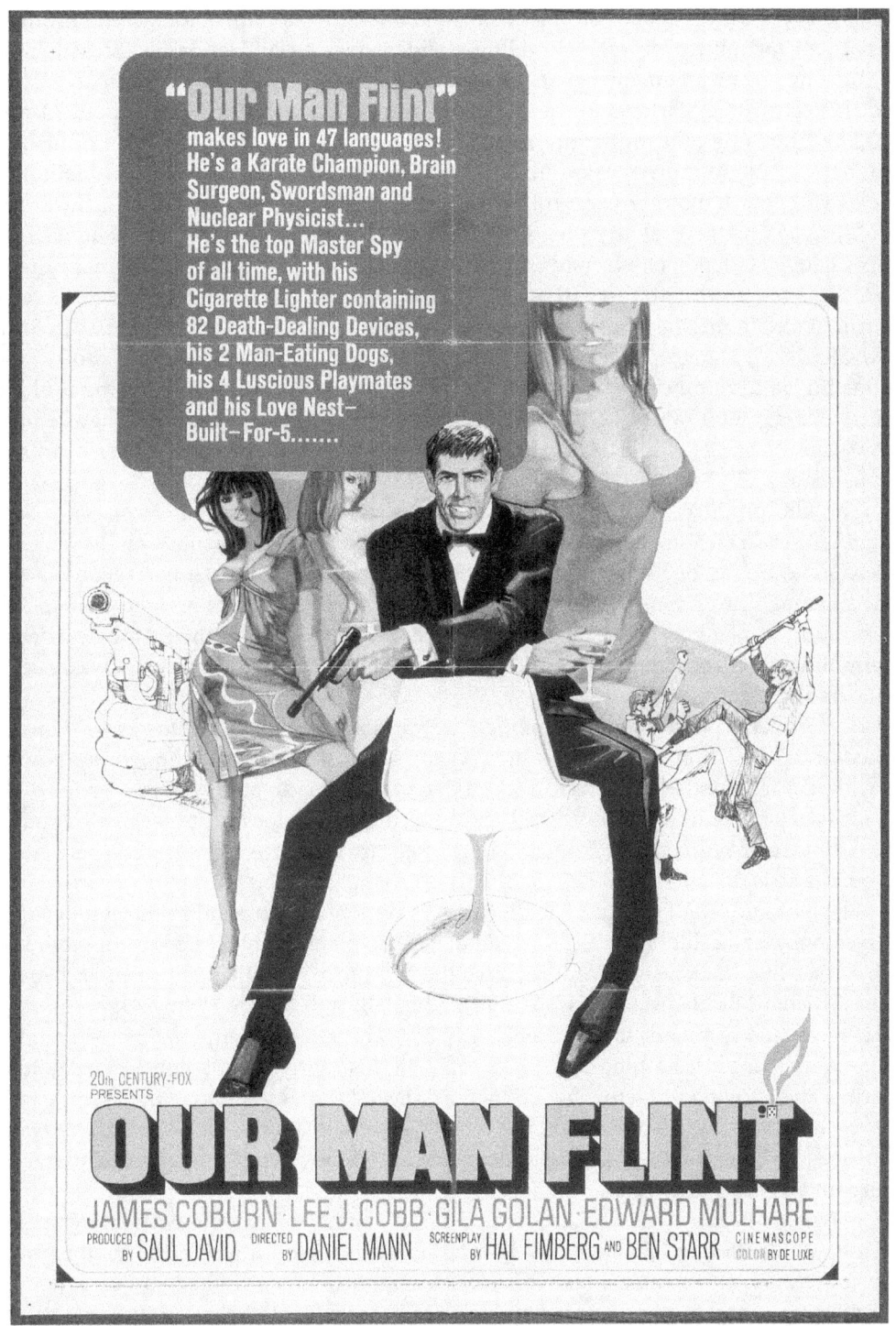

Well … maybe only 45 languages. James Coburn's portrayal of the gracefully athletic, unapologetically hedonistic and scientifically unrivaled Derek Flint remains the part for which he's best known (a long career's worth of other fine work notwithstanding). His secret agent derring-do gets additional pizzazz from Jerry Goldsmith's swingin' score.

useful, is left to our imagination.) Helm's insipid efforts to stop this plot are compromised by repeated encounters with the bumbling, accident-prone Gail Hendricks (Stevens), who may or may not be an enemy agent. America is saved during a climactic display of poor special effects, while Martin drops feeble double-entendres and quips about "booby traps."

The film's one redeeming quality is Elmer Bernstein's jovial score: one of his final great action jazz soundtracks (when it can be heard above Martin's relentless singing). The roaring, big-band jazz is on full display during the title sequence, with the credits unfolding against several strip-tease dancers (text handily covering all naughty bits). Helm's gadget-laden bachelor pad is introduced with a sexy reprise of the main theme, in an arrangement that boasts sweet solos on piano and sax. Big O agents hope to get their hands on a missile-control tape scheduled to be passed from a scientist to Sarita (Cyd Charisse), a singer/dancer at the Phoenix Slaygirl Club; this prompts another flirtatious big band number, as various models undress on the stage. Everything builds to a noisy climax, with rambunctious guitar, bass and percussion backing a chaotic blend of horns and strings, while Matt and Gail try to evade the cheesiest "laser beams" in movie history.

The film produced two soundtrack albums. *Dean Martin as Matt Helm Sings Songs from The Silencers* features eight vocals and four incidental instrumentals by the Mike Leander Orchestra (a poor substitute for Bernstein's ensemble). Bernstein's rerecorded score is far superior. The album-opening "Main Title" is a terrific blast of big-band swing; "Matt Helm Blues" is a languorous arrangement of the same theme, with the melody carried on Hammond organ; and "Showgirl Walk" builds into a Count Basie-esque display of sizzling trumpets and vigorous drum work.

The Silencers proved popular enough to warrant a sequel, and *Murderers' Row* was rushed into production only months later. It's the series' best entry—although that's damning with *very* faint praise—thanks to a script that offers some actual spycraft. Martin's dialog still reeks of lame puns and badly dated sexist humor, but he does treat his female companions with greater respect. The film's two best assets are co-star Ann-Margret—particularly her enthusiastic dancing—and Lalo Schifrin's excellent action jazz score.

The plot finds Matt grappling with another criminal mastermind in the employ of Big O: the monomaniacal Julian Wall (Karl Malden), who plans to obliterate Washington, D.C., with a laser-like "heliobeam." Wall requires the assistance of kidnapped scientist Norman Solaris (Richard Eastham), and also is waiting on delivery of some Helio-Magnesium X-4. Matt traces that shipment to the French Riviera, where he encounters Solaris' daughter, Suzie (Ann-Margret); he then runs afoul of Wall, his lovely companion Coco Duquette (Camilla Sparv), and their lethal henchman, Ironhead (Tom Reese), so named for the metal plate on his skull. Several brawls and a few hair's-breath escapes build to a protracted chase sequence involving the then-new Saunders-Roe SR.N6 hovercraft (apparently intended to amaze mid–1960s viewers).

Schifrin delivers a pulsating, uptempo instrumental title theme with energetic percussion and drumming, an aggressively exciting melody, and a wall of horns that grants even more intensity to the bridge. This segues smoothly into a military-esque action cue heard during a montage, as Ironhead systematically executes all the best agents working for ICE. All but one, that is; Wall and his Big O cohorts don't know how to find Matt. Subsequent cues include a tasty bossa nova number, the lyrical melody shared by flutes and vibes, during Matt's ICE briefing; and plenty of uptempo jazz/pop go-go source tunes, performed during Suzie's visits to various discos. The climactic battle involving Wall, Helm, Solaris,

Suzie and the fully functioning Heliobeam takes place against some appropriately exciting action jazz.

Schifrin's expanded soundtrack album arrangements deftly evoke the film's blend of action and larkish humor. Bud Shank covered one of the interior cues ("The Pin") on his 1967 album, *Bud Shank Plays Music from Today's Movies*.

Wanting to capitalize on the popularity of its television spy, MGM gave Robert Vaughn a big-screen starring assignment in between seasons of *The Man from U.N.C.L.E.* The result was a quickie cash grab that did little for Vaughn's résumé, since he was stuck in a pallid adaptation of Helen MacInnes' *The Venetian Affair*.

After a trusted American diplomat inexplicably triggers a suicide bombing at an international peace conference, former CIA agent Bill Fenner (Vaughn) is yanked out of retirement. The reason: His ex-wife Sandra (Elke Sommer), a suspected Communist sympathizer, is a prime suspect. The plot soon centers around a report prepared by the enigmatic Dr. Vaugiroud (Boris Karloff), which apparently will prove harmful to nefarious activities conducted by enemy agent Robert Wahl (Karl Boehm). The plot never makes any of this clear, instead detouring into experiments with a mind-controlling drug—giving Vaughn a chance to behave hysterically, in a padded cell—while killing off cast members at weirdly random moments.

The film offers little in the way of suspense, but it does boast a nifty soundtrack from the always reliable Schifrin, employing an instrumental palette that evokes both the Italian setting and the Cold War flavor of the story's vaguely defined Eastern European bad guys. Schifrin builds the score around two primary themes, the first of which debuts midway through the title credits; this swinging, midtempo cue gets its zest from an intriguing combination of harpsichord, zither, bass flute and marimba, all backing a melody carried by cimbalom. The second recurring cue is a love theme, first heard as a melancholy guitar and flute lament, when Bill's memories of Sandra are rekindled during a visit to her apartment. A mildly troubled reprise of this theme is heard when Bill believes that he has helped her to safety ... but such is not to be. The end credits roll up the screen against an inappropriately sentimental vocal version of this love theme: a bizarre way to conclude a story laced with such death and sorrow.

Schifrin's complete score finally appeared in 2010, as part of the box set *The Cincinnati Kid: Lalo Schifrin Film Scores Vol. 1 (1964–1968)*. Bonus tracks include a solo cimbalom version of the main theme, along with a longer version of the softly sensuous "Claire's Blues," titled after an American diplomat's secretary who succumbs to Bill's questionable charm.

At the bottom rung of spy spoofs, director Gerd Oswald's hilariously inept *Agent for H.A.R.M.* is bad enough to have been roasted by the 'bots of *Mystery Science Theater 3000*—season eight, episode 15—although its bargain-basement spyjinks are mildly enhanced by an enthusiastic jazz/surf rock score from Gene Kauer and Douglas Lackey. The film is flat-out unwatchable, but Kauer and Lackey do their best to suggest otherwise.

American secret agent Adam Chance (Mark Richman), an operative of the Human Aetiological Relations Machine, is assigned to protect defecting Soviet scientist Dr. Jan Steffanic (Carl Esmond), who has weaponized deadly spores attached to the remnants of a meteorite. Once turned into a liquid and subjected to "bacterial sporulation," any contact with skin transforms the victim into a grotesque human fungus. Steffanic and his niece Ava (Barbara Bouchet) are guarded by Chance at a beach safe house, while the good doctor tries to find an antidote; the ocean proximity gives Bouchet an excuse to spend most of the film in a bikini. Alas, neither Chance nor Steffanic knows that Ava is a Soviet spy working for Basil Malko (Martin Kosleck), who is determined to return his pet scientist to the Motherland.

The surprisingly slick title credits sequence is choreographed to fast-paced percussion, guitar and blazing horns, all of which give the film a Bondian allure that evaporates the moment Oswald slides into the first dramatic scene. Kauer and Lackey frequently repeat this uptempo waltz cue, generally leading with guitar and trumpet, as bumpers between scenes; at other times, a sexy jazz flute accompanies Ava's flirty efforts to distract Chance. The composers pull out all the stops during the climax, as Chance revs up a motorcycle to stop a crop-dusting plane that's about to pollute California's food crops with a powdered version of the deadly spores.

Amazingly, this turkey was intended as a TV series pilot; even more astonishing, somebody at Universal Studios decided on theatrical release instead.[15] Either way, Richman never had a Chance to repeat the role.

* * *

In the literary world, Ross Macdonald's Lew Archer bridged the transition from early, tough-talking private detectives—Dashiell Hammett's Sam Spade and Raymond Chandler's Philip Marlowe being the most famous examples—to the more thoughtful, angst-ridden investigators who followed in the 1960s and onward. Very few of Macdonald's 18 Archer novels and nine short stories have been adapted to film or television, despite the crowd-pleasing success of the first effort: *Harper*, adapted by William Goldman from 1949's *The Moving Target*. (Macdonald's detective is renamed Lew Harper here, thanks to star Paul Newman's then-fixation on "H" title films: *The Hustler*, *Hud* and *Hombre*.) Newman's snarky performance gives the world-weary gumshoe just the right blend of bitter self-loathing, shrewd intelligence, and foolish persistence. Johnny Mandel's similarly whimsical score offers cool bossa nova, traditional orchestral shading, and smoky jazz stylings.

The case begins when Harper is hired by wealthy, tart-tongued Elaine Sampson (Lauren Bacall) to find her wayward husband Ralph, an alcoholic womanizer prone to generous acts of fiscal imprudence. The Sampson estate is home base for Elaine's spoiled and flirty stepdaughter, Miranda (Pamela Tiffin), and her cheerful boyfriend, Allan (Robert Wagner), employed as the missing man's private pilot. The roster of suspicious characters includes alcoholic former starlet Fay Estabrook (Shelley Winters); drug-addicted lounge singer Betty Fraley (Julie Harris) and her vicious husband, Dwight Troy (Robert Webber); and a silver-tongued "holy man" (Strother Martin), who runs the cultish Temple in the Clouds on a prime chunk of mountaintop real estate given to him by Ralph. Harper gets roughed up quite a bit, while determining how many of these folks hide nasty secrets; he uncovers a few sidebar larcenies en route to solving the original case and identifying a most unexpected kidnapper/killer.

Harper is introduced during a droll title credits montage that deftly conveys his hand-to-mouth existence. Mandel's whimsical main theme is powered by inquisitive percussion and a sardonic melody—perfectly conveying Harper's dour mood—delivered by French horns and Hammond B3. The cue bursts into uptempo swing and brass during the bridge, then builds to a lusty, full-ensemble reprise of the primary melody, when Harper heads out to meet Elaine Sampson. His subsequent introduction to Allan and Miranda takes place alongside the lavish estate's back yard pool, while the latter boogies to an uptempo bossa nova/pop source cue reminiscent of Herb Alpert's Tijuana Brass. Most of Mandel's jazziest cues are source music, notably during a long evening when Harper gets Fay drunk

The soundtrack album for *Harper* includes two jazzy vocals that never appear in the film. The soggy "Quietly There" gains a bit of sex appeal from singer Ruth Price; "Sure As You're Born" is simply Harper's instrumental theme given bizarre lyrics by Marilyn and Alan Bergman, and performed by a crooner (Sam Fletcher) apparently trying to channel Bobby Darin's iconic cover of "Mack the Knife." Johnny Mandel's score screams for extended, more respectful treatment … but we're still waiting (courtesy Intrada Inc.).

enough to part with some useful information. A tasty piano trio is heard in the restaurant/bar where he first picks her up; they subsequently wind up at a go-go club (or two), gyrating to a couple of rock-inflected jump jazz tunes highlighted by heavy 4/4 drumming, saucy organ and a dynamic wall of brass.

When Harper eventually annoys various bad guys and gals, he lands in plenty of trouble; Mandel supplies a series of propulsive action jazz cues, heavy with brass, for a car chase, a stalking sequence, and a nasty encounter with Puddler (Roy Jenson), the saga's token towering thug. Goldman's audacious final scene—a freeze-frame, as Harper wonders what to do next—prompts a lively reprise of the main theme, as the end credits scroll up the screen.

The soundtrack LP is dominated by the film's vibrant source cues, reorchestrated into longer, listener-friendly arrangements; only three tracks are part of the underscore. There's no trace of Mandel's poignant love theme for Lew and his soon-to-be-ex-wife Susan (Janet Leigh); instead, we get two jazzy vocals that never appear in the film.

Newman reprised his role as Lew Harper a decade later, in 1975's *The Drowning Pool* (discussed in this book's companion volume).

Mystery also is at the heart of *Mister Buddwing*, director Delbert Mann's intriguing study of an amnesiac who, waking one morning on a bench in New York's Central Park, tries desperately to figure out who he is. The approach is vaguely *noir*, enhanced by Fredric Steinkamp's unsettling monochrome cinematography, which emphasizes the main character's disorientation and confusion. The title character is played by James Garner, who adopts the name "Buddwing" impulsively, after seeing a Budweiser beer truck and an airplane flying overhead. During the course of several days, he encounters three women who spark flashbacks of the life he built with his college sweetheart, Grace. Mann's artistic conceit is that this woman takes on the appearance, during these flashbacks, by each co-starring actress in turn: Katharine Ross, Suzanne Pleshette and Jean Simmons. As the story progresses, Buddwing fears that he's actually the murderous lunatic whose escape from a sanitarium is splashed across newspaper headlines.

Kenyon Hopkins' disquieting orchestral jazz score amplifies the story's bewilderment, although the cleverly composed cues also suggest hope. The plaintive main theme—with a 3-2-6-2 motif frequently used to bridge scenes—is a lovely, lonely ballad, introduced over the opening credits. That motif proves significant, midway through the film, when Buddwing suddenly remembers having *written* it. ("That's the slow movement from my jazz octet!") Source music cues include the trumpet- and organ-driven Latin swinger heard from inside a club that Buddwing passes late one evening; and buoyant bits of instrumental rock 'n' roll that emanate from various radios. Alternatively, a disorienting montage, when Buddwing suffers an excruciating headache, takes place against an edgy, fast-paced 5/4 cue driven by hard percussion and chaotic riffs from every instrument in the ensemble.

Hopkins heavily reorchestrated everything for the soundtrack LP. One rock-ish source cue ("Lunch Room") is expanded into a full-blown composition; another ("West Side Radio") becomes a dance-ready swinger powered by guitar, organ and trumpet, with choice licks traded between the latter two. Hopkins has the most fun with the main theme, constructing arrangements that are mysterious ("Mister Bee"), suspenseful ("The Bridge") and mildly optimistic ("12/8 Theme").

Hopkins' swinging contribution notwithstanding, the final word on *Mister Buddwing* definitely belongs to Garner, who—late in his career—called it "the worst picture that I ever made. What were they thinking? What was *I* thinking?"[16]

Meanwhile, Across the Pond…

The astoundingly prolific John Creasey wrote more than 600 novels—under his own name and 28 (!) pseudonyms—during a career that stretched from 1930 to his death in 1973. Most books feature a variety of series characters, including the Honorable Richard Rollison, better known as The Toff; Scotland Yard Commander George Gideon; and John Mannering, dubbed The Baron. ITC brought the latter to British television for a single season that debuted September 28, 1966. The music came from the equally indefatigable Edwin Astley, who produced a boldly brassy title theme and supplied underscores for all 30 episodes.

Mannering (Steve Forrest) is a fine arts dealer by day, with high-end establishments in London, Paris and Washington; by night he's an undercover operative for British Diplomatic Intelligence. His forté finds him handling cases involving insurance fraud, blackmail, theft and other crimes revolving around antiques and collectibles. Astley's mildly regal title theme opens with rapid guitar strums against a montage of exotic locales and Mannering's sepia-hued figure; an unexpected gunshot prompts fleeting action clips—including a quick glimpse of The Baron's sporty Jensen CV8 MkII roadster—against orchestral chaos, after which the title appears while Astley introduces the core 7-7 motif via energetic horns. The longer end credits arrangement inserts a brief soprano woodwind bridge.

Numerous underscore cues are variations of the title theme, and the episodes have a more pronounced "swing" element than most of the other shows on which Astley worked. He supplies choice little jazz cues for sequences of Mannering at rest or play, often bantering with impish gal pal—and Special Branch Diplomatic Agent—Cordelia Winfield (Sue Lloyd). Skulking sequences demand stealthy bass and percussion; skirmishes are backed by the same striking brass statements that characterize Astley's cues for similar scenes in *The Saint* and *Danger Man*. Vehicular pursuits take place against suspenseful bursts of action jazz.

Half a century passed before a soundtrack album—solely on vinyl (!)—finally debuted in 2015. Most of its nine tracks are stitched together from multiple cues; highlights include "Portrait of Louisa," a flamboyant bit of jazz/pop with a deliciously dirty sax melody; and portions of "Diplomatic Immunity," which feature some effervescent action jazz.

Wanting a slice of the popular espionage pie dominated by the likes of *The Baron*, *Danger Man* and *The Avengers*, the BBC introduced *The Spies* on New Year's Day 1966. British agents Richard Cadell (Dinsdale Landen) and Anthony Kelly (Simon Oates) are attached to the British Foreign Office's Department DI6, based in the tiny—and fictitious—European country of Amalia; many of their counterespionage activities find them in conflict with a Russian counterpart known only as Copic (Peter Arne). Little is known about this 15-episode series, beyond brief episode synopses retrieved from television guide listings; it's among the many shows wiped during the BBC tape purge. Only the final episode, "I Don't Even Volunteer," is known to exist ... somewhere.

The show's title theme came from veteran jazz pianist, composer and arranger Max Harris. Listening to his original arrangement is impossible, but the theme endures thanks to an excellent cover by the Cyril Stapleton Orchestra, issued by Pye a few weeks after the show debuted. It's a sly, rolling swinger with a mysterious 2-4-4-4 motif introduced by unison horns against bright brass highlights; a sparkling solo horn takes over during the bridge, and then the primary melody reprises until fading into an orchestral flourish. The theme conveys a suggestion of wistfulness that suits the lonely life endured by espionage agents rarely able to be candid with anybody.

The Spies was spun off from the earlier BBC series *The Mask of Janus*, which ran for 11 episodes following its debut on October 8, 1965. It focused mostly on the back-room protocol discussions and arguments required to maintain British and American democratic interests in Amalia, while thwarting incursions by the "Communist menace." Most episodes of *The Mask of Janus* also are lost, and—as with *The Spies*—the title theme came from Max Harris. Unfortunately, it wasn't covered by anybody, and therefore cannot be discussed.

Availability also is an issue—although not to the same degree—with another BBC series: one that allowed John Barry to once again employ the characteristic sound of a cimbalom. The instrument gives an exotic texture to his title theme for the crime series *Vendetta*, which debuted November 4, 1966. The drama was unusual for its time, given that its protagonist is an antihero at best, and quite possibly as ruthless as the foes he faces on a weekly basis. The series begins as Danny Scipio (Stelio Candelli), a former Mafioso from the days when Cosa Nostra members obeyed *something* of a code of conduct, is targeted by members of the "new Mafia"; they attempt to assassinate him with a car bomb, but succeed only in killing his family. The enraged Scipio announces a vendetta on all those responsible and spends three violent seasons seeking vengeance; he's assisted by Angelo James (Neil McCallum), an American whose wife also was killed by Mafia thugs.

Barry's unhurried, grimly mysterious theme uses the cimbalom for the core 2-5-2-2 motif, introduced over a low, growling rhythm section; the melody repeats, and then the brief, 35-second cue concludes with a plaintive, six-note fanfare via solo horn. Barry gave the tune more of a rhythmic beat for his expanded arrangement on a Pye single, released a few weeks prior to the show's debut. It opens with twitchy percussion effects; the melody line—again on cimbalom—is both familiar and yet different, sounding a bit more like some of the underscore cues used in *The Ipcress File*. This version of *Vendetta*'s theme—also called "The Danny Scipio Theme"—blossoms against a double-time rhythm section, with impudent counterpoint supplied by a solo muted trumpet, enigmatic flute touches and a final burst of bongos. The result is far jazzier than what TV viewers heard each week.

Barry handled only the title theme; episode underscores came from jazz pianist and BBC sound mixer John Baker, famed today as a pioneering electronic musician. His *Vendetta* cues range from brass-fueled mainstream swing to jarring bass lines and double-time percussion, along with deliberately weird and unsettling sound effects: electronic burps and hiccups often backed by a solo horn. Alternatively, some cues are quite pretty, as with several lovely solo flute passages in the episode "The Sugar Man."

Barry refreshed the title theme slightly for his 1972 compilation album *Theme from The Persuaders!* (CBS), and an assortment of Baker's underscore cues from four episodes were digitized in 2015. *Vendetta* was yet another casualty of the BBC's tape purge; only eight of the show's 36 episodes are known to exist.

On the big screen, Michael Caine once again donned Harry Palmer's cool spectacles for *Funeral in Berlin*. Director Guy Hamilton's touch is lighter than that found in the previous film, and Caine is a bit looser with mordant one-liners; even so, the overall tone still reflects author Len Deighton's signature cynicism, along with the cold-hearted opportunism that Palmer constantly encounters from friend and foe alike.

The story is a labyrinthine web of deception and double-cross, beginning as Palmer is sent to Berlin to arrange the defection of high-level Soviet intelligence officer Colonel Stok (Oskar Homolka). Palmer likes but doesn't trust the crusty old spy; Harry is equally suspicious of his "chance" encounter with Samantha Steel (Eva Renzil), a flirtatious model who immediately takes him to bed. The scheme grows more complicated with the participation of Johnny Vulcan (Paul Hubschmid), a longtime friend and colleague; and Otto Kreutzman (Günter Meisner), a West German "fixer" known to arrange full-proof escapes from the east side of the wall. The plan, involving swapped bodies in a funeral coffin, goes awry; the finale, true to Deighton's nature, once again leaves a bitter taste in Palmer's mouth.

German pianist/composer Konrad Elfers scored this sequel. John Barry's memorable cimbalom melody is sorely missed, but Elfers compensates with a vigorous, brass-laden title credits cue that sounds like a cheerful funeral march, and—in various jazz, orchestral and dissonant variations—becomes the film's signature theme. The quick cut to the next scene is startling: Palmer at his flat early on a Saturday morning, as salacious, sax-fueled swing lends emphasis to the delightful evening he's just enjoyed with the barely dressed babe who sashays in the foreground. Later, once in Berlin, a suspenseful blend of bass flute and bass shadows Palmer's introduction to Kreutzman, while the two men take each other's measure. The score's jazz elements vanish during most of what follows, until the aftermath; back in London, Palmer stalks angrily from his section head's office, as the end credits roll and Elfers reprises the title theme.

The soundtrack album includes a pop-oriented cover of the title theme, performed by The Puppets, which isn't used in the film.

Caine reprised the role in three more films—*Billion Dollar Brain* (1967), *Bullet to Beijing* (1995) and *Midnight in Saint Petersburg* (1996)—but none of those scores has the slightest trace of jazz. The latter two, shamefully low-rent dreck financed by schlockmeister Harry Alan Towers, feature atrociously inappropriate music by rock keyboardist Rick Wakeman.

Funeral in Berlin's dour tone is shared by director Michael Anderson's handling of *The Quiller Memorandum*, due to playwright Harold Pinter's brooding adaptation of Elleston Trevor's Edgar Award-winning novel, *The Berlin Memorandum*, first in what became a 19-book series about a spy code-named Quiller. The story finds him—an oddly cast George Segal, not even trying to affect an English accent—sent to Berlin, to replace an assassinated British agent who'd been on the verge of exposing a neo–Nazi organization known as Phoenix. The bad guys find Quiller first, and the bulk of the film concerns his cat-and-mouse skirmishes with Phoenix head Oktober (Max von Sydow), who wants to know how much the British have learned about their operation. Along the way, Quiller begins an unconvincing relationship with schoolteacher Inge Lindt (Senta Berger), which proves troublesome when the story builds to its climax.

John Barry took this assignment, with results that differ significantly from what he delivered for the similarly solemn *Ipcress*. His work here is mostly atmospheric and orchestral, with an unsettling, Eastern European flavor that reflects the story's bleak tone. Many of the cues derive from the primary theme, a nursery rhyme-styled ballad titled "Wednesday's Child," which Barry based on an 18th century lullaby; it's frequently performed with instrumentation that evokes theme park merry-go-rounds.[17]

The first burst of action jazz occurs when Quiller, having been drugged and captured by Oktober, attempts to escape from Phoenix's oddly palatial headquarters. Much later, during their final encounter, Quiller is given several hours to walk Berlin's late-night streets, while deciding whether to spill his secrets, to save Inge's life. Try as he might, he cannot escape his Phoenix chaperones; Barry supplies another action cue when Quiller cleverly dashes onto a departing subway ... but more Phoenix operatives await him at the next stop. He nonetheless manages a last-minute feint, which allows German authorities to round up all the neo–Nazis ... except, perhaps, one.

The soundtrack album includes Matt Monro's vocal on "Wednesday's Child," heard as radio source music during the film; the 2019 Twilight Time Blu-ray features an isolated score track.

Quiller reappeared in an eponymous 1975 BBC television series (discussed in this book's companion volume).

Descending back to the sub-basement of micro-budget Bondian rip-offs, Tom Adams' return as suave spy Charles Vine was no cause for celebration; *Where the Bullets Fly* is a hilariously inept disaster. This time out, Vine must outwit nefarious enemy agents who are determined to steal and then exploit a sample of ultra-light-weight metal dubbed "spurium." Rather unexpectedly—given the hapless acting, atrocious scripting (Michael Pittock) and impressively incompetent direction (John Gilling)—Kenny Graham's jazz-oriented score is reasonably solid. The best music sequence comes during Vine's lengthy pursuit of a baddie throughout London: a chase that concludes only when the villain finally escapes, despite having been dosed with laughing gas. (Don't ask.)

Graham's score never made it onto an album, but the title tune was released on the UK's Philips label. Vocalist Susan Maughan does her best to sound like Shirley Bassey, and the Bob Kingston/Ronald Bridges song opens with an unmistakably Bondian echo; the thoroughly enjoyable power anthem should have been attached to a far better movie.

This *still* wasn't the last we saw of Agent Vine, but Adams had to visit Spain to make 1968's *Somebody's Stolen Our Russian Spy* (aka *O.K. Yevtushenko*). The unreleased result sat around for years until being "found" and sold to television. The Ángel Arteaga score sounds like comedy movie sound effects; it certainly isn't jazz.

David Niven's debut entry in the spy genre is equally unsatisfying, mostly because director Val Guest can't decide whether he's orchestrating a straight drama or a gentle spoof. *Where the Spies Are* is adapted from James Leasor's *Passport to Oblivion*, the first in a series of books about country doctor-turned-secret agent Jason Love. Although MGM, Niven and Guest hoped to begin a franchise, *Where the Spies Are* got no Love at the box office, and the character never returned to the big screen.[18]

By virtue of his World War II espionage efforts, mild-mannered Dr. Love is recruited by British Intelligence officers desperate to learn what happened to one of their agents in Beirut; Love's cover is his participation at a medical conference. A brief stop in Paris is made to meet his contact, Vikki (Françoise Dorléac). Once in Beirut, Love liaises with fellow agent Parkington (Nigel Davenport); the two uncover a Communist plot to assassinate the pro–British prince of Zahlouf, which would destabilize UK oil interests. Although the assassination is foiled, Love winds up in the hands of Russian spies who don't buy his repeated protests. ("I'm a doctor, not a secret agent!") Worse yet, Vikki turns out to be a double agent in Communist employ … until she succumbs to the humble doctor's charms and helps him escape certain death.

As befits a movie that can't decide whether to play it straight or satirical, the score suffers from similar indecision. The bulk of Italian composer Mario Nascimbene's work is the symphonic stuff of melodramas. The film's sassier cues, however, are backed by a small combo that features Jimmy Smith on Hammond organ. These occasional bursts of action jazz supply some suspenseful bounce that is sorely absent from the rest of the film. The Beirut agent's abduction, during a prologue, unfolds against a tense blend of percussion and organ; the jaunty cue turns triumphant, as he seems to escape … but then doesn't. Much later, while Love and Parkington track down their colleague's killers, a skirmish unfolds against some equally lively swing. Love's eventual foiling of the assassination triggers a lengthy montage set to uptempo organ and percussion, as he flees the Russians, then gets caught, then gets drugged and flown to the snowy Canadian wilderness. (Whew!)

No soundtrack album appeared, although two tracks—"Main Titles" and "Fight/Vikki"—eventually appeared in 1996, on DRG's double-CD *Mario Nascimbene Anthology: Classic Hollywood Soundtracks*. Smith released his own versions of the title theme on a Verve 45. The uptempo arrangement became popular with lounge fans over time, and can be found on anthology albums such as *Come Spy with Us*.

Niven's occasionally inane antics notwithstanding, few British spy spoofs were sillier than *Modesty Blaise* … although that's not how the character was conceived by creator Peter O'Donnell. She debuted as a *London Evening Standard* comic strip on May 13, 1963; the series became wildly popular, ultimately running in newspapers for close to four decades. Beginning in 1965, O'Donnell also featured the character in an ongoing series of novels and short stories. Modesty and her constant companion, Willie Garvin, are cut from the classic bad girl/tough guy mold, and their exotic adventures have the hard-edged, often lethal spy/caper atmosphere of Ian Fleming or Donald Hamilton.[19]

Fans therefore must've blinked at how O'Donnell's classy *femme fatale* leaped to the big screen. *Modesty Blaise* is a mod spoof dominated by Jack Hildyard's cockeyed cinematography and Richard Macdonald's wacky, day-glo production design. The screenplay doesn't make a lick of sense, despite uncredited assists from O'Donnell and Harold Pinter; on-screen events are little more than an excuse for star Monica Vitti to prance about in Beatrice Dawson's hilariously improbable dresses and costumes. The resulting pop-art asylum is run by its cast of lunatics, all of whom overact atrociously ... except for Vitti, who doesn't act at all. She merely poses, pouts and bats her eyelashes.

John Dankworth had little choice but to follow this frivolous lead, and most of his score is the sort of orchestral pop/jazz that Burt Bacharach delivered for his British film work. One notable exception comes during Modesty's assignation in a Playboy-esque bachelor pad, where Dankworth delivers a delightful combo swinger; the film could have used more like it. The only other highlight is Modesty's groovy main theme, which surfaces numerous times and in a variety of styles: straight orchestral, mambo, and a go-go arrangement to accompany her visit to the villainous Gabriel's (Dirk Bogarde) yacht.

The soundtrack LP was digitized in 2010. Dankworth gave Modesty's theme a much peppier big band jazz spin on his 1974 compilation album, *Movies 'n Me*; it's a shame he didn't use that version in the film.

Mod sensibilities are similarly prevalent in the much more successful *Kaleidoscope*, which gets much of its effervescent bounce from a larkish big band jazz score from pianist/arranger/composer Stanley Myers. This frothy adventure bridges multiple genres—romantic comedy, heist flick and even mild spyjinks—while also serving as a love letter to London at its swinging '60s finest. Credit also goes to the incandescent pairing of up-and-coming stars Warren Beatty and Susannah York, along with an ingeniously quirky original script, complete with witty banter and the sauciest of one-liners.

Jet-setting playboy Barney Lincoln (Beatty) devises the perfect scheme to beat the house at Europe's grandest gambling palaces. He breaks into the Kaleidoscope Playing Card Company's Geneva-based manufacturing plant and alters the plates from which all decks are produced. Now able to "read" the backs of every card used at casinos supplied by Kaleidoscope, Barney becomes an unbeatable *chemin de fer* player. By coincidence, he has begun a tenuous relationship with ditzy Angel McGinnis (York), who brings his card prowess to the attention of her father, Scotland Yard Inspector Manny McGinnis (Clive Revill). After deducing the secret of Barney's success, Manny blackmails him into entering a high-stakes poker game hosted by notorious drug smuggler Harry Dominion (Eric Porter), whose private casino also uses Kaleidoscope cards. If Barney can financially eviscerate Dominion, Manny reasons, the master criminal will be forced into desperate actions that'll make him an easier target for Scotland Yard.

Myers' cues are an audaciously jaunty mix of spy jazz, playful '60s rock and psychedelic-hued Indian melodies, with affectionate nods to ceremonial British marching bands and classic English dance hall music. It all works, thanks to the care with which Myers associates each style to specific characters and situations. The swirling, kaleidoscopic title credits sequence—another great job by Maurice Binder—takes place against a triple-meter blast of big band jazz; the melody is led by Eddie Mordue's snarky tenor sax and Howard Blake's swinging Hammond organ, backed by impish harpsichord and percussion.

The *Kaleidoscope* soundtrack album's liner notes include a brief bio of composer Stanley Myers, who proudly notes that his first major musical accomplishment was playing 15th clarinet in the Band of the Royal Berkshire Regiment. Years later, following a run of television projects, *Kaleidoscope* marked the debut of what became an enormously successful quarter-century film-scoring career (courtesy Film Score Monthly).

Staccato drums and suspenseful strings accompany Barney's late-night infiltration of the Kaleidoscope plant. A hypnotic Indian cue—on sitar (Diwan Motihar), tabla (Keshave Sathe) and tambura (John Mayer)—adds suspense as the camera looks over Barney's shoulder, while he carefully alters the card plates. He turns on a transistor radio and dons an earplug; without missing a beat, Myers transforms the exotic, non-diegetic Indian cue into the tinny source music leaking from the earplug: a crazed, uptempo pop vocal by a German rock 'n' roll band. After a few bars, Myers again breaks the music's fourth wall by ramping up the volume and turning the source cue back into a non-diegetic anthem. The song's instrumental bridge expands into a percussive blast of brass-fueled action jazz, when—the following day—the presses roll, spitting out thousands upon thousands of Barney's marked decks. His subsequent trips to Monte Carlo, Baden-Baden and London, made in his beloved Aston Martin DB6, take place as montages against a breezy jazz waltz delivered alternately by sax and trumpet, with occasional organ and harpsichord shading. Myers shifts to gentle bossa nova when Barney and Angel become an item; lush jazz flute leads a midtempo melody backed by cooing vocalese, gentle harpsichord riffs and a nifty beat laid down by drummer Tony Kinsey.

The reorchestrated soundtrack album features three unused cues; one of those, a rock-inflected tune ("Barney") that deftly suits Beatty's debonair performance, is a cheerful, pop-oriented blend of trumpet and Hammond B3 anthem.

Kaleidoscope wasn't the year's sole valentine to the hedonistic '60s. Italian director Michelangelo Antonioni made his English-language debut with *Blow-Up*, and its similar depiction of the era's mod, unapologetically sybaritic London scene remains a fascinating time capsule. That said, the maddeningly vague and aggressively weird narrative has become even more irritating today, than when viewers first confronted the film in late 1966. The story *per se* is a few days in the life of a successful fashion photographer named Thomas, played by David Hemmings at his scornful, misanthropic best. Rarely have women been so ornamentally objectified, as vacant-eyed dolly-birds who can't wait to shed their knickers. (Actually, most of them don't bother with knickers, so it's just a matter of slipping out of loose sheath dresses.) While wandering through a park one afternoon, Thomas snaps some candid shots of a young woman (Vanessa Redgrave, as Jane) flirting with an older man. Later that evening, while developing the results, he spots unexpected details in several of the photos; after enlarging certain sections, he realizes that he has stumbled upon what appears to be a murder. Or is it? Antonioni never tells; rather than address increasingly vexing details, he devotes great chunks of screen time to sidebar encounters and dull, irrational conversations that often start and stop in the middle of stray sentences, as if the actors have forgotten their haphazard lines.

The film's score, however, is anything *but* dull. Antonioni sought out jazz pianist/composer Herbie Hancock, then midway through a six-year stint as a member of Miles Davis' iconic quintet. This became Hancock's first film scoring assignment, and—not knowing any better—he delivered a series of fully structured melodies, rather than cues better suited to the desires of Antonioni and his editor. No surprise, then, that Hancock was disappointed by the way his music was truncated to brief, often fleeting bursts in the finished film. "I couldn't hear my music," Hancock lamented. "Antonioni had buried it."[20]

Even so, Hancock's presence is striking. The title credits unfold to an aggressive main theme that opens with sizzling rock 'n' roll guitar and organ, then morphs into a lazy, horn-driven ballad. "It's kind of a blues-based melody," Hancock explained. "The drums work at double-time speed, but I made the bass line slower, almost at half-tempo, in a circular pattern to the harmonic structure. It's kind of related to the bass line in 'Maiden Voyage,' which I'd written and recorded by then, but I made the drums faster, because I wanted to get that churning feeling, an undercurrent."[21]

The story begins with one of Thomas' typical photo shoots, as he sexually teases professional model Veruschka von Lehndorff into a series of provocative poses: a sequence given more of an erotic edge by Hancock's smoldering, gut-bucket theme. Later, when Jane tracks Thomas to his studio, their sexually charged sparring takes place against a sweet, seductive melody ("Jane's Theme") led by guitarist Jim Hall. During their flirtation, Thomas puts an LP on his record player—we see the distinctive black Verve label—and plays an uptempo swinger ("The Thief") guaranteed to send listeners to the nearest dance floor. After Jane departs, Thomas begins to study his photos; he pulls out another LP, and this time the source music is a bongo-driven burst of energy, with horns adding a layer of tension. That's pretty much the end of Hancock's input, until a frantic reprise of the main title theme, over the closing credits.

The soundtrack album features Hancock's themes in their full majesty. The digitally remastered 1986 release adds a tune by John Sebastian and two unused tracks by the 1960s British psychedelic rock band Tomorrow. (Antonioni decided against their work, instead subbing a live club performance by The Yardbirds toward the end of the film.)

Elsewhere in the World

Not all Eurospy entries were cheap, incomprehensible and poorly dubbed, even if it often seems that way. *Se tutte le donne del mondo... (Opperazione Paradiso)*, released in the States as *Kiss the Girls and Make Them Die*, is a lavish production with opulent sets, a droll tone, and a star who looks great in a dinner jacket, and knows how to toss off a quip. Mike Connors was one short year from name-brand fame on television's *Mannix* when he made this Italian/American co-production. The approach is spy-spoofy; Connors' CIA agent never seems to be in serious trouble, even if director Henry Levin and co-director Arduino Maiuri do their best to suggest as much.

The madcap plot, set in Rio De Janeiro, finds Connors' Kelly investigating the odd behavior of wealthy industrialist Ardonian (Raf Vallone), who surrounds himself with beautiful women who subsequently disappear. The CIA's concern proves valid; Ardonian has developed a radical solution to world population control, involving the total elimination of male libido via radioactive rays generated by an orbiting satellite. He'll become the sole man able to reproduce: a task he'll tackle with the help of numerous lovelies he has placed in suspended animation. Preventing this catastrophe requires Kelly to team with posh British MI-6 agent Susan Fleming (Dorothy Provine) and her amazingly capable chauffeur (Terry-Thomas), whose vintage Rolls-Royce is equipped with enough gadgets to stuff a dozen Aston Martin DB5s. The bonkers climax takes place in Ardonian's vast underground lair, a stunning set that must've blown half the budget.

The film's only weak link is Mario Nascimbene's score, which at first listen is a pleasant blend of soft jazz and bossa nova; unfortunately, Levin and Maiuri beat the main theme to death via constant repetition. No matter what the mood—*mano a mano* skirmishes, car chases, flirty banter between Kelly and Susan—we get nearly identical instrumental arrangements of that title song. The backing rhythm ostinato becomes as aggravating as a dentist's drill. That's a shame, because it's a lovely little tune, and Howard Greenfield's lyrics—warbled by Lydia MacDonald, behind the title credits—are a hilarious tribute to the essential role played by film villains.

MacDonald's rendition of the title song was issued as a 45, but a full soundtrack didn't appear until 1998. The album offers more variety than the film, thanks to the inclusion of several unused small-combo cues. "Suzanne [sic] and Kelly" is a sparkling swinger, and "Guaracha (Version 1)" is a fizzy little bossa melody.

Director Sergio Grieco—hiding beneath the Anglicized pseudonym "Terence Hathaway"—gets reasonably close to the 007 vibe with *Password: Uccidete agente Gordon (Password: Kill Agent Gordon)*, and American actor Roger Browne displays the necessary *savoir faire* in this Spanish/Italian co-production. The plot is more topical than many, with CIA agent Douglas Gordon (Browne) assigned to infiltrate a criminal gang attempting to smuggle weapons to the Viet Cong. Midway through a mission that takes Gordon from Paris to

Tripoli and then Madrid, he achieves détente by teaming up with the equally capable Karin (Helga Liné), a Russian agent whose innocent-looking mascara pencil actually conceals a deadly laser weapon.

Piero Umiliani's score goes for the John Barry/*Goldfinger* orchestral jazz touch, starting with a power ballad—"You Play to Win"—bellowed lustily by Carol Danell. But as with *Kiss the Girls*, Umiliani relies too heavily on that title theme; instrumental arrangements—with regional variations appropriate to Gordon's various ports of call—become rather ubiquitous. A suspensefully thoughtful reading backs Gordon early on, when he searches a casino office for clues; a brassy action jazz version adds spice to a climactic car chase. Source cues include an unseen jazz piano combo supplying music at the aforementioned casino; and a tasty solo piano cover of the main theme heard in a nightclub, when Gordon attempts to get some information from a *femme* most *fatale*.

Despite the popularity of Umiliani's scores, *Password: Uccidete agente Gordon* has yet to produce a soundtrack album.

The handsomely mounted *Agent 505: Todesfalle Beirut* (*Agent 505: Death Trap in Beirut, From Beirut with Love*) also follows the 007 template reasonably well. It offers saucy one-liners, a jazz-inflected score by Ennio Morricone—one of his very few spy-fy assignments—and a suave turn by star Frederick Stafford. On the other hand, the plot is incomprehensibly silly.

Richard Blake (Stafford) is summoned to help Beirut police after two women—and their killer—die mysteriously, with nary a mark on their bodies. Suspects abound: wealthy philanthropist Omar Abdullah (Willy Birgel); nightclub performer Monique (Gisella Arden); and a mysterious, four-fingered mastermind known only as "The Sheikh." The film is laden with nasty gadgets—telephones, stage lights—that shoot bullets and equally lethal frozen liquid oxygen darts. Blake eventually finds his way into an underground laboratory where Abdullah intends to transform desert sand dunes into arable farmland; alas, the operation has been hijacked by The Sheikh and his army of thugs. They intend to poison the entire city of Beirut with a cloud of radioactive mercury—or radioactive potassium; the English dubbing is a bit sloppy—as a means of extorting a huge ransom from the rest of the world. (Seriously?)

Morricone's score is built from three primary themes, beginning with the propulsive, brass-heavy 2-3-3 fanfare that dominates the title credits; it develops into a jazz swinger that reprises during action sequences. The second theme is a throbbing 1-1-1-3 guitar cue generally complemented by flute counterpart, heard when various baddies are up to no good. Neither of these two action-oriented cues is used during Blake's early *mano a mano* skirmish with a thug, or his partner Bob's similar melee with a different ruffian, or a lengthy car/motorcycle chase; all these sequences occur without any music (to their detriment). The third primary cue is a soft, Latin-inflected romantic ballad dominated by a five-note flute motif, a whistled melody and saucy fanfares from unison muted trumpets.

The soundtrack album didn't appear until 2007.

Director Mino Loy's *Furia a Marrakech* (*Fury in Marrakesh*) is an impressively silly entry suggested by an actual historical premise: Hitler's plan to destroy the U.S. and British economies by flooding both countries with undetectably perfect forged bank notes. Fledgling CIA agent Bob Dixon (Stephen Forsyth) is sent into action when an international criminal organization revives this scheme, having found stacks of the counterfeit bills in Hitler's hitherto undiscovered Swiss Alpine bunker. Following an equipment briefing with gadgets even crazier than anything James Coburn's Derek Flint employs, Dixon evades death traps while following clues from New York to Morocco, and finally to the Swiss Alps. Ludicrous action sequences are (more or less) choreographed to Carlo Savina's frequently overwrought jazz score. His main theme is a hilariously opulent big band swinger with an *oom-pah* go-go beat, initially heard over the title credits and echoed a few times throughout the film.

The best action jazz cues are heard during a car chase along mountain roads, and a climactic ski chase toward the film's conclusion. Source music includes Moroccan dance music at a nightclub, where Dixon hopes to meet a contact; and a brief jazz vibes combo, heard at a ski chalet while he and British Intelligence colleague Alexander Keane (Jacques Ary) compare notes.

No soundtrack emerged from this ludicrous mess, which is just as well.

Things are even crazier in director/scripter Umberto Lenzi's *Kriminal*, which owes as much to American television's *Batman* as the crime *noir* genre it uneasily inhabits. The film is based on a popular Italian *fumetti neri* (comic book) serial of the same title, starring a master thief/cat burglar who dresses in a black-and-yellow costume with a grotesque skull face. Lenzi's live-action adaptation is bookended by title and end credit sequences that employ a comic book art motif, complete with *Batma*n-style sound effects balloons. The Italian/Spanish co-production boasts a surprisingly varied score by Romano Mussolini and Roberto Pregadio, which ranges from frivolous pop to tasty bossa nova and full-blown big band jazz.

The wildly complicated plot kicks off when Kriminal (Glenn Saxson) narrowly escapes execution in prison and is pursued by the relentless Inspector Milton (Andrea Bosic). Kriminal learns of a valuable diamond shipment being overseen by Lady Gold (Esmeralda Ruspoli) and twin couriers Inge and Trude (both played by Helga Liné), all of whom are up to no good. Kriminal's efforts to steal those gems are helped—and hindered—by both twins; it turns out that the triple-crossing Inge has teamed with nasty skunk Alex Lafont (Ivano Staccioli), although she's actually in league with late-entry lover Frank (Dante Posani) … while allowing herself to be romanced by Kriminal on the side. (My, my.) The globe-trotting story begins in London and proceeds to Rome, Madrid and Istanbul; Kriminal's talents for disguise and assumed identities are put to good use throughout, and everything builds to a reasonably suspenseful—and richly ironic—climax atop a moving train.

The sizzling jazz/pop title theme opens with a burst of brass, as throbbing rhythm guitar establishes an ostinato beat that introduces the primary 4-1 statement. The theme develops via more brass, and then the orchestration kicks into a swing-time bridge; the melody repeats first on an acid vox continental organ, then guitar, the latter fading and halting quite abruptly. It's a masterpiece of 1960s lounge-style kitsch, and Lenzi finds ample use for variations as the film proceeds. Vigorous big band action jazz is heard when Kriminal initially evades police pursuit, having just escaped the hangman's noose; and during the climax, while he tries to escape the police officers who have swarmed onto the train that he believes will take him to safety. On a lighter note, Kriminal's initial encounter with Lady Gold—in a nightclub—takes place as an unseen band performs some tasty, flute-driven bossa nova. A final bit of jazz/pop—with tasty solos on organ and vibes—is heard as source music emanating from a portable radio, when Kriminal, having escaped yet again, chances upon a seemingly compliant young woman … who has other intentions.

No soundtrack album emerged until 2006; highlights include a few jazz-hued compositions left unused in the film, along with longer versions of other cues.

Music also is the best part of *Le spie uccidono in silenzio* (aka *Spies Strike Silently*). The script is as clumsily haphazard as the villainous Dr. Rashid's machinations. He initially kills world scientists for no discernable reason; later, he wants to "burn his will into the mind of everyone on Earth." Bland Canadian actor Lang Jeffries is barely tolerable as good guy secret agent Michael Drum.

But Francesco De Masi's swinging jazz score is sensational throughout, starting with a lively main theme introduced behind a title credits sequence that evokes Maurice Binder's 007 credits. Solo muted trumpet and a toe-tapping rhythm section kick off against a colored, checkerboard-style moiré pattern; unison horns introduce the primary 1-3-3 motif as the film's title and Jeffries' name appear. A touch of vibes supports the muted trumpet until unison brass takes over; the intensity increases when De Masi's credit appears over a fancy pistol held by an unseen killer, and the entire ensemble hits a crescendo against director Mario Caiano's name (not that he deserves such a fanfare). There's scarcely a pause, and then sax, trumpets and vibes fuel a swinging cue as one car follows another through the streets of Beirut.

The mission takes Drum from Beirut to London and Madrid, and then back to Beirut and London; along the way, various gun battles, brawls and vehicular chases are spotted by terrific action jazz cues that favor vibes and trumpet. Slower, sexier sax ballads are employed when Drum encounters various lovelies. Numerous arrangements of the title theme enhance action sequences, leading up to the final confrontation with the megalomaniacal Rashid, and our hero's triumphant helicopter ride to safety. Source cues include a tasty swinger played by an unseen combo, when Drum visits a Beirut casino.

Sadly—tragically!—no soundtrack LP was produced.

Pietro Umiliani's energetic jazz- and bossa-hued score also is the sole attraction in director Sergio Sollima's *Requiem per un Agente Segreto* (*Requiem for a Secret Agent*), a thoroughly loathsome entry that appears to have been made on a budget of $1.97. Worse yet, the primary character—played by fading American B-star Stewart Granger—is a repugnant, unrepentant, sexist cad. The wafer-thin story concerns a global league of assassins known as The Society, whose members have been killing American spies. The U.S. government hires mercenary Jimmy Merrill (Granger) to liaise with callow Norwegian operative Erik (Giulio Bosetti) in Tangiers, where Society VIP Oscar Rubeck (Peter van Eyck) is believed to be based. Merrill suffers through incompetently staged skirmishes with Rubeck's various minions, and co-star Daniela Bianchi's ill-defined *femme fatale* fares quite badly.

Although the title credits claim that the music is by Antonio Pérez Olea, the score actually is composed, conducted and arranged by Umiliani. He wastes no time establishing a sizzling action jazz tone, with a rhythmic blend of percussion, brass and electric guitar; this shadows the first American agent dispatched by Society goons. Slower, darker variations of this melody later pop up when Merrill and Erik encounter Rubeck's minions, and when Merrill endures a brutal beating. Umiliani shifts to light-hearted and/or sexy bossa nova source cues for protracted strip club routines.

No soundtrack album appeared until 2001.

The convoluted spyjinks of *Sicario 77, vivo o morto* similarly are made more palatable by full-throttle action jazz from Federico Martínez Tudó and Mario Sensi. They favor a midsize combo approach that leans heavily on flute, vibes, trumpet and a low-octave electric guitar; the result is a propulsive, oft-employed title theme and plenty of underscore cues in a variety of jazz stylings.

Secret agent Lester (Rod Dana, aka Robert Mark) is dispatched by British Intelligence to investigate U.S. dollar bills which—bearing messages written in invisible ink—

are used to convey information among latter-day Nazis determined to further Hitler's goal of transforming the world into an Aryan-dominated Fourth Reich. Lester immediately suspects Rudolf King (José Bódalo), a local underworld figure who runs a Mayfair jazz spot called the Kit Kat Club; several vicious skirmishes eventually lead our hero to King's high-tech lair, concealed within a massive cathedral being renovated in the heart of Madrid.

The throbbing title theme sounds like something Ennio Morricone would have written for a spaghetti Western, with a moody electric guitar melody against quiet organ comping. Swinging action jazz backs Lester's battle with one baddie; rhythmic percussion and an uptempo walking bass highlight his dockside skirmishes with other thugs; jazz flute and organ deliver softer bossa nova when Lester surreptitiously snatches one of the "special" dollar bills from a sidebar cutie. A lengthy first act sequence in the Kit Kat Club grants plenty of space for source combo jazz, with a variety of vibes, guitar and trumpet solos highlighting different tunes as events progress. But director Mino Guerrini and his editors got rather sloppy in postproduction; one scene clearly shows a solo jazz pianist entertaining the crowd, but the soundtrack's source cue emanates from a vibes combo!

No soundtrack album was produced.

* * *

On paper, the heist comedy *Caccia alla volpe* (*After the Fox*) sounded like a sure thing: a cast headed by Peter Sellers, Britt Ekland and Victor Mature—the latter coaxed out of semi-retirement to spoof his own career—working from a script by Neil Simon (his first project written specifically for the big screen), with everything helmed by famed Italian director Vittorio De Sica. Sadly, the results are quite disappointing. The film gets its sole bounce from Burt Bacharach's effervescent blend of buoyant pop and soft jazz; he spots many scenes with full-fledged melodies, rather than short cues. For the most part, De Sica lets the music run uninterrupted behind dialogue and action, which helps some of the film's weaker scenes.

The story concerns master thief Aldo Vanucci, dubbed "The Fox" (Sellers), who agrees to smuggle 300 bars of gold into Italy: the haul from a Cairo heist masterminded by the sinister Okra (Akim Tamiroff). Vanucci concocts a plan to impersonate a movie director—dubbed Federico Fabrizi—shooting a film titled *The Gold of Cairo* in the tiny coastal village of Sevalio. The film will star Tony Powell (Mature) and Vanucci's star-struck younger sister, Gina (Ekland). When the ship carrying Okra's stolen bullion reaches the bay, the townsfolk—all hired as extras—will help load it into a waiting getaway truck, believing they're handling prop gold. Naturally, things don't quite work out that way.

Bacharach wrote several character themes, most notably the lively tune designed for Vanucci: a rhythmic 4/4 swinger powered by a robust trumpet melody and backed by Bacharach on Hammond B3. The tune pops up frequently, initially behind Maurice Binder's cute animated credits sequence. Two Italian cops pursuing Vanucci get their own jazzy theme each time they appear: a heavy 2/2 blend of distorted electric guitar, harpsichord, noodly B3 riffs and backing horns. When the action moves to Sevalio, an evening of romantic hijinks is fueled by a sultry clarinet melody with swooping strings, gentle percussion, lyrical piano comping and Hindi-style shading. It's an odd mix of instruments, but the result is quite sexy.

The film concludes with a manic vehicular chase, set to a lively blend of clarinet, trumpets, crashing cymbals and heavy drums, all powered by a strong 2/2 beat; the result strongly anticipates Bacharach's "Bond Street," which he'd soon write for the spoof film *Casino Royale*.

Interestingly, the film's Italian release features an entirely different score by composer Piero Piccioni. His score never was issued, but Bacharach's efforts became a popular soundtrack album.

11

Home, James, Don't Spare the Horses: 1967

Quincy Jones scored five big-screen features this year—three of which are discussed in this chapter—along with the TV-movie pilot of *Ironside* and 10 of that series' first 15 episodes, and two episodes of another series (*Hey, Landlord*). Lalo Schifrin scored four big-screen features—three also discussed herein—along with three TV-movies, eight episodes of *T.H.E. Cat*, and the pilot episode of *Mannix*.

One wonders when either of them ate or slept...

The Small Screen

Authenticity was the goal of *N.Y.P.D.*, a rugged ABC police procedural made with the full cooperation of the New York City police department and then-mayor John Lindsay. Many of the fast-paced half-hour episodes are adapted from actual cases, with equal time devoted to the personal lives of plainclothes detectives Mike Haines (Jack Warden), Jeff Ward (Robert Hooks) and Johnny Corso (Frank Converse). Voice-over narration allows us to eavesdrop on their private thoughts—investigative notions, ruminative observations, anxieties—while they pursue a case or prepare for a potentially dangerous confrontation. The series debuted September 5 and ran for two seasons.

Charles Gross' pulse-pounding title theme grabs the viewer with throbbing timpani and jagged brass statements, against a montage of New York's cityscape. The melody rises via horns and shrill woodwind counterpoint, as the camera descends to ground level and "hitches a ride" on the back of a speeding police cruiser. (This portion of the credits sequence was lampooned mercilessly by ABC's 1982 comedy, *Police Squad!*) Bold brass "pops" are timed to the superimposed title, which appears one letter at a time: *N ... Y ... P ... D*. Timpani, brass and woodwind continue their duel for dominance as the cast members are identified; the image then blurs out against a final explosion of unison horns.

The show's frequent use of montages—undercover stakeouts, tailing suspects, conducting interviews on the street—grant Gross the space for playful or saucy action jazz cues that suggest the urban funk soon to characterize many film and TV scores. Such cues also can be jangly, dissonant and unsettling, which heightens the show's atmosphere of nervous anxiety. Alternatively, the tension is broken during lighter moments—say, cops gently squabbling with each other—backed by droll jazz flute cues. At still other times, Gross' cues play against a scene, as with the gentle little piano trio swinger heard immediately after a young man guns down two cops, and then—gruesomely delighted by his actions—saunters cheerfully down the street.

No soundtrack album was produced, although the title theme was covered by The Wooden Trumpet (Amy) and jazz organist Johnny "Hammond" Smith (Prestige).

Perhaps unhappy with the violent direction TV cop shows were taking, Jack Webb revived *Dragnet* for a four-season run on NBC. Harry Morgan stepped in as Joe Friday's new partner Bill Gannon, but otherwise the formula remained unchanged from when the original run concluded in 1959. Walter Schumann's iconic title theme is retained, sounding very much like it had years earlier. The episode underscores, divided between Frank Comstock and Lyn Murray, bear no trace of jazz; many cues are no more than brief drum rolls. That said, the show's reappearance prompted a vibrant, Latin-hued cover by Stan Kenton and his Orchestra, issued as a single by Capitol.

Cops suddenly were all over the tube.

Quincy Jones got a call one day from colleague Stanley Wilson, then head of creative activities at Revue Studios. Three new television shows were up for scoring grabs—*Marcus Welby, M.D.*, *I Love a Mystery* (which never went further than its pilot film) and *Ironside*— and Wilson gave Jones his choice. He picked the latter, and musical history was made.[1]

Raymond Burr had been off the air for only a single year, after his nine-season run as *Perry Mason*, when his eight-season reign on NBC's *Ironside* began September 14; it was the opening salvo in what became a subgenre of "gimmick investigator" dramas. The back-story finds longtime veteran San Francisco police detective (and former chief) Robert Ironside forced to retire after an assassination attempt puts him in a wheelchair, paralyzed from the waist down. Unwilling to abandon the job he loves, Ironside pulls strings to become a "special consultant" assisted by former colleagues Sgt. Ed Brown (Don Galloway) and Policewoman Eve Whitfield (Barbara Anderson). Low-level felon Mark Sanger (Don Mitchell) gets a shot at redemption as Ironside's personal aide and bodyguard.

Quincy Jones scored the pilot movie, delivered a title theme and also contributed full or partial underscores for 12 of the first 17 episodes. The workload quickly proved overwhelming. "*Ironside* was especially tough," he recalled, "with car chases, love scenes and all sorts of last-minute changes. When I first began scoring it for a 44-piece orchestra, I'd fill my score paper with 16th and 32nd notes, whatever came to mind. Henry Mancini and/or Benny Carter would sometimes drop by and look over my scores and say, 'Are you crazy? You're writing like it's for a feature film. This is TV, Q; use whole notes, long-sustained passages with your strings and horns. Let a solo instrument, your rhythm section, or your bass player do the dancing on top. Don't try to write Stravinsky's *Firebird Suite* for every episode, or you'll never live through the year.' I finally got the message, but it was still a crushing workload.

"The rule of thumb for scoring a weekly hour-long show was to write an average of about 35 to 40 minutes of music a week. You write a detailed, six-line, condensed sketch score for the full orchestra, then you may have to change everything at the last minute to reduce or heighten the intensity according to editing cuts. The film editor could kill you by cutting just 30 or 40 seconds out of a car chase at the last minute. You had to make it work, and quickly. Nobody gave a damn about what you went through to make it happen, either. It's all part of the job."[2]

Jones set the show's forceful tone with an electrifying 40-second main theme sharply synchronized to the title credits sequence. The ensemble was sizable: five trumpets and flugelhorns, five trombones, soprano sax, flute, two guitars, keyboards, organ, two synthesizers, string bass, electric bass, drums, vibes, percussion and Toots Thielemans' whistling.[3] The cue begins with what sounds like wailing police sirens against insistent drumming; unison horns crescendo when Ironside's dark figure—silhouetted against a blood-red background—is gunned down by a sniper's bullet. The 5-4/5-4 melody is introduced via dramatic brass; Jones adds a bit of funk with *wah-wah* guitar and a pulsating rhythm section. Cast members are identified as the silhouetted figure resolves to Burr, now in a wheelchair; the theme builds to a final six-note brass climax that hangs in the air without resolving.

Not *too* much funk, though. "At the beginning," Jones chuckled, "they told me this [was] for Midwestern shut-ins. We don't *want* to get too jazzy and too hip here; we don't need all that funk!"[4]

Jones had the last laugh, when he expanded and added *serious* funk to a fresh arrangement of the title theme for his 1971 album *Smackwater Jack*. "I did my own version, how I'd *like* to hear it. It wasn't two minutes later, that they bought that version and put it on the air."[5]

The cue's initial "police sirens" were a groundbreaking innovation produced by a Moog synthesizer: the first time this gadget was used during a Hollywood scoring session. "Johnny Mandel, Dave Grusin and I used to go to Paul Beaver's house, to search for new, fresh 'color' sounds, because being distinctive is a very important thing in background scoring. And he said, 'Here's a thing I just got from Robert Moog; try it out.' It looked like a telephone switchboard. Paul Beaver played on that session, and I think it's the first time the public ever heard a synthesizer."[6]

Jones got a bonus while scoring the fourth episode, "Eat, Drink and Be Buried": his on-screen acting debut as Les Appleton, owner of a San Francisco jazz club called The Key of C. Ironside's aide Mark wanders in for a daytime chat about 14 minutes into the episode, while the resident sax/piano quartet rehearses some cool sounds. (Stan Getz is on sax, Shelly Manne on drums.) Jones, at the piano, pauses long enough to discuss the questionable cred of a former jazz drummer who may be a chief suspect.

Much as Jones enjoyed the assignment, the crushing responsibility became too onerous. Midway through the first season, he passed the gig to jazz saxophonist, clarinetist and composer Oliver Nelson, who made his name with the legendary 1961 album *The Blues and the Abstract Truth*; that led to arranging gigs for jazz heavyweights such as Buddy Rich, Wes Montgomery and Cannonball Adderley. Nelson ultimately scored 69 episodes through the end of the show's run. Marty Paich came on board in 1972; Benny Carter, David Shire and Robert Prince contributed a few scores here and there. All maintained the show's increasingly hip, jazz- and funk-flavored atmosphere. Sadly, none of this music endures outside of its television origins.

Burr and his core co-stars united for a 1993 reunion TV film, *The Return of Ironside*; composer John Cacavas dutifully retained the iconic main theme in his suitably dynamic score. Two decades later, NBC revived and updated *Ironside* for the 2013–14 season, with Blair Underwood taking over for Raymond Burr. The revival was a colossal flop, with only four episodes aired before cancelation.

One bullet was enough to put Robert Ironside in a wheelchair. During the 194 cases Mike Connors' Joe Mannix solved over the course of an eight-season CBS run that began September 16, 1967, he was shot 17 times and knocked unconscious 55 times, and always bounced back for more.[7] Mannix was one of television's best ultra-cool detectives: a perfect blend of Peter Gunn's *savoir faire* and Philip Marlowe's hard-charging man of action. "We do it *my* way," Mannix often insists, when confronted with intransigence. Connors fit the role perfectly, becoming one of the last old-school TV private eyes: before feminism, sensitivity training and psychological profiling transformed his successors into ... well, something else.

Not that *Mannix* was *entirely* traditional. As originally conceived, Joe Mannix is an awkward fit at Intertect, a futuristic detective agency whose investigators are expected to embrace best-case scenarios generated by the massive banks of computers that fill a central room. Mannix scoffs at such soulless nonsense, and viewers apparently agreed; the show didn't become a hit until its second season, when Mannix abandoned Intertect and hung up his own shingle. As was the case with the concurrently airing *Mission: Impossible*, much of Mannix's "cool" comes from the Lalo Schifrin soundtrack against which he swaggers. "[Producer] Bruce [Geller] said he had heard something on the radio, listening to a jazz station," Schifrin recalled. "They were playing something like a waltz, and it really was very syncopated. He tried to sing it for me, and right away I knew what he wanted."[8]

"A private detective in three-quarter time?" Geller later queried, entirely in jest.[9]

"Why not?" Schifrin insisted. "A syncopated jazz waltz was so different for this medium.[10] [That] gave it a different kind of life."[11]

Schifrin's buoyant jazz waltz adds just the right vigor and elegance to Mannix. Geller already had an opening credits sequence: a split-screen approach that begins as the episode teaser's final frame freezes, shrinks and becomes the upper-right corner of a three-by-three pattern. Schifrin kicks off with a bold, four-note brass motif followed by a roll of timpani; this repeats as various squares slide and pop onto the screen, all with clips of Mannix in action-laden scenes. Unison saxes introduce the fast-paced 3/4 melody, with trombones supplying counterpoint; the various squares coalesce into a single image of Connors running hell-for-leather across the Port of Los Angeles' Commodore Schuyler F. Heim Vertical-Lift Bridge. The words "Mike.... Connors ... is" pop onto the screen; the image shifts (during the first season) to an Intertect computer that spits out a punch card reading MANNIX. The primary melody returns against another round of split-screen action clips, followed by a final timpani roll and explosion of brass. This title sequence *dared* viewers to leave the room. Most didn't.

From the second season onward, the brief Intertect portion was replaced by a sequence of six checkerboard boxes showing Mannix at work and during down time, each image superimposed by a letter that ultimately spells the show's title. Beginning in the third season, Schifrin altered his title theme slightly, replacing the horn/string bridge—while the letters spell MANNIX—with a saucy piano solo.

Schifrin also wrote a full score for the debut episode, along with seven more as the years passed. Much the way he linked *Mission: Impossible* scenes with crisp, martial-style drumming, tense moments in *Mannix* are accompanied by taut brush work on snare drums. Additional underscores came from top-notch action/crime show talent: Jerry Fielding, Jack Urbont, Richard Hazard, Richard Markowitz, Joseph Mullendore, Benny Golson and others. All maintained the show's swinging jazz touch, and all were required to reference Schifrin's title theme throughout.

The soundtrack album contains only a few themes expanded from underscore cues; the rest are original compositions, many arbitrarily titled after TV episodes. The new material certainly "feels" like *Mannix*, and the result is a first-rate jazz album. Schifrin's longer title theme is highlighted by an expanded bridge that boasts one of the coolest piano solos he ever laid down. Sizzling big band action cues include the brass-fueled "Hunt Down" and the positively ferocious "Endgame"; the droll "Girl Who Came in with the Tide" wreaks havoc with time signatures, sliding effortlessly from 5/4 to 4/4 and 3/4. Decades later, when Schifrin wasn't able to coax a digital reissue from Paramount, he rerecorded the entire album on his own Aleph label, with an entirely different ensemble. Alas, this disco-hued 1999 retread has none of the fire-breathing intensity that made the original LP so memorable.

The Big Screen

James Coburn's return as super secret agent Derek Flint was inevitable. *In Like Flint* delivers the same over-the-top spyjinks and female pulchritude, and the escapades again are highlighted by opulent sets and another of Jerry Goldsmith's sublime action jazz scores. This sequel's music is a bit more orchestrally "elegant" than its predecessor, in part because the score is dominated by variations of its jazz-waltz title theme, "Your Zowie Face." Goldsmith also was savvy enough to include reprises of the first film's swinging, samba-hued title theme, along with the dynamic action cue that always signals Flint's gymnastic skirmishes.

Flint's sophomore adventure is triggered by events at a Virgin Islands–based beauty farm, Fabulous Face, whose owners have an insidious plan to switch the U.S. president with a puppet lookalike; he'll discredit the ZOWIE intelligence agency and then threaten the world by arming an orbiting space platform with nuclear weapons. The ultimate goal: to replace global patriarchy with feminist rulers who will (but of course) do a far superior job.

The alluringly sexy title credits sequence, which opens in Fabulous Face's steam-laden massage/sauna chamber, introduces a smoldering arrangement of the new title theme; this blossoms into a cheeky, uptempo samba with the melody carried by synth, reeds and strings, ultimately climaxing with a heroic brass fanfare. Flint eventually infiltrates Fabulous Face by swimming in via the sauna chamber: an excellent excuse for a voluptuous sax reprise of this title theme. When the beauty farm's leaders are betrayed by one of their male associates, Flint assaults the ZOWIE launch site with a flotilla of dinghies, rafts and small boats, all laden with bikini-clad Amazons. Goldsmith backs this droll "invasion" with a nautical-hued arrangement of the title theme, introduced via soprano reeds and military-style snare drums; the cue builds into full-blown orchestral jazz fury, as the group overpowers the guards, allowing Flint to save the world (again!).

The soundtrack album includes a vocal version of "Your Zowie Face" not heard in the film.

Flint reappeared one final time, in 1976's genuinely dreadful ABC-TV pilot, *Dead on Target*, which recast him as a private detective played unpersuasively by Ray Danton. About which, no more need be said.

At least the big-screen Flint went out with style. Dean Martin's Matt Helm hit rock bottom with 1967's *The Ambushers*, a pathetic assortment of inept sci-fi, laughably bad process shots and more wincingly sexist attempts at humor. The bonkers plot opens as the U.S. government launches a prototype "flying saucer" that can be piloted only by women, because its "electromagnetic force" is deadly to all males. The craft is hijacked via a long-distance tractor beam wielded by Big O criminal mastermind Jose Ortega (Albert Salmi), who conceals it in the Central American jungle. Matt and fellow ICE agent Sheila Sommers (Janice Rule) head to Acapulco, following a lead that connects Big O with the city's Montezuma Beer

Brewery. Ortega ultimately perishes when he attempts to fly the saucer, and Matt rescues the kidnapped Sheila seconds before her certain death.

Whereas the first two films boasted cool jazz scores, *The Ambushers* opens with a bikini-baiting pop tune that would have been better placed in a Frankie Avalon/Annette Funicello beach musical. Hugo Montenegro's underscore is relentless: laden with mickey-mousing and the orchestral equivalent of drum pops to help sell Martin's smug one-liners. Only a few cues veer dangerously close to jazz. The first is a sultry, strip club-style arrangement of the title theme, heard when Matt and his faithful secretary—series regular Lovey Kravezit (Beverly Adams)—enjoy a sexy sauna together. Solid action jazz (finally!) lends mild excitement to a chase and gunfight at the Montezuma Brewery; and then again during the climax, as Matt roars along on a motorcycle while trying to catch the saucer, fastened to a railroad flatcar and rolling toward a high cliff.

No soundtrack LP appeared. No loss.

The results aren't much better in *The Scorpio Letters*, a slapdash MGM quickie that turns British author Victor Canning's 1964 crime novel into an insufferably talky and confusing secret agent flick. Studio heads took one look at the mess director Richard Thorpe had made, and—rather than granting it big-screen release—instead slotted *Scorpio* as an ABC-TV movie on February 19, 1967. (It nonetheless was released theatrically in Europe and the UK.) This version obviously is chopped down from a longer director's cut; chunks of exposition are missing, and sidebar characters drift in for no reason, never to be seen again. Dave Grusin apparently wasn't inspired; his by-the-numbers score offers no suspense, and modest jazz cues do little to enhance the laughably inept action scenes.

Former American police detective Joe Christopher (Alex Cord) lives in London, where he works for an unspecified British intelligence agency. While investigating the unexpected suicide of a fellow agent, Joe uncovers an extensive blackmail operation masterminded by a shadowy villain dubbed Scorpio (Oscar Beregi, Jr.). Joe is assisted by Phoebe Stewart (Bond girl Shirley Eaton), an operative from a rival British spy network;

The Scorpio Letters should have become the first big-screen credit for jazz musician/composer Dave Grusin, at the time quite busy on MGM's franchise spin-off, *The Girl from U.N.C.L.E.* Alas, fate—and wiser studio heads—had other plans. Sharp-eared listeners will detect a strong similarity between this film's primary action cue and the music that propelled April Dancer's weekly adventures (courtesy Film Score Monthly).

they naturally fall in love while tracking Scorpio to his lair, dodging a few pathetically incompetent assassins along the way. More often than not, it looks like Scorpio and his minions intend to *lecture* Joe and Phoebe to death.

Grusin's oft-heard action cue is a staccato blend of percussion, piano and trumpet fanfares; it sounds remarkably similar to "Follow the THRUSH," one of his many cues for *The Girl from U.N.C.L.E.* Joe's theme is a lighthearted jazz flute cue, introduced when he gets this assignment from his oh-so-veddy-British superior (Laurence Naismith). A second jazz flute cue is a mischievous, saucy swinger that introduces Miss Gunther (Ilka Windish), whose involvement in this story remains bafflingly vague.

Grusin's soundtrack was digitized in 2007 and paired on a disc with Jerry Goldsmith's scores for 1971's *The Last Run* and *Crosscurrent*.

Paranoia-laced conspiracy thrillers became quite the rage during the post–Watergate era, but 1967's *The President's Analyst* beat them by nearly a decade. This savage, anti-authoritarian satire is more burlesque than espionage drama, but its spy-laden narrative and sinister undercurrent put it in the same scathingly *noir* territory as *The Manchurian Candidate*, if on a more farcical note. No targets are spared in writer/director Theodore J. Flicker's outrageous—and eerily prophetic—indictment of citizen surveillance, political extremists and government overreach.

Dr. Sidney Schaefer (James Coburn) is vetted by Central Enquiries Agency (CEA) spy/assassin Don Masters (Godfrey Cambridge), who puts the final stamp of approval on his appointment as the U.S. president's personal psychiatrist. Sidney soon succumbs to mounting paranoia, convinced that every seemingly suspicious person is a spy assigned to kidnap him, to extract what he now knows about U.S. secrets. As it happens, Sidney *is* being followed by clandestine agents from various world powers. He goes AWOL, hiding out with the "average American" Quantrill family, and later with a wandering hippie rock band; alas, he's ultimately kidnapped by the all-powerful TPC (The Phone Company). Masters and Russian spy V.I. Kydor Kropotkin (Severn Darden), longtime comrades despite their Cold War divide, team up to spring Sidney from TPC's sci-fi lair, where he has learned of an insidious plot to implant a cerebrum communicator in the brain of every man, woman and child in the United States.

Lalo Schifrin's title theme opens with a faux-patriotic drumbeat and brass fanfare, then slides into a brisk slice of trumpet- and flute-laden spy jazz; the camera follows a disguised Masters making his way along New York City's grimy streets, pausing long enough to kill an Albanian spy. Schifrin abruptly shifts the mood as we cut to the office-bound Sidney, treating a variety of patients; the title credits zip across the screen to a breezy jazz flute interlude, laced with tack piano and sizzling electric guitar. This montage cuts back and forth between Sidney and Masters, Schifrin obligingly switching from mod to militaristic with each edit; the result is as wild, wooly and flamboyant as Coburn's ear-splitting grin.

Additional musical highlights include the AWOL Sidney's effort to escape dueling spies; his panicked flight takes place against the pounding bongos, pulsating drums, brass fanfares and low-end piano riffs that characterize Schifrin's signature action jazz. Sidney's sojourn with the Quantrills is spotted by source music that scathingly ridicules their "all-American" values: Their car radio delivers a pair of trumpet-laden bossa nova cues that clearly mimic Herb Alpert's Tijuana Brass, beloved by 1960s conservatives trying to hang onto "their" music amid the growing rock cacophony. Later, the family's surround-sound stereo system belts out a droll spoof of the equally conformist pop jazz that Burt Bacharach pumped out in between Top 40 hits.

The soundtrack finally was issued in 2015.

The President's Analyst endures as a scathing satire, but *Fathom* is merely a limp spy spoof: little more than an excuse to slide star Raquel Welch into revealing bikinis. She plays American skydiving champion Fathom Harvill, who is approached by Douglas Campbell (Ronald Fraser), of a top-secret spy organization dubbed HADES (Headquarters Allied Defences, Espionage & Security). He spins some confusing nonsense about a jeweled relic known as the Fire Dragon: actually a nuclear triggering mechanism that must not fall into the wrong hands. It has gone missing somewhere in the Mediterranean and is being sought by a dodgy Armenian named Sergi Serapkin (Clive Revill) and wealthy adventurer Peter Merriwether (Tony Franciosa). Fathom stumbles and bumbles her way into and out of the clutches of each, in turn; various contrived escapes allow Welch to puff, pout and give poor readings to the inane dialogue.

John Dankworth's score is much like what he delivered for *Modesty Blaise*, including an inane title theme with insipid lyrics. The jazz content improves once the title sequence cuts to a montage of Fathom's fellow jumpers, who descend to Earth against a slowly swinging sax cue. Fathom's subsequent jump is spotted by an instrumental reprise of the title theme, with a smooth jazz flute handling the melody. Later, after getting caught by Merriwether, Fathom talks herself out of the sticky situation and walks to the nearby village square; this stroll is spotted by a tasty bossa nova cue, with a soft trumpet handling the melody. When all the competing factions finally reveal themselves, Fathom bounces through a series of silly chase scenes that gain minor suspense from Dankworth's action jazz.

The soundtrack album is a pale reflection of the film score. Dankworth's rerecordings purge almost all of the tasty jazz content, turning most of the cues into easy-listening orchestral pap.

* * *

Happily, we can always expect great things from Henry Mancini and Blake Edwards.

Peter Gunn went off the air in September 1961, but the 114 episodes proved quite popular in syndicated reruns; sensing momentum, Paramount gave Edwards the opportunity to put the character on the big screen.[12] He duly brought Mancini and star Craig Stevens onto the team; the other key roles—Pete's gal pal Edie, Lt. Jacoby and Mother, owner of their nightclub hangout—went to newcomers Laura Devon, Edward Asner and Helen Traubel. The resulting film, *Gunn*, has the same blend of crime-laden suspense and whimsical romantic comedy that made the TV show a hit.

The story's setting once again is the dingy, crime-laden waterfront community that Pete prowled in the TV series, little having changed aside from an acknowledgment of the rising youth culture. Mancini opens the film with a fresh, smokin'-hot arrangement of "Fallout!" as thugs board a yacht belonging to crime lord Julio Scarlotti, killing everyone on board. A quick cut to an op-art title credits sequence is propelled by a sizzling arrangement of the iconic "Peter Gunn" theme, with rock-inflected sass supplied by fuzz guitar and Plas Johnson's solo on Selmer Varitone electric sax.

As Pete tries to determine who killed Scarlotti, much of the film's humor revolves around his repeated discovery of the very naked Samantha (Sherry Jackson) in his apartment. Pianist Jimmy Rowles gives a droll country/western hue to Mancini's midtempo "Theme for Sam," a gently swaying ballad that includes a lovely vibes solo and builds to three final, Basie-esque notes. Much of Pete's "down time" takes place in Mother's, where flirty banter between Edie and Pete takes place while the off-camera band offers a lovely

The most amusing diegetic cue Henry Mancini contributes for *Gunn* occurs when the suave PI visits a gambling ship anchored just offshore; the venue's solo jazz pianist, surrounded by a bevy of underdressed escorts—all twins—is none other than Mancini himself (Photofest).

vibes ballad ("Silver Tears") given moody thoughtfulness by Bob Bain's guitar solo. Later, a sparkling "walking four" melody ("A Quiet Happening") is highlighted by solos from Ted Nash (alto sax) and Bud Shank (baritone sax).

The soundtrack album is a treasure, with full-length arrangements of the film's key melodies, although "Fallout!" is left behind. In its place, Mancini offers two unused tracks: "A Lovely Sound," a slow ballad led by Dick Nash's trombone; and "Night Owl," a leisurely, sultry swinger again showcased by Ted Nash's sax.

Edwards and Mancini would revisit Pete 'n' Edie one final time, in a 1989 TV movie (discussed in this book's companion volume).

Perhaps envious of Dean Martin's Matt Helm franchise, fellow rat-packer Frank Sinatra signed up for the big-screen adaptation of Marvin H. Albert's 1960 novel *Miami Mayhem*: the first of three books about chronic gambler and hard-nosed private investigator Tony Rome, who lives in a small houseboat dubbed *The Straight Pass*. Richard L. Breen's script for *Tony Rome* minimizes the rough stuff in deference to Sinatra's laid-back image; events begin with a distraught young socialite found passed out in a hotel. After Rome is hired to take her home, he gets mixed up in a complicated case involving stolen jewels, blackmail, drugs and a steadily mounting pile of bodies. Fans of Albert's novels found little to admire.

Billy May's lively but simple score didn't stretch his talents; relentless variations of the same four-note character theme follow Tony's dogged discoveries of fresh questions that need answers. May displays more aggressive jazz chops when Tony chases a thug along a beach laden with bikini babes; and when he later pursues a junkie who might be able to answer some of those open questions. May also collaborated with fledgling lyricist Randy Newman on a couple of songs that pop up as source music: notably during one of the embarrassing "go-go club" scenes that became obligatory in mid- to late 1960s movies, inserted by studio squares trying to entice the youth market.

The film did well enough to generate a sequel, *Lady in Cement*—about which, more later—but failed to produce a soundtrack album. Both films finally were paired on a 2016 Blu-ray, which includes isolated score tracks.

In another case of music serving as a film's lone saving grace, Lalo Schifrin's bouncy score is the sole attraction in *Who's Minding the Mint?*, an inane heist comedy apparently aimed at very young children. Harry Lucas (Jim Hutton), an employee at the Washington, D.C., Bureau of Engraving and Printing, accidentally destroys $50,000. With an audit coming up, he and sympathetic co-worker Verna (Dorothy Provine) concoct a plan to slip a retired Mint press operator—Walter Brennan, as Pop—into the building overnight, to print the necessary bills before they're missed. The scheme expands to include a deaf safecracker (Jack Gilford); a pawnbroker (Milton Berle); a public works employee (Joey Bishop); a maritime buff who can design a vessel that'll fit through a manhole (Victor Buono); an ice cream truck vendor (Bob Denver); and Pop's very pregnant beagle (Inky). Naturally, chaos ensues.

Schifrin's main theme opens with teletype-style percussion, as the title credits appear over images of the U.S. bank notes in circulation at the time, from the $1 bill to the $100,000 bill; the energetic melody is carried by a spirited *bah-da-bah* female chorus backed by furious bongos, drum rolls and brass fanfares. This sequence is much more clever than anything that follows. Schifrin's secondary theme—a sly, stealthy blend of walking bass, jazz flute, harpsichord and expectant percussion—is a light-hearted riff on the various "heist" cues he wrote for TV's *Mission: Impossible*; it recurs while Harry and his dim-bulb cohorts rehearse their caper, and (later) try to sneak past various Mint guards. Source cues include several lush bossa nova melodies heard on Harry's phonograph.

No soundtrack album appeared.

Schifrin had much better luck with *Cool Hand Luke*, although the jazz content is minimal; he felt the 1950s Florida setting would be represented better by a blend of bluegrass, thoughtful blues and Aaron Copland-esque symphonic themes. Even so, enough jazz creeps in to warrant acknowledgment. The film is based on Donn Pearce's 1965 novel of the same title; the four Oscar nominations included one for Schifrin (the first of his six Academy Award nods).

The story is simple but heavily symbolic: laden with religious songs, Christian imagery and a palpable suggestion that Newman's character is a Jesus surrogate. Decorated World War II veteran Lucas "Luke" Jackson (Newman) is sentenced to two years at a Florida chain gang prison, for the minor offense of decapitating parking meters after a night of heavy drinking. Luke quickly butts heads with the prisoners' unofficial leader, the hulking Dragline (George Kennedy); they later become friends. The restless, nonconformist Luke isn't wired to follow the rules laid down by the warden (Strother Martin, as Captain) and his grim-faced "walking bosses." Luke escapes once, gets caught and then escapes again; after being dragged back this second time, Captain and the walking bosses break his spirit ... or so they believe.

"Music and film have something in common: the rhythm," Schifrin observed. "The mission of the composer is to find the rhythm of the film. In the case of *Cool Hand Luke*, we found a parallel rhythm."[13]

"We discussed the theme music for Luke," director Stuart Rosenberg recalled, "and what was needed was a sense of loneliness for the non-conformist that he was, and the honesty of an existential hero who is to be judged not by what he says, but by what he does. Lalo's theme captured the sweetness and truthfulness of Luke."[14]

"My best ideas come when I see the film—the visuals—and I write them when they come," Schifrin added. "They showed me the dailies, and the theme came right there. I didn't even have music paper, but I made a staff and wrote it out. And you know, [at first] I tried to improve it. I said, 'It's too simple.' But that was the theme, and I was nominated for an Oscar."[15]

That main theme is a quietly heartbreaking bluegrass ballad, introduced over the title credits and then frequently heard as the story proceeds, the melody most often taken by guitar or harmonica. Solid jazz elements surface in the bass- and percussion-laden action cues that accompany Luke's various escape attempts, with an impish harmonica adding melodic touches. The sweetest bit of jazz, however, is a sensuous swinger that accompanies a scantily clad young woman (Joy Harmon) who teases the chain gang by soapily washing her car within their view; Schifrin's samba-hued cue is a lyrical, trumpet- and guitar-driven melody with tasty solos on piano and organ.

The soundtrack album includes several jazz-laden cuts not heard in the film. "Arletta Blues," apparently intended for a scene where Luke's mother visits, is a bluesy swinger that boasts Ray Brown's walking bass line and some tasty guitar licks. A saucy instrumental version of the spiritual "Just a Closer Walk with Thee" is highlighted by driving percussion and some wicked keyboard chops on a Dixieland-style piano.

It sometimes seemed, at this point, that every other film and TV show was scored by either Schifrin or Quincy Jones. *In the Heat of the Night* is the big-screen classic that cemented the latter's Hollywood reputation as a force to be reckoned with. Director Norman Jewison's savvy, subtle blend of murder mystery and prickly Deep South race relations is adapted from John Ball's 1965 novel, which kicked off an ongoing series featuring police detective Virgil Tibbs. The film takes place in the fictitious flyspeck town of Sparta, Mississippi, where Philadelphia-based homicide detective Tibbs (Sidney Poitier)—in transit after attending his mother's funeral—has the bad luck to be present when the body of a murdered real estate developer is discovered. Delighted by an opportunity to outsmart white cops, he accepts the challenge to solve the crime. This decision weighs heavily on local sheriff Bill Gillespie (Rod Steiger), who eventually swallows his knee-jerk animosity after perceiving Tibbs' savvy investigative skills. Trouble is, Tibbs' mere presence in this community is enough to rile up many of the lynch-minded locals.

Jones' soulful, jazz- and blues-inflected score is employed sparingly. The music often is angry and ominous, reflecting the hovering atmosphere of menace; specific themes define the primary characters, most notably the disconcerting blend of bass, cimbalom, harmonica and flute that enhances Poitier's superbly depicted chill politeness and repressed, indignant fury. Jones also delivers contrasts: a bit of urban fusion to suggest Virgil's Philadelphia origins, against the straight blues we'd expect would be the anthem of a small rural town. The smoky, soulful title song is performed with gospel-hued passion by Ray Charles; it's introduced over the title credits, as a train deposits Tibbs in Sparta, in the dead of night. Subsequent establishing scenes take place without any underscore, and Jewison maintains this pattern; Jones' music is used primarily for character embellishment, as opposed to event enhancement.

One action-oriented exception is titled "Shag Bag, Hounds & Harvey," a raucous orchestral piece that accompanies the mobilized police pursuit of the luckless Harvey (Scott Wilson), initially suspected of the crime. Even here, Jones isn't satisfied with traditional "chase music," opting instead for a jangly, percussive-heavy cue dominated by horn pops, drums, jagged strings and even tambourine.

The soundtrack album has been popular since its debut, and Poitier's Virgil Tibbs would return in two big-screen sequels (about which, more later).

Jones moved in an entirely different direction just a few months later, with *In Cold Blood*. His nervous, fingernails-on-blackboard opening theme blends jittery percussion, frantic strings, agitated bass and brass riffs, along with chords that are oddly sustained or unexpectedly chopped off. Viewers would have been unsettled, with good reason; director/scripter Richard Brooks' approach is every bit as grim and horridly fascinating as Truman Capote's mesmerizing 1966 nonfiction best-seller. Academy Award-nominated Conrad L. Hall's monochrome cinematography juxtaposes empty, even forlorn Kansas landscapes with the claustrophobic horrors of the murder site.

Jones almost didn't get the assignment. "Richard Brooks kicked ass for me, when Columbia Pictures and Truman Capote wanted to hire Leonard Bernstein," Jones recalled. "Brooks was furious about it. He told Columbia, 'Up yours. Quincy Jones is doing my score.' I'll never forget that. After the New York premiere of the film, Capote called me, speaking slowly, in a low voice, and crying apologetically."[16]

The film opens with a five-minute jazz symphony in several movements. Wailing horns accompany the title, after which disturbing bass riffs signal a match flare that illuminates the face of just-released ex-con Perry Smith (Robert Blake) during a late-night bus ride. He's traveling to reunite with Dick Hickock (Scott Wilson), whom we meet as he loads his car with what we know will become the murder weapons; his attitude is giddy. Jones shifts to a swinging, disturbingly cheerful blend of finger-snapping percussion, dirty horns and—most particularly—arresting bass licks. The mostly wordless prologue continues as Brooks shifts to the Clutter family, going about their ordinary business; Jones characterizes their purity with a sweeping orchestral waltz that evokes modern classical works such as Ferde Grofé's *Grand Canyon Suite*. As Brooks and editor Peter Zinner cut between these three tableaux—Perry, Dick and the Clutters—Jones does the same, leaving us breathless and increasingly agitated.

Once the two men hit the road, driving 400 miles to gain access to the money-filled wall safe that Dick is certain Herbert Clutter has in his home office, Jones returns to the restless bass, percussion and finger-snaps that signal the ghastly enthusiasm with which Dick, in particular, anticipates their little "adventure." Those details remain undisclosed for a time; instead, we later catch up with Perry and Dick, having the time of their lives during a buying spree financed by a trail of bad checks. Jones inserts a distressingly upbeat theme ("Hanging Paper") that amplifies the horror of watching these two men enjoy themselves, despite what they've just done. The mood shifts abruptly, once they're caught and trapped into confessing; we finally experience the multiple murders that Brooks withheld, earlier in the film. Years pass quickly, in montage; Jones eventually supplies a slow-march bass and percussion dirge as we focus on Perry, waiting his turn for the walk to the gallows that he knows has just claimed Dick's life.

Brooks' faith in Jones was rewarded when the film score garnered an Academy Award nomination: the first for an African American composer. (He lost to Elmer Bernstein's conventional work on *Thoroughly Modern Millie*.) Jones reorchestrated his primary themes for the soundtrack album.

* * *

Johnny Mandel barely flexes his jazz muscles in *Point Blank*, a *most* unusual crime thriller. The film is based on 1962's *The Hunter*, the first of Donald E. Westlake's hard-boiled Parker novels. Unfortunately, director John Boorman's surrealistic adaptation is self-consciously arty, particularly during the nearly incoherent first act, and is laden with flashbacks and flash-forwards, irritating sound effects, monochromatic set designs, dream visions and weird camera angles.

The plot is bare-bones: Lee Marvin's Walker—legal issues precluded using the name Parker—gets double-crossed during a heist, is shot and left for dead by "good friend" Mal Reese (John Vernon). As a further twist of the knife, the betrayal involves Walker's wife, Lynne (Sharon Acker). Ah, but our antihero survives; after recovering, he goes after Reese and everybody else further up the ladder of the mysterious "Organization" that controls all crime in Los Angeles and San Francisco. Walker isn't out for revenge *per se*; he merely wants the $93,000 he should have gotten from the original heist. People keep refusing, so he keeps killing them.

Mandel's score is dissonant and unsettling, and deliberately so: much the way Boorman begins the film by limiting the palette to washed-out browns and grays, then slowly adds brighter colors as the story proceeds. "I made it a serial score, all 12-tone," Mandel explained, "in order to disorient anyone in the audience from the center of gravity you get from ordinary diatonic music."[17]

(Arnold Schoenberg's 12-tone compositional structure involves creating a theme from all 12 of an octave's pitches, in a given order, and then expanding upon that theme by reversing and transposing the initial sequence.)[18]

The few exceptions are diegetic: two sultry jazz cues played on Reese's penthouse stereo system, when Walker sends Lynne's sister (Angie Dickinson) to distract him; and some brief, Basie-esque combo swing heard on a fancy tape deck in a plush hillside home, while Walker waits to confront the next kingpin (Carroll O'Connor) further up the Organization's chain of command. The soundtrack album features expanded arrangements of all three, although it didn't arrive until 2002.

The line between television and film production began to blur in the 1960s, with established tube stars sometimes "borrowing" studio colleagues for big-screen projects. Such is the case with *Warning Shot*, which kept David Janssen busy between the third and fourth seasons of *The Fugitive*. He stars as LAPD Sgt. Tom Valens, who confronts an armed figure during the foggy, late-night stakeout of an upscale apartment complex. Valens kills the suspect in self-defense, after which it's discovered that the dead man, James Ruston, is a well-respected physician and humanitarian. Worse yet, there's no sign of the gun that Valens insists Ruston was holding. Placed on suspension and charged with manslaughter by an arrogant prosecutor, Valens struggles to clear his name by looking into Ruston's private life. Nobody is willing to help, although he eventually gains the sympathy of the doctor's nurse, Liz Thayer (Stefanie Powers). Bits and pieces slowly emerge; when Valens barely survives an attempt on his life, he knows that he's getting close to the truth.

Jerry Goldsmith's score is a riveting blend of the suspense and action cues that he'd been writing for *Thriller* and *The Man from U.N.C.L.E.*, and his main theme for *Warning Shot* is very much in the latter mold. The lurid title credits pop onto the screen against an opening salvo of brass, followed by a swinging waltz melody carried by guitar, organ and a bank of trumpets. The cue builds to a climax and then retreats, as we meet Valens and his partner Musso (Keenan Wynn) during their midnight stakeout at the Seascape apartments. Suspenseful percussion and brass follow Valens when he chases the suspect; the horns turn shrill as he shoots the man. Most of the subsequent jazz cues are variations on the primary waltz theme, although the discovery of another murder victim prompts a provocative guitar/synth/percussion cue that could have been borrowed from Goldsmith's work on *Our Man Flint*. That isn't the only "lift"; Valens endures a vicious beating against a brass-laden cue which is strikingly similar to "Mince & Cook Until Tender," from *In Like Flint*.

Goldsmith's score suffered an odd fate, when it came time for a soundtrack album. The assignment went instead to trombonist/big band jazz leader Si Zentner, who reorchestrated the title theme and five underscore cues for a Liberty LP with the catalog-unfriendly title of *Si Zentner Plays Music from the Original Motion Picture Score of Warning Shot and Other Themes Composed by Jerry Goldsmith*. It's an excellent jazz album, with swinging arrangements by Bob Florence and Donald D. Dimick, although the half-dozen *Warning Shot* cues don't really convey the film's complex emotional sweep. Goldsmith's original score finally was released in 2012.

Meanwhile, Across the Pond...

It's not unusual for popular actors to earn their own shows after playing breakout supporting characters in an earlier series. Such is the case with William Mervyn's Scotland Yard Chief Inspector Charles Rose, who debuted during the third series of *The Odd Man*, a serio-comic ITV police/detective series than ran through September 1963. Mervyn's Rose subsequently was paired with co-star Keith Barron's Detective Sgt. Swift, in the much edgier *It's Dark Outside*, which ran through April 1965. Starting February 17, 1967, Mervyn and his popular character then moved on to ITV's *Mr. Rose*, which finds the now-former chief inspector attempting to enjoy a well-earned retirement in Eastbourne. Alas, a surfeit of intriguing cases transforms him into a reluctant private detective.

The title theme came from Derek Hilton, working under the pseudonym John Snow. It's a charming, uptempo jazz waltz, with a droll unison string and woodwind melody set against a swinging rhythm section dominated by cool piano riffs. The series didn't use music beyond that theme, given each episode's (mostly) studio-bound settings and live-to-film production. Hilton never released a commercial version, although two arrangements are included on 1971's *Swivel*, an LP of De Wolfe library cues. Roy Budd issued a jazzy cover as a Pye single.

Hilton also tagged along when bookish espionage agent-turned-criminologist Edwin G. Oldenshaw (Richard Vernon) and colleague Ian Dimmock (Michael Aldridge) returned to British television on May 15, 1967, in Granada's *The Fellows (Late of Room 17)*. Now ensconced at Cambridge University, Oldenshaw and Dimmock continue to solve crimes behind closed doors, as part of a Peel Research Fellowship tasked with anticipating how crime—and criminals—will adapt during "a period of rapid social change" (in other words, 1960s London). Their intellectual successes continue over the course of two brief seasons, often involving confrontations with an increasingly annoyed gangster, Spindoe (Ray McAnally).

Hilton's finger-snapping swing theme is powered by plenty of bass and percussion; it's heard over a rather peculiar credits sequence built from odd bits of woodcuts, hand-drawn images and fleeting chunks of animation. Unfortunately, the melody is carried by mixed-chorus vocalese, and the *doodly-doos* haven't aged well; one longs for solo sax or brass. As with *Mr. Rose*, music is almost entirely absent during each episode; Hilton's theme is heard solely during the title and end credits sequences.

No official single exists. Oldenshaw and Dimmock retired after solving their final case, but—in an intriguing twist—McAnally's Spindoe later graduated to *his* own series (about which, more later).

Meanwhile, much the way *The Fugitive's* Dr. Richard Kimble was accused and pursued for a murder he didn't commit, former American CIA Agent McGill (Richard Bradford) winds up in London after being charged with a treasonous act that he insists was a set-up. ITV's *Man in a Suitcase* debuted September 27, for a single season of 30 episodes. (The show migrated to the States the following year, airing on ABC from April through September.) Wanting to ply his tradecraft in some manner, McGill hires himself out as a private investigator. Cases range from conventional criminal activity to situations tinged with espionage, the latter always reminding the resentful McGill of the life he lost. Bradford gives McGill a cynical, hardened exterior that rarely permits friendships; he's a loner who lacks both a country and the career he loved.

Ron Grainer's brief but striking title theme features a core 3-4 horn motif anchored by insistent percussion. It plays against a simple animated credits sequence: fleeting "snapshots" of McGill, a gun, spent bullets and bank notes framed within a blood-red suitcase. The longer end credits arrangement includes more of the rhythmic vamp during the bridge.

Grainer supplied only the title theme. Albert Elms scored a dozen episodes, and Freddie Phillips handled one; the rest were tracked with Elms' existing cues, occasionally supplemented by a few new bits, along with material from the Chappell music library. Elms' approach leans mostly toward orchestral pop/rock and atmospheric percussion. Exceptions include a saucy blend of walking bass and expectant flute for the episode "All That Glitters"; numerous percussion-heavy action cues in "Variations on a Million Bucks"; and a particularly throbbing melody in "The Bridge," which also features a haunting solo piano ballad.

Grainer recorded an expanded arrangement of his title theme for a Pye 45; an entirely new bridge adds a keyboard and brass countermelody before returning to the core melody. Alexander Stone later turned the theme into an unlikely vocal, for a fuzz/funk-heavy, dance-friendly Gemini single. A 2008 five-disc box set features all 332 of the series' themes, cues and alternate takes.

Grainer's efforts for *Man in a Suitcase* and many other British shows notwithstanding, his fame may be linked forever with *The Prisoner*. Some view this 17-episode ITV series as a descendant of Patrick McGoohan's earlier *Danger Man* adventures, with John Drake prevented from retiring from the British Intelligence agency he served so loyally, because the knowledge he possesses makes him too tempting a target for "the opposition." Others speculate that the allegorical content—McGoohan created the show—is a means of thumbing his nose at an industry (television) that demeans compliant actors willing to be "pushed, filed, stamped, indexed, briefed, debriefed [and] numbered." Whatever the truth, *The Prisoner* proved both exhilarating and confounding when unleashed on September 29, 1967. (American viewers got it during the summer of 1968.) Some episodes are classics of twisty spycraft and double/triple-crossing espionage; others—most notably the notorious finale—are head-scratching marvels of self-indulgent, avant-garde surrealism.

The title credits sequence is a sharply edited mini-movie that depicts, in montage, the events leading to the quite unusual incarceration of McGoohan's never-named espionage agent: a drive to HQ, an angry resignation, the return home and hurried packing, the knockout gas that renders him unconscious ... and his subsequent awakening in The Village, which is filled with other, similarly "displaced" former spies. This sequence, repeated in front of each episode, runs slightly longer than two minutes and is synchronized precisely to Grainer's suspenseful jazz theme. It opens with a clap of thunder and a "distant" solo brass fanfare against expectant bongos; the core melody is stated by both brass and sizzling electric guitar. Percussive vamps and additional thunderclaps shadow McGoohan's movements; the melody repeats as he's followed home. Another brief rhythmic vamp foreshadows the cloud of knock-out gas entering via his flat's keyhole; McGoohan loses consciousness as Grainer builds his theme to a final barrage of bongos, brass and guitar.

Grainer supplied only the title theme; the bulk of the series' underscores came from Albert Elms, Wilfred Josephs and Robert Farnon. Given the variable nature of the deliberately weird scripts—one episode is a faux Western!—the music is all over the genre map. Because of the numerous efforts made to confuse McGoohan's character, many cues are disorienting, dissonant blends of unsettling strings and strange percussion instruments. Bits of swing do pop up—notably in "Dance of the Dead"—but they're fleeting exceptions to a musical tapestry that defies categorization.

Two decades passed before a soundtrack album debuted under quite unusual circumstances: as an LP commissioned by the fan-based Prisoner Appreciation Society. Additional albums followed, along with a 2008 box set containing all surviving cues.

The Prisoner was "re-imagined" in an updated 2009 miniseries that pleased few viewers. Rupert Gregson-Williams' disorienting synth score came nowhere near jazz.

As far as many British espionage fans were concerned, the only important event during the summer of 1967 was the big-screen return of James Bond.

The sweeping grandeur of John Barry's music for *You Only Live Twice* suits the story and its Japanese locales but is considerably removed from the aggressive spy jazz sound of his previous Bond efforts. Barry indulged a growing fondness for the lush orchestral elements that would characterize his most memorable future scores: "Strings are the most expressive instrument in the world, and I love them. They touch you. The vividness and variety of expression that you can get out of the strings is quite astonishing. Next to the human voice, it's the most expressive instrument; that's why I use them."[19]

You Only Live Twice accelerates the series' march toward gadgets and gibes, with a space-faring plot that begins when a massive spacecraft literally swallows an orbiting American capsule: a horrifying act that the Americans reflexively blame on the Russians. When the same thing later happens to an orbiting Soviet capsule, the world is poised on the brink of World War III: an outcome being engineered by SPECTRE's insidious Ernst Stavro Blofeld (Donald Pleasence). Bond teams with Japanese Secret Service head Tiger Tanaka (Tetsurô Tanba) and his two gorgeous associates, Aki (Akiko Wakabayashi) and Kissy Suzuki (Mie Hama); subtle clues point to a remote Japanese island supposedly populated only by fishermen and ama divers. The island's dormant volcano actually conceals the massive SPECTRE rocket base, site of the film's climactic battle between Blofeld's goons and Tanaka's ninja warriors, while Bond struggles to destroy the "space gobbler" before it swallows a second orbiting American capsule.

The bulk of the film's score is built from three new themes, starting with the dreamily lush title song. The second recurring cue, unofficially known as the "Space March," is heard whenever the SPECTRE rocket goes into action; this theme opens as a subtly threatening orchestral "shimmer" that gains menace and volume via an ominous, repeating 5-3-2 brass motif. The final new piece is a sweet, Japanese-hued love theme with a melodic 8-8 motif, employed during Bond's romantic encounters. This lyrical melody's delicate charm comes courtesy of John Leach, on the 13-string koto; and Hugo D'Alton, on mandolin.

The film isn't entirely bereft of jazz. Bond's early investigative activities take place against leisurely, contemplative arrangements of "The James Bond Theme," with Vic Flick's

Billboard anticipated great things for the music that fueled 007's fifth big-screen outing, in a review published June 10, 1967: "Take one James Bond film, have the title song done by Nancy Sinatra, and a score by John Barry [both above], and what do you have? A winning soundtrack album." Sinatra's title song also was released as a 45 single by Reprise, but it wasn't the version heard in the film; guitarist Billy Strange re-cast the tune as a rock-inflected anthem, with plenty of reverb, keyboard comping, background singers and a double-tracked lead vocal. By today's standards, the song is grotesquely overproduced (United Artists/Photofest).

pulsating guitar counterpointing a soft flute reading of the melody. The first blast of action jazz hits during a car chase choreographed to sharp, staccato blasts of percussion and brass; the cue abruptly shifts into an orchestral jazz waltz when the pursuing baddies are dispatched in a thoroughly satisfying (if wholly impractical) manner. A magnificently staged fight scene follows quickly, as Bond races across the rooftops of buildings at the Kobe Docks; he dodges, bludgeons and outruns dozens of thugs, while the camera pulls back for a stunning aerial shot, all against Barry's exciting, brass-laden arrangement of the title song. Much later, hints of Barry's familiar "007" theme accompany the assembly of the "Little Nellie" autogyro; when Bond's aerial reconnaissance of the dormant volcano attracts the attention of four SPECTRE helicopters; the subsequent skirmish is scored against repeated takes of Barry's original 1962 arrangement of "The James Bond Theme."

The soundtrack album includes one unused track: "Tanaka's World," a lyrical, mildly enigmatic flute melody that Barry wrote for Bond's droll and unexpected introduction to Tiger. The album rested comfortably on *Billboard's* Top LPs Chart for 26 weeks. Billy Strange's rock-inflected arrangement of Nancy Sinatra's title theme—grotesquely overproduced, by today's standards—spent 11 weeks on the UK's Top 100 chart. The song subsequently was covered by dozens of vocalists, including Anthony & The Imperials, Coldplay, Robbie Williams, Björk and (of course) Shirley Bassey.

The subsidiary "Bond Music Machine" continued full-tilt, with United Artists' 1967 release of *The Incredible World of James Bond*, a compilation LP that assembled covers and original John Barry tracks from the first three films. Roland Shaw's third album of orchestral jazz covers, *Themes from the James Bond Thrillers, Vol. 3*, was a more up-to-date package; its 12 tracks included three from *You Only Live Twice*.

Mention also must be made of *The Bedside Bond*, a rather unusual 1966 Decca album produced in association with *Penthouse Magazine*. Its dozen tracks have nothing to do with Barry's film scores, but instead are whimsically titled melodies—"Case for Tiffany," "The In-Spectre," "No Quarrel" and so forth—intended to evoke, as the liner notes promise, "James Bond as seen through the eyes of the *Penthouse Magazine* readers." This dubious creative premise notwithstanding, it's a terrific big band action jazz album performed by "some of the finest jazz musicians in all of England," who lamentably aren't identified. (Might they have worried about the association with *Penthouse*?) All we know is that the recording sessions were conducted by British musician, bandleader and producer Des Champ, who also arranged all the tracks, and co-wrote them with producer James Economides, Jr. It's worth seeking.

Bond producers Albert Broccoli and Harry Saltzman had made a point of securing the rights to all of Ian Fleming's stories and novels, but they weren't able to get *Casino Royale*, which was held by rival producer Charles K. Feldman. Unable to compete with any sort of "straight" Bond adventure, he opted for a parody that barely references the original novel. The result is a patchwork shambles helmed by six credited directors working independent of each other, from a sorta-kinda script that apparently changed by the hour: an overblown, star-studded mess that makes virtually no sense.

Even so, Burt Bacharach's score is sensational: a lively, larkish blast of hip jazz/pop powered by a swinging title theme. It's the ultimate in bachelor pad exotica; even the short, incidental cues that bridge scenes display plenty of jazzy vigor, while adding a layer of continuity the film scarcely deserves. The score's thematic strength derives, in part, from the fact that *Casino Royale* initially was intended as a musical (!); when that concept was scuppered, Bacharach reworked some of the songs-in-progress into bold jazz instrumentals.

The outlandish narrative finds the venerable Sir James Bond (David Niven) coming out of retirement to deal with an insidious SMERSH plot to eliminate all secret agents belonging to MI6, the CIA, the KGB and France's Deuxième Bureau. In addition to following his own line of investigation, Sir James "cleverly" renames *every* remaining MI6 operative as "James Bond," to confuse the enemy (and viewers). The SMERSH mastermind, Dr. Noah, turns out to be Sir James' nephew, Jimmy Bond (Woody Allen). A deranged climactic fracas at France's famed Casino Royale concludes when the entire place explodes, sending everybody to heaven … except for Jimmy, who winds up in a place "where it's terribly … hot."

Bacharach's breezy main theme gets additional bounce from Herb Alpert's overdubbed trumpet melody, and the brassy cue is synchronized perfectly to Richard Williams' whimsical "animation montage" title credits. Bacharach then cuts directly to some traveling jazz—an uptempo flugelhorn melody backed by harpsichord and swinging percussion, which climbs the scale during several repeats—as the heads of the four secret service agencies converge, via chauffeured limos, on Sir James' massive estate. Once Sir James is on the case, a madcap grouse shoot turns deadly when female SMERSH agents hurl bomb-laden mechanical birds toward him. Bacharach spots the comic tension of this trap with a mildly naughty orchestral and brass reprise of the main theme, which climaxes with (in Bacharach's words) a "high, screeching effect on trumpets."[20]

Additional key themes include the voluptuously carnal "The Look of Love," initially heard as a purring tenor sax instrumental when mild-mannered baccarat expert Evelyn Tremble (Peter Sellers) succumbs to the charms of retired spy Vesper Lynd (Ursula Andress); and an energetic blast of sax and organ action jazz—which Bacharach expanded and released as a single titled "Bond Street"—that spots an East Berlin fracas involving Sir James' love child, Mata Bond (Joanna Pettet). The whacked-out finale at Casino Royale is backed by a virtual rhapsody of primary themes, incidental action jazz cues and comic stingers, somehow held together by *oom-pah* percussion, unison soprano saxes, organ, an incidental brass band waltz and even bugle calls.

Bacharach reorchestrated and blended some of the cues for the soundtrack album; other cues—notably the main theme—are lifted directly from the film. The album spent 21 weeks on *Billboard's* Top LPs chart. Alpert and his Tijuana Brass released their cover of the title theme as an A&M single, which spent nine weeks on *Billboard's* Hot 100 chart (and went all the way to No. 1 on *Billboard's* Adult Contemporary chart). "The Look of Love" subsequently was covered by hundreds of vocalists and instrumentalists, and remains one of the most enduring hits in the Bacharach/David canon.

A 1991 issue of *The Absolute Sound* magazine hailed the original Colgems LP as one of the finest albums ever produced, for testing cutting-edge audio equipment. "The legend is that the original master tape had 'mad' levels on it," noted the magazine's Harry Pearson. "They used a supposedly very fancy grade of tape, and the engineers really pushed it, so the meters were typically running deep into the red: plus one, plus two, plus three, plus four. It can lead to disaster, but in the case of *Casino*, it doesn't. There's no saturation, no distortion. The record is clean as a whistle."[21]

The ever-expanding "Bond effect" had become so pervasive, that characters from other genres were transformed into secret agents. British author Herman Cyril "Sapper" McNeile's long-admired Hugh "Bulldog" Drummond, already a well-established character in British cinema, jumped into the spy age with *Deadlier Than the Male*. The derivative elements are blatant: Richard Johnson's suitably suave Drummond, reimagined here as an insurance investigator, answers to an M-like boss (Laurence Naismith, as Sir John Bledlow), who is guarded by a Moneypenny-esque receptionist (Justine Lord, as Miss Ashenden). The villain of the piece (Nigel Green, as Petersen) boasts a hulking, mute accomplice (Milton Reid) who is Oddjob in all but name. The plot concerns an unseen investor who attempts to force a merger with British-based Phoenician Oil, with the ultimate goal of winning the concession to develop newly discovered oil fields in the fictitious Middle Eastern country of Akmata. The narrative climaxes on the Mediterranean coast, where Peterson has arranged to kill Akmata's young King Fedra (Zia Mohyeddin), who refuses to allow *any* outside parties to develop his country's resources.

Veteran film and TV composer Malcolm Lockyer's wall-to-wall jazz score is great fun from its opening notes: a swinging cue that accompanies the lethal Irma (Elke Sommer), disguised as an airline hostess, as she dispatches an oil tycoon, sets a bomb, and then watches the plane explode while parachuting to safety. Similarly high-spirited cues accompany various bikini-clad lovelies as they execute intractable Phoenician Oil board members; one cue evokes John Barry's "007" theme, complete with Vic Flick-esque guitar riffs. Drummond's propulsive character theme surfaces often, notably during the climactic fight with Petersen, amid the life-size robotic pieces on the latter's huge chess board.

Maddeningly, we still await a soundtrack album. Johnson's Drummond returned for one more big-screen adventure, in 1969's *Some Girls Do* (about which, more later).

Henry S. Maxfield's debut novel, 1958's *Legacy of a Spy*, is regarded as a minor espionage classic; the same cannot be said of director Franklin J. Schaffner's big-screen adaptation. *The Double Man* borrows almost nothing from the book, and instead concocts a feeble scenario for star Yul Brynner, wholly out of his comfort zone. The Cold War plot kicks off when Soviet scientist Col. Berthold (Anton Diffring) orchestrates a skiing death for the estranged teenage son of top American spy Dan Slater (Brynner). Slater travels to the Austrian Alps and uncovers evidence that the so-called "accident" actually was murder. It's a trap by Berthold, who intends to replace Slater with a perfect double, thereby inserting the ideal mole into the American intelligence machine. But too much time is wasted on Slater's weirdly clumsy effort to befriend and/or interrogate a chalet employee (Britt Ekland) who may have been the last person to see his son alive. Once the switch is made, Berthold's plan never even gets off the ground, due to the actual Slater's escape; the third act is laden with dumb chases and action scenes.

The score was assigned to Ernie Freeman, a jazz/R&B keyboardist, arranger and bandleader who achieved modest chart success in the late 1950s and early '60s, and orchestrated songs for Frank Sinatra and Dean Martin. Freeman's work on *The Double Man* is primarily orchestral: uninspired shading and relentless mickey-mousing, which Schaffner employs with little imagination. That said, the title credits gain some pizzazz from a vigorous, trumpet-driven main theme. Freeman also delivers a tasty swinger—dynamic walking bass, trumpet and piano riffs—when Slater finally confronts his double.

No soundtrack album was produced.

Unlike Maxfield, John Le Carré has fared quite well with film adaptations. His debut novel, 1961's *Call for the Dead*, introduced career British Intelligence agent George Smiley, whose subsequent adventures would mesmerize readers for the next three decades. Smiley's big-screen debut came as a supporting presence in the 1965 adaptation of *The Spy Who Came in from the Cold*; as a result—since Paramount controlled the rights to the character—he had to be renamed when *Call for the Dead* was filmed in 1967 as *The Deadly Affair*. James Mason may be called Charles Dobbs, but he's Smiley to the core, and Paul Dehn's script is quite faithful to Le Carré's novel. Unfortunately, director Sidney Lumet tolerated a level of florid overacting that badly undercuts the suspense. Quincy Jones' score is similarly awkward; his gentle, bossa nova-flavored cues seem to have been written for an entirely different film. Astrud Gilberto delivers the seductive title song, "Who Needs Forever," which Lumet repeats too frequently in a drama that otherwise uses very little music.

The story begins as Dobbs probes the background of Foreign Office operative Samuel Fennan (Robert Flemyng). Their chat goes well, and Dobbs is satisfied with the man's loyalty. He's therefore bewildered when Fennan kills himself; surprise turns to suspicion when the section head orders the case closed. Dobbs quits the service to pursue an inquiry on his own, assisted by Mendel (Harry Andrews), a retired police inspector. Their investigation soon focuses on Fennan's widow, Elsa (Simone Signoret), a concentration camp survivor caught in a seemingly innocuous lie: one that convinces Dobbs that Fennan was murdered. The truth proves even worse.

Jones supplies genuine action cues only twice: a swinging blend of sax and horns that adds minor tension when Dobbs attempts to evade a car that's following him through London; and a pulsating sax solo, against trumpet fanfares, during a third-act surveillance montage.

The soundtrack album suffers from the score's redundancy.

* * *

Scottish musician, arranger and composer Johnny Keating found time for only three big-screen films during an impressively busy career, and his big band jazz cues for *Robbery* greatly enhance the film's taut action sequences. The drama is based loosely on what came to be known as the "Great Train Robbery": the carefully planned theft of £2.6 million from a Royal Mail train, during the early hours of August 8, 1963. The film meticulously depicts the events of the heist itself, but—to avoid lawsuits—fictionalizes the participants and everything leading up to the crime.

The story opens with the clever theft of diamonds from a gem courier. Crime boss Paul Clifton (Stanley Baker) uses the money from this haul to assemble a team and purchase the equipment required for a much more ambitious strike: the bags of cash known to be carried within a Royal Mail train, on its overnight journey from Glasgow to London. The eventual heist proceeds like clockwork; the gang then spends several days in the fallout shelter at a disused air base, while an intense police manhunt takes place above them. Most of the gang members eventually are arrested, but Clifton gets away; a final shot shows him entering New York with a fresh look and a new identity, having abandoned his wife, Kate (Joanna Pettet), back in London.

The title credits unfold against Keating's sensational 3/4 main theme, with repeating 2-4-4-4 piano riffs mimicking the spinning wheels of the mail train, as it hurtles along. This fast-paced cue grows more intense with hypnotic drumming, brass fanfares and unexpected explosions from the entire bank of horns. After Clifton and three accomplices hit the diamond courier, they're noticed by a passing police car; the subsequent chase roars through London streets while Keating's wall of horns builds to ferocious intensity and a final screaming blast. Music is absent during the planning of the train heist; once the scheme is put into action, Keating supplies a frisky waltz while the mail car attendants are subdued, the bags of cash then passed down a line of masked men and stuffed into several waiting vans. Much later, angry horns reflect the frustration of crooks who've never had the opportunity to spend any of their loot.

The soundtrack album includes some unused tracks, notably "Kate's Theme": a gorgeous lament, almost classical in nature, for Clifton's abandoned wife.

The larceny is less serious in *The Jokers*, a cheeky blast of British young-punk anarchy that's also a heist comedy. Aristocratic twentysomethings David and Michael Tremayne (Oliver Reed and Michael Crawford) impulsively decide to steal Britain's Crown Jewels from the Tower of London, just to make a public "grand gesture." Their intended Get Out of Jail Free card is the foreknowledge that one cannot be charged with theft unless one "intends to permanently deprive the owner of their property." Since David and Michael plan to return the jewels during a later media flourish, they anticipate nothing but headlines cheering their audacity. Alas, things don't turn out that way.

The film marks the big-screen scoring debut of Johnny Pearson, a celebrated British pianist, composer and orchestra leader who rocketed to Top 40 fame as a member of the Sounds Orchestral combo, and subsequently led Britain's Top of the Pops Orchestra for 16 years. His score for *The Jokers* is a sassy blend of pop anthems and big band jazz, starting with the energetic, brass-laden swinger that debuts behind the title credits. Once David and Michael hatch their bold scheme, they clarify their non-larcenous intentions by sending sealed letters to Scotland Yard and other legal entities; this flurry of typing takes place against a jocular blast of big band swing, highlighted by some mischievous piano riffs. The heist takes place the night that Michael's girlfriend Sarah (Ingrid Boulting) hosts a party; it features a high-spirited combo that performs plenty of cheerful cocktail jazz in the mold of Herb Alpert's Tijuana Brass.

Alas, when it's time to return the jewels, David and Michael are horrified to discover that they've been *re*stolen by unknown parties. A couple of diegetic cues—lively combo jazz, followed by a jolt of uptempo big band swing—power the story to its cheeky finale.

No soundtrack LP was produced.

Elsewhere in the World

The swinging Bob Adams/Joe Kentridge score is the sole attraction of *The Cape Town Affair*, a South African cheapie that clumsily rips off—scene for scene!—the 1953 *noir* classic *Pickup on South Street*. The story begins when pickpocket Skip McCoy (James Brolin, taking on Richard Widmark's role) snatches a few items from the purse of Candy (Jacqueline Bisset, an equally poor replacement for Jean Peters). The stolen goodies include a film strip that contains top-secret plans coveted by "the Reds," for whom the unsuspecting Candy's male companion, Joey (John Whiteley), works as a courier. Skip and Candy subsequently team up to help government agents "fight Communism." (This subtext was more timely in *Pickup on South Street*.) Everything builds to a listless showdown that loses track of the story's "Commie mastermind."

Adams and Kentridge give this incompetent debacle a degree of class that it scarcely deserves. Their title credits theme is a smoky, sax- and trumpet-driven cue with solid solos on piano and electric guitar; it later repeats behind a few limp action scenes. Skip and Candy's wary courtship unfolds against a playfully sexy sax ballad, although his perky character theme is close enough to "The Baby Elephant Walk" to interest Henry Mancini's lawyers. Between such eyebrow-lifting "homages" and the film's microscopic budget, it's no surprise that a soundtrack album wasn't in the cards.

Moving 6,000 miles east, Australia's first espionage TV show also was one of the first big-budget dramas produced by the country's fledgling television industry.[22] *Hunter* adopts many of the Bond/*U.N.C.L.E.* characteristics, but creator/director/scripter Ian Jones takes a serious approach; some episodes of *Hunter* are surprisingly bleak. The series focuses on the espionage activities of John Hunter (Tony Ward), an operative for SCU3 (Special Clandestine Unit 3) of COSMIC (the Commonwealth Offices for Security and Military Intelligence Coordination). He and various colleagues answer to Charles Blake (Nigel Lovell). Many assignments involve foiling the activities of CUCW (the Council for Unification of the Communist World), whose chief agent is Kragg (Gerard Kennedy). The show debuted July 4, 1967, ultimately running for 65 episodes.

The title theme and all episode underscores came from Australian jazz alto saxophonist Frank Smith. He and his fellow musicians created their "mixture of modern jazz and a double-mod rhythm section" by doubling up on drums and electric bass, along with an electric guitar for "strength and power," and a quartet of trumpets for "special impact."[23]

The pulsating, uptempo title theme has *plenty* of impact; it also runs much longer than American themes, clocking in at roughly 80 seconds. Smith opens with throbbing guitar and dramatic brass statements of the melody's primary 1-4 motif, vamping beneath clips of Ward and a grim narrator who explains the show's premise. As he finishes, blasts of brass are timed to the rifle crosshairs that appear over Hunter's standing figure. The show's title appears; sax and high reeds begin an improvisational countermelody while the cast members are introduced, and an even louder brass explosion finally concludes the theme. Underscore cues run the gamut: fast-paced action jazz, suspenseful atmospheric cues and softer romantic themes. A particularly lovely ballad, with gentle sax and piano, backs Hunter's flashback memories of a prior love affair in the episode "A Dark Reunion."

No soundtrack album was produced.

Moving back to Western Europe, Alain Delon's sizzling performance highlights director Jean-Pierre Melville's *Le Samouraï*, a suspenseful blend of 1940s Hollywood *noir* and 1960s French New Wave sensibilities. The film also established a template for numerous future crime dramas that focus on stoic, lone-wolf assassins. Rising young composer François de Roubaix blends his jazz roots with some (for the time) innovative electronic keyboard cues.

Career assassin Jef Costello (Delon) is hired to execute the owner of a Parisian nightclub; the hit is successful but attracts the attention of resident pianist Valérie (Cathy Rosier). During a subsequent line-up orchestrated by the dogged police commissioner (François Périer), she unexpectedly insists that Jef isn't the killer, despite having looked right at him. The commissioner nonetheless remains convinced that Jef *is* the guy; worse yet, the assassin's original employer decides it would be prudent to remove him, as a compromised loose end. Jef therefore must dodge both police surveillance and threats to his own life, while trying to figure out why Valérie lied ... and what to do about her.

The title credits unspool as we see Jef at rest, lying on his bed in a frugal apartment. De Roubaix's primary theme opens with malevolent strings and spare piano chords, which segue to the assassin's anthem: a 4-4 motif that debuts on Hammond B3. That cue follows Jef out of the apartment, and during his trip to the club. As he enters, Valérie is leading a trio in a lively little swinger; when she finishes, her combo yields the stage to an equally peppy quintet of sax, trombone, piano, bass and drums. After the murder and subsequent lineup, unable to get Valérie's baffling alibi out of his head, Jef returns to the club and listens to her trio play a sweet little ballad with a midtempo 4/4 beat and plenty of tasty bass. She lets him take her home: an expensively appointed apartment where she meditatively improvises a jazzy little theme on a gorgeous grand piano. When the story moves to its suspenseful climax, once again in the club, Valérie and her trio begin a slow, melancholy ballad as Jef approaches and draws his gun; she blinks but never stops playing. In the aftermath, a mournful sax segues to a reprise of Jef's 4-4 theme, once again on B3; the sax returns when the cue resolves to a final chord.

Philips released a 7-inch vinyl soundtrack EP with six cuts; additional tracks were added when the score was digitized in 2005.

In nearby Italy, this would be the final great (?) year for Eurospy releases.

The back-story leading to *Operation Kid Brother*—also known as *OK Connery*, *Operation Double 007* and *Secret Agent 00*—is far more entertaining than the film itself, which ranks as one of the most hilariously inept flicks ever made. Sean Connery's younger brother Neil—a union plasterer with virtually no acting experience—was heard on Scottish radio in the mid–1960s by director Terence Young, who was struck by how much he sounded like his famous sibling. Young shared this nugget of information with Italian film producer Dario Sabatello, who immediately hired Neil to star in a hastily mounted Bond spoof.[24] Wanting to further enhance the film's ersatz Bond credentials, Sabatello filled supporting roles with Anthony Dawson (*Dr. No*), Daniela Bianchi (*From Russia with Love*), Adolfo Celi (*Thunderball*) and—much to the displeasure of both Sean Connery and "real" Bond producers Albert Broccoli and Harry Saltzman—Bernard Lee and Lois Maxwell, playing thinly disguised versions of their iconic roles as M and Moneypenny.

The icing on the cake is an action jazz score by Ennio Morricone, who—with an assist from Bruno Nicolai—did his best to riff John Barry's Bond sound, without actually ripping it off. The energetic music couldn't save the stunningly dreadful result, which was mocked mercilessly years later, in an episode of TV's *Mystery Science Theater 3000* (season 6, episode 8). The final irony? Neil Connery's voice was dubbed by somebody who didn't sound the slightest bit like the non-actor's older brother.

The story finds famed plastic surgeon and hypnotist Neil Connery—yes, playing a character with his own name—"drafted" by the British Secret Service, while their "top agent" (you-know-who) is tied up with other matters. Neil, also a champion archer and accomplished lip-reader, is assigned to infiltrate Thanatos: a criminal organization run by Alpha (Dawson) and Beta (Celi), which intends to steal an "atomic nucleus" to complete a diabolical contraption that will incapacitate every mechanical gadget "from New York to Moscow." Thanatos' street-level activities are supervised by bad girl Maya (Bianchi) and her bevy of underdressed associates, all of whom eventually shift allegiance and help Dr. Connery save the day.

The film's title song, "The Man for Me," is a dreadful bit of brass-heavy Europop performed lustily by Maria Cristina Brancucci (aka Christy). A more satisfying blast of spy jazz follows, with Barry's familiar four-note bass line from "The James Bond Theme" powering a slinky trumpet melody while Max (Maxwell) awaits the arrival of a fellow agent. Much of the subsequent action is spotted by furious bongos and screaming brass: a combination that director Alberto De Martino reprises until we're well and truly sick of them. Fortunately, a few additional cues interrupt that redundant flow: a slinky, bass- and trumpet-laden swinger, heard when Thanatos agents kidnap a young woman; an uptempo burst of bongos, brass and guitars, when Dr. Connery joins a gaggle of blind rug weavers (!); and several swinging instrumental arrangements of the title theme.

Christy's vocal version of "The Man for Me" was released as a 45 single by Italy's Parade label, but a soundtrack album didn't appear until 2004.

Riz Ortolani's energetic jazz/pop score similarly is the best part of *Tiffany Memorandum*, a lackluster effort featuring American C-actor Ken Clark. The story begins in an illicit French casino, where journalist Dick Hallam (Clark) strikes up a chance acquaintance with a visiting El Salvadorian presidential candidate. That poor fellow is assassinated; Hallam's coincidental presence prompts the forces of evil—supervised by a nefarious clockmaker dubbed Shadow (Grégoire Aslan) and his *femme fatale* assistant (Loredana Nusciak)—to assume that he has retrieved Something Important from the body. Bad guys spend the rest of the film pursuing Hallam, to retrieve whatever it is, and he hasn't the faintest notion what they're on about. Further distractions are supplied by the mysterious Sylvie (Irina Demick), who is cheerfully willing to fall into bed with our hero.

Ortolani's title theme is a bouncy rhythmic ostinato, with a four-bar rising/falling motif that quickly becomes an infectious earworm; this segues to a swing bridge of smooth orchestral jazz, then slides back to the ostinato, now backed by unison horn counterpoint. Variations of this cue add a bit of sizzle to subsequent action sequences: when Hallam is beaten up by casino thugs; when he attempts to escape from a paint factory; and during a car chase. Many of director Sergio Grieco's other scoring decisions are totally daft; most notoriously when he drops a sexy sax swinger into a scene where a terrified Sylvie is forced to strip at gunpoint (*hardly* the right mood!).

Decades passed before four score tracks were included on the 1996 anthology album *Beat at Cinecittà*, released on the (I'm not making this up) Crippled Dick Hot Wax! label. The following year, a more respectable nine tracks appeared on an Ortolani compilation album that includes his scores for 1969's *Una Sull'Altra* and 1972's *Teresa La Ladra*.

Happily, director/scripter Marcello Ciorciolini's *Tom Dollar* is a solid cut above the average Eurospy entry, even if the story slides into *Perils of Pauline*-style nonsense. Events begin as when Iranian prince is murdered en route to signing a treaty with the U.S. government. His successor, Princess Samia (Giorgia Moll), is similarly inclined to proceed with the treaty; a clever CIA scheme to protect her involves transforming another woman—via plastic surgery and makeup—into the princess' double. This faux princess is escorted around Tehran by seasoned secret agent Tom Dollar (Maurice Poli), in an effort to expose the assassins, who operate on behalf on a ritualistic, alabaster-masked secret society. These nefarious baddies repeatedly capture Tom and his karate-savvy associate (Sojiro Kikukawa), and—rather than killing them—let them go each time!

Mario and Giosy Capuano provide a cool action jazz score that favors swing cues dominated by unison horns, saxes, flutes and aggressive keyboard work. Ciorciolini gives them plenty of room to stretch; most of the action scenes and brawls run at considerable length, and with no dialog. The first is one of the best, when Tom foils his own kidnapping and then chases a gun-toting goon across a hieroglyph-laden hillside covered with Persian rugs that are being dyed and dried: a marvelously staged sequence given additional pizzazz by the music. On a lighter note, when Tom inexplicably pauses his secret agenting long enough to escort girlfriend Lady Barbara Crane (Erika Blanc) throughout the city, this lengthy romantic montage is highlighted by cheerful bongos, horns and electric guitar.

No soundtrack album appeared, although Italy's Durium label issued a 45 single with Rocky Roberts' vocal title theme—a power ballad titled "If He Could"—and an underscore cue titled "Lady Barbara."

The action is equally intense in director/co-scripter Sergio Corbucci's *Bersaglio Mobile* (*Death on the Run*, *Moving Target*), a solid thriller that straddles the genre line between classic Eurospy and the nastier cop dramas soon to dominate 1970s Italian cinema. The package is complemented by a sizzling big band jazz score from Ivan Vandor and an uncredited Fiorenzo Carpi; their brass-heavy action and suspense cues add considerable urgency to a saga that literally hits the ground running.

Career criminal Jason (Ty Hardin), flown into Greece on an outstanding warrant, escapes police custody with unexpected assistance from a criminal gang; they want him for a tricky assignment that involves extracting a tooth from a heavily guarded corpse. Jason succeeds brilliantly and discovers that the tooth contains microfilmed information wanted by all manner of nasty characters; the worst is a stone-cold killer known as The Albanian (Gordon Mitchell). To further complicate matters, Jason's activities are monitored by Maj. Worthington Clark (Michael Rennie), a high-level British agent granted considerable leverage by the Greek police. But is Clark a good guy, or is he playing all sides against each other?

Suspenseful rhythm, furious walking bass and bold brass statements highlight the main theme, which plays against a silhouetted, Bond-style title credits sequence of a handcuffed Jason fleeing across an airport runway. Subsequent action cues spot a late-night car chase, and a well-staged melee among the ruins of the Acropolis. Jason has one ally: Billy "Pizza" (Vittorio Caprioli), the well-connected owner of the Gold Star nightclub, where the featured attraction is a stripper dubbed Rumba (Graziella Granata). Her performances are an excuse for several saucy source cues: lively combo jazz with cool solos on vibes and brass, alternating with softer bossa nova. Ferocious blasts of brass, bass and percussion fuel the climax, when Jason must rescue Pizza from The Albanian and his men.

The film failed to generate a soundtrack album, although the title theme turned up on the 2003 compilation album *Mademoiselle de Sade/E i Suoi Vizi*.

12

Shifting Gears: 1968

Both the secret agent frenzy—and its copycat Eurospy craze—began to wane this year, and the subsequent drop-off quickly became exponential. Within two years, public taste would shift to meatier crime and suspense films.

The Small Screen

Baby-boomers vividly remember this quote, immortalized by Malachi Throne during the way-cool title credits sequence for *It Takes a Thief*: "Oh, look, Al; I'm not asking you to spy. I'm just asking you to *steal*." It's the ultimate irresistible premise: Debonair playboy Alexander Mundy (Robert Wagner), actually an adept cat burglar and pickpocket, agrees to ply his trade on behalf of the U.S. government's Secret Intelligence Agency. Chaperoned by SIA handler Noah Bain (Throne), Mundy grudgingly accepts all manner of dangerous assignments that involve theft, misdirection or other larcenous activity.

The ABC series continued for a healthy three seasons, and Dave Grusin's swinging title theme—a heavily percussive, midtempo waltz deftly synchronized to mod-esque title credits—has a lot to do with the show's atmosphere of breezy sophistication. Dazzling percussion kicks off the 3/4 tempo, as the signature 1-4-4-4 motif debuts against a blend of brief heist clips and still shots of Wagner. The theme pauses after horns climb the scale, allowing Throne his iconic line, then resumes as unison brass boldly restates the melody.

"It's like writing a headline, as opposed to a story," Grusin explained, when asked about the importance of a catchy title theme. "Producers and directors want something that sounds like it's going to bring you back into the room, during the commercial break between shows. It's crucial to make it identifiable."[1]

As it happened, Grusin wasn't part of the initial team. The series was sold on the basis of a 90-minute pilot movie—*A Thief Is a Thief Is a Thief*—scored by Ernie Freeman. His title theme is more mysterious, opening with a rising four-note ostinato and suspenseful brass, which yield to a vaguely defined 4/4 melody. It's a vibrant bit of orchestral jazz, but hard to hum and not terribly memorable: no surprise, then, that Grusin was brought in to deliver something catchier.

Grusin also provided the initial episode's underscore—his only assignment for the series—which includes conventional, string-laden orchestral cues; midtempo bossa nova source melodies, performed by a small combo at a casino; and sleek swing cues, for Mundy's frequent reconnaissance sequences. The latter often continue at length, as montages, granting plenty of time for the music. Over time, the jazz ambiance was maintained by Benny Golson, Oliver Nelson, Lyn Murray, Billy Goldenberg and numerous others. Grusin freshened up his title theme for season two, adding a stronger synthesizer line to the melody, against a new credits sequence that relies more heavily on split-screen action clips. Brass fanfares became more prevalent when Grusin again tweaked the theme during the third season.

No soundtrack album appeared, but Grusin did record a full-length arrangement of his title theme for a Decca 45 single. Subsequent covers came from The Little Big Horns (Capitol); the UK's Des Champ Orchestra (Page One); and Dave Sealey (DJM), who turned the theme into a raucous rock/pop *vocal*, thanks to lyrics supplied by Zack Laurence. (Cole Porter had nothing to worry about.)

Grusin delivered another hit theme that autumn when NBC's *The Name of the Game* established a programming subgenre descended from the anthology series that had dominated 1950s television. The format underwent a slight change and resurfaced as "umbrella shows," and *The Name of the Game* captivated viewers during three compelling seasons. The 90-minute episodes are more akin to mini-movies, with rotating stars—Gene Barry, Robert Stack and Tony Franciosa—who are linked by virtue of their employment at the Los Angeles–based publishing empire built and run by Glenn Howard (Barry). Dan Farrell (Stack) is senior editor of *Crime Magazine*; Jeff Dillon (Franciosa) is the intrepid investigative reporter for *People Magazine* (six years before the Meredith Corporation created the actual *People* magazine). Each episode features one of the three stars, who divided every season more or less evenly.

This series also began with a pilot film—*Fame Is the Name of the Game*—which aired two years earlier, on November 26, 1966. Benny Carter gave it a solid jazz vibe that was retained when NBC okayed the series. Wanting a more vibrant main theme, the network turned to Grusin; he responded with an electrifying blast of uptempo jazz that perfectly suits the animated credits sequence. Each star's name *swooshes* onto the screen multiple times, the text sliding back and forth, and ultimately resolving into a graphic image of the actor in question. The melody's 4-8 motif is introduced via solo horn against lively synth keyboard comping, and a funk-laden rhythm section; the theme gains intensity with the third actor's credit, the melody now taken by unison horns. The music builds to a crescendo of rising brass triplets as the show's title appears multiple times; the text compresses into just a single line, and then "explodes" outward as Grusin brings the music to a climactic finish.

"I don't think I was very analytical about it," Grusin later admitted. "To try to make something—in 35 or 45 seconds—complete or maybe a little memorable, in terms of having something strong. It's like writing a short story, as opposed to a novel, where you have a limited number of words, and you have to make your point quickly."[2]

Grusin supplied an underscore for only one episode; subsequent assignments went to Carter, Oliver Nelson, Dominic Frontiere, Billy Goldenberg and many others. Combo jazz tends to be the go-to diegetic cue during meetings and interviews in restaurants and bars, although the winds of musical change also dictated occasional bursts of rock 'n' roll. Frontiere delivers some saucy jazz organ cues in the first season episode "Pineapple Rose"; Ralph Burns adds plenty of sassy R&B to a second season episode aptly titled "A Hard Case of the Blues."

The show didn't produce a soundtrack album, but Grusin did record a longer, heavily funkified arrangement of his title theme for a Decca 45 single. Derry O'Leary covered it for Uni.

* * *

Mischievous serendipity had struck back in early 1967, when CBS requested a TV series about a high-tech private investigator. Rival producers Paul Monash and Bruce Geller prepared competing pilot episodes, and both hired composer Lalo Schifrin.

"The whole situation was one of the funniest things that could happen, only in Hollywood," Schifrin recalled. "I had time to do both, because there was a one- or two-week difference in the deadline. Both had almost the same story.[3]

"From my point of view it was great, because it is not easy to sell a pilot, and develop it into a series. So I had nothing to lose. On the contrary, it was 'heads I win, tails I win.'"[4]

Gellar's show was *Mannix*, discussed in the previous chapter. Monash's effort, *Braddock*, is set a decade in the future, in a high-tech realm of lapel radios, picture phones and snazzy cars. Tom Simcox stars in the title role; he and partner Tratner (Stephen McNally) dodge assassins while trying to prevent bad guys from getting their hands on a portable laser weapon.

Schifrin's title theme opens with a recurring xylophone phrase that he had used as a brief cue for *Cool Hand Luke*, and which he'd rework again for 1983's *The Osterman Weekend*. (Current events junkies will recognize it as the urgent melody that has introduced all manner of TV *Eyewitness News*–style programs ever since.) It suggests the show's high-tech milieu, particularly with unison horn fanfares and attention-getting drum ba-*bumps*. Subsequent underscore cues deliver a flavor of *Mission: Impossib*le-style suspense, with plenty of bongos, inquisitive flute solos, and unison horns.

Mannix became an eight-season hit, but *Braddock* went no further than a pilot episode; it aired only once on July 22, 1968, as an installment of *Premiere*, CBS' summer anthology refuge for wannabe shows. Scores for failed pilots rarely achieve commercial release, but *Braddock* was more fortunate than most. Schifrin's roughly 25 minutes of music were stitched into five tracks and included with the 2008 release of his score for the 1966 Jerry Lewis bomb, *Way.... Way Out*.

This was a strong year for attention-grabbing title credits sequences, and few shows possessed anything more dynamic than what opened *The Mod Squad*: a (literally) hard-charging montage accompanied by Earle Hagen's equally ferocious jazz theme, highlighted by an aggressive beat and forceful brass. It leaves viewers as breathless as the show's stars—Michael Cole, Clarence Williams III and Peggy Lipton—as they run hell-for-leather down a darkened, rain-soaked alleyway, ultimately collapsing into each other's arms.

The show is an audacious blend of youth culture and mainstream crime drama, with three "social dropouts"—Pete Cochran (Cole), Linc Hayes (Williams) and Julie Barnes (Lipton)—given a shot at redemption as members of an undercover squad headed by veteran police Capt. Adam Greer (Tige Andrews). The team's goal: to infiltrate counterculture, underground and activist organizations to identify nefarious adults taking advantage of gullible flower children. (Ratting out their peers wouldn't have been cool, donchaknow.) The ABC series became a five-season hit.

Hagen's *Mod Squad* theme is meticulously synchronized to the aforementioned montage. Although he composed to the already edited set of visuals, that didn't make the job easier. "The show started with a teaser," he explained, "and the music that came out of the teaser had to go right into the main title, and resolve into that bounding chord. [Additionally,] I was married to some action and freeze frames. You'd see Clarence Williams running down the street, and they'd come close-up on him and freeze. And the same thing with Peggy, and the same thing with Michael, and finally Tige Andrews. And in blocking out those freezes, and where they occurred, it didn't fall into any given pattern. [So] that theme

12. Shifting Gears: 1968

wound up being a tempo layout of 4/4, 7/8, 6/8, 4/4. It suggested a musical pattern that seemed appropriate, and I went with it. It was a good title, in that the music didn't necessarily sound like it was accommodating the picture, if you listened to the track alone, but it accommodated *everything* in the picture."[5]

Hagen got an assist from Shorty Rogers on the 90-minute pilot episode. "He wrote the end theme, which I thought was wonderful. We used it every week, as the 'walk off into the sunset' theme."[6] Rogers' piece is a lyrical jazz ballad with the melody generally introduced by guitar against either synth keyboard or a lonely sax, and then—depending on the episode's atmosphere—sometimes expanding into brilliant brass backed by the entire band. It's slow, somber and a touch wistful, reflecting stories that usually conclude agreeably, but not necessarily happily.

Jazz isn't evident in the underscores. "Rock worked real well in the car chases and fights, and all of that stuff; it was great. But for scoring, rock 'n' roll isn't harmonically very sophisticated, and unless you have rhythm going, it doesn't really work well as a dramatic entity. By the third show, I tried mixing in serial music: 12-tone. I expected to get some screams of pain, and I didn't, and we wound up doing the rest of the shows in 12-tone."[7] Hagen brought in Billy May as an ongoing collaborator; between the two of them, they scored 77 episodes during the show's five-year run.

The series failed to produce a soundtrack album.

* * *

Sometimes the past comes back to haunt an actor.

After his single-season run in the 1962–63 Western drama *Stoney Burke*, Jack Lord was just another hard-working actor accepting one-off guest roles and hoping for a fresh shot at steady employment. He came close with *The Faceless Man*, a potential series pilot broadcast on May 4, 1966, as an episode of *Bob Hope Chrysler Theatre*. Lord stars as BOSS (Bureau of Secret Services) agent Don Owens, assigned to infiltrate the Los Angeles waterfront to discover who has been killing defecting foreign seamen. By posing as a contract assassin with sniper skills, Owens works his way into a gang led by ruthless crime boss Rajeski (Joseph Wiseman), at which point he betrays the baddies. Alas, the pilot remained unsold. Two years after its one-and-done broadcast, Universal added supplemental footage and released the now 95-minute thriller theatrically in late spring 1968, under the misleading title *The Counterfeit Killer*.

The Faceless Man had marked the first television assignment for Quincy Jones, then looking to expand on his big-screen work. His score feels like that of a composer seeking his own sound. No unifying melody serves as a linking thread; each cue is its own animal, ranging from a bouncy, bluesy keyboard swinger—barely heard above the ambient noise of the title credits sequence—to furious action jazz, to riffs that employ the vocalese Jones soon would use to far greater effect, when collaborating with the Don Elliott Voices on films such as *$ (Dollars)*. Aggressive free jazz pops up when Owens decoys some surveillance thugs; a dynamic, sax-fueled action cue erupts during the climax, set at the Los Angeles International Airport. The best cue, however, is a pleasant bit of combo source jazz heard during a meeting in a hotel lobby: smooth piano chops followed by equally fine solos on vibes and guitar.

No soundtrack album emerged. Universal execs must've kicked themselves, upon realizing they had missed the opportunity to release this film *after* what happened to Lord's career, just a few months later.

Hawaii Five-O was an immediate cultural phenomenon, and a Top 10 show for many of its 12 seasons. (It became television's longest-running crime/cop drama until *Law & Order* later beat that record.) The show's music fueled this popularity; The Ventures' cover of Mort Stevens' iconic title theme enjoyed a 14-week run on *Billboard's* Hot 100 chart, rising to No. 4 on May 10, 1969. The theme is instantly recognizable, from the opening drum roll backdropped by a massive ocean wave.

The show is spearheaded by the forceful (if tight-lipped) Jack Lord, giving the performance of his career as former Naval Intelligence officer Steve McGarrett, now the head of a special unit of the Hawaiian State Police. His team initially includes Danny Williams (James MacArthur), Kono Kalakaua (Zulu) and Chin Ho Kelly (Kam Fong). The crew tackles cases too complex, politically sensitive or overwhelming for the traditional police force; the list of powerful syndicate baddies is topped by Chinese criminal mastermind Wo Fat (Khigh Dhiegh), who debuted with the series' two-hour pilot. Stevens scored that episode and roughly 40 more during the series' run.

"After I left CBS, I still worked on the show," he admitted. "Jack Lord came in and said, 'Morty, we want you to give us at least five shows a year. Please,' and I said yes, because it was important."[8]

As for that memorable title theme…

"It took 11 minutes to get the basics down," Stevens recalled. "The simplicity of it, and the driving force of instruments rather than simply the drums, made it into a popular rhythmic entity. With two trumpets playing the melody, and two trumpets playing the same melody an octave lower, it sounded like a blunderbuss coming at you."[9]

Most episode teasers build to a climax—often involving some nefarious act—accompanied by a rising orchestral chord that resolves into the initial drum roll and massive ocean wave of title designer Reza S. Badiyi's tautly edited credits sequence. The melody's primary 6-5 motif erupts against staccato clips of ocean, beach front and a cityscape of tall, densely packed buildings, until an accelerated helicopter swoop

As executive producer Leonard Freeman explained in the soundtrack album's liner notes, "The value of a great one-minute theme to any television series is inestimable, and I wanted one for my then-brand-spanking-new *Hawaii Five-O*. No ukuleles or steel guitars or falsetto singers or overused bongos, but a kind of melding of the Polynesian, the classic, the jazz and—most of all—the pop sound of today." Mort Stevens definitely delivered the goods; his theme remains iconic (courtesy Film Score Monthly).

leads to a close-up of McGarrett, standing atop one of the structures: a smash-cut against a blast of brass. The theme continues for another 20 seconds of cityscape—cars, planes, people, a hula dancer and much more, all timed precisely to Stevens' exciting beat—until the other three cast members are introduced. The final drum roll coincides with Freeman's credit, superimposed atop a police car speeding along late-night streets: all in all, a breathtaking 60 seconds.

Many episode underscores feature similarly exhilarating, rock-inflected jazz cues, balanced by softer themes that "feel" appropriate to the gorgeous locations. Stevens handled most of the first-season assignments, with assists from Harry Geller and Richard Shores. Later seasons feature scores by John Cacavas, Bruce Broughton, Pete Rugolo, Mundell Lowe and Richard Markowitz, among others. By way of acknowledging The Ventures, Stevens arranged for three of the band's members—Gerry McGee (guitar), Bob Bogle (bass) and Mel Taylor (drums)—to perform in the first season's 15th episode, "Up Tight."

Eschewing the tradition of rerecording fresh arrangements of meatier cues, the soundtrack album features music from actual episode recording sessions. The menu includes hard-charging action jazz ("The Floater," "Front Street," "Call to Danger"), bluesy swingers ("Operation Smash") and a tasty bossa nova anthem ("McGarrett's Theme"). Stevens earned three Emmy Award nominations during the show's run and won twice. As an indication of the caliber of music written for the show, *all three* of the 1973–74 Emmy nominations were for *Hawaii Five-O* episodes. The title theme quickly became the University of Hawaii's unofficial "fight song," frequently heard during Battle of the Bands competitions.[10]

Decades later, when composer Brian Tyler was hired to score the show's 2010 revival, he insisted on returning to Stevens' original arrangement. "That theme is so iconic, it's in the culture," he insisted. "If you take it out of the instrumentation and change it up, you might have interesting music, but it isn't *Hawaii Five-O*."[11]

Hard-charging cops like McGarrett notwithstanding, the tube still had room for the occasional old-school gumshoe.

"My name is David Ross. I'm a private investigator, and you may be wondering how I got into a situation like this."

Every episode of *The Outsider* begins as star Darren McGavin speaks something similar in narrative voice-over, while the camera freezes on a scene of peril. The bulk of the story then unfolds via flashback, eventually catching up to—and moving beyond—the teaser. This all-but-forgotten NBC series is a minor classic of then-contemporary private eye *noir*. McGavin's Ross is a world-weary underdog without friends or family, who nonetheless possesses moral certainty and a strong sense of justice. He's a proto–Jim Rockford—both came from creator Roy Huggins—down to idiosyncratic quirks such as Ross' habit of keeping his telephone in the refrigerator. (Rockford kept his gun in a cookie jar.) McGavin fits the role perfectly, his morose demeanor emblematic of a guy forever trying to retain a little dignity. Viewers didn't give him much; the show barely limped through its single season.

Pete Rugolo's title theme is a midtempo jazz ballad with a somber guitar melody against occasional flashes of brass; it plays over a montage of Ross enduring a breakfast of burnt toast and sour milk. Reeds and strings add a brief countermelody before a concluding brass fanfare. The show's underscores are unremarkable, likely built from library cues. Rugolo never recorded the theme; it's as lost today as the series itself.

The Big Screen

Dean Martin's Matt Helm series came to an abysmal conclusion with *The Wrecking Crew*, a thoroughly inept—and aptly titled—flick that looks like it was assembled with a meat cleaver. The script relentlessly debases Martin's female co-stars, most notably the klutzy character played by Sharon Tate. The plot finds Matt assigned to retrieve $1 billion in gold bullion snatched by the nefarious Count Massimo Contini (Nigel Green), who hopes to wreck the world's economy. Matt's allies include Gypsy dancer Lola Medina (Tina Louise) and Danish tourism bureau agent Freya Carlson (Tate).

Matters aren't helped by Hugo Montenegro's flimsy score. Most of the cues sound like inane cartoon music, with so-called melodies supplied by a male chorus chanting the repetitive cue: "*Ba-ba-baaah ... ba-ba-baah!*" (For the sake of novelty, they sometimes switch to *woo-woo-woo*.) Even the occasional action jazz cues are an exercise in lazy writing: endless reprises of the same four-bar motif, with little changes in arrangement or instrumentation.

No soundtrack album emerged, for which the world should be grateful.

Fellow Rat Packers Sammy Davis Jr. and Peter Lawford must've been jealous, so they teamed up for their own spy spoof. The cringe-worthy result, *Salt & Pepper*, has aged quite badly; many of its sexist and racist one-liners now elicit groans. The plot concerns a renegade British Cabinet's effort to hijack the actual government by threatening to blow up one million citizens with a nuclear missile; details of this scheme fall into the hands of Charles Salt (Davis) and Christopher Pepper (Lawford), who run a Playboy-esque club in a posh part of London. Plenty of *Carry On*-esque shenanigans ensue, with Salt and Pepper managing unlikely escapes, thanks to the former's fondness for spy flicks. ("I saw this movie once, where...")

Composer John Dankworth apparently was instructed to supply relentless mickey-mousing. Such aural overkill notwithstanding, he manages a few choice cues, starting with the lively, trumpet- and organ-fueled jazz/rock title theme. Additional jazz highlights include a sly, percussive swing cue heard while the duo attempts to escape from a mocked-up Polaris sub; and the lengthy, horn-laden jazz march that fuels a climactic assault on a military training college.

The soundtrack LP is a much better showcase for Dankworth's music. Along with lively renditions of the title theme, the album boasts a sax- and piano-driven version of an incidental love theme.

Amazingly, Lawford and Davis managed to con Hollywood into a sequel (about which, more later).

Even more amazing, the micro-budgeted *A Man Called Dagger* is even worse than *Salt & Pepper*. Paul Mantee is the stiffest secret agent ever placed in front of a camera; no wonder he gets billed fourth, behind 1960s pin-up cuties Terry Moore and Sue Ane Langdon, and comedian Jan Murray, improbably cast as the master villain. The plot finds agents Richard Dagger (Mantee) and Harper Davis (Moore) assigned to take down SS Col. Rudolph Koffman (Murray). He has figured out how to "completely subjugate the human mind," thereby turning beautiful young women into soulless assassins. Sometimes the process kills the subjects, whereupon Koffman—whose secret lair is concealed within a meat-packing plant—carves up the bodies and sells them as "Andes boar meat." (Yep, this tawdry little flick traffics in cannibalism.)

And yet the music is no joke; it's a solid, Barry-esque score by celebrated actor/comedian/talk show host and musician Steve Allen, who took the assignment far more seriously than the film deserves. Consider the opening sequence: a late-night melee between Dagger and half a dozen thugs, staged so poorly that it's impossible to tell who's doing what to whom. Thanks to Allen's rousing, bass- and sax-driven action cue, we can at least *imagine* that something exciting is happening. The propulsive 2/2 title theme is powered by Joe Leahy's trumpet; a later car chase is spotted with equal aplomb, Leahy's trumpet trading licks with electric guitar. Future Bond co-star Richard Kiel pops up as a hulking henchman; Dagger's two brawls with this man-mountain take place against unhurried trumpet fanfares, suggesting the baddie's bulk and slow, menacing movements.

Remarkably, this bomb produced a soundtrack LP, no doubt trading on Allen's fame. The standout track is a swinging version of "Dagger's Theme," with Allen's keyboard work nicely complemented by some cool walking bass.

* * *

Robert Vaughn enjoyed a *Venetian Affair* in between seasons of television's *Man from U.N.C.L.E.*, so nobody was surprised when David McCallum was granted a similar big-screen sojourn in Mexico. Alas, *Sol Madrid* is a lamentably clumsy crime thriller, noteworthy for little beyond Lalo Schifrin's solid score. The plot finds Interpol narcotics agent Sol Madrid (McCallum) assigned to track down Mafia accountant Harry Mitchell (Pat Hingle), who has stolen $500,000 from his bosses and fled to Acapulco in the company of Stacey Woodward (Stella Stevens), longtime girlfriend of Mafia lieutenant Dano Villanova (Rip Torn). Madrid travels to Mexico, where he liaises with undercover investigator Jalisco (Ricardo Montalban), to set up a sting that will entrap Villanova's long-hated rival, Emil Dietrich (Telly Savalas); the rather vague notion is that this, in turn, will lead to Villanova. Very few people are left alive by the time Madrid ties up all loose ends.

Schifrin's vibrant title theme is full-blown orchestral fury, with drum rolls and heavy percussion building to a trumpet fanfare, followed by a chaotic assault of free jazz over a montage that depicts heroin's journey from poppy fields to a junkie's dingy apartment. Madrid and Stacey begin an uneasy alliance while entering Mexico via boat: a journey made to a dazzling mélange of vibrant percussion and mariachi-style horns. The clever means by which a shipment of heroin moves across the border and into the United States is spotted by classic Schifrin action jazz in his *Mission: Impossible* mode.

His source cues are the most fun: several high-spirited mariachi bands; bouncy Cuban *charanga* melodies with a strong flute line; and slower, Tijuana Brass–style dance music highlighted by a sweet trumpet.

The soundtrack album features fresh arrangements of the film's primary themes.

A few months later, Schifrin began what would blossom into a highly successful association with Clint Eastwood. Unfortunately, premise trumped execution in *Coogan's Bluff*. The "country cop navigating the big city" concept is sure-fire, and Eastwood can't be blamed; he's equal parts chiseled and charismatic as impetuous Arizona detective Walt Coogan, sent to New York to extradite wanted fugitive James Ringerman (Don Stroud). But the script has dated hilariously, particularly when it deals with the rising counterculture scene. All the young twentysomethings are giggling, babbling fruit bats; this is particularly true of Stroud, who overacts atrociously.

Schifrin's score is cool and impressively diverse: energetic action themes and jazz cues, with some softer seductive ballads and a flavor of Americana, for the Arizona desert vistas that open the film. The title credits unspool in two parts—bisected by some narrative action—with the first half dominated by gentle guitar: our first exposure to the primary

"Coogan theme" that anchors Eastwood's character. The instrumentation expands to include rolling percussion—Shelly Manne and Earl Palmer on drums—and then switches keys for the peppier second half, with flute and ukulele yielding to driving piano (Artie Kane and Mike Melvoin). Drum pops yield to horns and strings, which segue back to another round of attention-demanding piano chops.

Schifrin contributes a softer theme when Coogan and a bleeding-heart probation officer (Susan Clark) begin a flirty relationship; their playful banter unfolds against a lyrical piano melody, with a guitar comping gently in the background. The intensity ramps back up during the exciting climax, when Coogan finally locates and pursues Ringerman through the pathways and staircases of uptown Manhattan's expansive Fort Tyron Park: first on motorcycles, and then on foot. Schifrin opens with tense piano riffs, plucked strings and plenty of percussion pizzazz; then shifts to energetic vibes and bass, with horn accents accelerating the suspense; and finally climaxes with a frantic 4/4 blend of piano, horns, percussion and bongos, climbing the scale from one key to the next.

A decade passed before an abbreviated score of seven tracks arrived on a 1978 LP—*Coogan's Bluff*—that includes music from three other films. Schifrin's full 50-minute score finally was digitized in 2012. (Sharp-eared listeners will recognize one cue—"Get Out"—as an only slightly modified arrangement of "End Game," a track from Schifrin's *Mannix* soundtrack album.)

A mere two weeks after *Coogan's Bluff* hit theaters, Schifrin's involvement with another cop thriller made a much stronger impact at the box office. *Bullitt* became the year's fifth-highest box-office hit: equal parts methodical police procedural and suspense-laden action flick, while granting star Steve McQueen several stunt-laden opportunities to demonstrate his athletic grace. The unfolding story focuses on a mob informant—who narrowly eludes assassins during the title credits—brought to San Francisco as a star witness groomed by condescending local politician Walter Chalmers (Robert Vaughn); he hopes to further his career at a Senate subcommittee hearing on organized crime.

Schifrin's score is one of his best, starting with a killer main theme synchronized to Pablo Ferro's stylish title credits. Schifrin begins the cue gently, almost teasingly: a sustained note backstopped by brushed cymbals and drum kicks, until shrill horns erupt. The percussive elements settle into a swinging, midtempo 2/2 beat, as a guitar takes the melody, accompanied by horn fanfares. Saxes take over, and the percussion becomes more intense; the sax line yields to flutes and screaming trumpets ... by which point, viewers know that whatever comes next is gonna *rock*. Director Peter Yates paces the subsequent drama shrewdly, with lengthy exposition sequences interrupted by bursts of action or violence; he's also parsimonious with the music and doesn't use anywhere near all the cues Schifrin provided, making scenes *with* music that much more effective.

A terrific diegetic cue surfaces when Frank Bullitt (McQueen) and his girlfriend Cathy (Jacqueline Bisset) enjoy dinner at a restaurant; a sleek quartet dubbed Meridian West—Julie Iger (flute), Larry Vogt (guitar), Nat Johnson (bass) and Allan Pimental (drums)—performs a lengthy, fast-paced jazz waltz. A subsequent non-diegetic cue sets up the film's iconic car chase: Frank, spotting a tail, executes some fast maneuvers, and the pursuing bad guys become the pursued. Schifrin's taut, expectant 2/2 cue builds tension as the goons consider their options. Horns and saxes supply terse counterpoint as Yates holds ... holds ... holds ... holds even more ... and then the bad guys buckle their seat belts and accelerate. The chase is on ... and Schifrin goes silent. The chase roars along without music, which would have been superfluous.

Schifrin returns for the suspenseful climax, set amid the chaos of holiday travelers at San Francisco Airport. In the aftermath, he concludes with a bleak guitar and flute reading of the main theme, while Frank stares at his reflection in a mirror, wondering if he has become as hard and soulless as those he pursues.

Schifrin turned the soundtrack album into a jazz spectacular, reorchestrating various film cues into sizzling tracks. Even a few minor cues—such as "Hotel Daniels," heard only as source music on a hotel radio—are expanded into full-blown big band fury. As a final whimsical touch, Schifrin also includes a swing version of the Sonny Burke/Paul Francis Webster Christmas carol, "The First Snowfall," briefly heard over the airport PA system during the film's climax.

Lalo Schifrin's main theme for *Bullitt* was given lyrics by Norman Gimbel, and the resulting tune—"The Great Divide"—was recorded by pop singer Joanie Sommers for a 1968 Warner Bros. single. It's available digitally on Sommers' *The Complete Warner Bros. Singles*: a fascinating alternate reading of a theme that almost everybody knows solely as an instrumental (courtesy *Film Score Monthly*).

On the gumshoe front, Frank Sinatra's second and final outing as Miami houseboat-based gambler and occasional private investigator Tony Rome—*Lady in Cement*—is a pathetic embarrassment. The script is painfully sexist and homophobic; women are present solely as naked tarts, and Sinatra repeatedly belittles mincing gay characters. The story begins when Tony, attempting to find undersea treasure, spots the body of a dead blonde, her feet encased in a concrete block. He gets hired by a man-mountain named Waldo Gronsky (Dan Blocker), whose behavior and motivation echo Moose Malloy, from Raymond Chandler's *Farewell, My Lovely*. Attempts to determine the blonde's identity, and who killed her, involve alcoholic heiress Kit Forrest (Raquel Welch); a retired gangster (Martin Gabel) with a vicious son (Steven Peck); a "cool" artist (Richard Deacon) with a fondness for painting nudes; and a go-go dancer (Lainie Kazan) who works in a sleazy club. The film is as inane as Hugo Montenegro's score, and no cliché is left behind; it's no surprise when he inserts the *Bonanza* theme during one of Tony's conversations with Gronsky.

The title credits unspool against a horn-driven cue ("Tony's Theme"), the first few bars of which subsequently repeat—relentlessly—as musical bumpers between scenes. Other cues are intentionally comic: a sleazy strip anthem for a brief encounter in a burlesque club, and droll riffs on standards such as "Give Me the Simple Life," "You Make Me Feel So Young" and "Love Is a Many Splendored Thing."

The soundtrack album was digitized in 2002, adding alternate takes and an interview with Welch and Blocker. The title theme unexpectedly became a kitsch staple, often included on lounge anthology CDs.

Sinatra—and viewers—didn't fare any better with his other 1968 release. Scripter Abby Mann's adaptation of Roderick Thorp's 1966 novel, *The Detective*, is appallingly homophobic and sensationalistic; while the adult content may have been viewed as "progressive" in the late 1960s—lurid sex crimes, nymphomania—the tone has since become exploitative and wincingly offensive. The film deserves mention solely due to Jerry Goldsmith's slight but effective jazz score: an obvious precursor to the more ambitious work he'd later do for *noirish* projects such as *Chinatown* and *L.A. Confidential*.

New York City police detective Joe Leland (Sinatra) investigates the brutal murder of Teddy Leikman, beaten to death and mutilated. The victim's sexual preferences lead to former roommate Felix Tesla (Tony Musante), who is coerced into a confession. Tesla goes to the electric chair; Leland gets a promotion. A few years later, an apparently open-and-shut suicide by Colin MacIver (William Windom) comes to Leland's attention when the man's wife, Norma (Jacqueline Bisset), complains that her efforts to probe the case are being rebuffed by unknown "people with connections." Smelling a high-level conspiracy, Leland investigates and finds that a certain psychiatrist—Dr. Wendell Roberts (Lloyd Bochner)—also is a link to the Leikman murder.

The title credits are choreographed to Goldsmith's bluesy main theme: a strutting, midtempo jazz waltz backed by a strong rhythmic beat and a world-weary melody carried by a mournful trumpet. Clarinets, trombones and strings bring the cue to an orchestral finale while Leland drives to the apartment where Leikman's body awaits. Later, when Tesla has been located, the suspect's brief attempt to flee is spotted with a tense blast of pizzicato bass, slashing guitar, screaming flute and horn pops. Lengthy flashbacks chart the collapse of Leland's relationship with his ex-wife Karen (Lee Remick): melancholy memories that Goldsmith amplifies with numerous reprises of the main theme. The variations include a doleful single trumpet line accompanied by Artie Kane's gentle piano comping; and an equally sad tenor sax and bass flute similarly backed by keyboard noodling. Leland ultimately is faced with painful choices; with the decision made, the end credits appear and Goldsmith reprises the main theme's initial orchestration, until the trumpet unexpectedly screams in triumph.

Diegetic cues are mostly mellow combo jazz heard as background music in restaurants: first during a flashback involving Leland and Karen; and second when Leland meets Norma, to learn more about her late husband's financial affairs. A final source cue is deliberately overstated: a sleazy blend of organ and stripper-style trumpet, serving as the backdrop to a "disgusting" gay nightclub.

Goldsmith's score remained unreleased until being digitized in 2004, when it was included in the box set *Jerry Goldsmith at 20th Century–Fox*. The 2015 Blu-ray includes an isolated score track.

Although *Jigsaw* is just as lurid, it's interesting in one respect: Quincy Jones got to score a remake of one of his own earlier projects, because this tawdry clunker is an overcooked retread of 1965's *Mirage*. The story begins when Jonathan Fields (Bradford Dillman) regains consciousness in an apartment, unable to remember his name or anything else; he flees after finding a dead woman in the bathtub. He hires private detective Arthur Belding (Harry

Guardino) to help figure out what's going on; back-tracking eventually reveals that Fields is a scientist at Thought Corp., a hush-hush entity that determines whether individuals are psychologically stable enough to push the button that'll start World War III. Fields learns that he was dosed with LSD in a weird plot by Lew Haley (Pat Hingle), a colleague who wants his job.

Given the story's focus on the escalating drug culture, Jones's score is appropriately unsettling: lots of slashing strings, wavering brass and tune glasses, the latter frequently used as "stings" each time Fields remembers something. The only solid jazz cue is the title theme: a suspenseful 4/4 swinger that opens with tick-tock percussion, and blossoms into a melody carried by urgent brass and reeds. No soundtrack album appeared.

The drama is less exploitative in *Madigan*, another effort to add emotional depth to police officers too often depicted as soulless, *Dragnet*-style automatons. This adaptation of author/journalist Richard Dougherty's 1962 novel, *The Commissioner*, begins on a Friday morning, when New York City cops Daniel Madigan (Richard Widmark) and Rocco Bonaro (Harry Guardino) attempt to collect known felon Barney Benesch (Steve Ihnat) for routine questioning. Benesch flips out, steals Madigan's gun and escapes. Police Commissioner Russell (Henry Fonda), appalled by this incompetence, gives Madigan and Bonaro 72 hours to bring Benesch back in ... or else. The subsequent manhunt is interspersed with soapy personal melodrama: various infidelities, and Russell's realization that his best friend and longtime colleague, Chief Inspector Kane (James Whitmore), accepted a bribe.

The scoring assignment went to guitarist, record producer, arranger and conductor Don Costa, one year into a modest film and TV soundtrack career. His roots as a session musician—and big band orchestrator for vocalists such as Frank Sinatra, Sarah Vaughan and Tony Bennett—are amply evident in his energetic jazz cues. The film's title theme is dominated by uptempo 4/4 action jazz, although a core melody is difficult to distinguish. The rooftop chase following Benesch's escape is backed by an equally propulsive cue, and solid swing is employed as "traveling music" each time Madigan and Bonaro drive across the city. Unfortunately, these pleasant bursts of jazz are overshadowed by persistent mickey-mousing, when director Don Siegel employs orchestral blasts to (needlessly) emphasize pregnant dialogue.

Nobody was surprised by the absence of a soundtrack album.

Widmark later reprised his character for NBC's 1972–73 *Mystery Movie* umbrella series: a neat trick, since Madigan gets killed at the end of this film!

Resurrection isn't unheard of, in Hollywood; neither is transformation. Author Donald E. Westlake's Parker was played by Lee Marvin, in 1967's *Point Blank*; when the character returned in *The Split*—based on Westlake's seventh Parker novel—the role was shaped for former NFL superstar-turned-actor Jim Brown. On top of which, Parker was renamed again, this time becoming McClain. (Westlake's fans must've been *quite* bewildered.)

McClain returns to Los Angeles after an undefined absence, hoping to arrange a big score; on the advice of longtime associate Gladys (Julie Harris), he decides to steal the ticket and concession sales during an upcoming, sold-out football playoff game at the Los Angeles Coliseum. McClain assembles a crew—getaway driver Harry Kifka (Jack Klugman), marksman Dave Negli (Donald Sutherland), electrical expert Marty Gough (Warren Oates) and muscled thug Bert Clinger (Ernest Borgnine)—and the heist takes place without a hitch. But then alliances are shattered by numerous double-crosses, and McClain survives only with the assistance of Brill (Gene Hackman), a bent police detective looking to keep some of the loot. When McClain eventually departs Los Angeles, once again alone, he carries only as much of the cash that he feels is rightfully his.

No complaints can be made about Quincy Jones' tense and vigorous jazz score. Our first glimpse of Brown's imposing physique is backed by a bold orchestral statement that segues to a swinging, mid-tempo trumpet fanfare; this introduces the sleek, R&B title song—lyrics by Ernie Shelby, sung by Billy Preston—and five-note refrain ("Gotta get away") which, as an instrumental motif, becomes McClain's primary cue throughout the film. Jones gets ample opportunity for action jazz when McClain "auditions" each of his potential accomplices; the best of these bizarre little interludes comes when he tests Kifka's driving prowess, against dynamic sax, organ riffs and a sizzling 2/2 rhythm section. Once assembled, the crew prepares for the heist during

New Yorker film critic Pauline Kael was particularly taken by Quincy Jones' score for *The Split*, clearly preferring his music to the film itself: "It's a relief to hear the Quincy Jones music, which goes along independently, at its own rhythm," she noted, on **Nov. 23, 1968**. "Flemyng's direction is so uninteresting, that without the kind of music that makes points and emphasizes climaxes and intensifies the changes in mood, one tends to forget about what is going on, on the screen" (courtesy Film Score Monthly).

a series of montages that grant Jones plenty of space for restless percussion, rumbling bass and anxious, muted horns. A climactic, late-night shoot-out at the docks is spotted by a slow, throaty reprise of the primary theme's percussion line, building the five-note motif through various instruments—bass, organ and electric guitar, with disturbing bursts of trumpet—as McClain's colleagues meet their demise, one by one.

Jones' score finally was digitized in 2009: a gorgeous album that grants much better exposure to the music, than that provided within the film.

Kirk Douglas would have made an excellent Parker, during his younger days. Alas, Douglas scraped the bottom of the barrel when he starred in the laughably awful *A Lovely Way to Die*. It warrants mention here solely because (a) it's a crime drama, of sorts; and (b) it offers the final, faintly jazz notes of Kenyon Hopkins' scoring career, before he was forced into the bland ghetto of mundane television projects.

The plot follows hot-headed ex-cop Jim "Sky" Schuyler (Douglas), as he accepts an assignment to bodyguard Rena Westabrook (Sylva Koscina), a recent widow on trial for having conspired with a lover to kill her husband. Director David Lowell Rich and Douglas take a leering approach to Rena and all the other objectified women in this pathetic "mystery," with Sky eventually stumbling his way to a gang of greedy thieves who've killed the reclusive owner of the adjacent estate, to loot the place at their leisure. It turns out they also killed Rena's husband, because he happened upon their activities by sheer chance.

Most of Hopkins' score is mickey-mousing of the worst sort, including saucy orchestral pops inserted every time some babe bends over. He nonetheless manages a few bursts of former glory: some sexy walking bass, early on, when the promiscuous Sky wakens in a strange bed; a fragment of action jazz when Sky confronts a masked killer late one night; and a series of fast-paced action cues during the climactic car/helicopter chase/gun battle that ends with the most unconvincing lovers' clinch in cinema history.

The film failed to produce a soundtrack album, although vocalist Jackie Wilson's funk-laden title song did make it onto a 45 single.

The larceny and heist elements are much sleeker in *The Thomas Crown Affair*, a perfect marriage of incandescent star power, directorial flourish, clever scripting and mood-enhancing music. Audiences were dazzled by director Norman Jewison's innovative use of split-screen images, as a means of conveying simultaneous action in multiple locales. Steve McQueen plays the title character, a jaded, Boston-based millionaire businessman who masterminds an ingenious bank robbery. Crown never sets foot near the bank in question; he clandestinely hires five strangers—who know neither him nor each other—to handle different aspects of the $2.6 million caper. The insurance company brings in their best investigator, the voluptuous Vicki Anderson (Faye Dunaway). She deduces key details, seizes upon Crown as the likely ringleader, and cheekily confronts him; Crown, amused by her impudence, revels in the challenge. The blossoming romance is undercut by the fact that he knows that she knows, and *she* knows that he knows that she knows. What, then, will each do?

Composer Michel Legrand's collaboration with Jewison remains one of Hollywood's most captivating musical sagas. Legrand's first exposure to the film was a five-hour work print that hadn't yet been trimmed, so he made a radical suggestion: He'd write roughly 90 minutes of music, with lengthy compositions based entirely on impressions he derived from the unfinished print. Only then, he proposed, should the film be edited down to roughly two hours, with scenes timed to the music (a totally reversal of the usual process, where composers synch their themes to the final edit).[12] Jewison and supervising editor Hal Ashby agreed, and even allowed Legrand to participate in the editing process; this is why, as the film progresses, so many of Legrand's longish cues continue through multiple scenes.

"I adored Michel's method," Jewison recalled, decades later. "I can see us now, using his music to structure the famous chess game scene. The script described it in only three words: Chess with sex. It was the ideal marriage of music and pictures: no dialogue, just pure cinematic storytelling."[13]

Legrand also contributed two songs. The first, with lyrics by Alan and Marilyn Bergman, was intended to back Crown's glider flight, as he enjoys the quiet isolation of the empty sky. But Jewison so admired Noel Harrison's wistful vocal on "The Windmills of Your Mind," that it also became the film's opening theme. Legrand's vocal on the second tune—"His Eyes, Her Eyes"—never made it into the finished film, although it does appear on the soundtrack album.

The enticing Vicki debuts striding purposefully through an airport terminal, against a full-blown, big-band swinger that matches Dunaway's come-hither smile. A bit later, having deduced that Crown is her man, she watches him play polo during one of the film's split-screen montages: a sequence complemented by a robust arrangement of "His Eyes, Her Eyes"—trumpet fanfares accompanied by Legrand's lightning-quick keyboard runs—that matches the intensity of the aggressive polo action. Once invited to Crown's home, Vicki prowls his study to Ray Brown's wicked walking bass, augmented by erotic sax and muted trumpet. The subsequent chess game is scored to gentle guitar licks, softly brushed drums and plucked strings; the cue builds in intensity, morphing into a slow, sensual reading of "His Eyes, Her Eyes," which matches the steamy glances exchanged by McQueen and Dunaway. (Watch for the sharp burst of brass, when Vicki caresses one of her bishops in a most lascivious manner.)

The tension soon wears on Crown, who is determined to go down fighting. Jewison builds to a nail-biting climax, and Legrand enhances the suspense with nervous piano runs that ascend and descend the entire length of the keyboard.

Legrand rearranged and expanded his cues for the soundtrack album, which he rerecorded in France with an entirely different band. He was nominated for a Grammy Award, for his instrumental arrangement of "Windmills," but lost to the Mike Post/Mason Williams hit, "Classical Gas." Legrand fared better at the Academy Awards, securing nominations for both score and original song; he won the latter, sharing the Oscar with the Bergmans. "The Windmills of Your Mind" subsequently was covered by all manner of vocalists, from Vic Damone and Neil Diamond, to Dusty Springfield and Barbra Streisand. Sting performed it for the 1999 remake of *The Thomas Crown Affair*; alas, Bill Conti's fresh score isn't jazz.

Meanwhile, Across the Pond…

When *The Avengers* returned to UK television on September 25, 1968, the show's producers orchestrated a graceful transition from Diana Rigg's Emma Peel to Steed's new female companion: the perky and much younger Tara King (Linda Thorson). The latter passes Emma on the stairs, as she departs Steed's flat for the final time. Tara then bounds into Steed's flat, accompanied by the debut of her theme: a mildly wistful muted trumpet melody. A fresh end credits sequence completes the transition, Macnee now sharing cutaway scenes with Thorson; Laurie Johnson's iconic title theme kicks into life, with Tara's theme inserted as counterpoint via solo horn against the core melody. The big band jazz swinger otherwise reprises as before, complete with its saucy bridge.

Tara ultimately assisted Steed in 32 cases during Series 6. The adventures grew progressively crazier, sliding more frequently into science-fiction; each episode also concludes with a droll tag scene (which has nothing to do with the preceding story). Johnson wrote a delectably swooning romantic theme for the latter sequences, with a muted trumpet playing the sensuous melody between two countermelody bridges: first via harpsichord/harp, then soft horns.

Johnson also supplied fresh underscore cues for each episode, until other demands proved overwhelming. He therefore shared *Avengers* responsibilities with Howard Blake, who'd been playing keyboards in Johnson's band. Blake scored 10 episodes, and even careful listeners sometimes having trouble distinguishing his work from that of his mentor. Soft brass and a saucy sax solo highlight a suspenseful sequence in "All Done with Mirrors"; bongos, brass fanfares and a picked solo bass guitar add an unsettling atmosphere to "My Wildest Dream"; numerous bluesy swing cues highlight "Take Me to Your Leader."

Johnson never released an album devoted specifically to his work on Series 6, although his freshened title theme—with Tara King's countermelody—and the "tag theme" can be found on 1998's Redial/PolyGram anthology CD, *The Professional: The Best of Laurie Johnson*. Blake was more generous; his 2011 two-disc *The Avengers: Original Tara King Season Score* includes cues from all 10 of his scores.

Although the show went into hibernation for seven years, Steed, Johnson and numerous key production people would return in the fall of 1976, when *The New Avengers* tweaked the formula yet again. (See this book's companion volume.)

Toward the end of the 1960s, the British television industry seemed willing to float *any* espionage/spy series concept, no matter how ill-conceived or poorly executed. The eye-rolling premise of ITV's *The Champions* concerns three agents assigned to a United Nations intelligence outfit dubbed Nemesis—Craig Stirling (Stuart Damon), Sharron Macready (Alexandra Bastedo) and Richard Barrett (William Gaunt)—who complete a clandestine mission in China, only to crash-land in the Himalayas while flying back to England. A Tibetan shaman grants the trio "enhanced abilities" such as strength, intelligence, hearing and vaguely defined ESP powers. In theory, these gifts should help the Nemesis trio make short work of future assignments; in practice, the show's sloppy scripts rarely find reason to tap into the special powers that make *The Champions* ... well ... champions.

Happily, the show's music is a different matter. Tony Hatch's title theme is a thoughtful, midtempo jazz march, with a woodwinds/brass melody given momentum by a rolling rhythm section. Hatch left underscores to the indefatigable Edwin Astley, with support from Robert Farnon and Albert Elms; the latter uncorks several smokin' swing cues in his episodes. No concurrent soundtrack album appeared, although Hatch's title theme was released as a 45 single; he adds a feisty sax solo and saucy walking bass during a swing bridge. A 2014 box set includes all of the show's 223 cues by all four composers.

Not all of 1968's new UK shows focused on flamboyant heroes. It will be recalled that criminologists Edwin G. Oldenshaw (Richard Vernon) and Ian Dimmock (Michael Aldridge) spent two earlier programs—*The Man in Room 17* and *The Fellows (Late of Room 17)*—putting bad guys in prison, before finally retiring in August 1967. A sequel-of-sorts focuses on one of those incarcerated criminals, Alec Spindoe (Ray McAnally). Granada's six-part *Spindoe*, which debuted April 19, 1968, begins when Alec is released from prison after a five-year stretch. He discovers that his former associate Eddie Edwards (Anthony Bate) has taken over his criminal empire; worse yet, Spindoe's wife Shelagh (Colette O'Neil) has climbed into Edwards' bed. The subsequent drama depicts Spindoe's ruthless determination to regain what he perceives as rightfully his.

The miniseries gets a swinging main theme from Derek Hilton (aka John Snow). The title credits sequence is restricted to bland graphics that open with the jagged line of a heartbeat monitor; the first few notes of Hilton's theme add counterpoint to the monitor sound effects, and then the ensemble segues into a frisky jazz waltz when the show's title appears. The rhythmic melody is carried by muted trumpet against a lively rhythm section; jazz flute adds perky counterpoint, until the theme fades out when each episode's action begins. The end credits arrangement is quite different, opening with soprano woodwinds against unison horns and a faster tempo; the full ensemble then slides into the primary theme, with a concluding—and slightly ominous—drum roll that backs a brief hint of the next installment.

The live-to-film production precludes much in the way of underscores, although Spindoe's occasional visits to bars and other hangouts are backed by faint jazz band source cues, likely from the De Wolfe Music Library. Although Hilton's *Spindoe* theme never achieved mainstream release, it is included on 1969's *Newsdesk: The Modern Sound*, an LP of De Wolfe library cues.

* * *

On the big screen, the Bond phenomenon still prompted plenty of action-laden imitators, but discriminating viewers could find Cold War–era spycraft treated seriously. *A Dandy in Aspic*, adapted from Derek Marlowe's 1966 novel, held that potential; the twisty plot concerns a British Intelligence agent known as Eberlin, actually a deep-cover Russian spy. Things get complicated when the Brits—aware that a KGB agent named Krasnevin has killed several of their agents—assign Eberlin to identify and kill the man. But Eberlin actually *is* Krasnevin, and therefore must find a way to pin that label on some other British operative, who can be executed instead. Sadly, the film can't match the book's absorbing plot and atmosphere. Director Anthony Mann died during production, and star Laurence Harvey took over; his cold, clinical style—very much like his chilly portrayal of Eberlin/Krasnevin—doesn't mesh well with the previously completed footage. The result is contrived and manipulative, much like the string puppet that is cruelly jerked about (an obvious metaphor) during the title credits.

Quincy Jones' score relies heavily on electronic keyboard and cimbalom. The puppet-laden credits sequence begins with unsettling tick-tock synth effects, which coalesce into a catchy, "galloping" keyboard and cimbalom melody. This theme reprises during subsequent action sequences: a bungled British attempt to catch a low-level KGB agent; and when Eberlin tries to save one of his undercover Russian colleagues from being kidnapped. Other notable cues include a lyrical jazz ballad—"If You Want Love," sung by Shirley Horn—which becomes the theme for Caroline (Mia Farrow), a photographer who falls for Eberlin; and a bit of cheerful jazz heard a bit later, when Eberlin and Caroline are followed by an inept agent of unknown loyalty.

Sharp-eared listeners will recognize another theme from a different source. Midway through the film, Eberlin meets a young British agent (Peter Cook) in the restaurant atop Berlin's Fernsehturm Tower; the background source music is a leisurely jazz arrangement of "The Spell You Spin," which Jones uses prominently in his score for the 1969 romantic comedy *Cactus Flower*.

No soundtrack album arrived, although Shirley Horn's "If You Want Love" was released as a 45 single.

After spending five seasons as American TV's Dr. Ben Casey, square-jawed Vince Edwards traveled across the pond to make the graceless *Hammerhead*. He stars as American spy Charles Hood, recruited by British Intelligence to safeguard a nuclear defense report code-named Operation Watchdog. The document is coveted by a criminal mastermind named Hammerhead (Peter Vaughan), a wealthy collector of erotic art who schemes to replace Britain's NATO delegate, Sir Richard Calvert (Michael Bates), with a look-alike who thus will gain access to the report. Hood is distracted throughout by the ditsy and underdressed Sue Trenton (Judy Geeson), while doing his best to outwit bad girls Kit (Diana Dors) and Ivory (Beverly Adams).

British songwriter/arranger David Whitaker made his film scoring debut, with uneven results. His John Barry-esque title theme is solid: big and brassy, with Madeline Bell belting out lyrics clearly intended to evoke Shirley Bassey's sensuous reading of the title theme for *Goldfinger*. Most of the subsequent, percussion-laden action cues are fast and furious, when

Hood is attacked by nameless thugs at various points during his pursuit of Hammerhead. A few gentler cues are pleasant, salsa-inflected or Vegas-style swingers, such as those heard during Hood's clandestine exploration of the villain's opulent yacht.

But we can't help judging a movie by its opening scenes. The hapless Whitaker is forced to provide some atonal weirdness for a laughably repulsive "Chelsea Happening" that takes place behind the title credits—while Hood watches incredulously from the wings—and the film never recovers from this bizarre prologue. Things get even worse during the climax, when Whitaker's bubbly, horn-driven cues sound like something borrowed from a *Carry On* comedy.

The soundtrack album's few jazz cues are buried amid what frequently sounds like cartoon music.

The mocking tone is better modulated in *Sebastian*, a quirky little film that suggests the sort of code-breaking activities that took place behind Bletchley Park's super-secret closed doors. That premise is updated into an odd blend of Cold War–era spyjinks, colorful 1960s London pop fashion and design, and uneasy romance between two quite dissimilar characters. Dirk Bogarde plays the title character: a brilliant but socially challenged cryptographer assigned to British Intelligence, who heads a team of 100 hand-picked analysts—all women—who work rotating shifts around the clock, to break Russian and Chinese ciphers. His newest recruit is Rebecca Howard (Susannah York), who proves quite adept at this secret "civil service" work; she also falls for her perpetually distracted boss. Sebastian has other problems: a "chatty" Sputnik satellite; and an aggressive Head of Security (Nigel Davenport), who has grown suspicious of the left-wing Communist sympathies of the team's senior decoder, Elsa Shahn (Lilli Palmer).

Jerry Goldsmith ingeniously concocted a spy-jazz score with a math/computer undercurrent, satisfying all of the whimsical film's varied elements. (Several cues sound similar to what he'd recently written for the two *Flint* entries.) Sebastian's character theme opens with a quirky blend of percussion, strings and harpsichord; it bursts into life with sax and electric guitar, when he has a fateful meet-cute encounter with Rebecca. Goldsmith then adds swinging, midtempo percussion, electric guitar and horns as the movie's credits debut: an imaginative sequence with cast and production names unscrambling, as if on a computer. It's one of Goldsmith's all-time coolest title themes.

He also has fun with the classics, Sebastian's music of choice in the office; Bach's Partita No. VI gets jazzed up with an expanding piano line and accelerating bass and drums. Once Rebecca begins her romantic pursuit, Goldsmith contributes an even bouncier version of Sebastian's theme—almost comical, with flute touches—when she strips his apartment's ghastly wallpaper, in an effort to bring some color into his life. Much later, ominous percussion, nervous strings and edgy sax enhance Sebastian's realization that he's in genuine danger.

Goldsmith reorchestrated his primary cues for the lively soundtrack LP; the later digital release adds 12 tracks of electronic "Sputnik themes."

Computers are similarly prominent in *Hot Millions*, a quirky heist comedy replete with dry British wit and a plum starring performance from Peter Ustinov. He stars as serial fraudster Marcus Pendleton, who assumes the identity of a computer programmer to obtain a high-level position at an investment firm, where he subsequently penetrates the company mainframe's security system. After setting up three dummy corporations at mail drops in France, Italy and Germany, Pendleton arranges for regular checks to be sent to their corporate heads … all actually his own self. Ah, but his increasingly unusual behavior is noticed by security chief Willard C. Gnatpole (Bob Newhart), which leads to a delightful final confrontation in Rio de Janeiro.

Laurie Johnson's title theme is a big band swinger that opens with martial percussion, strings and trumpet fanfares, until a ferocious drum roll kicks off the primary melody: a fast 2/2 strut with reeds carrying the melody against sizzling string accompaniment. The cue evokes the clattering behavior of a computer spitting out paperwork; unison trumpets take over until a bridge repeats the patriotic march motif. Another drum roll reintroduces the primary melody, which builds to a rousing blast of unison horns. Numerous arrangements of this theme recur, most whimsically with French, Italian and German instrumental touches when Pendleton creates each of his international money drops. A lighter, secondary love theme surfaces—again, fast-paced and buoyant—when Pendleton begins a relationship with Patty (Maggie Smith).

The rest of the score is more orchestral pop than jazz, and there wasn't enough music to warrant a soundtrack album.

The "mod London vibe" also is evident in *Duffy*, a bizarre slice of late 1960s psychedelia masquerading as a heist flick; any semblance of plot continuity frequently takes a back seat to Philip Harrison's baroque art direction and set design. The thin plot finds half-brothers Stefane (James Fox) and Antony (John Alderton) conspiring to steal £1 million from their insufferably condescending father, Charles (James Mason), when he sends the cash overseas—by ship—to settle a dodgy business debt. The guys enlist the aid of Duffy (James Coburn), who has some experience in covert operations; eye candy is provided by Segolene (Susannah York), a sexy, free-spirited libertine who flits between Stefane and Duffy, as her mood dictates. Much of the action takes place in a sunbaked Southern Spanish beach resort, where clothing remains as loose as everybody's morals.

The setting allows Ernie Freeman to slide from jazz and R&B to sensual bossa nova. Most of the cues are tight combo affairs led by electronic keyboard, bass and drums; flute and electric guitar occasionally shade the action. Music is ubiquitous; numerous sequences are staged as wordless montages, allowing Freeman's cues to run several minutes. Many longer cues are arrangements of "I'm Satisfied," the R&B anthem lustfully growled by Lou Rawls when Coburn—and his broad smile—enter the story. Duffy's initial reaction to the crazed scheme is understandably negative, but he weakens after inviting the trio to his spacious home in Tangier. Freeman gets the longest uninterrupted cue here: nearly four minutes of sassy, keyboard- and guitar-driven swing against a four-bar bass ostinato, while the trio eyes the opulent pad's lunatic art installations.

Additional choice cues include some saucy keyboard trio work, when Segolene taunts Duffy while taking a soapy shower; and the 5-3-5 motif that highlights the veritable jazz symphony which powers the lengthy heist sequence. In the film's funniest music gag, this cue cuts off abruptly, midmeasure, when Stefane—having been supplied with the wrong combination—initially is unable to open the safe.

Freeman's thoroughly enjoyable score screamed for release, but no soundtrack album ever emerged.

* * *

Producer Walter Mirisch erred badly when he continued the *Pink Panther* series without director Blake Edwards, star Peter Sellers and composer Henry Mancini. *Inspector Clouseau* was dead on arrival, because nobody wanted to see Clouseau played by anybody other than Sellers. To make matter worse, the klutzy, language-mangling policeman is saddled with a series of James Bondian gadgets, in a failed attempt to cash in on cinema's spy craze. Ken Thorne's effervescent score nonetheless injects an appropriate air of mischief. The former big band jazz pianist was just beginning his successful film career, and he honors his roots with a couple of swing cues that put some bounce into this Clouseau's ungainly steps.

Scotland Yard's inability to halt a crime wave has been attributed to a mole within the police force, so Commissioner Braithwaite (Patrick Cargill) and Supt. Weaver (Frank Finlay) request the assistance of Clouseau (Alan Arkin), who—as an outsider—can be trusted as a reliable ally. He eventually bumbles his way into suspecting escaped convict Addison Steele (Barry Foster), while fending off romantic overtures from Weaver's promiscuous wife (Beryl Reid), and trying to determine whether the sensuous Lisa Morrel (Delia Boccardo) is friend or foe. The criminal gang devises a plan to simultaneously rob 13 Swiss banks, pinning the blame on Clouseau by virtue of lifelike face masks, and then escaping the continent by concealing the loot as wrapped Lindt candy bars.

Thorne opens his title theme with a brass-heavy, Mack Sennet–style silent movie prologue that segues into an orchestral jazz waltz with a 4-4-8 melodic motif; the cue shifts to sparkling big band swing as the credits conclude. Variations of this theme support Clouseau's subsequent antics; the best arrangement comes during a montage, as the villains' numerous vehicles—camouflaged to resemble Lindt delivery vans, each driven by an ersatz Clouseau—snatch the cash from all those Swiss banks. Thorne kicks up the tempo with muted trumpet, against a suspenseful, finger-snapping rhythm section; the cue explodes into ferocious action jazz, a wall of brass taking the melody against some sparkling Hammond B3 comping.

The soundtrack album includes a few unused cues that suggest scenes cut from the film; the best is "Bossa Nova (in the Restaurant)," a lovely bit of midtempo Latin swing.

Elsewhere in the World

Rapporto Fuller Base Stoccolma (*Fuller Report*) is an unusual Eurospy entry, in that the protagonist is a bewildered civilian in the classic Hitchcock mold, rather than a gadget-laden secret agent. The hapless fellow is professional race car driver Dick Worth (Ken Clark), who gets caught between American, Russian and unknown third-party agents. They all believe he's a fellow spy, and they all seek a document known as the "Fuller Report," somehow linked to a planned assassination that involves defecting Russian ballerina Svetlana Golyadkin (Beba Loncar). The result is an entertaining thriller that gets a solid boost from Armando Trovajoli's big band/combo jazz score.

The title credits unfold against a power ballad—"The Touch of a Kiss," given melodramatic heft by bold brass fanfares and chanteuse Lara Saint Paul—that deserved to become a lounge classic. Instrumental arrangements of this tune, with plenty of bass flute and organ touches, become ubiquitous; the secondary theme is a 5/4 action cue with a catchy rhythm line strongly influenced by Desmond/Brubeck's "Take Five." Mistaken identities and repeated threats against Dick's life soon lead him to Svetlana, whom he believes holds the key to the whole mess. Subsequent skirmishes give Trovaioli's 5/4 action cue plenty of exercise, often with bongos and sax licks serving as counterpoint behind the suspenseful brass melody: most notably during a gun-laden melee in a lumberyard.

On a gentler note, some cool-school sax, muted trumpet and organ bossa nova is heard as PA source music, during Dick's later rendezvous with Svetlana in the Stockholm

Calidarium (public bathhouse). Harp glissandos, low flutes and spooky solo sax add tension as the third act builds to a surprise-laden climax, and the 5/4 action cue gets a final reprise when Dick puts his driving skills to good use.

Trovaioli's score finally was released in 2007.

Basil Kirchin's fizzy jazz score is a similar highlight in *Assignment K*, an otherwise limp adaptation of British crime novelist Leopold Horace Ognall's gritty source novel. To the world at large, Philip Scott (Stephen Boyd) is the head of Howsco Toys Ltd., which gives him the freedom to roam Europe in search of product. To British Intelligence, he's also Agent Mercury, head of a courier network that transports valuable intel on microfilm artfully concealed within toys and dolls. His successes have enraged Mr. Smith (Leo McKern), heading a team of East German Stasi agents; he's determined to expose and shut down Mercury's network. Most of the resulting surveillance time is spent watching Scott meet, flirt and fall in love with perky Toni Peters (Camilla Sparv); Smith kidnaps her and demands the identities of everybody in Scott's network.

Kirchin, a well-established British jazz musician/composer, cut his teeth playing drums in his father's big band; *Assignment K* is his sole spy-jazz score. The lengthy title credits sequence unfolds as a wordless montage that depicts the ingenuity of Scott's courier network: the perfect opportunity for Kirchin's first jazz cue, which opens with Ron Prentice's smooth solo on acoustic double bass. The initially random riffs coalesce into the rhythm of a passenger train, an exploratory trumpet noodling its way toward an actual melody; that theme emerges on vibes and guitar and segues to a wall of brass. A solo trumpet takes over, with cool riffing at the bridge; the cue concludes with a roar from the entire orchestra, suggesting a level of excitement that the film never delivers.

Scott and Toni begin their relationship at a nightclub, where revelers dance energetically to vibrant diegetic tunes by a resident clarinet/organ combo. Back in London, she moves into Scott's flat; their relationship is cemented by a cheerful bossa-nova romantic theme, the melody shared by keyboards and tasty horns, and backed by more of Prentice's silky bass riffs. Kirchin's efforts are absent during the kidnapping and most of what follows. In the aftermath, a pensive drum roll segues to a slow orchestral reading of the main theme; melancholy horns follow Scott, when he drives away.

The film failed to produce a soundtrack album, so fans must be content with a digitized bootleg that debuted in 2014.

A potentially clever heist thriller is buried beneath the desert sand of *They Came to Rob Las Vegas*, but it's betrayed by budgetary constraints, clumsy editing and poor dubbing. This multinational production has the gruff momentum and grade-B overacting of early Sergio Leone spaghetti Westerns, although star Gary Lockwood doesn't have a trace of Clint Eastwood's charisma. Even so, the film gets substantial momentum from French-Armenian composer/songwriter Georges Garvarentz's vigorous big band jazz score.

The complex plot, based loosely on French crime/espionage author André Lay's *Les hommes de Las Vegas*, begins with the reunion of Las Vegas blackjack dealer Tony Ferris (Lockwood) and his older brother, prison escapee Gino (Jean Servais). Their happy get-together is brief; Gino is killed during the bungled hold-up of an armored van fortified by ruthless security measures overseen by Steve Skorsky (Lee J. Cobb). Vowing revenge, Tony mounts a more carefully planned heist and assembles a crew; they hit another of Skorsky's armored vans while it traverses the barren Five Palms Road in the desert outside of Las Vegas. They then maneuver the van into a large underground vault beneath the desert sand, making it appear that the huge vehicle has vanished into thin air; this gives

Tony and his comrades plenty of time to burn their way into its heavily armored interior. Alas, this particular van isn't carrying only cash; Skorsky has been using occasional runs on behalf of the Mexican Mafia. And *nobody* knows that the entire operation is under the watchful gaze of U.S. Treasury Inspector Douglas (Jack Palance).

Garvarentz opens the film with plenty of exhilarating brass, when Gino breaks out of prison. Once safely away, Gino's long-awaited reunion with Tony plays against a gentle solo guitar cue ("The Wordless Song") that reprises frequently: often as ironic counterpoint, and also as a love theme for Tony and Ann (Elke Sommer). Garvarentz spots the subsequent title credits with a bluesy, unexpectedly mournful trumpet theme, which foreshadows the pitfalls to come. Gino's doomed raid on a Skorsky armored van kicks off against swinging drums and bass, which build into big band fury; a lively sax solo emerges from the wall of brass, until everything goes awry.

The Five Palms Road assault on the Skorsky van is the film's showpiece. Garvarentz highlights this sequence with an extended jazz symphony, starting with a suspenseful blend of percussion and strings; this builds to a 6-6 brass motif that becomes yet another of the film's primary themes. Tempo and orchestral intensity shift when the van approaches the point where it will be attacked; the subsequent assault is backed by a rolling blast of percussion and trumpets, the dynamic melody shared by strings and brass, and highlighted by a kick-ass organ solo. Later, newly arrived members of the Mexican Cosa Nostra get their own theme: a stealthy, midtempo swinger with a menacing melody delivered by unison flutes, organ and electric guitar. The story climaxes during a violent finale—Garvarentz builds to a suspenseful frenzy with yet another full-blown, big band swinger—when everybody converges at the desert site.

The soundtrack album is highlighted by the lengthy jazz opus heard during the desert assault on the van.

13

This Never Happened to the Other Fella: 1969

In a disturbing indication of things to come, no jazz-scored American crime or spy shows debuted this year.

On a related note, Dennis Hopper's counterculture hit, *Easy Rider*, would prove to have an enormous impact on Hollywood's approach to film scoring. Hopper's reliance on a soundtrack built entirely from hits by Steppenwolf, The Byrds, The Band, Jimi Hendrix and other rock 'n' roll icons—the film lacks any sort of instrumental underscore—was as audaciously innovative as the film itself. When the soundtrack roared up the *Billboard* album chart and was certified gold after only five months, studio execs couldn't help taking notice.

Jazz and orchestral session musicians began to sleep uneasily.

The Big Screen

Raymond Chandler wrote seven novels starring Philip Marlowe, and all but one—1958's *Playback*—have been made into films at least once. The eponymous *Marlowe* is adapted from the author's fifth novel, 1949's *The Little Sister*; screenwriter Stirling Silliphant did a masterful job of retaining the book's plot, attitude and mordant one-liners—all delivered archly by James Garner—while bringing the plot into the swinging '60s. The action is propelled by a feisty big band jazz score from pianist, composer and arranger Peter Matz.

Marlowe is hired by whiny Kansas country girl Orfamay Quest (Sharon Farrell) to find her brother Orrin, who has gone missing somewhere in Los Angeles. The young man's last known address is a seedy hotel, where Marlowe chats with a shady manager and a shifty tenant; shortly thereafter, both are murdered with an ice pick. Additional clues lead Marlowe to popular TV actress Mavis Wald (Gayle Hunnicutt), who is chaperoned by her best friend, exotic dancer Dolores Gonzáles (Rita Moreno). Mavis' mobster boyfriend, Sonny Steelgrave (H.M. Wynant), proves troublesome; Marlowe gradually realizes that Orrin was involved in a blackmail plot. But how does all of this involve Mavis' manager/agent, Crowell (William Daniels), or the sinister Dr. Vincent Lagardie (Paul Stevens)?

The psychedelic title credits are accompanied by a lively rock 'n' roll tune—"Little Sister," honoring the source novel—performed by the short-lived sunshine pop quartet Orpheus. The song's final verse becomes a diegetic cue heard on Marlowe's car radio, as he pulls up to a seedy residence hotel dubbed The Infinite Pad, where Orrin Quest supposedly lives. Without missing a beat, Matz segues into a sparkling instrumental jazz arrangement of the title song—the melody traded between flute and guitar, against soft bongos—while

Marlowe searches for the establishment's manager. Jazz flute remains Matz's instrument of choice, although numerous short, sax-fueled combo swingers are used as "traveling music," each time Marlowe drives to—or arrives at—a fresh location.

Other disgetic cues include a tasty samba tune performed by an unseen jazz trio, when Marlowe takes his girlfriend Julie (Corinne Camacho) to the Steelgraves' fancy restaurant; a cute jazz swinger emanating from Crowell's car radio, when Marlowe wins permission to investigate matters officially; and the debauched, drum- and horn-laden strip numbers performed by the house band where Dolores and her fellow dancers doff their duds each night.

No soundtrack album was produced.

Garner's shot at Chandler's iconic gumshoe was one of the year's cinematic treasures; director Bernard L. Kowalski's tawdry adaptation of Harold Robbins' *Stiletto* is hack filmmaking in nearly every respect. The sole attraction is Sid Ramin's vigorous jazz score, anchored by Dave Grusin's stylish keyboard work.

Alex Cord stars as Count Cesare Cardinali, a sports car-racing playboy who "moonlights" as a blade-wielding assassin for the Mafia. Cesare's immoral tendencies are exposed during a nasty flashback prologue, when he rapes a young woman and then kills one of her defenders; he's saved from an angry mob by Mafia underboss Emilio Matteo (Joseph Wiseman). Years later, with Cesare now established as a jet-setting aristocrat, he's ordered to kill a series of witnesses scheduled to testify against Matteo and two Mafia colleagues. Cesare develops second thoughts; that naturally puts him in the Mafia's crosshairs. At the same time, New York City–based investigator George Baker (Patrick O'Neal), long determined to nail Matteo, blackmails Cesare's girlfriend Illeana (Britt Ekland) into turning informant. Everything climaxes within the corridors of Puerto Rico's 16th century Castillo San Felipe del Morro.

Ramin's main theme—introduced as the title credits unfold against a lively casino montage, where Cesare smoothly claims his first victim—opens with gentle bossa nova percussion, then accelerates into a vibrant trumpet melody against Grusin's lovely Hammond B3 comping. The momentum pauses during a bridge, with Grusin all over the keyboard; the wall of brass resumes and rises to a screaming climax when Cesare slides the knife home. His subsequent coupling with Illeana introduces Ramin's love theme: a gentle bossa nova melody anchored by soft reeds and strings. Cesare's eventual effort to make amends with Matteo leads to the climax in Puerto Rico; Ramin supplies a Schifrin-esque action cue—bongos, heavy bass and a wall of brass—when Baker follows the other two men to the ancient castle.

Ramin also contributes several diegetic cues, mostly bossa nova and dance band arrangements of the main theme. A particularly lively cover comes from the resident quartet of a Harlem club, during a sidebar plotline that introduces lethal crime baron Hannibal Smith (Lincoln Kilpatrick).

Ramin's title theme earned a rowdy surf rock cover by Chico Rey and the Jet Band, for a single on the UK's Pye label.

Meanwhile, Across the Pond...

English playwright/author Francis Henry Durbridge's popular amateur detective, Paul Temple, finally came to television in a popular BBC series that debuted November 23. The original scripts update the characters to the swinging '60s; Francis Matthews stars as the unfailingly urbane Temple, with Ros Drinkwater as his equally sleuthful wife, Steve. Ron Grainer's catchy, gently swinging title theme opens with a hypnotic 3-5 brass vamp against harpsichord riffs, then reprises the melody via full orchestra. The end credits arrangement is slower, with a lone sax carrying the melody against a solo horn countermelody. Dudley Simpson's minimal "incidental music" for episode underscores is little more than fleeting harpsichord riffs.

Paul Temple was all but obliterated by the BBC's tape purge; only one episode survives from the first two seasons, along with roughly a dozen (combined) from seasons three and four.

Grainer recorded an expanded version of his title theme for a 45 single; it eventually was digitized as part of the 1994 compilation album, *Doctor Who & Other Classic Ron Grainer Themes*.

Temple would have been mocked by members of the London Metropolitan Police's anti-terrorism and anti-espionage department. *Special Branch*, a taut ITV investigative procedural, debuted September 17, 1969; it took a hiatus after two seasons and returned in an entirely new iteration in the spring of 1973. Various actors cycled through different roles over time, although the focus remained on the police officers tasked to work collaboratively with England's intelligence and security services (i.e., MI5).

The initial run—featuring Derren Nesbitt's DCI Elliot Jordan—is dominated by studio-based videotape shoots with occasional filmed "on location" inserts. Underscores are sparse and restricted to occasional diegetic cues from radios or phonographs; the sole continuing melody is the main theme heard over the title and end credits sequences. Norman Kay contributed the first-season theme: an initial barrage of jarring brass that segues to a melodic 3-4 motif on electric guitar. Background brass elements crescendo when the show's title is "stamped" onto the screen; the melody then repeats, builds to a final brass climax and fades as the episode begins. The upgraded second season title sequence features a new theme by Robert Sharples (aka Robert Earley). It's much more effective: an uptempo jazz waltz that wreaks havoc with time signatures, while powered by suspenseful unison trumpets against throbbing bass. The theme fades as the bass repeats a nine-note ostinato.

The entire cast and production team were dumped during the transition that led to the third season, with the action now centered around DCI Alan Craven (George Sewell); a greater reliance on film allowed the increased use of underscores. These are mostly synth shading, soft jazz or bossa tunes; the absence of a "score by" credit suggests that episodes were tracked with library cues. That said, Earley's yet again new title theme is an even more dynamic blast of brass against wandering tempos and time signatures, with a countermelody delivered by a particularly dirty sax. The end credits version is a different arrangement: Expectant electric guitar licks segue to the primary melody, carried by unison brass and sax against a noodly synth ostinato.

Kay's first-season theme wasn't issued as a mainstream recording. Sharples/Earley's efforts remained similarly unavailable until the release of 2015's vinyl compilation album *Themes for TV Drama: The Music of Robert Earley*.

Sharples also was involved with ITV's *Fraud Squad*, which was considered groundbreaking at the time: one of the first mainstream British police procedurals to feature a female detective in a leading role (as opposed to fantasy-oriented shows such as *The Avengers*). Viewed today, *Fraud Squad* is so gently quaint that it becomes charming. Patrick O'Connell and Joanna Van Gyseghem star as DI Gamble and DS Vicky Hicks, the sole members of the hilariously tiny Metropolitan Police Fraud Squad, where they investigate cases involving embezzlement, forgery, con artists, tax fiddles, bent politicians, savings swindles, dodgy "memorial funds" and—in one grim episode—a doctor exploiting ailing patients for his own financial gain. The dialogue-heavy approach focuses more on character interaction than active field work, during the course of two 13-episode seasons that debuted May 20, 1969.

The title theme is another ear worm from Sharples, this time concealed behind the pseudonym "E. Ward" (and not even acknowledged in the opening or end credits). The cue kicks off with a four-note brass ostinato against a pulsating rhythm section, as the show's title appears via black-and-white graphics that resolve into a close-up of O'Connell; unison horns introduce the catchy 2-3-4/2-3-3 motif that powers the melody, when DI Gamble hops into a car driven by Hicks, who smiles rather too broadly for her tight close-up. They drive off; the episode title is revealed, and the music fades as the drama begins.

There are no underscores; aside from the short brass bumpers heard between acts, episodes unfold without musical backing. Sharples' main theme never achieved mainstream release but is included—along with the bumpers—on 1971's *Swivel*, an LP of De Wolfe library cues.

Fraud Squad was practically cozy: a descriptor that never could have been applied to *Big Breadwinner Hog*. Granada TV's switchboard lit up like a Christmas tree after this serial's debut episode was broadcast on April 11, 1969; staid British viewers choked on their Maltesers when the show's title character threw a bottle of hydrochloric acid into the face of a rival hooligan. This nasty, eight-part crime saga charts the ruthless rise of hip young gangster Hogarth—known as "Hog" (Peter Egan)—as he tries to take over a long-established London criminal syndicate ruled by the equally cold-blooded Lennox (Timothy West). The arrogant Hog leads a smug, gleefully homicidal band of trendy "cool kids" determined to depose the "stuffy old guys" who've dominated the underworld for too long.

Hog's mod affectations demand an equally trendy pop/rock soundtrack, and most source music—from car radios, or heard in bars—is drawn from Top 40 hits of the day. But Derek Hilton's main theme is hard-charging combo jazz, anchored by flute riffs as saucy as Hog himself. The wildly rhythmic cue opens with four rising notes carried by unison horns; the melody's "call and response" motif is introduced via four flute notes, with the eight-note answer handled by unison brass. This repeats over rudimentary text and graphics, sometimes giving way to sassy jazz flute solos. Although each episode begins against the core melody, Hilton varies the arrangement; sometimes the music fades quickly, as the drama begins, while other times the flute and/or brass solos continue at length over an action montage. The flute soloist really cooks during the more impertinent end credits arrangement, which runs at greater length.

Hilton also supplies occasional underscore cues. One of the best is heard when Hog and his gaggle of light-fingered friends are introduced in episode one, during a brazen shoplifting montage; Hilton spots this sequence with an impudent, gently swinging jazz waltz that occasionally echoes the main theme, but more frequently grants plenty of space for cheeky solos by all of the musicians.

Hilton never recorded any of this show's music for mainstream release; it can be enjoyed only by watching the serial.

British viewers scandalized by such depictions of "true" crime likely were relieved by the latter seasons of *The Avengers*, which prompted a wave of similar shows featuring uniquely qualified individuals and government departments tasked with solving "bizarre" cases. Retired criminologist Adam Strange (Anthony Quayle) operates out of his own Paddington flat in ITV's *Strange Report*, from which he and colleagues Hamlyn Gynt (Kaz Garas) and Evelyn McClean (Anneke Wills) employ cutting-edge methodology to solve "open file" investigations abandoned by conventional detective entities. That premise notwithstanding, the cases were fairly routine criminal matters—murder, kidnapping, counterfeiting, a cholera epidemic—during a 16-episode run that began September 21.

The title theme and underscores came from British songwriter and jazz pianist Roger Webb, who favors gentle combo arrangements rather than the big band bluster of Laurie Johnson and Edwin Astley. Webb's title theme opens with an ominous three-note horn statement, after which the 1-5-3-4 motif is introduced via unison strings and brass, against a rhythmic eight-note ostinato. Additional brass touches herald the credits for Quayle and Garas; Wills, as the team's lone woman, gets a "softer" bridge countermelody against harpsichord comping. Some episodes offer a bit of swinging combo jazz—a soft vamp with the melody traded between reeds and piano—for a post-credits sequence that reveals episode title, writer and director. Webb's underscores mix atmospheric suspense and action cues with jazz-inflected arrangements of the title theme and some sleek combo cues. Diegetic touches range from raucous jazz/rock to original pop tunes.

Webb recorded the title theme for a 45 single, although it wasn't released until July 1971, well over a year after the show had been canceled. The 2009 box set *Strange Report: The Original Soundtrack* contains 61 tracks from six episode scores along with unused and alternate takes.

The action leans more toward the bizarre in ATV's *Department S*, where investigators handle genuine mysteries: a passenger airplane landing six days late, with nobody aboard aware of this passage of time; an entire village whose inhabitants disappear, save for one person; and a chauffeured passenger whose body vanishes, leaving behind only a skeleton. The three-person team—former American FBI agent Stewart Sullivan (Joel Fabiani), field investigator/computer expert Annabelle Hurst (Rosemary Nicols) and playboy novelist Jason King (Peter Wyngarde)—answer to Sir Curtis Seretse (Dennis Aba Peters), head of Interpol's unconventional Department S. (The "S" doesn't seem to stand for anything.)

The show gets its musical bounce from Edwin Astley, who supplied both an attention-grabbing title theme and underscores for the 28-episode season that began March 9. "The basis for the theme came from my son Jon, who was tinkering with the piano at home in Stanmore one day," Astley recalled. "He came up with a double-note sting, and I liked the sound of it, and asked if he minded me using it. He didn't, and it became the starting point for my theme to *Department S*."[1]

The title theme's eight-note synth ostinato always begins as an episode title, writer and director are superimposed over the teaser's conclusion; Astley then introduces the melody's 2-6 motif via strings and horn fanfares, as the credits sequence kicks off. A brass countermelody builds anticipation when the camera ultimately focuses on a "Department S" folder containing the unit's next assignment, after which a reprise of the synth ostinato slows into silence. Many underscore cues are built from this melody; the synth ostinato enhances viewer apprehension when transformed into suspensefully edgy cues. Underscores include plenty of bold action jazz cues that favor more fully developed melodies, and generally lack the staccato sharpness of what Astley wrote for *The Saint* and *Danger Man*.

Astley's title theme was covered by Cyril Stapleton for a 45 single. The 2008 box set *Department S Original Soundtrack* features all of Astley's 195 title theme variations and underscore cues.

13. This Never Happened to the Other Fella: 1969

Not quite two years after *Department S* solved its final "impossible" case, Wyngarde's Jason King was spun off into his own series. (See this book's companion volume.)

* * *

On the big screen, James Bond's new face wasn't the only innovative element within *On Her Majesty's Secret Service*. John Barry broke new ground by making Moog synthesizers a dominant part of his orchestral mix: the first time a major studio film had featured this electric keyboard so prominently.[2] Barry also had a very specific and subtler assignment: to ensure that audiences accepted new star George Lazenby as the "real" 007.

"What I felt was, well, we've lost Sean," Barry recalled, years later. "And so I have to stick my oar in the musical area double-strong, to make the audience try and forget that they don't have Sean. What I did was to over-emphasize everything that I'd done in the first few movies, and just go over the top, to try and make the soundtrack strong. To do Bondian beyond Bondian."[3] Barry and director Peter Hunt didn't miss a trick. When an early squabble between Bond and M (Bernard Lee) prompts the former to consider resigning, his memories of past missions are accompanied by brief quotes of themes from *Doctor No*, *From Russia with Love* and *Thunderball*.

As the film opens, the iconic gun-barrel's snippet of "The James Bond Theme"—at a slightly slower tempo—is delivered not by Vic Flick's throbbing guitar, but by Moog. A robust orchestral arrangement presents the full theme immediately thereafter—traditional brass taking the first verse and then handing the melody off to the electronic keyboard—when Bond (his face not yet revealed) saves a suicidal young woman and winds up in a nasty brawl; the latter is set to Barry's aggressive, brass and string action cue. This, in turn, segues to Maurice Binder's sexy title credits sequence, backed by a dynamic four-note descending bass line and a bold, rhythmic main theme: the last time a Bond film would open with a jazz instrumental. (The lengthy title was impossible to work into a lyric.)

This exhilarating cue also is used during the action showpieces, starting with Bond's initial escape—on skis, with dozens of baddies right behind him—from Piz Gloria, the Alpine retreat where the megalomaniacal Blofeld (Telly Savalas) has cooked up an ambitious plot to threaten the world via biological warfare. The cue repeats when the pursuit expands into a vehicular chase in the village below, where Bond is rescued by Tracy (Diana Rigg), the woman he earlier saved. Hunt inserts the classic 1962 "James Bond Theme" when 007 returns to Piz Gloria in the company of forces allied with Tracy's father, to rescue her and destroy Blofeld's lab.

Such action cues aside, Barry's score also grants plenty of space to a contemplative song—"We Have All the Time in the World"—which serves as the romantic theme that brings Bond and Tracy together. It debuts via forlorn solo flute, when they spend their first night together, and reprises frequently: most prominently with Louis Armstrong crooning the lyrics, during a montage that shows Bond and Tracy falling in love.

The soundtrack album's *Billboard* chart run was modest, at 13 weeks. Decades later, "We Have All the Time in the World" was revived in the UK as the anthem for a trippy TV commercial on behalf of Guinness Beer. The tune's renewed popularity prompted a fresh 45 single, which climbed all the way to No. 3 during a 19-week run.

Even sporting a new face, Bond didn't lose any momentum. The same cannot be said of Richard Johnson's second and final outing as Hugh "Bulldog" Drummond, in *Some Girls Do*. This slapstick farce sorely lacks its predecessor's clever touches, and Charles Blackwell's mild jazz score is an equally poor substitute for Malcolm Lockyer's previous effort.

The erratic story finds Drummond investigating a series of "accidents" that have befallen various individuals and ground-support teams working on England's prototype supersonic jet, the SST1. These incidents have been orchestrated by an identity-switching baddie eventually revealed as Carl Petersen (James Villiers), who commands a coterie of

Director Peter Collinson wanted Quincy Jones to handle the music for *The Italian Job*, so the composer and his family flew across the Atlantic for a spell. Jones delivered a lively, larkish bossa nova score that relies heavily on harpsichord and harmonica, and perfectly suits the film's tone. The results don't swing quite as much as other assignments to be found within these pages; several harpsichord- and string-laden themes instead convey a droll sense of Merrie Olde England (Columbia Pictures/Photofest).

lethal lovelies from a stronghold in the Mediterranean. Most of the nasty work is done by Helga (Daliah Lavi) and Pandora (Beba Loncar); the rest of Petersen's gun-toting babes turn out to be robots (possibly the inspiration, decades later, for Austin Powers' similarly deadly Fembots). Drummond is saddled with a dim-bulb tag-along: the kooky, shrill-voiced Flicky (Sydne Rome), introduced via one of Blackwell's gently sexy jazz cues. The composer cooks up a more aggressively erotic melody for a dumb sequence when Petersen asks Drummond to educate his robots in "the art of seduction." Later action cues are backed by jazz arrangements of the movie's title theme.

Although the film failed to generate a soundtrack album, Trinidadian soul/rock singer Lee Vanderbilt's salacious delivery of the title song was released as a 45 single.

On a far more successful note, *The Italian Job* boasts Michael Caine's energetic starring performance, Peter Collinson's vibrant direction, and Quincy Jones' lively bossa nova score. The climactic, wildly entertaining car chase remains famous, in part because it gave many viewers their first glimpse of BMC's adorable Mini Cooper S. That chase caps a caper that begins when enterprising Cockney criminal Charlie Croker (Caine) assembles a crew to steal $4 million in gold from an Italian armored courier. Charlie secures the blessing and financial backing of London criminal kingpin Mr. Bridger (Noël Coward), still living a life of luxury despite being behind prison bars. But the Italian Mafia, personified by boss Altabani (Raf Vallone), isn't about to let a bunch of British invaders succeed, so Charlie's plan must thwart the Turin police *and* the mob.

Jones' score relies heavily on harpsichord and harmonica—Ross Garren on the latter—and perfectly suits the film's madcap tone. The title tune, "On Days Like These," is romantic cheese when sung by Matt Monro, but subsequent instrumental variations swing quite nicely, often via Peter King's smoldering alto sax solos. A secondary action cue—"It's Caper Time"—is driven by mischievous percussion, bongos and an irreverent melody played on both harmonica and bass reeds. This theme roars into life when the gold-laden Mini Coopers evade, out-maneuver and just plain outfox the larger, clunkier police pursuit vehicles. The lengthy instrumental cue eventually is supplemented by a male chorus composed of Caine and his lads—triumphantly billing themselves as "the *self*-pre-ser-*va*-tion so-*ci-e-ty*!"—and chanting in time to Jones' bonkers blend of bongos, harmonica, soprano sax, flutes, tambourine and all manner of percussion madness.

The initial soundtrack LP was produced in *very* limited quantities, which prompted frustrated fans to assemble at least two bootlegs. That problem finally was solved with a 2000 digital release that includes a bonus track reprise of "On Days Like These." Better yet, in December 2019 Quartet issued a 50th anniversary "expanded edition" that includes Jones' complete score, along with numerous bonus tracks.

The film was remade in 2003; although director F. Gary Gray orchestrates equally entertaining results with a clever variation on the original heist scheme, John Powell's score (alas) does not qualify as jazz.

Elsewhere in the World

Bent cops don't come much more corrupt than Commissario Stefano Belli, the crooked investigator who propels the action in Italian director Romolo Guerrieri's *Un Detective* (known in the States as either *Ring of Death* or *Detective Belli*). The twisty murder mystery begins when Belli (Franco Nero) is hired by wealthy criminal attorney Avvocato Fontana

(Adolfo Celi) to "fix" an inconvenient liaison between his son, Mino (Maurizio Bonuglia), and expat British fashion model Sandie Bronson (Delia Boccardo). Belli soon learns that Sandie previously was associated with Romanis (Marino Masé), a young man killed by an unknown assailant. The case expands to include Emmanuelle (Susanna Martinková), an aloof model with a heroin habit; Claudio (Roberto Bisacco), an arrogant photographer; and Fontana's youthful wife, Vera (Florinda Bolkan). Belli coldly plays these suspects against each other, particularly when some of them can enrich his own bank account.

The music assignment went to celebrated Italian singer/songwriter Alfredo "Fred" Bongusto, just beginning a parallel career as a soundtrack composer. His score veers wildly from big band jazz to gentle solo piano, with bits of bossa nova thrown in for good measure. The title credits appear against a svelte jazz waltz ("The World of the Blues") that opens with a lyrical horn solo, then blossoms into a big band swinger; tasty solos on trumpet and vibes are backed by brass fanfares. The cue builds to a crescendo that cuts off abruptly, when Romanis is shot dead. When Belli later discovers the body, Bongusto introduces his mildly unsettling "Mystery Theme," the melody carried by a melancholy solo trumpet. This establishes a pattern: Belli uncovers a new piece of evidence, against another arrangement of the "Mystery Theme"; he then interrogates one of the suspects, against a reworking of either the title theme or a quieter love theme.

Depending on which version of the film one watches, Belli ultimately is killed, as vocalist Shirley Harmer belts out a lusty version of "The World of the Blues" … or he survives, badly wounded, against an instrumental reprise of that same theme.

No soundtrack album appeared until 1997, when most of the score was digitized, along with incidental source cues and two takes of Harmer's vocal on the title theme.

14

Soul Flower: 1970

Although it could be argued that Sidney Poitier's Virgil Tibbs helped pave the way—with *In the Heat of the Night*—Hollywood's "blaxploitation" subgenre truly exploded with the release of director/co-scripter Ossie Davis' rollicking, big-screen adaptation of *Cotton Comes to Harlem*. It's based on the seventh novel in Chester Himes' hard-boiled crime series, featuring New York City Police detectives Gravedigger Jones and Coffin Ed Johnson. The film lightened Himes' grim tone, with a sassy atmosphere that occasionally borders on burlesque. But the formula worked: *Cotton* became a huge box-office hit, and—coupled with the subsequent release of *Shaft*—the resulting subgenre would dominate movie screens for much of the decade.

All of which is discussed at length in this book's companion volume.

The Small Screen

Burt Reynolds' *Dan August* is a home-grown police lieutenant prowling the streets of fictitious Santa Luisa, Calif. The ABC series limped through a single 26-episode season, although rival network CBS got some mileage out of airing reruns during the summer of '73 and spring of '75, in the wake of Reynolds' rising big-screen fame. August is a hard-charging cop who nonetheless possesses a softer side, because he often knows and empathizes with the locals who pop up as victims, suspects or perps. Each episode features tautly choreographed action scenes that find Reynolds running, jumping and diving after baddies foolish enough to attempt flight.

Dave Grusin's slick title theme opens with a "droning" ostinato against which a 6-6 motif debuts via flutes; sharp brass elements play over clips of Reynolds at his action-oriented best. The theme expands into a propulsive swinger with a pounding rhythm section and strong 2/2 drum beat, the primary motif repeated by unison brass. The bridge is dominated by a string countermelody, after which the tempo picks up again; the orchestra climbs the scale and climaxes with a bold brass statement. It's one of Grusin's best themes, but—as with all Quinn Martin productions—the music is marred by a voice-over narrator. The end credits arrangement plays without such distraction.

"The music was very arresting," recalled postproduction supervisor John Elizalde. "Dave was the one who came up with playing that buzz kalimba for our opening credits. It's an African instrument: a hollow sound board, with usually four or five flattened-out nails on the board. When you strike it, you get a very distinctive, twangy sound. You get a varying pitch, depending on how you tweak it."[1]

Grusin also wrote full scores for three episodes. Each displays plenty of the composer's funkified pizzazz; melodies often are carried by Echoplex flutes or electric keyboards, with peppy brass fanfares against vibrant rhythmic backing. Many cues run long, and action jazz is plentiful; the stories also give Grusin opportunities for softer swing cues led by gentle reeds or acoustic piano. Tom Scott supplies a similar blend of funk bass, vibrant horns and synth keyboards for two episodes, but neither he nor those who followed—Richard Markowitz, Duane Tatro, Don Vincent and Patrick Williams—come close to Grusin's intensity.

Grusin's title theme and two full episode underscores—"The King Is Dead" and "When the Shouting Dies"—finally were digitized and released in 2019, as part of *The Quinn Martin Collection, Volume 1: Cop and Detective Series*.

Reynolds didn't fare any better with *Hunters Are for Killing* (aka *Hard Frame*), a made-for-TV movie that gives him another of the interchangeable action roles that characterized his résumé during this period; his aloof, angst-ridden protagonists often are misunderstood and/or mistrusted, sometimes anxious to atone for past mistakes. That's the case with L.G. Floran, who returns to the California wine country town of Ballisten, after serving a prison stretch for a DUI incident that killed his younger brother. Although family ties, lost love and other melodramatic entanglements dominate the baroque screenplay, it deserves mention here for a sidebar murder for which Floran is wrongly accused, and for Jerry Fielding's jazz score.

Fielding concentrated on television work during the 1960s, which initially gave little indication of the rugged jazz and action film scores for which he'd soon become known. His big breaks came with the one-two punch of 1969's *The Wild Bunch* and this telefilm, both of which get considerable snap from their robust music.

Fielding's riveting main theme for *Hunters* debuts after Floran drives into town behind the wheel of a convertible he "borrows" from two punks who try to rob him. A drum roll kicks off a blazing 5/4 beat laden with percussion, walking bass and a slick brass melody; Fielding plays with the meter as the title credits burst onto the screen, the cue eventually diminishing when Floran parks and strides into the local diner, where he immediately runs afoul of the owner and local police Chief Hamilton (Martin Balsam).

(Fielding clearly liked this melody and used it again for two future projects: the 1975 pilot film for the short-lived *Matt Helm* TV series; and Robert Mitchum's second outing as Philip Marlowe, in 1978's *The Big Sleep*. Both are discussed in this book's companion volume.)

Sassy drums power a bluesy melody when Floran gives a lift to an underage sexpot (Jill Banner) who hopes to score, only to be sent on her way; he has eyes only for Barbara (Suzanne Pleshette), a former love now married to somebody else. When a local man turns up dead, a gun-toting posse of townsfolk—hastily assuming Floran is guilty—chases him into the surrounding hillside. Fielding spots this prolonged pursuit with unsettling drum rolls, dissonant reeds, slashing strings and cacophonous brass elements; the lengthy cue lends considerable tension to our hero's desperate plight. In the aftermath, Fielding reprises the main theme when Floran thanks the friends who saved his life, and then—his conscience clear—drives out of town, leaving Barbara behind.

Very few early TV movies produced soundtrack albums, but Fielding's complete score finally was digitized in 2010.

The Big Screen

In between television work on *Ironside*, *It Takes a Thief* and *The Name of the Game*, Oliver Nelson found time to score a few big-screen features, the last of which was *Zig Zag*.

14. Soul Flower: 1970

This twisty mystery opens as insurance executive Paul Cameron (George Kennedy) endures a grim, step-by-step booking process en route to a prison cell. His predicament emerges via flashback, where we learn that he has framed *himself* for a long-unsolved kidnap/murder. Cameron has a brain tumor and knows he'll die soon; this elaborate plot is his means of supplying financial security for his family, by enabling his wife (Anne Jackson) to get the still-unclaimed $250,000 reward for "information leading to an arrest." Cameron is duly convicted at trial, but then lucks into a breakthrough emergency surgery that removes the tumor and saves his life. Now the only means of proving his innocence requires identifying the actual killer, who has eluded police for so long.

The initial booking sequence unfolds without music. Once Cameron is thrust into a cell, an angry assault of bongos builds to a ferocious, trumpet- and percussion-driven main theme that promises more excitement than the film delivers. This primary cue repeats often: even as diegetic music, when Cameron—during a flashback—pops an eight-track tape into his car stereo. Following his miracle cure, Cameron escapes from his hospital room against a taut bass and scratcher cue, which segues to another rousing arrangement of the title theme—powered by flute, bass and percussion—while he maneuvers through service elevators and hallways. When the story builds to its climax, Nelson reprises the main theme one final time, during a confrontation that answers all questions.

The film gets additional juice from a co-starring appearance by famed jazz chanteuse Anita O'Day, cast as a singer at a club where Cameron once played drums in her band. She delivers a delectable cover of "On Green Dolphin Street," backed by a gently swinging orchestral combo (which obviously is much too large for the venue).

The soundtrack album boasts longer arrangements that deliver far more of the solid jazz Nelson could only hint at, in his score; highlights include a terrific expansion of a diegetic cue (now titled "Earphones"), fueled by Artie Kane's kick-ass piano chops; and an ultra-cool quintet variation of the love theme.

Sidney Poitier's Virgil Tibbs may have closed the case at the conclusion of *In the Heat of the Night*, but his character was too charismatic to abandon. He was resur-

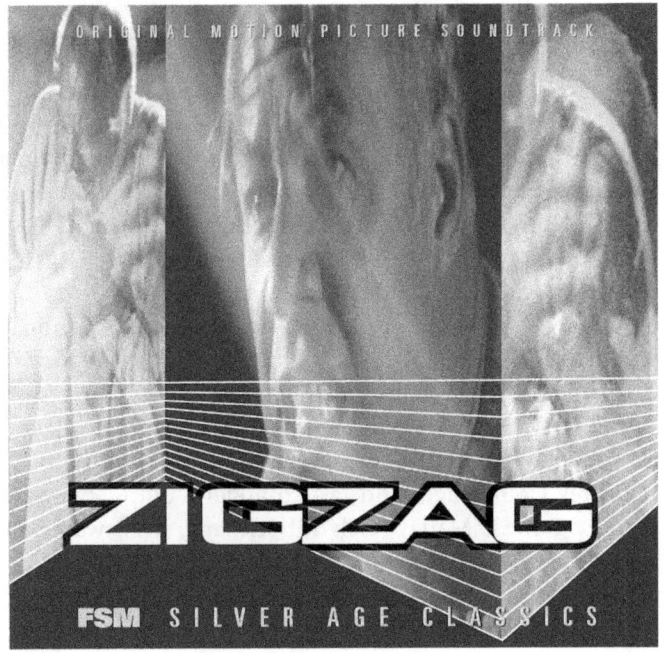

Jazz saxophonist, clarinetist and composer Oliver Nelson made his name with the legendary 1961 album *The Blues and the Abstract Truth*, which introduced the world to his iconic composition, "Stolen Moments." Following the trail blazed by Quincy Jones and Benny Carter, Nelson became one of the first African American composers to earn respect—and plenty of assignments—in Hollywood. Despite his impressive résumé, *Zig Zag* remains the only one of his film or TV scores granted commercial release (courtesy Film Score Monthly).

rected three years later in an original thriller titled after Poitier's signature line in the earlier film: *They Call Me MISTER Tibbs!* Rather oddly, this sequel behaves as if the first film never existed; Tibbs is in San Francisco, where we're told he has been with their police department for at least 12 years (!). He's also given a wife, Valerie (Barbara McNair), and two young children. Poitier once again slips comfortably into the role; good friend Quincy Jones also reupped for the sequel, which boasts a vibrant, funky sound completely different than the first film's laid-back, Deep South sensibilities. "We took a whole other attack, because we're in San Francisco," Jones explained. "There's much more of an urban feel to it, orchestration-wise."[2]

The story opens with the murder of a high-end call girl. Tibbs catches the case and learns that one of her frequent visitors was his longtime friend, the Rev. Logan Sharpe (Martin Landau). Their bond aside, Tibbs also is reluctant to charge Sharpe because he's a popular liberal street preacher and political activist, who backs a city proposition that would return development control to local neighborhoods. Other likely suspects turn up: Rice Weedon (Anthony Zerbe), the smarmy owner of the apartment building where the dead woman lived; Woody Garfield (Edward Asner), the businessman paying her rather expensive rent; and Mealie Williamson (Juano Hernandez), the janitor who found the body. Tibbs' investigation is intercut with his strained family life, particularly with respect to his misbehaving son (a dynamic that no longer plays, given the way Tibbs smacks him across the face several times).

Jones' lively title theme—Tibbs' theme—opens with vibrant trumpets that segue into a hard-charging R&B power groove, with horns punctuating a cool electric keyboard melody line. It's another of Jones' great title themes, thanks also to a swinging 4/4 beat laid down by Emil Richards. When Tibbs later has Garfield tailed by plainclothes cops, the lengthy pursuit sequence gives Jones plenty of room to stretch; he obliges with a lively blend of percussion and nervous piano riffs. The sleekest cue comes when Tibbs heads to a basement pool hall, hoping to find Mealie; this sequence is scored against slow-groove organ and guitar, backed by Richards' gentle drumming.

Jones reorchestrated and expanded much of his music for the soundtrack album. The pool hall cue ("Blues for Mister Tibbs") runs a delicious 6:27, with an improvisational blend of organ and guitar that sounds like the backdrop to a sexy seduction.

Tibbs probably wouldn't have known what to make of Gravedigger Jones and Coffin Ed Johnson. *Cotton Comes to Harlem* begins as the patient, often smirking Gravedigger (Godfrey Cambridge) and fast-to-anger Coffin (Raymond St. Jacques) have their eye on the Rev. Deke O'Malley (Calvin Lockhart), who swans into Harlem selling shares—at $100 a pop—to devoted followers wanting to join his "Back to Africa" movement. The two detectives smell a scam, but their suspicions are interrupted by the arrival of masked gunmen who steal $87,000 from the reverend's armored car. A furious vehicular chase concludes with an explosion and no sign of the money; it was concealed within a bale of cotton positioned as cover for the gunmen and lost during the pursuit. Gravedigger and Coffin's investigation is hampered by their unsympathetic precinct captain (John Anderson); constant lies from the smooth-talking O'Malley; the reverend's jealous girlfriend, Iris (Judy Pace); and even a local Mafia kingpin.

Consider: a black director, adapting a novel by a black author, which features black protagonists, brought to the screen with a primarily black cast. So who handled the music? The very white Canadian American Galt MacDermot, best known—then and now—as the composer of the hit rock musical *Hair*. (In fairness, MacDermot specialized in African music while studying at South Africa's Cape Town University, and he subsequently released numerous jazz and funk/R&B albums.)[3]

The instrumental underscore shares screen time with half a dozen R&B and gospel tunes; at times, the film borders on becoming a musical. MacDermot's first blast of action jazz—Gravedigger and Coffin's primary theme—comes during the gun-popping car chase resulting from the initial money snatch: a pursuit kicked off by Martin Banks' sassy trumpet licks, with background percussion and electric guitar occasionally pausing for some slapstick business involving astonished bystanders. Later, bluesy guitar and *wah-wah* trumpet showcase a late-night montage of Harlem's mean streets, while Gravedigger and Coffin search for suspects. MacDermot is equally adept at saucier cues: Banks' trumpet sounds positively naughty when Iris sheds her clothes in an effort to escape the dim-bulb white cop guarding her. Once the case wraps up, Gravedigger and Coffin cheerfully head into the metaphorical sunset, as MacDermot's full band signals the end credits with a raucous reprise of their theme.

The soundtrack album blends MacDermot's instrumental cues and an equal number of vocals. Gravedigger and Coffin would return, in *Come Back, Charleston Blue* (discussed in this book's companion volume).

As tough cop thrillers and blaxploitation flicks began to rise, the sun finally set on 007 knockoffs ... and the end couldn't come quickly enough.

Dorothy Gilman's Emily Pollifax may have enjoyed a healthy, 14-book literary run, but her sole big-screen outing is a groaning embarrassment. *Mrs. Pollifax—Spy* was a vanity project for Rosalind Russell, who in her mid–60s was just the right age to play the character: a bored New Jersey widow who impulsively spices up her life by joining the CIA. Alas, Russell wrote the screenplay herself—concealed behind the pseudonym C.A. McKnight—and director Leslie H. Martinson couldn't breathe life into the flaccid result.

Russell and Martinson nevertheless did one thing right: They hired Lalo Schifrin, and he obliged with a score that opens with a terrific assortment of Latin and spy jazz cues. The main theme is particularly cool, set against a cute animated credits sequence: Suspenseful percussion kicks off an organ melody backed by blasts of brass, with a flute taking over the bridge. It's a swinging echo of Schifrin's efforts for *The Man from U.N.C.L.E.* and *Mission: Impossible.*

Alas, this two-minute sequence is the film's highlight.

Mrs. Pollifax marches into CIA headquarters precisely when assignment chief William Carstairs (Dana Elcar) needs somebody who can behave like an ordinary tourist while visiting a bookstore in Mexico City, to exchange a few code words and collect a book containing top secret microfilm. The mission couldn't be easier, but Mrs. Pollifax doesn't know that the store owner has been killed and "replaced" by the villainous Gen. Raul Perdido (Albert Paulsen), who seeks the microfilm for his own nefarious purposes. A drugged Mrs. Pollifax wakes up in a cell alongside veteran CIA agent John Sebastian Farrell (Darren McGavin); they're being held in a remote prison outpost in the People's Republic of Albania. She charms the outpost's Gen. Berisha (Nehemiah Persoff), Col. Nexdhet (Harold Gould) and young Sgt. Lulash (John Beck); she also discovers where the microfilm has been hidden, after which she and Farrell manage an unlikely escape.

Schifrin's breezy jazz cues are ubiquitous as the film begins, and Mrs. Pollifax's trip to Mexico City is an obvious excuse for numerous Latin cues. Slow bossa nova follows her first approach to the bookstore; a taut, suspenseful jazz shuffle accompanies her return, at which point she succumbs to a drugged cup of coffee. Once in Albania, though, the spy jazz and bossa nova are left behind; even a potentially suspenseful truck chase is anticlimactic, backed solely by a mild orchestral cue. Schifrin inserts a final bossa nova swinger only when the end credits roll.

No soundtrack album appeared.

Speaking of popular of book characters, if anybody wonders why John D. MacDonald's 21-novel Travis McGee series never made a significant big-screen splash, look no further than the dreadful adaptation of 1966's *Darker than Amber*. Although star Rod Taylor is a credible McGee, scripter Ed Waters' slash-and-burn approach to the novel trivializes supporting characters and abridges the plot to the point of absurdity. The resulting stinker warrants mention solely because of John Carl Parker's modest jazz score. Perhaps recognizing that this music is his film's strongest asset, director Robert Clouse frequently intensifies the volume, thereby (thankfully) obscuring some of the lifeless dialogue.

Travis and best friend Meyer (Theodore Bikel), fishing beneath a bridge one evening, are horrified when a bound and weighted young woman is tossed into the water from above. Travis manages to rescue Vangie (Suzy Kendall), who confesses her involvement in a prostitution/robbery scheme that targets rich, lonely men on cruise ships. The gang is masterminded by a sociopathic bodybuilder (William Smith, as Terry) who decided to kill Vangie when she resisted adding a lethal element to their activities. Despite the watchful embrace of Travis' beach community, Terry manages to snuff Vangie anyway; this prompts a furious McGee to flush out the killer by following him—and a fresh female accomplice—onto a cruise ship and posing as a wealthy victim. The film then rushes its unsatisfying conclusion, as if the studio abruptly ran out of money.

Parker's energetic opening cue begins with screaming brass, synthesizer countermelody and a rolling rhythm section; unison horns introduce a 2-1-1/4/2-1-1 motif that segues into a driving action melody when the film's title is revealed. Sleek solo sax takes over as a grim-faced Terry takes Vangie on what he intends to be her last ride; the terrified young woman crouches in the passenger seat, one foot weighted with a dumbbell. Parker builds to a piercing orchestral blast when Terry stops the car and tosses Vangie over the bridge: a breathtaking blend of mesmerizing action jazz and macabre violence unmatched by anything this pallid thriller subsequently offers.

Gentler, romantic sax cues dominate the first act, as Travis and a repentant Vangie fall in love; Terry's reappearance revives the unsettling percussion and horns, which amplify the shock when he kills her. Travis' subsequent scheme is backed by steel drums and other calypso touches, when he boards the cruise ship and makes himself a target. Taylor looks lost, stumbling his way through what follows; Parker inserts another round of propulsive action jazz when McGee finally confronts the now-berserk Terry. A tedious epilogue leads to the end credits, which unspool against a laughably awful vocal ballad.

No soundtrack album appeared.

Darker than Amber is merely bad; Sammy Davis Jr. and Peter Lawford's return as Charles Salt and Christopher Pepper—in the aptly titled *One More Time*—is a train wreck. While the first film legitimately qualifies as a spy spoof, this sequel barely pokes fun at high crime; it's mostly a weak excuse for shameless mugging by both stars.

The so-called plot removes Salt and Pepper from their London nightclub, dumping them instead into a colossal mansion owned by the latter's wealthy, identical twin brother, Lord Sydney Pepper. He's killed early on, so the financially strapped Christopher impersonates Sydney amid a scheme involving Interpol, various baddies and a fortune in stolen diamonds. The scattershot attempts at humor even include cameos by Peter

Cushing and Christopher Lee, in their iconic Victor Frankenstein/Count Dracula roles. A break-the-fourth-wall finale finds the two stars discussing "their next picture" with us viewers: an unduly optimistic proposal that (mercifully) never came to pass.

The score is no better, dominated by bland orchestral comedy cues from Les Reed, who gets no chance to display the far superior chops he exercised during his earlier stint as a jazz pianist for The John Barry Seven. Reed's score also is laden with mickey-mousing, no doubt in an effort to enliven director Jerry Lewis' feeble efforts at visual humor. Traces of jazz surface only a few times: during a strip club-esque cue, to introduce the voluptuous Miss Tomkins (Maggie Wright); and when Davis croons a lively pair of obligatory vocals. No soundtrack album was produced, although the aforementioned vocals landed on a 45 single.

Elsewhere in the World

Writer/director Jean-Pierre Melville's *Le Cercle Rouge (The Red Circle)* was treated disgracefully upon its initial release in the States, when the 140-minute crime thriller was chopped down to an incomprehensible 99 minutes. American viewers couldn't enjoy Melville's original cut until Criterion's 2003 digital release, which is criminal; *Le Cercle Rouge* is a terrific heist thriller, which takes its time to introduce the three felons who collaborate on an "impossible" jewelry store robbery at Place Vendome, and the dogged police officer who pursues them. Melville's style and execution owe much to 1955's *Rififi*, notably with the actual robbery, which similarly unfolds without dialogue or music.

After the imprisoned Corey (Alain Delon) is released early for good behavior, he learns about a "sure-fire" jewelry robbery that could be handled with the right crew. Elsewhere, a handcuffed prisoner named Vogel (Gian Maria Volontè) is being transported to Paris by Inspector Mattei (André Bourvil); Vogel escapes and evades pursuit when—completely by coincidence—he hides in the trunk of Corey's car. The two men bond; the plan's requirement for a marksman is fulfilled by Jansen (Yves Montand), an alcoholic ex-cop grateful for the opportunity. Unfortunately, Corey's movements are shadowed by a vengeful gangster (André Ekyan, as Rico); Inspector Mattei, in turn, obtains information by applying pressure to Santi (François Périer), owner of the jazz nightclub where Corey first meets Jansen. After the heist goes down, it's only a matter of time before the three conspirators will be found by Rico or Mattei. Or both.

The music assignment went to jazz pianist/composer Éric Demarsan. "It's an icy film about people's trajectories," he explained. "Melville asked me for a minimalist piece of music in the orchestral spirit of the Modern Jazz Quartet. To guide my inspiration, Melville had me listen to a 35mm tape of the mixed soundtrack to Robert Wise's *Odds Against Tomorrow*. 'That's the color I need,' he said to me. Hence, the main theme for *Le Cercle Rouge*: brass chords and a jazz quintet for a simple melody drawn back into itself. The score for the film, as a whole, is run through with anxiety. The music gives you the feeling of being trapped, the idea of Fate."[4]

Demarsan's percussive jazz score relies heavily on vibes, bass and horns, but Melville uses it only sparingly. There's no music at all for the first 24 minutes, and also none during the lengthy heist sequence; the primary theme that Demarsan designed so carefully, in the mold of John Lewis and the MJQ, isn't heard in full glory until the end credits. Non-diegetic underscore cues are limited mostly to moody, unmelodic strings and bass riffs: more sound effects than music.

On the other hand, the numerous diegetic cues are glorious, big-band swing anthems, particularly during visits to Santi's club. The resident band backs a lively troupe of scantily clad dancers, the mood evolving as the plot progresses. The first performance—a cheerfully sassy bit of 1950s midtempo swing, with peppy horn and piano solos—is heard when Mattei initially forces Santi to become a snitch. Later, when Corey meets Jansen in the same club, the women are in different outfits; the band performs exciting, uptempo jump jazz, with aggressive horns backed by thumping, double-time drumming.

All club scenes are lengthy, allowing full exposure to Demarsan's vibrant cues. He also provides lovely jazz compositions for the source cues heard on car radios, or as background in the various bars that Mattei visits, while he doggedly probes for leads. "Melville wanted to personalize places by using specific themes," Demarsan continued, "jazz radio in the car, a musette waltz for a tart's hotel, big band for the nightclub."[5] One such cue is a lovely jazz ballad, with Demarsan's piano melody nicely complemented by gentle horn fanfares and a lyrical vibes solo.

The initial soundtrack LP failed to include two of Demarsan's slower, vibes-and-piano source cues: an oversight remedied by the 2000 digital release.

Appendix A: Instrument Abbreviations

ab *acoustic bass*
acc *accordion*
as *alto sax*
b *bass*
bcl *bass clarinet*
bh *baritone horn*
bj *banjo*
bo *bongos*
bs *baritone sax*
bt *bass trombone*
c *cornet*
cbc *contra-bass clarinet*
ce *cello*
cim *cimbalom*
cl *clarinet*
cng *congas*
d *drums*
eb *electric bass*
elg *electric guitar*
ep *electric piano*
f *flute*
Fb *Fender bass*
fh *flugehorn*
Frh *French horn*
g *guitar*
h *harmonica*

HB3 *Hammond B3*
ho *horns*
hps *harpsichord*
key *keyboards*
md *mandolin*
o *oboe*
org *organ*
p *piano*
per *percussion*
pic *piccolo*
r *reeds*
sax *sax*
sg *slide guitar*
ss *soprano sax*
syn *synthesizer*
t *trumpet*
tb *trombone*
timp *timpani*
ts *tenor sax*
tuba *tuba*
v *vocal*
vib *vibraphone*
vtb *valve trombone*
ww *woodwinds*
x *xylophone*

Appendix B: Discography

Films discussed in this book—but not present here—did not generate a soundtrack album or 45 single. If no digital release is cited, one does not (as yet) exist. Participating musicians are cited when known, but in many cases—particularly with session musicians—such records weren't kept. A starred entry (★) is a must-have album that deserves pride of place in a dedicated fan's library. Finally, this discography is limited to soundtracks and scores by the composer(s) who wrote and performed the original title themes and/or underscores, and does not include cover albums or singles by different artists, which instead are cited in the text.

* * *

À bout de souffle
- Gatefold double 45s by Martial Solal: "Duo"/"La Mort," "Poursuite"/"Dixieland" (Columbia, 1966).
- *À bout de souffle: Bande Originale du Film* (EmArcy CD, 2002).
- *À bout de souffle: Musique de Martial Solal* (Doxy LP, 2012). Includes bonus tracks and alternate takes. Roger Guérin (t); Pierre Gossez (as); Martial Solal (p); Michel Hausser (vib); Paul Rovère (b); Daniel Humair (d)

After the Fox
- *After the Fox: Original Motion Picture Soundtrack* (United Artists, 1966; Rykodisc CD, 1998).
- 45 single by The Hollies: "After the Fox"/"The Fox Trot" (Burt Bacharach instrumental) (United Artists, 1966).

Agent 505: Todesfalle Beirut
- *Agent 505: Todesfalle Beirut/Il Successo: Colonne Sonore Originali* (GDM CD, 2007).

Agent Secret FX-18
- Michel Colombier: *Capot Pointu* (Play Time CD, 2005). Includes three tracks from *Agent Secret FX-18*. Eddie Louis (org); Raymond Gimenes (g); Francis Darizcuren (b); Andy Arpino (d).

Agente X1-7 Operazione Oceano
- *Agente X1-7 Operazione Oceano: Original Motion Picture Soundtrack* (Beat CD, 2013).

The Alfred Hitchcock Hour
- *The Alfred Hitchcock Hour: Original Television Soundtrack, Volumes 1–3* (Varèse Sarabande CDs, 2011–12). Conte Candoli (t); Dick Nash and Frank Rosolino (tb); Ronny Lang (sax); Paul Horn (f); Laurindo Almeida (g); Red Mitchell (ab); Alvin Stoller (d).

★ Anatomy of a Murder
- *Anatomy of a Murder: From the Sound Track of the Motion Picture* (Columbia, 1959; Rykodisc CD, 1987). Grammy Awards for Best Performance by a Dance Band, Best Musical Composition First Recorded and Released in 1959, and Best Sound Track Album. Cat Anderson, Shorty

Baker, Herbie Jones, Ray Nance, Clark Terry and Gerald Wilson (t); Quentin Jackson and Britt Woodman (tb); John Sanders (vtb); Jimmy Hamilton (cl, ts); Johnny Hodges (as); Russell Procope (cl, as); Paul Gonsalves (ts); Harry Carney (cl, bs); Duke Ellington and Billy Strayhorn (p); Jimmy Woode (b); James Johnson (d).
- 45 single by Duke Ellington: "Anatomy of a Murder"/"Flirtibird" (Columbia, 1959).
- *Anatomy of a Murder: From the Sound Track of the Motion Picture* (Columbia CD, 1999). Includes 13 bonus tracks.

Any Number Can Win, see *Mélodie en sous-sol*.

Arabesque
- *Arabesque: Music from the Film Score* (RCA Victor, 1966; CD, 1999). Grammy Award nomination, for Best Original Score Written for a Motion Picture or Television Show: 1967. Manny Klein and Jack Sheldon (t); Dick Nash (tb); Vince DeRosa (Frh); Ted Nash (as); Ethmer Roten (f); Jimmy Rowles (p); Henry Mancini (autoharp); Shelly Manne (d).
- 45 single by Henry Mancini: "Arabesque"/"We've Loved Before" (RCA Victor, 1966).

Ascenseur pour l'échafaud
- *Ascenseur pour l'échafaud* (Fontana, 1958; CD, 1988). Miles Davis (t); Barney Wilen (ts); René Urtreger (p); Pierre Michelot (ab); and Kenny Clarke (d).
- *Miles Davis: Jazz Track* (Columbia, 1958). Miles Davis (t); Barney Wilen (ts); René Urtreger (p); Pierre Michelot (ab); Kenny Clarke (d).

The Asphalt Jungle (1950 movie)
- *Miklós Rózsa Treasury 1949–68* (Film Score Monthly CD box set, 2010). Includes all five cues from *The Asphalt Jungle*.

The Asphalt Jungle (TV series)
- 45 single by Duke Ellington: "Asphalt Jungle Theme (Part I)"/"Asphalt Jungle Theme (Part II)" (Columbia, 1961).
- *Duke Ellington: Duke 56/62, Volume 2* (CBS, 1984). Includes the "Asphalt Jungle Suite." Willie Cook, Fats Ford, Moon Mullins and Ray Nance (t); Lawrence Brown, Juan Tizol, Booty Wood and Britt Woodman (tb); Jimmy Hamilton (cl, ts); Johnny Hodges and Russell Procope (as); Paul Gonsalves (ts); Harry Carney (bs); Aaron Bell (b); Sam Woodyard (d).

Assault on a Queen
- *Assault on a Queen: Music from the Motion Picture* (Dragon's Domain CD, 2016). Cat Anderson, Conte Candoli, Al Porcino, Ray Triscari and Cootie Williams (t); Milt Bernhart, Hoyt Bohannon, Murray McEachern and Ken Shroyer (tb); Jimmy Hamilton (ts, cl); Buddy Collete and Bud Shank (as, f); Johnny Hodges (as); Paul Gonsalves (ts); Harry Carney (bs, cl); Tommy Tedesco (g); Duke Ellington (p); John Lamb (ab); Louis Bellson (d).

★ *Assignment K*
- *The Shuttered Room/Assignment K* (bootleg CD, 2014). Includes 13 tracks from *Assignment K*.

Assignment: Vienna
- *TV Omnibus: Volume One (1962–1976)* (Film Score Monthly CD box set, 2010). Includes title theme variations and five full underscores from *Assignment: Vienna*.

Audace colpo dei soliti ignoti
- *Audace colpo dei soliti ignoti* (Four Flies LP, 2016). Chet Baker and Nini Rosso (t); Bill Gilmore (tb); Livio Cerveglieri (ts); Marcello Boschi (as); Gino Marinacci (bs, f); Piero Umiliani (p); Roberto Pregadio (org); Enzo Grillini (g); Berto Pisano (b); Jimmy Pratt (d); Franco Chiari (marimba, per).

The Avengers (1961)
- 45 single by John Dankworth: "Avengers Theme"/"Chano" (Columbia, 1961). Derrick Abbott, Gus Galbraith, Dickie Hawdon and Kenny Wheeler (t); Eddie Harvey, Ray Premru and Tony

Russell (tb); Dankworth (as); Art Ellefson, Pete King, Danny Moss and Ronnie Moss (r); Alan Branscombe (p); Spike Heatley (b); Ronnie Stephenson (d).

The Avengers (1962)
- 45 single by John Dankworth: "The Avengers"/"Off the Cuff" (Fontana, 1963).

★ *The Avengers* (1965)
- 45 single by Laurie Johnson: "Theme from the TV Series *The Avengers*"/"Minor Bossa Nova" (Pye, 1965). Kenny Baker and Stan Broderick (t); Jackie Armstrong, Lad Busby and Don Lusher (tb); Alan Civil and Barry Tuckwell (Frh); Frank Reidy (cl, ts, cbc); Howard Blake and rock impresario Rick Wakeman (key).
- *Original Television Scores: The Avengers* (Unicorn-Kanchana, 1980).
- *The Music of Laurie Johnson, Volume 1: The Avengers* (Edsel CD box set, 2007). Includes the title themes and underscore cues from 16 episodes.

The Avengers (1968)
- *The Avengers: Original Tara King Season Score* (Silva Screen CD, 2011).

Baby Doll
- *Baby Doll: A Soundtrack Recording* (Columbia, 1956; DRG CD, 2003).

The Baron
- 45 single by Edwin Astley: "The Baron"/"Drop Head" (Decca, 1966).
- *The Baron: Original Soundtrack* (Network LP, 2015; CD, 2019).

Batman (TV series)
- 45 single by Neal Hefti: "Batman Theme"/"Batman Chase" (RCA, 1966). Eight weeks on *Billboard's* Hot 100 Chart, peaking at No. 35 on March 12, 1966. Grammy Award for Best Instrumental Composition: 1967.
- *Batman Theme and 11 Hefti Bat Songs* (RCA, 1966; Razor & Tie CD, 1997).
- *Hefti in Gotham City* (RCA, 1966; Razor & Tie CD, 1997).
- *Batman: Exclusive Original Television Soundtrack Album* (20th Century–Fox, 1966).

Batman: The Movie (1966)
- *Batman: Original Motion Picture Soundtrack* (Film Score Monthly CD, 2000).

Big Deal on Madonna Street, see *I Soliti Ignoti*.

The Big Knife
- Gatefold double 45s by Frank DeVol: "Theme from *The Big Knife*"/"Two's a Crowd" and "Upstairs"/"That's Love, That's Love" (Columbia, 1955).

Blow-Up
- *Blow-Up: The Original Sound Track Album* (MGM, 1966; CD, 1987). Two weeks on *Billboard's* Top LPs chart, at No. 192 on May 13 and 20, 1967. Freddie Hubbard and Joe Newman (t); Phil Woods (as); Joe Henderson (ts); Jim Hall (g); Paul Griffin (org); Herbie Hancock (p); Ron Carter (b); Jack DeJohnette (d).

Bourbon Street Beat
- *Bourbon Street Beat (The Sound That's Rocking TV)* (Warner Bros., 1959; Jazz on Film CD, 2014).
- 45 single by Don Ralke: "Bourbon Street Beat"/"Theme from "Summer Place" (Warner Bros., 1959).

Braddock
- *Way, Way Out* (Film Score Monthly CD, 2008). Includes Lalo Schifrin's score for *Braddock*.

Breathless, see *À bout de souffle*.

★ *Bullitt*
- *Bullitt: Original Motion Picture Soundtrack* (Warner Bros., 1968; CD, 1996). John Audino, Bud

Brisbois and Tony Terran (t, fh); Milt Bernhart, Dick Noel, Lloyd Ulyate and Lew McCreary (tb); Gene Cipriano, Ronnie Lang, Jack Nimitz, Bill Perkins and Bud Shank (r); Bob Bain, Mike Deasy and Howard Roberts (g); Mike Melvoin (p, org); Ray Brown (b); Max Bennett and Carol Kaye (eb); Stan Levey (d); Larry Bunker (per).
- 45 single by Lalo Schifrin: "Bullitt"/"That Night" (Warner Bros., 1969).
- *Bullitt* (Aleph CD, 2000). Rerecording of the score, with fresh arrangements by Schifrin, performed by the WDR Big Band.
- *Bullitt* (Film Score Monthly CD, 2009). Includes Schifrin's original score cues, along with the LP tracks.

Burke's Law
- *Instrumental Themes from the Original Soundtrack Recording of Burke's Law* (Liberty, 1964; Harkit CD, 2012). Digital edition includes Joseph Mullendore's soundtrack for *Honey West*.

★ Casino Royale
- *Casino Royale: An Original Motion Picture Soundtrack* (Colgems, 1967; Varèse Sarabande CD, 1990). Twenty-one weeks on *Billboard's* Top LPs, chart, peaking at No. 22 on July 15, 1967. One week on the UK's Top LPs chart, at No. 35 on July 22, 1967. Grammy Award nominations for Best Instrumental Arrangement, Best Instrumental Performance, Best Instrumental Theme, and Best Original Score Written for a Motion Picture or Television Show: 1968. Academy Award nomination for Best Original Song: 1968.
- 45 single by Herb Alpert and the Tijuana Brass: "Casino Royale"/"The Wall Street Rag" (A&M, 1967). Nine weeks on *Billboard's* Hot 100 chart, peaking at No. 27 on May 27, 1967. Fourteen weeks on the UK's Top 40 chart, peaking at No. 27 on May 3, 1967.
- 45 single by Dusty Springfield: "The Look of Love"/ "Give Me Time" (Philips, 1967). Fifteen weeks on *Billboard's* Hot 100 chart, peaking at No. 22 on November 4, 1967.
- 45 single by Burt Bacharach: "Bond Street"/"Alfie" (A&M, 1967).
- *Casino Royale: An Original MGM Motion Picture Soundtrack* (Kritzerland CD, 2011). Includes several bonus tracks.
- *Casino Royale: An Original Motion Picture Soundtrack* (Quartet CD, 2012). Two-disc set with the original score cues, and a remastered digital version of the LP.

★ Le Cercle Rouge
- *Le Cercle Rouge: La Bande Originale du Film* (Les Disques Pierre Cardin, 1970; Universal Music Jazz France CD, 2000). Digital edition includes 11 bonus tracks. Raymond Guiot (f); Joss Baselli (acc); Georges Arvanitas (p); Bernard Lubat (vib); Guy Pedersen (ab); Daniel Humair (d).

The Champions
- 45 single by Tony Hatch: "Who-Dun-It"/"The Champions" (Pye, 1969).
- *The Champions Original Soundtrack* (Network CD, 2014). Three-disc set with all 223 of the surviving cues and alternate takes by Robert Farnon, Edwin Astley, Albert Elms and Tony Hatch.

★ Charade
- *Charade: Music from the Motion Picture* (RCA, 1963; CD, 1988). Forty-two weeks on *Billboard's* Top LPs Chart, peaking at No. 6 on February 22 and 29, 1964. Ray Davis, Tommy McQuater and Stan Roderick (t); Jackie Armstrong, Don Lusher, Tony Russell and Jimmy Wilson (tb); Tommy Whittle (ts); Bob Burns (cl); Phil Goody and Johnny Scott (f); Frank Horrox (p); Dave Goldberg (g); Jack Emblow (acc); Martin Slavin (vib); Joe Muddel (ab); Bobby Midgeley and Barry Morgan (per).
- 45 single by Henry Mancini: "Charade" (instrumental)/"Orange Tamouré" (RCA, 1963). Thirteen weeks on *Billboard's* Hot 100 Chart, peaking at No. 36 on February 1, 1964.
- *Charade: Original Motion Picture Score* (Intrada CD, 2012). Mancini's original score cues (as opposed to the LP reorchestrations).

★ Checkmate
- 45 single by John Williams: "Theme from *Checkmate*"/"The Black Knight" (Columbia, 1960).

- *Checkmate* (Columbia, 1961; Film Score Monthly CD, 2006). Grammy Award nomination, for Best Sound Track Album: 1962. Frank Beach, Pete Candoli, Conrad Gozzo and Ollie Mitchet (t); Dick Nash, Richard Noel and Lloyd Ulyate (tb); John Cave, Vince DeRosa and Richard Perissi (ho); Gene Cipriano, Charles Gentry, Ronald Langinger and Ted Nash (sax); Jimmy Rowles (p); Bob Bain (g); Joe Mondragon (b); Shelly Manne and Jerry Williams (per).

★ *The Cincinnati Kid*
- *The Cincinnati Kid: Music from the Original Sound Track* (MGM, 1965; CD, 1988). Al Porcino (t); Milt Bernhart (tb); Bill Holman (sax); Justin Gordon (cl); John Kitzmiller (tuba); Al Hendrickson and Tommy Tedesco (g); Tommy Morgan (h); Keith Mitchell (b); Victor Feldman and Stan Levey (d, per); Ray Charles (v).
- 45 single by Lalo Schifrin: "The Cincinnati Kid"/ "So Many Times"(MGM, 1965).
- 45 single by Ray Charles: "The Cincinnati Kid"/"That's All I Am to You" (ABC-Paramount, 1965).
- *Lalo Schifrin Film Scores: 1964–68* (Film Score Monthly CDs, 2011). Includes the contents of the MGM album, along with Schifrin's 14 original score cues.

City of Fear
- *City of Fear: Original Motion Picture Soundtrack* (Intrada CD, 2011). Robert Di Vall and Maurice Harris (t); Louis Castellucci, Robert Marsteller and Lloyd Ulyate (tb); Fred Fox, Sinclair Lott and Richard Perissi (Frh); Roy D'Antonio and Dominick Fera (cl); Merritt Buxbaum (b cl); Morris Bercov (f); John(ny) Williams (p); Phil Stephens (ab); Frank Flynn, Milt Holland and Lee Perrin (per).

Cloportes, see *La métamorphose des cloportes*.

Compartment Tueurs
- Gatefold double 45s by Michel Magne: "Compartment Tueurs"/"Tempo Danger," "No Smoking"/"The Killing Train" (Barclay, 1965).
- *Michel Magne: Compartment Tueurs/De La Part Copains* (Universal Music France CD, 2004). Includes the four tracks from the 1965 EP.

Concrete Jungle, see *The Criminal*.

★ *The Connection*
- *The Music from The Connection* (Blue Note, 1960; CD, 1994). Jackie McLean (as); Freddie Redd (p); Michael Mattos (b); Larry Ritchie (d).
- *Music from The Connection* (Felsted, 1960; Boplicity CD, 1995). Howard McGhee (t); Tina Brooks (ts); Freddie Redd (p); Milt Hinton (b); Osie Johnson (d).

★ *Coogan's Bluff*
- *Coogan's Bluff: Original Soundtrack Recording* (Temple, 1978). Partial score of seven tracks, along with music from three other films.
- *Coogan's Bluff* (Intrada CD, 2012). Full score, with eight bonus tracks. Dick Nash, Richard Noel, George Roberts and Lloyd Ulyate (tb);Vince DeRosa, David Duke and Richard Perissi (Frh); Caesar Giovannini and Mike Lang (hps); Ralph Grierson (org); Paul Beaver (ep); Artie Kane and Mike Melvoin (p); Chuck Berghofer and Ray Brown (b); Carol Kaye (Fb); Larry Bunker, Shelly Manne, Earl Palmer, Emil Richards, Alvin Stoller and Ken Watson (per).

Cool Hand Luke
- *Cool Hand Luke: Original Soundtrack Recording* (Dot, 1967; MCA CD, 1995). Academy Award nomination for Best Original Music Score: 1968. Howard Roberts and Tommy Tedesco (g); Tommy Morgan (h); Mike Melvoin (p); Ray Brown (ab); Earl Palmer (d); Emil Richards (per).
- *Cool Hand Luke: Oscar Nominated Score* (Aleph CD, 2001). Includes seven bonus tracks.

★ *The Cool World*
- *Original Score from The Cool World* (Philips, 1964; Verve CD, 2008). Dizzy Gillespie (t); James Moody (ts, f); Kenny Barron (p); Chris White (b); Rudy Collins (d).

Cotton Comes to Harlem
- *Cotton Comes to Harlem: Original Motion Picture Score* (United Artists, 1970; Beyond CD, 2001).

Crime in the Streets
- *Crime in the Streets* (Decca, 1956; Varèse Sarabande CD, 2009). Includes Franz Waxman's three primary themes from *I, the Jury*. Pete Candoli (t); Jack Dumont (as); Charles Gentry (ts, bs); Ray Turner (p); Joe Mondragon (b).

The Criminal
- Gatefold double 45s by John Dankworth: "Riverside Stomp"/"Freedom Walk," "After the Party"/"Treasure Drive" (Columbia, 1960; Jazz on Film CD, 2015). Digitized as part of Jazz on Film's *The New Wave II* box set. Gus Galbraith, Dickie Hawdon and Kenny Wheeler (t); Eddie Harvey, Ian McDougall and Tony Russell (tb); Art Ellefson and Danny Moss (ts); John Dankworth and Pete King (as); George Tyndale (bs); Ron Synder (tuba); Dudley Moore (p); Spike Heatley (b); Kenny Clare (d).

★ Dan August
- *The Quinn Martin Collection, Volume 1: Cop and Detective Series* (La-La Land CDs, 2019). Includes title themes and two episode underscores for *Dan August*.

A Dandy in Aspic
- 45 single by Shirley Horn: "If You Want Love"/"The Spell You Spin" (Bell, 1968).

Danger Man (1960)
- *Danger Man: Original Soundtrack* (Network CDs, 2008). Two-disc set with all 91 of Edwin Astley's surviving cues and alternate takes.

Danger Man (1964)
- *Secret Agent Meets the Saint* (RCA, 1965; CD 2002). Includes six tracks from each of the two shows.
- 45 single by Edwin Astley: "Danger Man"/"The Saint" (RCA, 1965).
- *Secret Agent: Music from the TV Series* (RCA, 1966; BMG/Razor & Tie CD, 1997).
- *Danger Man: Original Soundtrack* (Network CDs, 2008). Five-disc set with all 388 of Edwin Astley's surviving cues and alternate takes.

The Deadly Affair
- *The Original Sound Track Album of The Deadly Affair* (Verve, 1966; CD, 1996). Digital edition includes Quincy Jones' score for 1964's *The Pawnbroker*.

Department S
- *Department S Original Soundtrack* (Network CDs, 2008). Three-disc set with all 195 of Edwin Astley's surviving cues and alternate takes.

The Detective
- *Von Ryan's Express/The Detective* (Intrada CD, 2013). Includes 12 tracks from *The Detective*. John Clyman, Robert Fowler and Cappy Lewis (t); Edward Kusby, Ray Klein and Phillip Teele (tb); Russell Cheever, Justin Gordon, Harry Klee, Abe Most and William Ulyate (cl); Bob Bain (g); Artie Kane (p); Red Mitchell, Mike Rubin and Kenneth Winstead (b); Richard Cornell, Shelly Manne and Hal Rees (d).

★ Un Detective
- 45 single by Fred Bongusto: "Un Detective"/"Un Detective (Part 2)" (Seven Seas, 1970).
- *Un Detective* (Avanz CD, 1997).
- *Un Detective* (Quartet CD, 2019). Resequenced and remastered edition.

Detective Belli, see *Un Detective*.

★ *Deux Hommes dans Manhattan*
- *Deux Hommes dans Manhattan: Bande Originale du Film* (Columbia France, 1959). Bernard Hulin (t); Albert Raisner (h); Christian Chevallier (vib); Art Simmons and Martial Solal (p); Paul Rovère (ab); Kansas Fields (d).
- *The New Wave II* (Jazz on Film CDs, 2015). Includes four tracks from *Deux Hommes dans Manhattan*.

Dr. No
- *Dr. No: Original Motion Picture Sound Track Album* (United Artists, 1962; Capitol CD, 1991). Ten weeks on *Billboard's* Top LPs chart, peaking at No. 82 on August 17, 1963.
- 45 single by John Barry: "The James Bond Theme"/"The Blacksmith Blues" (Columbia, 1962). Eight weeks on the UK's Top 40 Singles chart, peaking at No. 13 on December 8, 1962.
- *Dr. No: 50th Anniversary Edition Original Soundtrack* (Harkit CD, 2012). Includes five bonus tracks.

Duffy
- 45 single by Lou Rawls: "Down Here on the Ground"/"I'm Satisfied (The Duffy Theme)" (Capitol, 1968).

★ *East Side/West Side*
- *East Side/West Side: Music from the CBS Television Network Series* (Columbia, 1963; Sony CD, 2013).

Echo Four Two
- 45 single by Laurie Johnson: "Sucu Sucu"/"Echo Four Two" (Pye, 1961). Twelve weeks on the UK's Top 40 Singles chart, peaking at No. 9 on October 4, 1961.

Elevator to the Gallows, see *Ascenseur pour l'échafaud*.

Experiment in Terror
- *Experiment in Terror: Music from the Motion Picture* (RCA Victor, 1962; CD, 1997). Six weeks on *Billboard's* Stereo Album chart, peaking at No. 37 on June 30, 1962. Pete Candoli, Don Fagerquist, Conrad Gozzo and Manny Klein (t); John Halliburton, Dick Nash and Jimmy Priddy (tb); Karl De Karske (bt); Gene Cipriano, Justin Gordon, Plas Johnson, Ronnie Lang and Ted Nash (sax); Jimmy Rowles (p); Bob Bain and Howard Roberts (g); Rollie Bundock and George Duvivier (ab); Larry Bunker and Shelly Manne (d, per).

Fathom
- *Fathom: Original Motion Picture Soundtrack Album* (20th Century–Fox, 1967; Harkit CD, 2009).

Les félins
- *Les félins: Bande Originale du Film* (Universal Music Jazz France CD, 2004). Grammy Award for Best Original Jazz Composition ("The Cat"): 1965. Roger Guérin (t); Raymond Guiot (f); Jeanne Lorid (key); Pierre Michelot (ab).

Des Femmes Disparaissent
- *Art Blakey & The Jazz Messengers: Des Femmes Disparaissent* (Fontana, 1958; CD, 2003). Lee Morgan (t); Benny Golson (ts); Bobby Timmons (p); Jimmy Merritt (ab); Art Blakey (d).

Fiasco in Milan, see *Audace colpo dei soliti ignoti*.

From Beirut with Love, see *Agent 505: Todesfalle Beirut*.

★ *From Russia with Love*
- *From Russia with Love: Original Motion Picture Sound Track* (United Artists, 1963; EMI/Capitol CD, 2003). Twenty-eight weeks on *Billboard's* Top LPs chart, peaking at No. 27 on August 22, 1964.

- 45 single by John Barry: "From Russia with Love"/"007" (Ember, 1963). Three weeks on the UK's Top 40 Singles chart, peaking at No. 39 on November 27, 1963.
- 45 single by Matt Monro: "From Russia with Love"/"Here and Now" (Liberty, 1964)

The Fugitive
- *The Fugitive: Original Television Series Soundtrack* (Silva Screen CD, 2000).

Fuller Report, see *Rapporto Fuller Base Stoccolma*.

Funeral in Berlin
- *Funeral in Berlin* (RCA Victor, 1967; CD, 2001).
- *Funeral in Berlin: Music from the Motion Picture* (Intrada CD, 2014). Includes four bonus tracks.

The Girl from U.N.C.L.E.
- *The Girl from U.N.C.L.E.: Music from the Television Series* (MGM, 1967; Varèse Sarabande CD, 2008).
- *The Man from U.N.C.L.E. Volume 3, The Girl from U.N.C.L.E.* (Film Score Monthly CD, 2004).

The Girl Hunters
- 45 single by Eddie Calvert: "Velda"/"Girls Are…" (Columbia UK, 1963).

★ Goldfinger
- *Goldfinger: Original Motion Picture Soundtrack* (United Artists USA, 1964). Seventy weeks on *Billboard's* Top LPs Chart, peaking at No. 1 for three weeks beginning March 20, 1965. Grammy Award nomination for Best Original Score Written for a Motion Picture or Television Show: 1965.
- *Goldfinger: Original Motion Picture Soundtrack* (United Artists UK, 1964). Includes four tracks not on the U.S. LP. Five weeks on the UK's Top 20 Albums Chart, peaking at No. 14 on November 7, 1964.
- 45 single by Shirley Bassey: "Goldfinger"/"Strange How Love Can Be" (United Artists, 1964). Thirteen weeks on *Billboard's* Hot 100 chart, peaking at No. 8 on March 27 and April 3, 1965. Nine weeks on the British Top 40 chart, peaking at No. 21 on October 21, 1964.
- 45 single by John Barry: "Goldfinger" (instrumental)/"James Bond Back in Action Again" (United Artists, 1965).
- *Goldfinger: Original Motion Picture Soundtrack* (EMI/Capitol CD; 2003). Includes all tracks from the U.S. and UK LPs.

The Green Hornet
- 45 single by Al Hirt: "Green Hornet Theme"/"Strawberry Jam" (RCA, 1966).
- *The Green Hornet: Original Television Score* (20th Century–Fox, 1966; Harkit CD, 2006).

★ Gunn
- *Gunn: Music from the Film Score* (RCA, 1967; CD, 1999). Pete Candoli (t); Dick Nash (tb); Ted Nash (as, bs, f); Bud Shank (bs); Plas Johnson (bs); Vince DeRosa (Frh); Bob Bain (g); Larry Bunker (vib); Jimmy Rowles (p); Ray Brown (b); Shelly Manne (d).

Hammerhead
- *Hammerhead: Music from the Film Score* (Colgems, 1968).

Hard Frame, see *Hunters Are for Killing*.

Harper
- *Harper: Original Sound Track Recording* (Mainstream, 1966; Intrada CD, 2018).

★ Hawaii Five-O
- *Hawaii Five-O: Original TV Soundtrack* (Capitol, 1969; Film Score Monthly CD, 2010). Emmy Awards for Outstanding Music Composition for a Series: 1970 and '74. Emmy Award nomination for Outstanding Achievement in Musical Composition: 1969.
- 45 single by Mort Stevens: "Hawaii Five-O"/"McGarrett's Theme" (Capitol, 1969).

Hawaiian Eye
- *Hawaiian Eye* (Warner Bros. 1960; Collectables CD, 2006).

★ Honey West
- *Honey West: Original Music from the Soundtrack* (ABC-Paramount, 1965; Harkit CD, 2005). Don Fagerquist, Carroll Lewis, Larry Sullivan and George Werth (t); Albert Anderson, Dick Nash, Barrett O'Hara, Tommy Pederson, William Schaeffer and Tom Shepard (tb); Buddy Collette, William Green, Plas Johnson, Wilbur Schwartz and William Ulyate (sax); John Gray and Barney Kessel (g); Paul Smith (p); Red Callender (b) Larry Bunker, John Cyr, Milt Holland and Alvin Stoller (per).

Hong Kong
- *Exciting Hong Kong* (ABC-Paramount, 1961).

How to Steal a Million
- *How to Steal a Million: Original Motion Picture Score Album* (20th Century-Fox Records, 1966; Intrada CD, 2008). Digital edition includes the contents of the re-orchestrated LP, along with all of John Williams' original score cues.

Hunters Are for Killing
- *Hunters Are for Killing: Original Television Soundtrack* (Film Score Monthly CD, 2010). John Audino, Pete Candoli, Cappy Lewis, Vito Mangano and Clyde Reasinger (t); Milt Bernhart, Gilbert Falco, Joe Howard, Charles C. Loper, Dick Nash, George M. Roberts, William Schaefer, Thomas Shepard and Lloyd Ulyate (tb); James A. Decker and Henry Sigismonti (Frh); Tommy Morgan (h); Al Hendrickson, Tony Rizzi, Tommy Tedesco and Al Viola (g); Artie Kane and John Jack Latimer (p); Red Callender, Milt Kestenbaum and Joe Mondragon (b); Larry Bunker, John Cyr, John Guerin, Shelly Manne and Ken Watson (per).

★ The Hustler
- *The Hustler: The Original Sound Track* (Kapp, 1961; Intrada CD, 2017). Digital edition includes 20 bonus tracks and alternate takes. Bernie Glow, Doc Severinsen and Joe Wilder (t); Jimmy Cleveland and Frank Rehak (tb); Richard Hixson (bt); Tony Miranda (Frh); Phil Bodner, Romeo Penque, Jerome Richardson, Lew Stern and Phil Woods (r); Hank Jones and Bernie Leighton (p); Joe Venuto (vib); Joseph Barry Galbraith (g); Milt Hinton (b); Osie Johnson (d).
- 45 single by Kenyon Hopkins: "Theme from The Hustler"/"Bert's Theme" (Kapp, 1961).

I Promised to Pay, see Payroll.

★ I Spy
- *I Spy: Music from the Television Series* (Warner Bros., 1966; Film Score Monthly CD, 2011). Emmy Award for Outstanding Achievement in Musical Composition: 1968. Emmy Award nominations for Outstanding Individual Achievement in Music: 1966 and '67. Pete Candoli (t), Dick Nash (tb), Ronnie Lang and Ted Nash (sax and fs), Pete Jolly (p) Emil Richards (per).
- *I Spy: Music from the Television Series* (Capitol, 1967; Film Score Monthly CD, 2011).
- 45 single by Earle Hagen: "I Spy"/"Sophia" (Capitol, 1968).
- *I Spy: Original Television Soundtrack* (Film Score Monthly CD, 2002). Includes underscores from five episodes.

I, The Jury (1953)
- *Crime in the Streets* (Decca, 1956; Varèse Sarabande CD, 2009). Includes Franz Waxman's three primary themes from *I, the Jury*.

★ I Want to Live
- *Johnny Mandel's Great Jazz Score: I Want to Live!* (United Artists, 1958; Rykodisc CD, 1999). Ed Leddy, Al Porcino and Jack Sheldon (t); Milt Bernhart and Frank Rosolino (tb); Dave Wells (b t, bt); John Cave, Vince DeRosa, Sinclair Lott and Dick Parisi (Frh); Harry Klee (f, pic); Abe Most (cl); Pete Jolly (p); Al Hendricksen (g); Red Mitchell (ab); Larry Bunker, Mel Lewis, Mike Pacheco, Milt Holland and Shelly Manne (d, per).
- *The Jazz Combo from I Want to Live!* (United Artists, 1958; Rykodisc CD, 1999). Both 1958

albums are included on the 1999 digital release. Art Farmer (t); Frank Rosolino (tb); Gerry Mulligan (bs); Bud Shank (as, f); Pete Jolly (p); Red Mitchell (b); Shelly Manne (d).
- 45 single by the Gerry Mulligan Combo: "Theme from I Want to Live"/"Black Nightgown" (United Artists, 1958).

In Cold Blood
- *In Cold Blood: Music from the Film Score* (Colgems, 1967). Academy Award nomination for Best Original Music Score: 1968. Buddy Childers (t); Frank Rosolino (tb); Gene Cipriano, William Green and Bud Shank (ww); Howard Roberts (g); Dave Grusin (clavinet); Ray Broan and Andy Simpkins (ab); Carol Kaye (eb); Shelly Manne and Earl Palmer (d); Don Elliott and Emil Richards (per).
- *The Cinema of Quincy Jones* (Decca CDs, 2016). Includes all tracks from *In Cold Blood*.

In Like Flint
- *In Like Flint: Original Motion Picture Score* (20th Century–Fox, 1967; Intrada CD, 2014). Digital edition includes Jerry Goldsmith's score for 1967's *In Like Flint*. Dick Nash (tb); Plas Johnson (ts); Ronnie Lang (as); Red Mitchell (b); Shelly Manne (d).
- 45 single by Jerry Goldsmith: "Your Zowie Face"/"Ladies Will Kindly Remove Their Hats" (20th Century–Fox, 1967).
- *In Like Flint/Our Man Flint: Original Motion Picture Soundtracks* (Varèse Sarabande CD, 1998). Goldsmith's original score cues for both films (as opposed to the LP reorchestrations).

In the Heat of the Night
- *In the Heat of the Night: Original Motion Picture Soundtrack* (United Artists, 1967; Rykodisc CD, 1998). Grammy Award nomination for Best Original Score Written for a Motion Picture or Television Show: 1968. Digital edition includes Quincy Jones' score for 1970s *They Call Me MISTER Tibbs*. Don Elliott (t); Bud Shank (r); Roland Kirk (f); Toots Thielemans (h); Mike Post (g); Glen Campbell (g, bj); Billy Preston (HB3); Bobby Scott (tack piano); Ray Brown (ab); Carol Kaye (Fb); Ray Charles (v).
- 45 single by Ray Charles: "In the Heat of the Night"/"Something's Got to Change" (ABC, 1967). Seven weeks on *Billboards's* Hot 100 chart, peaking at No. 33 on September 30, 1967.

Inspector Clouseau
- *Inspector Clouseau: Original Motion Picture Score* (United Artists, 1968; Kritzerland CD, 2009).

International Detective
- *International Detective* (Ember, 1959; Harkit CD, 2004).

★ Intrigo a Los Angeles
- *Intrigo a Los Angeles: Colonna Sonora Originale* (CAM, 1964). Chet Baker and Nini Rosso (t); Bill Gilmore (tb); Livio Cervegleiri (ts); Gino Marinacci (bs); Enzo Grillini (g); Piero Umiliani (p); Franco Chiari (vib); Berto Pisano (ab); Jimmy Pratt (d).
- *Chet Baker: Italian Movies* (Jazz on Film CDs, 2013). Includes the contents of the 1964 album, along with two bonus tracks from *Intrigo a Los Angeles*.
- *Intrigo a Los Angeles: Colonna Sonora Originale* (Contempo LPs, 2015). Includes almost twice as much music as the 2013 CD.

Intrigue in Los Angeles, see *Intrigo a Los Angeles*.

The Ipcress File
- *The Ipcress File: Original Sound Track Album* (Decca, 1965; MCA CD, 1995).
- 45 single by John Barry: "A Man Alone (Latin Version)"/"A Man Alone (Jazz Version)" (Decca, 1965).
- 45 single by John Barry: "A Man Alone"/"Barbara's Theme" (Columbia, 1965).

Ironside
- 45 single by Quincy Jones: "Theme from *Ironside*"/"Cast Your Fate to the Wind" (A&M, 1972). Emmy Award nomination for Outstanding Music Composition for a Series: 1973.

It Takes a Thief
- 45 single by Dave Grusin: "It Takes a Thief"/"The Name of the Game" (Decca, 1968).

The Italian Job
- *The Italian Job: Music from the Original Motion Picture Soundtrack* (Paramount, 1969; MCA CD, 2000). Digital edition includes one bonus track. Pete King (as); Tubby Hayes (ts); Ross Garren (h).
- 45 single by Matt Monro: "On Days Like These"/"Lily M'Lady" (Capitol, 1969).
- *The Italian Job: 50th Anniversary Expanded Edition* (Quartet CD, 2019). Includes the 1969 album, Jones' complete score and numerous bonus tracks.

El Jefe
- Gatefold double 78s by Lalo Schifrin: "El Jefe"/"Mima," "Blues Para Berger"/"Buenos Aires Minuet" (Disc Jockey, 1958). Ruben Barbieri (t); Gato Barbieri (ts); Lalo Schifrin (p); Alfredo Remus (b); Eduardo Casalia (d).

Jericho
- *Jericho: Original Television Soundtrack* (Film Score Monthly CD, 2005). Includes John(ny) Williams' score for the failed TV pilot *The Ghostbreaker*.

★ *Johnny Cool*
- *Johnny Cool: Billy May's Original Motion Picture Score* (United Artists, 1963; Rykodisc CD, 1999). Bud Brisbois, Don Fagerquist and Billy May (t); Justin Gordeon (ts); Sammy Davis Jr. (v).

Johnny Staccato, see *Staccato*.

Joy House, see *Les félins*.

Kaleidoscope
- *Kaleidoscope: Original Motion Picture Soundtrack* (Warner Bros., 1966; Film Score Monthly CD, 2007). Digital edition includes Johnny Keating's score for 1967's *Hotel*. Eddie Mordue (ts); Diwan Motihar (sitar); Keshave Sathe (tabla); John Mayer (tambura); Howard Blake (HB3); Ron Prentice (ab); Tony Kinsey (d).

King of the Roaring 20s: The Story of Arnold Rothstein
- *Captains Courageous: The Frank Waxman Collection* (Intrada CDs, 2017). Includes the complete score and one unused cue from *King of the Roaring 20s*.

Kiss the Girls and Make Them Die
- 45 single by Lydia McDonald: "Kiss the Girls and Make Them Die"/"Fools Have All the Fun" (Parade, 1966).
- *Kiss the Girls and Make Them Die* (Avanz CD, 1998).

Knife in the Water
- Gatefold double 45s by Krzysztof Komeda: "Typish Jazz"/"Crazy Girl," "Cherry"/"Ballad for Bernt" (Polskie Nagrania Muza, 1961). Bernt Rosengren (ts); Krzysztof Komeda (p); Roman Dylag (b); Leszek Dudziak (d).
- *Cul-de-Sac/Knife in the Water: Original Soundtracks* (Harkit CD, 2005). Includes eight bonus tracks from *Knife in the Water*.
- *Jazz in Polish Cinema: Out of the Underground 1958–1967* (Jazz on Film CDs, 2014). Includes a further expanded score from *Knife in the Water*.

★ *Kriminal*
- 45 single by Robert Pregadio and Romano Mussolini: "Kriminal"/"Il Cobra" (Beat, 1967).
- *Kriminal: Original Soundtrack Music from the Motion Picture* (Beat CD, 2006).

Lady in Cement
- *Lady in Cement: Original Motion Picture Soundtrack Album* (20th Century–Fox, 1968; Harkit CD, 2002). Digital edition includes two bonus tracks.

★ *Les Liaisons Dangereuses*
- *Art Blakey's Jazz Messengers Avec Barney Wilen: Les Liaisons Dangereuses 1960* (Fontana, 1960; Universal Music Jazz France CD, 2003). Digital edition includes one bonus track. Lee Morgan (t); Barney Willen (ts, ss); Bobby Timmons (p); Jimmy Merritt (b); Art Blakey (d); John Ridriguez (bng); Tommy Lopez and William Rodriguez (cng).
- Gatefold double 45s by Art Blakey's Jazz Messengers: "No Problem"/"Prelude in Blue (À L'Esquinade)," "No Hay Problema"/"Prelude in Blue (Chez Miguel)" (Fontana, 1960).
- *Duke Jordan: Les Liaisons Dangereuses* (Charlie Parker, 1962; CD, 1997). Sonny Cohn (t); Charlie Rouse (ts); Duke Jordan (p); Eddie Kahn (b); Art Taylor (d).
- *Thelonious Monk: Les liaisons dangereuses 1960* (Sam/Saga Jazz LP and CD, 2017). Includes numerous alternate takes. Charlie Rouse and Barney Wilen (ts); Thelonious Monk (p); Sam Jones (ab); Art Taylor (d).

Licensed to Kill
- 45 single by Bertram Chappell: "Main Theme"/"Charles Vine's Theme" (Seven Seas, 1966).

The Lineup
- *Jerry Goldsmith: The Early Years, Volume One* (Prometheus CD, 2007). Includes 12 cues from the sixth-season episode, "Wake Up to Terror."

The Liquidator
- *The Original Sound Track Album of The Liquidator* (MGM, 1965). Ronnie Scott (sax); Tubby Hayes (f); Tony Crombie (d).
- 45 single by Shirley Bassey: "The Liquidator"/"Sunshine" (United Artists, 1966).
- *The Liquidator: Original Motion Picture Soundtrack* (Film Score Monthly CD, 2006). Lalo Schifrin's original score cues, along with three of the LP reorchestrations.

A Lovely Way to Die
- 45 single by Jackie Wilson: "A Lovely Way to Die"/"Soulville" (Coral, 1968).

★ *M Squad*
- *The Music from M Squad* (RCA, 1959; BMG CD, 2001). Grammy Award nomination, for Best Sound Track Album: 1959. Digital edition includes Skip Martin's soundtrack for *Mickey Spillane's Mike Hammer*. Frank Beach, Pete Candoli and Don Fagerquist (t); Milt Bernhart, Pete Carpenter, Joe Howard and Frank Rosolino (tb); Benny Carter and Marshall Royal (as); Bill Green (r); Al Hendrickson and Howard Roberts (g); Jimmy Rowles, John Williams and Stan Wrightsman (p); Joe Comfort, Red Mitchell and Joe Mondragon (ab); Earl Palmer and Alvin Stoller (d).

★ *A Man Called Dagger*
- *A Man Called Dagger: Music from the Original Soundtrack* (MGM, 1968; Demon S&C CD, 2011). Digital edition includes 29 bonus tracks.

★ *Man from Interpol*
- *Man from Interpol* (Top Rank, 1960; Harkit CD, 2005). Harold McNair (sax, f); Tubby Hayes, Ronny Scott, Don Rendell and Bobby Wellins (r); Gordon Beck (p); Malcolm Cecil (b); Tony Crombie (d).
- *Man from Interpol: Soundtrack Music from the AR-TV Series* (Ember, 1960; Harkit CD, 2005).
- 45 single by Tony Crombie: "Man from Interpol Main Theme," "Interpol Cha Cha"/"Interpol Chase" (Top Rank, 1960).

★ *The Man from U.N.C.L.E.*
- *Original Music from The Man from U.N.C.L.E.* (RCA, 1965; CD 1998). Twenty weeks on

Billboard's Top LPs chart, peaking at No. 52 on May 28, 1966. Emmy Award nomination for Outstanding Individual Achievement in Music: 1966. Grammy Award nomination, for Best Original Score Written for a Motion Picture or Television Show: 1966.
- *More Music from The Man from U.N.C.L.E.* (RCA, 1966; CD 1998).
- *The Man from U.N.C.L.E., Volumes 1-3* (Film Score Monthly CDs, 2002-04).
- *The Spy with My Face: Music from The Man from U.N.C.L.E. Movies* (Film Score Monthly CD, 2006).

Man in a Suitcase
- 45 single by Ron Grainer: "A Man in a Suitcase"/"Andorra" (Pye, 1967).
- *Man in a Suitcase: Original Soundtrack* (Network CDs, 2008). Five-disc set with all 332 of Grainer and Albert Elms' surviving cues and alternate takes.

★ The Man with the Golden Arm
- *Music from the Soundtrack of The Man with the Golden Arm* (Decca, 1956; MCA CD, 1992). Sixteen weeks on *Billboard's* Top Pop Albums chart, peaking at No. 2 April 7–21, 1956. Academy Award nomination for Best Music, Scoring of a Dramatic or Comedy Picture: 1956. Conte Candoli, Pete Candoli, Buddy Childers, Bob Fleming, Ray Linn and Cecil Read (t); Shorty Rogers (fh); Albert Anderson, Harry Betts, Milt Bernhart, Jimmy Henderson, George Roberts, Frank Rosolino and Ray Sims (tb); Joe Eger, Arthur Frantz and Richard Perissi (Frh); Martin Ruderman and Sylvia Ruderman (f); Nick Fera and Mitchell Lurie (cl); Jerome Kasper and Bud Shank (as); Bob Cooper, Bill Holman and Jack Montrose (ts); Jimmy Giuffre (bs); Chauncey Haines (novachord); Pete Jolly, Lou Levy and Ray Turner (p); Abe Luboff and Ralph Peña (b); Shelly Manne (d); Milt Holland and Lee Previn (per).
- 45 single by Elmer Bernstein: "Main Title from The Man with the Golden Arm"/"Clark Street" (Decca, 1956). Thirteen weeks on *Billboard's* Hot 100 chart, peaking at No. 32 on April 28, 1956.

★ The Manchurian Candidate
- *The Manchurian Candidate: Complete Soundtrack Recording* (Premier CD, 1997). Joe Gordon and Carmel Jones (t); Lou Blackburn and Dick Leith (tb); David Amram (Frh); Paul Horn (as, f); Harold Land (ts); Jack Nimitz (bs); David Amram (p, per).
- *David Amram's Classic American Film Scores 1958-2016* (Jazz on Film CDs, 2016). Includes an expanded presentation of *The Manchurian Candidate*.

★ Mannix
- *Mannix: Themes from the Original Score of the Paramount Television Show* (Paramount, 1968; Collector's Choice Music CD, 2008). John Audino, Bobby Bryant, Conte Candoli and Graham Young (t, fh); Milt Bernhart, Dick Nash, George Roberts and Lloyd Ulyate (tb); Gene Cipriano, Plas Johnson, Ronny Lang, Jack Nimitz and Bud Shank (r); Mike Melvoin (key); Howard Roberts and Tommy Tedesco (g); Carol Kaye (g, eb); Max Bennett (ab); Francisco Aguabella, Larry Bunker, Emil Richards and Ken Watson (per).
- 45 single by Lalo Schifrin: "Mannix"/"End Game" (Paramount, 1969).
- *Mannix Soundtrack* (Aleph CD, 1999). Rob Bruynen, Andry Haderer, Rick Kiefer, John Marshall and Klaus Osterloh (t, fh); Dave Horler, Bernt Laukamp and Ludwig Nuss (tb); Lucas Schmid (bt); Elmar Frey, Jens Neufang, Olivier Peters, Rolf Römer, Harald Rosenstein and Heiner Wiberny (r); Paul Sigihara (g); Frank Chastenier (key); John Goldsby (b); Wolfgang Haffner (d); Egmont Kraus, Romanus Schöttler, Thomas Steiner and Janos Szudy (per).

Martin Kane, Private Eye
- 10-inch 78 rpm disc by Charles Paul: "Martin Kane Theme"/"Love" (MGM, 1953).

Mélodie en sous-sol
- 7-inch EP by Michel Magne: "Hymne a L'argent," "Hold Up," "Palm Beach" and "Deconfiture" (Barclay, 1963; Universal Music France CD, 2006). Digital edition includes bonus tracks, along with Magne's score for 1962's *Un singe en hiver*.

La métamorphose des cloportes
- *La métamorphose des cloportes: Bande Originale du Film* (Verve, 1965; EmArcy CD, 2002). Jimmy Smith (org); Quentin Jackson (g); William Hart (d).

Mickey One
- *Music from the Sound Track of Mickey One Played by Stan Getz* (MGM, 1965; Verve CD, 1998). Digital edition includes nine bonus tracks. Grammy Award nomination for Best Original Jazz Composition: 1966. Clark Terry (t, fh); Al DeRisi, Joe Ferrante and Bobby Nichols (t); Eddie Bert, Johnny Messner, Eph Resnick and Sonny Russo (tb); Tommy Mitchell (bt); Bob Abernathy, Ray Alonge, Richard Berg, James Buffindton, Earl Chapin (Frh); Stan Getz (ts); Ray Shiner (ts, cl); Harvey Estrin (as, cl, f); Wally Kane (b sax, cl, boon); Barry Galbraith (g); Roger Kellaway (p); Richard David (ab); Mel Lewis (d); Elden C. Bailey, Herbie Harris, Phil Kraus, Walter Rosenberg and Joe Venuto (per).

★ *Mickey Spillane's Mike Hammer*
- *The Music from Mickey Spillane's Mike Hammer* (RCA, 1959; BMG CD, 2001). Digital edition includes Stanley Wilson's soundtrack for *M Squad*. Pete Candoli, Don Fagerquist and Cappy Lewis (t); Joe Howard and Frank Rosolino (tb); Ted Nash and Bud Shank (as, f); Richie Kamuca (ts); Pete Jolly (p); Alvin Stoller (d).

Mirage
- *Mirage: Original Motion Picture Score* (Mercury, 1965).
- *The Cinema of Quincy Jones* (Decca CDs, 2016). Six-disc box set includes all tracks from *Mirage*.

★ *Mission: Impossible*
- *Music from Mission: Impossible* (Dot, 1967; Hip-O CD, 1996). Forty-seven weeks on *Billboard's* Top LPs chart, peaking at No. 47 on April 13, 1968. Grammy Awards for Best Instrumental Theme, and Best Original Score Written for a Motion Picture or Television Show: 1968. Grammy Award nomination for Best Instrumental Performance: 1968. Emmy Award nominations for Outstanding Achievement in Musical Composition: 1967–69. Uan Rasey and Stu Williamson (t); Dick Nash (tb); Bud Shank (as, f); Lalo Schifrin (key); Mike Melvoin (p); Red Mitchell (ab); Larry Bunker and Emil Richards (per).
- 45 single by Lalo Schifrin: "Mission: Impossible"/"Jim on the Move" (Dot, 1967). Fourteen weeks on *Billboard's* Hot 100 chart, peaking at No. 41 on March 2 and 9.
- *More Mission: Impossible* (Paramount, 1969).
- *The Best of Mission: Impossible, Then and Now* (GNP Crescendo CD, 1992).
- *Mission: Impossible, The Television Scores* (La-La Land CDs, 2015). Six-disc box set with full and partial scores by all 16 composers who worked on the original series.
- *Mission: Impossible, Music from the 1988 Television Series* (La-La Land CD, 2018).

Mr. Broadway
- 45 single by Dave Brubeck: "Toki's Theme"/"Mr. Broadway" (Columbia, 1964). Grammy Award nomination for Best Original Jazz Composition: 1965.
- *Jazz Impressions of New York* (Columbia, 1965; CD 1990). Paul Desmond (as); Dave Brubeck (p); Eugene Wright (b); Joe Morello (d).

Mister Buddwing
- *Mister Buddwing: Music from the Original Soundtrack* (Verve, 1965).

★ *Mr. Lucky*
- *Music from Mr. Lucky* (RCA, 1960; CD, 1999). Seventy-eight weeks on *Billboard's* Top LPs chart, peaking at No. 5 on May 23, 1960. Grammy Awards for Best Arrangement, and Best Performance by an Orchestra: 1961. Grammy Award nomination, for Best Soundtrack Album: 1961. Don Fagerquist (t); Karl de Karske, John Halliburton, Dick Nash and Jimmy Priddy (tb); Gene Cipriano, Lloyd Hildebrand, Jules Jacob, Henry Klee, Ronald Langinger and Howard Terry (sax); John Cave, James Decker, Vince DeRosa, John Graas and Richard Perissi (Frh);

Buddy Cole (org); John Williams (p); Bob Bain, Al Hendrickson and Trefoni Rizzi (g); Roland Bundock (b); Milt Holland and Shelly Manne (d); Frank Flynn (per).
- 45 single by Henry Mancini: "Mr. Lucky"/"Floating Pad" (RCA, 1960). Thirteen weeks on *Billboard's* Hot 100 chart, peaking at No. 21 on May 2, 1960.
- *Mr. Lucky Goes Latin* (RCA, 1961; CD, 1999). Twenty-nine weeks on *Billboard's* Top LPs chart, peaking at No. 46 on August 14, 1961. Digital edition includes both albums. Dick Nash (tb); Ronald Langinger (sax); Vince DeRosa (Frh); Jimmy Rowles (key); Robert Hammack (org); Laurindo Almeida (g, md); Bob Bain (g); Roland Bundock and Keith Mitchell (b); Larry Bunker, Frank Flynn, Milt Holland and Shelly Manne (per).

Modesty Blaise
- *Modesty Blaise: Original Motion Picture Soundtrack Album* (20th Century–Fox, 1966: Harkit CD, 2001). Digital edition includes eight bonus tracks.

Murder, Inc.
- *Original Sound Track from "Murder Inc"* (Canadian American, 1960; Fresh Sound CD, 2013). May Britt and Sarah Vaughan (v) and the Jeff Alexander Orchestra. Digital edition includes Alexander Courage's score for 1957's *Hot Rod Rumble*.

Murderers' Row
- *Murderers' Row: An Original Soundtrack Recording* (Colgems, 1967). Plas Johnson and Bud Shank (r); Mike Deasy, Howard Roberts and Tommy Tedesco (g); Carol Kaye (ab); Earl Palmer (d); Emil Richards (per).

The Naked City
- *The Naked City* (Colpix, 1959; Jazz on Film CD, 2014).

The Name of the Game
- 45 single by Dave Grusin: "It Takes a Thief"/"The Name of the Game" (Decca, 1968). Emmy Award nomination for Outstanding Music Composition for a Series: 1971.

No Sun in Venice, see *Sait-on jamais*.

Nowhere to Go
- Gatefold double 45s by the Dizzy Reece Quartet: "Main Title (Nowhere to Go)"/"The Escape and the Chase," "The Search (On the Scene)"/"The Sunset Scene (Nowhere to Go)" (Tempo, 1959). Included in Jazz on Film's 2015 box set, *The New Wave II*. Dizzy Reece (t); Tubby Hayes (ts, bs); Lloyd Thompson (ab); Phil Seamen (d).

Nóz w wodzie, see *Knife in the Water*.

★ *Odds Against Tomorrow*
- *Odds Against Tomorrow: Original Music from the Motion Picture Soundtrack* (United Artists, 1959; Signature CD, 1991). Melvyn Broiles, Bernie Glow, Joe Wilder and John Ware (t); John Clark and Thomas McIntosh (tb); Raymond Alonge, Paul Ingram, Al Richman and Gunther Schuller (Frh); Harvey Phillips (tuba); Robert DiDomenica (f); Jim Hall (g); Milt Jackson (vib); Bill Evans (p); Percy Heath (b); Connie Kay (d); Richard Horowitz (timp); Walter Rosenberger (per).
- *Music from Odds Against Tomorrow* (United Artists, 1959; Blue Note CD, 1990). John Lewis (p); Milt Jackson (vib); Percy Heath (b); Connie Kay (d).

OK Connery
- 45 single by Christy/Bruno Nicolay: "The Man for Me"/"N-A-50–33–11" (Parade, 1967).
- *OK Connery: Operation Kid Brother* (Digitmovies CD, 2004).

On Her Majesty's Secret Service
- *On Her Majesty's Secret Service: Original Soundtrack Recording* (United Artists, 1969; EMI CD, 1988). Thirteen weeks on *Billboard's* Top LPs chart, peaking at No. 103 on March 21, 1970.

- 45 single by Louis Armstrong: "We Have All the Time in the World"/"Pretty Little Missy" (United Artists, 1969). Nineteen weeks on the UK's Top Singles chart, peaking at No. 3 on November 19, 1994 (!).
- *On Her Majesty's Secret Service* (EMI/Capitol CD, 2003). Includes 10 bonus tracks.

★ Once a Thief
- *Music from the Motion Picture "Once a Thief" and Other Themes* (Verve, 1965). Includes three reorchestrated themes from *Once a Thief*. Conte Candoli (t); Dick Nash and Frank Rosolino (tb); Buddy Collette and Ronnie Lang (sax); Paul Horn (f); Red Callender (tuba); Howard Roberts (g); Artie Kane (p); Red Mitchell (b); Shelley Manne (d).
- *Lalo Schifrin Film Scores: 1964–68* (Film Score Monthly CDs, 2011). Five-disc box set includes the entire score from *Once a Thief*, along with the contents of the Verve album.

One More Time
- 45 single by Sammy Davis Jr.: "Where Do I Go from Here"/"One More Time" (United Artists, 1970).

Operation Kid Brother, see *OK Connery*.

Our Man Flint
- *Our Man Flint: Original Motion Picture Score* (20th Century–Fox, 1966; Intrada CD, 2014). Three weeks on *Billboard's* Top LPs chart, peaking at No. 118 on October 22, 1966. Digital edition includes Jerry Goldsmith's score for 1967's *In Like Flint*. Dick Nash (tb); Plas Johnson (ts); Ronnie Lang (as); Red Mitchell (b); Shelly Manne (d).
- 45 single by Jerry Goldsmith: "Our Man Flint"/"Leave it to Flint" (20th Century–Fox, 1966).
- *In Like Flint/Our Man Flint: Original Motion Picture Soundtracks* (Varèse Sarabande CD, 1998). Goldsmith's original score cues for both films (as opposed to the LP reorchestrations).

Our Man in Beirut, see *Le spie uccidono a Beirut*.

Paul Temple
- 45 single by Ron Grainer: "The Paul Temple Theme"/"The Jazz Age" (RCA, 1969).

The Pawnbroker
- *The Pawnbroker: Explosive Motion Picture Score* (Mercury, 1965; Verve CD, 1996). Digital edition includes Quincy Jones' score for 1966's *The Deadly Affair*. Freddie Hubbard (t); J.J. Johnson (tb); Oliver Nelson (as, ts); Jerry Dodgion (as); Anthony Ortega (ss); Don Elliott (vib); Bobby Scott (p); Kenny Burrell (g); Tommy Williams (b); Elvin Jones (d); Ed Shaughnessy (per).

Payroll
- 45 single by Reg Owen: "Payroll"/"Swing-A-Ling-Ling" (Palette, 1961).

Pete Kelly's Blues (1955 film)
- *Music from Jack Webb's Pete Kelly's Blues* (Columbia, 1955). Dick Cathcart (c); Moe Schneider (tb); Eddie Miller (ts); Matty Matlock (cl); George Van Eps (g); Ray Sherman (p); Jud Denaut (b); Nick Fatool (d).
- *Pete Kelly's Blues* (RCA Victor, 1955; Collector's Choice CD, 1999). Dick Cathcart (c); Moe Schneider (tb); Eddie Miller (ts); Matty Matlock (cl); George Van Eps (g); Ray Sherman (p); Jud Denaut (b); Nick Fatool (d).
- *Songs from Pete Kelly's Blues* (Decca, 1955; CD, 1999).

Pete Kelly's Blues (TV series)
- *Pete Kelly's Blues: The Authentic Music from the Television Production* (Warner Bros., 1959). Grammy Award nomination for Best Sound Track Album: 1959. Frank Beach (t); Moe Schneider (tb); Eddie Miller (ts); Dick Cathcart (c); Matty Matlock (cl); George Van Eps (g); Ray Sherman (p); Jud De Naut (b); Nick Fatool (d).

★ Peter Gunn

- *The Music from Peter Gunn* (RCA, 1959; RCA/BMG CD, 1988). 107 weeks on *Billboard's* Top LPs chart, hitting No. 1 for 10 weeks beginning February 3, 1959. Emmy Award nomination for Best Musical Contribution to a Television Program: 1959. Grammy Awards for Best Album of the Year, and Best Arrangement: 1959. Grammy Award nomination, for Best Sound Track Album: 1959. Frank Beach, Pete Candoli, Conrad Gozzo, Ray Linn and Uan Rasey (t); Milt Bernhart, Karl de Karske, Dick Nash and Jimmy Priddy (tb); John Cave, Vince DeRosa, John Graas and Richard Perissi (ho); Plas Johnson, Ronald Langinger and Ted Nash (sax); Bob Bain and Al Hendrickson (g); Johnny Williams (p); Larry Bunker (vib); Roland Bundock (b); Jack Sperling (d).
- 45 single by Henry Mancini: "Peter Gunn Theme"/"The Brothers Go to Mother's" (RCA, 1959).
- *More Music from Peter Gunn* (RCA, 1959; RCA/BMG CD, 1988). Twenty-four weeks on *Billboard's* Top LPs chart, peaking at No. 7 on August 3, 1959. Grammy Award nominations for Best Album of the Year, Best Arrangement, Best Jazz Performance—Group, Best Musical Composition, Best Performance by an Orchestra, and Best Soundtrack Album: 1959. Frank Beach, Pete Candoli, Conrad Gozzo and Graham Young (t); Hoyt Bohannon, Karl de Karske, John Halliburton, Dick Nash and James Priddy (tb); John Cave, Vince DeRosa, John Graas and Richard Perissi (ho); Gene Cipriano, Plas Johnson, Ronald Langinger and Ted Nash (sax); Bob Bain (g); Johnny Williams (p); Victor Feldman (vib); Roland Bundock (b); Shelly Manne and Alvin Stoller (d).
- *Dreamsville* (Columbia, 1959; Flare CD, 2009). Vocal album by TV co-star Lola Albright, including her versions of six Mancini compositions heard as instrumentals during the show. Backing band conducted by Mancini, with Dick Nash (tb); Ronny Land and Ted Nash (f); Tony Rizzi (g); John Williams (p); Victor Feldman (vib); Bob Bain (g); Ronnie Bundock and Red Mitchell (b); Shelly Manne and Jack Sperling (d).

The Pink Panther (1963)

- *The Pink Panther: Music from the Film Score* (RCA Victor, 1963; CD 1989). Eighty-seven weeks on *Billboard's* Top LPs chart, parking at No. 8 on August 15 and 22, 1964. Academy Award nomination for Best Music Score—Substantially Original: 1964. Grammy Awards for Best Instrumental Composition, Best Instrumental Arrangement and Best Instrumental Performance (Other Than Jazz): 1965. Grammy Award nominations for Album of the Year, Best Engineered Recording, and Best Original Score Written for a Motion Picture or Television Show: 1965. Frank Beach, Pete Candoli, Conrad Gozzo and Ray Triscari (t); Lew McCreary, Dick Nash, Jimmy Priddy and Lloyd Ulyate (tb); Plas Johnson (ts); Gene Cipriano, Harry Klee, Ronny Lang and Ted Nash (sax); Bob Bain and Howard Roberts (g); Jimmy Rowles (p); Larry Bunker (vib, per); Carl Fortina (acc); Red Mitchell (b); Shelly Manne (d).
- 45 single by Henry Mancini: "The Pink Panther Theme"/"It Had Better Be Tonight" (RCA Victor, 1963)

Point Blank

- *Point Blank/The Outfit* (Film Score Monthly CD, 2002). Includes Jerry Fielding's score for 1973's *The Outfit*. Buddy Childers, Uan Rasey, George Werth and James C. Zito (t); Kenneth Shroyer (tb); Jack Cave, George W. Hyde, Arthur Maebe, Jr., Richard Perissi and Alan I. Robinson (Frh); Tommy Tedesco (g); Paul Beaver, William Mitchell Byers, Artie Kane and Ray Sherman (key); Ray Brown, Monty Budwig, Red Callender, Red Mitchell and Joe Mondragon (b); Hugh Anderson, Frank L. Carson, Victor Feldman, Mel Lewis, Emil Richards and Charlie Shoemake (d).

The President's Analyst

- *Man on a Swing/The President's Analyst* (Quartet CD, 2015). Includes Lalo Schifrin's score for 1974's *Man on a Swing*.

The Prisoner

- 45 single by Ron Grainer: "The Prisoner"/"Happening Sunday" (RCA, 1967).

- *The Prisoner: Original Soundtrack Music from the TV Series* (Bam-Caruso, 1986; Silva Screen CD, 1989).
- *The Prisoner Files, Volumes 1–3* (Silva Screen CDs, 2002–03).
- *The Prisoner: Original Soundtrack* (Network CDs, 2008). Three-disc set with all 235 of the surviving cues and alternate takes.

★ *Private Hell 36*
- *Original Score from the Soundtrack of the Motion Picture Private Hell 36* (Coral, 1954; Fresh Sound CD, 2005). Digital edition includes Leith Stevens' score for 1953's *The Wild One*. Pete Candoli, Charlie Grifford, Carlton MacBeth and Shorty Rogers (t); Milt Bernhart and Harry Betts (tb); Bob Enevoldsen (vtb); George Roberts (bt); Sal Franzella (cl, as); Lennie Niehaus (as); Bob Cooper and Jimmy Giuffre (ts); Bob Gordon (bcl, bs); Bud Shank (bs); John Graas (Frh); Paul Sarmento (tuba); Claude Williamson (p); Joe Mondragon (ab); Shelly Manne (d).

The Prize
- *The Prize Plus Music from These Other Great Motion Pictures* (MGM, 1963). Includes four reorchestrated themes from *The Prize*.
- *The Prize: Original Motion Picture Soundtrack* (Film Score Monthly CD, 2002). The complete score, along with the four tracks from the MGM album.

The Quiller Memorandum
- *The Quiller Memorandum: The Original Sound Track Recording* (Columbia, 1966; Varèse Saranbande CD, 1989).
- 45 single by Matt Monro: "The Lady Smiles"/"Wednesday's Child" (Capitol, 1967).

★ *Rapporto Fuller Base Stoccolma*
- *Rapporto Fuller Base Stoccolma: Original Soundtrack Music by Armando Trovaioli* (Beat CD, 2007).

Rear Window
- *Hitchcock: Master of Mayhem* (Pro-Arte Audio+ CD, 1990). Includes a four-movement suite of cues from Franz Waxman's score for *Rear Window*.

The Red Circle, see *Le Cercle Rouge*.

The Reporter
- *The Reporter: The Original Music from the CBS Television Network Series* (Columbia, 1964). Joe Newman, Ernie Royal, Nick Travis and Joe Wilder (t); Wayne Andre, Jimmy Cleveland, Dick Hixson and Frank Rehak (tb); Phil Woods (as, cl); Zoot Sims (ts); Romeo Penque and Jerome Richardson (sax, f); Ray Alonge, Dick Berg, Jimmy Buffington and Morris Secon (Frh); Bernie Leighton (p); Barry Galbraith (g); Joe Venuto (vib and bng); George Duvivier (b); Ed Shaughnessy (d).

Repulsion
- *Notti di Terrore/Repulsione* (CAM, 1966). Includes four tracks ostensibly from *Repulsion*. Jimmy Woods (as, f); Gabor Szabo (g); Albert Stinson (b); Chico Hamilton (d).
- *The Film Music of Chico Hamilton: Sweet Smell of Success and Repulsion* (Harkit CD, 2008). Includes the four tracks from the CAM album, along with a fifth bonus track from *Repulsion*.

Requiem per un Agente Segreto
- *Requiem per un Agente Segreto: Original Motion Picture Soundtrack* (GDM CD, 2001).

Return from the Ashes
- 45 single by John Dankworth: "Return from the Ashes"/"Piano Theme" (Fontana, 1966).

★ *Richard Diamond*
- *The Music from Richard Diamond* (Mercury, 1959; Fresh Sound CD, 2002). Digital edition includes Pete Rugolo's soundtrack for *Thriller*. Pete Candoli, Ollie Mitchell, Joe Triscari and

Stu Williamson (t); Milt Bernhart, Francis "Joe" Howard, George Roberts and Frank Rosolino (tb); Paul Horn and Bud Shank (pic, f and as); Bob Cooper and Chuck Gentry (r); Bernie Mattison (vib); Jimmy Rowles (p); Al Viola (g); Red Mitchell (b); Shelly Manne (d).
- 45 single by Rugolo: "Thin Man Theme"/"Richard Diamond Theme" (Mercury, 1959).

The Road to Shame, see *Des Femmes Disparaissent*.

The Roaring 20's [sic]
- *The Roaring 20's* (Warner Bros., 1960; Sepia CD, 2011). Forty-two weeks on the UK's Top Albums chart, peaking at No. 3 on December 2, 1961.
- 45 single by Dorothy Provine: "Don't Bring Lulu"/"Whisper Song" (Warner Bros., 1961). Twelve weeks on the UK Singles chart, peaking at No. 17 on December 13, 1961.
- 45 single by Dorothy Provine: "Crazy Words, Crazy Tune"/"Bye Bye Blackbird" (Warner Bros., 1962). Three weeks on the UK Singles chart, peaking at No. 45 on July 4, 1962.
- *Dorothy Provine: The Vamp from The Roaring 20's* (Warner Bros., 1961; Sepia CD, 2011). Seven weeks on the UK's Top Albums chart, peaking at No. 9 on February 10, 1962.

★ ***Robbery***
- *Robbery: Original Sound Track* (Decca/London, 1967; Vocalion CD, 2008).
- 45 single by Jackie Lee: "Born to Lose"/"Saying Goodbye" (Decca UK, 1967).

The Rogues
- *Original Music from The Rogues* (RCA, 1964; Vocalion CD, 2017). John Audino, Lewis Carroll, Vito Mangano and Shorty Sherock (t); Dick Nash, Tommy Pederson and Thomas Shepard (tb); George Roberts (bt); William Hinshaw and Vince DeRosa (Frh); Gene Cipriano, Lloyd Hildebrand, Plas Johnson, Harry Klee, Wilbur Schwartz and Warren Webb (sax, ww); Jimmy Rowles and Ray Sherman (p); Bob Bain and Barney Kessel (g); Joe Comfort and Edward Gilbert (b); Irving Cottler (d); Frank Flynn (per).

Route 66
- 45 single by Nelson Riddle: "*Route 66* Theme"/"Lolita Ya Ya" (Capitol, 1962). Twelve weeks on *Billboard's* Hot 100 chart, peaking at No. 30 on August 11, 1962. Grammy Award nominations for Best Instrumental Theme, Best Instrumental Arrangement and Best Engineering Contribution: 1963.

***The Saint* (1962)**
- *Secret Agent Meets the Saint* (RCA, 1965; CD 2002). Includes six tracks from each of the two shows.
- 45 single by Edwin Astley: "Danger Man"/"The Saint" (RCA, 1965).
- *Music from the TV Series The Saint* (RCA, 1966; BMG/Razor & Tie CD, 1997).
- *The Saint Original Soundtrack* (Network CDs, 2010). Four-disc set with all 238 of Edwin Astley's surviving cues and alternate takes.

★ ***Sait-on jamais***
- *The Modern Jazz Quartet Plays One Never Knows: Original Film Score for "No Sun in Venice"* (Atlantic, 1958; CD, 1998). John Lewis (p); Milt Jackson (vib); Percy Heath (b); Connie Kay (d).

Salt & Pepper
- *Salt & Pepper: Original Motion Picture Score* (United Artists, 1967).

Le Samouraï
- *Le Samouraï: Bande Originale du Film* (Philips, 1967).
- *Les Aventuriers/Le Samouraï: Bandes Originale du Film* (Universal Music France CD, 2005). Includes six additional tracks from *Le Samouraï*.
- *Le Samouraï: Bande Originale du Film* (Rambling CD, 2015). The full 21-track score.

★ ***Satan in High Heels***
- *Satan in High Heels: Original Soundtrack* (Charlie Parker, 1961; Collectables CD, 1997). Bernie

Glow, Joe Newman, Ernie Royal, Doc Severinsen and Clark Terry (t); Jimmy Cleveland, Buster Cooper and Urbie Green (tb); Jim Buffington (Frh); Ray Beckenstein (as, f); Walter Levinsky (as, cl); Phil Woods (as); Al Cohn, Al Klink and Oliver Nelson (ts); Gene Allen and Sol Schlinger (bs); Barry Galbraith and Mundell Lowe (g); Eddie Costa (p, vib); George Duvivier (b); Ed Shaughnessy (d).
- *Blues for a Stripper, and Other Exciting Sounds* (Charlie Parker, 1962; Modern Harmonic CD, 2016). Identical contents as the "official" soundtrack, despite the misleading title.

The Scorpio Letters
- *The Last Run/Crosscurrent/The Scorpio Letters* (Film Score Monthly CD, 2007).

Sebastian
- *Sebastian: Music from the Original Motion Picture Score* (Dot, 1968; Harkit CD, 2009). Digital edition includes 12 bonus tracks.
- *Sebastian* (Intrada, 2013). Jerry Goldsmith's original score cues, along with all tracks from the previous editions.

Secret Agent, see *Danger Man*.

Secret Agent Fireball, see *Le spie uccidono a Beirut*.

Seven Golden Men, see *7 uomini d'oro*.

7 Uomini d'Oro
- *7 Uomini d'Oro: Colonna Sonora Originale* (CAM, 1965; Seven Seas CD, 1992).

77 Sunset Strip
- *77 Sunset Strip: Music from This Year's Most Popular New TV Show* (Warner Bros., 1959; CD, 2000). Twenty-eight weeks on *Billboard*'s Top LPs chart, peaking at No. 3 on May 11, 1959.
- Gatefold double 45s by Warren Barker: "Swingin' on the Strip"/"Blue Night on the Strip," "77 Sunset Strip Cha Cha"/"Kookie's Caper" (Warner Bros., 1959).
- *77 Sunset Strip and Other Selections* (Jubilee, 1959). Frankie Ortega (p); James Nottingham, Richard Perry, Ernest Royal and Charlie Shavers (t); Lawrence Brown, Rod Levitt and Frank Sarraci (tb); Seldon Powell and Sam Taylor (ts); George Dorsey (as); Daniel Bank and Dave McRae (bs); Phil Bodner (cl); Kenny Burell and Al Chernet (g); Bert Hanson (b); Donald Lamond and Walter Sage (d).

Shadows
- *Beat, Square & Cool* (Jazz on Film CDs, 2012). Includes the four tracks Charles Mingus expanded from his film cues. Willie Dennis (tb); Shafi Hadi (ts, f); Booker Ervin (ts); John Handy (as); Charles Mingus (b, p, per); Horace Parlan and Richard Wyands (p); Dannie Richmond (d).

★ The Silencers
- *The Silencers: An Original Soundtrack Recording* (RCA Victor, 1966; Vocalion CD, 2016).
- 45 single by Vikki Carr: "The Silencers"/"Santiago" (Liberty, 1966).

The Sleeping Car Murders, see *Compartiment Tueurs*.

Sol Madrid
- *Sol Madrid: Music from the Original Sound Track* (MGM, 1968). Uan Rasey and Tony Terran (t); Randall Miller, Dick Noel and Don Waldrop (tb); Vince DeRosa, William Hinshaw and Art Maebe (Frh); Ronnie Lang and Bud Shank (f); Al Hendrickson and Tommy Tedesco (g); Bob Bain and Howard Roberts (elg); Paul Beaver (org); Artie Kane, Ray Sherman and Ray Turner (p); Red Mitchell (ab); Frank Carlson, Shelly Manne and Emil Richards (d).
- *Lalo Schifrin Film Scores: 1964–68* (Film Score Monthly CDs, 2011). Five-disc box set includes all 23 score cues from *Sol Madrid*, along with the contents of the 1968 LP.

I Soliti Ignoti
- Gatefold double 45s by Piero Umiliani: "Blues for Gassman: Parte I"/"Blues for Gassman: Parte II," "Tema D'Amore"/"Finale" (RCA Italiana, 1958). Included in Jazz on Film's 2013 box set, *Chet Baker: Italian Movies*. Bill Gilmore (tb); Baldo Maestri (cl); Marcello Boschi (as); Gino Marinacci (bs); Piero Umiliani (p); Franco Chiari (vib); Berto Pisano (ab); Roberto Zappulla (d).

Some Girls Do
- 45 single by Lee Vanderbilt: "Some Girls Do"/"Dark in the City" (United Artists, 1969).

Special Branch
- *Themes for TV Drama: The Music of Robert Earley* (Network CD, 2015).

★ *Le spie uccidono a Beirut*
- *Le spie uccidono a Beirut: Colonne Sonore Originali* (CAM, 1965; digital download, 2008).

The Split
- *The Split* (Film Score Monthly CD, 2009). Buddy Childers, Uan Rasey, Raymond Triscari and Graham Young (t); Robert Knight, Lewis Melvin McCreary, Richard Noel, Barrett O'Hara, Frank Rosolino, Kenneth Shroyer, Ernie Tack and Donald G. Waldrop (tb); Eugene S. Di Novi, Artie Kane, Mike Lang, Don Randi and Michael Rubini (p); Paul Beaver, Mitchell H. Ellis and Billy Preston (org); Max R. Bennett, James E. Bond Jr., Ray Brown, Clyde Hoggan, Stephens LaFever and Joe Mondragon (b); Larry Bunker, Frank L. Carlson, Ralph Collier, Richard Cornell, Gene Paul Estes, Paul N. Humphrey, Shelly Manne, Emil Richards and Jerry D. Williams (d).
- 45 single by Billy Preston: "It's Just a Game, Love"/"The Split" (MGM, 1968).

★ *Staccato*
- *Staccato* (Capitol, 1959; Jazz on Film CD, 2014). Pete Candoli and Don Fagerquist (t); Milt Bernhart, Dick Nash and Si Zentner (tb); Gene Cipriano, Ronnie Lang, Ted Nash and Dave Pell (r); Johnny Williams (p); Al Hendrickson, Barney Kessel and Howard Roberts (elg); Larry Bunker and Red Norvo (vib); Red Mitchell (ab); Shelly Manne (d).
- 45 single by Elmer Bernstein: "Staccato"/"The Jazz at Waldo's" (Capitol, 1960). Eight weeks on the UK's Best Selling Pop Records chart, peaking at No. 4 on January 18, 1960.

Stakeout on Dope Street
- Gatefold double 45s by Richard Markowitz: "Stakeout"/"Love Dream," "Withdrawal"/"Needle in a Stack" (RCA Victor, 1958). Ollie Mitchell (t); Phil Gray (tb); Dick Houlgate (bs, f); Rubin Leon (as, p); Robert Drasnin (cl); Mel Pollan (ab); Gene Estes (x, timp); Ritchie Frost (d).

Stiletto
- *Stilleto: Selections from the Sound Track* (CBS/Columbia, 1969; Vocalion CD, 2014).
- 45 single by Sid Ramin: "Stiletto"/"Sugar in the Rain" (CBS, 1970).

★ *The Strange One*
- *The Strange One: Music from the Sound Track* (Coral, 1957).

Strange Report
- 45 single by Roger Webb: "Strange Report"/"Summer Fancy" (Columbia, 1971).
- *Strange Report: Original Title and Incidental Music* (Network CD, 2009).

A Streetcar Named Desire
- *A Streetcar Named Desire: Music from the Original Soundtrack* (Capitol, 1951; Soundtrack Factory CD, 1999). Academy Award nomination, for Best Music, Scoring of a Dramatic or Comedy Picture: 1951. Digital edition includes Bernard Herrmann's score for 1943's *Jane Eyre*. Larry Sullivan and Ziggy Elman (t); Hoyt Bohannon (tb); Archie Rosate (cl); Les Robinson (as); Babe Russin (ts).

★ Sweet Smell of Success
- *Sweet Smell of Success: Music from the Soundtrack* (Decca, 1957; CD, 2017). Pete Candoli (t); Frank Rosolino and Lloyd Ulyate (tb); Herb Geller and Ted Nash (sax); Sinclair Lott (Frh); Mitchell Lurie (cl); Martin Ruderman (f); Jack Marshall (g); Ernie Hughes and Johnny Williams (p); Curtis Counce (ab); Shelly Manne (d); Milt Holland (per, vib).
- *The Chico Hamilton Quintet: Sweet Smell of Success* (Decca, 1957; CD, 2017). Paul Horn (r); John Pisano (g); Fred Katz (ce); Carson Smith (ab); Hamilton (d). Both 1957 albums are included on the 2017 digital release.

Un témoin dans la ville
- *Un témoin dans la ville: Bande Originale* (Fontana, 1959; CD, 2003). Kenny Dorham (t); Barney Wilen (ts, ss); Duke Jordan (p); Paul Rovère (b); Kenny Clarke (d).

They Call Me MISTER Tibbs
- *They Call Me MISTER Tibbs: Original Motion Picture Score* (United Artists, 1970; Rykodisc CD, 1997). Digital edition includes Quincy Jones' score for 1967's *In the Heat of the Night*.

★ They Came to Rob Las Vegas
- *They Came to Rob Las Vegas: Original Soundtrack of the Film* (Philips, 1969; Harkit CD, 2002).
- 45 single by Georges Garvarentz: "The Wordless Song"/"Last Trip of the Truck" (Riviera, 1969).

The Thin Man
- 45 single by Pete Rugolo: "Thin Man Theme"/"Richard Diamond Theme" (Mercury, 1959).

The Thomas Crown Affair (1968)
- *The Thomas Crown Affair: Original Motion Picture Score* (United Artists, 1968; Rykodisc CD, 1998). Six weeks on *Billboard's* Top LPs chart, peaking at No. 182 on September 28, 1968. Academy Award for Best Original Song: 1969. Academy Award nomination for Best Original Score: 1969. Grammy Award nomination for Best Instrumental Arrangement: 1969. Digital edition includes two bonus tracks. Vince DeRosa (Fh); Louise DiTullion (f); Bud Shank (sax); Tommy Tedesco (g); Michel Legrand (p); Ray Brown (ab); Carol Kaye (eb); Shelly Manne (d); Emil Richards (per).
- 45 single by Noel Harrison: "The Windmills of Your Mind"/"Leitch on the Beach" (Reprise, 1968). Fourteen weeks on the UK's Top Singles chart, peaking at No. 8 on March 4, 1969.
- *The Thomas Crown Affair: Expanded Original MGM Motion Picture Soundtrack* (Quartet CD, 2014). Includes Michel Legrand's film score cues, along with the contents of the 1968 LP.

Thriller
- *The Music of Thriller* (Time, 1961; Fresh Sounds CD, 2002). Digital edition includes Pete Rugolo's soundtrack for *Richard Diamond*. Frank Beach, Don Fagerquist, Ollie Mitchell and Uan Rasey (t); Red Callender (tuba); James Decker, Vince DeRosa and Richard Perissi (Frh); Milt Bernhart, Dick Nash, Frank Rosolino and George Roberts (tb); Harry Klee and Bud Shank (as, f, pic); Gene Cipriano (ts, f, pic); Bob Cooper (ts); Ronny Lang (bs, f); Caesar Giovannini and Jimmy Rowles (p); Jack Cockerly (org); Bob Bain (g); Red Mitchell and Joe Mondragon (b); Alvin Stoller (d); Larry Bunker, Frank Flynn, Milt Holland and Lou Singer (vib, per).
- Jerry Goldsmith: *Thriller* (Tadlow CD, 2017).
- Jerry Goldsmith: *Thriller 2* (Tadlow CD, 2018).

★ Thunderball
- *Thunderball: Original Motion Picture Sound Track* (United Artists, 1965; EMI CD, 1988). Twenty-seven weeks on *Billboard's* Top LPs chart, peaking at No. 10 on March 5, 1966.
- 45 single by Tom Jones: "Thunderball"/"Key to My Heart" (Parrot, 1965). Nine weeks on *Billboard's* Hot 100 chart, peaking at No. 24 on January 22, 1966. Four weeks on the UK's Top 40 chart, peaking at No. 35 on January 19, 1966.
- *Best of James Bond 30th Anniversary Edition* (EMI, 1992). Includes a bonus "Thunderball Suite" not on the original album.

- *Thunderball* (EMI/Capitol CD, 2003). Expanded edition with all tracks from both previous albums.

Tiffany Memorandum
- *Una Sull'Altra/Teresa La Ladra/Tiffany Memorandum: Original Soundtrack Music* (Beat CD, 1997). Includes nine tracks from *Tiffany Memorandum*.

Tom Dollar
- 45 single by Rocky Roberts: "If He Could"/"Lady Barbara" (Durium, 1967).

Tony Rome
- 45 single by Nancy Sinatra: "Tony Rome"/"This Town" (Reprise, 1967).

Top Secret
- 45 single by Laurie Johnson: "Sucu Sucu"/"Echo Four Two" (Pye, 1961). Twelve weeks on the UK's Top 40 Singles chart, peaking at No. 9 on October 4, 1961.

Touch of Evil
- *Touch of Evil: Music from the Sound Track* (Challenge, 1958). Includes only three Henry Mancini score cues.
- *The Wild Side of Henry Mancini* (Challenge, 1962). A "stealth" soundtrack album, exclusively devoted to Mancini's score cues from *Touch of Evil*.
- *Touch of Evil: Original Motion Picture Soundtrack* (Varèse Sarabande CD, 1993). Includes all tracks from the two Challenge albums.

The Twilight Zone
- *The Twilight Zone: Volumes 1–5* (Varèse Sarabande, 1983–85; Silva Treasury CDs, 1999).

Two Men in Manhattan, see *Deux Hommes dans Manhattan*.

The Untouchables
- *Original Music from the TV Show The Untouchables* (Capitol, 1960; Jazz on Film CD, 2014). Grammy Award nomination, for Best Soundtrack Album: 1961.
- 45 single by Nelson Riddle: "The Untouchables"/"The Untouchables Strike Back" (Capitol, 1960).

Vendetta
- 45 single by John Barry: "Vendetta"/"The Danny Scipio Theme" (CBS, 1966).
- *The Vendetta Tapes* (Buried Treasure LP and CD, 2015).

The Venetian Affair
- 45 single by Lalo Schifrin: "Our Venetian Affair"/"Venice After Dark" (MGM, 1966).
- *Lalo Schifrin Film Scores: 1964–68* (Film Score Monthly CDs, 2011). Five-disc box set includes the entire score from *The Venetian Affair*, along with bonus tracks. Laurindo Almeida, Barney Kessel and Tommy Tedesco (g); Sam Chianis (cim); Artie Kane and Mike Lang (p, hps); Red Mitchell (b); Shelly Manne and Emil Richards (per).

Warning Shot
- *Si Zentner Plays Music from the Original Motion Picture Score of Warning Shot and Other Themes Composed by Jerry Goldsmith* (Liberty, 1967).
- *Warning Shot: Music from the Motion Picture* (La La Land CD, 2012). Includes Jerry Goldsmith's original film cues, along with the contents of the 1967 LP.

Where the Bullets Fly
- 45 single by Susan Maughan: "Where the Bullets Fly"/"I'll Never Stop Loving You" (Philips, 1966).

★ *The Wild One*
- *Jazz Themes from The Wild One* (Decca, 1953). Maynard Ferguson, Conrad Gozzo, Ray Leen,

Tom Reeves and Shorty Rogers (t); Harry Betts and Jimmy Knepper (tb); Bob Enevoldsen (vtb); John Graas (Frh); Paul Sarmento (tuba); Herb Geller and Bub Shank (as); Bill Holman and Bill Perkins (ts); Bob Cooper and Jimmy Giuffre (bs); Russ Freeman (p); Joe Mondragon (b); Shelly Manne (d).
- 45 single by Leith Stevens' All Stars: "The Wild One"/"Blues for Brando" (Decca, 1954).
- *The Wild One* (RCA Victor, 1953). Maynard Ferguson and Shorty Rogers (t); Milt Bernhart (tb); Bud Shank (sax, f); Bob Cooper (ts); Jimmy Giuffre (sax, cl); Russ Freeman (p); Carson Smith (b); Shelly Manne (d).
- *Jazz Themes from The Wild One* (Bear Family CD, 2001). Includes all tracks from both 1953 albums.

The Wild Wild West
- *The Wild Wild West: Music from the Television Series* (La La Land CDs, 2017). Four-disc set includes full or partial scores from 26 episodes.

A Witness in the City, see *Un témoin dans la ville*.

The Yellow Canary
- *The Yellow Canary: Music from the Motion Picture* (Verve, 1963). Joe Newman and Clark Terry (t); Billy Byers, Dick Lieb and Jimmy Cleveland (tb); Zoot Sims (ts); Romeo Penque and Jerome Richardson (r); Kenny Burrell (g); Lalo Schifrin (p); Bill Costa (vib); George Duvivier and Milt Hinton (b); Ed Shaughnessy (d).

You Only Live Twice
- *You Only Live Twice: Original Motion Picture Soundtrack* (United Artists, 1967; EMI CD, 1988). Twenty-six weeks on *Billboard*'s Top LPs chart, peaking at No. 27 on September 16, 1967.
- 45 single by Nancy Sinatra: "You Only Live Twice"/"Jackson" (Reprise, 1967). Ten weeks on *Billboard*'s Hot 100 chart, peaking at No. 44 on June 24, 1967. Nineteen weeks on the UK's Pop Singles chart, peaking at No. 11 on July 11, 1967.
- *You Only Live Twice* (EMI/Capitol CD, 2003). Includes seven bonus tracks.

The Young Savages
- *The Young Savages: An Original Sound Track Recording* (Columbia, 1961; Intrada CD, 2014).

★ Zig Zag
- *Zig Zag: Original Motion Picture Score* (MGM, 1970; Chapter III CD, 2001). Digital edition includes Riz Ortolani's score for 1968's *The Biggest Bundle of Them All*. Albert Aarons, Bobby Bryant, Conte Candoli, Buddy Childers and Paul T. Hubinon (t); Louis Blackburn, James Cleveland, James L. Johnson and George M. Roberts (tb); William E. Green, Plas Johnson, Andreas Kostelas, Ronny Lang, Jack Nimitz, Sylvia Ruderman, Thomas W. Scott, Bud Shank and Ernie Watts (f); Dennis Budimir, William Pitman and Louie Shelton (g); Artie Kane, Pearl Kaufman and Joseph L. Sample (p); Ray Brown, Mario Camposano, Morty Corb, Wilton L. Felder, Abraham Luboff and Peter Mercurio (b); Hugh Anderson, Jack Arnold, Larry Bunker, Frank L. Carlson, Don Cunningham, Victor Feldman, John Guerin, Paul N. Humphrey and Gene Pello (d).
- *Zig Zag/The Super Cops* (Film Score Monthly CD, 2006). Includes Oliver Nelson's original score cues, along with the contents of the MGM LP.

Chapter Notes

Preface

1. Irwin Bazelon, *Knowing the Score: Notes on Film Music* (New York: Van Nostrand Reinhold, 1975), 14.

Prologue

1. Anonymous, "George Raft in *The Case of Mr. Ace*," *The Billboard*, June 28, 1947, 10.
2. Kevin Burton Smith, "Eddie Drake," *The Thrilling Detective Web Site*, accessed Aug. 13, 2019, http://www.thrillingdetective.com/more_eyes/eddie_drake.html.
3. "CBS Invests 300G in Indie Tele-Pix Deal," *The Billboard*, Aug. 28, 1948, 3 and 15.
4. "*Drake* Film Series Ready for CBS Tele," *The Billboard*, Nov. 20, 1948, 15.
5. "Kiss Me Kate," *Broadway Musical Home*, accessed Aug. 13, 2019, http://broadwaymusicalhome.com/shows/kate.htm.

Chapter 1

1. Jerry Franken, "Barney Blake, Police Reporter," *The Billboard*, May 1, 1948, 11.
2. Kevin Burton Smith, "Flashgun Casey," accessed July 30, 2019, http://www.thrillingdetective.com/flashgun.html.
3. Ibid.
4. Michael J. Hayde, *My Name's Friday: The Unauthorized but True Story of Dragnet and the Films* (Nashville: Cumberland House, 2001), 70.
5. "The Line-Up," accessed July 30, 2019, http://www.digitaldeliftp.com/DigitalDeliToo/dd2jb-Line-Up.html.
6. Nat Hentoff, "Miles: A Trumpeter in the Midst of a Big Comeback Makes a Very Frank Appraisal of Today's Scene," *Down Beat*, Nov. 2, 1955, 14.
7. K.C. Spence, "From Big Band to Be-Bop: Jazz Digest," *Film Comment*, November/December 1988, 42.
8. Gene Lees, *Friends Along the Way: A Journey Through Jazz* (New Haven: Yale University Press, 2003), 32–33.
9. Cynthia Millar, "Elmer Bernstein: An Interview," *The Guardian*, October 9, 2002.
10. "Music on Film: Elmer Bernstein in Conversation with Ken Barnes," bonus feature video included with the 50th anniversary DVD and Blu-ray release of *The Man with the Golden Arm* (Hart Sharp Video, 2005).
11. John W. Waxman, "*Crime in the Streets*: Program Notes," accessed July 31, 2019, http://franzwaxman.com/music-performance/crime-in-the-streets/.
12. Bruce Elder, "Kenyon Hopkins," accessed July 31, 2019, http://www.allmusic.com/artist/kenyon-hopkins-mn0000086822/biography.
13. Jay Carr, "Bob le Flambeur," accessed July 31, 2019, http://www.tcm.com/tcmdb/title/69262/Bob-le-Flambeur/articles.html.

Chapter 2

1. "Richard Diamond," accessed January 20, 2020, https://thrillingdetective.wordpress.com/2019/08/31/richard-diamond/.
2. Fred Steiner, video interview by Karen Herman on June 26, 2003, accessed July 31, 2019, http://www.emmytvlegends.org/interviews/people/fred-steiner.
3. Jon Burlingame, "Dave Kahn Dies," filmmusicsociety.org, July 14, 2008, accessed July 31, 2019, http://www.filmmusicsociety.org/news_events/features/2008/071408.html?isArchive=071408.
4. Lee Zhito, "Hollywood," *The Billboard*, Nov. 9, 1959, 35.
5. Henry Mancini with Gene Lees, *Did They Mention the Music?* (New York: Cooper Square, 2001), 87.
6. Jon Burlingame, *TV's Biggest Hits* (New York: Schirmer, 1996), 31.
7. Mancini and Lees, *Did They Mention the Music?*, 90.
8. Burlingame, *TV's Biggest Hits*, 34.
9. Teddy Reig and Edward Berger, *Reminiscing in Tempo* (Lanham, MD: Scarecrow, 1995), 55.
10. Burlingame, *TV's Biggest Hits*, 34.
11. John S. Wilson, "Benny Carter, 95, Jazz Musician and Arranger, Dies," *The New York Times*, July 14, 2003, accessed July 31, 2019, http://www.nytimes.com/2003/07/14/obituaries/benny-carter-95-jazz-musician-and-arranger-dies.html.
12. Burlingame, *TV's Biggest Hits*, 36.

13. *Ibid.*, 37.

14. Kliph Nesteroff, "The Rise and Fall of Dino's Lodge," *WFMU's Beware of the Blog*, accessed July 31, 2019, https://blog.wfmu.org/freeform/2011/07/dining-at-dinos-lodge.html.

15. Cynthia Millar, "Elmer Bernstein: An Interview," *The Guardian*, Oct. 9, 2002.

16. Bill Milkowski, "Chico Hamilton: The Sweet Smell of Success," *JazzTimes*, Nov. 1, 2001, accessed July 31, 2019, https://jazztimes.com/archives/chico-hamilton-the-sweet-smell-of-success/.

17. Gideon Bachmann, "An Interview with Kenyon Hopkins," *Film and TV Music*, Nov. 5, 1957, accessed July 31, 2019, https://cnmsarchive.wordpress.com/2013/08/14/kenyon-hopkins/.

18. *Ibid.*

19. John Tynan, liner notes for the soundtrack album *Johnny Mandel's Great Jazz Score: I Want to Live!* (United Artists, 1958).

20. Kathleen A. O'Shea, *Women and the Death Penalty in the United States, 1900–1998* (Santa Barbara, CA: Praeger, 1999), 70.

21. Johnny Mandel, video interview by Linda Danly on Aug. 1, 2007, accessed July 31, 2019, https://www.filmmusicfoundation.org/interviews.html.

22. Johnny Mandel, interview by Patrick McGilligan in September 1998, for the liner notes for the CD reissue of *Johnny Mandel's Great Jazz Score: I Want to Live!* (Rykodisc, 1999), 2–3.

23. P.K. Scheuer, "Anxiety Jazz Killer-Diller," *Los Angeles Times*, April 14, 1958.

24. Johnny Mandel, liner notes for the soundtrack album *Johnny Mandel's Great Jazz Score: I Want to Live!* (United Artists, 1958).

25. Mandel and McGilligan, liner notes, 7.

26. Mancini and Lees, *Did They Mention the Music?*, 78.

27. John Caps, *Henry Mancini … Reinventing Film Music* (Chicago: University of Illinois Press, 2012), 39.

28. Kevin Mulhall, liner notes for the CD reissue of the soundtrack album *Touch of Evil* (Varèse Sarabande, 1993).

29. Mancini and Lees, *Did They Mention the Music?*, 82.

30. Clifford Allen, "Dizzy Reece: From In to Out," *allaboutjazz.com*, March 7, 2006, accessed Aug. 1, 2019, https://www.allaboutjazz.com/dizzy-reece-from-in-to-out-dizzy-reece-by-clifford-allen.php?pg=3.

31. Selwyn Harris, booklet notes for *Sait-on jamais*, in the box set *French New Wave* (Jazz on Film, 2013), 12.

32. John Lewis, quoted in Gary Kramer's liner notes for *Sait-on jamais* (Atlantic, 1958).

33. Selwyn Harris, booklet notes for *Ascenseur pour l'échafaud*, in the box set *French New Wave* (Jazz on Film, 2013), 19–20.

34. Miles Davis and Quincy Troupe, *Miles* (New York: Simon and Schuster, 1989), 217.

35. Jerry Tallmer, "Cinematic Retrospective of Louis Malle," *The Villager*, June 28, 2005, accessed Aug. 1, 2019, https://www.thevillager.com/2005/06/cinematic-retrospective-of-louis-malle-2/.

36. Piero Umiliani, "1958–1961," *Piero Umiliani: The Official Website*, accessed Aug. 1, 2019, http://www.umiliani.eu/1958-1961.html.

37. "Biography," schifrin.com, accessed Aug. 1, 2019, http://www.schifrin.com/biography.htm.

38. Mark Russell and James Edward Young, *Film Music* (Waltham, Massachusetts: Focal Press, 2000), 85.

Chapter 3

1. Mark Hasan, "The Man with the Jazzy Sound," *Film Score Monthly*, February 2002, 16.

2. Peter J. Levinson, *September in the Rain: The Life of Nelson Riddle* (New York: Billboard, 2001), 196.

3. *Ibid.*

4. *Ibid.*

5. Herschel Burke Gilbert, video interview by Jon Burlingame on April 30, 2001, accessed Aug. 1, 2019, https://interviews.televisionacademy.com/interviews/herschel-burke-gilbert.

6. Henry Mancini with Gene Lees, *Did They Mention the Music?* (New York: Cooper Square, 2001), 96.

7. *Ibid.*, 95–96.

8. United States Congress House Committee on Interstate and Foreign Commerce, *Investigation of Television Quiz Shows. Hearings before a Ssubcommittee of the Committee on Interstate and Foreign Commerce, House of Representatives, Eighty-Sixth Congress, First Session* (Washington: U.S. Government Printing Office, 1960), 624.

9. Mancini and Lees, *Did They Mention the Music?*, 97.

10. Duke Ellington, 1959 open-ended interview presented as a bonus track on the soundtrack album *Anatomy of a Murder* (Sony, 2009).

11. *Ibid.*

12. Scott Yanow, *Jazz on Film: The Complete Story of the Musicians and Music Onscreen* (New York: Backbeat, 2004), 142.

13. Matt Schudel, "Buddy Bregman, Gifted Hollywood Musical Arranger and Conductor, Dies at 86," *The Washington Post*, January 10, 2017, accessed Aug. 1, 2019, https://www.washingtonpost.com/local/obituaries/buddy-bregman-musical-arranger-of-ellas-first-song-book-albums-dies-at-86/2017/01/10/c399284a-d6b2-11e6-b8b2-cb5164beba6b_story.html.

14. Steve Ross, *Hollywood Left and Right: How Movie Stars Shaped American Politics* (Oxford: Oxford University Press, 2011), 206.

15. Gunther Schuller, *Musings: The Musical Words of Gunther Schuller* (Oxford: Oxford University Press, 1986), 114.

16. Letter to John Lewis from Robert Wise, March 11, 1959; Robert Wise Collection, Special Collections, USC Cinema and Television Library; as

quoted in David Butler's *Jazz Noir* (Westport, CT: Praeger, 2002), 152.

17. Eugene B. Bergmann, *Excelsior, You Fathead: The Art and Enigma of Jean Shepherd* (New York: Applause, 2005), 153–54.

18. "William J. Burns," fbi.gov, accessed Aug. 1, 2019, https://www.fbi.gov/history/directors/william-j-burns.

19. Selwyn Harris, booklet notes for *Des Femmes Disparaissent*, in the box set *French New Wave* (Jazz on Film, 2013), 31–32.

20. Robin D.G. Kelley, *Thelonious Monk Sessionography*, accessed Aug. 1, 2019, http://www.monkbook.com/sessionography/sessionography-1958-1962/.

21. Robin D.G. Kelley, *Thelonious Monk: The Life and Times of an American Original* (New York: Simon and Schuster, 2009), 269–71.

Chapter 4

1. *Man on the Beach*, Internet Movie Database, accessed Aug. 1, 2019, https://www.imdb.com/title/tt5024042/trivia?ref_=tt_ql_2.

2. John Williams, interviewed by Donald Macleod on BBC Radio 3's *Composer of the Week*, Jan. 14, 2013.

3. Jon Burlingame, *TV's Biggest Hits* (New York: Schirmer, 1996), 38.

4. Jeff Eldridge, booklet notes for the soundtrack album *Checkmate* (Film Score Monthly, 2006), 9.

5. Peter J. Levinson, *September in the Rain: The Life of Nelson Riddle* (New York: Billboard, 2001), 199.

6. "An Important Contributor to British Jazz," *The Scotsman*, 1999, accessed Aug. 1, 2019, http://www.jazzhouse.org/gone/lastpost2.php3?edit=940658024.

7. "Police Surgeon," theavengers.tv, accessed Aug. 1, 2019, http://theavengers.tv/police/history.htm.

8. Edwin Astley, quoted by Andrew Pixley in the booklet notes for the two-disc set *Danger Man: Original Soundtrack (B/W)* (Network, 2008), 3.

9. Tise Vahimagi, "The Danzigers," *BFI screen online*, accessed Aug. 1, 2019, http://www.screenonline.org.uk/people/id/773807/.

10. John Dankworth, *Jazz in Revolution* (London: Constable & Robinson, 1999), 154.

11. Guillaume Lagrée, "The Music of Breathless," *CitizenJazz*, Jan. 6, 2008, accessed Aug. 1, 2019, https://www.citizenjazz.com/La-musique-d-A-bout-de-souffle.html.

12. *Ibid.*

13. *Ibid.*

Chapter 5

1. Jake Rossen, "Wipe Out: When the BBC Kept Erasing Its Own History," *Mental Floss*, Aug. 8, 2017, accessed Aug. 2, 2019, http://mentalfloss.com/article/501607/wipe-out-when-bbc-kept-erasing-its-own-history.

2. A.H. Lawrence, *Duke Ellington and His World* (Abingdon-on-Thames, UK: Routledge, 2001), 357.

3. Ken Vail, *Duke's Diary* (Lanham, MD: Scarecrow, 2002), 161, 180.

4. Jonathan Etter, *Quinn Martin, Producer* (Jefferson, NC: McFarland, 2008), 27.

5. Richard Harland Smith, "The Gist," tcm.com, accessed Aug. 2, 2019, http://www.tcm.com/this-month/article/209790%7C0/The-Gist-Blast-of-Silence.html.

6. Allan Kozinn, "Meyer Kupferman, Composer in Many Forms, Is Dead at 77," *The New York Times*, Dec. 3, 2003, accessed Aug. 2, 2019, at https://www.nytimes.com/2003/12/03/arts/meyer-kupferman-composer-in-many-forms-is-dead-at-77.html.

7. Ira Gitler, liner notes for the soundtrack album *The Connection* (Blue Note, 1960).

8. Pat Dowell, "Shirley Clarke's Connection: Will It Click at Last?," npr.org, June 23, 2012, accessed Aug. 2, 2019, https://www.npr.org/2012/06/23/155513524/shirley-clarkes-connection-will-it-click-at-last.

9. "David Amram's Biography," accessed Aug. 2, 2019, at https://kyhote.com/davidamram/biography.php.

10. Derek Alger, "David Amram," *pif Magazine*, January 2008, accessed Aug. 2, 2019, at https://www.pifmagazine.com/2008/01/david-amram/.

11. David Amram, liner notes for the soundtrack album *The Young Savages* (Columbia, 1961).

12. David Amram, *Vibrations: A Memoir* (Abingdon, UK: Routledge, 2015), 377.

13. "Echo Four-Two," *Action TV*, accessed Aug. 2, 2019, http://www.startrader.co.uk/Action%20TV/guide60s/echo42.htm.

14. Richard McGinlay & Alan Hayes, *With Umbrella, Scotch and Cigarettes* (Hidden Tiger, 2014), 45–46.

15. *Ibid.*, 191–192.

16. Mike Gross, liner notes for the album *Manhattan Spiritual* (Palette, 1958).

17. Marc Myers, "Johnny Mandel," *jazzwax.com*, Oct. 24, 2008, accessed Aug. 2, 2019, https://www.jazzwax.com/2008/10/interview-joh-5.html.

Chapter 6

1. William Grimes, "John Barry Dies at 77; Composed for Bond Films," *The New York Times*, Jan. 31, 2011, accessed Aug. 3, 2019, https://www.nytimes.com/2011/02/01/movies/01barry.html?_r=1&scp=1&sq=john%20barry&st=cse.

2. John Caps, *Henry Mancini ... Reinventing Film Music* (Chicago: University of Illinois Press, 2012), 69.

3. Henry Mancini with Gene Lees, *Did They Mention the Music?* (New York: Cooper Square, 2001), 118.

4. Rich Kienzle, "The Guitarist Behind Chiller Theater: Al Caiola," [Pittsburgh] post-gazette.com, Nov. 22, 2016, accessed Aug. 3, 2019, http://communityvoices.post-gazette.com/arts-entertainment-

living/get-rhythm/item/40535-the-guitarist-behind-chiller-theater-al-caiola.

5. David Amram, *Vibrations: A Memoir* (Abingdon, UK: Routledge, 2015), 398.

6. Ibid., 399.

7. Marc Myers, "Mundell Lowe," *jazzwax.com*, Jan. 17, 2008, accessed Aug. 3, 2019, https://www.jazzwax.com/2008/01/mundell-lowe--3.html.

8. Jon Burlingame, *The Music of James Bond* (Oxford: Oxford University Press, 2012), 6–12.

9. Geoff Leonard, Pete Walker and Gareth Bramley, *John Barry: The Man with the Midas Touch* (Bristol, UK: Redcliffe, 2008), 80.

10. Burlingame, *The Music of James Bond*, 14.

11. "Biography," *Vic Flick: The Official Website*, accessed Aug. 3, 2019, http://vicflick.com.

12. Leonard, Walker and Bramley, *John Barry: The Man with the Midas Touch*, 79.

13. Burlingame, *The Music of James Bond*, 15.

14. John Barry, quoted in director John Cork's *The Bond Sound: The Music of 007* (2000), a bonus feature included in the "ultimate edition" DVD reissue of *A View to a Kill* (MGM, 2006).

15. Booklet notes for the CD reissue of the soundtrack album *Knife in the Water* (él, 2012), 3–4.

Chapter 7

1. Jon Burlingame, "Pete Rugolo and *The Fugitive*," liner notes for the soundtrack album *The Fugitive: Original Television Series Soundtrack Music*, 2000.

2. "Fugitive Gets Huge Rating in Last Show," *Chicago Tribune*, Aug. 31, 1967, C-19.

3. Ed Robertson, *The Fugitive Recaptured* (Berkeley: Pomegranate, 1993), 36–37.

4. Ibid., 37.

5. Jon Burlingame, "*The Fugitive* Music Debacle: Why It Happened," The Film Music Society website, Aug. 15, 2008, accessed Aug. 4, 2019, http://www.filmmusicsociety.org/news_events/features/2008/081508.html.

6. Herschel Burke Gilbert, video interview by Jon Burlingame on April 30, 2001, accessed Aug. 1, 2019, https://interviews.televisionacademy.com/interviews/herschel-burke-gilbert.

7. David McGee, "I'm a Romantic Guy," *The Bluegrass Special*, January 2011, accessed Aug. 4, 2019, http://www.thebluegrassspecial.com/archive/2011/jan2011/henry-mancini-blake-edwards.php.

8. Jon Burlingame, "Teaching an Old Cat a New Song," *The New York Times*, June 12, 2005, accessed Aug. 4, 2019, https://www.nytimes.com/2005/06/12/movies/teaching-an-old-cat-a-new-song.html.

9. John Caps, *Henry Mancini … Reinventing Film Music* (Chicago: University of Illinois Press, 2012), 92–93.

10. "Pop Spotlight: *Charade*," *Billboard*, Dec. 21, 1963, 25.

11. Murray Schumach, "Low-Budget Film Planned for Fox," *The New York Times*, Nov. 5, 1962, 37.

12. *The Cool World*, Playbill Broadway Database, accessed Aug. 4, 2019, http://www.playbill.com/production/the-cool-world-eugene-oneill-theatre-vault-0000004744.

13. "Complete National Film Registry Listing," U.S. Library of Congress website, accessed Aug. 4, 2019, https://www.loc.gov/programs/national-film-preservation-board/film-registry/complete-national-film-registry-listing/.

14. Dizzy Gillespie, *To Be, Or Not—to Bop* (New York: Doubleday, 1979), 462.

15. Robert Hoshowsky, "The Gstaad Memorandum: John Barry," *Film Score Monthly*, Nov. 1996, 13.

16. Jon Burlingame, *The Music of James Bond* (Oxford: Oxford University Press, 2012), 28.

17. Ibid., 33.

18. David Arnold, quoted in director John Cork's *The Bond Sound: The Music of 007* (2000), a bonus feature included in the "ultimate edition" DVD reissue of *A View to a Kill* (MGM, 2006).

19. David Picker, Ibid.

Chapter 8

1. Peter J. Levinson, *September in the Rain: The Life of Nelson Riddle* (New York: Billboard, 2001), 215.

2. "Pop Special Merit: *The Reporter*," *Billboard*, Nov. 28, 1964, 30.

3. Dave Brubeck, liner notes for the album *Jazz Impressions of New York* (Columbia, 1965).

4. Dave Brubeck, liner notes for the album *Jazz Impressions of Japan* (Columbia, 1964).

5. Jon Burlingame, *TV's Biggest Hits* (New York: Schirmer, 1996), 201.

6. Jon Burlingame, booklet notes for the CD box set *The Cincinnati Kid: Lalo Schifrin Film Scores Vol. 1 (1964–1968)* (Film Score Monthly, 2010), 8.

7. Gerald Fried, video interview by Karen Herman on June 23, 2003, accessed Aug. 4, 2019, https://interviews.televisionacademy.com/interviews/gerald-fried.

8. Michael McKenna, *The ABC Movie of the Week: Big Movies for the Small Screen* (Lanham, MD: Scarecrow, 2013), xviii.

9. Sidney Lumet, *Making Movies* (New York: Knopf, 1995), 175.

10. Ibid., 176.

11. Biography, Quincy Jones Productions website, accessed Aug. 4, 2019, http://www.quincyjones.com/about.

12. Paul de Barros, "Reissuing *The Pawnbroker* and *The Deadly Affair*," liner notes for the digital soundtrack album, 1996.

13. Lumet, *Making Movies*, 176.

14. Quincy Jones, *Q: The Autobiography of Quincy Jones* (New York: Doubleday, 2001), 178.

15. Andrew Pixley, booklet notes for the five-disc set *Danger Man: Original Soundtrack (Color)* (Network, 2008), 3–5.

16. Jon Astley, quoted in director Geoff Wonfor's

documentary film, *Astley's Way*, broadcast by BBC2 on Jan. 1, 2001.
   17. Jon Burlingame, *The Music of James Bond* (Oxford: Oxford University Press, 2012), 35.
   18. Eddi Fiegel, *John Barry: A Sixties Theme* (London: Constable, 1998), 136.
   19. Burlingame, *The Music of James Bond*, 41.
   20. Fiegel, *John Barry: A Sixties Theme*, 139.
   21. Lalo Schifrin, *Music Composition for Film and Television* (Boston: Berklee, 2011), 112.
   22. Lalo Schifrin, *Mission Impossible: My Life in Music* (Lanham, MD: Scarecrow, 2008), 55.

Chapter 9

   1. James Chapman, *Licence to Thrill: A Cultural History of the James Bond Films* (New York: Columbia University Press, 2000), 120.
   2. Lukas Kendall, "Tennis and Trouble," booklet notes for the soundtrack album *I Spy: Original Television Soundtrack* (Film Score Monthly, 2002), 5.
   3. Earle Hagen, video interview by Jon Burlingame on Nov. 17, 1997, accessed Aug. 4, 2019, https://interviews.televisionacademy.com/interviews/earle-hagen.
   4. *Ibid*.
   5. Earle Hagen, "Earle Hagen on *I Spy*," The Best of All Worlds: Official Earle Hagen Website, accessed Aug. 4, 2019, http://www.earlehagen.net/hagenonispy.htm.
   6. Jon Burlingame, *TV's Biggest Hits* (New York: Schirmer, 1996), 204.
   7. Hagen, video interview, Nov. 17, 1997.
   8. Hagen, http://www.earlehagen.net/hagenonispy.htm.
   9. Susan E. Kesler, *The Wild Wild West: The Series* (Downey, CA: Arnett, 1988), 16.
   10. Jon Burlingame, "The Wild Wild Music of The Wild Wild West," booklet notes for the four-disc set, *The Wild Wild West: Music from the Television Series* (La-La Land, 2017), 33.
   11. Lalo Schifrin, *Mission Impossible: My Life in Music* (Lanham, MD: Scarecrow, 2008), 122–23.
   12. Bob Kenselaar, "Stan Getz: I'm Gonna Blow the Walls Down," *allaboutjazz.com*, March 20, 2012, accessed Aug. 5, 2019, https://www.allaboutjazz.com/stan-getz-im-gonna-blow-the-walls-down-stan-getz-by-bob-kenselaar.php?page=1.
   13. John Wriggle, "Eddie Sauter's Film Score for Mickey One," *American Music Review*, Spring 2012, accessed Aug. 5, 2019, http://www.brooklyn.cuny.edu/web/academics/centers/hitchcock/publications/amr/v41-2/wriggle.php.
   14. Quincy Jones, *Q: The Autobiography of Quincy Jones* (New York: Doubleday, 2001), 188.
   15. Associated Press, "Shorty Rogers, 70, Jazz Trumpeter," *The New York Times*, Nov. 9, 1994, accessed Aug. 5, 2019, https://www.nytimes.com/1994/11/09/obituaries/shorty-rogers-70-jazz-trumpeter.html.
   16. Laurie Johnson, "The Avengers Series and Its Music," booklet notes for the three-disc set *The Music of Laurie Johnson: The Avengers* (Edsel, 2007), 4.
   17. Laurie Johnson, *Noises in the Head* (New Romney, UK: Bank House, 2003), 108–09.
   18. Eddi Fiegel, *John Barry: A Sixties Theme* (London: Constable, 1998), 187.
   19. Lalo Schifrin, quoted in Lukas Kendall's booklet notes for the digital reissue of the soundtrack album *The Liquidator* (Film Score Monthly, 2006), 7.
   20. *Ibid*., 4.
   21. Geoff Leonard, Pete Walker and Gareth Bramley, *John Barry: The Man with the Midas Touch* (Bristol, UK: Redcliffe, 2008), 124.
   22. Fiegel, *John Barry: A Sixties Theme*, 170.
   23. David Meeker, "La Métamorphose Des Cloportes," *Jazz on Screen*, accessed Aug. 5, 2019, https://www.loc.gov/item/jots.200017657.

Chapter 10

   1. Forrest Patten, "Interview with Neal Hefti," *Journal into Melody*, March 2006, 38–42, accessed Aug. 6, 2019, http://www.nealhefti.com.
   2. Jon Burlingame, "Inside Jericho," booklet notes for the soundtrack album *Jericho: Original Television Soundtrack* (Film Score Monthly, 2005), 6.
   3. Jon Burlingame, "Impossible Missions Force," booklet notes for the six-disc box set *Mission: Impossible—The Television Scores* (La-La Land, 2015), 8.
   4. *Ibid*.
   5. *Ibid*., 9.
   6. Lalo Schifrin, video interview by Jon Burlingame on Oct. 3, 2008, accessed Aug. 6, 2019, http://www.emmytvlegends.org/interviews/people/lalo-schifrin#.
   7. Lalo Schifrin, quoted in director Pascale Cuenot's 2012 documentary, *In the Tracks of Lalo Schifrin*.
   8. Bruce Geller, liner notes for the soundtrack album *Music from Mission: Impossible* (Dot, 1967).
   9. Patrick J. White, *The Complete Mission: Impossible Dossier* (London: Boxtree, 1996), 50.
   10. Aljean Harmetz, "Writers Ratify Contract, Ending Longest Strike," *The New York Times*, Aug. 8, 1988, accessed Aug. 6, 2019, https://www.nytimes.com/1988/08/08/movies/writers-ratify-contract-ending-longest-strike.html.
   11. Mike Matessino, "Genius Rising: John Williams and Twentieth Century-Fox," booklet notes for the soundtrack album *How to Steal a Million* (Intrada, 2008), 14.
   12. Derek Elley, "John Williams," *Films and Filming*, July/August 1978, accessed Aug. 6, 2019, http://www.jw-collection.de/misc/interview/elley.htm.
   13. Jon Burlingame, booklet notes for the soundtrack album *Assault on a Queen: Music from the Motion Picture* (Dragon's Domain, 2016), 4.
   14. A.H. Lawrence, *Duke Ellington and His World* (Abingdon-on-Thames, UK: Routledge, 2001), 368.
   15. Larry Langman, *Destination Hollywood: The Influence of Europeans on American Filmmaking* (Jefferson, NC: McFarland, 1999), 106.

16. James Garner and Jon Winokur, *The Garner Files: A Memoir* (New York: Simon & Schuster, 2011), 256.
17. Eddi Fiegel, *John Barry: A Sixties Theme* (London: Constable, 1998), 175.
18. Sheridan Morley, *The Other Side of the Moon: The Life of David Niven* (New York: Harper & Row, 1985), 235.
19. Peter O'Donnell, "Modesty, The Beginning," *modestyblaiseltd.com*, accessed Aug. 6, 2019, https://modestyblaiseltd.com/Modesty-The-Beginning.
20. David Fricke, booklet notes for the soundtrack album *Blow-Up: Original Motion Picture Soundtrack* (Rhino, 1996), 15.
21. *Ibid.*, 12.

The Taking of Pelham One Two Three (Retrograde/Film Score Monthly, 1996).
19. Eddi Fiegel, *John Barry: A Sixties Theme* (London: Constable, 1998), 202.
20. Jon Burlingame, *The Music of James Bond* (Oxford: Oxford University Press, 2012), 66.
21. Richard Panek, "*Casino Royale* Is an LP Bond with a Gilt Edge," *The New York Times*, July 28, 1991, accessed Aug. 7, 2019, https://www.nytimes.com/1991/07/28/movies/casino-royale-is-an-lp-bond-with-a-gilt-edge.html?pagewanted=all.
22. Don Storey, "Hunter," *Classic Australian Television*, 2013, accessed Aug. 7, 2019, https://www.classicaustraliantv.com/Hunter.htm.
23. *Ibid.*
24. Neil Connery, interviewed by Brian Smith in "Bond of Brothers," *Cinema Retro*, September 2008.

Chapter 11

1. Quincy Jones, video interview by Jon Burlingame on Nov. 13, 2002, accessed Aug. 7, 2019, https://interviews.televisionacademy.com/interviews/quincy-jones#.
2. Quincy Jones, *Q: The Autobiography of Quincy Jones* (New York: Doubleday, 2001), 193–94.
3. Clarence Bernard Henry, *Quincy Jones: His Life in Music* (Jackson: University Press of Mississippi, 2013), 103.
4. Jones, video interview, 2002.
5. *Ibid.*
6. *Ibid.*
7. Neely Tucker, "Mannix Was the Man," *The Washington Post*, Nov. 18, 2007, accessed Aug. 7, 2019, http://www.washingtonpost.com/wp-dyn/content/article/2007/11/16/AR2007111600181.html?hpid=features1&hpv=national.
8. Jon Burlingame, booklet notes for the album *Mannix Soundtrack* (Aleph, 1999), 2.
9. Bruce Geller, liner notes for the soundtrack album *Mannix: Themes from the Original Score of the Paramount Television Show* (Paramount, 1968).
10. Burlingame, *Mannix Soundtrack*, 1999.
11. Lalo Schifrin, video interview by Jon Burlingame on Oct. 3, 2008, accessed Aug. 6, 2019, http://www.emmytvlegends.org/interviews/people/lalo-schifrin#.
12. Sam Wasson, *A Splurch in the Kisser: The Movies of Blake Edwards* (Middletown, CT: Wesleyan University Press, 2009), 121.
13. Lalo Schifrin, quoted in Pascale Cuenot's 2012 documentary, *In the Tracks of Lalo Schifrin*.
14. Stuart Rosenberg, liner notes for the digital reissue of the album *Cool Hand Luke: Original Soundtrack Recording* (Aleph, 2001).
15. Doug Adams, "Schifrin Rushes In," *Film Score Monthly*, September 1998, 21.
16. Quincy Jones, *Q: The Autobiography of Quincy Jones* (New York: Doubleday, 2001), 189.
17. Johnny Mandel, video interview by Linda Danly on Aug. 1, 2007, accessed Aug. 6, 2019, https://www.filmmusicfoundation.org/interviews.html.
18. Doug Adams, booklet notes for the album

Chapter 12

1. Dave Grusin, video interview by Jon Burlingame on March 22, 2011, accessed Aug. 7, 2019, https://www.filmmusicfoundation.org/interviews.html.
2. Jon Burlingame, *TV's Biggest Hits* (New York: Schirmer, 1996), 151.
3. Jon Burlingame, booklet notes for the soundtrack album *Way… Way Out* (Intrada, 2008), 6.
4. Lalo Schifrin, *Mission Impossible: My Life in Music* (Lanham, MD: Scarecrow, 2008), 114.
5. Earle Hagen, video interview by Jon Burlingame on Nov. 17, 1997, accessed Aug. 7, 2019, https://interviews.televisionacademy.com/interviews/earle-hagen.
6. *Ibid.*
7. *Ibid.*
8. Jon Burlingame, "Morton Stevens Revisited," Film Music Society, Aug. 20, 2010, accessed Aug. 7, 2019, http://www.filmmusicsociety.org/news_events/features/2010/082010.html?isArchive=082010.
9. Burlingame, *TV's Biggest Hits*, 50.
10. Teri Okita, "A Battle of the Bands over the Hawaii Five-O Theme Song," Hawaii News Now, Sept. 2, 2010, accessed Aug. 7, 2019, https://www.hawaiinewsnow.com/story/13094750/a-battle-of-the-bands-over-the-hawaii-five-o-theme-song/.
11. Burlingame, "Morton Stevens Revisited," 2010.
12. Stéphane Lerouge, "Michel Legrand: The Windmills of His Mind," booklet notes for the digital album *The Thomas Crown Affair: Expanded Original MGM Motion Picture Soundtrack* (Quartet, 2014), 6–9.
13. *Ibid.*, 9.

Chapter 13

1. Andrew Pixley, booklet notes for the three-disc set *Department S: Original Soundtrack* (Network, 2008), 3.

2. Jon Burlingame, *The Music of James Bond* (Oxford: Oxford University Press, 2012), 84–85.

3. Eddi Fiegel, *John Barry: A Sixties Theme* (London: Constable, 1998), 219.

Chapter 14

1. Jonathan Etter, *Quinn Martin, Producer* (Jefferson, NC: McFarland, 2008), 113.

2. Doug Adams, booklet notes for the soundtrack album *In the Heat of the Night/They Call Me MISTER Tibbs* (Rykodisc, 1995), 5.

3. "Galt MacDermot: Biography," accessed Aug. 7, 2019, http://www.galtmacdermot.com/bio.html.

4. Éric Demarsan quoted in an interview by Stéphane Lerouge, included in the booklet notes for the soundtrack album *Le Cercle Rouge* (Universal Music Jazz France/EmArcy, 2000), 9.

5. *Ibid.*

Bibliography

Books

Amram, David. *Vibrations: A Memoir.* Abingdon, UK: Routledge, 2015.

Bergmann, Eugene B. *Excelsior, You Fathead: The Art and Enigma of Jean Shepherd.* New York: Applause, 2005.

Brooks, Tim, and Earle Marsh. *The Complete Directory to Prime-Time Network and Cable TV Shows: Ninth Edition.* New York: Ballantine, 2007.

Burlingame, Jon. *The Music of James Bond.* Oxford: Oxford University Press, 2012.

Burlingame, Jon. *TV's Biggest Hits.* New York: Schirmer, 1996.

Butler, David. *Jazz Noir.* Westport, CT: Praeger, 2002.

Caps, John. *Henry Mancini ... Reinventing Film Music.* Chicago: University of Illinois Press, 2012.

Chapman, James. *Licence to Thrill: A Cultural History of the James Bond Films.* New York: Columbia University Press, 2000.

Dankworth, John. *Jazz in Revolution.* London: Constable & Robinson, 1999.

Davis, Miles, and Quincy Troupe. *Miles.* New York: Simon & Schuster, 1989.

Etter, Jonathan. *Quinn Martin, Producer.* Jefferson, NC: McFarland, 2008.

Fiegel, Eddi. *John Barry: A Sixties Theme.* London: Constable, 1998.

Garner, James, and Jon Winokur. *The Garner Files: A Memoir.* New York: Simon & Schuster, 2011.

Gillespie, Dizzy. *To Be, Or Not—to Bop.* New York: Doubleday, 1979.

Hayde, Michael J. *My Name's Friday: The Unauthorized but True Story of Dragnet and the Films.* Nashville: Cumberland House, 2001.

Henry, Clarence Bernard. *Quincy Jones: His Life in Music.* Jackson: University Press of Mississippi, 2013.

Johnson, Laurie. *Noises in the Head.* New Romney, UK: Bank House, 2003.

Jones, Quincy. *Q: The Autobiography of Quincy Jones.* New York: Doubleday, 2001.

Kelley, Robin D.G. *Thelonious Monk: The Life and Times of an American Original.* New York: Simon & Schuster, 2009.

Kesler, Susan E. *The Wild Wild West: The Series.* Downey, CA: Arnett, 1988.

Langman, Larry. *Destination Hollywood: The Influence of Europeans on American Filmmaking.* Jefferson, NC: McFarland, 1999.

Lawrence, A.H. *Duke Ellington and His World.* Abingdon-on-Thames, UK: Routledge, 2001.

Lees, Gene. *Friends Along the Way: A Journey Through Jazz.* New Haven: Yale University Press, 2003.

Leonard, Geoff, Pete Walker and Gareth Bramley. *John Barry: The Man with the Midas Touch.* Bristol, UK: Redcliffe, 2008.

Levinson, Peter J. *September in the Rain: The Life of Nelson Riddle.* New York: Billboard, 2001.

Lumet, Sidney. *Making Movies.* New York: Knopf, 1995.

Mancini, Henry, and Gene Lees. *Did They Mention the Music?* New York: Cooper Square, 2001.

McGinlay, Richard, and Alan Hayes. *With Umbrella, Scotch and Cigarettes.* Hidden Tiger, 2014.

Morley, Sheridan. *The Other Side of the Moon: The Life of David Niven.* New York: Harper & Row, 1985.

O'Shea, Kathleen A. *Women and the Death Penalty in the United States, 1900–1998.* Santa Barbara, CA: Praeger, 1999.

Reig, Teddy, and Edward Berger. *Reminiscing in Tempo.* Lanham, MD: Scarecrow, 1995.

Robertson, Ed. *The Fugitive Recaptured.* Berkeley: Pomegranate, 1993.

Ross, Steve. *Hollywood Left and Right: How Movie Stars Shaped American Politics.* Oxford: Oxford University Press, 2011.

Russell, Mark, and James Edward Young. *Film Music.* Waltham, MA: Focal, 2000.

Schifrin, Lalo. *Mission Impossible: My Life in Music.* Lanham, MD: Scarecrow, 2008.

Schifrin, Lalo. *Music Composition for Film and Television.* Boston: Berklee, 2011.

Schuller, Gunther. *Musings: The Musical Words of Gunther Schuller.* Oxford: Oxford University Press, 1986.

United States Congress House Committee on Interstate and Foreign Commerce. *Investigation of Television Quiz Shows. Hearings before a Subcommittee of the Committee on Interstate and Foreign Commerce, House of Representatives, Eighty-Sixth Congress, First Session.* Washington: U.S. Government Printing Office, 1960.

Vail, Ken. *Duke's Diary.* Lanham, MD: Scarecrow, 2002.

Wasson, Sam. *A Splurch in the Kisser: The Movies of Blake Edwards.* Middletown, CT: Wesleyan University Press, 2009.

White, Patrick J. *The Complete Mission: Impossible Dossier.* London: Boxtree, 1996.

Yanow, Scott. *Jazz on Film: The Complete Story of the Musicians and Music Onscreen.* New York: Backbeat, 2004.

Interviews

Fried, Gerald. Video interview by Karen Herman on June 23, 2003. https://interviews.televisionacademy.com/interviews/gerald-fried.

Gilbert, Herschel Burke. Video interview by Jon Burlingame on April 30, 2001. https://interviews.televisionacademy.com/interviews/herschel-burke-gilbert.

Grusin, Dave. Video interview by Jon Burlingame on March 22, 2011. https://www.filmmusicfoundation.org/interviews.html.

Hagen, Earle. Video interview by Jon Burlingame on November 17, 1997. https://interviews.televisionacademy.com/interviews/earle-hagen.

Jones, Quincy. Video interview by Jon Burlingame on November 13, 2002. https://interviews.televisionacademy.com/interviews/quincy-jones#.

Mandel, Johnny. Video interview by Linda Danly on August 1, 2007. https://www.filmmusicfoundation.org/interviews.html.

Schifrin, Lalo. Video interview by Jon Burlingame on October 3, 2008. http://www.emmytvlegends.org/interviews/people/lalo-schifrin#.

Steiner, Fred. Video interview by Karen Herman on June 26, 2003. http://www.emmytvlegends.org/interviews/people/fred-steiner.

Williams, John. Interviewed by Donald Macleod on BBC Radio 3's *Composer of the Week,* January 14, 2013.

Index

Numbers in ***bold italics*** indicate pages with illustrations

À bout de souffle 87
Abbott, John 177
Acker, Sharon 212
Adams, Beverly 205, 242
Adams, Bob 221
Adams, Don 148
Adams, Nick 153
Adams, Tom 158, 189-190
Adderley, Cannonball 202
After the Fox 198-199
Agent 505: Todesfalle Beirut 195, 266
Agent for H.A.R.M. 183-184
Agent Secret FX-18 142
Agente X1-7 Operazione Oceano 165
Albert, Herman 16
Albert, Marvin H. 208
Albertini, Adalberto 142
Albright, Lola 36, 130, 141, 282
Alderton, John 244
Aldrich, Robert 24-25
Aldridge, Michael 154, 213, 241
Alexander, Ben 170
Alexander, Jeff 72, 110, 148
The Alfred Hitchcock Hour 101-102
Alfred Hitchcock Presents 101
Algren, Nelson 26
Allégret, Catherine 163
Allen, Marc 137
Allen, Steve 232-233
Allen, Woody 218
Almeida, Laurindo 44, 58, 60, 132, 148, 266, 280, 288
Alpert, Herb 184, 206, 218, 221, 269
Alton, John 23
Ambler, Eric 74
The Ambushers 204-205
Amram, David ***95***-97, 104, 278
Amsterdam, Morey 81
Anatomy of a Murder ***27***, 38, 62-63, 89, 266-267
Anderson, Barbara 201
Anderson, Cat 63, 266-267
Anderson, John 260
Anderson, Michael 189
Anderson, Warner 17
Andress, Ursula 109, 218
Andrews, Edward 96
Andrews, Harry 220
Andrews, Tige 228

Anka, Paul 76
Ann-Margret 149-150, 158, 182
Anthony, Ray 17, 19, 36-37
Antonioni, Michelangelo 193-194
Any Number Can Win see *Mélodie en sous-sol*
The Applejacks 57
Appleyard, Peter 80
Arabesque 176, 267
Archer, Lew 184
Arden, Gisella 195
Arkin, Alan 245
Armendariz, Pedro 126
Armstrong, Louis 20-22
Arne, Peter 187
Arnold, David 127
Arnoul, Françoise 49
The Art of Noise 37
Ary, Jacques 196
Ascenseur pour l'échafaud 50-51, 267
Aslan, Grégoire 86, 224
Asner, Edward 110, 207, 260
The Asphalt Jungle (1950 movie) 19, 267
The Asphalt Jungle (1961 TV series) 89-90, 99, 267
Assault on a Queen 178-179, 267
Assignment K 246, 267
Astley, Edwin 7, 66, 83-85, 107-108, 138-139, 186-187, 241, 252, 268-269, 271, 284
Atterbury, Malcolm 28
Audace colpo dei soliti ignoti 70-71, 143, 267
Auger, Claudine 158
Auld, Georgie 60
Auric, Georges 30
Avalon, Frankie 205
The Avengers (1961) 83, 97-98
The Avengers (1962) 106-107, 146
The Avengers (1965) 146, 155-157, 187
The Avengers (1968) 240-241, 250-251, 267-268
Ayala, Fernando 52
Aznavour, Charles 164

Baby Doll 29, 268
Bacall, Lauren 130, 184
Badel, Alan 176
Bailly, Michèle 67

Bain, Barbara 39, 173
Bain, Bob 79, 103, 176, 180, 208, 269-273, 280, 282, 284, 285, 287
The Baja Marimba Band 120
Baker, Carroll 29
Baker, Chet 9, 71, 142, 267, 275, 286
Baker, Diane 122, 152
Baker, John 188
Baker, Stanley 85, 220
Balaban, Burt 81
Ball, John 210
Balsam, Martin 258
Banks, Martin 261
Banner, Jill 258
Barclay, Eddie 31, 142
Bardem, Rafael 165
Barker, Warren 34, 39, 40, 56, 60, 90, 146, 285
Barney Blake, Police Reporter 15
Barnum, H.B. 134
The Baron 186-187, 268
Baron, Allen 91-92
Barretto, Ray 158
Barri, Steve 139
Barron, Keith 213
Barron, Kenny 124, 270
Barry, Gene 115, 227
Barry, John 2, 5, 87, 101, 108-110, 120, 125-127, 139-140, 157, 159-161, 165, 179, 187-189, 195, 215-217, 219, 223, 232, 242, 253, 263, 272, 275, 288
Basie, Count 34, 37-38, 46, 61, 82, 90, 110, 136, 158, 182, 207, 212
Bass, Saul ***27***, 28, 62, 81
Bassey, Shirley 139-140, 157, 160, 165, 190, 217, 242, 273, 277
Bastedo, Alexandra 241
Bate, Anthony 241
Bates, Michael 242
Batman 133, 167-169, 196, 268
Baxter, Les 2, 104
Bay, Francis 60
Bazelon, Irwin 6
Beat Girl 108-109
Beatty, Warren 152, 191, 193
Beaver, Paul 202, 270, 282, 285, 286
Beck, John 261
Beeson, Paul 48-49
Belafonte, Harry 64

Index

Bell, Aaron 37, 123, 267
Bell, Madeline 242
Bellaver, Harry 57
Bellson, Louis 118, 267
Belmondo, Jean-Paul 87, 111
Benedek, Laslo 22
Beneke, Tex 59
Bennett, Tony 237
Beregi, Oscar, Jr. 205
Berger, Senta 189
Berghofer, Chuck 76, 270
Bernardi, Herschel 36
Bernhart, Milt 22, 27, 37, 267, 269, 270, 274, 277, 278, 282-284, 286, 287, 289
Bernstein, Elmer 7, 26-28, 41, **42**, 55, 182, 278, 286
Bernstein, Leonard 45, 94-95, 211
Bersaglio Mobile 224-225
Berthier, Jacques 68
Bertin, Yori 51
Bezzerides, A.I. 25
Bianchi, Daniela 126, 197, 223
Bianchi, Eleanora 165
Big Breadwinner Hog 251
Big Deal on Madonna Street see *I soliti ignoti*
The Big Knife 25-26
The Big Sleep 8, 258
Bigard, Barney 20
Bikel, Theodore 262
Billboard 12, 15, 17, 28, 36, 37, 40, 58, 60, 79, 80, 110, 119, 120, 128, 130, 134, 139-141, **151**, 158, 174, 175, **216**-218, 230, 248, 253, 268, 269, 272, 273, 275, 278-282, 284, 285, 287, 289
Billion Dollar Brain 189
Binder, Maurice 39, 109, 120, 176, 191, 197, 253
Biraud, Maurice 164
Birgel, Willy 195
Bisacco, Roberto 256
Bishop, Joey 81, 209
Bisset, Jacqueline 221, 234, 236
Bivona, Gus 61
Black, Don 157
Blackboard Jungle 22, 28
Blackman, Honor 106, 146, **156**
Blackwell, Charles 253, 255
Blain, Estella 68
Blake, Howard 191, 240, 268, 276
Blake, Jean 80
Blake, Robert 211
Blakey, Art 68-70, 272, 277
Blanc, Erika 224
Blanchard, Terence 120
Blast of Silence 91-92
Blettery, Maurice 30
Blindfold 175-176
Blocker, Dan 235-236
Blow-Up 193-194, 268
Blue Light 171-172
Bob Hope Presents the Chrysler Theatre 117-118, 229
Bob le Flambeur 30-31
Boccardo, Delia 245, 256
Boccia, Tanio 165

Bochner, Lloyd 76, 236
Bódalo, José 198
Bodner, Phil 80, 274, 285
Boehm, Karl 183
Bogarde, Dirk 191, 243
Bogle, Bob 231
Bolkan, Florinda 256
Bond, James 2, 5, 6, 39, 72, 108-110, 113, 125-127, 129, 131, 139-140, 142, 144, 157-158, 159-160, 165, 172, 179, 215-218, 223, 253
Bond, Jimmy 218
Bond, Julian 83
Bonfá, Luiz 152
Bongusto, Alfredo "Fred" 256, 271
Bonuglia, Maurizio 256
Boone, Pat 122-123
Boorman, John 212
Borgnine, Ernest 237
Boschero, Dominique 166
Boschi, Marcello 71, 267, 286
Bosetti, Giulio 197
Bosic, Andrea 196
Boswell, Connee 54
Bouchet, Barbara 183
Boulting, Ingrid 221
Bourbon Street Beat 55-56, 268
Bourvil, André 263
Boyd, Stephen 246
Boyer, Charles 18, 129
Boyer, Jo 31
Braddock 228, 268
Bradford, Richard 214
Brando, Marlon 20, 22, 73
Bray, Robert 43
Breathless see *À bout de souffle*
Bregman, Buddy 64
Brennan, Walter 209
Bricusse, Leslie 139, 157
Brisbois, Bud 122, 268-269, 276
Britt, May 81, 280
Brody, Merrill S. 91
Brolin, James 221
Brooks, Richard 211
Brooks, Tina 93, 270
Broughton, Bruce 231
Brown, Fredric 18, 19, 45
Brown, Jim 237-238
Brown, Les 37, 117
Brown, Ray 118, 210, 240, 269, 270, 273, 275, 282, 286, 287, 289
Browne, Roger 194
Brubeck, Dave 111, 130-131, 245, 279
Brynner, Yul 219
Buckner, Teddy 135
Budd, Roy 213
Budwig, Monty 36, 282
Bullet to Beijing 189
Bullitt 141, 234-**235**, 268-269
Bunker, Larry 37, 132, 269, 270, 272-274, 278-280, 282, 286, 287, 289
Buono, Victor 209
Burke, Alfred 154
Burke, Paul 57
Burke's Law 115-116, 146, 269
Burnett, W.R. 19, 89

Burns, Ralph 227
Burns, William J. 66
Burr, Raymond 33-34, 201-202
Bushkin, Joe 73
Byrd, Donald 61
The Byrds 248
Byrnes, Edd 40

Caan, James 101
Cabot, Sebastian 75
Cacavas, John 202, 231
Caccia alla volpe see *After the Fox*
Cage, John 136
Cahn, Edward L. 64
Cahn, Sammy 37, 81, 122, 158
Caiano, Mario 197
Caine, Michael 160, 177, 188-189, 255
Cain's Hundred 110-111
Caiola, Al 2, 16, 103, 116, 140, 168
Call for the Dead 219
Call Mr. D. see *Richard Diamond, Private Detective*
Calvert, Eddie 125, 273
Camacho, Corinne 249
Cambridge, Godfrey 206, 260
Camden, Joan 19
Campbell, Glen 110, 275
Campbell, Royce 119
Candelli, Stelio 187
Candoli, Conte 36, 76, 266, 267, 278, 281, 289
Candoli, Pete 22, 27, 37, 55, 60, 61, 270-274, 277-279, 282, 283, 286, 287
Canning, Victor 205
The Cape Town Affair 221
Capote, Truman 211
Capp, Frank 37
Caprioli, Vittorio 225
Capuano, Giosy 224
Capuano, Mario 224
Cardiff, Jack 159
Cardinale, Claudia 51, 175
Carey, Philip 45, 56-57
Cargill, Patrick 98, 245
Carlyle, Richard 16
Carmel, Roger C. 102
Carney, Art 130
Carotenuto, Memmo 51
Carpenter, Pete 38, 277
Carpi, Fiorenzo 225
Carricart, Robert 172
Carson, Johnny 5
Carter, Benny 20, 38, 102, 118, 135, 201, 202, 227, **259**, 277
Carter, Ron 93, 268
The Case of the Dangerous Robin 79-80
The Cases of Eddie Drake 12-13, 17
The Cases of Mr. Ace 12
Casey, Jack "Flashgun" 16
Casino Royale (1967) 217-218
Cassavetes, John 28, 55, 65-66
Castle, Peggie 23
Cathcart, Dick 26, 54, 281
Celi, Adolfo 223, 256
Centenero, Ramón 142

Index

Le Cercle Rouge 263-264, 269
Cerval, Claude 142
The Challengers 134
Champ, Des 217, 227
The Champions 241, 269
Chandler, Raymond 15, 18, 33, 40, 56, 73, 91, 154, 184, 235, 248-249
Chaney, Jan 43
Chapman, Robin 154
Chappell, Herbert 158, 277
Charisse, Cyd 182
Charles, Ray 136, 210, 270, 275
Chayefsky, Paddy 18
The Cheaters 85
Checkmate 74-76, 269-270
Chevallier, Christian 67, 272
Chevron Hall of Stars 32
Childers, Buddy 61, 275, 278, 282, 286, 289
Chinatown 236
Christy 223, 280
The Cincinnati Kid 150-**151**, 270
Ciorciolini, Marcello 224
City of Fear 63-64, 270
Clanton, Hampton 123
Clare, Kenny 86, 271
Clark, Ken 142, 224, 245
Clark, Susan 234
Clarke, Kenny 50, 70, 267, 287
Clarke, Shirley 92, 123-124
Clayton, Adam 175
The Clee-Shays 134
Cleveland, Jimmy 61, 94, 274, 283, 285, 289
Clune, Peter 91
Cobb, Lee J. 179, 246
Coburn, James 110, 120, 179, **181**, 195, 204, 206, 244
Cochran, Steve 23
Cole, Buddy 59, 280
Cole, Cozy **21**
Cole, Dennis 170
Cole, Eddie 55-56
Cole, Michael 228
Cole, Nat King 25, 56, 57
Collins, Joan 82
Collins, Rudy 124, 270
Collinson, Peter **254**, 255
Colombier, Michel 142, 266
Comfort, Mady 25
The Commissioner 237
Compartiment Tueurs 163-164, 270
Comstock, Frank 60, 178-179, 201
Concrete Jungle see *The Criminal*
Condon, Richard 103-104
The Connection 92-93
Connery, Neil 223
Connery, Sean 6, 109, 113, 125, 139
Connors, Mike 54, 194, 202-203
Conrad, Robert 56, 147-148, 153
Constant, Marius 72
Constantine, Eddie 162
Conte, Richard 178
Conti, Bill 240
Converse, Frank 200
Coogan's Bluff 233-234, 270
Cook, Peter 242
Cook, Willie 89, 267

Cool Hand Luke 209-210, 270
The Cool World 123-124, 270
Cooper, Bob 27, 61, 278, 283, 284, 287, 289
Cooper, Gladys 129
Cooper, Maxine 25
Copeland, Alan 174
Corbett, Glenn 78
Corbucci, Sergio 224
Cord, Alex 205, 249
Corey, Weldell 25
Corman, Roger 44
Cosby, Bill 144
Costa, Bill 123, 289
Costa, Don 237
Costa, Eddie 61, 80, 105, 285
Costa-Gavras 163
Costanzo, Jack 55, 58, 79
Cotton Comes to Harlem 257, 260-261, 271
The Counterfeit Killer 118, 229
Coupland, Diana 108-109
Courage, Alexander 42-43, 79, 280
Coutard, Raoul 162-163
Covington, Warren 56
Coward, Noël 255
Coxe, George Harmon 16
Craig, Michael 99
Crane, Bob 148
Crawford, Broderick 18, 90
Crawford, John 86
Crawford, Michael 221
Creasey, John 186
Cresci, John, Jr. 37
Crime in the Streets 23, 28, 271
Crime Photographer 16
The Criminal 85-86, 271
Crombie, Tony 82-83, 277
Crosby, Floyd 123
Cruise, Tom 175
Culp, Robert 135, 144-145, 174
Curtis, Tony 41

Dacqmine, Jacques 68
Dali, Fabienne 111
Dalton, Abby 45
D'Alton, Hugo 216
Damon, Stuart 241
Damone, Vic 21, 240
Dan August 257-258, 271
Dan Raven 76
Dana, Rod 197
Dandridge, Dorothy 110-111
A Dandy in Aspic 242, 271
Danell, Carol 195
Danger Man 83-85, 138-139, 187, 214, 252, 271
Daniels, William 248
Dankworth, John(ny) 82, 85-86, 97-98, 106, 161-162, 191, 207, 232, 267, 268, 271, 283
Dante 77
Dante, Michael 82
"Dante's Inferno" (*Four Star Playhouse*) 18-19
Danton, Ray 204
Darden, Severn 206
Darin, Bobby 76, 120, **185**

Darker Than Amber 262
Dassin, Jules 29-30, 34
Davenport, Nigel 190, 243
David, Mack 40, 56, 79
Davis, Bill 59
Davis, John E. 116, 175
Davis, Miles 2, 20, 50, 193, 267
Davis, Ossie 257
Davis, Richard 152
Davis, Sammy, Jr. 81, 122, 159, 232, 262, 276, 281
Dawson, Anthony 223
Deacon, Richard 235
Dead Heat on a Merry-Go-Round 179
Dead on Target 204
Deadlier Than the Male 218-219
Dean, James 43
De Angelis, Peter 168
Death on the Run see *Bersaglio Mobile*
Decaë, Henri 30, 68
DeFrancesco, Papa John 142
Deighton, Len 160, 188
Delon, Alain 127, 141, 149, 222, 263
DeLugg, Milton 57, 134
Demarest, William 20
De Marlo, Eddie 26
Demarsan, Éric 263-264
De Martino, Alberto 223
De Masi, Francesco 197
De Mendoza, Alberto 52
Demick, Irina 224
Deneuve, Catherine 162
Dennis, Willie 80, 285
Denver, Bob 209
Department S 252-253
Dernick, Irina 164
de Rosa, Vincent 176
de Roubaix, François 222
De Sica, Vittorio 198
Desilu Playhouse 57
Desmond, Johnny 44
Desmond, Paul 37, 111, 131, 245, 279
The Detective 236
Un Detective 255-256, 271
The Detectives 58-59
Deutsch, Adolph 8
Deux Hommes dans Manhattan 67, 272
De Vol, Frank 25, 32, 39, 81
Devon, Laura 207
Devon, Richard 44
Dhiegh, Khigh 230
Diamond, Neil 240
Diamond, Richard 32, 39-40, 61, 94, 283-284
The Dick Powell Show 116
Dickinson, Angie 81, 212
Dietrich, Marlene 48
Diffring, Anton 219
Dillman, Bradford 236
Dirty Harry 141
Dixon, Ivan 110, 146
Dmytryk, Edward 152
Dr. No 5, 6, 108-110, 125, **126**, 223, 272

Index

Doleman, Guy 160
Doménech, Amédée 142
Donati, William 90
Donen, Stanley 119-120, 176
Donohue, Jack 178
Dorham, Kenny 69-70, 287
Dorléac, Françoise 190
Dors, Diana 242
Dorsey, Jimmy 46
Dorsey, Tommy 56, 99
Double Indemnity 8
The Double Man 219
Dougherty, Richard 237
Douglas, Craig 127
Douglas, Kirk 238
Douglas, Robert 100
Le Doulos 111-112
Dragnet (1952 TV series) 16-17, 26, 33, 54
Dragnet (1967 TV series) 201, 237
Drake, Eddie 12-13
Drake, John 72, 84, 138, 214
Drasnin, Robert 133-134, 147, 174, 286
Drew, Kenny 93
Dreyfus, Liliane 87
Drinkwater, Ros 250
Drummond, Hugh "Bulldog" 218-219, 253-255
Duchesne, Roger 30
Duering, Carl 176
Duff, Howard 23, 77, 170
Duffy 244
Duggan, Andrew 55
Dunaway, Faye 239-240
Duncan, Pamela 43
Duning, George 35, 54, 57
Dunne, Philip 175-176
Dunstedter, Eddie 17
Durbridge, Francis Henry 249
Duvivier, George 80, 105, 272, 283, 285, 289
Dylag, Roman 112, 276

East Side/West Side 117, 130, 272
Eastham, Richard 182
Eastwood, Clint 233-234, 246
Easy Rider 248
Eaton, Shirley 125, 205
Echo Four Two 97
Eddy, Duane 37
Eden, Barbara 123
Edwards, Blake 18-19, 32, 34, 37, 59, 77, 102, 118, 134, 207-208, 244
Edwards, Vince 63, 242
Egan, Peter 251
Eggar, Samantha 161
Eisinger, Jo 12
Eisley, Anthony 56
Ekberg, Anita 45
Ekland, Britt 198, 219, 249
Ekyan, André 263
Elcar, Dana 261
Elevator to the Gallows see *Ascenseur pour l'échafaud*
Elfers, Konrad 188
The Elgin Hour 28
Elizalde, John 91, 257

Ellington, Duke 19, 28, 38, 62-63, 82, 89-90, 102, 136, 178-179, 267
Ellington, Mercer 89
Elliot, Biff 23
Elliott, Don 137, 229, 275, 281
Ellis, Don 174
Elms, Albert 214-215, 241, 269, 278
Engel, Roy 44
Ericson, John 146-147
Esmond, Carl 183
Estrin, Harvey 152, 279
Evans, Bill 65, 280
Evans, Gil 136
Evans, Nora 55
Evans, Ray 59
Evell, Julian 124
Experiment in Terror 102-103

Fabiani, Joel 252
The Faceless Man 118, 229
Fagerquist, Don 61, 122, 272, 274, 276, 277, 279, 286, 287
Falk, Peter 81, 148-149
Fame Is the Name of the Game 227
Farewell, My Lovely 235
Farnon, Robert 215, 241, 269
Farr, Lee 58
Farrell, Sharon 248
Farrow, Mia 242
Fast, Howard 152
Fathom 207, 272
Feldman, Charles K. 217
Feldman, Victor 36, 82, 148, 270, 282, 289
Feldon, Barbara 148
Les félins 141, 272
Fell, Norman 135
The Fellows (Late of Room 17) 155, 213, 241
The Felony Squad 170
Felton, Norman 133-134, 170
Des Femmes Disparaissent 68, 272
Ferrara, Romano 142
Fiasco in Milan see *Audace colpo dei soliti ignoti*
Fickling, G.G. 146
Fielding, Jerry 174, 203, 258, 282
Fields, Kansas 67, 272
Finlay, Frank 245
Finnerty, Warren 81, 92
Fitzgerald, Barry 34
Fitzgerald, Ella 26, 63, 78
Fitzgerald, Geraldine 137
Fitzpatrick, Bob 61
Fleming, Art 66
Fleming, Ian 125, 191, 217
Flemyng, Robert 220
Fletcher, Lucille 175
Fletcher, Sam **185**
Fleury, Colette 67
Flick, Vic 5, 108-109, 125, 140, 165, 216, 219, 253
Flicker, Theodore J. 206
Flint, Derek 179-180, **181**, 195, 204
Fonda, Henry 19, 237
Fonda, Jane 141
Fong, Kam 230
Ford, Glenn 102

Forrest, Steve 123, 186
Forsyth, Eddie 58
Forsyth, Stephen 195
Foster, Barry 245
Foster, Dianne 95
The Four Freshmen 120
Four Star Playhouse 32, 77
Fox, James 244
Franciosa, Tony 178, 207, 227
Francis, Anne 146-147
Franciscus, James 34
Francks, Don 170
Frankenheimer, John 96, 104
Franklyn, William 98
Fraser, Ronald 207
Fraud Squad 250-251
Freberg, Stan 5, 17, 169
Frechter, Colin 116
Frederick, Geoffrey 155
Freeman, Ernie 56, 219, 226, 244
Freeman, Leonard **230**, 231
Freeman, Russ 36, 37, 43, 61, 76, 289
Fried, Gerald 73, 132-134, 174
Friedhofer, Hugo 145
Fröbe, Gert 140
From Beirut with Love see *Agent 505: Todesfalle Beirut*
From Russia with Love 29, 125-126, 129, 223, 253, 272-273
Frontiere, Dominic 82, 91, 227
Frost, Richie 43
The Fugitive 113-115, 212, 214, 273
Fuller Report see *Rapporto Fuller Base Stoccolma*
Funeral in Berlin 188-189, 273
Funicello, Annette 205
Furia a Marrakech 195-196
Furneaux, Yvonne 162

Gabel, Martin 235
Gabin, Jean 127
The Gallants 134, 168
Gallo, Tullio 176
Galloway, Don 201
Gambit 177-178
Ganley, Allan 85
Garas, Kaz 252
Garcia, Russell 148
Gardner, Erle Stanley 33-34
Gardner, John 159
Gargan, William 15
Garland, Red 38
Garner, James 186, 248-249
Garner, Pam 37
Garren, Ross 255, 276
Garriguenc, René 72
Garrone, Riccardo 71
Garton, Robin 116
Garvarentz, Georges 246-247, 287
Gassman, Vittorio 51, 71
Gastaldi, Ernesto 165
Gaunt, William 241
Gayson, Eunice 109
Gazzara, Ben 43, 62
Geeson, Judy 242
Gelber, Jack 92
Geller, Bruce 173, 203, 228

Index

Geller, Harry 231
Geller, Herb 36, 61, 287, 289
George, Anthony 75
Géret, Georges 164
Gershwin, George 24, 28, 67, 79, 128
Get Shorty 48
Get Smart 148, 166
Getz, Stan 135-136, 151-152, 202, 279
Gibson, John 16
Gidding, Nelson 46
Gilbert, Herschel Burke 58-59, 115-116, 129
Gilberto, Astrud 135-136, 220
Gilberto, João 152
Gilford, Jack 209
Gillespie, Dizzy 52, 96, 108, 117-118, 123-124, 137, 141, 270
Gilling, John 189
Gilman, Dorothy 261
Girard, Bernard 179
The Girl from U.N.C.L.E. 169, **205**-206, 273
The Girl Hunters 124-125, 273
Gist, Robert 110
Giuffre, Jimmy 27, 278, 283, 289
Glass, Ned 120
Gleason, Jackie 94
Godard, Jean-Luc 87
Golan, Gina 180
Goldberg, Mel 110
Goldenberg, Billy 226-227
Goldfinger 139-140
Goldman, William 184-185
Goldsmith, Jerry 18, 39, 63-64, 72-74, 111, 114, **121**-122, 131-134, 169, 170, 179-**181**, 204, 206, 212-213, 236, 243, 275, 277, 281, 285, 287, 288
Golson, Benny 68, 203, 226, 272
Gonsalves, Paul 89, 267
Goodman, Benny 34, 99, 105, 148, 152
Gordon, Dexter 93
Gordon, Justin 122, 270-272, 276
Gould, Harold 261
Goulet, Robert 171
Gozzo, Conrad 22, 270, 272, 282, 288
Graham, Barbara 46-47
Graham, Kenny 189-190
Grainer, Ron 214-215, 250, 278, 281, 282
Granata, Graziella 225
Granger, Stewart 197
Granier-Deferre, Pierre 164
Grant, Cary 59, **119**-120, 176
Grasset, Pierre 67
Graves, Peter 5, 173, 175
Greco, Buddy 158
Green, Bennie 93
Green, Johnny 33, 37
Green, Nigel 219, 232
Green, Philip 86, 125
Green, Urbie 80, 285
The Green Hornet 168-169, 273
Greene, Graham 160

Gregg, Virginia 32
Gregory, John(ny) 34, 97, 98
Grieco, Sergio 194, 224
Griffith, Hugh 176
Grignon, Marcel 70
Gross, Charles 200
Grusin, Dave 8, 148, 169, 172, 202, **205**-206, 226-227, 249, 257-258, 275, 276, 280
Guaraldi, Vince 60, 93, 158
Guardino, Harry 130, 236-237
Guarnieri, John 16
Guerrieri, Romolo 255
Guest, Val 190
Guffey, Burnett 45
Guida, Wandisa 166
Gunn 138, 207-**208**, 273
Gunn, Peter 35-36, 40, 55, 138
Guns Girls and Gangsters 64
Guthrie, Carl E. 94

Hackman, Gene 117, 170, 237
Hagen, Earle 8, **145**-146, 228-229, 274
Hagen, Jean 25
Haggerty, Don 12
Hail, Mafia see *Je vous salue, mafia!*
Hall, Cliff 16
Hall, Conrad L. 211
Hall, Ginger 67
Hall, Grayson 105
Hall, Jim 65, 193, 268, 280
Hama, Mie 215
Hamilton, Chico 42, 162, 283, 287
Hamilton, Donald 180, 191
Hamilton, Dran 23
Hamilton, Guy 188
Hamilton, Jimmy 63, 89, 267
Hamilton, Ray 90
Hammer, Mike 23, 25, 34, 42-43, 61, 90, 124-125
Hammerhead 242-243, 273
Hammett, Dashiell 18, 33, 91, 184
Hammond, Earl 105
Hampton, Lionel 96, 136
Hancock, Herbie 193-194, 268
The Hanged Man 135-136
Hanson, Bert 41, 285
Hard Frame see *Hunters Are for Killing*
Hardin, Ty 225
Harmer, Shirley 256
Harmon, Joy 210
Harper 184-186, 273
Harris, Julie 184, 237
Harris, Max 187
Harris, Steve 123
Harrison, Noel 239, 287
Harrison, Richard 166
Harrison, Susan 41
Hart, Billy 164
Hartnell, William 86
Harvey, Laurence 104, 242
Hasse, O.E. 49
Hatch, Tony 34, 58, 241, 269
Hathaway, Henry 82
Haven, Alan 126-127

Hawaii Five-O 171, **230**-231, 273
Hawaiian Eye 56, 274
Hawk 169-170
Hayer, Nicolas 67, 111, 164
Hayers, Sidney 99
Hayes, John Michael 24
Hayes, Tubby 49, 276, 277, 280
Hayward, Susan 46
Hazard, Richard 203
Haze, Jonathan 44
Heath, Percy 50
Heath, Ted 84, 99
Heatley, Spike 85, 268, 271
Heflin, Van 149
Hefti, Neal 107, 167-168, 268
Heindorf, Ray 20, 26, 29
Helm, Matt 179-180, 182, 204, 208, 232
Hemmings, David 193
Hendrickson, Al 180, 270, 274, 277, 280, 282, 285, 286
Hendrix, Jimmy 248
Hendry, Ian 83, 97, 106
Henki, Mel 41
Henry, Robert 100
Hepburn, Audrey 119, 176-177
Herman, Woody 152, 153
Hernandez, Juano 260
Herrmann, Bernard 72, 101, 286
Heston, Charlton 47-**48**
Highway Patrol 17-18, 90
Hildyard, Jack 191
Hill, Steven 5, 173
Hilton, Derek 154-155, 213-214, 241-242, 251
Himes, Chester 257
Hines, Earl "Fatha" 20-**21**
Hingle, Pat 233, 237
Hinton, Milt 37, 93, 123, 270, 274, 289
Hirschenson, Bernard 104
Hirt, Al 168-169, 273
Hitchcock, Alfred 24, 101-102, 109, 121, 162, 245
Hixson, Dick 80, 283
Hjerstedt, Gunnar 141
Hodges, Johnny 62, 89, 267
Holland, Milt 55, 270, 274, 278, 280, 287
Holman, Bill 27, 270, 278, 289
Holmes, LeRoy 66, 140
Holt, Seth 48-49
Homeier, Skip 76
Homolka, Oskar 188
Honey West 146-147, 169, 269, 274
Hong Kong 76-77, 274
Hooks, Robert 200
Hopkins, Kenyon 29, 43-44, **93**-94, 117, 123, 130, 169-170, 186, 238-239, 274
Hopper, Dennis 248
Horn, Paul 42, 55, 60, 61, 266, 278, 281, 284
Horn, Shirley 242, 271
Hossein, Robert 49, 68
Hot Millions 243-244
How to Steal a Million 176-177
Howard, Trevor 159

Howe, Bob 37
Howell, Arlene 55
Hubbard, Freddie 136-137, 268, 281
Hubschmid, Paul 188
Hudson, Rock 175
Huggins, Roy 40, 113, 231
Hunnicutt, Gayle 248
Hunter 221-222
Hunter, Evan 96
Hunter, Kim 20
Hunters Are for Killing 258, 274
The Hustler **93**-94, 184, 274
Huston, John 19
Hutton, Jim 209
Hyde, Alexander 19

I Deal in Danger 172
I Promised to Pay see *Payroll*
I Spy 144-146, 174, 274
I, the Jury (1953) 23, 271, 274
I Want to Live! 46-47, 50, 274-275
Iger, Julie 234
Ihnat, Steve 237
In Cold Blood 211, 275
In Like Flint 204, 213, 275, 281
In the Heat of the Night 210-211, 257, 259, 275, 287
Inspector Clouseau 244-245, 275
International Detective 66, 275
Intrator, Jerald 104
Intrigo a Los Angeles 142-143, 275
The Ipcress File 120, 160-161, 188, 189, 275
Ireland, John 85
Ironside 200-202, 258, 275
Issenhuth, Dale 61
It Takes a Thief 226-227, 258, 276, 280
The Italian Job **254**-255, 276
It's Dark Outside 213

Jackson, Anne 259
Jackson, Calvin 89
Jackson, Charlie 124
Jackson, Howard 40
Jackson, Milt 50, 280, 284
Jackson, Sherry 207
James, Harry 38
Janssen, David 32, 39, 94, 113, 115, 212
Japrisot, Sébastien 163
Jarre, Maurice 177
Jason, Rick 79
Jazz Messengers 68-70, 272, 277
Je vous salue, mafia! 162-163
El Jefe 52-53, 276
Jeffries, Lang 165, 197
Jenson, Roy 185
Jerico 170-**171**, 276
Jessup, Richard 150
Jewison, Norman 150, 210, 239-240
Jigsaw 236-237
Jobin, Antônio Carlos 152
John, Errol 178
Johnny Cool 122, 276
Johnny Midnight 73
Johnson, James 63, 267
Johnson, J.J. 137

Johnson, Laurie 5, 97-99, 155, 157, 240-241, 244, 252, 268, 272, 288, 289
Johnson, Nat 234
Johnson, Osie 93, 270
Johnson, Plas 2, 5, 118, 175, 180, 207, 273-275, 278, 280-282, 284
Johnson, Richard 218-219, 253
Johnstone, Bill 17
The Jokers 221
Jones, Elvin 137, 281
Jones, Hank 37, 274
Jones, Ian 222
Jones, Quincy 60, 117-119, 136, 152-153, 200, 201, 210-211, 220, 229, 236, **238**, 242, 254-255, **259**, 260, 271, 275, 281, 287
Jones, Ron 175
Jones, Sam 38, 69, 277
Jones, Spike 17, 148
Jordan, Duke 69-70, 93, 277, 287
Josephs, Wilfred 215
Joy House see *Les félins*

Kahn, Dave 34, 125
Kaleidoscope 191-**192**, 193, 276
Kamuca, Richie 76, 279
Kane, Artie 132, 234, 236, 259, 270, 271, 274, 281, 282, 285, 286, 288, 289
Kane, Martin 13, 15, 278
The Kane Triplets 174
Kardos, László 20
Karloff, Boris 169, 183
Katz, Fred 42, 287
Kauer, Gene 183-184
Kay, Charles 86
Kay, Connie 50, 280, 284
Kay, Norman 250
Kaye, Sammy 178
Kazan, Elia 19, 29
Kazan, Lainie 236
Keating, Johnny 220, 276
Keene, Mike 105
Keith, Brian 34
Kellaway, Roger 152, 279
Kelly, Grace 24
Kelly, Wynton 116
Kendall, Suzy 262
Kennedy, George 120, 209, 259
Kennedy, Gerard 222
Kenton, Stan 37, 74, 101, 108, 113, 125, 153, 201
Kentridge, Joe 221
Kerr, Anita 120
Kershner, Irvin 44
Kessel, Barney 55, 274, 284, 286, 288
Khan, Chaka 140
Kiel, Richard 233
Kikukawa, Sojiro 224
The Killers 17
Kilpatrick, Lincoln 249
King, Peter 255
King, Zalman 101
King of Diamonds 90
King of the Roaring 20s: The Story of Arnold Rothstein 94-96

Kirchin, Basil 246
Kirk, Phyllis 33
Kiss Me Deadly 24-25, 124
Kiss the Girls and Make Them Die 194-195, 276
Kitt, Eartha 146
Kitzmiller, John 109
Kjellin, Alf 178
Klee, Harry 47, 271, 274, 282, 284, 287
Klein, Manny 132, 267, 272
Kluger, Irv 61
Klugh, Earl 140
Klugman, Jack 72-73, 123, 162, 237
Knife in the Water 112, 276
Koenig, Walter 101
Kole, Ronnie 168
Komeda, Krzysztof 112, 276
Koscina, Sylva 238
Kosleck, Martin 184
Kowalski, Bernard L. 249
Kraft Television Theatre 18
Kramer, Allen 44
Kriminal 196, 276
Kroeger, Berry 82
Kruschen, Jack 76
Kupferman, Meyer 91-92

L.A. Confidential 236
Lackey, Douglas 183-184
Lady in Cement 209, 235-236, 277
Laine, Cleo 86
Lancaster, Burt 41, 96
Landau, Martin 173, 260
Landen, Dinsdale 187
Lander, Eric 97
Lang, Ronnie 37, 55, 180, 269, 272, 274, 275, 281, 285, 286
Langdon, Sue Ann 232
Laszlo, Ernest 24-25
Lateef, Yusef 123-124
Lathrop, Philip H. 102
Laura 8
Laurie, Piper 94
Lavi, Daliah 180, 255
The Lawbreakers 99-100
Lawford, Peter 33, 81, 102, 232, 263
Lawrence, Marc 122
Lazenby, George 253
Leach, John 161, 216
Leahy, Joe 233
Leander, Mike 182
Leaper, Bob 138
Leasor, James 190
Le Breton, Auguste 30
Le Carré, John 160, 219-220
Lee, Bernard 49, 223, 253
Lee, Bruce 168
Lee, Carl 92, 123
Lee, Gypsy Rose 45
Lee, Peggy 2, 26, 46, 63
Lee, Russell 150
Legrand, Michel 239-240, 287
Lehman, Ernest 121
Leigh, Glenda 67
Leigh, Janet 47-**48**, 104, 185
Leigh, Vivien 20
Lenard, Melvyn 125

Lenzi, Umberto 196
Leonard, Sheldon 144-*145*
Leroy, Philippe 165
Le Sage, William A. "Bill" 85
Lesou, Pierre 111, 162
Levin, Henry 194
Levitt, Rod 80, 285
Lévy, Raoul 49, 162
LeWars, Marguerite 109
Lewis, Jerry 228, 263
Lewis, John 49-50, 65
Lewis, Mel 152, 279, 280, 282
Lewis, Monica 22
Leyton, John 170
Les Liaisons Dangereuses 69-70, 277
Licensed to Kill 158-159, 277
Lieberman, Frank 155
Linder, Cec 140
Liné, Helga 195, 196
The Lineup 17, 38-39, 277
Linn, Ray 61, 278, 282
Lipman, Jerzy 112
Lipton, Peggy 228
The Liquidator 159-160, 277
Lisi, Virna 178
The Little Big Horns 227
The Little Sister 248
Livingston, Jay 60
Livingston, Jerry 40, 56, 79
Lloyd, Sue 161, 187
Lockhart, Calvin 260
Lockwood, Gary 246
Lockyer, Malcolm 219, 253
Loggia, Robert 172
Lom, Herbert 177
Loncar, Beba 245, 255
London, Julie 76
Long, Richard 55
Lontoc, Leon 115
Lopez, Tommy 69
Lord, Jack 109, 118, 229-230
Lord, Justine 219
Loren, Sophia 176
Loring, Lynn 102
Losey, Joseph 85
Louise, Tina 232
Love Is a Many-Splendored Thing 7
Lovell, Nigel 222
Lovelle, Herbie 124
A Lovely Way to Die 238, 277
Lowe, Mundell 61, 80, 105, 148, 231, 285
Loy, Mino 195
Loy, Myrna 33
Loy, Nanni 70
Ludovisi, Vicky 71
Luger, Mary 142
Lumet, Sidney 136-137, 220
Lupino, Ida 18, 23
Lupus, Peter 173
Lynch, Ken 100

M Squad 33, 37-*38*, 74-75, 90, 277, 279
MacArthur, James 230
MacDermot, Galt 260-261
MacDonald, John D. 262

Macdonald, Ross 91, 184
MacInnes, Helen 183
Mackendrick, Alexander 42
Mackintosh, Ken 18
MacLaine, Shirley 177
Macnee, Patrick 97, 106, 155-*156*, 240
Maddow, Ben 19
Madigan 237
Magne, Michel 128, 163, 270, 278
Maharis, George 78
Maher, Wally 17
Malanowicz, Zygmunt 112
Malden, Karl 29, 150, 182
Malle, Louis 50-51
The Maltese Falcon 8
A Man Called Dagger 232-233, 277
Man from Interpol 82-83, 277
The Man from U.N.C.L.E. 116, 121, 129, 131-134, 147, 148, 167, 169, 183, 212, 233, 261, 277-278
Man in a Suitcase 214, 278
The Man in Room 17 154-155, 241
The Man with the Golden Arm 7, 26-28, 41, 131, 278
The Manchurian Candidate 103-104, 206, 278
Mancini, Henry 5-7, 35-37, 47, *48*, 59, 60, 66, 76, 80, 83, 100, 102, 103, 113, 116-120, 123, 130, 134, 135, 141, 142, 146, 153, 176, 177, 201, 207, **208**, 221, 244, 267, 269, 280, 282, 288
Mandel, Johnny 46-47, 90, 100, 184-*185*, 202, 212, 274-275
Manfredi, Nino 71
Mankiewicz, Don 46
Mann, Abby 18, 236
Mann, Anthony 242
Mann, Claude 163
Mann, Daniel 179
Mann, Delbert 186
Mann, Herbie 61, 180
Manne, Shelly 22, 27, 36, 43, 55, 60, 61, 74, 76, 132, 176, 180, 202, 234, 267, 270-275, 278, 280-289
Mannix 194, 200, 202-203, 228, 234, 278
Mantee, Paul 232
Mantel, Joe 72, 73, 110
Manuel, Robert 30
March, Phillipe 111
Mariano, Charlie 43
Marini, Luciano 142
The Marketts 168
Markham, Monte 34
Markowitz, Richard 44-45, 56-57, 147, 203, 231, 258, 286
Marlier, Carla 127
Marlo, Steven 44
Marlowe 248-249
Marlowe, Derek 242
Marquand, Christian 49
Marshall, Jack 103, 287
Marterie, Ralph 34, 61
Martin, Dean 2, 40, 81, 179-180, 204, 208, 219, 232
Martin, Grady 17

Martin, Quinn 90, 113, 257
Martin, Ray 149
Martin, Ross 59, 102, 147
Martin, Skip 34, 60-61, 277
Martin, Strother 184, 209
Martin Kane, Private Eye 13, 15-16, 278
Martinková, Susanna 256
Martino, Luciano 165
Martinson, Leslie H. 261
Marvin, Lee 33, 73, 212, 237
Masé, Marino 170, 256
The Mask of Janus 187
Mason, James 219, 244
Mastroianni, Marcello 51
Mathis, Johnny 153
Matthau, Walter 120, 153
Matthews, Francis 249
Mattos, Michael 92, 270
Mature, Victor 198
Matz, Peter 248-249
Maughan, Susan 190, 288
Maxfield, Henry S. 219
Maxwell, Lois 223
May, Billy 2, 57, 76-77, 122, 168, 208, 229, 276
May, Donald 79
Mayer, John 192, 276
McAnally, Ray 213-214, 241
McBain, Ed 96
McCallum, David 131, 134, 233
McCallum, Neil 188
McCarthy, Molly 91
McClure, Doug 75
McCook, Tommy 180
McFerrin, Bobby 119
McGavin, Darren 16, 34, 125, 231, 261
McGee, Gerry 231
McGee, Travis 262
McGhee, Howard 57, 93, 270
McGivern, William P. 64
McGoohan, Patrick 72, 83-84, 138-139, 214-215
McIntire, John 34-35
McKern, Leo 246
McLean, Jackie 92, 270
McMahon, Horace 57
McNair, Barbara 260
McNally, Stephen 228
McNeile, Herman Cyril "Sapper" 218
McQueen, Steve 150, 234, 239-240
Meeker, Ralph 25
Meet Flash Casey 16
Meet McGraw 32-33
Meisner, Günter 188
Mélodie en sous-sol 127-128, 141
Melville, Jean-Pierre 30-31, 67, 87, 111, 222, 263-264
Melvoin, Michael 234, 269, 270, 278, 279
Merrill, Buddy 168
Merrill, Dina 96
Mervyn, William 213
La Métamorphose des Cloportes 164, 279
Michelot, Pierre 50-51, 267, 272

Mickey One 151-152
Mickey Spillane's Mike Hammer 34
Midgeley, Bobby 120, 269
Midnight in Saint Petersburg 189
Miles, Vera 100, 135
Milestone, Lewis 81
Miller, Bob 41
Miller, Glenn 17, 32, 34, **48**
Miller, Warren 123
Milner, Martin 41-42, 78
Mineo, Sal 28
Mingus, Charlie 66, 96, 285
Minnelli, Liza 130
Mirage 152-153
Misraki, Paul 111-112
Mission: Impossible 172-175
Mr. Ace 11-12
Mr. Broadway 130-131
Mister Buddwing 186
Mr. Lucky 19, 59-60, 77, 103, 176, 279-280
Mr. Rose 213-214
Mitchell, Don 201
Mitchell, Gordon 225
Mitchell, Red 37, 55, 60, 61, 132, 180, 266, 271, 275, 277, 281, 282, 284, 285, 288
Mitchell, Tommy 152
Mobley, Mary Ann 153
The Mod Squad 228-229
Modern Jazz Quartet 49-50, 65, 263, 284
The Modernaires 60
Modesty Blaise 190-191, 207, 280
Möhner, Carl 30
Mohr, Gerald 64
Mohr, Hal 22
Mohyeddin, Zia 219
Molinaro, Édouard 68-69
Moll, Giorgia 224
Monash, Paul 228
Mondragon, Joe 61, 270, 271, 274, 277, 282, 283, 286, 287, 289
Monicelli, Mario 51, 70
Monk, Thelonious 69-70, 277
Monro, Matt 126-127, 189, 255, 273, 276, 283
Montalban, Ricardo 233
Montand, Yves 163, 263
Montenegro, Hugo 134, 180, 205, 232, 235
Montgomery, Elizabeth 122
Montgomery, Wes 202
Moody, James 119, 124, 270
Moon, Keith 83
Moore, Dudley 86, 271
Moore, Mary Tyler 39
Moore, Roger 106-107
Moore, Terry 232
Mordue, Eddie 191, 276
Moreau, Jeanne 51, 70
Morello, Joe 131, 279
Moreno, Rita 248
Morgan, Barry 120, 269
Morgan, Harry 201
Morgan, Henry 81
Morgan, Lee 68, 272, 277
Morgan, Terence 86

Morgan, Tommy 150, 270, 274
Morison, Patricia 12-13
Morricone, Ennio 195, 198, 223
Morris, Greg 173
Morrow, Buddy 17, 18, 34, 55, 61, 80
Morse, Barry 113
Morse, Terry O. 153-154
Motihar, Diwan 192, 276
Mottola, Tony 16
Moving Target see *Bersaglio Mobile*
Mrs. Pollifax—Spy 261-262
Muldaur, Maria 63
Mullen, Larry, Jr. 175
Mullendore, Joseph 116, 146-147, 172, 203, 269
Müller, Werner 56
Mulligan, Gerry 46-47, 63, 275
Murder Inc. 80-81, 280
The Murder Men 110-111
Murderers' Row 182-183, 280
Murgia, Tiberio 50, 71
Murray, Jan 232
Murray, Lyn 72, 101, 201, 226
Musante, Tony 101, 236
Mussolini, Romano 196, 276
My Gun Is Quick 42-43
Myers, Stanley 191-**192**
Myles, Meg 105

Nader, George 49
Nahon, Philippe 111
Naish, J. Carrol 135
Naismith, Laurence 206, 219
The Naked City (1948 film) 29
The Naked City (1958 TV series) 34-35, 280
Naked City (1960 TV series) 57-58, 78, 129
The Name of the Game 227, 258, 276, 280
Nance, Ray 63, 89, 267
Nascimbene, Mario 190, 194
Nash, Dick 37, 132, 180, 208, 266, 267, 270, 272-275, 278-282, 284, 286, 287
Nash, Ted 37, 176, 208, 267, 270, 272-274, 279, 282, 286, 287
Nelson, Oliver 137, 202, 226, 227, 258-259, 281, 285, 289
Nelson, Ralph 149
Nero, Franco 255
Nesbitt, Derren 250
The New Breed 90-91
The New Perry Mason 34
Newborn, Ira 38
Newhart, Bob 244
Newley, Anthony 139
Newman, Alfred 7
Newman, Joseph M. 94
Newman, Lionel 76, 167
Newman, Paul 93-94, 121, 184-185
Newman, Randy 209
Newmar, Julie 78
Nicolai, Bruno 223
Nicols, Rosemary 252

Nielsen, Leslie 90
Niemcyzk, Leon 112
Night and the City 12
Niven, David 18, 19, 119, 129, 190, 218
No Sun in Venice see *Sait-on jamais*
Nolan, Jeanette 12
Nolan, Lloyd 15, 125
Norman, Monty 108-110
North, Alex 19-20, 41
North by Northwest 121
Norvo, Red 45, 55, 81, 105, 152, 286
Nowhere to Go 48-49, 280
Nóz w wodzie see *Knife in the Water*
Nusciak, Loredana 224
N.Y.P.D. 200-201

Oakland, Simon 46
Oates, Simon 187
Oates, Warren 237
O'Brien, Edmund 73, 135
O'Brien, Erin 40
Ocean's Eleven (1960)
O'Connell, Patrick 81-82
O'Connor, Carroll 117, 212
O'Day, Anita 259
The Odd Man 213
Odds Against Tomorrow 64-65, 263, 280
Odets, Clifford 25, 83
O'Donnell, Peter 190-191
OK Connery see *Operation Kid Brother*
Oliver, Thelma 137
On Her Majesty's Secret Service 253, 280-281
Once a Thief 149-150, 281
One More Time 262-263, 281
O'Neal, Patrick 249
O'Neil, Colette 241
Operation Kid Brother 223
Oranj Symphonette 120, 135
Orbital 108
Ortega, Frankie 40-41, 90, 285
Ortolani, Riz 224, 289
Osborne, Frances 23
The Osterman Weekend 228
Oswald, Gerd 45, 183-184
O'Toole, Peter 177
Our Man Flint 179-180, 213, 281
Our Man in Beirut see *Le spie uccidono a Beirut*
Out of the Past 8
The Outsider 231
Owen, Reg 99, 281

Pace, Judy 260
Paich, Marty 202
Palance, Jack 25, 149, 247
Pallem, Fred 128
Palmer, Earl 134, 234, 270, 275, 277, 280
Palmer, Harry 160-161, 188-189
Palmer, Lilli 243
Parker, Charlie 93, 105
Parker, John Carl 262

Index

Parnell, Jack 17, 41
Password: Uccidete agente Gordon 194-195
Paul, Charles 15, 278
Paul Temple 249-250, 281
Paulsen, Albert 261
The Pawnbroker 136-137, 153, 271, 281
Payne, Cecil 93
Payne, Don 61
Payroll 99, 281
Pearce, Donn 209
Pearson, Johnny 221
Peck, Gregory 152-153, 176
Peck, Steven 235
Pederson, Tommy 61, 274, 284
Pell, Dave 61, 286
Peña, Ralph 27, 278
Penn, Arthur 151
Périer, François 222, 263
Perkins, Bill 22, 269, 289
Perrin, Jacques 163
Perry Mason 33-34
Persip, Charlie 93
Pete Kelly's Blues (1955 film) 26, 281
Pete Kelly's Blues (1959 TV series) 54, 281
Peter Gunn 7, 19, 35-37, 46, 48, 54, 59, 60, 76, 77, 100, 103, 116, 117, 120, 122, 123, 130, 131, 141, 146, 147, 172, 176, 207, 282
Peters, Brock 137
Peters, Dennis Alaba 252
Pettet, Joanna 218, 220
Petty, Tom 140
Pevney, Joseph 101
Pfau, Stefano 142
Philip Marlowe 56-57, 147
Philip Marlowe, Private Eye 12
Philipe, Gérard 70
Phillips, Freddie 214
Phillips, Paul 58
Phillips, Stu 179
Piccadilly Third Stop 86-87
Piccioni, Piero 199
Piccoli, Michel 111
Pickup on South Street 221
Pigozzi, Luciano 166
Pimental, Allan 234
The Pink Panther 118-119, 134, 282
Pisacane, Carlo 51, 71
Pisano, Berto 71, 267, 275, 286
Pisano, John 42, 287
Platt, Edward 148
Playhouse 90 18
Pleasence, Donald 215
Pleshette, Suzanne 186, 258
Podestà, Rossana 165
Point Blank 212, 237, 282
Poitier, Sidney 210-211, 257, 259-260
Polanski, Roman 112, 162
Poli, Maurice 224
Police Squad! 38, 200
Police Surgeon 83
Ponce, Poncie 56
Porter, Cole 12, 79, 227

Porter, Eric 191
Posani, Dante 196
Post, Mike 38, 240, 275
Poujouly, Georges 51
Powell, Dick 18, 32, 77, 116
Powell, William 33
Powers, Stefanie 102, 169, 212
Pratt, Lloyd 21
Pregadio, Roberto 196, 267, 276
Preminger, Otto 26-27, 62
Prentice, Ron 246, 276
The President's Analyst 206-207, 282
Preston, Billy 140, 238, 275, 286
Previn, André 19, 46, 122
Prévost, Françoise 99
Price, Dennis 86
Price, Red 84
Price, Sherwood 63
Priddy, Jimmy 59, 272, 279, 282
Prince, Robert 202
The Prisoner 214-215, 282-283
Private Hell 36 23-24, 28, 61, 283
The Prize **121**-122, 283
Procope, Russell 62, 267
Provine, Dorothy 79, 194, 209, 284
Public Eye 154
Purdy, Stan 23

Quayle, Anthony 251-252
The Quiller Memorandum 189, 283

Raft, George 11
Ralke, Don 40, 56, 268
Ramin, Sid 149, 249, 286
Randazzo, Teddy 169
Rapporto Fuller Base Stoccolma 245-246, 283
Rasey, Uan 61, 132, 279, 282, 285-287
Raskin, David 8
Rawls, Lou 244, 272
Ray, Don B. 8
Raymond, Gene 135
Rear Window 24, 94, 283
Reason, Rex 79
The Red Circle see *Le Cercle Rouge*
Redd, Freddie 92, 93, 270
Redfield, William 92
Redgrave, Vanessa 193
Reece, Alphonso Son "Dizzy" 49, 282
Reed, Les 107, 263
Reed, Oliver 221
Reese, Tom 182
Reggiani, Serge 111
Rehak, Frank 80, 274, 283
Reid, Beryl 245
Reid, Carl Benton 116
Reid, Milton 219
Reig, Teddy 37
Reinhardt, Django 162
Remick, Lee 62-63, 102-103, 236
Rennie, Michael 225
Renzil, Eva 188
The Reporter 130, 283
Repulsion 162, 283
Requiem per un Agente Segreto 197, 283

Rescher, Gayne 81
Return from the Ashes 161, 283
Revill, Clive 191, 207
Rey, Alejandro 175
Rey, Chico 249
Reynolds, Burt 169-170, 257, 258
Reynolds, Dick 17
Reynolds, Stan 54
Reynolds, William 54
Rich, Buddy 46, 202
Rich, David Lowell 238
Richard Diamond, Private Detective 32, 39-40, 94, 283-284
Richards, Emil 132, 260, 270, 275, 278-280, 282, 285-289
Richman, Mark 110, 183-184
Riddle, Nelson 2, 16, 57-58, 61, **77**-79, 81-82, 129-130, 133, 167-168, 284, 288
Rififi 30
Rigg, Diana 146, 155-**156**, 240, 253
Rilla, Wolf 86
Ring of Death see *Un Detective*
Ring of Fear 23
Ritchie, Larry 92, 270
Riviera Police 155
Rivkin, Allen 20
The Road to Shame see *Des Femmes Disparaissent*
The Roaring 20's [sic] 79, 284
Robards, Jason 130
Robbery 220-221, 284
Robbins, Harold 249
Robert Montgomery Presents 18
Roberts, George 61
Roberts, Lynne 12
Roberts, Rocky 224
Robinson, Edward G. 82, 122, 150
Robson, Mark 121
Rodgers, Gaby 25
Rodriguez, John 69
Rodriguez, William 69
Rodríguez, Yolanda 124
Rogers, Shorty 22, 27, 63, 153, 170, 229, 278, 283, 289
The Rogues 129-130, 284
Romano, Marcel 68, 69
Rome, Sydne 255
Romero, Cesar 81
Ronet, Maurice 51
Rooney, Mickey 20-**21**
Rose, David 18, 80, 133
Rose, Reginald 18, 28
Rosenberg, Stuart 81, 210
Rosengren, Bernt 112, 276
Rosenman, Leonard 72
Rosier, Cathy 222
Rosolino, Frank 27, 37, 60, 61, 266, 274, 275, 277-279, 281, 284, 286, 287
Ross, Katharine 186
Ross, Ronnie 85
Rossen, Robert 93-94
Rosson, Harold 19
Rostaing, Hubert 162-163
Roten, Ethmer 176, 267
Rothwell, Alan 98
Rouse, Charlie 69, 277

Route 66 35, 58, **77**-79, 113, 129, 284
Rovère, Paul 67, 70, 266, 272, 287
Rowles, Jimmy 37, 60, 61, 103, 118-119, 130, 176, 207, 267, 270, 272, 273, 277, 280, 282, 284, 287
Rózsa, Miklós 8, 17, 19, 267
Rugolo, Pete 20, 37, 39, 74, 80, 113-115, 170, 172, 231, 283-284, 287
Rule, Janice 204
Ruspoli, Esmeralda 196
Russell, Rosalind 261
Ryan, Robert 64
Rydell, Mark 28

Saad, Margit 85
Sabatello, Dario 223
Safranski, Eddie 16
Sage, Walter 41, 285
The Saint 106-108, 284
St. Jacques, Raymond 260
Saint Paul, Lara 245
Sait-on jamais 49-50, 284
Salmi, Albert 204
Salt & Pepper 232, 284
Salvatori, Renato 51, 71
Le Samouraï 222-223, 284
San Francisco Beat 17
Sanchez, Jamie 137
Sanders, George 135
Satan in High Heels 104-106, 284-285
Sathe, Keshave 192, 276
Saul, Oscar 19
Sauter, Eddie 151-152
Savalas, Telly 233, 253
Savina, Carlo 165-166, 196
Saxson, Glenn 196
Schaffner, Franklin J. 219
Scharf, Walter 132, 134, 148, 174
Schell, Maximilian 161
Schifrin, Lalo 5, 6, 52-53, 102, 117-118, 123, 132-134, 141, 149-150, **151**, **159**-160, 170-175, 182-183, 200, 203-204, 206, 209, 210, 228, 233-**235**, 249, 261-262, 268-270, 276-279, 281, 282, 285, 288, 289
Schoen, Vic 54
Schoenberg, Arnold 212
Schüfftan, Eugen 94
Schuller, Gunther 65, 280
Schumann, Walter 5, 16-17, 201
The Scorpio Letters **205**-206, 285
Scott, Bobby 137, 275, 281
Scott, Brenda 135
Scott, George C. 62, 94, 117
Scott, John 140
Scott, Nathan 16
Scott, Pippa 59
Scott, Raymond 148
Scott, Ronnie 82, 277
Scott, Tony 61
Scourby, Alexander 82
Screaming Mimi 45
Se tutte le donne del mondo... see *Kiss the Girls and Make Them Die*
Sealey, Dave 227
Sears, Fred F. 44

Sebastian 243, 285
Sebastian, John 194
Seberg, Jean 87
Secret Agent see *Danger Man*
Secret Agent Fireball see *Le spie uccidono a Beirut*
Sedlar, Jimmy 158
Segal, George 189
Sellers, Peter 118, 134, 198, 218, 244
Selzer, Milton 123
Sensi, Mario 197
Serling, Rod 18, 63, 72, **121**, 122, 178
Servais, Jean 30, 246
Seven Golden Men see *7 uomini d'oro*
Seven Thieves 82
7 uomini d'oro 165, 285
77 Sunset Strip 40-41, 55, 56, 61, 79, 90, 285
Sewell, George 250
Shadows 65-66
Shank, Bud 22, 27, 61, 118, 179, 183, 208, 267, 269, 273-275, 278-280, 283-285, 287, 289
Sharples, Robert 154, 250-251
Shaughnessy, Ed 61, 80, 130, 281, 283, 285, 289
Shaw, Artie 99, 148, 152
Shaw, Arvell 21
Shaw, Robert 126
Shaw, Roland 140, 158, 217
Sheldon, Jack 176, 267, 274
Shelton, Dean 92
Sheridan, Margaret 23
Shire, David 202
Shonteff, Lindsay 158
Shores, Richard 39-40, 73, 134, 148, 169, 171, 231
A Shot in the Dark 134-135
Sicario 77, vivo o morto 197-198
Sidney, Sylvia 11
Siegel, Don 23, 28, 135-136, 237
Signoret, Simone 220
The Silencers 180, 182, 285
Silva, Henry 122, 162
The Silvertones 180
Simcox, Tom 228
Simmons, Art 67, 272
Simmons, Jean 186
Simms, Hank 90
Simpson, Dudley 250
Sinatra, Frank 1, 27, 46, 57, 78, 81, 104, 123, 131, 136, 178, 208, 219, 235, 236, 237
Sinatra, Nancy **216**-217, 288, 289
Singer, Hal 124
Singer, Lou 61, 287
Skiles, Marlin 42-43
Slaney, Ivor 83, 138
The Sleeping Car Murders see *Compartiment Tueurs*
Sloan, P.F. 139
Sloane, Everett 72
Smart, Ralph 138
Smith, Carson 42, 287, 289
Smith, Frank 222
Smith, Jimmy 128, 140, 141, 164, 174, 190, 279

Smith, Johnny "Hammond" 201
Smith, Maggie 49, 244
Smith, Roger 40
Smith, William 262
Sol Madrid 233, 285
Solal, Martial 67, 87, 266, 272
I soliti ignoti 51-52, 286
Sollima, Sergio 197
Some Girls Do 219, 253, 255, 286
Somebody's Stolen Our Russian Spy 190
Sommer, Elke 121, 135, 183, 219, 247
Sommers, Joanie **235**
Sounds Orchestral 140, 158, 221
Sparv, Camilla 179, 182, 246
Special Branch 250, 286
Le spie uccidono a Beirut 165-166, 286
Le spie uccidono in silenzio 196-197
The Spies 187
Spies Strike Silently see *Le spie uccidono in silenzio*
Spillane, Mickey 23, 24, 124-125
Spindoe 241-242
Spink, Brian 155
The Split 237-**238**, 286
Springfield, Dusty 240, 269
The Spy Killers see *Le spie uccidono a Beirut*
Staccato 54-55, 286
Staccioli, Ivano 196
Stack, Robert 57, 227
Stafford, Brendan J. 83
Stafford, Frederick 195
Stage 7 32
Stakeout on Dope Street 44-45, 286
Stand By for Crime 15
Stander, Lionel 91
Stapleton, Cyril 18, 99, 187, 252
The Star and the Story 19
Steiger, Rod 25, 82, 136, 210
Steiner, Fred 33-34, 72
Steiner, Max 8, 101
Steinkamp, Fredric 186
Stepanek, Karel 158
Steppenwolf 248
Stevens, Connie 56
Stevens, Craig 35, 130-131, 207
Stevens, Julie 106
Stevens, Leith 22-24, 61, 77, 283, 289
Stevens, Mark 15
Stevens, Mort(on) 8, 74, 111, 132, 134, 170, 230-231, 273
Stevens, Paul 248
Stevens, Stella 180, 182, 233
Stewart, Alexandra 152
Stewart, David J. 81
Stewart, Ernest 99
Stewart, James 24, 62-63
Stewart, Paul 25
Stiletto 249, 286
Stine, Harold E. 40
Sting 240
Stinson, Albert 162, 283
Stoll, George 20
Stoller, Alvin 37, 266, 270, 274, 277, 279, 282, 287

Stone, Alexander 214
Stone, Peter 176
Stoney Burke 229
Stott, Wally 60
Stover, Hal 21
Stradling, Harry 20
Strange, Billy 140, 148, 158, 180, **216**-217
The Strange One 43-44, 286
Strange Report 251-252, 286
A Streetcar Named Desire 19-20, 28, 41, 286
The Streets of San Francisco 17
Streisand, Barbra 240
The Strip 20-22
Stroud, Don 233
Stroyberg, Annette 69-70
Surfside 6 56
Suspense (TV anthology series) 18
Sutherland, Donald 237
Sweet Smell of Success 41-42, 287
Sykes, Eric 159
Sylvester, Victor 41
Szabo, Gabor 162, 283
Szathmary, Irving 148, 166

Tamiroff, Akim 198
Tanba, Tetsurô 215
Tani, Yolo 86
Tate, Sharon 232
Tatro, Duane 258
Taylor, Arthur (Art) 38, 69, 123, 277
Taylor, Don 32, 34
Taylor, Mel 231
Taylor, Robert 58
Taylor, Rod 76, 159, 262
Teagarden, Jack 20-21, 148
Tedesco, Tommy 132, 267, 270, 274, 280, 282, 285, 287, 288
Un témoin dans la ville 68-69, 287
Templar, Simon 106-108
Terri, Vincent 37
Terry, Clark 80, 93, 123, 152, 267, 279, 285
Terry-Thomas 194
Tevis, Walter 94
T.H.E. Cat 172
They Call Me MISTER Tibbs! 260, 287
They Came to Rob Las Vegas 246-247, 287
A Thief Is a Thief Is a Thief 226
Thielemans, Toots 202, 275
Thieves' Highway 29
The Thin Man (TV series) 33, 37
The Thomas Crown Affair 239-240, 287
Thompson, Bob 41
Thompson, J. Lee 161
Thompson, Lloyd 49, 280
Thorne, Ken 245
Thornton, Teri 58, 79
Thorp, Roderick 236
Thorpe, Richard 205
Thorson, Linda 240
Thorson, Russell 58
Thriller 73-74, 287

Throne, Malachi 226
Thulin, Ingrid 161
Thunderball 140, 157-158, 253, 287-288
Tiffany Memorandum 224, 288
Tiffin, Pamela 184
Tightrope 54
Timmons, Bobby 68, 272, 277
Tom Dollar 224, 288
Tony Rome 208-209, 288
Toomey, Regis 18
Top Secret 98-99, 288
Tormé, Mel 46, 63
Torn, Rip 150, 233
Touch of Evil 47-**48**, 64, 288
Townes, Harry 45
Tracy, Lee 15
Traubel, Helen 207
Trevarthan, Noel 155
Trevor, Elleston 189
The Trials of O'Brien 148-149
Triscari, Joe 61, 283
Trovajoli, Armando 165, 245-246, 283
Tudó, Federico Martínez 197
Tully, Tom 17
Twelve-tone compositional structure 43-44, 92, 212, 229
The Twilight Zone 63, 72-73, 114, **121**, 288
Two Men in Manhattan see *Deux Hommes dans Manhattan*
Tyler, Brian 231
Tyson, Cicely 117

Umecka, Jolanta 112
Umiliani, Piero 51, 70, 142, 165, 195, 267, 275, 286
The Untouchables 57, **77**, 79, 288
Urbont, Jack 174, 203
Urtreger, René 50-51, 267
Ustinov, Peter 243

Vadim, Roger 49-50, 69-70
Valérie, Jeanne 69-70
Vallone, Raf 194, 255
Van Cleave, Nathan 73, 178
Vanderbilt, Lee 255, 286
Vandor, Ivan 225
Van Doren, Mamie 64
van Eyck, Peter 197
Van Gyseghem, Joanna 250
Vaughan, Peter 242
Vaughan, Sarah 60, 81, 136, 138, 237, 280
Vaughn, Billy 79
Vaughn, Robert 131, 134, 183, 233, 234
Velona, Tony 149
Vendetta 187-188, 288
The Venetian Affair 183, 233, 288
Ventura, Lino 51, 69, 164
The Ventures 110, 119, 134, 168, 230-231
Verneuil, Henri 127-128
Vernon, John 212
Vernon, Marie 150
Vernon, Richard 154, 213, 241

Vicario, Marco 165
Villiers, James 254
Vincent, Don 258
Vine, Charles 158-159, 189-190
Vinnegar, Leroy 43
Viola, Al 61, 274, 284
Vitti, Monica 191
Vivyan, John 59
Vogel, Nicolas 70
Vogt, Larry 234
The Volcanos 54
Volontè, Gian Maria 263
von Sydow, Max 189

Wagner, Robert 119
Wagner, Wende 168, 184, 226
Wakabayashi, Akiko 215
Waldron, Mal 123-124
Walker, Carole 142
Wall, Jean 51
Wallace, Irving 121
Wallach, Eli 29, 82
Wallant, Edward Lewis 136
Wanamaker, Sam 85
Ward, Burt 167
Ward, Tony 222
Warden, Jack 100, 175, 200
Warning Shot 212-213, 288
Warren, Quentin 164
Warwick, Dionne 157
Washington, Ned 35
Waters, Benny 31
Watt, Tommy 116
Waxman, Franz 20, 23, 24, 28, 72, 94-95, 274, 276, 283
Waxman, John W. 28
Webb, Jack 5, 16, 26, 33, 41, 54, 201
Webb, Roger 252, 286
Webb, Roy 8
Webber, Robert 184
Webster, Ben 118
Weidman, Jerome 130
Welch, Raquel 207, 235-236
Weld, Tuesday 150
Welles, Orson 47, 92
Wesson, Dick 90
West, Adam 167
West, Timothy 251
Westinghouse Studio One 18
Westlake, Donald E. 212, 237
Wexler, Haskell 44
Wexler, Yale 44
Where the Bullets Fly 189-190, 288
Where the Spies Are 190
Whitaker, David 242-243
White, Chris 124, 270
Whiteley, John 221
Whitman, Stuart 81
Whitmore, James 237
The Who 83
Who's Minding the Mint? 209
Widmark, Richard 221, 237
Wiggins, Gerald 134
The Wild Bunch 258
The Wild One 22-23, 28, 73, 288-289
The Wild Wild West 44, 147-148, 289

Index

Wilder, Joe 37, 274, 280, 283
Wilhoit, Ken 114
Willen, Barney 50, 277
Williams, Andy 120
Williams, Clarence III 123, 228
Williams, John (Johnny, John T.) 18, 38, 42-43, 55, 74-76, 117, 171, 176-177, 269-270, 276, 277, 280, 282, 287
Williams, Keith 61
Williams, Mason 240
Williams, Patrick 258
Williams, Richard 218
Williams, Tennessee 19, 29
Williams, Tommy 137, 281
Williams, Van 168
Williamson, Stu 43, 279, 284
Willingham, Calder 43
Wills, Anneke 252
Wilson, Eileen 25
Wilson, Elizabeth 117
Wilson, Jackie 239, 277
Wilson, Scott 211
Wilson, Stanley 33, 37-38, 74-75, 118, 201
Wilson, Teddy 16
Winchell, Walter 41
Windish, Ilka 206
Windom, William 236
Winstone, Eric 140
Winters, Jonathan 73
Winters, Shelley 25, 96, 184
Wise, Robert 46, 64, 263
Wiseman, Joseph 109, 229, 249
A Witness in the City see *Un témoin dans la ville*
Women Are Trouble 16
Woode, Jimmy 63, 267
Woods, Jimmy 162
Woods, Phil 94, 130, 268, 274, 283, 285
Woolrich, Cornel 18, 24
Wooten, Red 45
Wray, Link 168
The Wrecking Crew 232
Wright, Gene 131
Wright, Maggie 263
Wrightson, Stan 61, 277
Wyble, Jimmy 45
Wyler, Richard 82-83
Wyler, William 176-177
Wynant, H.M. 248
Wyngarde, Peter 252-253
Wynn, Keenan 213

The Yardbirds 194
Yates, Peter 234
The Yellow Canary 122-123, 289
York, Susannah 191, 243, 244
You Only Live Twice 215-217, 289
Youmans, Vincent 79
Young, Gig 129
Young, Lester 118
Young, Terence 109, **126**, 223
Young Dillinger 153-154
The Young Savages **95**-96, 289
Younis, Richard 52
Yuro, Robert 105

Zentner, Si 213, 286, 288
Zerbe, Anthony 260
Zetterling, Mai 86
Zig Zag 258-**259**, 289
Zimbalist, Efrem, Jr. 40-41
Zulu 160